Teaching Middle School Physical Education

A Standards-Based Approach for Grades 5-8

THIRD EDITION

Bonnie S. Mohnsen, PhD

Bonnie's Fitware, Inc.

HUMAN KINETICS

Library of Congress Cataloging-in-Publication Data

Mohnsen, Bonnie S., 1955-
    Teaching middle school physical education : a standards-based approach for grades 5-8 /
Bonnie S. Mohnsen. -- 3rd ed.
            p. cm.
    Includes bibliographical references and index.
    ISBN-13: 978-0-7360-6849-9 (soft cover)
    ISBN-10: 0-7360-6849-X (soft cover)
    1.   Physical education and training--Study and teaching (Middle school)--United States.
I. Title.
    GV365.M65 2008
    796.071--dc22

                                                    2007035700

ISBN-10: 0-7360-6849-X
ISBN-13: 978-0-7360-6849-9

The Web addresses cited in this text were current as of October 24, 2007, unless otherwise noted.

Acquisitions Editor: Scott Wikgren; **Developmental Editor:** Melissa Feld; **Assistant Editor:** Martha Gullo, Bethany J. Bentley, and Jackie Walker; **Copyeditor:** Julie Anderson; **Proofreader:** Anne Meyer Byler; **Indexer:** Craig Brown; **Permission Manager:** Dalene Reeder; **Graphic Designer:** Nancy Rasmus; **Graphic Artist:** Denise Lowry; **Cover Designer:** Bob Reuther; **Photographer (cover):** Top photo reprinted, by permission, from Source Distributors, Inc.; bottom photos © Human Kinetics; **Photographer (interior):** © Human Kinetics unless otherwise noted; **Photo Asset Manager:** Laura Fitch; **Photo Office Assistant:** Jason Allen; **Art Manager:** Kelly Hendren; **Associate Art Manager:** Alan L. Wilborn; **Illustrators:** Keri Evans and Kelly Hendren, chapters 3-12; Keri Evans and Patrick Griffin, chapters 14-17; **Printer:** Versa Press

Printed in the United States of America   10   9   8   7   6   5   4   3   2   1

Human Kinetics
Web site: www.HumanKinetics.com

United States: Human Kinetics, P.O. Box 5076, Champaign, IL 61825-5076
800-747-4457
e-mail: humank@hkusa.com

Canada: Human Kinetics, 475 Devonshire Road Unit 100, Windsor, ON N8Y 2L5
800-465-7301 (in Canada only)
e-mail: info@hkcanada.com

Europe: Human Kinetics, 107 Bradford Road, Stanningley, Leeds LS28 6AT, United Kingdom
+44 (0) 113 255 5665
e-mail: hk@hkeurope.com

Australia: Human Kinetics, 57A Price Avenue, Lower Mitcham, South Australia 5062
08 8372 0999
e-mail: liaw@hkaustralia.com

New Zealand: Human Kinetics, Division of Sports Distributors NZ Ltd., P.O. Box 300 226 Albany, North Shore City, Auckland
0064 9 448 1207
e-mail: info@humankinetics.co.nz

This book is dedicated to Carolyn Thompson,
for her constant professional and personal support.

It is further dedicated to Karen Mendon, for her professional and personal support
as well as for sharing her middle school students with me.

Finally, it is dedicated to my father, Earl H. Mohnsen,
for showing me how important it is to live each day to the fullest.

Contents

PART III   Travel Toward Your Destination

PART IV   Discover Your Destination

Preface

Much has changed since the writing of the second edition of *Teaching Middle School Physical Education*. Most notable is the second edition of the NASPE national physical education standards along with the publication of the CDC's Physical Education Curriculum Analysis Tool, the second edition of the *Shape of the Nation Report,* and assessment examples from NASPE for evaluating student performance related to the physical education standards. Additionally, there have been changes in publications from various state agencies and tremendous growth in some physical education programs thanks to grants such as the Carol M. White grant. The increased emphasis on after-school programs and coordinated school health programs has also had a direct impact on the quality of our physical education programs.

Teaching middle school students is still a frustrating—and most rewarding—experience, as noted in the first and second editions of this text. We still have a tremendous opportunity to affect students' lives as we help them transform into responsible, physically active adults. The original text was the first comprehensive practical resource for designing quality middle school physical education programs that both addressed the specific needs of middle school students and prepared them for our rapidly changing world.

This new edition continues where the previous two editions left off with some exciting new additions. Most significant is the inclusion of the following:

- Recommended equipment packages to make your job easier when implementing this program (see chapter 4 and the CD-ROM)
- More detailed lesson outlines to help you present the information to your students
- A CD-ROM with examples of task cards and daily detailed lesson plans that can be purchased to accompany the text

- Unit plans realigned to reflect the new national standards

The book is written specifically for middle school physical education teachers. It has also been adopted by colleges as a methods book for teaching middle school physical education and teaching secondary physical education. Curriculum planners; physical education supervisors, coordinators, and consultants; general professional development planners; and district and school administrators also use the text in curriculum development and for professional development seminars. Designed around the metaphor of a journey, this text provides a blueprint for the development of environment, curriculum, instruction, and assessment for middle school based on high-quality physical education guidelines.

In part I of *Teaching Middle School Physical Education*, Prepare for Your Journey, we look at society, technology, health, and education changes and how these changes can shape middle school physical education programs for the better. We examine the development of middle schools, current reform efforts, and examples of quality middle school physical education programs. I encourage you to buy your ticket by becoming an equal partner in the entire education program of your school in order to gain equal funding, administrative support, and equitable class size and instructional time. In addition, I show you ways to increase respect for your program through developing extracurricular activities and coordinating an integrated, coordinated school health program. To conclude part I, I discuss the physical and psychological components of a quality physical education environment.

In part II, Map Out Your Journey, I guide you through the development of a physical education curriculum step by step, from start to finish. We discuss how to select a curriculum committee and how to define a physically educated person.

Then I show you how to translate this definition into exit standards and how to create grade-level standards (benchmarks) in alignment with the exit standards. Unlike other curriculum textbooks that may be collecting dust in your office, this book goes beyond ideals, as I show you how to select instructional units, integrate physical education with other subject areas, and develop unit and lesson plans. But the book doesn't stop there. We examine the benefits of alternative assessment and grading in physical education, including how to create rubrics and help students develop performance portfolios. We look at several assessment tools that focus on student strengths and uncover student weaknesses in ways that are not demeaning or unfair, including structured observations, written tests, logs and journals, role-playing, reports, and projects.

In part III, Travel Toward Your Destination, I share insights into the needs of middle school learners and the corresponding teaching behaviors, instructional styles and strategies, instructional materials, and new technologies that are especially effective in middle school. We discuss ways to motivate your students and reach all types of learners by engaging both your students and yourself. Specifically, we look closely at why and how to select a particular teaching style or strategy, based on the content standard you're teaching and the learning styles of your students. I conclude part III by encouraging you to continue to grow as a physical educator by attending in-services, conferences, or graduate school and by expanding your knowledge base through peer coaching, doing committee work, supervising a student teacher, becoming board certified, or visiting other schools.

In part IV, Discover Your Destination, I outline sample physical education programs for fifth, sixth, seventh, and eighth grades. In each unit, I include an overview, a list of unit standards linked directly to the grade-level standards, and a day-by-day lesson outline. In addition, I suggest assessment tool ideas for each unit so that you can be sure that your students have accomplished the standards.

The book concludes with three appendixes, each designed to provide you with valuable additional information. Appendix A provides you with an in-depth look at the characteristics of middle school students. Appendix B includes the content for each of the grade-level standards described in chapters 6 and 7 and addressed in chapters 14 through 17. Appendix C contains contact information for vendors who supply materials for middle school physical education.

The enclosed CD-ROM is not a software program but rather contains examples of resources for physical education teachers such as bulletin boards, a curriculum model, lesson plans, a student handbook, student and teacher worksheets, task cards, Web booklets, and a document listing software available for trial download. Please see the User Instructions for CD-ROM page at the back of this book for more information on using the CD-ROM.

Designed with both you and your students in mind, *Teaching Middle School Physical Education* is a comprehensive yet flexible resource guide for creating a quality middle school physical education program at your school. It contains quality, up-to-date information that is practical and usable for both the veteran and new teacher. If we have learned anything over the past decades, it is that gains in student performance require educators to stay the course over an extended period of time.

So, let the journey continue . . .

PART I

Prepare for Your Journey

Physical education does not take place in isolation. In part I, we examine the middle school setting, the larger educational system, American society, and the global community. In **chapter 1**, we explore the many changes that are occurring in society, technology, health care, and education as well as their impact on quality physical education. In **chapter 2**, we examine the middle school reform movement's attempts to meet the special needs of middle school students, and we discuss the positive contributions that quality physical education programs can make as an equal partner in the middle school setting. In **chapter 3**, I define the role of physical education in the instructional setting, extracurricular program, and the coordinated school health system. I also provide information on how to promote your program both in school and throughout the community. In **chapter 4**, I outline what makes an efficiently run physical education department that provides students with safe facilities and adequate equipment. And in **chapter 5**, we discuss the composition of physical education classes as well as how to create a psychologically safe environment in which all students are treated and disciplined respectfully.

Physical Education in a Changing World

Think for a moment about the physical education program you had as a student in middle or junior high school. Now think about the physical education program at the school where you currently teach or one that you have recently observed. How are the two programs similar and different? Are the differences for the better? Has physical education moved into the future at the same pace as the rest of the world? And what about the world in which your students will live as adults? What knowledge, skills, and attitudes learned in middle school physical education will your students be able to use when they are in their 30s, 40s, 50s, and beyond?

Today's physical educator must keep pace with changes in technology, society, health, and education. In *Teaching Middle School Physical Education, Third Edition,* I provide a blueprint for quality physical education programs in a changing world, a foundation on which you can build an ideal program. But physical education does not occur in isolation, and we must know what is going on in the world around us. Everything is interconnected, and if we take a myopic view of our role as physical educators, we will do an injustice to our students. In this chapter, we begin our journey by exploring some of the changes in technology, society, health, and education and their implications for physical education in the 21st century.

In times of change, learners inherit the earth, while the learned find themselves beautifully equipped to deal with a world that no longer exists.

Futurist Eric Hoffer

Our Changing Technology

In the last two decades, technology has changed the way in which we teach physical education. In many classes across the United States, physical educators now use heart monitors, pedometers, electronic blood pressure devices, handheld computers, instructional software, and quasi–virtual reality physical activities such as Revolution, GamePad, GameBike, and EyeToy (see figure 1.1). In 1988, I asked a group of physical educators if they thought they would ever have a computer in their offices, and the answer was a resounding no. Today, these same physical educators are walking around with computers in their pockets. And now, with the introduction of the $150 laptop computer with Internet access, their students will also be carrying a computer from class to class.

Between 1994 and 2003, the number of schools with Internet access jumped from 35% to 100%, and between 1998 and 2003 the ratio of computers to students increased from 1:12 to 1:3 (National Center for Education Statistics 2005). The use of technology in the home has also increased rapidly. The percentage of households with a computer jumped from 8% in 1984 to 56% in 2001 to 62% in 2003, whereas the percentage of households with Internet access jumped from 18% in 1997 to 50% in 2001 to 55% in 2003 (National Center for Education Statistics 2005).

The abundance of information on the Internet is phenomenal. We already have more information than we could possibly read in one lifetime, and with wireless access, the information is at our fingertips. The dilemma is no longer how to access information but how to sift through it to find the most appropriate and accurate information. Databases and Internet search engines can now assist with searching for and filtering data, but eventually you'll be able to customize your computer as a personal assistant or reference librarian. This active software agent will select and store pieces

a

b

Reprinted, by permission, from Source Distributors, Inc.

Figure 1.1 Using products that combine technology and physical activity, like the (a) GamePad and (b) GameBike, motivates students to perform to the best of their ability.

of information that it determines you will want to read or have read to you by the computer.

To accommodate such an enormous quantity of information, storage systems are becoming even more compact. Drives no larger than the size of your thumb can hold 16 GB of information or close to seven million pages of text. These devices also can hold pictures, audio, and video, so that all of your important resources can be carried with you.

Moreover, as computers continue to evolve, they will do more than provide you access to the Internet and your storage devices. As noted by Perelman (1992), "Hans Moravec, director of the Mobile Robot Laboratory at Carnegie Mellon University, anticipates . . . by the year 2030, compact, PC-like machines will be able to reason, perceive, and act on their environment with full human equivalence" (p. 29). These computers will take over numerous chores currently performed by humans, and they will be capable of learning from their experiences. As a result, even your toaster will learn whether you like your bread toasted dark or light and will serve it up accordingly.

Other futurists predict that televisions and monitors will be replaced by holography (Negroponte 1995). A hologram is a three-dimensional image made up of all possible views of a scene collected into a single plane of modulated light patterns. Imagine that instead of watching a football game on a television, your children or grand-children will watch a football game by moving the coffee table aside and letting 8-inch-high players run around the living room passing a half-inch football back and forth! Not only will holographic images like this play football on our living room floor; they may also run around our desk organizing our work. They may, in fact, become the next generation of the computer interface. The holographic images will listen to our speech and implement our directions.

Programmers have already developed a technology that allows the user to transcend the barrier of keyboard and screen and become immersed in an interactive experience generated by a computer. This is called virtual reality (VR). As early as 1985, a programmer developed a VR system so he could learn to juggle. With virtual goggles over his eyes and virtual gloves on his hands, both connected to the computer, the programmer picked up the virtual balls and practiced juggling. The programmer created a new artificial world in which the balls moved downward in slow motion, altering physics to suit his needs. This allowed him more time to react accurately; indeed, each of his tosses and catches needed to be accurate because the computer responded to the force and release angle of each throw. The better the programmer juggled, the faster he had the virtual balls move until the speed matched that of reality. Eventually, the programmer removed the virtual equipment and began juggling real balls. Today,

The Times Are Changing

WHAT THEY WERE SAYING . . .

Teacher's Conference, 1703: Students today can't prepare bark to calculate their problems. They depend on their slates, which are more expensive. What will they do when the slate is dropped and it breaks? They will be unable to write!

Principal's Association, 1815: Students today depend on paper too much. They don't know how to write on a slate without getting chalk dust all over themselves. They can't clean a slate properly. What will they do when they run out of paper?

National Association of Teachers, 1907: Students today depend too much on ink. They don't know how to use a pen knife to sharpen a pencil. Pen and ink will never replace the pencil.

Federal Teachers, 1950: Ballpoint pens will be the ruin of education in our country. Students use these devices and then throw them away. The American values of thrift and frugality are being discarded. Businesses and banks will never allow such expensive luxuries.

From the collection of Father Stanley Bezuska, reported in Thornburg (1992).

WHAT THEY ARE SAYING . . .

2008: Physical education cannot be learned from the Internet! What about physical activity?

one can visit Epcot to see many VR-based sport technologies including VR bicycles and VR rafting, with less expensive versions suitable for use in the home.

Other technologies hitting the scene today include white boards, response systems, distance learning systems, biometric identification devices, and movement tracking systems. Maybe you're thinking, "What does technology have to do with my classroom? These ideas would be too difficult and expensive to incorporate." Yet educators of every generation have learned to cope with new technologies. In the 19th century, teachers were given the chalkboard. Like many new things, it was at first rejected by teachers as being too difficult to use. After all, in 1850 classes contained students in several different grades, and teachers had little use for a board on which to write an assignment or lesson for all to see. It wasn't until schools began to divide students by grade level that the chalkboard became an important device. Tomorrow, you may teach your students through distance learning, take roll using biometric devices, and teach orienteering with a global positioning system (GPS). We must be aware of the technological advances that are occurring and consider their role in a quality physical education program.

Our Changing Society

In the late 1800s, society moved from an agrarian model to an industrial model. At that time, everything reflected the industrial model, including the schools. Indeed, students were moved in an assembly-line fashion from period 1 to period 2 without any attempt to pull the information together. During the late 1900s, our industrialized society developed into an information-based society, and now, with the impact of the Internet and wireless devices, we are moving into a communication-based society. During the industrial age, we moved from the farm to the assembly line; in the information age, we moved from the assembly line to the office; during the communication age, we will go back home to work. These developments in our society have changed the way we live and work; however, our schools—with their assembly-line approach—have essentially remained in the industrial age.

We must move all aspects of education, including physical education, into the communication age. The amount of information available is doubling every year; and information experts predict

that between the years 2010 and 2020, information will double every *70 days*. With currently available communication systems, this information can circle the globe almost instantaneously. This increasing information base will change the work we perform as well. Our students will hold several different jobs during their lifetimes. They will need to learn new and more demanding skills in order to work in globally competitive industries. These jobs will require more white-collar workers as technologies replace many blue-collar jobs. Businesses will need to create and implement on-the-job training strategies that will develop highly skilled workers who continuously upgrade their skills and retrain in response to new markets and technologies.

Concerned about the lack of significant change in schools, the Department of Labor's Secretary's Commission on Achieving Necessary Skills (SCANS) in 1991 identified five competencies that businesses expected from students graduating from high school. In 2000, this list was updated to address the continuing changes in society:

Effective workers can productively use

- resources—they know how to allocate time, money, materials, space, and staff;
- interpersonal skills—they can work on teams, teach others, serve customers, lead, negotiate, and work well with people from culturally diverse backgrounds;
- information—they can acquire and evaluate data, organize and maintain files, interpret and communicate, and use computers to process information;
- systems—they understand social, organization, and technological systems; they can monitor and correct performance; and they can design or improve systems; and
- technology—they can select equipment and tools, apply technology to specific tasks, and maintain and troubleshoot equipment.

Competent workers in the high-performance workplace need

- basic skills—reading, writing, arithmetic and mathematics, speaking, and listening;
- thinking skills—the ability to learn, reason, think creatively, make decisions, and solve problems; and
- personal qualities—individual responsibility, self-esteem and self-management, sociability, and integrity.

These competencies are needed in our changing society, and each will continue to have an impact on the selection of educational standards for students and teachers. Physical educators as well must take these competencies into consideration as they design physical education curricula.

Interpersonal skills may be the most important of the competencies when you consider that 36% of all job listings explicitly mention *teamwork* as a requirement for the job (Thornburg, 2002) (figure 1.2). Interpersonal skills and personal qualities are significant attributes in view of our increasingly multicultural society. In such a society, beliefs differ dramatically and there are conflicting norms of behavior. It becomes increasingly important that teachers familiarize themselves with the norms of the minority cultures represented by their student population. This allows the educator to model appropriate behavior and interpersonal skills based on the differing perspectives of their students. It also provides the teacher with insight regarding the different learning styles of the students.

When schools fail to teach interpersonal skills, businesses must assume the responsibility. When businesses want upper-level managers to work more efficiently together, they sometimes put the managers through physical challenges like an Outward Bound experience to promote team building. During these experiences, participants must work together in groups, organize and allocate resources, use information, and analyze complex interrelationships in order to be successful with the physical challenge—much like what is done in high-quality physical education programs today.

Our society also is seeing an increase in violence, including child and spouse abuse, gang-related incidents, drive-by shootings, and neighborhood riots. One third of all male students have reported carrying a weapon, and America has the highest murder rate in the world (Harrison, Blakemore, and Buck 2001). At school, incidents of bullying, violence, and harassment are often daily events. We can easily see a greater need to learn to work better together. Yet ironically, competition in our society is encouraged more than cooperation. Physical educators can help reverse this trend by including cooperative activities as well as competitive activities in our lessons.

Our Changing Health Issues

The current life expectancy in the United States is 77 years. However, the number of individuals living past 100 is increasing weekly, and futurists predict that we will see individuals living past 120

Figure 1.2 Activities that foster teamwork help students develop their interpersonal skills.

years. In 2003, the Human Genome Project (HGP) was completed. This 13-year project, coordinated by the U.S. Department of Energy and the National Institutes of Health, identified all of the approximately 20,000 to 25,000 genes in the human DNA and determined the sequences of the three billion chemical base pairs that make up human DNA. The follow-up analysis will continue for many years and will have a dramatic impact on molecular medicine and the quality of health care.

In addition, we are seeing evidence (Staff Writer 2002) of the development of ultrathin "micromachines" that are small enough to travel in the blood vessels of the human body and do repair work. Current prototypes use motors that are thinner than a human hair with gears even smaller. But improvement in health care does not tell the entire story when we examine the quality of life during the 21st century.

The cost of addressing health issues is taking its toll on the American economy. According to the National Coalition on Health Care (2006), health care costs reached $1.9 trillion in 2004 and are expected to reach 2.9 trillion in 2009. These statistics bring to light several questions related to health care advances:

Who should benefit from improvements in health care?

What is the responsibility of the individual for his health in terms of both prevention and intervention?

Should individuals who exhibit positive health behaviors have priority for improved medical care?

Heart disease kills more than 900,000 people annually (American Heart Association 2006). Although cardiovascular disease primarily affects the elderly, 5% of all heart attacks occur in individuals less than 40 years of age and 34% occur in individuals less than 75. Cardiovascular disease is also a significant contributor to physical disability, dramatically affecting the lives of many survivors. The economic cost of cardiovascular disease in 2006 was estimated at $403.1 billion (American Heart Association 2006). However, the American Heart Association noted that lifestyle choices, including smoking, alcohol abuse, poor nutrition, and physical inactivity, are the leading causes of cardiovascular disease. Heart disease caused by these lifestyle choices can be prevented.

Adolescents and children are also at risk from poor lifestyle choices. A report prepared in 2004 by the Division of Population Surveys, Office of Applied Studies, noted that 7.9% of American people aged 12 or older were current illicit drug users, 50.3% were current drinkers of alcohol, and 29.2% were current tobacco smokers. The percentage of young people who are overweight has more than tripled since 1980. Among U.S. children and teens aged 6 to 19, 16% are overweight (Hedley, Ogden, Johnson, et al. 2004). Approximately 60% of obese children ages 5 to 10 years have at least one cardiovascular disease risk factor, such as elevated total cholesterol, triglycerides, insulin, or blood pressure, and 25% have two or more risk factors (Freedman, Khan, Dietz, et al. 2001). It has been noted that children and adolescents who are overweight by the age of 8 are 80% more likely to become overweight or obese adults. The recommendations for lowering cholesterol level and body fat include a healthier diet and more exercise—again lifestyle choices.

On July 11, 1996, the U.S. Department of Health and Human Services (USDHSS) produced a report titled *Physical Activity and Health: A Report of the Surgeon General*. The report concluded that regular physical activity directly relates to improved health benefits and that there is a direct link between physical activity and physical fitness. The report recommended that moderate amounts of physical activity be performed on most days of the week. The report noted that by following this simple guideline, one can reduce the risk of death from coronary heart disease, hypertension, colon and ovarian cancer, and non-insulin-dependent diabetes along with the symptoms of anxiety and depression.

The National Association for Sport and Physical Education (2004b) recommends that school-age youth participate daily in 60 minutes or more of moderate to vigorous physical activity that is developmentally appropriate, is enjoyable, and involves a variety of activities. The current United Kingdom guidelines also recommend an hour of exercise; however, Professor Lars Bo Anderson (Norwegian School of Sports Sciences in Oslo) has challenged that amount, stressing a need for 90 minutes of daily exercise (BBC News 2006). Regardless, only about half of young people in the United States aged 12 to 21 years regularly participate in vigorous activity (USDHSS 1996).

In response to these issues, the U.S. Department of Health and Human Services developed *Healthy People 2010: Understanding and Improving Health* (2000). This document, comprising 467 objectives in 28 focus areas, represents our national systematic approach to health improvement. The objectives (see figure 1.3) promote the prevention of disease by increasing positive health practices. In addition, on June 20, 2002, President George W. Bush announced the *Healthier U.S. Initiative*, which is based on four principles of healthy living:

1. Be physically active every day.
2. Eat a nutritious diet.
3. Get prevention screenings.
4. Make healthy choices.

This initiative focuses attention on the importance of daily physical activity and, of equal importance, the risks associated with inactivity. Health-related initiatives will continue to evolve. To access up-to-date information, go to www.pesoftware.com/Middle/Resources.html.

As well-intentioned as *Healthy People 2010* and the *Healthier U.S. Initiative* may be, the responsibility for a healthy lifestyle still rests with the individual. Schools can help by becoming model health systems that provide smoke-free environments, healthy food, wellness centers for staff and community, counseling and other psychological services, opportunities for relaxation, and health services, alongside health education and physical education for all students. Seek to understand how the positive and negative changes in health and health care will affect your students' lives; then design physical education programs that will specifically meet their needs.

Our Changing Education System

The educational world is also changing; and often the physical educator, busy with coaching or other after-school duties, is not involved in or knowledgeable about these changes. More disturbing

---

Healthy People 2010 Physical Activity and Fitness Objectives

- Increase the proportion of adolescents who engage in moderate physical activity for at least 30 minutes 5 or more of the previous 7 days.
- Increase the proportion of adolescents who engage in vigorous physical activity that promotes cardiorespiratory fitness 3 or more days per week for 20 or more minutes per occasion.
- Increase the proportion of children and adolescents who view television 2 or fewer hours per day.
- Increase the proportion of trips made by walking.
- Increase the proportion of the nation's public and private schools that require daily physical education for all students.
- Increase the proportion of trips made by bicycling.
- Increase the proportion of adolescents who participate in daily physical education.
- Increase the proportion of adolescents who spend at least 50% of school physical education class time being physically active.
- Increase the proportion of the nation's public and private schools that provide access to their physical activity spaces and facilities for all persons outside of normal school hours (i.e., before and after the school day, on weekends, and during summer and other vacations).
- Increase the proportion of middle, junior high, and senior high schools that provide comprehensive school health education to prevent health problems in the following areas: unintentional injury, violence, suicide, tobacco use and addiction, alcohol or other drug use, unintended pregnancy, HIV/AIDS and STD infection, unhealthy dietary patterns, inadequate physical activity, and environmental health.

Figure 1.3 Your physical education department can play a role in meeting these objectives.

U.S. Department of Health and Human Services. *Healthy people 2010: Understanding and improving health.* Washington, DC: U.S. Department of Health and Human Services, Government Printing Office, 2000.

is the frequent exclusion of physical educators from professional development opportunities afforded to their colleagues in other subject areas because of misconceptions regarding physical education. Some physical educators meet only with other physical educators on the basis of the assumption that their in-service programs should directly relate only to physical education. Worse yet, physical educators may attend a staff-wide in-service but not see its relevance to physical education.

The time has come for us to see ourselves as an integral part of the education community. Join committees. Attend seemingly unrelated in-services, and apply the information you gather to your physical education program. Seek opportunities to learn from your colleagues in other subject areas and educate your colleagues and administrators about physical education. But, most important, stay abreast of educational trends.

From the *Elementary and Secondary Education Act* in 1964 to *Goals 2000: Educate America Act* to the *No Child Left Behind* legislation, federal policy has had a significant impact on America's schools. However, we continue to lag behind many other industrialized nations. The *No Child Left Behind* act focuses on four principles: strong accountability for results; greater flexibility for states, school districts, and schools in the use of federal funds; more choices for parents of children from disadvantaged backgrounds; and an emphasis on teaching methods that have been demonstrated to work. Although the name of the legislation and the president behind it will change, we can expect to see educational reform that focuses on these principles along with the following:

- Greater emphasis on addressing world-class standards
- Instruction that takes into account brain-based research related to student learning
- Interdisciplinary instruction
- Community-based learning and community service
- Professional development for teachers
- Students who are healthy and fit
- Increased high school graduation rates
- Students who are prepared to work in a global economy
- Increased use of technology in schools
- Real-life learning experiences using cooperative learning, constructivism, and problem-based learning

- Students who have equal access to instruction and information
- More curriculum that promotes lifelong learning
- Instruction that emphasizes active learning, where students learn by doing
- Greater emphasis on *learning how to learn*

Educational reform initiatives will continue to evolve. To access up-to-date information, go to www.pesoftware.com/Middle/Resources.html.

The rapidly changing world has forced even the most reluctant of us into the role of lifelong learners; thus, schools must become communities of learners in which students and teachers alike must learn, think, and create to stay abreast of current topics. Teachers in this setting become facilitators of learning rather than distributors of knowledge.

But keeping abreast of new ideas is not enough. You must also educate yourself about possible changes in the near future. Some educational futurists are discussing classrooms that will be accessible to children, adolescents, and adults 24 hours a day. This access may be via the Internet, cable television, or satellite dish, or it may be gained the old-fashioned way—by attending on-site classes. Today, the largest growing segment of education is the home school. When you consider the potential of the Internet, you can readily see the possibility of students spending at least part of their school day learning from home. Schools may become organized around clusters of ages and grades that provide students, when they do arrive at school, with cross-age and cross-grade tutoring and mentoring. Ironically, as physical educators begin to use student textbooks, futurists are predicting that we will see fewer and fewer textbooks in school. Replacing this medium will be a variety of software, Internet access, and virtual reality systems.

Our Changing Physical Education Programs

According to a study by Welsh researchers, pupils striving for academic success at school are far more likely to succeed if they take a full and active part in physical education lessons (Blake 2006). The researchers noted that physical education can improve literacy, numeracy, and technology skills. It also helps youngsters to improve their communication, personal, social, and learning skills. But, more than 20 years after the U.S. Congress (1987) passed Resolution 97 encouraging state and local governments and local educational agencies to provide high-quality daily physical education programs for all children in kindergarten through grade 12, and 10 years after the Surgeon General's report (United States Department of Health and Human Services 1996) called for "every effort . . . to encourage schools to require daily physical education in each grade and to promote physical activities that can be enjoyed throughout life" (p. 6), minimal progress has been made.

Only 33 of the 50 U.S. states mandate middle school and junior high school physical education. Only seven states mandate minutes per week for middle and junior high school, with only one of those states (Montana) meeting the national recommendation of 225 or more minutes per week (NASPE 2006a). However, all is not bleak. Forty-seven states along with the District of Columbia have developed state standards for physical education (NASPE 2006a). Eight states have developed or are developing comprehensive assessment for physical education (NASPE 2001b). Forty-three states require that the physical education grade be included in the grade point average. And forty-three states require all who teach middle school or junior high school physical education to be certified or licensed. In addition, the Carol M. White Physical Education Grant is helping to provide the necessary resources to improve physical education programs. These grants are designed to assist students in meeting state standards for physical education and to enable students in grades K–12 to participate in physical activities. Much of the process that we see comes from the involvement of physical educators in the legislative process. NASPE has a new state legislative center (www.naspeinfo.org—under Media and Advocacy menu) where you can monitor bills related to physical education in each of the 50 U.S. states and the District of Columbia.

We also are seeing changes in the perspectives of parents, students, and community members regarding physical education (figure 1.4). Ninety-five percent of parents nationwide said that physical education should be included in the school curriculum for all students in grades K–12. Eighty-five percent of parents and 81% of teachers believe that students should be required to take physical education every day at every grade level, and 92% of teens said that they should receive daily physical education (NASPE 2003).

As we look to the future, the fact that 25% of the states now allow required physical education credits to be earned through online physical education courses (NASPE 2006a) provides us with a glimpse of what physical education may look like. In the *Shape of the Nation Report* (2006a), NASPE and AHA recommended the following improvements:

1. Quality physical education is provided to all students as an integral part of K–12 education.

Railroads: A Lesson for Change

In the late 19th century, the railroad magnates believed that the purpose of their organizations was to move freight and passengers by rail. In brief, they viewed themselves as being in the railroad business, the rail freight business, and the rail passenger business. In the early part of the 20th century, mass-produced automobiles and trucks, an improved highway system, and, later, airplanes caused the railroads considerable trouble. In fact, competition from these sources, combined with other leadership failures, drove many rails into bankruptcy. If, as numerous management theorists contend, the leaders of the railroad industry had conceptualized the purpose of their business differently—if they had thought of their enterprise as the freight transportation business, for example—the results for railroads might have been quite different. If railroaders had thought of themselves as being in the transportation business, they would have viewed trucks and airplanes as new technologies for their business rather than as competition. They would have viewed an improved highway system as a subsidy (just as they viewed free land in the 19th century as a legitimate subsidy) and would have lobbied for improved highways rather than lobbying against them.

—*Phil Schlechty*

Reprinted, by permission from California School Leadership Academy, 1991, *Thinking/meaning-centered curriculum module* (Sacramento, CA: California School Leadership Academy).

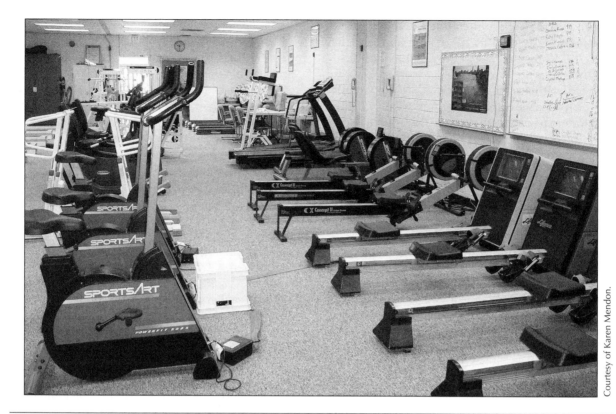

Courtesy of Karen Mendon.

Figure 1.4 Fitness centers inside schools can be used for physical education during the school day and by the community in the evenings.

2. Physical education is delivered by certified and licensed physical education teachers.

3. Adequate time is provided for physical education at every grade, K–12.

4. All states develop standards for student learning in physical education that reflect the national standards.

5. All states set minimum standards for student achievement in physical education.

6. Successfully meeting minimum standards in physical education is a requirement for high school graduation.

7. Other courses and activities that include physical activity are not substituted for instructional physical education.

8. Physical activity is incorporated into the school day, in addition to physical education, through school recess, physical activity breaks, physical activity clubs, and special events.

9. Parents monitor and support their children's physical education progress and regular participation in physical activity.

10. Communities provide and promote the use of safe, well-maintained, local sidewalks, bike paths, trails, and recreation facilities.

Physical educators need to stay abreast of the current recommendations from the National Association for Sport and Physical Education as well as other national and state agencies. We need to proactively take advantage of existing technology, such as computer software, the Internet, heart monitors, video analysis, and other devices. Finally, we need to contemplate future physical education trends so we can prepare ourselves and our students for the world in which they will live and be physically active.

Summary

In this chapter we have examined changes in technology, society, health, education, and physical education. We must continue to grow and change for the better, or our physical education programs will surely suffer the same fate as the

19th-century railroad industry. Some programs are already being challenged by decreases in the time allocated to physical education and by specialists from the fitness and recreation industries who are attempting to replace physical educators. We are currently at a crossroads, and the direction that we take now will determine the future of our profession. Now is the time for us to reevaluate our existence and our future as physical educators. We must look beyond our fear of change and accept the challenges that await us. *Teaching Middle School Physical Education, Third Edition,* provides a vision, along with the skills and techniques necessary to bring about these changes. So, let us start our journey. . . .

Reform Efforts in the Middle School

- Accomplished physical education teachers use their knowledge of students to make every student feel important. They communicate through a humane, sensitive approach that each child, regardless of ability, can succeed and will benefit from a physically active, healthy lifestyle.

  — National Board for Professional Teaching Standards

Early adolescence is a time of discovery, when young people have significantly greater capacity for complex thinking. They are more able to be out in the world, to participate in a wider universe of activities. They are better equipped to make important decisions affecting themselves and others, but their lack of experience leaves them vulnerable. They are better able to fend for themselves, yet they are caught up almost daily in a vortex of new risks.

Anthony W. Jackson and Gayle A. Davis, Turning Points 2000, p. 7

You only have to spend a small amount of time in a middle school to realize that middle school students are diverse. Throughout my years as a middle school teacher, I was constantly amazed by the heterogeneous mix of young adolescents. Each new class brought students as tall as I was who seemed mature and others who were half their peers' size, awkward, and immature. I saw fear in the eyes of some, extreme confidence in the eyes of others. Many of the students had already mastered the skills I planned to teach, whereas others weren't ready for the challenges. Indeed, middle school students are in transition from childhood to young adulthood—some closer to childhood and others closer to adulthood. This difficult transition makes most middle school students very self-absorbed and sometimes confused or depressed.

Does your physical education program meet the needs of this diverse group of students? Can you assess your current situation and determine the course you wish to pursue? In this chapter, I describe the characteristics of middle school students, explain the history and purpose of middle schools in the United States, summarize the characteristics of quality middle schools, and set a course for reforming the middle school program at your school.

Characteristics of Middle School Students

What most differentiates middle school students from other age groups is their wide range of intellectual, physical, psychological, social, and ethical developmental levels. In appendix A, I provide a detailed listing of common characteristics of this age group. Remember, however, that each middle school student has her own set of capabilities and needs.

Middle school students are not miniature adults. The learning and playing opportunities you provide these students should reflect their developmental levels. Learning activities must be active—not passive. Make physical education more meaningful by connecting the activities you select to real-life experiences of adolescents. Certainly, middle school is the appropriate time to begin explaining the *why* behind everything that we do in physical education. These youngsters are moving from concrete to abstract thinking and are capable of considering different viewpoints and drawing their own conclusions. Physical activities that promote social interaction and provide many varied opportunities for hands-on learning are most appropriate for young adolescents.

The Boston Middle School Leadership Initiative provides middle school students with social and physical challenges in situations relevant to their own lives. Through hands-on activities, students learn leadership, social, and cooperative skills (figure 2.1). The introduction to the program, held at the students' school, teaches the principles of leadership. The second part of the program, held on Thompson Island (an island in Boston Harbor that has a training facility for Outward Bound), involves students in activities of varying degrees of physical challenge. During the students' first visit, they participate in group activities designed to build self-confidence and trust in others. Common activities include figuring out how to pass each member of a group through a web of rope without touching the rope and walking the

Figure 2.1   Hands-on group activities are designed to build self-confidence, prosocial skills, and trust in others.

length of a balance beam suspended a few feet off the ground. During the second visit, students must experience the risks of leadership and stretch the limits of their courage when teachers ask them to climb a rope ladder, walk a cable 50 feet above ground, and ride a harness down a zipline from a platform to the ground. In the final phase of the Leadership Initiative, students rock climb at a nearby quarry. Throughout the exercises, students learn to help and support one another.

Because of the many changes that middle school students experience, they tend to doubt themselves, often relying on peer approval for their identities. Yet these same students are also looking for a significant adult in their lives. They want someone they can talk to who will validate their feelings of confusion and frustration about the changes they undergo—someone to help them deal with their tension. This significant adult may be a parent, a relative, or a teacher. If students are unable to deal with the tension associated with the changes they are experiencing, they are at risk of dropping out of school. Therefore, we must design middle schools—including physical education programs—to specifically meet these students' capabilities and needs.

History of Middle Schools in America

Many of us began our teaching careers in junior high schools, and some of you may still be in a junior high setting. Over the past 30 years, however, most junior highs have converted to the middle school model. Interestingly, the movement to provide a separate instructional setting for young adolescents dates back to 1913, when the National Committee on Economy of Time in Education (George, Stevenson, Thomason, and Beane 1992) first discussed a separate junior division of secondary education (seventh through ninth grades).

This junior division led to the creation of many 3-year junior high schools across the United States. The purpose of this division was to meet the unique needs of young adolescents by focusing on learning skills while emphasizing guidance, exploration, independence, and responsibility. The junior high experience was supposed to provide students with a transition between elementary school and high school. You may recognize these reasons as the same ones given for the move from junior high schools to middle schools.

Unfortunately, over time, many junior high schools became more and more like little high schools. The elusive goals of junior high education included flexible scheduling, interdisciplinary instruction, moderate class size, blocks-of-time instruction, and teachers prepared for and devoted to teaching young adolescents using new instructional strategies. The difficulty in attaining these goals led educators to issue a new call for the replacement of junior high schools with middle schools. By 1965, educators across the country were advocating schools that included fifth through eighth or sixth through eighth grades in order to achieve the 50-year-old goals of meeting the needs of young adolescents. Educators believed that without the ninth graders, these new schools could finally address the original reasons for establishing the junior high school model.

One of the first major documents to report on middle schools was the Association for Supervision and Curriculum Development's (ASCD) *The Middle School We Need* (1975). This publication emphasized the developmental characteristics of young adolescents and the need to respond appropriately to those characteristics. Unfortunately, the educational aims of middle school did not, in themselves, produce the necessary impetus for change. Instead, a decrease in the number of high school students and an increase in births primarily motivated administrators and boards of education to move ninth graders into high schools and sixth graders into middle schools.

By the late 1980s, states such as California were publishing their own educational agendas for middle school education in documents like *Caught in the Middle: Educational Reform for Young Adolescents in California Public Schools* (California Department of Education 1987). Several years later, the Carnegie Council on Adolescent Development published its vision of middle school education in *Turning Points: Preparing American Youth for the 21st Century* (Carnegie Council on Adolescent Development 1989). As more and more educators encountered positive experiences with the middle school concept, the total number of junior high schools (seventh through ninth grades) declined by approximately 53%, while the number of middle schools (fifth or sixth through eighth grades) increased by more than 200% between 1970 and 1990 (George et al. 1992).

During the 1990s, the move from junior high schools to middle schools, at least in name, continued. But as with the junior high movement, middle schools started to grow in number of students, and safety-related issues such as violence, gangs, and drugs became a new stimulus for change. Transitions into and out of middle school also remained an issue. In fact, some districts are now creating ninth grade schools to deal with overcrowding and transition. The documents of the 1980s have been updated with the publication in California of *Taking Center Stage* (California Department of Education 2008) and *Turning Points 2000* (Jackson and Davis 2000).

Quality Middle School Programs Today

Successful middle schools today provide students with strong academic programs that have personal meaning to them as well as the necessary health care, nutrition, counseling, and guidance services that help these students concentrate on their academic goals. Certainly, students who are sick, hungry, confused, or depressed cannot function well in school. Programs such as Healthy Start in California, which addresses the whole child by placing comprehensive support services at or near schools, are effective at keeping students in school because they meet the physical, psychological, social, and emotional needs of the students and their families. Drawing on the community's assessment of its needs and resources, Healthy Start programs are able to reduce the fragmentation and cost of service delivery through interagency collaboration.

Turning Points: Preparing American Youth for the 21st Century (Carnegie Council on Adolescent Development 1989) described a 15-year-old who has graduated from a quality middle school program as an "intellectually reflective person, a person en route to a lifetime of meaningful work, a good citizen, a caring and ethical individual, and a healthy person." The report focused on eight characteristics to define quality middle school programs. Using these eight characteristics as a blueprint for middle school reform, the Carnegie Council adopted a number of middle schools from across the United States, donating money to implement their vision. Educators involved in these schools noticed improvements in the knowledge, attitudes, and behavior of their students.

As *Turning Points 2000* (Jackson and Davis 2000) summarized the reform efforts, "If we have learned anything over the past ten years, it is that gains in student achievement and other positive outcomes for students require comprehensive implementation of reforms over an extended period of time. Moreover, a comprehensive reform is difficult work, fraught with unanticipated barriers, to say nothing of organized resistance. Nevertheless, there is mounting evidence that when educators stay the course of comprehensive reform, student outcomes do improve" (p. 16).

As part of the continuing evolution of middle schools, *Turning Points 2000* (Jackson and Davis 2000) focused on seven characteristics of quality middle school programs (figure 2.2). Throughout the rest of this book you will see various references to the concepts embedded in these seven characteristics. For now, let's look at a few key points to better understand these characteristics and the role that you and other physical educators can play in the middle school reform efforts.

Physical education needs to be viewed by all as part of the core curriculum. Therefore, it is crucial that you have identified physical education content standards (characteristic 1). These

standards must set the bar high to prepare your students to become healthy and active adults in the 21st century. By focusing on a few key content standards from kindergarten through high school, you can expect students to master those skills and knowledge, which in turn will have a significant impact on their lives.

Over the last decade, society has held educators accountable for student achievement and for documenting that achievement (characteristic 2). Physical educators must also be accountable for student achievement and its documentation. Not only will you have proof that learning has occurred, but you will also have proof that physical education is an equal partner with the other disciplines, putting physical educators on the same level of professionalism and accountability as other educators. Chapter 8 presents detailed information on developing and providing high-quality student assessment in physical education.

Characteristic 2 reinforces the need for high performance while focusing on the celebration of diversity. This characteristic addresses the elimination of tracking and the promotion of success for all students as another key element in quality middle schools. Yet historically, many physical educators have grouped students by ability. Teaching heterogeneous classes certainly can be more challenging than working with homogeneous groups; but by offering a variety of developmentally appropriate activities and by using a variety of instructional strategies, you can accommodate and promote successful experiences for all your students. For example, through cooperative learning strategies, you can better meet the social needs of middle school students, which is essential to their success in school (figure 2.3).

To create a school environment in which all of the desired characteristics can flourish, *Turning Points 2000* (Jackson and Davis 2000) insisted that both the teachers and principal be specifically prepared to work with and take responsibility for the education of students in fifth, sixth, seventh, and eighth grades (characteristic 3). Together, teachers and administrators must address the content areas of the core curriculum using a variety of instructional strategies and materials, emphasizing active learning, and keeping in mind the developmental characteristics of young adolescents. To be prepared to work with middle school students and take responsibility for their physical education, you are encouraged to apply for National Board Certification from the National Board for Professional Teaching Standards to demonstrate your expertise as a physical educator. Throughout this

Seven Characteristics of Quality Middle Schools

1. *Teach a curriculum grounded in rigorous public academic standards for what students should know and be able to do, relevant to the concerns for adolescents, and based on how students learn best.* Considerations of both excellence and equity should guide every decision regarding what will be taught. Curriculum should be based on content standards and organized around concepts and principles. A mix of assessment methods should allow students to demonstrate what they know and what they can do.

2. *Use instructional methods designed to prepare all students to achieve higher standards and become lifelong learners.* To be effective, instruction should mesh with three other aspects of teaching and learning: the standards and the resulting curriculum outlining what students should learn; the assessments students will use to demonstrate their knowledge and skills; and the needs, interests, and learning styles of the students themselves. Classes should include students of diverse needs, achievement levels, interests, and learning styles, and instruction should be differentiated to take advantage of the diversity, not ignore it.

3. *Staff middle grades schools with teachers who are expert at teaching young adolescents, and engage teachers in ongoing, targeted professional development opportunities.* Schools should hire staff specifically trained for the middle grades and should provide mentors and "induction" to teachers new to the profession or the school. Schools should also engage teachers in ongoing professional development—driven by results, based on standards, and embedded in their daily work—that yields improvements in student learning. A facilitator, either full- or part-time, should coordinate professional development opportunities.

4. *Organize relationships for learning to create a climate of intellectual development and a caring community of shared educational purpose.* Large schools should be divided into smaller learning communities, with teams of teachers and students as the underlying organizational structure. To ensure strong teams, schools must pay attention to the nature and quality of interactions among teacher and student team members, ensuring that teams continually concentrate their efforts on achieving high standards for both teaching and learning. Schools should also attend to critical elements affecting team success, such as team size, composition, time for planning, and continuity.

5. *Govern democratically, through direct or representative participation by all school staff members, the adults who know the students best.* All decisions should focus relentlessly on attaining the goal of success for every student and should be based on data drawn from various sources. Schools should be proactive, not reactive, in their efforts to ensure every student's success, using a "living" school improvement plan to direct actions in both the short and the long term.

6. *Provide a safe and healthy school environment as part of improving academic performance and developing caring and ethical citizens.* Healthy lifestyles and academic success are tightly interwoven—improvement in one leads to improvement in the other, both directly and indirectly. Positive intergroup relations are essential to a safe and healthy school. Middle grades schools, in partnership with the community, should support physical and mental health and fitness by providing a safe, caring, and healthy environment, health education, and access to health services.

7. *Involve parents and communities in supporting student learning and healthy development.* Schools and families must collaborate to establish continuity (e.g., similarly high expectations) and communication between home and school; to monitor and support students' schoolwork and academic progress; to create opportunities outside the school for safe, engaging exploration; and to improve the school itself through parent and community involvement on site. Schools and communities should forge connections to provide needed services to students, offer career exploration opportunities, expand learning beyond regular school hours and outside school walls, and advocate for the school improvements critical to ensuring success for every student.

Figure 2.2 Focusing on these seven characteristics will help in your own reform efforts.

Figure 2.3 The cooperative learning strategies used during coeducational intramurals can help meet the social needs of middle school students.

History of the National Board for Professional Teaching Standards

The National Board for Professional Teaching Standards was created in 1987 after the Carnegie Forum on Education and the Economy's Task Force on Teaching as a Profession released *A Nation Prepared: Teachers for the 21st Century* (May 16, 1986).

The report followed the landmark report, *A Nation at Risk: The Imperative for Educational Reform* (1983), developed by the President's Commission on Excellence in Education. *A Nation at Risk* set off alarms across the country with statements like "If an unfriendly foreign power had attempted to impose on America the mediocre educational performance that exists today, we might well have viewed it as an act of war." Educators, parents, business executives, and legislators awakened to the economic and social consequences of an education system failing to keep pace with a changing American and global society.

The Carnegie task force report, *A Nation Prepared,* offered solutions: "The key to success lies in creating a profession equal to the task—a profession of well-educated teachers prepared to assume new powers and responsibilities to redesign schools for the future." The task force urged the teaching profession to set the standards and certify teachers who meet those standards and called for the formation of the National Board for Professional Teaching Standards.

The members of the task force outlined a plan designed to retain, reward, and advance accomplished teachers through a system of advanced certification. The National Board for Professional Teaching Standards was created from the framework of these ideas. Many of the task force members remain involved in the continuing evolution of the National Board today.

The National Board's mission is to advance the quality of teaching and learning by

- maintaining high and rigorous standards for what accomplished teachers should know and be able to do,
- providing a national voluntary system certifying teachers who meet these standards, and
- advocating related education reforms to integrate National Board Certification in American education and to capitalize on the expertise of National Board Certified Teachers.

The National Board concentrates education reform efforts on the heart of education—the teacher. They believe that the single most important action the nation can take to improve schools and student learning is to strengthen teaching. As their founding chair Governor James B. Hun, Jr., of North Carolina succinctly states, "Improved student learning depends on one thing to start with—a quality teacher."

Quality Physical Education + Interdisciplinary Involvement = Support

Over the past several years, we have been upgrading our content and delivery systems. We are always looking for some ways to improve. We aren't afraid to risk anything new. The things that seem to work we keep; the ones that don't, we drop. Nothing is sacred except for the overarching philosophy that physical education is an academic subject worthy of the same respect and accountability as other subject areas. We lobby hard and often that physical education belongs in the academic core. We constantly seek equity with our teaching peers in all phases of the education process. We are on school and district committees. We invite department chairs from other subjects to visit us and discuss our commonalities. We show that physical education can support what is going on in other subjects on the campus. In short, we demonstrate through our daily work that physical education is an integral part of the total education of students and that to think otherwise is a disservice to the students and community we serve.

At a faculty meeting, the administration presented a new teaming model for the school. It was based on a four-subject interdisciplinary team: English, history, mathematics, and science. When the time came for questions and comments, the English department chair asked, "Where is physical education?" The administration responded, "It can't be done with physical education." The mathematics department chair stood up and said, "Without physical education, the mathematics department will not participate." The administration gave us 1 year to develop a way to include physical education on the teams. We did.

—*Physical educator Bill Silva, Kenilworth Junior High, Petaluma, California*

book, I share the National Board for Professional Teaching Standards for physical education with you along with the application process. You will find standards, related to each chapter's topic, listed at the beginning of chapters 2 to 13.

You also must establish your physical education program as an integral component of the total middle school program (characteristic 4). Specifically, as middle schools organize themselves as schools-within-schools or schools in houses, you must become involved (see Bill Silva's statement about the benefits above). In many schools the mathematics, science, language arts, history, and social science teachers share a group of students as well as a common planning period. The teachers may, in fact, instruct these same students throughout their middle school years in order to build significant teacher–student relationships. If at your school physical education is part of this kind of organization, you know how it facilitates teachers' working together on thematic or interdisciplinary units of instruction. If your school excludes physical education from interdisciplinary teaming, speak up. You and your colleagues can easily and meaningfully include physical education across the curriculum. Participating on an interdisciplinary team demonstrates that you are an equal partner in the school and gives you the opportunity to explain the physical, social, and intellectual benefits of physical education to your colleagues. In addition, many times there is the added benefit of smaller class sizes, because

every teacher on the team must have the same class size.

Being proactive (characteristic 5) is addressed in more detail in chapter 3, because it is such an important practice for physical educators. Physical educators must speak out on the importance of physical education and physical activity as they relate to the quality of life. Physical educators must constantly remind school staff members, as well as community members, that educational decisions made now will affect students throughout their lives.

The Carnegie Council's sixth characteristic suggests that schools can improve the academic performance of young adolescents through fostering health and fitness. Many Japanese and Chinese schools weave health and fitness into the class schedule. After every 40- to 50-minute academic period, students play vigorously during a recess. After formal classes have concluded for the day, all students spend an hour or more at school in extracurricular activities (Stevenson and Stigler 1992).

In the past, most sport programs in the United States were reserved for the gifted athlete. In today's middle schools, however, we are designing intramural programs to include all students and physical activity programs that include students and their families (characteristic 7). In so doing, we are extending the physical education instructional period into a practical application session, thereby extending the time allocated to physical

Middle School After-School Sport Program: What's the Goal?

I didn't think that I played good enough to participate in after-school sports. Then my teacher told us that the 3-on-3 basketball games were for everybody. She also said that we were going to play basketball after school because that was what we were learning in physical education. Now, I am having a lot of fun playing with my friends, and I'm even getting better at basketball.

—Anonymous, eighth grade student

education and, in turn, increasing student success in and out of physical education class (see "Middle School After-School Sport Program"). Perhaps even more important, parents and community members are becoming key players in the education of their youth instead of remaining on the sidelines.

Quality Middle School Physical Education

Now let's turn our attention specifically to our area of interest—quality middle school physical education programs. You must educate your colleagues about the many major benefits of physical activity that your school should make available to your students. Your colleagues need to know that physical activity

- enhances the function of the central nervous system by promoting healthier neuron function;

- aids cognitive development in many areas (learning strategies; decision making; problem solving; and acquiring, retrieving, and integrating information);

- improves aerobic fitness, muscle endurance, muscle power, and muscle strength;

- promotes a more positive attitude toward physical activity, leading to a more active lifestyle during unscheduled leisure time;

- enhances self-concept and self-esteem as indicated by increased self-confidence, assertiveness, emotional stability, independence, and self-control;

- creates a major force in the socializing of individuals during late childhood and adolescence; and

- deters mental illness and alleviates mental stress.

In light of these benefits, physical education needs a more revered place in the school curriculum! More and more, educators in all subject areas are viewing physical education as an essential element in any school curriculum designed to educate the whole person. Indeed, today's quality middle school physical education program aligns itself with the characteristics of quality middle schools in general. Beyond this, you must address the specific needs of *your* middle school students.

Use figure 2.4 to assess the effectiveness of your middle school physical education program. The tool addresses the key areas of a high-quality middle school physical education program: physical environment, psychological environment, curriculum, instruction, instructional materials, assessment, and professional development. Take some time now to complete this assessment (figure 2.4), because you will use the results when creating a vision for the future.

By assessing your middle school physical education program, you take the first step toward improving it. By becoming aware of the documents that can support your position for quality physical education (see figure 2.5) and sharing these documents with others, you invite all stakeholders to travel the path toward quality physical education with you. This book is aligned with all of the documents listed in figure 2.5.

Planning for Success

Now that you have determined where you are, you can decide where you want to go. What do you want your physical education program to look like? How many changes can you address in the next 3 years? Using the information we've discussed so far and the results of your assessment, write a scenario (see "Creating a Vision" on page 25 for an example) describing your program 3 years from today.

Self-Assessment: Middle School Physical Education Program

Place a mark next to those items that currently occur in your program. For all items not marked, read the chapter noted in parentheses.

Physical Environment (chapter 4)

_____ Class size in physical education is commensurate with other class sizes.

_____ The instructional period is of sufficient length for meaningful learning to occur.

_____ Policies are in place for handling accidents, uniform, fees, medical excuses, and other pertinent issues.

_____ Facilities are available to implement the curriculum.

_____ Equipment is available to implement the curriculum.

_____ Modified equipment is available to meet the needs of all students.

_____ Dressing areas, lockers, and showers are large enough to accommodate all students.

_____ All facilities are kept clean and free of safety hazards.

_____ All facilities are accessible to physically handicapped students.

_____ Adequate storage space is provided.

_____ Equipment and facilities are cared for by teachers and students.

_____ All facilities and equipment are checked regularly for safety hazards.

_____ Hazards are reported and corrected in a timely manner.

_____ Safety rules are clearly communicated to students.

_____ First-aid kits are readily available.

_____ Clothing appropriate for the activity is required.

_____ Showering is encouraged.

_____ Student medical information is shared with teachers.

_____ School system has a written policy for providing emergency first aid and reporting accidents to parents and school authorities.

Psychological Environment (chapter 5)

_____ Teachers know the names of all their students.

_____ A nonthreatening atmosphere is provided for all students.

_____ Emphasis is placed on cooperative activities.

_____ Everyone (e.g., administrators, teachers, students) demonstrates respect for others.

_____ All students are encouraged to succeed.

_____ All students (e.g., boys, girls, ethnic groups, disabilities, skill levels) are treated equitably.

_____ Positive social interaction skills are taught and practiced.

_____ Positive class management routines and discipline are employed.

Curriculum (chapters 6-7)

_____ There is a written curriculum.

_____ The curriculum includes a variety of movement forms: rhythms, dance, games, stunts and tumbling, individual and dual sports, team sports, aquatics, combatives, and outdoor education.

(continued)

Figure 2.4 Assessment of the effectiveness of your middle school physical education program.

From *Teaching Middle School Physical Education: A Standards-Based Approach for Grades 5–8, Third Edition,* by Bonnie S. Mohnsen, 2008, Champaign, IL: Human Kinetics.

(continued)

_____ All students participate in the physical education curriculum; there are no waivers or substitutes.

_____ The physical education curriculum is shared with other teachers, administrators, and the community.

_____ The curriculum provides for integration opportunities with other subject areas.

_____ Instructional activities are selected to help each student achieve standards.

_____ Instructional activities support a scope and sequence within each unit of instruction.

_____ Instructional activities support a scope and sequence from year to year.

_____ The curriculum provides a variety of fitness activities that enable all students to meet individual health-related fitness.

Instruction (chapters 9-11)

_____ Opportunities to learn are provided for all (e.g., boys, girls, exceptional students).

_____ A variety of teaching styles and strategies based on student need and content are used.

_____ Effective teaching behaviors that provide for maximum student learning are used by all teachers.

_____ Motivational techniques are used by all teachers.

_____ Instructional activities align with brain-based research.

_____ Motor learning principles are followed in each lesson.

_____ All lessons are planned ahead of time.

_____ All lessons are written and kept on file.

Instructional Materials (chapter 12)

_____ Resources are available to purchase necessary instructional material.

_____ Instructional materials are selected to help each student achieve standards.

_____ Instructional materials are evaluated before purchase.

Assessment (chapter 8)

_____ Grading is based on student achievement related to the grade level and unit standards.

_____ Specific criteria exist with which to grade student performance.

_____ Students understand how they will be evaluated.

_____ Evaluation of student performance is criterion based.

_____ The physical education grade is used when calculating the overall school grade point average (GPA).

_____ Recognized assessment and evaluation instruments (where available) are used to assess students.

Professional Development (chapter 13)

_____ All physical education teachers are certified in physical education.

_____ All teachers pursue professional growth.

_____ All teachers are members of professional physical education organizations.

_____ All teachers subscribe to professional physical education and educational journals.

Figure 2.4   _(continued)_

From _Teaching Middle School Physical Education: A Standards-Based Approach for Grades 5–8, Third Edition,_ by Bonnie S. Mohnsen, 2008, Champaign, IL: Human Kinetics.

Do You Have?

Comprehensive Physical Education

Centers for Disease Control and Prevention. 2002. *School health index for physical activity, healthy eating, and a tobacco-free lifestyle: A self-assessment and planning guide—middle school/high school version.* Atlanta: Author. Available at: www.cdc.gov/HealthyYouth/SHI/.

United States Department of Health and Human Services. 1996. *Physical activity and health: A report of the Surgeon General.* Atlanta: Author.

United States Department of Health and Human Services. 2000. *Healthy people 2010: Understanding and improving health.* Washington, DC: Author.

Physical Education Curriculum

Centers for Disease Control and Prevention. 2006. *Physical education curriculum analysis tool.* Atlanta: Author. Available at: www.cdc.gov/HealthyYouth/PECAT/index.htm.

Mohnsen, B.S., ed. 2003. *Concepts and principles of physical education: What every student needs to know.* Reston, VA: National Association for Sport and Physical Education.

National Association for Sport and Physical Education. 2004. *Moving into the future: National standards for physical education* (2nd ed.). Reston, VA: Author.

Physical Education Instruction

National Association for Sport and Physical Education. 2001a. *Appropriate practices for middle school physical education.* Reston, VA: Author.

National Board for Professional Teaching Standards. 1999. *Physical education standards.* Arlington, VA: Author.

Physical Education Environment

National Association for Sport and Physical Education. 2004a. *Opportunity to learn standards for middle school physical education.* Reston, VA: Author.

Physical Education Assessment

National Association for Sport and Physical Education. (in press). *Student assessment project.* Reston, VA: Author.

Figure 2.5 Numerous publications from the Centers for Disease Control and Prevention and the National Association for Sport and Physical Education can assist you with your vision and with bringing your program up to date. These publications belong in every physical educator's personal library.

Adapted from CDC, 2002, *School health index for physical activity, healthy eating, and tobacco-free lifestyle: A self-assessment and planning guide—middle school/high school version* (Atlanta, GA: CDC).

Creating a Vision

Although the scenarios must be individualized, the following scenario provided by Kranz Middle School in El Monte, California, provides you with one example. Remember, each program is at a different place on the change continuum, so your scenario or vision may look quite different.

Three years from today, our physical education department will have a fitness laboratory that uses technology and a Project Adventure component in the curriculum that addresses the social needs of our students. The fitness lab will be fully equipped with exercise bikes, treadmills, steppers, rowers, and computers. Testing equipment such as heart monitors, electronic blood pressure devices, and electronic skinfold calipers will be available to all students. The Project Adventure component will include a low ropes course along with cooperative initiatives that stress social development. Project Adventure will become a unit of instruction for our seventh graders as well as an ongoing program for our eighth graders.

Stanley Davis (1987), author of *Future Perfect,* says that we need to skip from the present to a date well into the future, design a system that makes sense for that time, and then make changes now that work toward the long-term view. Thus, using the scenario you just created, begin to think about the steps you will take this year, next year, and the third year, so that by the end of the third year, your program will be on target.

Summary

To align your physical education program with the current philosophy of middle school reform, be aware of both the specific needs of middle school students and the characteristics of quality middle school programs. In the preceding chapter, we discussed the general changes in society, technology, business, and education that you must consider as you design your middle school physical education program. In this chapter, I took this concept one step further to include monitoring the changes in the middle school reform efforts so that your middle school physical education program progresses in alignment with the other middle school changes designed to meet the needs of students.

The next 15 chapters will help you clarify your vision of a quality middle school program by presenting additional information and a blueprint for the future. I also give you information on the knowledge and skills necessary to implement your program. Keep the answers that you have written in response to the questions posed in this chapter and revisit them after completing the book. Then modify your plan based on your newfound knowledge, thereby creating your own personal blueprint for change.

The Role of Physical Education in Middle School

> - Accomplished physical education teachers create advocates for physical education by providing opportunities for family involvement and the involvement of the broader community in the physical education program.
> - Accomplished physical education teachers do not work in isolation but function as members of a larger learning community.
> - Accomplished physical education teachers recognize the multiple benefits of a physically active lifestyle and promote purposeful daily activities for all students that will encourage them to become lifelong adherents of physical activity.
>
> —*National Board for Professional Teaching Standards*

The middle school principal began his back-to-school address to the teachers and classified staff at his new middle school. As he explained his vision, he announced that all departments would be treated equally and receive the same amount of funding for instructional materials. In addition, the class size for all classes would be the same. The physical education teachers looked at one another, smiled, and realized that they finally had attained the respect and endorsement of a school administrator.

Does the story at the beginning of the chapter sound like a dream? It could happen at your school if you remember that physical education does not take place in a vacuum. It is part of a larger world, both within the middle school reform effort and the middle school site where it exists.

NASPE's (2001b) position paper "Physical Education Is Critical to a Complete Education" can provide you with support for this idea. However, to fully achieve the dream, you need to help your colleagues and community see the physical education program as part of the overall school setting. As a physical educator, you need to be seen as an equal partner in the educational program, you need equitable class size and instructional time, and you need sufficient funding to provide a quality program for your students. To receive what you want and need, however, you must first understand what the profession of physical education owes to the community at large.

Participation in various school-wide programs can earn your physical education department the respect and endorsement it needs from administrators, other teachers, community members, parents, and students—those individuals who already have a vested interest and a say in what goes on in the school. Gaining the respect of these stakeholders can give you the access to get what you want and need. In this chapter, I address the role of physical education in the school setting, specifically related to the instructional program, the extracurricular program, and the coordinated school health program. I also give you ideas on how to create positive public relations for your physical education program.

Physical Education and the Instructional Setting

Physical education is one of several subject areas required in most middle school curricula. As described in the opening scenario, schools should include physical education in all school-wide reform projects, allocating it equitable instructional time, class size, funding, and interdisciplinary participation. In other words, your school should allow and encourage students to apply knowledge and skills they have gained in physical education across the curriculum. For example, some middle schools require students to complete an eighth grade research project. If teachers expect the eighth graders to take an interdisciplinary approach, the project should certainly include both the physical educator and physical education content.

Instructional Time

Students in middle school should take physical education every semester or quarter for a total time equal to that allocated to other subject areas. If students spend 50 minutes a day in language arts, science, mathematics, and social science, then they should spend 50 minutes a day in physical education. If the school is on block scheduling and students spend 100 minutes every other day in language arts, science, mathematics, and social science, then they should spend 100 minutes every other day in physical education. The National Association for Sport and Physical Education (NASPE 2001b) recommends at the very least 225 minutes of physical education per week for middle school youngsters. For those of you who need assistance in transitioning from a more traditional schedule to a block schedule, NASPE (2000) has developed a resource paper titled *Teaching Physical Education in a Block Schedule*.

A few states mandate the number of minutes students must spend in physical education or the number of courses they must take. Work with your state professional association to change state laws that mandate time spent on physical education, and take advantage of any trend in your state that gives local school sites more freedom to make decisions regarding curriculum and instruction. As your school becomes involved with local (or site-based) decision making, seek to increase the instructional time allocated to physical education beyond state mandates.

Class Size

The class size and the grouping of students in physical education classes should also be the

Key Barrier

The large class sizes with which physical educators are often confronted are a key barrier to the implementation of quality physical education. Physical education should have the same class size as other subjects. Quality physical education must cover a great deal of content, and physical educators cannot do their jobs effectively or have enough time to work with individual students if classes are overcrowded. As one physical educator has said, "Try teaching English with 72 kids!"

Centers for Disease Control and Prevention (CDC), 2000a.

same as for other content areas. In some schools, counselors or computers first assign students to other classes and then put them into whatever physical education class fits into their schedules. As a result, you may have fifth, sixth, seventh, and eighth graders in the same class or very small classes in the morning and larger classes in the afternoon. A better approach is to determine the number of courses for each grade level that will be offered in physical education and then spread the students equally throughout the day. Next, determine the current class size average for physical education, add 5% to 10% to that number, and make that the limit for the number of students in each class. Now, it's up to the counselor or computer program to assign students to their appropriate classes, staying within the class size limits.

Funding

Even the best physical education teachers in the world will find it difficult to keep their students active during most of a physical education class if they don't have adequate amounts of equipment and supplies. Many schools don't have enough equipment or supplies to keep all students active during physical education class; consequently, many students waste valuable time standing in line and watching others play while they wait for a turn. Support for the purchase of physical education equipment and supplies has been identified as an urgent priority for many U.S. schools (CDC 2000a).

Does your school spend the same amount of money on instructional materials for physical education as it does for other subject areas? The instructional materials for physical education include equipment and supplies as well as the same types of instructional materials used in other classes, such as textbooks and technology. Equitable funding is evidence that your school and the community at large see physical education as a full member of the instructional program.

Gaining Administrative Support

Physical educators must gain the respect of their administrators and of colleagues in other subject areas before physical education will be fully included in the instructional setting. Butler and Mergardt (1994) found that gaining administrative support was the most significant factor in creating and maintaining effective physical education programs. Naturally, in schools in which administrators and colleagues respect the physical educators

and physical education, the physical education program benefits from more equitable treatment. Goodlad (1984) noted a direct correlation between the amount of time allotted for a subject and the respect it received from society as a whole, and specifically from the educational community.

What's the secret to gaining administrative support? First, provide a quality physical education program, including an articulated K–12 curriculum, such as the one I outline in this book, taught by qualified physical education teachers in a supportive environment. Continually assess your program and assess the performances of the students and yourself. In turn, use the data from these assessments to improve the instructional program.

The second step is to share your program and its benefits with the school's stakeholders. You must educate them about the positive influence of physical education on the lives of the students. The public relations information at the end of this chapter will assist you with promoting your program and educating your stakeholders.

The third step is to represent your department's interests on school-wide committees. Representation on funding, professional development, restructuring, and curriculum committees ensures equal access to resources and—sometimes more important—to information. By actively participating on decision-making committees as a representative of the physical education department and your students, you can play a vital role in restructuring your school. For example, if allocation of instructional time is a committee issue, work to ensure that the committee allocates equal instructional time to physical education. Otherwise, you'll have no guarantees and little chance for equitable treatment.

An example of the importance of representation on school-wide committees involves a curriculum committee that was given the task of creating additional electives for the eighth graders. In this school, a physical educator on the committee was able to add physical education electives to the required eighth grade physical education class. One elective class the committee added to this program was the junior physical education teacher class, in which the students learned the basics of teaching physical education. Part of the requirement for the class was to assist with teaching a fifth or sixth grade class—of great value to everyone involved. Would this committee have thought to include electives related to physical education without a physical educator's input? Probably not.

Other key committees at your school may require physical education representation as well. But how do you find time and energy for them all? Distribute the responsibility of serving on committees throughout the department, thereby reducing the pressure and time commitment on any one person as well as educating all staff members about the issues facing the school.

Committee membership provides two other benefits you may not have considered: You can more easily get to know your colleagues in other subject areas, and you can increase the opportunities you have to educate other stakeholders about the positive attributes of your physical education program. Likewise, your colleagues and other stakeholders will have a better chance to know and respect you personally. In short, committee membership creates valuable networking opportunities that may lead to more equitable treatment of your physical education program.

Physical Education and the Extracurricular Setting

Extracurricular physical activity programs provide students with additional opportunities to be active and to use the skills taught in physical education class. They also offer important social and psychological benefits: Studies have shown that participation in extracurricular activities is negatively associated with tobacco and other drug use and positively associated with good conduct, academic achievement, and staying in school (Wechsler, Devereaux, Davis, and Collins 2000). Moreover, middle school students need unstructured time for physical activity.

Physical education has a significant role to play in the offering of these extracurricular activities. All high-quality after-school programs aim to provide positive relationships with adults and peers, enriching activities, and a safe place. These programs can take the form of after-school physical education, fitness–wellness programs, fundraising events, and intramurals.

After-School Physical Education

The purpose of an after-school physical education program is to provide boys and girls with an opportunity to practice motor skills, increase their physical activity levels, extend their physical education learning, and participate in a wide variety of new and exciting activities. After-school programs should be open and inviting to all youngsters regardless of motor skill ability and fitness levels (see figure 3.1). Such programs provide a safe place where new skills are learned and familiar skills are reinforced, practiced, and used in fun games and recreational activities.

In many ways the after-school physical education program and the in-school physical education program are similar. However, the after-school

Figure 3.1   Boys and girls, including students with disabilities, benefit from well-organized after-school physical education programs.

program is less formal and provides more opportunities for student-initiated and -directed activities. The goals of an after-school physical education program are to

- reinforce the concepts addressed during in-school physical education;

- provide assistance to the youngster who needs extra help with motor skills;

- build on a youngster's natural desire to move and play (i.e., create intramural and recreational opportunities);

- help students develop a positive attitude;

- improve students' social skills when working with others in physical activities;

- provide opportunities for participation in activities of choice (i.e., orienteering); and

- provide students with moderate amounts of exercise as recommended by the 1996 Surgeon General's report on physical activity (United States Department of Health and Human Services 1996) (see "Examples of Moderate Activity").

Fitness–Wellness Programs

The International Consensus Conference on Physical Activity Guidelines for Adolescents established two main guidelines (Sallis and Patrick 1994). First, all adolescents should be physically active daily or nearly every day. Second, adolescents should engage in three or more sessions per week of activities that last 20 minutes or more and that require moderate to vigorous levels of exertion. The National Association for Sport and Physical Education (2004b) extended this recommendation, stating that school-age youth should participate daily in 60 minutes or more of moderate to vigorous physical activity.

Your physical education program can promote fitness and wellness by creating a fitness center to be available for student (and perhaps school and community) use during noninstructional times. Students who would like to improve their cardiorespiratory endurance, muscular strength and endurance, muscular flexibility, or body composition can drop in to the fitness center during recess, during lunch, or before or after school and participate in a personal fitness program that they have developed in consultation with a physical educator. Some schools include a fee for the fitness–wellness program as part of an optional student fee that allows participants to attend school events and, in this case, the fitness center. Other schools charge a "per-use" fee for participation in this optional activity or provide it free to their students. Those schools that provide the program free of charge often use money secured from grants to support the program or funds from jog-a-thons or other fundraisers.

Fundraising Events

Physical education is in a unique position when it comes to fundraising. Today, walk- and jog-a-thons are popular fundraising activities. Or you may think of something more creative and unusual. In any case, your physical education department can promote physical activity while simultaneously raising funds for your community, school, or physical education program. Although you'll probably use or adapt activities you've taught during physical education for the fundraising events, the actual events must take place outside the school day so they do not interfere with the instructional program.

The Jump Rope for Heart Program was developed by the American Heart Association and the American Alliance for Health, Physical Education,

Examples of Moderate Activity

Walking (3.5 mph)

Bicycling (<10 mph)

Dancing

Hiking

Golf (walking and carrying clubs)

Weightlifting (light workout)

Stretching

Examples of Vigorous Activity

Running or jogging (5 mph)

Bicycling (>10 mph)

Swimming

Aerobics

Walking (4.5 mph)

Weightlifting (vigorous)

Recreation and Dance. It is a fitness education and fundraising activity as well as a positive physical activity. Most physical educators hold this event as the culmination of a fitness or jump rope unit. Members of six-person jump teams take turns jumping during a 3-hour period. Students solicit pledges for the amount of time they jump. See figure 3.2.

Figure 3.2   A fundraising activity that requires students to engage in physical activity has multiple rewards.

The goals of the Jump Rope for Heart Program are to

1. promote the lifelong benefits of regular exercise;

2. provide an opportunity for students and parents to work together toward a common goal;

3. reinforce the merits of the physical education curriculum as well as provide visibility for physical education professionals in the community;

4. encourage teamwork by involving participants in working toward a common goal and instilling school pride; and

5. emphasize to participants and the community the importance of a healthy lifestyle, including proper nutrition, not smoking, and controlling high blood pressure.

For more information about the Jump Rope for Heart Program, contact your local American Heart Association or call 800-242-8721.

School wide jog-a-thons (or walk-a-thons, bike-a-thons, and the like) have the potential of bringing financial resources to the school and physical education program. Unlike candy drives, this form of fundraising both promotes positive health habits and develops in students a sense of responsibility for their school. Students secure and collect pledges for a certain monetary amount for each mile completed or a flat rate for participation in the event. The school or its physical education program receives the money.

Intramural Programs

The purpose of the physical education program is to provide instruction to all students so that they can accomplish the standards that I describe in part II of this book. Intramural programs, on the other hand, give students opportunities to apply the motor skills they have learned in physical education. Historically, many extracurricular programs were exclusive, involving only the most elite athletes on campus, but a model intramural program is open to and enjoyable for students with average and below-average motor skill ability as well.

The ideal intramural program is run by an intramural council composed of students and a faculty advisor. The council sets the schedule, decides on the activities and form of competition, and assigns the personnel—equipment monitors, officials, scorekeepers, and organizers who provide students with information as to where and when they are playing. You must train these individuals to understand and implement their roles in order to create and deliver an effective intramural program.

As you start to set up an intramural program, you will need to make decisions regarding the level of competition. We often think that competition promotes sportspersonship. Yet competition often impedes both learning and performance and can encourage negative attitudes and behaviors. Individuals who have had extended experiences in organized sport as children tend to display poorer attitudes of sportspersonship than nonparticipants (Seefeldt and Vogel 1986). The sport participants tend to be more concerned with winning, whereas the nonparticipants are more concerned with fair play. Looking for an alternative? Rotate players from team to team during a game so that no group can actually be declared the winner. A good intramural program emphasizes participation instead of competition. If you have ever watched students play a sport during recess or lunch, you've seen that they are, indeed, more interested in participation than competition. Students rarely maintain win–loss records beyond the immediate game, and yet back they come the very next day to play again. Ultimately, greater participation equals greater benefits.

Intramural programs can function at various times throughout the school day. In some schools, students have a free period during which they can select from alternative recreational activities, including intramural activities. Other schools create time during advisory periods, recess, nutrition, or lunch, or before or after school, including evenings, to ensure opportunities for all students to participate. When setting up the intramural program, however, make sure it does not compete with physical education for the use of facilities and equipment.

Select activities for the intramural program based on the activities you have recently covered in physical education, or you could use novel activities (see "Intramural Activities" for a few examples). Note, however, that the physical education program drives the intramural program—not vice versa. For example, because the instructional units should be different for each grade level in a middle school, it makes sense to have separate intramural programs for the various grade levels as well. The National Association for Sport and Physical Education and the Middle and Secondary School Physical Education Council have developed a position paper titled "Co-Curricular Physical Activity and Sport Programs for Middle School Students." This document can assist you with the development of your intramural program.

Physical Education and the Coordinated School Health Program

Another way physical education can contribute to and receive support from the school community is through a coordinated school health program. A coordinated school health program is a comprehensive approach to addressing the health status of students so that they are better prepared to learn in school. Such a program is not intended to simply tell students what constitutes a healthy lifestyle but rather to encourage them to practice good health habits that will remain with them for a lifetime. This approach consists of eight components designed to reinforce and build on one another. See www.cdc.gov/healthyyouth/cshp/.

The eight components of a coordinated school health program are

1. physical education,
2. health education,
3. health services,
4. nutrition services,
5. counseling and psychological services,
6. family and community involvement,
7. safe and healthy school environment, and
8. health promotion for staff.

Physical Education

A high-quality physical education program contributes to the coordinated school health system by providing a planned, sequential curriculum that includes cognitive content and learning experiences in a variety of activities and seeks to improve students' fitness levels. A fitness center is an exciting and effective approach to fitness. It becomes a source of pride for the middle school with a strong focus on coordinated school health.

Intramural Activities

Yo-yo events	Juggling events	Orienteering
Flying disc golf	Modified soccer	Modified team handball
Over-the-line	Pickleball	Rock or wall climbing
2-on-2 basketball	Miniature golf	In-line skating

Furthermore, it demonstrates your interest in the health of your students.

Physical educators at some schools also promote the inclusion of one or more fitness breaks during the school day in which the classroom teacher conducts stretching exercises, takes the class for a walk or jog, or provides some other type of aerobic activity. The physical educators in these schools serve as a resource for the types of activities that the classroom teacher may wish to provide. Periods of increased aerobic activity increase blood and oxygen flow to the brain and have proven to be effective in increasing student learning (Caine and Caine 1990, 1997a, 1997b; Jensen 1994, 1998).

Health Education

A quality health education program is similar to a quality physical education program in the sense that a sequential K–12 curriculum addressing the physical, mental, emotional, and social dimensions of health is taught by qualified health education teachers. A health education curriculum committee establishes both local exit standards and grade-level standards. Many states and districts begin their work by studying the National Health Education Standards (available at www.aahperd.org/aahe/pdf_files/standards.pdf). The committee also uses information from the following content areas to set the standards: community health, consumer health, environmental health, family life, mental and emotional health, injury prevention and safety, nutrition, personal health, prevention and control of disease, and substance use and abuse.

The purpose of health education is to motivate and help students to maintain and improve their health, prevent disease, and reduce health-related risk behaviors. Health education allows students to develop and demonstrate increasingly sophisticated health-related knowledge, attitudes, skills, and practices. Students in the middle grades should receive 2 to 3 hours a week of instruction in health education (Kane 1993). Health education appears to be more effective when health topics are taught as a separate discipline rather than covered in the context of other subject areas (Kane 1993; Lohrmann and Wooley 1998). Research indicates that students' gains in health knowledge and skills last into adulthood (Dusenbury and Falco 1995).

As in physical education and other subject areas, health education instructors must

- establish a positive learning environment;

- use instructional strategies designed to personalize information and engage students;

- provide age-appropriate and developmentally appropriate learning strategies, teaching methods, and materials;

- incorporate instructional strategies and materials that are culturally inclusive; and

- set up performance-based assessments.

It is also crucial that health education programs promote active student learning, critical thinking, and the development of positive health behaviors. Physical educators and health educators also must work together to integrate concepts addressed in both curricula.

Health Services

In addition to providing information regarding health issues, a coordinated school health system should provide students with health service support. Every school has established procedures for dealing with emergency health care situations as well as health care maintenance. Schools maintain accurate records of student immunizations and routine screenings. However, the health service program should take these services one step further and seek to identify health problems that may interfere with student learning. Health service workers should regularly administer hearing, dental, vision, height and weight, posture, and blood pressure screening.

One recent innovation that has proven to be highly effective in reducing student health problems is the school-based health clinic or school-linked health center. These health clinics or centers are located on or near school campuses and are often cosponsored by county health departments or private foundations. The advantages of health clinics include convenience for students, ease of follow-up care, integration with health education activities, and opportunities to address health issues specific to the adolescent population.

Nutrition Services

Nutrition services should reinforce the information students receive in the health education and physical education classes. Cafeterias can become the laboratory for students to see good eating habits in practice (figure 3.3). The school cafeteria

Figure 3.3 Students can practice good eating habits in the school cafeteria.

provides students with nutritionally balanced meals that follow the United States Dietary Association guidelines for foods high in fiber and low in fat, sugar, and salt. Certainly, proper nutrition plays an important role in preparing students for maximum learning during the school day.

Even schools that have nutrition-conscious cafeteria staff must contend with the selling of unhealthy foods by outside vendors, in the student store, and in candy- and soda-selling fundraisers. Banning the sale of unhealthy foods on school property and substituting healthy foods and fundraising activities help to improve schoolwide nutrition.

Counseling and Psychological Services

According to the Center for Mental Health Services, 20% of U.S. children and adolescents have a diagnosable mental disorder, and about two-thirds of these children and adolescents do not receive mental health care. Figures from 2005 published by the World Health Organization (WHO) estimated that approximately 877,000 suicides occur annually worldwide with approximately 200,000 of these occurring among individuals 15 to 24 years of age. The counseling and psychological staff promote the mental, emotional, and social health of both students and staff. By working in partnership with teachers, these specialized staff members develop plans for helping students cope with difficult situations through individual and group assessments, interventions, and referrals. Counseling and psychological staff also provide professional development for all teachers on the

warning signs of emotional stress, on staying sensitive to student well-being, and on knowing the appropriate steps to take when students are under emotional stress.

Students learn best in a psychologically safe environment (chapter 5). They need to sense that the school supports their needs not only for academic achievement but also for self-esteem and relationships. Students who have a forum for discussing concerns and a system through which they may receive assistance in making healthy decisions, dealing with depression, coping with crises, and setting goals are more ready to learn. In addition, the counseling and psychological professionals can provide support for students and their families after disasters or violence that occurs at or near the school.

Family and Community Involvement

Often physical educators complain that parents don't support their children's education in physical education class. When we involve family members and other community members in the school's coordinated health program, they will understand our goals and needs better and will be more likely to support the physical education and health programs. Family and community members make excellent guest speakers or volunteers in the physical education program. Invite them to your class to share their experiences, assist with activities, and learn more about your program. In addition, involving parents and other family members in the educational process increases student motivation (Henderson and Berla 1994), thereby presenting both parents and teachers with fewer discipline problems.

Unfortunately, many adults are unable to participate because of work schedules. However, you can include them by assigning homework that requires your students to work with their family or community members to extend the scope and depth of the physical education and coordinated health programs. For example, ask students to calculate target heart rate ranges for their entire family based on each individual's age and resting heart rate. This type of activity not only promotes positive health behaviors in your students but also educates the entire family and community about fitness concepts. You do, however, need to be sensitive to the role of the family as the student's primary caretaker. Understanding different family structures and the differences between various cultural and ethnic groups will ensure that you don't overstep your boundaries when assigning family homework. For example, many students come from nontraditional families (including single-parent families, families with same-sex parents), so be careful not to require the simultaneous participation of both mother and father.

Two other ways to involve others in your physical education program are physical activity nights and health fairs through which you bring students, family members, and community members together for wellness and physical activities at the school. In addition to conducting physical activities, provide learning experiences so that all participants leave the evening with a greater understanding of the concepts related to improving fitness. One alternative to your leading this activity is to have the students lead their parents through the physical activities and learning experiences. When students must do the teaching, they need to assimilate what they have learned well enough to pass it on to someone else—a highly effective teaching approach and assessment tool.

The school and community must work together to ensure a complementary recreation program for students and adults. Research has shown that parent activity levels have a positive effect on the activity levels of their children (Kalakanis, Goldfield, Paluch, and Epstein 2001). In schools without recreational programs, the community recreation department can provide activities for students during appropriate times of the day. Communities and schools also share facilities for the benefit of both programs. For example, fitness courses and swimming pools are often built in park and recreation facilities. These specialized facilities are often unavailable to students in school but provide opportunities for practice in the evenings, on weekends, and during vacations. Assign homework that encourages the use of these community facilities; students can report to the entire class about the benefits.

Community service is a new area in the educational arena. Ask your students to work with younger students in recreation programs, provide exercise breaks for persons who are elderly, or assist at community health fairs. Each of these activities extends students' physical education learning while giving something back to the community.

Safe and Healthy School Environment

Naturally, it is difficult to learn in an environment where fear and unsanitary conditions prevail. A healthy school environment provides students with a clean and safe (physically and psychologically) environment in which to learn. In such schools, maintenance of every area, including the school grounds, parking areas, the playground and its equipment, floors, stairs, classrooms, and physical education facilities, is a priority. Schools with healthy environments keep restrooms, which are especially vulnerable to vandalism, clean and supplied with soap and towels, eliminating graffiti and maintaining doors on individual stalls for student privacy. Such schools check all facilities for asbestos dust, radon, and lead-contaminated water. They adhere to legal regulations regarding lighting, heating, and ventilation.

Health Promotion for Staff

The last area of coordinated school health is health promotion for the staff. A large body of research links teacher stress with burnout. An on-site wellness program attracts qualified employees and enhances productivity and efficiency. It also reduces absenteeism related to stress, obesity, and cardiorespiratory disease. Schools with wellness centers often have a high level of school morale. A frequently unrecognized benefit is that teachers who are involved in fitness programs become models for the students within their care.

Model programs offer classes on weight management, smoking cessation, personal goal setting, aerobic workouts, and strength building. All participants new to the program undergo medical tests, receive appraisals of health and fitness status, set goals, and follow individually prescribed exercise routines. Often, if the school has a student fitness center, the staff uses it during noninstructional times.

Developing a Coordinated School Health System

Section 204 of the Child Nutrition Act Reauthorization of 2004 required that each school district participating in a reimbursable school lunch or breakfast program develop a local wellness policy. Congress placed responsibility of developing a wellness policy at the local level so that the individual needs of each district could be addressed. Policy had to be in place before the 2006–2007 school year. At a minimum, the wellness policies had to include goals for physical activity, nutrition education, and other school-based activities designed to promote student wellness in a manner that the local educational agency determined appropriate. The policies had to include nutrition guidelines for all foods available on campus and provide an assurance that guidelines for school meals were not less restrictive than those set by U.S. Department of Agriculture. The policy also had to include a plan for measuring the implementation of the local wellness policy. Parents, students, school food authority representatives, school board members, school administrators, and the public were required to be involved with the development of these policies. This legislation provided a catalyst for examining each school's coordinated school health system. But it was only a start.

To address the health status of each student, schools and districts need to establish coordinated school health committees composed of physical educators, health educators, school nurses, risk managers, principals, food service personnel, school counselors, custodial staff, and other teachers as well as parents and community members. Then the committee proceeds through the next four steps of institutionalizing a coordinated school health program (figure 3.4).

The committee members begin by creating a vision for the coordinated school health system. Next, they assess the current status of the eight components of coordinated health and set goals for improving each of these areas to realize their vision. The *School Health Index: A Self-Assessment and Planning Guide—Middle School/High School Version* (CDC 2005) will assist with this process. The document consists of eight modules aligned with the eight components of a coordinated school health program. Within the physical education module alone, 20 assessment points cover the learning environment, curriculum, instruction, and assessment. This step provides an opportunity for each group of professionals to learn about and respect the other areas related to school health. Then, the committee develops a 3-year plan for implementing the vision. Finally, the committee begins to implement the 3-year plan. Committee members will need to update and modify their plan as they progress through the implementation stage.

Many strategies can help to raise the awareness level of other faculty and community members to the issues surrounding coordinated school health. Professional development workshops and wellness fairs are two of the most helpful practices. A holistic approach to staff and student health also helps—such as creating a smoke-free workplace, screening for high blood pressure, serving healthy food in the cafeteria, and teaching relaxation techniques for stress reduction. To have a strong coordinated school health system, however, each of the eight components must deliver top-quality service.

Public Relations

A strong public relations program (see sidebar on page 38 for ways to promote physical education) communicates to all stakeholders the quality features of the school's physical education program; its relationship to the instructional program, extracurricular program, and coordinated school health program; and the positive benefits that students receive from physical education. Public relations is more than a one-time announcement or participation in a special activity like National Physical Education Week; instead, it must be an ongoing program to gain support for physical education from the various stakeholders.

Community members are an especially important group in which to instill a strong commitment to the physical education program. School

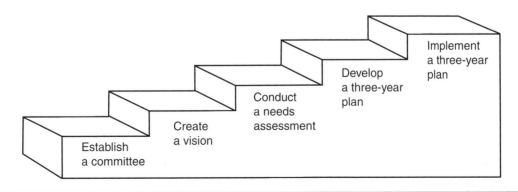

Figure 3.4   A five-step plan for developing a coordinated school health program.

administrators and teachers are often influenced by the community's beliefs, and parents, as part of a community, internalize many of the beliefs held by that community. Historically, the Olympic Games have—at least temporarily—heightened awareness of the efforts of physical education programs. More significantly, society has given more or less respect to physical education programs during times of war when a physically fit military is valued by society. Every day, however, opportunities arise for you to communicate with parents, teachers, business leaders, community members, and legislators about physical education.

Physical educators who put forth quality physical education programs and tell others about it are protecting their programs before any threat against them can occur. Placek's (1983) famous study of physical education teachers showed that many teachers and administrators think of a successful physical education lesson as one in which students are on-task, enjoying themselves, and not presenting discipline problems—in which students are "busy, happy, and good." That study demonstrated the need to refocus physical education on the business at hand—that of educating students through a quality middle school physical education program. Let others know how physical education programs have changed. Share with the community that physical educators no longer "throw out the ball." Let parents know how physical education promotes the health, physical fitness, and psychosocial growth of their children.

To get started, follow these three steps to develop a public relations program. First, determine your message, including information on your current program and your future needs. Second, use a variety of media—print, video, audio, and displays—to present your message. Third, don't give up—no matter what happens or doesn't happen. Keep delivering your message.

To determine and fine-tune your message, start with a public service announcement in your local newspaper. Make your public service announcement specific to your program. Say to your students' parents, "See what your kids are learning in physical education!" For example,

Parents, get involved! The U.S. Surgeon General confirms that physical activity reduces the risk, at all ages, of heart disease, high blood pressure, and diabetes. Active, fit young people also learn better. However, many students don't have access to daily physical education. Parents, get involved!

Crash Course in Public Relations: 10 Ways to Promote Physical Education

1. Create displays of student work for exhibition at special community and school events.

2. Make presentations at school board meetings, including student demonstrations.

3. Visit and write to local state legislators to solicit their support.

4. Describe your program in a physical education newsletter that goes home to parents and out to local businesses and community members.

5. Present adventure-based or other workshops for businesses, parents, and community members.

6. Put on student demonstrations at a local shopping center.

7. Make a fitness fact sheet and send it to community members.

8. Speak at a meeting of a local civic organization about your quality physical education program and its benefits to students.

9. Arrange for messages about quality physical education to be printed on grocery bags.

10. Write short public service announcements for local radio and television stations.

Talk to the physical education teacher and principal in your school. For free information about physical education, call 800-213-7193, extension 410. (NASPE 1999)

There are many ways to promote your physical education program, and NASPE publishes a notebook titled *NASPE Sport and Physical Education Advocacy Kit II* (NASPE 1999), which provides a complete public relations package. In addition, the PE4Life Web site (www.pe4life.com) contains numerous advocacy resources includ-

ing presentations and information on connecting with your legislators. To get you started, "Tips on Communicating With Your Legislators" and a sample letter (figure 3.5) to encourage continuing support for physical education funding are provided. As of the writing of this book, the Carol M. White Physical Education Program provides federal funds to local school districts to initiate and improve physical education in schools. The individual grants range from $100,000 to $500,000, and funds can be used to train teachers and purchase equipment.

452 Glenway Blvd.
Madison, WI 53717

September 10

Dear Senator Smithson:

I am writing to urge you to support the full funding for the _____ _____ grant, which will be included in the _____ _____ bill this year. This bill will promote physical education in schools. It will create a new incentive grant program for local school districts to develop programs that include minimum weekly requirements for physical education, and daily physical education, if possible.

The U.S. Surgeon General has recommended that daily physical education be provided to all students in kindergarten through 12th grade. According to a recent study, the percentage of young people who are overweight has more than tripled since 1980.

Only two states in the United States (Illinois and Massachusetts) require physical education in every grade, K–12, and both of these allow for exemptions. We are doing a disservice to our youth by not providing more and better opportunities in this area. And, as a nation, we are guaranteeing a huge health care bill in the future by not taking action now.

Participation in sports and fitness has many additional benefits. It aids social and emotional development, builds self-esteem, teaches desirable life lessons, and provides healthy outlets for young people's energy. Physical education is an ideal avenue to get kids who are not elite athletes involved in sports and fitness in an appropriate, healthy, and fun way.

I urge you to support this legislation. Now is the time to make a difference in kids' lives through the _____ grant.

Thank you.

Sincerely,

Timothy Dean
Physical Education Department
Jackson Middle School

Figure 3.5 Sample letter to a legislator to promote the funding of physical education.

Tips on Communicating With Your Legislators

Be brief during all communications (written or oral).

Identify yourself as a constituent who lives and does business in the legislator's district.

Explain how the proposed legislation affects your business and why you support or oppose it.

Call instead of writing or e-mailing, because calling is more effective.

Ask to speak directly to the legislator; if the legislator is not available, then speak to the administrative assistant or legislative aide.

Ask what the legislator's position is; if the legislator's position is the same as yours, then express agreement and thanks.

If the position differs, then politely express disappointment and offer some factual information to support your views.

Request that your legislator take a specific action by telling the legislator what you desire.

Keep all communications friendly and respectful.

Visit the legislator's district office to discuss a particular piece of legislation or just to get acquainted.

Adapted from "Contacting Your Legislators—Some Tips on Protocol," by K. Lynch, CAHPERD legislative advocate.

Summary

Imagine every school in the United States with a supportive principal like the one I described at the beginning of this chapter. Make that scenario a reality by aligning your physical education program with the total school environment, including the instructional setting, the extracurricular setting, and the coordinated school health program.

You can earn respect and support in a number of ways. Above all, provide quality physical education for all your students. Beyond this, work with other subject area teachers, administrators, and community members on numerous projects and committees through which you can share and augment your program. Finally, publicize your program through physical education newsletters, public service announcements, and school board presentations.

The Physical Education Environment

- Accomplished teachers of physical education create and sustain a welcoming, safe, and challenging environment in which students engage in and enjoy physical activity.

—*National Board for Professional Teaching Standards*

To learn in physical education, students need access to a quality physical education environment consisting of adequate and safe facilities, equipment, and supplies. Some physical educators are fortunate enough to already work in schools with excellent facilities. For example, Punahou School is a K–12 private school on the island of Oahu in Honolulu, Hawaii (figures 4.1 and 4.2). The physical education facilities include a four-story building, an outdoor swimming pool, a 440-meter track, court space, and all the open field space you could ever want. The building contains teachers' offices; locker rooms; laundry room; trainer's room; storage rooms filled with equipment and supplies; dance, weight training, gymnastics, and wrestling rooms; handball courts; classrooms; student health center; and gymnasium.

Unfortunately, we don't all work under these conditions. Yet many of your colleagues have created better physical education environments for their students under less than ideal circumstances. Although individual teachers can create quality physical education environments, the task

Through fundraising, we have developed our fitness lab using an empty woodshop room. The lab has been painted by the district, carpeted by fundraising, and outfitted with a cardiovascular exercise circuit, a classroom area, and a computer area by grants. The lab is used by the seventh and eighth grade students and is open to the staff and community after school hours.

—*physical educator Karen Mendon, Montebello Intermediate, Montebello, California*

Figure 4.1 Swimming pool at Punahou School.

Figure 4.2   Gymnastics room at Punahou School.

is much easier when all members of the physical education department (also known as the physical education team) work together. In this chapter, I discuss improving your physical education environment as well as successful strategies for organizing your department.

Facilities

The actual need for specific facilities is directly linked to the curriculum (refer to figure 4.3). For example, if the curriculum calls for aquatics, then you need a pool. But be creative in your choices as well. You'll probably think of many standard facilities, but have you ever considered adding a ropes course? A ropes course is a collection of

challenges (or elements) that students, working in small groups, must solve (figure 4.4). These challenges require the group to overcome anxiety and fear and learn to function together under stress to arrive at a solution. For more information on how to build a ropes course and for the different types of challenges, contact Project Adventure, 701 Cabot Street, Beverly, MA 01915; 800-468-8898.

Although most departments have little opportunity to change their facilities except during the construction of a new school or renovation projects, you can expand your facilities by exploring alternative locations, converting other school buildings, and using portable facilities. Alternative locations you should consider include nearby elementary or high schools, community recreation centers, and state parks. Typically, field space,

---

Facilities for a Middle School Program

Hard Surface Area

Basketball/team handball courts with standards

Racket sports courts

Unmarked surface for bowling and skill practice

Volleyball courts with poles and nets

Dirt and Turf Area

Football fields with goal areas

Golf and flying disc golf area

Long jump jump area

Running track (440 yards, or 400 meters)

Shot put and discus area

Soccer fields with goal areas

Softball diamond with 250-foot (76-meter) batting radius

Ultimate fields

Gymnasium or Multipurpose Room

Marked area for bowling (if conducted inside)

Matted area for self-defense, stunt, tumbling, gymnastic, and circus activities

Sound system (music player, speakers, wireless microphone) for dance, stunts, tumbling, or gymnastics

Swimming Pool

Fitness Center

Interactive aerobic equipment (a variety)

Muscular strength and endurance equipment appropriate for middle school students

Computers for data entry

Locker Rooms

Clothes dryer

Hair dryers

Lockers (with built-in locks that can be programmed with five different combinations)

Showers

Washing machine

Classroom

Chairs

Computers

Projection system

Tables

White board

Storage Rooms

Teachers' Offices

Figure 4.3 Suggested facilities based on the sample curriculum presented in this book.

Figure 4.4 Students at Montebello Intermediate School step onto the swinging log suspended 6 inches off the ground. Students must balance themselves so that the entire group remains stable on top of the log.

swimming pools, tennis courts, and gymnasiums are the most prized facilities. Some schools have also initiated in-line skating, hiking, and bicycling programs using trails in local or state parks. Other school agencies have worked effectively with local community governments to build new diamonds, gymnasiums, or pools that are available for school use during the day and for community recreation at night and on the weekends. Physical educators have secured free or low-cost services from businesses such as golf courses, bowling centers, skating rinks, and climbing centers for physical education classes during the school day. These businesses understand that students taught on their facilities are more likely to return with their families to use these facilities during their free time. Be open-minded and creative and see what's available in your area.

Another approach to increasing facilities is to appropriate empty buildings on campus and convert them into physical education facilities. The practice of converting woodshops into fitness labs, as described at the beginning of this chapter, is becoming very popular at many middle schools (see figure 4.5). Likewise, schools have successfully converted unused classrooms into physical education classrooms, dance rooms, or storage rooms. Should you have the opportunity to build new facilities, be sure to include all staff members in the planning.

Can't find what you need anywhere? Bring it in on wheels! An excellent example is the Los Angeles Unified School District summer swimming program, in which portable pools are moved from site to site to bring aquatics to students who otherwise would have limited access to swimming. But portable *pools?* It took an innovative, creative, and determined physical educator to make it happen.

You don't have to wait for new facilities, however, to improve your physical education learning environment. Start today by making your current facilities more attractive. Retire those drab posters and use your bulletin boards to communicate important messages to students. Make the messages and presentations informative, exciting, and relevant to your current physical education content. See the CD-ROM for examples.

Topical themes could include these:

- Back-to-school information
- Student fitness projects
- Athletes with physical challenges
- History of a sport
- Myths about diets
- The Olympics
- Social skills
- Physical fitness testing information

© Karen Mendon.

Figure 4.5 The fitness lab at Montebello Intermediate School is an example of a converted woodshop. It contains numerous cardiorespiratory stations including treadmills, stationary bicycles, steppers, climbers, and rowers.

- Water safety
- Analysis of a skill

Enriched environments promote dendrite growth and increase learning. You can even use student work to help convey your message. If you include any pictures, however, ensure that they represent boys and girls of various ethnicities.

Equipment and Supplies

Typically, we can classify "equipment" as items that cost more than $300 (the exact amount is determined by the local educational agency) and "supplies" as items that cost less than that amount. Often, the administration or local committee allocates funds specifically for equipment or supplies, limiting departments as to the amount they can spend in each category. In this section, we specifically discuss sporting goods from both the equipment and supply categories. We explore other instructional materials, such as textbooks, technological devices, and videos, in chapter 12.

As with facilities, the curriculum defines the need for various pieces of equipment and supplies (see the CD-ROM for equipment packages based on

the sample curriculum presented in this book). If the curriculum calls for a unit on softball, then you need backstops, gloves, softballs, bats, batting helmets, and catcher protective equipment (see figure 4.6). When you are purchasing or receiving donations of equipment and supplies, ensure that they are appropriate for middle school students. For example, sporting goods companies are beginning to produce softer balls, pucks, and projectiles of various sizes that are safer and facilitate more success for middle school students, making them more educationally sound for middle school physical education settings (see figure 4.7). Also, all donated equipment must be in good repair and your school board may need to approve the donation.

Increase the amount of equipment and supplies you have access to by sharing materials with other schools, community recreation programs, and local businesses. Lobby to have your district purchase items that you usually use only once or twice a year, such as golf clubs, unicycles, or gymnastics equipment, to be shared by a number of different schools. This system maximizes the use of materials, frees storage space, and, perhaps most important, frees funds for other materials. However, either the central office administrator or one physical educator needs to take responsibility for organizing and overseeing the program to make

Figure 4.6 Protective equipment must be sized appropriately to be effective.

Figure 4.7 Using softer balls, pucks, and projectiles during an activity makes it safer, and these supplies also help students be more successful in the activity.

sure everyone has a fair chance to use the equipment and to reduce the potential for loss or theft.

Don't forget free materials. Many agencies, such as the United States Tennis Association and the United States Bowling Congress, provide free supplies to schools to promote their sport. Local agencies, such as golf courses, bowling centers, and the American Heart Association, also have free supplies for the asking. Some physical educators have experienced great success writing letters (figure 4.8) to companies such as health clubs or fitness equipment companies and requesting donations of new or used equipment. Explore all of these avenues to augment your supplies and equipment.

Creating a Safe Environment

Providing students with a safe environment in which to learn is your moral and legal responsibility. You certainly don't want your students physically hurt in the process of learning new skills. You have legal obligations as well. In a litigious

society, it becomes the responsibility of professionals, including you and your colleagues, to protect yourselves and your school from being sued.

You are not responsible for student injuries if you have acted as a reasonable, prudent person would have acted during a similar situation. The basis for legal suits against a teacher is almost always negligence—the failure to exercise the care that a reasonable, prudent person would have taken. The law requires four elements to be present in order for negligence to be declared:

1. The teacher must have a responsibility to ensure the safety of the participant; this is implied in the teacher–student relationship.

2. The teacher must have violated this responsibility by either failing to perform a required duty (act of omission) or doing something that he or she should not have done (act of commission).

452 Glenway Blvd.
Culver City, CA 90230

September 10

Holiday Spa
11234 Sepulveda Blvd.
Culver City, CA 90230

To Whom It May Concern:

I am the physical education department chairperson at James Middle School in Culver City. My department is in the process of creating a fitness lab for our students on campus. We envision a room equipped with exercise machines, computers, and fitness testing devices. To make our vision a reality, we are requesting donations of any used equipment that is still in good working order that you may be replacing at this time or in the near future. Specifically, we are interested in treadmills, ergometers, and rowers.

As you are well aware, healthy behaviors are established at a young age. My department and I are eager to teach our students to participate regularly in a fitness program, so that as adults they will participate in health clubs such as yours and lead higher quality lives. We anticipate posting the names of our benefactors on one of the walls of our new fitness center to show our appreciation for their support. We hope that we can include your name in the listing. Thank you for your time, and I look forward to hearing from you soon.

Sincerely,

Timothy Dean
Physical Education Department
James Middle School

Figure 4.8   Sample letter to fitness equipment company requesting donated equipment.

3. An injury must have occurred while the student was under the care of the teacher.

4. The injury must be the result of the teacher's violating the responsibility for the safety of the student.

Students also have a responsibility to exercise care for their own welfare. In fact, courts many times attribute an injury to both parties (teacher and student) and make an award based on comparative negligence. To protect the institution from being sued, however, you must take active steps:

- Provide adequate supervision.
- Anticipate foreseeable risks and warn students of any inherent risks.
- Make sure the activity is suitable for the participants.

- Ensure that the activity takes place in a safe learning environment.

Although it is impossible to completely eliminate the risk of being sued, by following certain procedures you can reduce that risk.

Adequate Supervision

Failure to provide adequate supervision is the most common allegation of negligence (van der Smissen 1990). Adequate supervision includes considering the ratio of teachers to students, the teacher's training, the physical distance between the teacher and the students, and the establishment and implementation of safety rules. You and your department can use the issue of teacher-to-student ratio as you work to lower class size, because large classes can result in claims of inadequate supervision. Typically, courts look at the age, maturity, and skill level of the students before determining the appropriate ratio.

You can reduce the risk of a successful lawsuit against yourself and your school district by following certain supervision principles:

- Always be in the immediate vicinity (within sight and sound) of the students.

- Constantly screen the area for clues that may indicate a potentially dangerous situation.

- Secure an adequate replacement (not a paraprofessional, student teacher, or custodian) before leaving the area.

- Be aware of the health status of each student in your class.

- Provide a safe buffer zone between all play (don't use common boundary lines).

- Carefully match students for any activity involving potential contact.

- Keep all facilities clean and orderly.

- Disinfect all equipment that may expose students to communicable diseases.

- Obtain ongoing training on how to handle emergency situations.

- Create written supervision procedures that designate the responsible teacher (e.g., for the locker room, before class, after class).

- Develop written procedures for what to do if a problem or emergency arises.

- Have access to a phone or other communication device and post emergency phone numbers in a handy location.

- Do not use equipment for purposes other than those for which it was intended.

- Do not alter equipment in any manner.

- Do not allow students to use any equipment before receiving instruction on the safe use of the equipment.

But how do you prove you have adequately supervised your students? Document any injuries in writing, along with standard operating procedures; and make sure that all the physical educators in your department are trained by the American Red Cross in first aid and cardiopulmonary resuscitation and have current certification cards. Staff should also receive training in universal blood precautions. These precautions include infection and control measures that reduce the risk of transmission of blood-borne pathogens through exposure to blood or body fluids. Under the principle of universal precaution, blood and body fluids from all persons should be considered as infected, regardless of the known or supposed status of the person. For physical educators, this means that plastic gloves must always be available and used whenever there is the potential of exposure to blood or other body fluids. Documentation and certification are strong defenses against accusations of negligence pertaining to inadequate supervision and the handling of medical emergencies. For additional information on supervision and safety, read *Principles of Safety in Physical Education and Sport, Second Edition* (Dougherty 2002) and *Liability and Safety in Physical Education and Sport* (Hart and Ritson 2002).

Selection and Conduct of Activities

Another common area for allegation of negligence is the selection and conduct of activities. If you select units of instruction merely according to your own preference, you have little defense against charges of negligence when a student is injured. If you select units of instruction based on the sequence of grade-level standards, however, you can demonstrate that the activities are based on the age, size, physical condition, and ability of the students (figure 4.9). If physical educators in your district develop and implement a curriculum for kindergarten through 12th grade that progressively and appropriately develops skills, then your defense against negligence is even stronger. Refer to chapters 6 and 7 for more information on how to develop a progressive, developmentally appropriate curriculum for your district.

Although a written curriculum can provide a good defense in terms of what physical educators should be teaching, the defense for *how* you provide instruction rests with you, the individual. Daily written lesson plans including suitable activities and safety instruction, documentation of any injuries that occur, and adequate supervision provide you with a more than adequate defense against a lawsuit. Figure 4.10 provides a typical list of questions that are often asked of expert witnesses during litigation. If an injury occurred in your class, what answers might the expert witness give during trial?

Safety Issues

Beyond providing adequate facilities and materials (both equipment and supplies) for your students to use, you must ensure that the facilities

Considerations When Selecting Activities

✔ Are the skills properly sequenced so that all prerequisite skills have been taught before a new skill is introduced?

✔ For strenuous activities, are the students in sufficient condition before the introduction of the skill?

✔ Did you properly demonstrate and explain the skill's technique?

✔ Did you explain the safety rules related to the skill, activity, or game?

✔ Did you warn the students of any inherent risk involved in the skill?

✔ Did you demonstrate and discuss incorrect techniques that might result in injury?

✔ Did you provide proper equipment, including safety equipment, to the students?

✔ Did you provide instruction to students on how to use equipment?

✔ Did you provide a series of developmental drills for practicing the skill?

✔ Did you provide adequate feedback for students regarding their execution of the skill?

Figure 4.9   Keep these questions in mind as you're developing, selecting, and teaching activities.

Typical Questions Asked of Expert Witnesses

✔ Did the activity or drill in progress at the time of the injury have a legitimate educational objective or purpose?

✔ Is the activity or drill inherently dangerous?

✔ Are the participants appropriately grouped or matched?

✔ Is the activity or drill appropriate for the readiness level (i.e., the age, ability, maturity, mentality) of the injured participant?

✔ Did the teacher appropriately warn all the students about the inherent risks of the activity, telling them how to guard against injury as a result of those risks?

✔ Did the teacher provide the participant with appropriate feedback related to proper skill or activity execution so as to prevent injury?

✔ Did the teacher provide correct instruction?

✔ Were all necessary physical skills covered before the student's participation in the activity?

✔ Were all necessary progressions covered so that the participant could master essential simple skills before attempting complex skills?

✔ Did the teacher develop, communicate, and consistently enforce all necessary safety rules?

✔ Did the teacher adequately anticipate the hazards involved in the activity and take the necessary steps to provide reasonably for the participant's safety?

✔ Was the participant properly supervised at the time of the injury?

✔ Did the equipment play a role in the injury sustained by the participant?

✔ Did the facility contribute to the injury because of improper design or condition?

✔ Did the potential likelihood and potential severity of injury outweigh the teacher's reasons for conducting the activity in the way he or she did?

Figure 4.10   Consider what answers an expert witness might give to these questions if an injury were to occur in your class.

Adapted from G.R. Gray, 1995, "Safety tips from the expert witness," *Journal of Physical Education, Recreation and Dance* 66(1): 18-21.

and materials are clean, safe, and used appropriately. Specifically, you must establish, teach, and enforce safety rules. Create safety rules specific to your site; then include rules stating that students must use materials for their intended purpose only and that students must always use safety materials, such as catcher's protective equipment and shin guards for soccer. If an activity has an inherent risk (i.e., the risk of drowning during swimming), inform students of this possibility ahead of time and teach them ways to ensure their personal safety. Document all of this in your lesson plans.

Inspect facilities and materials daily, and document your inspection weekly using a checklist (figure 4.11). After completing the safety inspection, date the checklist and save it as written documentation. You also can instruct students to check for safety hazards before they use the facility or equipment. Report any defects in materials or facilities in writing to the appropriate administrator so that they can be corrected as soon as possible. Keep a copy of such reports for yourself. If the defect is severe enough, don't allow anyone to use the material or facility until the defect is corrected.

Probably the most frustrating situation for physical education staff is leaving a clean facility on Friday only to return to a littered, graffiti-covered, or vandalized facility on Monday. Many schools facing this issue have instituted community watch programs in which neighbors whose properties overlook the school facilities keep an eye on them during the evenings or over the weekends. Other schools have taken an additional step by hiring a custodian or watchperson to live on the school campus and maintain and watch the facilities. Still others use cleanup crews that work early Monday morning before most of the staff and students arrive.

Organizing the Program

Both teachers and students benefit when teachers work together instead of operating independently or at odds with one another. You'll discover that the more your department works as a team, the more you'll be able to accomplish, the more smoothly your program will run, and the more rewarding your work will be. In addition, students will respond more appropriately when they

---

Inspection Checklist

✔ Playground layout has been planned so that there are appropriate traffic patterns.

✔ Signs are posted informing users of any inherent risks involved with using the facility or material.

✔ Area is free of glass, vandalism, trash, gravel, and broken or misplaced equipment.

✔ At least 12 inches (30 centimeters) of sand lies under outdoor equipment.

✔ Top of all concrete footers is below the playing surface.

✔ Poles for volleyball and badminton are secured.

✔ No broken or worn-out parts exist.

✔ No wood is cracked or splintered.

✔ Paint is not rusted or peeling.

✔ Bearings are not worn.

✔ Locking devices are provided for all bolts.

✔ Exposed ends of bolts do not exceed one-half the diameter of the bolt.

✔ There are no open-ended S hooks.

✔ Bolts and nuts are screwed tightly.

✔ All connecting and covering devices are secured.

✔ No sharp edges or points exist.

Figure 4.11 Inspection checklist of middle school facilities and materials. For more information, read the United States Consumer Product Safety Commission's *Public Playground Handbook for Safety* (2005).

perceive consistency from one teacher to another. How can you and your colleagues work better together to support one another as you strive to provide an organized physical education program for your students?

Physical Education Department

The physical education department should be one department, including both male and female physical education teachers, with one teacher acting as chairperson or lead teacher. The chairperson should assume the role of facilitator or leader as opposed to commander or manager. The chairperson should not, as a manager or commander would, focus exclusively on the tasks at hand while ignoring the long-range goal of developing and maintaining a quality physical education program. Instead, such a leader must possess a clear vision of where the department is going and must work with the other physical educators to realize the vision. For more information on leadership, read *The New Leadership Paradigm for Physical Education: What We Need to Lead* (Mohnsen 1999).

One helpful way to work together is for department members to share responsibilities, thereby more efficiently using everyone's time. These managerial functions include organizing equipment for the upcoming instructional units, maintaining facilities, inventorying and ordering new equipment, developing and maintaining emergency plans, laundering and maintaining loaner uniforms, issuing and maintaining the locker system, conducting safety inspections, organizing the public relations campaign, serving on school-wide committees, and completing paperwork required by the school administration. Department members can select the task they would like to perform for the year and then rotate from year to year, so that everyone is aware of all the operational procedures required to run a physical education program. And what about the daily chores, such as locker-room duty, yard duty, checking out loaner clothes, and issuing forgotten locker combinations? Some schools are fortunate enough to have classified personnel who handle many of these responsibilities. If your school is not so lucky, the physical educators in your department should share them equally.

Naturally, department members must share facilities as well. A yearly schedule designating who will have which facility based on the curriculum prevents conflicts during the year. Department members must also work together to maintain programs during special days, including rain, snow, smog, and minimum-schedule days, retaining as much consistency with the regular program as possible. In some schools, all classes must share a common facility on a special day; however, with a little creativity many schools find alternative meeting areas, minimizing disruption of the learning process. Try using multipurpose rooms, classrooms not in use during certain class periods because of teacher preparation time, weight training rooms, locker rooms, libraries, and hallways. If it is not possible to continue with the current instructional unit, then prepare a special-day series of lessons ahead of time. Base this series on a cognitive standard, such as developing a fitness plan, or on a particular set of motor skills, such as dancing; or create any other lesson that you can conduct indoors.

Another way to create a positive working atmosphere relates to the hiring of new people in the department. As members of the department retire or leave for other positions, it is important to bring in new staff members who are qualified and who hold a philosophy of physical education consistent with the department. Lobby your administration to make sure that new staff members possess a university degree in physical education and that they have updated their skills through continual professional development. If allowed by local policies, the department chair or lead teacher should sit in on the interviews with the administrative staff. Along with being knowledgeable about physical education and instructional strategies, new staff members should possess the ability to work with others and should share your department's vision for implementing a quality physical education program.

Student Handbook

Creation of a student handbook by the department is evidence of working together as educators. It sends a clear message to students and other stakeholders that your department knows what it is trying to accomplish and that it will consistently apply standard procedures. Your students are, in effect, the customers for your physical education program. They are the end-users of the product (information) that you provide. A student handbook can introduce your students to the physical education program so that they may fully understand and participate in your department's vision. A sample student handbook is available on the

CD-ROM. A typical student handbook could have this table of contents:

Distribute the student handbook during the first few days of school and use it for a number of lessons that introduce the students to the physical education program. One homework assignment should involve taking the handbook home and reviewing it with parents or guardians. In addition, give the handbook to each new student who arrives after the school year is underway. The student handbook is further documentation that your department is actively seeking to provide adequate supervision and instruction.

Your department will need to allocate sufficient time to the creation of the student handbook. First, however, determine department policies, curriculum, and extracurricular events. Many times the student handbook makes for an excellent summer or off-track project. The specifics for many of these items need to be based on your own program (I discuss suggestions for many of them in detail throughout this book). But let's take a moment to discuss the items in sections VI through VIII, because these relate to the physical education environment and are common issues for physical educators.

Physical Education Uniform Policy

For sanitary and safety reasons, it is reasonable to require students to change their clothing for physical education. The most common concerns related to uniforms are what to do with students who forget their uniforms or refuse to wear their uniforms. A simple three-step process solves the problem. The first step is to require attractive

and suitable clothing, so that the students are not embarrassed to change into their physical education uniform. Many physical education departments have changed their required uniform for this reason. For example, most programs now allow longer shorts and a plain T-shirt with the option of sweats for inclement weather. One creative department had the name of the school along with the words *Fitness Center* printed on the front of each T-shirt. This simple act created positive feelings in the students about their physical education uniforms. The second step is to require that everyone dress every day with no exceptions. The third step is to provide "loaner" clothes for those students who forget their uniforms. These loaners must be laundered after each use, which is why you need a washer and dryer in the locker room or some other nearby area. This three-step process may sound too simple to work—especially for students who refuse to wear their uniforms—but it does. Simply treat refusing to wear the uniform as an act of defiance and deal with it like all other defiance issues that occur at school (e.g., students throwing textbooks on the floor, students refusing to follow directions). In schools that adamantly follow these three steps, there are very few problems related to changing clothes for physical education. But if students find a loophole in this process and one or two students refuse to change clothes for physical education, then the three-step process will fail.

Showering Options

It is important to provide showers in the middle school setting and encourage students to shower after physical activity. You should not require showers, however; instead, promote the use of showers by explaining the reasons for taking a shower after physical activity. Then take a look at your showering facilities. Would you want to shower there? Can you do anything to make the shower environment more inviting? Can you increase privacy within the showering facilities? Many middle school students are embarrassed by their bodies, and the more privacy you can provide, the more comfortable they'll be with changing clothes and showering.

Medical Excuses

As a physical educator you must address medical excuses that your regular classroom colleagues get to ignore. A typical policy that seems to work well for many departments is to require a parent signature for a 1- to 3-day excuse and the signature of a nurse (including the school nurse) or a doctor for longer medical excuses. Students should still be required to put on their uniforms (unless the medical situation prohibits the changing of clothes), participate in those activities that don't interfere with their medical situation, and complete alternative tasks when injury prohibits participating in the class activity.

Summary

A quality physical education environment provides the physical surroundings that promote student learning and enjoyment during physical education. Many times you inherit your facilities and equipment, but with a little creativity, your program can share facilities with other schools, community centers, or businesses. Businesses and community groups can help by purchasing, loaning, or donating adequate equipment and supplies. Work together as a department to accomplish the seemingly impossible to provide your students with an outstanding physical education setting.

The Psychological Environment

- Accomplished teachers of physical education create and sustain a welcoming, safe, and challenging environment in which students engage in and enjoy physical activity.

- Accomplished physical education teachers model and promote behavior appropriate in a diverse society by showing respect for and valuing all members of their communities and by having high expectations that their students will treat one another fairly and with dignity.

- Accomplished physical education teachers tenaciously maintain a stimulating, productive setting that encourages participation, discovery, goal setting, and cooperation and that holds all students to the highest expectations.

- Through their own passion for teaching and their personal example, accomplished physical education teachers inspire their students to learn and to participate in and appreciate physical education.

—National Board for Professional Teaching Standards

Our program stresses cooperation, integration of other subject areas, and motivation to succeed regardless of gender, age, size, and current level of ability or interest. This approach ensures that all students experience personal success and enjoyment from physical activities such as team sports, lifetime and leisure activities, physical conditioning, body management, safety skills, and circus arts.

—physical educator Jerry Ronk, Meany Middle School, Seattle, Washington

At least once a year a newspaper columnist receives a letter describing how, when the writer was a child, he was always picked last when teams were picked. The letter writer goes on to describe how this experience shattered his self-esteem and how he has always associated physical activity with this negative experience. Having personally observed classes where this practice continues, when I make presentations I often include a segment on not picking teams. After one presentation, a young professional came up to me and asked, "If teams should not be picked, then how should they be selected?" She couldn't imagine any other way. This reinforced for me that picking teams and other detrimental activities, such as elimination games, using students as targets (e.g., dodgeball), and using exercise as punishment, are still going on in our middle schools.

In contrast, a psychologically safe environment provides every student with the utmost respect and dignity. Physical educators learn and use students' names; take students' needs into consideration; listen to students; help students feel valued and recognized for who they are and what they are capable of doing; and set up a positive, warm, and cooperative climate. In a psychologically safe environment, physical educators never use sarcasm, choose teams using methods that lower students' self-esteem, or assign exercise as a form of punishment. Most important, they are sincere about wanting to establish a positive relationship with each of their students. Making these simple adjustments in your approach to conducting classes invites more students into the physical education learning environment and improves the image of physical education in society.

Ensuring psychological support in your classes not only benefits the students on an affective level; it also increases the potential for learning. And, unlike the physical environment, where physical educators may not have control over the situation, the psychological environment affords the physical educator with complete control. Following a code of ethics (see "Code of Ethics for Physical Education Teachers") ensures that every student is provided with a psychologically safe learning environment.

In this chapter, we look at promoting a psychologically safe environment through the total inclusion of all students in your classes, the teaching of prosocial skills, and the development of class management strategies that promote positive self-esteem in students. We examine the type of environment in which all students experience success

Figure 5.1 Students in a psychologically safe environment are more willing to risk participating in a new activity.

and demonstrate a willingness to risk participating in new activities and skills (figure 5.1).

Inclusion

If you don't even allow students access to your classes, you can't say that you are providing them with a psychologically safe environment. According to a number of legal mandates (figure 5.2), the composition of classes must include students with disabilities, boys and girls, and students representing different ethnicities and cultures. Simply placing students in a well-balanced class is, however, only the first step toward inclusion and meeting each student's needs.

If psychological safety refers to respect for students, then it must include respect for all students—boys and girls, black and white, Christian and Jew, homosexual and heterosexual, low income and high income, and lowly skilled and highly skilled. Students who are valued and who value one another are more likely to reach their academic and physical potentials (Williamson 1993). Therefore, the respect and psychological support must come not only from you, the teacher, but also from fellow students. You can use a number of strategies to ensure total inclusion of students from all groups

Code of Ethics for Physical Education Teachers

I promise to . . .

always provide quality instruction;

assign appropriate and safe exercises to my students;

respect the diversity of my students including their gender, sexual orientation, race, culture, and language dominance;

closely monitor my students for any signs of abuse (e.g., bruises, hunger, poor hygiene, behavior extremes);

include all my students (highly skilled, poorly skilled) in the learning process;

never sell candy or sodas or give these as rewards;

assign teams, never allowing students to pick teams;

have and maintain a vision and implementation plan for a quality curriculum; and

never use exercise as punishment.

in your classes. These strategies include establishing class norms that support the rights of all students, providing direct instruction on social skills, sharing information on the contributions of various groups of people, and ensuring that instructional materials are inclusive of various groups.

Class norms need to focus on students' treating one another with respect, including not allowing "put-downs" or comments based on stereotypes. One junior high in a Chicago suburb expanded on this concept and established its own bill of rights (see sidebar), outlining specifically what students are entitled to and how students should be treated. As you think about developing your own class norms, why not include some of these rights or, better yet, let your students establish their own set of class norms?

Along with establishing class norms, you must actively teach social skills. Just as motor skills do not develop on their own, prosocial skills will not

Public Laws Mandating Inclusion

Public Law 94-142, Education for All Handicapped Children Act of 1975 (Updated 1990—Individuals With Disabilities Education Act [IDEA]) (Updated 1997 PL 105-17)

To the maximum extent appropriate, children with disabilities, including children in public and private institutions or other care facilities, are educated with children without disabilities, and that special classes, separate schooling or other removal of children with disabilities from regular educational environments occur only when the nature or severity of the disability is such that education in regular classes with the use of supplementary aids and services cannot be achieved.

Section 504 of the Rehabilitation Act of 1973, Reauthorized Public Law 99-057 of 1986

No otherwise qualified handicapped individual shall, solely by reason of his handicap, be excluded from participation in, be denied the benefits of, or be subject to discrimination under any program or activity receiving federal financial assistance.

Educational Amendment Act of 1972 (Title IX)

No person in the United States shall, on the basis of sex, be excluded from participation in, be denied the benefits of, or be subjected to discrimination under any education program or activity receiving federal financial assistance.

Figure 5.2 Three legal mandates provide the basis for inclusion.

Sample Student Bill of Rights

1. The right to develop one's own personality (so long as it does not interfere with the rights of others) without disrespectful criticism or pressure from cliques.
2. Freedom from physical abuse and mental abuse such as name calling, intimidation, or harassment.
3. Freedom from being set apart or mocked because of race, sex, religion, physical strength, size, features, friendship groups, age, culture, disability, financial status, clothing, or classroom performance.
4. The right of privacy and freedom from being harassed in the classroom; the right to be treated respectfully.
5. The right to an education, which means that the teacher should be free to teach and students free to learn without being interrupted by inconsiderate students.
6. The right to have personal and school property respected. Our school should be a safe place for property as well as people.

Reprinted, by permission, from K.M. Williamson, 1993, "Is your inequity showing? Ideas and strategies for creating a more equitable learning environment," *Journal of Physical Education, Recreation and Dance* 64(8): 20.

occur by chance. I discuss specific strategies for teaching social skills in a separate section later in this chapter. In chapter 11, I discuss cooperative learning, which provides an opportunity for students to not only master content but also improve their social skills.

Including instruction on the contributions of different groups of people including women, ethnic minorities, and people with disabilities in physical education, sport, and other areas will help your students recognize that all individuals have something to offer. Weave this instruction throughout the instructional process, or create separate units that focus on one or more groups. The common practice of designating time periods as opportunities to focus on a group, like Black History Month (February), Women's History Month (March), or the Special Olympics, ensures that the contributions of these groups are highlighted. Relate this information to ongoing instruction and make an even more significant impact on your students.

Portraying positive images of individuals from all groups along with descriptions of their unique contributions is especially important when it comes to instructional materials. This practice will heighten your students' awareness of the significant contributions of these various groups and provide the students with models of inclusion. Moreover, when students see pictures of men and women participating in sport activities together, they learn that a particular sport is not the exclusive domain of one gender. Remember, bulletin board displays are an excellent forum for setting

an inclusive atmosphere. In addition, be willing to give students time for discussion when issues of race, gender, and other differences arise.

Commit yourself to making all students feel included and valued in the physical education class. Let's look at special considerations for including students representing different ethnic groups, genders, special needs, skill levels, and at-risk groups.

Including Ethnic Groups

As our culture becomes more diverse, we must become more tolerant of individual differences. To adequately address the ethnic and cultural diversity in your classes, you must look first at your own cultural background and understand how your own biases affect your interactions with students. Then, you must examine the backgrounds and needs of your students as well as their cultural biases. Here are 10 tips for working in a multicultural environment:

1. Become aware of cultural differences (i.e., the meaning associated with eye contact).
2. Treat students as individuals, not as members of groups.
3. Have students work in small heterogeneous groups.
4. Encourage students to research their cultures and share dances and games from their cultures.

5. Avoid stereotypical language (i.e., "throws like a girl," "white lie").

6. Learn to pronounce students' names correctly.

7. Vary instructional approaches to meet different learning styles.

8. Set high expectations for all students.

9. Analyze instructional materials for stereotypes.

10. Accept students' native language and help students to develop their English language skills.

Sometimes the cultural backgrounds of students may run counter to what you're trying to accomplish in physical education. This type of situation can result either in a conflict between the school and family or in a compromise that meets the needs of both the physical education program and the culture. For example, some cultures do not allow girls to wear shorts. In such cases, physical educators have allowed the girls to wear culottes (a divided skirt) instead of shorts. The culottes met the needs of the culture as well as the safety and hygiene requirements of the physical education program. Williamson (1993) identified four stages that individuals experience on the way to accepting a multicultural environment:

1. Isolate stage—identify with one's group.

2. Inquiry stage—acknowledge the existence of difference and recognize the complex process of culture.

3. Contact stage—accept the validity of differences and put into perspective strengths and weaknesses of culture.

4. Integration stage—master knowledge and skills to feel comfortable and to communicate effectively with people of any culture in cross-cultural situations.

To help students advance from the isolate stage all the way to the integration stage, you must provide students with critical thinking skills that help them challenge social inequalities and promote cultural diversity. By becoming aware of how students within various cultures perceive physical education, physical activity, and interpersonal relationships, you can integrate issues related to social change into the physical education program (see lesson agendas in chapters 14-17 for examples).

Including Boys and Girls

One of the most hotly debated topics in physical education is coeducational classes. In U.S. society, most teachers would never think of segregating students by ethnic group, but some still have a hard time accepting students from different gender groups in the same classes. Some teachers argue that the students learn more in gender-segregated classes; however, a recent comprehensive study (Asthana 2006) found that teaching girls in single-sex schools makes no difference in their educational attainment. In addition, segregated classes prevent boys and girls from interacting with one another and learning how to work and play together (figure 5.3). Segregation by gender limits opportunities for boys and girls to reconsider their stereotypical assumptions in the physical domain.

Placing boys and girls in the same physical education class is only the first step toward giving students the opportunity to examine their preconceived ideas about the opposite gender. Figure 5.4 shows six steps to equity. Not every teacher needs to pass through all six steps; however, you should be able to identify the step you currently occupy. Step 6 is complete equity, including opportunities for both genders to demonstrate skills, answer questions, receive feedback, and feel respect from the teacher and other students. It also includes an environment in which the teacher uses inclusive language (referring to the class as "students" instead of "you guys") and omits stereotypical phrases (e.g., "You throw like a girl").

Reaching step 6 does not occur haphazardly. To arrive at step 6, first write down your concerns about coeducational physical education so you can examine and deal with each concern one at a time. Second, visit programs in which coeducational physical education has become the norm. During the visit, observe the types of strategies and curricula that work in middle school coeducational settings. Ask questions about how the schools were able to make the transition.

As you progress through steps 2 to 5, continually reflect on your own teaching behaviors. When boys and girls appear to not be working well together, examine the learning environment and determine what might be causing the problem. Often, I hear physical educators state that the boys won't let the girls touch the ball. Sometimes the physical educator says that she has even made a rule that a girl must touch the ball before the team can score. When I question the teacher as to

Figure 5.3   Physical education classes that include both genders, as well as ethnic minorities and individuals with disabilities, provide students the opportunity to learn how to live and play together, regardless of individual differences.

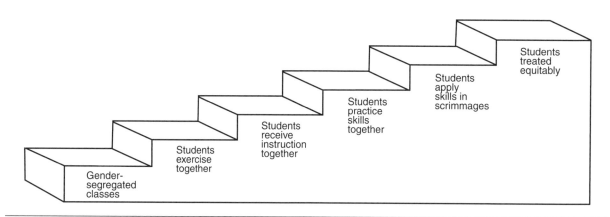

Figure 5.4   Six steps to gender equity.

whether all the boys in her class refuse to share, she typically responds, "No, it's a few aggressive boys." This tells me that the situation has little to do with coeducational physical education, because these same boys are also preventing the other boys from touching the ball. The remedy is either to make a rule that everyone must touch the ball, or better yet, to reduce the size of the teams so that everyone on the team must be involved for the team to be successful. Requiring that a girl must touch the ball before scoring sends the message that girls need special treatment, which only reinforces the stereotype that girls are not as competent as boys.

Including Students With Disabilities

The term *inclusion,* as it relates to students with disabilities, means placing these students in regular education classes at the school they would attend if they did not have a special need. Special education and other services are brought to the student, rather than having the student go to these services in separate classes or schools. Considerable evidence from the past 20 years suggests that segregation of these students can harm their academic performance and social adjustment. Indeed, all students have a legal right to placement in a regular physical education class, even

Coeducational Physical Education

I have found coeducational physical education to be highly successful, for both girls and boys. Certainly the skill levels of girls have improved. . . . The boys, too, have benefited from exposure to a greater diversity of activities, experienced more opportunities to be successful, and learned more social skills—with no decline in their learning of movement skills.

—Jean Flemion, 1990 NASPE Secondary Physical Education Teacher of the Year

if they have special needs and require extra support to be successful. Support for the student can come from a special educator, adapted physical educator, parent, peer tutor, volunteer, or teacher assistant. Let's take a look at two steps that can greatly improve the quality of the physical education program for your inclusion students.

The first step toward inclusion requires that you develop a positive attitude and a willingness to work with students with disabilities. Frequently students with disabilities may take longer to learn skills, drills, and routines; however, if you believe that all students can learn given enough time, then the situation will be less stressful for both you and the student. In addition, you can visit other schools and classes where inclusion is working. Don't hesitate to join the Individualized Education Program (IEP) team so that you can give input regarding the student's level of placement.

The second step is to understand the characteristics of the disabilities of your special needs students. By understanding the nature of each disability, you will have a better idea of the instructional styles and strategies that will work best with each student and of any appropriate modifications. Base modifications on the lifelong needs of each student with disabilities, always ensuring that the modifications do not embarrass the student. These modifications can include

adaptations to equipment, rules, and instructional strategies as well as additional prompts and cues. Specific modifications can include lowering or increasing the size of targets, reducing the size of the playing area, adjusting the weight or size of the manipulative or striking implement, allowing students to play positions that entail less mobility, and providing assistive devices (e.g., ramps, switches, beeping balls, batting tees).

Block (2000) suggested that you ask yourself four questions regarding any modification:

1. Does the change allow the student with a disability to participate successfully yet still be challenged?

2. Does the modification make the setting safe for the student with a disability as well as for students without disabilities?

3. Does the change affect students without disabilities?

4. Does the change cause an undue burden on the regular physical education teacher?

Although most students with disabilities should have a chance to try regular physical education classes, it's possible that regular physical education may not be appropriate for all students. If a student is not receiving any benefit from regular physical education, is disruptive to other

Inclusion

I believe that having differently abled students in the class, socializing and trying the activities, is very important. My student aides usually help these students with the class activity. I enjoy watching while these students blend in with the rest of the class. The regular education students tell them where to stand, give them the ball for a chance, and really work hard at including them. The regular education students also really get on someone who does not include or tries to bully them. It has taken us a couple of years to get to this place. I have had to change the way I think. I now see how meaningful it is to include these students.

—physical educator Marcia Troutfetter, South Middle School, Salina, Kansas

students, or poses a severe threat to the safety of the other students, then the IEP team, with input from you, should consider an alternative placement (Block 2000). One alternative short of segregating the student completely is to allow the student limited time in regular physical education with support from an adapted physical educator or another individual. Martin Block's *A Teacher's Guide to Including Students With Disabilities in General Physical Education, Second Edition* (2000), is an excellent resource for working with inclusion students.

Including All Skill Levels

In all areas of the curriculum, educators are debating the concepts of tracking (assigning students to classes based on ability) and ability grouping within a class. So it's not surprising that these concepts are also an issue in physical education. As a physical educator, you may very well come from a background of athletics in which you were the most highly skilled and in which you participated with and competed against others who were also highly skilled, perhaps predisposing you to a philosophy that leans toward homogeneous groupings. Little evidence, however, supports this philosophy or the claim that tracking or grouping by ability produces greater overall achievement than heterogeneous grouping (Berliner and Casanova 1993; Gamoran 1992; Kuykendall 1992; Slavin 1990). In fact, the research shows that tracking and ability grouping practices are detrimental to low-ability students.

Another related issue, which I described in the opening scenario for this chapter, is the practice of having captains stand in front of the class to pick teams. Even though the end result is heterogeneous teams, the emotional impact on the last student picked and the amount of instructional time spent on the process argue against this practice in the educational world. I am often asked about various alternatives to picking teams, such as having captains pick teams in private or having captains pick two or three players while the rest of the students get to choose their teams themselves. I believe these are, in fact, variations on the same theme, and even if they shelter the dignity of the last student, we can never be sure that a captain will not share with a student that he or she was picked last. My second concern is the amount of time invested in these activities when we already have such limited time for instruction. Instead, save time and feelings and choose from a variety of appropriate methods for assigning groups. These

include randomly assigning students to teams before class; lining students up by birth month or favorite ice cream flavor; or assigning students to teams so that each team consists of high-, medium-, and low-skilled students.

Including At-Risk Students

At-risk students are the fastest growing group of special needs students. These students are more likely to experiment with drugs and participate in gangs and are less likely to put effort into their school work. Research has identified several factors that predispose students to becoming at-risk. The greater the number of risk factors present within a student's life (figure 5.5), the greater is the likelihood that the student will be at risk.

More important than the risk factors are the protective factors (see figure 5.5). If present, these factors help students develop individual resiliency and strength, making them less likely to participate in at-risk activities. The more protective factors present in a student, the less likely it is that the student will be at risk. You can help your students develop resiliency by creating opportunities for all students to be successful. Help students set realistic and manageable goals by helping them problem solve in difficult situations, by creating a trusting atmosphere in which to learn, by reducing stress, and by helping students develop positive self-esteem. Interestingly, these are many of the same strategies that the major middle school reform documents have identified as being important for all middle school students.

Developing Social Skills

Naturally, the teaching of prosocial skills is an effective strategy for helping students deal with inclusion issues. Suggested prosocial skills for middle school students include

- compliments,
- compromises,
- courtesy,
- disagreement that is positive,
- encouragement,
- helpfulness,
- kindness,
- listening, and
- sharing.

Factors That Put Students at Risk

Peer Factors

Early antisocial behavior

Alienation and rebelliousness

Antisocial behavior in late childhood and early adolescence

Favorable attitudes toward drug use

Early first use (of drugs)

Greater influence by and reliance on peers rather than on parents

Friends who use tobacco, alcohol, or other drugs or sanction their use

School Factors

Lack of a clear school policy regarding the use of tobacco, alcohol, or other drugs

Availability of tobacco, alcohol, or other drugs

School transitions

Academic failure

Lack of involvement in school activities

Little commitment to school

Community Factors

Economic and social deprivation

Low neighborhood attachment and high community disorganization

Community norms and laws favorable to the use of tobacco, alcohol, or other drugs

Availability of tobacco, alcohol, or other drugs

Family Factors

Family management problems (lack of clear expectations of children's behavior, lack of monitoring, inconsistent or excessively severe discipline, lack of caring)

Use of tobacco, alcohol, and other drugs by parents or parents' positive attitudes toward use

Low expectations of children's success

Family history of alcoholism

Factors That Protect Students From Risk

Effectiveness in Work, Play, and Relationships

They establish healthy friendships.

They are goal-oriented.

Healthy Expectancies and Positive Outlooks

They believe that effort and initiative will pay off.

They are oriented to success rather than to failure.

Self-Esteem and Internal Locus of Control

They feel competent, have a sense of personal power, and believe that they can control events in their environment rather than being passive victims.

Self-Discipline

They have the ability to delay gratification and control impulsive drives.

They maintain an orientation to the future.

Problem-Solving and Critical Thinking Skills

They have the ability to think abstractly, reflectively, and flexibly.

They are able to define alternative solutions to problems.

Humor

They can laugh at themselves and situations.

Figure 5.5 Although it is hard to control some of the risk factors, you can help develop protective factors.

Reprinted, by permission, from *Not schools alone: Guidelines for schools and communities,* copyright 1991, California Department of Education, 515 L Street #250, Sacramento, CA 95814.

Students who demonstrate prosocial skills are better able to communicate and work with a variety of peers. The establishment of a psychologically safe environment, including your modeling of prosocial skills, is the first step to introducing students to prosocial skills.

Often, students do not know the prosocial skills that we expect them to demonstrate. Therefore, you must teach these skills to students much as you teach motor skills. When teaching motor skills, you probably recognize that each student goes through stages: describes the skill, forms a mental image of the skill, practices the skill, executes the skill correctly, and applies the skill in a variety of settings. The same process applies to the development of social skills:

Aware—knows that the skill exists

Knowledgeable—knows when and how the skill should be used

Self-conscious—feels awkward when performing the skill because it is new

Phony—applies the skill only because he or she is being monitored

Habitual or mechanical—internalizes the skill for use in certain situations

Natural—exhibits the skill appropriately in a wide variety of situations

In the past, we have simply put students into situations and told them to play fairly. We now recognize that this is not enough. When teaching students prosocial skills, you must

- introduce the social skill,
- ask students to identify what it looks like, sounds like, and feels like (figure 5.6),

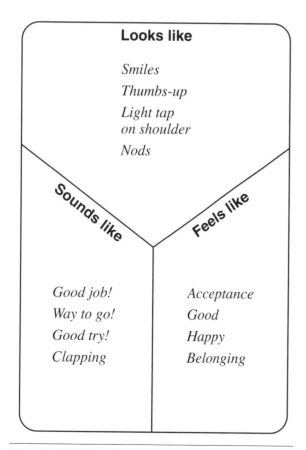

Figure 5.6   Y chart for encouragement.

- instruct students to demonstrate the social skill as they practice the motor skill in a drill or activity, and
- provide feedback to the students as they attempt to use the social skill.

Once students have begun to develop their prosocial skills, they are ready to learn how to negotiate and resolve conflicts instead of getting into fights or ignoring issues. Johnson and Johnson (1991, 1998) identified a two-step negotiation process for students. In the first step, each student describes what she wants out of the negotiation and then together the students involved specifically define their conflict. In the second step, each student presents his reasons for what he wants, and then the parties clarify their differences before exploring possible solutions that are in the mutual interest of both. Once a solution is agreed upon, both parties must agree to stick to it. After the solution is implemented, you can ask the students, "Is the solution working?" If not, students can reexamine possible solutions.

To solve the conflict, especially a minor conflict, the parties can take turns or share the resources, compromise, or resolve the conflict by chance. Chance may involve flipping a coin or playing Rock, Scissors, Paper. In Rock, Scissors, Paper, students pound their fist into the palm of their other hand two times and then form a rock (fist), scissors (extended index and middle fingers), or paper (hand flat). Winning is based on the following order: Rock beats scissors, scissors beats paper, and paper beats rock.

Positive Class Management

Waiting in lines, feeling afraid of ridicule, and suffering from being put down by others often lead to severe disruptions. Few disruptions occur, however, when you create a learning environment that makes students feel psychologically safe, that provides intellectual and physical challenges, that includes interesting and relevant activities, that fosters prosocial skills, that uses a variety of instructional strategies, and that allows students to contribute to the class. Often when we think about effective class managers, the image of the military-style instructor who demands the attention of the students comes to mind. As a physical educator, however, you should command the attention of the students through clearly stated high expectations and firmness combined with attitudes and actions that demonstrate concern for the students as individuals.

Because of large class sizes and the early adolescent predisposition to challenging authority, a few precautions in the form of routines, rules, and a plan for handling discipline problems can ensure an effective learning environment. Research supports actively teaching students routines, rules, and consequences during the first several days of the school year. Although this may seem to waste instructional time, in fact it saves class time in the long run by reducing the likelihood of disruptive behavior. So invest early and reap the dividends throughout the school year.

Routines

Establish class routines (figure 5.7) to effectively organize your classes. Most teachers use routines, and students eventually learn them. More effective teachers, however, take the time at the beginning of the year to teach their routines.

Another effective technique for class order is the use of routine or leadership groups. To use this strategy, assign every student in the class to a group. Each group is then responsible for handling one of the classroom routines. Sample assignments include

- exercise leaders who lead their groups in warm-up exercises,

---

Class Routines

Starting Class

Students sit down on their numbers as the teacher approaches the class, so the teacher can readily see which students are absent.

Students write in their journals in response to a prompt (e.g., "Describe a social skill that you demonstrated during the last 24 hours.") while the teacher takes attendance.

Students write a summary of the previous day's activities in their journals as the teacher takes attendance.

Students read directions (task analysis of a skill or rules for an activity) on a chalkboard or task card while the teacher takes attendance.

Students begin exercising while the teacher goes from group to group checking attendance.

Warm-Up Exercises

Students get into small groups; each group forms a circle around their exercise leader, who takes them through their warm-up exercises.

Students rotate through exercise stations set up around the physical education area.

Getting and Putting Away Equipment

One student from each group hands out and collects equipment.

Equipment monitors hand out and collect equipment for all the groups.

Gaining Student Attention

Slap a tambourine once to indicate to students that you have additional directions. The students stop what they are doing, put down their equipment, and listen.

Blow a whistle once to indicate to students that you have additional directions. The students stop what they are doing, put down their equipment, and listen.

Ending Class

Students sit down on their numbers for the closure of the lesson.

Students sit down in their practice groups for the closure of the lesson.

Figure 5.7 Suggestions for effective class routines.

- junior teachers who learn a skill from the teacher and then teach it to their groups,
- greeters who are responsible for welcoming and answering questions posed by visitors,
- equipment managers who are responsible for distributing and collecting equipment,
- conflict resolution managers who assist with disputes,
- homework checkers who monitor homework completion, and
- assistants to substitute teachers who welcome substitutes and help them learn the class rules and routines.

Rotate membership in these groups frequently so that students have the opportunity to learn a variety of organizational tasks.

Establishing Rules

In addition to establishing class routines, state a few specific rules in a positive way. To be effective, however, make sure your rules are fair and enforceable. Some teachers have had great success with guiding their students in creating their own rules. Other departments have created rules for the entire physical education department to ensure consistency between the physical educators. Sample classroom rules include the following:

- Arrive on time.
- Dress appropriately for participation.
- Listen when the teacher or another student is talking.
- Respect yourself and others.
- Treat equipment and facilities with care.

Regardless of who creates the rules, they must be communicated to both the students and their parents. First, make the rules the focus of each lesson for the first several days of the school year. Post the rules where students can see them, and send copies home so that parents also become familiar with them. Teach the rules and their reasons. Next, make sure students understand the rules. Then enforce the rules, having students practice rules throughout the instructional period, while you remind and reinforce as needed.

Reinforcing the rules is important throughout the year but especially during the first several weeks of school, because rules that are not mentioned are quickly forgotten. I believe that one of the main reasons that many physical educators, as well as other teachers, have more discipline problems in their afternoon classes is that they are too tired to follow up on minor rule infractions. If you really want your students to obey the rules, you must consistently identify all rule violations. When pointing out misbehavior, preserve students' dignity and show the students that they are responsible for their own actions. In addition, you must follow through, so that the student ends up following the rule.

Dealing With Disruptions

Although planning and establishing rules and routines will reduce the number of discipline problems in the class, nothing can be done to completely eliminate all disruptions. There will always be one or two students in your classes who want to challenge the system no matter what. How should the teacher handle these situations? Two important guidelines involve respect for the student and follow-through (see sidebars).

In the past, many thought that punishing misbehavior and rule violations was the answer. Punishment refers to any action that embarrasses, threatens, physically hurts (including using exer-

---

Remember Your Students' Dignity!

Sara and Jose are whispering while the teacher, Ms. Smith, is giving directions for the next activity.

Ms. Smith: "Sara and Jose, what are you doing?"

Jose: "Why are you picking on us?"

Ms. Smith: "I would like to know if there has been a violation of one of our rules."

Sara: "Rule number 3: 'Listen when the teacher or another student is talking.'"

Ms. Smith: "Jose, why do we have this rule?"

Jose: "So that we know what to do in the next activity."

Sara: "Also, so that other people can hear you and know what to do in the next activity."

Remember to Follow Through!

John arrives for class at the last minute, out of breath, and wearing his street clothes.
Mr. Garcia: "John, where is your physical education uniform?"
John: "I forgot it at home."
Mr. Garcia: "What are you supposed to do when you forget your uniform?"
John: "Borrow from the office."
Mr. Garcia: "So, why didn't you borrow today?"
John: "Because I was late getting to the locker room."
Mr. Garcia: "What can you do tomorrow so you are not late?"
John: "Not stop by my locker on the way to physical education."
Mr. Garcia: "Okay, for now go get dressed so that you can participate in class today."

cise as punishment), or otherwise reduces self-esteem. Punishment, however, does not work. If it did work, then teachers who use it would not continue to experience disruptive events in their classes.

What is often less obvious to many teachers is that rewards can also be detrimental to students. Lepper and Green (1978) showed that using rewards and praise to motivate learning increases the students' dependency on others for learning, instead of helping them find the learning inherently satisfying. As Kohn (1999) described, "No behavioral manipulation ever helped a child develop a commitment to becoming a caring and responsible person" (p. 161).

So what can you do when a student is disruptive or violates a rule? First, make sure that you are implementing the suggestions for teaching prosocial skills, providing a psychologically safe environment, using effective instructional strategies, and establishing rules and routines. Second, be prepared for disruptions so you are not caught off guard. Third, constantly monitor student behavior. Fourth, deal directly with the student who is being disruptive.

When monitoring student activity during the class period, position yourself where you can constantly watch and be aware of the activities of all students, even when working with an individual or small group. This is sometimes referred to as "back to the wall," because in order to see all students you must position yourself around the perimeter of the activity area instead of in the center of the class. In addition, if you constantly move around the instructional area in unpredictable patterns, you can spot and stop inappropriate behavior more quickly. Many times, simply calling out the student's name respectfully or moving

closer to the student who is misbehaving will put an end to the misbehavior.

When the student does not immediately stop the misbehavior, quietly remind the student of the rule and the reasons for it (e.g., "What is the rule about respecting equipment? Does hanging on the volleyball net violate this rule? What damage occurs when someone hangs on the net?"). This encourages the student to examine her own behavior and the consequences of her behavior. If the misbehavior continues, provide a time-out for the student and ask the student to think about how she can change her behavior (e.g., "What will help you to remember not to hang on the volleyball net? How can you better spend your time?"). This provides students with an opportunity to find possible solutions for themselves. Initially, time-outs should last no more than 5 minutes; then give the student the opportunity to share how she is going to change her behavior. If the misbehavior continues after the time-out, then call the parents to solicit their involvement. Keep your sense of humor and don't let your ego become involved in a confrontation with the student.

The student who constantly challenges your authority is probably challenging authority in all his classes. In this situation, look for underlying reasons. Determine if the student is having a problem with learning the material, with other students in the class, or in his family. It may become necessary in these cases to temporarily remove such a student from the class while you investigate and work on the underlying problems. The need to remove more than one or two students on a continuous basis, however, should cause you to reflect on what is occurring in the class and to concentrate more on preventing problems.

Summary

A psychologically safe environment sets the stage for learning. When all students—regardless of their group affiliation—have the opportunity for success, they are more willing to risk trying new skills, and the potential for learning increases. When you provide instruction on social skills and related social issues, you not only eliminate many behavior problems but also prepare your students to live in a multicultural society. Social skills instruction along with consistent enforcement of routines, rules, and consequences reduces the amount of class time you spend on student misbehavior and creates an environment in which learning is the focus.

PART II

Map Out Your Journey

In part II, I address curriculum development and assessment from kindergarten through high school, focusing mainly on the middle school program. In **chapter 6**, I start leading you through the curriculum development process from selecting the curriculum committee to developing the appropriate assessment tools. In **chapter 7**, I complete this discussion by showing you how to select instructional units through developing lesson plans. In **chapter 8**, I outline a variety of alternative assessment tools and appropriate grading practices and apply them to physical education. In effect, I create a road map from start to finish for your journey toward an effective middle school physical education program.

Creating the Curriculum Foundation

- Accomplished physical education teachers have a deep and broad understanding of the content and principles of physical education, which enables them to devise sound and developmentally appropriate instructional activities.
- Accomplished physical education teachers select, plan, and evaluate curriculum in a continuous process meant to ensure a sensible, properly structured, positive physical education program that meets students' needs and results in student learning.

—*National Board for Professional Teaching Standards*

"Will you please tell me which way I ought to go from here?"
"That depends a great deal on where you want to get to," said the Cat.
"I don't care much where," said Alice.
"Then it doesn't much matter which way you go," said the Cat.

—*Lewis Carroll, Alice's Adventures in Wonderland, 1865*

As you begin your journey toward quality middle school physical education, you must create a map of where you want to go. The map is your curriculum; it identifies what you will teach. As you create your map, you must consider the future in which your students will live and the needs that they will have as they become adults during the 21st century.

Historically, many have criticized physical education curricula for problems such as a lack of sequential progressions, inclusion of too many objectives and too much or too little content, redundant instruction, units that were too long or too short, activities unrelated to the objectives, and too much emphasis on teacher preference. To provide effective instruction, you must establish a curriculum foundation that can stand up to these criticisms. You must provide middle school students with activities that progressively increase their competence, that improve their feelings about themselves, and that have relevance to their lives. Challenging? Yes, but a well-planned curriculum is well worth the effort.

The development of a curriculum is typically prompted by one of several events: a new state framework or standards, a curriculum reform movement, or a group of teachers who are interested in improving their program. Regardless of the catalyst, the development of a district or county physical education curriculum instead of an individual school curriculum is in the best interest of your students. A curriculum that encompasses several elementary, middle, and high schools allows for articulation (sharing of information) and a variety of opinions while still allowing local control. If your district or county is not interested but your school wants to create a new curriculum, then you should still follow the curriculum development process I outline here.

To develop a curriculum, ask yourself, "What do my students need to know? To feel? To be able to do?" Beginning at the end (known as "backward mapping") forces you to take a broader look at the entire educational process. Then, after choosing your goals, work backward to develop a program that focuses on what your students need and what is relevant and meaningful and that includes prioritizing components to make the most of the short time set aside for physical education (figure 6.1). In doing so, you will ensure that your program will produce physically educated individuals rather than physically trained individuals—individuals who understand movement and move efficiently, instead of individuals who leave school fit but

have no understanding of how to maintain their fitness.

There are 12 steps in the curriculum development process:

1. Select a committee.
2. Prepare a committee.
3. Define a physically educated person.
4. Review NASPE's content standards.
5. Develop exit standards.
6. Develop grade-level standards.
7. Determine criteria for competence.
8. Select instructional units.
9. Develop unit standards.
10. Integrate with other subject areas.
11. Determine the yearly plan.
12. Develop unit plans and lesson plans.

Let's look now at the first seven steps. The remaining five are addressed in chapter 7. Familiarize yourself with the terms listed in the sidebar before beginning the process.

Select a Committee

The central office either appoints the committee or asks for volunteers. The committee should be composed of elementary teachers (elementary physical education teachers if they are available), middle school physical education teachers, high school physical education teachers, adapted physical education teachers, site and central office administrators, parents, community members, and students. Why do you need elementary and high school teachers if you're developing a middle

Middle Grade Education

The main purpose of middle grades education is to promote young adolescents' intellectual development. It is to enable every student to think creatively, to identify and solve meaningful problems, to communicate and work well with others, and to develop the base of central knowledge and skills that is the essential foundation for these "higher order" capacities. As they develop these capacities, every young adolescent should be able to meet or exceed high academic standards. Closely related goals are to help all students develop the capacity to lead healthful lives, physically and mentally; to become caring, compassionate, and tolerant individuals; and to become active, contributing citizens of the United States and the world. But above all else, and to enable all these other goals to be realized, middle grades schools must be about helping all students learn to use their minds well.

G.A. Davis and A.W. Jackson, 2000, *Turning Points: A Decade Later*, 10-11.

Figure 6.1 Focus on your goals when developing a curriculum, and work backward from there.

Terms for Understanding Curriculum Development

alignment—The process of linking content and performance standards to assessment, instruction, and learning.

content standards—Expectations of what all students should know and be able to do in particular subjects and grade levels. The content standards describe knowledge, skills, and understanding that students should have to attain high levels of competency.

curriculum—A body of material that defines the content to be taught (what) and the methods to be used (how and when).

exit standards—Expectations of what all students should know and be able to do on graduation from high school.

grade-level standards—Expectations of what all students should know and be able to do at the end of a grade level. These are sometimes referred to as benchmarks.

performance based—Based on a determination of how good is good enough related to the expectations of what all students should know and be able to do in particular subjects and grade levels.

scope—The content that is to be covered.

sequence—The order in which the content is presented and studied.

standards—Essential knowledge and skills that guide the development of curriculum.

standards based—Based on standards, indicating that a clear and direct relationship exists among any combination of instructional materials, instructional processes, and assessments.

standards-based curriculum—A curriculum designed to produce student understanding and work that demonstrates achievement of the standards.

unit standards—Expectations of what all students should know and be able to do at the end of an instructional unit. These are sometimes referred to as benchmarks.

school curriculum? Ideally, the committee is responsible for developing a kindergarten through 12th grade curriculum; however, even if you are developing only a middle school curriculum, still include representatives from the elementary schools and high schools so that during the initial steps of the curriculum development process you can develop a K–12 perspective. Then shift your focus to the specifics of the middle school curriculum in the later stages of the process, creating a curriculum that both builds on what your students learned in elementary school and prepares them for high school.

The central office administration usually selects members for the curriculum committee in one of two ways. One way is to select only those individuals who are knowledgeable about educational reform and who agree with the direction that the leadership wishes to take in the development of the physical education curriculum. This choice eliminates most of the potential for dissension as the committee moves forward with its work. However, this option usually results in a document that is not well received or readily implemented by most physical educators. The second option is seeking out individuals with a variety of opinions. This option will create a very diverse group and the possibility of many heated debates during the developmental process. This second option, however, is more likely to produce results that all physical educators will implement. The heated debates will also bring more physical educators up to date with reform issues and solutions. Thus, I recommend this second option. To further facilitate the implementation of a new curriculum, I recommend that, whenever feasible, the committee include a representative from each school. The representative reports to the school staff after each committee meeting and solicits any concerns or questions so that everyone is both well-informed and heard from during the developmental process.

Prepare a Committee

Spend some time preparing and educating committee members for the task at hand. The amount of time you devote to this step will reap dividends in the steps to follow. The committee needs to understand the curriculum development process, current educational reform issues related to curriculum development, the district's holistic goals, and the current body of physical education knowledge (research). Depending on the general knowledge level of your committee, you may complete this step relatively quickly, or you may have to educate committee members throughout the entire curriculum development process.

Current Educational Reform Issues

To assist you with preparing the committee, a variety of materials are available on educational reform, technology, and the future of education, such as those covered in chapters 1 and 2. In addition, the Association for Supervision and Curriculum Development (see appendix C for address) has many excellent resources on these topics.

The committee members will definitely need to understand the current state of educational reform as it relates to standards, curriculum, instruction, and assessment.

The current thinking is that a well-designed curriculum gives students interactive learning experiences in which they can construct their own meanings by considering and processing ideas and concepts. Specifically, the curriculum (1) allows students to form their own meaning out of the information presented, instead of telling them what they should think; (2) asks students to make their own connections between the information presented and their current and future out-of-school endeavors; (3) has students apply the new information to meaningful projects; (4) helps students connect the new information to what they already know; and (5) encourages students to take responsibility for their own learning. Contrast this to a more traditional curriculum that focuses on an "information in—information out" approach. To be successful during the 21st century, individuals must be able to apply the information they learn. This type of curriculum also aligns with our understanding of how adolescents learn.

Applying this reform to physical education results in a standard such as "Applies movement concepts and principles to the learning and development of motor skills" instead of "Identifies the critical features in 10 movement patterns." Stated the first way, the objective expresses the expectation that students will take the information learned from movement concepts and principles and create their own learning plans. The ability to create learning plans has significance both now and in the future. For example, suppose, at 40, a former student wants to take up golf. Given what the student has learned as a result of this standard, the student (now an adult) should be able to create a practice plan for learning golf or at least be able to select a competent golf instructor and know whether the information that the golf instructor is conveying is accurate. Stated the second way, the objective simply expresses the expectation that students will reiterate the key elements of a throw, kick, catch, or the like—not that they will use that information to make meaning out of it for themselves.

Holistic Goals

If your state, district, or county has a description of an educated person stated in holistic terms, the committee will need to see this document so that the physical education curriculum can support it. For example, the state of Kentucky (Kentucky Department of Education 1990) established six goals for learning, which the writers stated holistically, based on an open-ended survey of citizens, businesses, and industry. These goals (which are still in effect today) represent what the writers believe to be most important for an educated person to know and be able to do when exiting high school:

1. Use basic communication and math skills.
2. Understand core concepts and principles: math, science, social studies, practical living, arts and humanities, and vocational education.
3. Become a self-sufficient individual.
4. Become a responsible group member.
5. Use thinking and problem-solving skills.
6. Integrate knowledge.

The second goal addresses the content standards for health, physical education, and home economics. However, you can relate many of the national physical education standards (NASPE 2004c) to the other goals. Certainly, the more links you can make between physical education and such holistic goals, the more established the position of physical education is in the K–12 educational program.

Physical Education Content

The committee must have a solid base of understanding about physical education. I have listed textbooks in the bibliography that will help broaden committee members' understanding of the various subdisciplines of physical education. These are some examples:

Motor learning: *Motor Learning and Control: Concepts and Applications* (Magill 2007)

Biomechanics: *Basic Biomechanics* (Hall 2007)

Exercise physiology: *Physiology of Sport and Exercise* (Wilmore and Costill 2004)

Historical perspectives: *A History and Philosophy of Sport and Physical Education: From Ancient Civilizations to the Modern World* (Mechikoff and Estes 2006)

In addition, NASPE has published a book titled *Concepts and Principles of Physical Education: What Every Student Needs to Know, Second Edition* (Mohnsen 2003a), based on the national standards for physical education (NASPE 2004c). By reading this book, committee members will bring themselves up to date on important physical education information.

Refrain from giving the committee any official definition of a physically educated person or any exit content standards for physical education, although it is tempting to do so at this point. Committee members should first determine what they value and believe about a physically educated person before you give them another group's work.

Define a Physically Educated Person

Once the committee begins to understand the curriculum development process, understands the educational reform issues related to curriculum, has read the holistic goals for your educational system, and has completed some readings and discussions on the current content of physical education, it's time to begin writing. The committee must first define for themselves what they believe is a physically educated person. In other words, what should students on graduation day from high school know, feel, and be able to do as a result of their physical education experience? The following is an example of such a definition:

Students graduating from high school are individuals who can plan their own lifelong fitness and wellness programs, develop their own learning plans for acquiring new motor skills, and analyze their own movement performances by applying biomechanical principles. These individuals can also explain the purpose of physical education and give a historical perspective; they understand and appreciate skillful movement from both a personal and social perspective. As adults, they will be able to apply their understanding of developmentally appropriate activities for the children within their care.

The committee needs sufficient time to brainstorm their definition, because they will base all other decisions on it. Interestingly, the groups I have worked with (more than 100) have developed results very similar to each other and to the national standards.

Review NASPE's Standards

After the committee members have had a chance to share and reflect on their definition, they should study NASPE's (2004c) national physical education standards:

Standard 1: Demonstrates competency in motor skills and movement patterns needed to perform a variety of physical activities.

Standard 2: Demonstrates understanding of movement concepts, principles, strategies, and tactics as they apply to the learning and performance of physical activities.

Standard 3: Participates regularly in physical activity.

Standard 4: Achieves and maintains a health-enhancing level of physical fitness.

Standard 5: Exhibits responsible personal and social behavior that respects self and others in physical activity settings.

Standard 6: Values physical activity for health, enjoyment, challenge, self-expression, or social interaction.

Moving Into the Future: National Standards for Physical Education, 2nd Edition (2004) reprinted with permission from the National Association for Sport and Physical Education (NASPE), 1900 Association Drive, Reston, VA 20191-1599.

These standards may be used to stimulate further thought as the committee works to refine and complete its definition. The formatting, with either lists or paragraphs, should match the formatting used by the central office for other curricular areas. But keep in mind that the strength of the committee members' belief in their definition counts the most—not the format.

Develop Exit Standards

The next step involves taking the definition of a physically educated person and turning this statement into a list of exit or content standards for physical education. The exit standards should be broad-based, challenging, demonstrable, and relevant. Indeed, the standards must be set at a world-class level so that your students will be successful in the global society during the 21st century. Therefore, the standards need to focus on securing and applying new information and on learning a few central concepts instead of memorizing many unrelated facts, such as the rules of games that may soon be outdated.

The committee may review NASPE's content standards again to stimulate further discussion before the committee finalizes its list of exit or content standards. Take a moment now and compare NASPE's content standards with the concepts discussed in chapter 1; you'll see that they are in good alignment with the Department of Labor's Secretary's Commission on Achieving Necessary Skills (SCANS) 2000 report and many of the other future trends discussed in chapter 1, such as lifelong learning. In fact, 47 of the U.S. states (NASPE 2006a) have state standards: 47 states have a standard that aligns with national standard 1, 46 have a standard that aligns with national standard 2, 45 have a standard that aligns with national standard 3, 47 have a standard that aligns with national standard 4, 46 have a standard that aligns with national standard 5, and 44 have a standard that aligns with national standard 6. So for the purposes of this book, I use NASPE's content standards as the exit standards. Your exit standards will probably align with these content standards but they won't be stated verbatim.

If the goal is for your committee to develop standards similar to those of NASPE, why not simply adopt the national standards? It is valuable for your committee to recognize that, in fact, their beliefs are similar to those expressed in the national standards. Going through the steps in the curriculum development process will increase the probability that the curriculum will be implemented, rather than left on shelves collecting dust. For this reason, the committee should share its work with as many other teachers in the district or county as possible and as often as possible. In fact, the greater the number of teachers who go through these last three steps (defining a physically educated person, reviewing NASPE's documents, and developing the exit standards), the greater is the possibility of implementation. This is where it comes in handy to have teacher representatives from every school in the district on the committee. If it's not possible to have non-committee members go through the process, then at least solicit their reactions along the way.

Develop Grade-Level Standards

Once the committee identifies and agrees on exit standards, the next step—developing grade-level standards—falls easily into place. Simply put, for each exit standard, the committee must determine how much of it can be learned at each grade level at which physical education is taught. The grade-level standards must be developmentally appropriate, relevant to the students' lives, directly related to corresponding exit standards, and performance based. Performance-based standards tell us what students will do with the learning—not

just that they learned it. During the 21st century, students must be able to apply information—not simply reiterate it.

Let's look at an example of the development of K–12 grade-level standards (figure 6.2) for national standard 5, "Exhibits responsible personal and social behavior that respects self and others in physical activity settings." This standard has two components: social interaction and personal responsibility. We examine the social aspects here. The progression develops from simple to complex issues: working alone, sharing space, working with a partner, working in a small group, working cooperatively with a group, solving problems, and demonstrating leadership and personal responsibility. Each grade-level standard builds on the previous grade-level standard, and all of the grade-level standards align with the exit standard. Moreover, this progression is developmentally appropriate because it parallels the social development of the student. For example, at the middle school level, this progression takes into consideration the students' capacity for abstract thought (see appendix A).

Sample K–12 Grade-Level Standards Related to the Social Area of National Standard 5.1

Kindergarten—Plays alone in personal space without interfering with others.

1st grade—Shares space and equipment with others in physical activity settings.

2nd grade—Works cooperatively with another to complete an assigned task in physical activity settings.

3rd grade—Supports and encourages a partner, both male and female, in physical activity settings.

4th grade—Respects the rights of others and their property in physical activity settings.

5th grade—Works with an individual who is differently abled in physical activity settings.

6th grade—Works cooperatively with a small group in physical activity settings.

7th grade—Applies problem-solving techniques when working with another person in physical activity settings.

8th grade—Collaborates with others to solve group problems in physical activity settings.

9th grade—Uses the strengths of each individual in the group during physical activity.

10th grade—Displays leadership skills during physical activity.

11th grade—Resolves group conflicts with sensitivity to the rights and feelings of others in physical activity settings.

12th grade—Exhibits responsible social behavior in a physical activity setting.

Figure 6.2 These sample K–12 grade-level standards show the progression of the standard from grade to grade.

To develop my sample, I consulted *Moving Into the Future: National Physical Education Standards, a Guide to Content and Assessment* (NASPE 2004c), *Physical Education Curriculum Analysis Tool* (CDC 2006), and *Concepts of Physical Education: What Every Student Needs to Know, Second Edition* (Mohnsen 2003a). Your committee's progression may be different for the fifth standard; simply make sure that it is logical, meets the criteria for grade-level standards, and works for your situation.

The strategy that I recommend you follow to complete this task is to start with the exit standard and work backward, answering the following questions in succession: What does this look like in 12th grade? 11th grade? 10th grade? . . . Kindergarten?

For each exit standard, your committee must also write kindergarten through 4th grade and 9th through 12th grade standards. I am including grade-level standards for all the grades for exit standard 5.1 (social aspect); however, I am including only the standards directly related to the middle school program for the others (see figure 6.3). Notice that exit standards 2, 3, 4, and 6 also contain two or more aspects. Standard 2 has five grade-level standards (2.1, 2.2, 2.3, 2.4, and 2.5), standard 3 has two grade-level standards (3.1, 3.2), standard 4 has two grade-level standards (4.1, 4.2), standard 5 has two grade-level standards (5.1, 5.2), and standard 6 has four grade-level standards (6.1, 6.2, 6.3, and 6.4). These exit standards embody more than one major concept. For example, exit standard 2 contains the motor

---

Sample Grade-Level Standards

National standard 1: Demonstrates competency in motor skills and movement patterns needed to perform a variety of physical activities.

1.0

5 Demonstrates speed, accuracy, and control using the mature form for fundamental movement and manipulative skills.

6 Demonstrates the mature form for specialized skills and combinations during cooperative activities; lead-up or simple target, invasion, field, and net activities; stunts and tumbling; and dance activities.

7 Demonstrates the mature form for specialized skills and combinations during individual and dual activities.

8 Demonstrates the mature form for specialized skills and combinations during modified team and dance activities.

National standard 2: Demonstrates understanding of movement concepts, principles, strategies, and tactics as they apply to the learning and performance of physical activities.

2.1

5 Explains the types of practice that improves motor skill performance for speed and accuracy.

6 Explains how to provide appropriate feedback to a partner who is developing or improving specialized skills.

7 Explains the process of setting appropriate goals, conducting appropriate practice, and monitoring changes in the development of specialized skills.

8 Analyzes the effect of positive transfer on specialized skill improvement.

2.2

5 Describes how to generate and absorb force when performing movement and motor skills.

6 Explains ways to use force to increase speed or distance of a body or propelled object.

7 Explains how force can make an object spin.

8 Explains how force can be used to alter the outcome of a skill performance.

Figure 6.3 Sample grade-level standards for grades 5 through 8 related to the exit standards.

NASPE Standards: Moving into the Future: National Standards for Physical Education, 2nd Edition (2004) reprinted with permission from the National Association for Sport and Physical Education (NASPE), 1900 Association Drive, Reston, VA 20191-1599.

2.3

5 Describes how the qualities of movement (e.g., space, time, force) are used in basic game tactics.
6 Describes offensive strategies for cooperative and bowling activities and offensive and

defensive strategies for simple invasion, field, and net activities.
7 Explains offensive and defensive strategies for individual net and target sports.
8 Explains offensive and defensive strategies for invasion, net, and field sports.

2.4

5 Describes changes from birth through puberty along with their impact on physical performance.
6 Describes the characteristics of physical activities appropriate for early adolescents.

7 Explains individual differences and how these differences impact performance in physical activities.
8 Analyzes the role of physical abilities in the performance of specialized skills.

2.5

5 Describes critical elements of fundamental movement and manipulative skills.
6 Describes the critical elements of specialized skills and combinations in cooperative activities; lead-up or simple target, invasion, field, and net activities; stunts and tumbling; and dance activities.

7 Explains the critical elements of specialized skills and combinations used in individual and dual sports.
8 Explains critical elements of specialized skills and combinations used in team sports.

National standard 3: Participates regularly in physical activity.

3.1

5 Engages in moderate physical activity for 60 minutes 5 days each week.
6 Engages in moderate and vigorous physical activity for 60 minutes 5 days each week.

7 Engages in moderate and vigorous physical activity for 60 minutes 6 days each week.
8 Engages in moderate and vigorous physical activity for 60 minutes 6 days each week.

3.2

5 Describes opportunities in the school setting for regular participation in physical activity.
6 Describes opportunities in the local community for regular participation in physical activity.

7 Describes opportunities in the larger community for participation in individual and dual physical activities.
8 Explains ways of increasing physical activity in routine daily activities.

National standard 4: Achieves and maintains a health-enhancing level of physical fitness.

4.1

5 Works toward a health-enhancing level of physical fitness.
6 Works toward a health-enhancing level of physical fitness.

7 Works toward a health-enhancing level of physical fitness.
8 Works toward a health-enhancing level of physical fitness.

4.2

5 Designs a cardiorespiratory and body composition fitness plan including a warm-up and cool-down for 1 day.
6 Designs a 1-day personal health-related fitness plan.

7 Designs a 1-week personal health-related fitness plan.
8 Designs a 2-week personal health-related fitness plan taking into account the possibility of inclement weather, minor injury, or travel.

(continued)

Figure 6.3   *(continued)*

(continued)

National standard 5: Exhibits responsible personal and social behavior that respects self and others in physical activity settings.

5.1

5 Works with an individual who is differently abled in a physical activity.
6 Works cooperatively with a small group in physical activity settings.

7 Applies problem-solving techniques when working with another person in physical activity settings.
8 Collaborates with others to solve group problems in physical activity settings.

5.2

5 Accepts responsibility for personal safety during physical activity.
6 Accepts responsibility for safely completing assigned role when working with a small group during physical activity.

7 Accepts responsibility for individual improvement during challenging physical activity.
8 Accepts responsibility for one's own actions and decisions during physical activity.

National standard 6: Values physical activity for health, enjoyment, challenge, self-expression, and social interaction.

6.1

5 Describes the development and role of movement-related activities in the United States during the 17th and 18th centuries.
6 Describes the development and role of movement-related activities in the ancient world and their influences on physical activities today.

7 Describes the development and role of movement-related activities in medieval times and their influences on physical activities today.
8 Explains the development and role of movement-related activities in the United States (19th to 20th centuries) and their influence on physical activities today.

6.2

5 Expresses personal feelings through a movement-based routine.
6 Expresses personal feelings through a manipulative or movement-based routine.

7 Appreciates one's own stylistic approach to creating a routine.
8 Appreciates others' stylistic approaches to creating a dance or routine.

6.3

5 Chooses to engage in skill competencies at a level that leads to personal satisfaction, success, and enjoyment.
6 Chooses to engage in new physical activities.

7 Chooses to engage in physical activities at the appropriate level of physical challenge.
8 Chooses to engage in physical activities at the appropriate level of social, physical, and emotional challenge.

6.4

5 Describes the physical benefits of regular participation in physical activity.
6 Describes the health benefits of regular participation in physical activity.

7 Describes the social benefits of regular participation in physical activity.
8 Explains the cognitive and psychological benefits of regular participation in physical activity.

Figure 6.3 *(continued)*

learning principles (learning how to learn), scientific or biomechanical principles, motor development principles, the critical elements of skills, and game strategy. Included in exit standard 6 are the concepts of historical perspectives, aesthetics, enjoyment and challenge, and valuing the benefits of physical activity. Every committee must decide how to divide the standards for its curriculum. Your group may decide to have only one grade-level standard for each exit standard.

The grade-level standards presented here are based on the premise that the elementary feeder school or schools are focusing their physical education programs on kindergarten through 4th grade–level standards, which cover basic locomotor skills, nonlocomotor skills, basic manipulation, qualities of movement, learning speed and accuracy in movement, appropriate practice of skills, aesthetic features of movement, origin of activities in the local community, enjoyment and participation in movement, physical changes occurring in the child, and scientific principles of movement. If this is not occurring at your feeder schools, your grade-level standards may need to be different from the ones I am presenting. For example, the K–10 grade-level standards (2.2) are based on the sequencing of scientific principles of movement from simple to complex (figure 6.4) and are aligned with the type of physical activity taught at each grade level. If elementary teachers are not teaching the simpler scientific principles (such as stability and using force to manipulate

the body and an object) at the elementary school, then you, a middle school physical educator, must adjust the fifth, sixth, seventh, and eighth grade-level standards accordingly. In addition, the committee may choose to cover the biomechanical principles in a different sequence altogether or cover all of them each year in increasing complexity.

Consider, also, other variables that may warrant the creation of different grade-level standards, including the types of local recreation, the amount of instructional time set aside for physical education, and the content taught in other subject areas. For example, for grade-level standard 6.1, I have chosen to teach students about movement-related activities in the United States (17th and 18th centuries) in fifth grade, in the ancient world in sixth grade, in medieval times in seventh grade, and in the United States (19th and 20th centuries) in eighth grade, paralleling the content that students in my state are studying in their history and social science classes. However, your history and social science classes may be different, and I recommend that you adjust your grade-level standards accordingly. Furthermore, the sample grade-level standards for 6.1 also line up with the motor skills identified in grade-level standard 1 for fifth, sixth, seventh, and eighth grade. For example, many of the team sports we play in the United States either became popular or were invented during the late 1800s. Thus, we have a match: United States history (19th and 20th centuries) and team

Scientific Principles Related to National Standard 2.2

Kindergarten—Stabilizing the body during nonlocomotor skills

1st grade—Stabilizing the body during locomotor skills

2nd grade—Using speed, velocity, and acceleration during locomotor skills

3rd grade—Using force to start and stop movement of the body

4th grade—Using force to manipulate an object

5th grade—Generating and absorbing the force of an object

6th grade—Using force to increase speed or distance

7th grade—Using force to create spin

8th grade—Using force to alter the outcome

9th grade—Understanding the impact of drag and air resistance

10th grade—Application of levers

Figure 6.4 The K–10 grade-level standards for 2.2 move from simple to complex and are aligned with the type of physical activity taught at each grade level.

sports in the eighth grade. (I discuss aligning with other subject areas in more detail in chapter 7.) Certainly, it is possible to show meaningful connections between physical education and other subject areas while still maintaining the integrity of your physical education curriculum, thereby integrating physical education across the curriculum and, in so doing, making the entire school curriculum more relevant and interesting.

Once the committee finishes writing the grade-level standards, it must review each one to ensure that it is performance based, developmentally appropriate, important, and related to the exit standard. Committee members must also double-check the sequencing of grade-level standards for each exit standard to ensure that it is logical and that it works for your situation. The curriculum committee should begin to address assessment at this point in the process (see chapter 8 for more on assessment). The committee must ask the key question, "Can teachers assess the grade-level standard?" For example, grade-level standard 4.2 for seventh grade states, "Designs a 1-week personal health-related fitness plan." Can this be assessed? Yes, each student can create a calendar, videotape, or an essay outlining the fitness plan so that the teacher can assess each student's understanding (see chapter 8). The committee must rewrite any grade-level standard that is not performance based, important, and related to the exit standard.

Determine Grade-Level Criteria for Competence

For each approved grade-level standard, the committee needs to determine the appropriate level of competence. This step is sometimes referred to as a task analysis.

For example, standard 2.1 for sixth grade states, "Explains how to provide appropriate feedback to a partner who is developing or improving specialized skills." For students to demonstrate achieving this standard, they must understand the content outlined in figure 6.5. Appendix B provides sample criteria for all the grade-level standards I've discussed in this chapter. Yes, this step is very tedious, but it helps everyone implement the new curriculum because it clarifies the grade-level standard and provides information necessary to develop student assessment (chapter 8).

Now that you have the grade-level standards and their level of competence for each exit standard (sometimes referred to as the *sequence*), resort the standards by grade level so that everyone can see all the standards for each grade level (the scope). The CD shows a sample database of the grade-level standards. Using a database allows you to easily sort by standard (sequence) and grade level (scope).

The committee must now consider the reality of physical education time constraints. For example, I created the sample grade-level standards identi-

Criteria for Competence: Standard 2.1—Sixth Grade

Students can explain the following:

- Feedback improves the learning of motor skills by providing error detection and motivation for the learner.
- Feedback is based on the critical elements for each skill.
- Only one or two corrections should be identified for feedback after each performance.
- Feedback is delayed for a few seconds after the performance to give the performer an opportunity to reflect on her own performance.
- Feedback is given when the performer cannot see the result of the performance (e.g., technique).
- Feedback is not given when the performer can see the result of the performance (e.g., accuracy, speed, or distance).
- Feedback is most helpful when it is specific and meaningful.
- Feedback should be given frequently in the early stages of learning and then tapered off.

Figure 6.5 Developing criteria for competence not only clarifies the grade-level standard but also provides information necessary for developing student assessment.

fied in this chapter for daily physical education classes, 30 to 40 minutes long. Ask yourselves, "Is there sufficient time in our program to accomplish the listed standards?" By implementing the reform concept of "less is more" (meaning that it's better to focus on a few important standards) in defining the exit standards, by working backward when developing curriculum, and by being aware of your time constraints throughout the curriculum development process, you should be able to answer yes to this question. If by chance, however, the answer is no, then the committee must determine its priorities and either eliminate those standards (exit and grade level) of lower priority or rewrite the exit or grade-level standards, narrowing their focus.

The work done during this step is definitely committee work and does not require the participation of all teachers in the district. However, all teachers should give input to the committee before the committee members make final decisions about the grade-level standards and competency. Therefore, near the end of this step—as throughout the development process—the committee should share its work with as many teachers as possible.

Summary

In this chapter, we have begun to map out our curriculum journey from kindergarten through high school with special emphasis on the middle school program. This process included selecting and educating the physical education curriculum development committee, defining a physically educated person, and translating the definition into exit standards to creating grade-level standards in alignment with the exit standards. In the next chapter, we continue our journey by creating unit standards (figure 6.6). We also select instructional units, look at integrating with other subject areas, and outline the yearly plan. As throughout this process, we focus on the major concepts or big ideas that will prepare students for the skills they will need as adults in the 21st century.

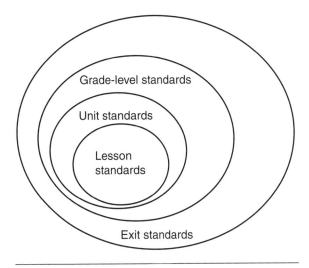

Figure 6.6 The relationship between standards.

Planning a Course of Study

* Accomplished physical education teachers have a deep and broad understanding of the content and principles of physical education, which enables them to devise sound and developmentally appropriate instructional activities.
* Accomplished physical education teachers select, plan, and evaluate curriculum in a continuous process meant to ensure a sensible, properly structured, positive physical education program that meets students' needs and results in student learning.

—National Board for Professional Teaching Standards

I am really proud of the work we've been doing in tying physical education to other subjects. We always begin with our physical education curriculum outcomes, but we have the other subject area teachers tell us about their program, so that we can try to support them as well. We have found that physical education is a natural medium for interdisciplinary learning and the kids often have that "aha!" look in their eyes.

—physical educator Cindy Kuhrasch, Barneveld Schools, Barneveld, Wisconsin

Once the curriculum development committee completes the exit and grade-level standards, you have a map that shows the route to be followed during each year of middle school. In this chapter, we examine the remaining steps of the curriculum process. We look at selecting instructional units, developing unit standards, integrating with other subject areas, determining the yearly plan, and developing unit and lesson plans.

Select Instructional Units

Unfortunately, when committee members begin to determine the units of instruction for each grade level, they often completely forget about the exit and grade-level standards. Everyone must remember that the purpose of the units is to deliver the standards. For example, in language arts, the purpose of language arts is not to read *Moby Dick* but rather to develop competent readers and writers. *Moby Dick* is simply one book that assists in the development of competent readers and writers. Likewise, in physical education, our purpose is not to teach basketball but rather to develop competent and knowledgeable movers. We use basketball as a vehicle with which to reach certain standards.

Beyond selecting units that teach to the standards and competencies, you should provide your students with a variety of different movement experiences. Just as language arts teachers don't have students read *Moby Dick* every year, you don't need to teach basketball every year. Some students will be successful in some activities and some in others. By providing a wide variety of activities, including a balance between the different types of activities (dance; combatives; individual, dual, and team sports; cooperative games; aquatics; tumbling; and adventure), you provide opportunities for all students to experience success while still strengthening their skills in weaker areas. Moreover, when selecting instructional units, consider which instructional units the feeder elementary schools have covered. As when developing grade-level standards, build on what students already know. Then include a variety of activities to create more interest and greater chances for success.

Finally, when selecting instructional units, ask, "What type of units (sometimes referred to as organizing centers) do I want to offer?" You can organize your instructional units with many different approaches (figure 7.1), including skills theme, process, social, activity, fundamentals of movement, or standards (which includes one

Instructional Units Approaches

Skills Theme Approach
Physical fitness

Body management

Locomotor skills

Throwing and catching

Striking with body parts

Striking with objects

Process Approach
Making choices

Problem solving

Resolving conflicts

Developing strategies

Decision making

Social Approach
Adventure and risk

Cultural preservation

Games in the city

Socialization through sports

New games

Activity Approach
Volleyball

Golf

Track and field

Square dancing

Soccer

Swimming

Fundamentals of Movement Approach
Buoyancy

Force

Laws of motion

Spin

Stability

Velocity

Standards Approach
Movement skills

Movement concepts

Daily physical activity

Fitness development

Personal and social behavior in physical activity

Enjoyment, challenge, and self-expression

Figure 7.1 You can organize your instructional units using many different approaches.

instructional unit on each grade-level standard) approaches.

You might think that the standards approach is the way to go because it emphasizes the standards, making it easy for you to see if you are meeting them. You can, however, deliver the standards through one of the other approaches. In figure 7.2a, each unit of instruction addresses one standard, so that during the sixth grade personal and social behavior unit, you use a variety of social initiatives and new games as the physical activities addressing sixth grade standard 5.1, "Works cooperatively with a small group in physical activity settings." In figure 7.2b, each unit of instruction is an activity through which you address each of the standards—at least to some extent. For example, during volley-

ball, teach the skills and the movement concepts and cover fitness development, social skills, and so on. As illustrated by figure 7.2c, the skills theme approach uses thematic instructional units to address each of the standards (to some extent) in each skill area. For example, during the unit on striking with objects, you address all six standards through skills and activities that involve striking with a racket, bat, and club. You can also select units combining approaches.

Grade-Level Themes

When selecting the type of instructional units and then the specific instructional units, I have found it helpful to first identify grade-level themes for

Standards Delivered Through Various Approaches

		STANDARD					
		1	2	3	4	5	6
a.	**Standards delivered through the standards approach**						
	Movement skills (standard 1)	X					
	Movement concepts (standard 2)		X				
	Daily physical activity (standard 3)			X			
	Fitness development (standard 4)				X		
	Personal and social behavior in physical activity (standard 5)					X	
	Values physical activity (standard 6)						X
b.	**Standards delivered through the activity approach**						
	Volleyball	X	X	X	X	X	X
	Golf	X	X	X	X	X	X
	Track and field	X	X	X	X	X	X
	Square dancing	X	X	X	X	X	X
	Soccer	X	X	X	X	X	X
	Swimming	X	X	X	X	X	X
c.	**Standards delivered through the skills theme approach**						
	Physical fitness	X	X	X	X	X	X
	Body management	X	X	X	X	X	X
	Locomotor skills	X	X	X	X	X	X
	Throwing and catching	X	X	X	X	X	X
	Striking with body parts	X	X	X	X	X	X
	Striking with objects	X	X	X	X	X	X

Figure 7.2 To deliver the standards you don't have to follow the standards approach shown in figure 7.1.

tying the grade-level standards together under a common umbrella. Several other sources have also begun to do this as well. For example, in the Kendall/Hunt series *Essentials of Physical Education* (Spindt et al. 2002a, 2002c, 2002e), the sixth grade book is titled *Moving With Confidence,* the seventh grade book is titled *Moving With Skill,* and the eighth grade book is titled *Moving as a Team.* The Physical Education Framework for California Public Schools (California Department of Education 1994b) identifies grade-level themes for kindergarten through 12th grade. The theme for fifth grade is Manipulating Objects Efficiently and Effectively, the sixth grade theme is Working

Cooperatively to Achieve a Common Goal, the seventh grade theme is Accepting Appropriate Challenges Through Problem Solving, and the eighth grade theme is Working as a Team to Solve Problems.

For my sample curriculum, I have selected Manipulating Objects Efficiently and Effectively as the fifth grade theme, Learning Skills Through Cooperation as the sixth grade theme, Taking Acceptable Risks Through Problem Solving as the seventh grade theme, and Working as a Team to Develop Strategies for Success as the eighth grade theme (figure 7.3). You may choose four different grade-level themes, even if you are using the same

Approaches to Units of Instruction

Fifth Grade: Skills Theme Approach (Manipulating Objects Efficiently and Effectively)

1. Introduction (3 weeks)
2. Cooperative Activities (3 weeks)
3. Body Management (3 weeks)
4. Locomotor Skills (3 weeks)
5. Throwing and Catching (3 weeks)
6. Throwing and Catching With Implements (3 weeks)
7. Striking With Hand(s) (3 weeks)
8. Striking With Feet (3 weeks)
9. Striking With Implements (3 weeks)
10. Early American Dances (3 weeks)
11. Early American Games (3 weeks)
12. Closure (3 weeks)

Sixth Grade: Activity Approach (Learning Skills Through Cooperation)

1. Introduction (3 weeks)
2. Cooperative Activities (3 weeks)
3. Stunts and Tumbling (3 weeks)
4. Folk Dance (3 weeks)
5. Target Sport: Bowling (3 weeks)
6. Target and Invasion Sport: Flying Disc (3 weeks)
7. Invasion Sport: 3-on-3 Basketball (3 weeks)
8. Net Sport: Pickleball (3 weeks)

9. Field Sport: Three-Team Softball (3 weeks)
10. Ancient Games (3 weeks)
11. Circus Skills (3 weeks)
12. Closure (3 weeks)

Seventh Grade: Activity Approach (Taking Acceptable Risks Through Problem Solving)

1. Introduction (3 weeks)
2. Tumbling and Gymnastics (5 weeks)
3. Outdoor Education: Orienteering (4 weeks)
4. Net Sport: Tennis (4 weeks)
5. Aquatics (4 weeks)
6. Target Sport: Golf (4 weeks)
7. Self-Defense (5 weeks)
8. Medieval Times Activities (4 weeks)
9. Closure (3 weeks)

Eighth Grade: Activity Approach (Working as a Team to Develop Strategies for Success)

1. Introduction (3 weeks)
2. Problem-Solving Activities (4 weeks)
3. Team Invasion Sports (11 weeks)
4. Team Net Sports (5 weeks)
5. Team Field Sports (5 weeks)
6. Square Dancing (5 weeks)
7. Closure (3 weeks)

Figure 7.3 Units of instruction from the sample curriculum presented in this book.

exit and grade-level standards that I selected. As long as you select grade-level themes thoughtfully and logically, aligning them with the grade-level standards and thereby setting the stage for the selection of the specific instructional units, then you have many options for the specific grade-level themes. First, however, I'll explain my rationale for the grade-level themes that I selected.

The theme Manipulating Objects Efficiently and Effectively addresses fifth graders at their level of development. It emphasizes practicing with a variety of objects for accuracy and speed as identified in grade-level standards 1.0, 2.1, and 2.2. The theme stresses individual achievement and small-group cooperation over competition, with students achieving personal success with object manipulation.

My sixth grade theme, Learning Skills Through Cooperation, emphasizes sixth grade standard 1.0, which includes learning specialized skills, and the many sixth grade standards that require cooperation. For example, notice that even standard 2.1 focuses on cooperation as the students learn to provide appropriate feedback to a partner (see figure 6.2 and appendix B). Most important, however, an emphasis on social interaction early in the middle school experience can make both the physical education and school climate a positive experience for all throughout the middle school years.

The theme Accepting Appropriate Challenges Through Problem Solving suits seventh graders especially well because they like to experiment with new challenges and, unless the school curriculum provides challenging activities in a safe environment, they are likely to take unacceptable risks on their own (see appendix A for more information). This theme teaches students the difference between appropriate and inappropriate risk-taking activities. Furthermore, this theme encompasses the seventh grade standards that emphasize problem solving as well as setting and monitoring goals, participating in personally challenging activities, and accepting personal responsibility for individual improvement during challenging activities. Concerned about interdisciplinary aspects? The challenge theme works well with seventh grade's history and social science emphasis on medieval times and the adventurous activities that predominated in that era.

My eighth grade theme, Working as a Team to Develop Strategies for Success, helps students combine their motor skills into more complex patterns and strategies as they use the skills in team situations. By the eighth grade, students have the

capacity for the abstract thought (see appendix A for more information) that effective offensive and defensive strategies require—especially necessary in team sports. During this stage of mental development, students are able to consider various aspects of a situation simultaneously. For example, an offensive player in Speed-a-Way who is approaching the goal line must assess the situation to determine whether to run across the goal line or drop the ball and go for the higher score. If you delay introducing students to the content of modified team sports until this point, they are less likely to experience the frustration felt by younger students who are not capable of mentally dealing with the number of variables involved with many of the team activities. The link to the grade-level standards is found in the transfer of learning, because there are many similarities in skills and strategies between different team sports; the emphasis on collaborative problem solving; and the growth of team sports during the 19th and 20th centuries—the period that the students are studying in their U.S. history and social science classes.

Instructional Units

Each year includes an introductory unit that focuses on learning class rules and routines, including exercises and participating in the fitness preassessment while encouraging students to get to know one another. A closing unit concludes each grade and includes fitness postassessment and the completion of class projects to assess student understanding of the grade-level standards.

I selected a skills theme approach for fifth grade because my grade-level theme focuses on improving manipulative skills and because my feeder elementary schools don't have an exceptionally strong program (lack of elementary specialists). The first instructional unit after the introductory unit targets cooperative skills acquisition to get fifth graders off to a good start on personal interactions skills. Then for the next seven units, students work on seven different skill themes. Unit 10 focuses on dances from the United States during the 17th and 18th century—which is the time period being studied in history or social science. Unit 11 reviews all the skill units and challenges the students need to increase proficiency in an especially fun way, as they learn games from early America.

I selected a lead-up activity approach for sixth grade because my grade-level theme focuses on applying skills in a variety of lead-up games and activities. The first instructional unit after the introductory unit targets small-group cooperative activities. This is followed by a stunts and tumbling unit and a folk dance unit that teaches dances from countries studied in history or social science. Then for the next five units, students work on manipulative skills in a variety of activities, including bowling, Frisbee, 3-on-3 basketball, Pickleball, and three-team softball. Unit 10, ancient games, offers a direct link to the students' area of study in history and social science. During this unit, students participate in activities from ancient times. Unit 11 reviews all the skill units and challenges the students to increase proficiency in an especially fun way as they work on circus skills.

I have applied an eclectic approach (primarily activity-based) for unit selection in the seventh grade because many of the traditional activities that involve risk taking are new to my students. Instructional units such as tennis, golf, self-defense, orienteering, tumbling and gymnastics, aquatics, and medieval games provide my students with the challenges that they need while simultaneously preparing them for a variety of lifetime activities from which to choose. In addition, aquatics, orienteering, and self-defense involve life

skills that every individual must possess (figure 7.4). Individual and dual sports also help students learn to set goals and monitor their own progress (figure 7.5), whereas activities such as tumbling and gymnastics and self-defense help students learn to apply the biomechanical principles of rotation. Even the medieval times activities unit brings together all of the seventh grade standards, as you'll see as I begin to develop unit standards. Yet, we could categorize the medieval times activities unit as a standards approach instructional unit, because it specifically addresses standard 6.1. From this perspective, my selection of seventh grade instructional units mixes approaches.

Because the eighth grade-level theme focuses on team strategies, I have selected an activity approach with an emphasis on team sport units, along with a unit on problem solving, which involves problem-solving activities for teams and square dancing, which requires a group approach to dancing. Through these instructional units, students learn team strategies and how to apply basic skills to sport-specific skills in a variety of everyday team sports and activities that they can enjoy throughout their lives. More important, these activities highlight the same major movement concepts, encouraging students to transfer

Figure 7.4 An instructional unit on self-defense provides a challenge for students and teaches them an important life skill.

Figure 7.5 Individual sports such as rock climbing help students learn to set their own goals and monitor their progress.

learning from one activity to another. Team sports, problem-solving activities, and square dancing all address (1) how force can be used to alter the outcome of a performance, (2) the effect of physical abilities on skill performance, and (3) the appreciation of another's stylistic approach to performance. Thus, the activity approach in eighth grade creates a program that meets all the grade-level standards.

Even if you choose the same exit standards, grade-level standards, and grade-level themes that I have selected, you must base your specific instructional units on your own situation. Take into account the type of elementary school program feeding your program, local interests, local geography and climate (e.g., snow, water), whether you are on a traditional or year-round

calendar, whether your school is in a rural or urban area, and your philosophy regarding the type of instructional units better suited for middle school. Perhaps, philosophically, you choose the skills theme approach for every grade level. A common practice in Florida is to base most of the instructional units in middle school on skills theme units such as throwing and catching, striking with objects, and striking with body parts. This helps students develop competence in motor skills while applying them to a wide variety of movement forms. Or, let's say you choose the same themes and types of units I did for my sample curriculum, but, depending on your geographic location, you can select in-line skating, sailing, downhill skiing, or water skiing as a seventh grade unit. Depending on community interests, you select an eighth grade unit on cricket, lacrosse, or ice hockey. If you choose to include grade-level themes, as your standards committee work proceeds, you will probably find yourself jumping back and forth between selecting units of instruction, finalizing your grade-level themes, and refining your grade-level standards.

No matter what grade-level themes (if you use them), what types of instructional units, or what specific units you select, you must ask, "Can we deliver the grade-level standards through the units we select?" For example, if class A learns the standards through the skills theme approach and class B in the same grade learns the standards through the activity approach, then that is what is important. Interestingly, some schools are conducting "action research" projects to see what really works best with students. Wouldn't it be interesting to teach the sixth grade class this year with the skills theme approach and the sixth grade class next year with the activity approach and then compare the results?

As you finalize your selection of instructional units, you will also need to determine the optimal length of time required to complete a unit. First, consider how often and how long your physical education classes meet. My instructional units assume daily 30- to 40-minute classes. Yet there is no definitive answer to the question "What is the ideal length of an instructional unit?" Motor learning research does tell us that if you use units of very short duration, it will be impossible for students to learn enough to realize whether they like the activity (Schmidt and Wrisberg 2000). So, ensure that the unit is long enough so that students can accomplish the unit standards (see the next section). Remember, fundamental motor

Depth or Breadth?

A colleague of mine went to visit a local school district. The first day he visited the middle school. The teachers showed him their program, which consisted of new activities every week. When my colleague asked why they changed units so frequently, the teachers responded that they wanted to expose the students to a wide variety of activities. The next day, he visited the high school. Again, the teachers showed him their program, which, in the high school's case, consisted of new activities every other week. When he asked why they changed units so frequently, the teachers responded that they wanted to expose the students to a wide variety of activities. After his second visit, he called me to ask whether anyone in this school district actually taught anything or whether they all spent all of their time exposing students to the curriculum.

skills require 120 to 180 minutes of practice to reach the competency level. So most instructional units at the middle school level will last from 4 to 6 weeks, allowing enough time to develop new skills. Additionally, the average length of the units will become progressively longer from grade to grade as the students' attention spans and depth of understanding increase.

Develop Unit Standards

Once the committee has determined the units of instruction, it must determine how to address each of the grade-level standards within each unit. The strategy for determining unit standards from grade-level standards is similar to the strategy used to determine the grade-level standards from the exit standards. Obviously, if the committee has selected the type of units based on the standards approach, then each unit addresses one grade-level standard. For example, if I include a fitness unit, which could occur in either the standards approach or mixed approach, then I could deal exclusively with standard 4 during that unit.

But because most middle schools do not use the standards approach for their unit selection, let's discuss how to determine how much of each grade-level standard you can teach in each unit. By the end of the school year, the majority of your students should be able to demonstrate all the standards. But don't be concerned that some units focus primarily on one or two grade-level standards; you can cover the other standards in other units. During this process, it may become obvious that certain units of instruction need to come before others. Remember this when you make your interdisciplinary and yearly plan.

As we examine the exit standards, certain patterns emerge as we begin to determine which part of a grade-level standard belongs in each unit. Figure 7.6 shows the unit standards related to grade-level standard 4.2 for seventh grade. Each unit addresses a different part (flexibility, muscular endurance, muscular strength, cardiorespiratory endurance, and body composition) of health-related fitness. I have taken into consideration the parts of health-related fitness that are most improved through each of the activities. For example, swimming requires cardiorespiratory endurance; tumbling and gymnastics require flexibility; and self-defense requires muscular strength. Just as easily, I could have addressed all five parts of fitness in each instructional unit, beginning with simple ideas and progressing to more advanced ideas through the year. Either way works.

For grade-level standard 5.1 in eighth grade, students could build their collaboration skills by going from the simple to the complex (figure 7.7) by collaborating with one other person, then demonstrating the conflict resolution process, and then collaborating with team members during invasion, net, and field sports. In this situation, the order of the first two units is important, because each unit builds on previously covered problem-solving skills. In contrast, for standard number 4.1, the order was not as important. We will consider this issue when we develop our yearly plan. Check the competencies (see appendix B) of each standard for a breakdown of the grade-level standards, which you can then assign to appropriate units of instruction.

Once you establish unit standards for each grade-level standard and each unit, you can reorganize the information to see what needs to be accomplished in each unit (see figure 7.8). You will find all the specific unit standards in chapters

---

Sample Unit Standards for Seventh Grade Related to Grade-Level Standard 4.2

Grade-Level Standard: Designs a 1-week personal health-related fitness plan.

Introduction

Define the terms warm-up, cool-down, progression, overload, and specificity.

Tumbling and Gymnastics

Creates a 1-week flexibility plan.

Outdoor Education: Orienteering

Creates a 1-week nutrition plan.

Net Sport: Tennis

Creates a 1-week body composition plan.

Aquatics

Creates a 1-week cardiorespiratory plan.

Target Sport: Golf

Creates a 1-week muscular endurance plan.

Self-Defense

Creates a 1-week muscular strength plan.

Medieval Times Activities

Designs a 1-week personal health-related fitness plan.

Closure

Refines 1-week personal health-related fitness plan.

Figure 7.6 Each unit has a standard related to standard 4.2, and the unit achieves this standard by focusing on a different part of health-related fitness.

Sample Unit Standards for Eighth Grade Related to Grade-Level Standard 5.1

Grade-Level Standard: Collaborates with others to solve group problems in physical activity settings.

Introduction

Demonstrates collaboration with a partner.

Problem-Solving

Demonstrates the steps for conflect resolution.

Invasion Sports

Collaborates with team emebers during invasion sports.

Net Sports

Collaborates with team members to solve problems during net sports.

Field Sports

Collaborates with team members to solve problems during field sports.

Square Dancing

Collaborates with others to solve group problems in physical activity settings.

Closure and Fitness Assessment

Callaborates with others to sove group problems in physical activity settings.

Figure 7.7 In this example, problem solving moves from the simple to the complex and the units build on each other.

14, 15, 16, and 17 as well as sample unit plans. The committee should not finalize the units of instruction until it has completed the unit standards and can therefore verify the validity of the selection of the instructional units against the unit standards. Now is also the time for the committee to make sure that it has allocated sufficient time to each unit, enabling the majority of students to attain the unit standards.

As you can see, many options exist for each stage of curriculum development. Choose those that work best for your situation.

Seventh Grade Self-Defense Unit Standards

1.0   Demonstrates the mature form for stance, stomps, knee kicks, front snap kick, side kick, rear kick, elbow strike, palm–heel strike, side falls, wrist release, front choke release, rear choke release, hair release.

2.1   Explains the process of setting appropriate goals, conducting appropriate practice, and monitoring changes in the development of self-defense skills.

2.2   Explains how magnitude affects spin or rotation of the body or an object.

2.3   Explains the use of strategy in self-defense.

2.4   Explains individual differences and how these differences affect self-defense performance.

2.5   Explains the critical elements for stance, stomp, knee kick, front snap kick, side kick, rear kick, elbow strike, palm–heel strike, ear slap, side falls, wrist release, front choke release, rear choke release, hair release.

3.1   Engages in moderate and vigorous physical activity for 60 minutes 6 days each week.

3.2   Describes opportunities in the larger community for participation in self-defense activities.

4.1   Works toward a health-enhancing level of physical fitness.

4.2   Creates a 1-week muscular strength plan.

5.1   Applies problem-solving techniques when working with another person in self-defense activities.

5.2   Accepts responsibility for individual improvement during self-defense activities.

6.1   Describes combative activities during medieval times.

6.2   Not applicable.

6.3   Chooses to engage in self-defense activities at the appropriate level of personal challenge.

6.4   Describes the social benefits of regular participation in self-defense.

Figure 7.8   Sorting the standards by unit shows you exactly what needs to be taught in each unit.

Integrate With Other Subject Areas

Now that your committee has identified the units of instruction based on unit standards, it's time to ask, "How can we integrate physical education with other disciplines?" Before finalizing the sequence of units in the yearly plan, you and your physical education colleagues should meet with teachers from other subject areas to identify interdisciplinary possibilities. Caine and Caine (1991, 1997a, 1997b) identified two reasons why interdisciplinary teaching is important:

- The brain searches for common patterns and connections.

- Every experience actually contains within it the seeds of many, and possibly all, subject areas, and one of the keys to understanding is what is technically known as redundancy, or revisiting information through different experiences and perspectives.

Interdisciplinary teaching adds more meaning to learning while, at the same time, approaching learning from a real-life perspective. When your students go out into the world as adults, they don't apply their science knowledge for an hour, then apply their language arts skills for an hour, and then apply their understanding of human movement for an hour. Rather, real-world situations integrate disciplines. Interdisciplinary instruction is the wave of the future, and we must join in.

Yet, let's not engage in interdisciplinary activities for the sake of engaging in interdisciplinary activities. To avoid this pitfall, keep focused on your physical education exit, grade-level, and unit standards while looking for meaningful links to other subject areas.

Let's examine four models (sequenced, shared, integrated, and webbed) for connecting subject areas. (Note: Consider interdisciplinary connections using any one of the first three models at this point in the process; however, when using the fourth model, the webbed model, conduct the interdisciplinary step just before selecting instructional units.)

Sequenced Model

The sequenced model (figure 7.9) encourages teachers from various disciplines to rearrange the order of topics so that similar units coincide with each other, synchronizing the content of two related subject areas. In this way, the content and activities in each class enhance the learning in both. This model is an easy way to initiate an interdisciplinary approach because it requires little articulation between teachers.

Let's examine some examples of how to apply the sequenced model to physical education. You could coordinate your teaching of body composition with the health educator's teaching of nutrition. Of course, the connections between health and physical education are easy to see, but what about connections between physical education and other subject areas? Try timing a medieval times activities unit to occur when the history teacher is specifically covering medieval times. By learning two units simultaneously, students will begin

to see relationships between concepts, helping them make more sense out of the content of both classes. Keep it simple when planning, though; you don't necessarily have to go into the details of how each of you will approach the unit using this model—simply offer the units at the same time.

Shared Model

The shared model (figure 7.10) encourages two teachers to look for overlaps in subject matter content. This approach is most appropriate when subject content is clustered into broad themes, such as humanities or practical arts. Each subject area in the shared model relates its curriculum to the common theme. For example, physical educators provide instruction on dance while music educators provide instruction on theater music to create a thematic unit on the performing arts. In another example, physical educators provide instruction on health-related fitness and health educators provide instruction on personal health to create a unit on wellness. The two teachers involved in this model plan their instruction together, so that their lessons complement each other. Although the shared model takes more effort to plan than the sequenced model, the benefits are greater because students see more connections between the content taught in the two classes. This approach is an appropriate intermediary step between the sequenced model and the integrated model.

Integrated Model

The integrated model (figure 7.11) involves interdisciplinary sharing among four or more subject areas. To follow this model, each subject area must

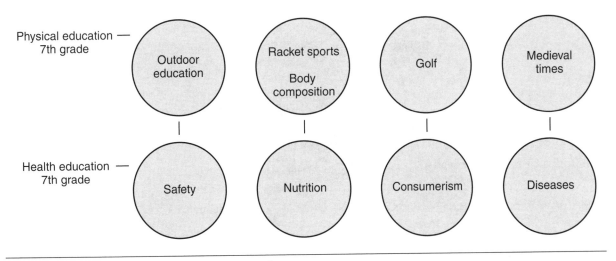

Figure 7.9 Sequenced model for interdisciplinary planning.

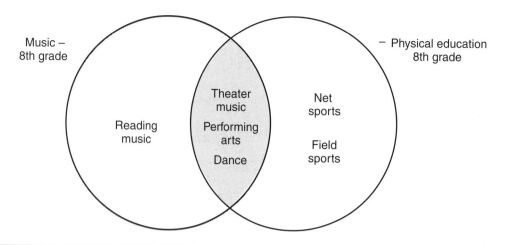

Figure 7.10   Shared model for interdisciplinary planning.

first set its own priorities. Then, all participating teachers look for the skills, attitudes, and concepts that overlap between those subject areas. One example of this model is a thematic unit on Life Under Water.

In this unit, the physical education instruction focuses on swimming and skin diving, the science instruction is on the laws of physics below sea level, the mathematics instruction is on performing calculations on the laws of physics below sea level, and the language arts instruction is on the writing process through which students describe what it would be like to live under water. Because this approach is very time consuming and requires the total commitment of all teachers involved, I recommend that you start small with a 3- to 4-week unit before attempting to develop a semester- or year-long plan. As you continue to work together and learn more about each other's subject areas, you can then plan longer instructional units.

Webbed Model

The webbed model is a thematic approach that integrates subject content from several disciplines, beginning with a theme such as inventions or consumer ideas. The theme becomes the overlay for the other subject areas. This approach is also very time consuming; you should start with one unit of instruction before attempting a semester- or year-long plan. Common themes that work well when including physical education include transitions, change, social skills, and taking acceptable risks. Figure 7.12 illustrates a webbed model focusing on taking acceptable risks.

The webbed model differs from the others in that the theme does not necessarily come from within one or more of the other subject areas; instead, the theme is simply a common area of interest for teachers or students. And unlike the other three models, you must design your web

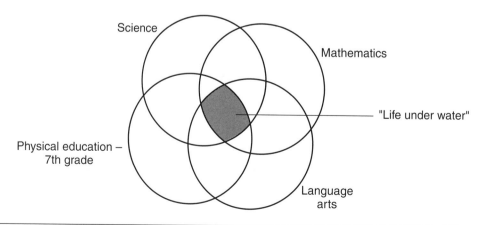

Figure 7.11   Integrated model for interdisciplinary planning.

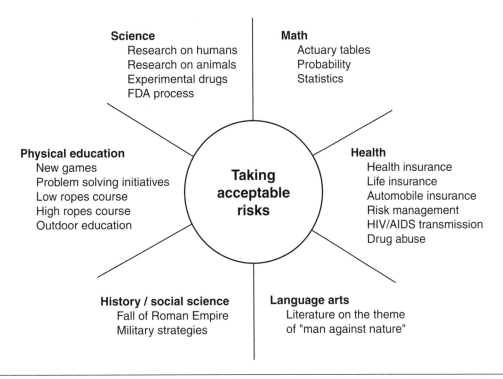

Science
    Research on humans
    Research on animals
    Experimental drugs
    FDA process

Math
    Actuary tables
    Probability
    Statistics

Physical education
    New games
    Problem solving initiatives
    Low ropes course
    High ropes course
    Outdoor education

Taking acceptable risks

Health
    Health insurance
    Life insurance
    Automobile insurance
    Risk management
    HIV/AIDS transmission
    Drug abuse

History / social science
    Fall of Roman Empire
    Military strategies

Language arts
    Literature on the theme
    of "man against nature"

Figure 7.12   Webbed model for interdisciplinary planning.

before—not after—choosing instructional units. As with the first three models, physical educators must remember to stay devoted to their own grade-level standards, joining a web only when participating in it helps students meet the physical education standards.

Determine the Yearly Plan

Next, you must decide the order in which you'll teach the units of instruction you have chosen. Consider the following aspects when determining the yearly plan: sequencing of instructional units, interdisciplinary possibilities, and use of facilities. Make sequencing issues your top priority when designing your yearly plan. Ask, "Why should one unit come before another?" Look back at any notes you made regarding sequencing issues while writing unit standards. For example, in eighth grade, the fifth standard (see figure 7.7) clearly presented sequencing issues, because the unit standards moved from simple to complex. For units for which sequencing can be more flexible, look closer at the interdisciplinary possibilities. By choosing and sequencing your units before looking at interdisciplinary possibilities, you ensure that the goals of physical education receive top priority.

After sequencing your units, you must set up a yearly schedule for sharing facilities and equipment within the physical education department. Unfortunately, this often becomes a limiting factor

Caught in a Web!

To coincide with our Heart Adventures Challenge Course (see chapter 12), the music department developed a unit where all music heard, sung, or played related to the heart, with additional emphasis on the beat (relating to the heartbeat). Social studies classes studied countries that have high rates of heart disease. Home economics students studied healthy foods, and math students learned how to calculate heart level percentages in the target zone.

Reprinted, by permission, from B. Kirkpatrick and M.M. Buck, 1995, "Heart Adventures Challenge Course: A lifestyle education activity," *Journal of Physical Education, Recreation and Dance* 66(2): 17-24.

when planning sequencing and interdisciplinary units. Sometimes, limited facilities and equipment make ideal sequencing of units impossible. For example, if the seventh grade class needs the gymnasium during the second unit for gymnastics and the eighth grade class needs the gymnasium during the second unit for dance, and only one class at a time can use the gymnasium, then either one of the grade levels will have to change the unit sequence or one of the grade levels will need to find an alternative location for the unit of instruction. Some sequences are more easily accommodated than others, such as introductory units, which you can teach in a variety of locations and don't require a specific facility. Be creative and work out facility sharing and rotation, keeping students' needs at the forefront.

Don't lock yourself into teaching units of instruction during the corresponding sport season. Not only does this approach tie you down to an activity-based approach, but it also tends to ignore important educational considerations, such as appropriate sequencing. Although this traditional approach can have some positive benefits, such as allowing students to watch the activity on television to better understand the game concept, let them enjoy the flexibility created by recording instead. Focus on educational considerations and, if you're able to teach basketball skills during the NCAA finals in March, great, but don't let that restrict your yearly plan to the detriment of students' overall skill acquisition.

In many counties and districts, the development of yearly plans as well as the development of unit plans and lesson plans is left to the individual teacher. Yet, regardless of who develops the yearly, unit, and lesson plans, all three must occur. As the saying goes, "What is not planned for is not taught, and what is not taught is not learned."

Develop Unit Plans and Lesson Plans

Congratulations—you've made it this far in the curriculum development process! Now it's time to put all your hard work into developing the actual unit plans. Chapters 14, 15, 16, and 17 contain sample unit plans for each of the suggested units of instruction. Remember, when developing the grade-level standards, we worked backward from the exit standards. When developing the unit stan-

dards, we worked backward from the grade-level standards. Now, as we develop unit plans, we must align all instruction with the unit standards.

When I provide direct assistance for a physical education department, I always recommend that they work cooperatively to develop unit plans, because unit plans can take a long time to develop well. When creating a unit plan, be sure to list the unit standards on the first page to keep them foremost in your mind as you plan. Next, begin to create a day-by-day unit outline showing the unit standards and competencies you'll address and the skills and activities you'll include. Constantly go back and forth between the skills, activities, competencies, and unit standards to ensure that you are, in fact, addressing each standard so that your students will be able to demonstrate their understanding of it by the end of the unit. In addition, note the type of facility, equipment, media, and other resources you'll need for the unit. Finally, determine how you will assess student learning at the end of the unit (see chapter 8).

Once you complete a unit plan, ask, "Do the competencies, skills, and activities match the unit standards?" Make sure the unit competencies line up with the exit, grade-level, and unit standards. But you're not quite ready to teach yet. If curriculum is the map (or the *what),* then instruction is the vehicle of transportation (or the *how);* before entering the classroom, you must create lesson plans, the delivery vehicles of the curriculum. We discuss lesson planning in part III.

Summary

In chapters 6 and 7, we discussed a 12-step process for curriculum development in a linear fashion. You, however, will probably find that as you begin to work through these steps you'll tend to jump back and forth between determining grade-level standards, selecting instructional units, and integrating with other subject areas. Each of these areas influences the other, so avoid a lockstep approach. The task of curriculum development is arduous; however, the benefits for you and your students are many. Now, with our map laid out, we can see our destination. But before we begin our journey, let's make sure we clearly understand the destination (student learning) and how we will know whether the students have arrived (assessment). Thus, in the next chapter, we examine student assessment.

Assessing and Grading Your Students

• Accomplished physical education teachers design assessment strategies appropriate to the curriculum and to the learner. They use assessment results to provide feedback to the learner, to report student progress, and to shape instruction.

—National Board for Professional Teaching Standards

When I began to try self- and partner assessments in class, kids learned more. I believe that it helped to make clearer for them the specifics of what I was asking them to learn, and it touched every area a learner might be more proficient in.

—physical educator Francesca Zavacky, Clark School, Charlottesville, Virginia

In many physical education programs, we have forgotten the intended purpose of grading and have begun to use it as a means of reward or, worse, punishment. Grading of this kind short-changes the students, whereas a well-thought-out assessment plan is likely to cultivate higher-order thinking and problem-solving capacities in your students. You may put a lot of energy into your teaching, but only assessment can tell you if the students are learning. In this chapter, we look at standards-based assessment and the role of grading in physical education.

We have already seen that the purpose of curriculum is to map out student learning: cognitive (knowledge based), psychomotor (skill based), and affective (belief based). The purpose of assessment, then, is to determine whether students have learned in these three areas. More specifically, assessment is the process of gathering evidence and documenting a student's learning related to the standards. The matching of assessment to the curriculum is known as *alignment.*

According to NASPE (2006a), 15 states require student assessment in physical education. Nine require assessment of motor and movement skills (national standard 1), 11 require assessment of physical fitness (national standard 4), 10 require assessment of content knowledge (national standards 2 and 4), and three require assessment of participation in physical activity outside of school (national standard 3). As accountability continues to be a critical issue in education reform, these numbers will rise.

Some of you may wonder why we are discussing assessment before instruction. First, you must identify for students, up front, what you expect from them and how you will assess their learning. Let's say, for example, that you are grading a student on a headstand at the end of your seventh grade tumbling and gymnastics unit. The student performs a tripod (inverted position with knees resting on elbows) and remains balanced for 4 seconds. What grade would you give this student? I have asked this question often in workshops, and I get answers ranging from a B (very good) to an F (failing). But then I present the participants with my criteria for the headstand:

A: Performs a headstand and balances on own for at least 3 seconds.

B: Performs a headstand but receives support from a partner to remain balanced for 3 seconds.

C: Performs a tripod and balances on own for at least 3 seconds.

D: Initiates a tripod but is unable to balance on own.

F: Fails to initiate a tripod.

On seeing the criteria, most teachers readily agree the student deserved a grade of C. The teachers have performed what is known as criterion-referenced grading. Sharing this information with students at the beginning of a unit provides motivation because it gives them something to work toward. In addition, when you announce a student's grade, the student will understand why he received that grade, eliminating unnecessary conflict.

Another reason I'm addressing assessment now is that part of standards-based assessment involves what is called *embedded assessment*. This means assessing students while they are actually practicing—as part of the instruction or simultaneously with instruction. The assessment can take place periodically throughout the unit (formative assess-

ment) or at the conclusion of the unit (summative assessment). Perhaps a student is initially unable to perform a headstand, and you record an F. Then, during the first 2 weeks of practice, you observe the student in a balanced tripod, and you record a C. Finally, during the last week of practice, you observe the student extending her legs over her head with her partner assisting, and you record a B. This type of documentation provides evidence of student growth over the instructional unit. In addition, the B (the end result) becomes the final grade for the headstand, and you have not made the student nervous by telling her you're assessing her. We discuss later in this chapter a better approach to documenting skill growth—one that uses rubrics instead of grades.

Assessment

Traditionally, physical educators have based assessment and grading on standardized motor skill tests for accuracy and distance; on written tests of rules, history, and strategy; and on physical fitness tests. With the move toward standards-based curricula, physical educators have begun to use alternative assessment tools, including structured observations, written tests with an emphasis on open-ended questions, student logs and journals, role-playing and simulations, research and reports, and projects. These tools require students to use higher-order thinking skills and to actually apply what they have learned (performance-based assessment).

Authentic assessment goes one step further in that it resembles a real-life situation in which students must apply skills, knowledge, and attitudes in scenarios that reflect the ambiguities of life. Students engaged in authentic assessment are often more motivated to perform because the value of the work goes beyond the demonstration of competence in school and relates to their lives and futures.

The exit, grade-level, and unit standards that I identify in chapters 6, 7, and 14 through 17 set the stage for assessment. If your curriculum committee writes the standards so that they are observable and measurable and require evidence of students' abilities to create new knowledge or apply motor skills in new situations, then it will be relatively easy to construct assessment tools. In fact, the tools should be self-evident. Remember, there must be a match between an assessment tool and each standard. You must be able to clearly show

Terms for Understanding Assessment

alignment—Clear and direct relationship among standards, curricula, instructional materials, instructional methods, and assessments.

alternative assessment—Assessment tools that engage students in the learning process and assess higher-order cognitive processes. This type of assessment requires students to generate a response to a question rather than choose from a set of responses given to them.

analytic rubric—A procedure in which performances are evaluated for selected dimensions, with each dimension receiving a separate score.

anchor—A sample of student work that exemplifies a specific level of performance.

assessment—Process of acquiring qualitative or quantitative information.

authentic assessment—Process of acquiring evidence and documentation of a student's learning in ways that resemble real life.

criterion-referenced grading—Assessment based on comparison to a criterion.

critical features—Those elements (e.g., stepping forward on the opposite foot when throwing) of performing a skill deemed necessary for its correct execution.

dimensions—Subcategories used in assessment of a task.

embedded assessment—Assessment that occurs simultaneously with instruction.

exit standards—Expectations of what all students should know and be able to do at graduation from high school.

formative assessment—Ongoing assessment that can provide information to guide instruction and improve performance.

grade-level standards—Expectations of what all students should know and be able to do at the end of a grade level. These are sometimes referred to as benchmarks.

grading—The process of assigning a symbol (grade) to denote progress.

holistic rubric—Scoring based on an overall impression (several dimensions) of the student's performance.

mature form—The most efficient pattern of movement (e.g., stepping forward on the opposite foot when performing an overhand throw) for performing a skill.

open-ended question—A question for which there is not a single correct answer. There will, however, be effective responses to the question that meet an identified criterion.

performance-based assessment—Direct observation and judgment of student products or performances. These assessments replicate the actions required for actual performance of the task rather than reference the tasks indirectly. They require students to construct a response, create a product, or perform a demonstration.

performance standard—Standard that defines how good is good enough related to the expectations of what all students should know and be able to do in particular subjects and grade levels.

portfolio—Collection of student work aligned to the standards.

process assessment (psychomotor)—Assessment of the technique used to perform the skill.

product assessment (psychomotor)—Assessment of the outcome of the movement (i.e., number of volleyball serves that land in the court).

rubric—A set of scoring guidelines for assessing student work.

scope—The content that is to be covered during a particular time period (usually 1 year).

standards-based assessment—Process of determining whether and to what extent a student can demonstrate the standards.

summative assessment—Culminating assessment for a unit or grade level, providing a status report on the degree of mastery according to identified standards.

how students are progressing toward each of the grade-level standards. Regardless of the type of assessment, provide students with relevant and timely feedback focusing on their strengths and on aspects of their performance that may need improvement.

Assessment Tools

Let's turn now to specific assessment tools appropriate for physical education. Although one or more types of assessment can be effective, you must ensure that your choices match one or more grade-level or unit standards. In fact, you may opt to allow students with different primary intelligences (see chapter 9) to select different assessment tools in order to use their strengths. For example, say you are assessing seventh grade students on standard 4.2, "Designs a 1-week personal health-related fitness plan." The student could

- design a chart showing his 1-week fitness plan,
- write an essay describing his 1-week fitness plan,
- create a multimedia project showing his 1-week fitness plan,
- create a video project showing his 1-week fitness plan, or
- create a rap describing his 1-week fitness plan.

The products created by students are then assessed using a rubric and placed in the student's portfolio—but more on rubrics and portfolios later.

Structured Observations

In a subject area such as physical education in which you can see so much of what students learn, structured observations are a key assessment tool. Teachers, peers, or students themselves can observe and assess performance of motor skills, exercises, routines, and demonstrations of appropriate social interaction skills, including helping a peer learn a new skill (figure 8.1, *a-b*). When assessing performance based on an observation, use a checklist, a scale, a rubric (see later section), or a simple counting system, such as number of encouragements or number of curl-ups. In some situations it's appropriate to use several assessment strategies: self-assessment, peer assessment, and teacher assessment. For example, students may first assess themselves and then have a

peer validate their observations; only then is the teacher brought in to make a final assessment.

Assessments from observations are sometimes difficult to justify because there is no concrete product for both you and the student to review. Once the observation period is over, there is no way to replay the performance to verify the observer's assessment. Or is there? Recording the performance provides a permanent record of the incident. You can save video clips either on videotape or in digitized form (see electronic portfolios later in this chapter) for use on a computer. Either way, you can document growth over time, saving the information for future review.

Observations work especially well with grade-level standards 1 and 5. For example, taking sixth grade standard 1.0, "Demonstrates the mature form for specialized skills and combinations during cooperative activities; lead-up or simple target, invasion, field, and net activities; stunts and tumbling; and dance activities" and specifically targeting an overhand softball throw, a peer, teacher, or both use a checklist of critical features (figure 8.2) to assess performance. Looking at the checklist after her performance, the student will see her softball overhand throwing strengths and weaknesses. In keeping with the embedded assessment concept, many of these assessment tools work well not only as assessment tools but also as instructional activities.

Written Tests

For assessing cognitive understanding, written tests are still appropriate tools. A shift has taken place, however, from emphasizing true–false questions, multiple choice, and short answers to essay and open-ended questions. Other subject area educators often refer to this change as going "beyond the bubble"—going beyond filling in a scantron sheet to using higher-order thinking skills to answer questions. Although true–false questions, multiple choice, and short answers will sometimes be appropriate, we must shift our emphasis to essay and open-ended questions.

The way in which a standard is written will often tell you the appropriate type of question to ask. For example, if the standard begins with the verb *choose,* then a multiple choice question is appropriate. If the standard begins with the verb *list,* then a short-answer test item is appropriate. If the standard begins with the verb *explain,* then an essay question is appropriate.

When writing true–false questions, avoid trivial information such as the exact year a sport was

Figure 8.1 Structured observation by *(a)* the teacher or *(b)* a student, performed properly, is an effective assessment method.

invented and focus on significant, standards-based information. Equally important is avoiding broad generalizations and ambiguous statements. Remember to

- have only one idea per question,

- have similar numbers of true–false statements,

- avoid creating patterns with true–false answers,

- keep true–false statements about the same length, and

- avoid words like *never, always, often, usually,* and *sometimes.*

The key to writing good multiple choice items is to make the item as clear and straightforward as possible. The purpose is to test learning, not reading skill, mind reading, or puzzle solving. When you are writing multiple choice items,

- make the content meaningful and relative to the unit standards;

- don't test trivial or unimportant facts;

- write short, clear items, including as much item content in the stem (the part of the question before the answers) as possible;

- construct the stem so that it conveys a complete thought;

Structured Observation Checklist for an Overhand Throw

Sixth Grade: Demonstrates the mature form for specialized skills and combinations during cooperative; lead-up or simple target, invasion, field, net; stunts and tumbling; and dance activities.

Unit standard: Demonstrate the mature form for the softball overhand throw.

- Keeps nonthrowing side and arm toward target.
- Places weight on back foot.
- Swings throwing arm backward in preparation.
- Steps forward with foot on opposite side of body from throwing arm.
- Makes forward body rotation occur through lower body, then upper body, and then shoulders.
- Transfers weight to foot on opposite side of body from throwing arm.
- Leads the way with the elbow for the arm movement, followed by forearm extension, and ending with a wrist snap.
- Follows through in the direction of the target.

Figure 8.2 The checklist can be used by a peer, teacher, or both.

- have distractors (incorrect answers) that are parallel in form, of the same length, and grammatically consistent with the stem;
- avoid overusing *always, never, all of the above,* and *none of the above* in the distractors;
- randomly select the position of the correct answer;
- avoid stereotyped phrases and negative statements;
- have only one correct or best answer; and
- design three well-written, plausible alternative answers.

Short-answer questions require a learner to supply a single word, a few words, or a brief sentence in response to an incomplete statement or a question. *Fill in the blank* or *completion* are also used to refer to this type of constructed-response question. When writing these types of questions, remember that

- the question should elicit responses higher than mere recall,
- only one desired answer should be clear from the question,
- the question should be very specific, and
- context should be included if required to make the question more specific.

By answering essay questions, students can demonstrate deeper understanding of the content. For example, instead of asking a series of true–false or multiple choice questions on strategies related to volleyball, instruct students to "Describe the game of volleyball and explain how three different offensive and defensive strategies are used to gain an advantage in the game." Or, instead of asking matching or fill-in-the-blank questions on the FITT (frequency, intensity, time, and type) concepts, ask, "How would you go about improving your flexibility?" When using essay questions,

- be very specific about the information you're requesting,
- inform students of the grading criteria and conditions (i.e., expected length of answer),
- keep questions short,
- make an answer key for what should be included in the student's response,
- score all responses to one question before proceeding to the next question, and
- score responses anonymously.

Open-ended questions (figure 8.3) differ from essay questions in that essay questions measure what students know whereas open-ended questions measure both what students know and what they can do with that knowledge. Open-ended questioning evaluates students' ability to apply, analyze, and synthesize. Thus, many different, yet valid, answers should result. When creating an open-ended question, ask the question in such a way that the students are able to approach it from many different angles. For example, asking why the ball may be veering left in tennis gives students an opportunity to share different reasons, including the effect of spin. In addition, ask questions in such a way that students can be confident that they have provided a complete answer. To do this, either specify the amount of information you're requesting (e.g., "Name one . . . ") or include this information in the grading rubric. Also, remember to:

- specify the criteria for assessment,
- award partial credit or give a separate score for using correct procedures when the final answer is incorrect,
- construct a model answer for each problem that indicates the amount of credit to be awarded for work at different stages, and
- determine a real-world context in which to use the knowledge.

Keep in mind that you're using each assessment item to collect data for one or more grade-level (or unit-level) standards. Thus, you must ensure that your questions originate from the standards themselves. Don't simply think up open-ended questions to fill a category; to assess student understanding, you must specifically design questions to match certain standards. Thus, one test may address several standards.

Student Logs and Journals

Use student logs and journals to document the accomplishment of standards that relate to a performance of a physical activity and feelings surrounding that experience. Logs and journals differ from open-ended and essay questions in that students record data (figure 8.4) or their feelings instead of answering a single question. Often in situations in which logs and journals are kept, students take notebooks or steno pads and a pencil or pen to class with them, or the teacher stores the notebooks rather than relying on students to keep track of them. In a few schools, each student has a tablet or handheld computer in which to record information.

Specifically, students can maintain a log of the various kinds of physical activity that they perform outside the school day. The log can show the frequency, intensity, time, and type of exercise. In some cases, students record and verify their own involvement. In other situations, you may wish to ask parents or guardians to verify student participation. After several weeks of record keeping, students can evaluate their improvement and compare the results with their out-of-school participation in physical activity (figure 8.5). Data of this type can demonstrate growth over time,

---

Ideas for Open-Ended Test Questions

Eighth Grade: Analyzes the effect of positive transfer on specialized skill improvement.

1. Name three similarities between soccer and Speed-a-Way skills. How can these similarities help you learn Speed-a-Way if you already know how to play soccer? (standard 2.1)

Sixth Grade: Describes the development and role of movement-related activities in the ancient world and their influences on physical activities today.

2. Name one of the movement-related activities in the ancient world. What influence has this activity had on modern-day games and sports? (standard 6.1)

Seventh Grade: Applies problem-solving techniques when working with another person in physical activity settings.

3. Two players on your basketball team are constantly arguing about the best offensive and defensive strategies to use. How would you assist your teammates in working out their differences? (standard 5.1)

Figure 8.3 Open-ended questions measure what students know and what they can do with that knowledge.

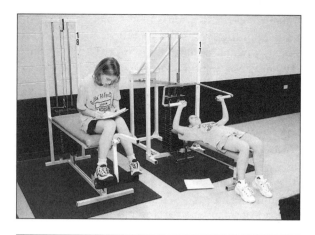

Figure 8.4 Student logs capture chronological data related to the performance of a physical activity, allowing students to evaluate their progress in that activity.

specifically as it relates to grade-level standards 2.1, 3.1, and 4.1.

Students can also maintain a journal in which they describe events and their feelings. Journal writing is especially effective after a cooperative learning or social skill activity, aligning well with standards 5.1 and 6.3. The teacher needs to supply a prompt (see figure 8.6) for journal entries. Students can describe their abilities to demonstrate certain social skills as well as the feelings that participation as an active team member aroused.

Through the journal-writing process, students can document their own growth over time as well as develop goals for future growth. This can occur during the cool-down at the end of a lesson or can be assigned as homework.

Role-Playing and Simulations

In chapter 12, I discuss virtual reality technology in which students experience "semirealistic" situations controlled by a computer. Once in these situations, students respond as if they were in the real situation. Putting students into virtual reality situations in which they must demonstrate skills and apply knowledge is a truly authentic assessment. Short of having the software and hardware for virtual reality, we can ask students to role-play or perform in simulations that we create. For example, some students are confined to a chair and asked to play the role of persons who are mobility impaired while the other students find ways to include these students in the sport or activity.

Other role-playing assessment activities include asking students to

- resolve simulated conflicts;
- create performances for simulated gymnastic meets (see figure 8.7);
- practice dances for simulated recitals;

Ideas for Logs

Seventh Grade: Works toward a health-enhancing level of physical fitness.

- *Evidence of work:* Maintain a record of your health-related fitness test scores along with the physical activities you perform out of school over [a designated period of time]. (standard 4.2)

Seventh Grade: Explains the process of setting appropriate goals, conducting appropriate practice, and monitoring changes in the development of specialized skills.

- *Evidence of experiencing the process:* Maintain a record of your improvement for [a given skill] along with your practice schedule. (standard 2.1)

Eighth Grade: Works toward a health-enhancing level of physical fitness.

- *Evidence of progress:* Maintain a record of your resting heart rate, training heart rate, and recovery heart rate for [a designated period of time]. (standard 4.1)

Sixth Grade: Explains ways to use force to increase speed or distance of a body or object.

- *Evidence to support response:* Participate in a variety of lab situations involving [manipulatives (e.g., release the ball at various angles, release the ball after involving various body segments, or the like)] and record your results. (standard 2.2)

Figure 8.5 Log entries usually involve recording data.

Prompts for Journal Entries

Fifth Grade: Chooses to engage in skill competencies at a level that leads to personal satisfaction, success, and enjoyment.

- How do you feel when you participate in a physical activity after a stressful event in your life? (standard 6.3)

Fifth Grade: Works with an individual who is differently abled in physical activity settings.

- Describe a situation in which you encouraged an individual who is differently abled during a physical activity. How did it make you feel? (standard 5.1)

Sixth Grade: Works cooperatively with a small group in physical activity settings.

- Describe examples of your behavior in which you displayed cooperative skills and examples in which you did not display cooperative skills during a physical activity.
- Describe how each event made you feel. (standard 5.1)

Figure 8.6 Journal entries allow students to record feelings and describe events.

- participate in a simulated on-campus orienteering experience; and
- participate in a simulated round of golf by using hula hoops for the holes, long jump pits for sand traps, and benches for obstacles.

Authentic assessment asks students to demonstrate their learning in real-life situations; however, this is not always possible, so role-playing and participating in simulations may be the next best option. These types of assessments are especially effective for determining if students are meeting standards 1 and 5.

Reports

A common element of real-life work is the ability to research a topic and write a summary. Student reports have been a feature of education for the last century; however, it is becoming increasingly important for students to be able to search through a variety of resources (e.g., DVDs, books, the Internet) and find the most accurate, up-to-date information on a topic. Another important report

Ideas for Gymnastics Routines

Sixth Grade: Expresses personal feelings through a manipulative or movement-based routine.

1. Create a tumbling routine that has a beginning pose, three changes of level (high, medium, low), three changes in direction (forward, backward, sideways), three changes of pathways (straight, zigzag, curved), and an ending pose that expresses your personal feelings. (standard 6.2)

Seventh Grade: Appreciates one's own stylistic approach to creating a routine.

2. Create a beam routine that demonstrates a beginning pose, two static skills, two rotations, three different locomotion skills, two different levels, two different directions, a landing skill, and an ending pose that illustrates your own style. (standard 6.2)

Fifth Grade: Expresses personal feelings through a movement-based routine.

3. Create a rhythmic routine that has a beginning pose, four different rhythmic steps, sequences that repeat at least three times, sequences performed in time to music, and an ending pose that expresses your personal feelings. (standard 6.2)

Figure 8.7 Creating gymnastics routines is one example of a simulated performance.

resource is the interview. In this case, students interview someone who is considered an expert on a particular issue as a means of research. Because information is doubling yearly, the availability of information is not the issue; the issue is selecting the most appropriate and accurate information.

NASPE (1995a) provides several examples of research topics:

- Critical elements of a motor skill (e.g., overhand throw, instep kick)

- Practice ideas (e.g., amount of feedback, whole or partial skill practice) for improvement of a motor skill

- Physiological responses (e.g., strength improvements, lactic acid production) of the body to exercise

- History of a sport or dance

- Why people exercise

Research is a viable option related to every standard that has a cognitive component. As a physical educator, however, you must be sure that students possess the necessary skills to conduct the research. Student reports provide an ideal arena for interdisciplinary efforts, because the language arts teacher can ensure that students learn to search the Internet, find information on DVDs and in books, and conduct interviews. You, in turn, can provide students with specific resources and guidance to complete their research. Students then produce documents to share with the rest of the class. Including additional subject areas also encourages students to look at a topic from many perspectives. For example, students can explore the topic "why people exercise" from a financial and health insurance perspective (mathematics), a health perspective (science, health, and physical education), and the meeting of social needs perspective (history and social science). Students can produce these reports as individuals or in a cooperative group. As you did with open-ended and essay questions, communicate to students your expectations and grading guidelines for the reports.

Projects

Take student reports one step further and assign projects (see figure 8.8) in which students (working alone or in small groups) create products from their research other than a written report. These products can take the form of a video, multimedia presentation (using a computer), chart, speech, demonstration, publication, or lesson. One example of a project is a movement pattern video presentation with an introduction to the movement pattern followed by video clips of different sport skills that use that pattern. When assigned the task, one group of students in my class chose the overhand throw and, after an introduction to that pattern, videotaped the volleyball overhand serve, the football forward pass, the softball throw, and the team handball pass. Projects motivate students because they can select their own topics for study, use skills associated with their primary intelligences (see chapter 9), and use their creativity.

Ideas for Projects

Seventh Grade: Designs a 1-week personal health-related fitness plan.

1. Develop a week-long health-related personal fitness plan and present it in a chart. (standard 4.2)

Seventh Grade: Explains how force can be used to make an object spin.

2. Create a multimedia presentation on how force can be used to create topspin, backspin, and sidespin. (standard 2.2)

Eighth Grade: Explains offensive and defensive strategies for invasion, net, and field sports.

3. Create a new invasion game, along with appropriate offensive and defensive strategies, and teach it to a small group of peers. Explain how the offensive and defensive strategies can be applied to other invasion, net, and field sports. (standard 2.3)

Sixth Grade: Describes opportunities in the local community for regular participation in physical activity.

4. Design a brochure on the physical activity opportunities in the community. (standard 3.2)

Figure 8.8   Projects can involve creating products rather than a written report.

Both research reports and projects require a great deal of time. Yet, through them, students not only learn in-depth information regarding their selected topics but also learn time and resource management, social skills, technological skills, proper telephone use (for conducting interviews), and how to conduct original research—the process skills that students need to know in the 21st century.

Ideas for different projects are limited only by your imagination. Simply make sure they relate to specific standards. Notice in the samples provided (figure 8.8) that project 1 relates to standard 4.2, project 2 to standard 2.2, project 3 to standard 2.3, and project 4 to standard 3.2. Projects are far-reaching in that you can use them to address most, if not all, standards. Even though the sample projects specify the media (e.g., video, multimedia, paper), you may prefer to have students select their own media or to rotate students through the various media. If you have only one digital video camera, for example, then for one project, group A has access to it; for the next project, group B has access to it, and so on.

A new area for projects is community service. Although community service is more common at the high school level, middle school students can benefit from giving something back to the community as well. Keeping in mind the desired outcomes of physical education, students provide one of the following services to demonstrate their learning of one or more of the grade-level standards. Students could

- teach a new motor skill to elementary school students,
- visit nursing homes and take the residents through simple stretching exercises,
- help out at a park and recreation center by teaching younger participants new games,
- invite a parent or another adult who does not regularly exercise to participate in an aerobic activity, or
- work as conflict managers on the middle school playground during recess and lunch.

In some middle schools, students must complete an eighth grade project. The school sets the parameters for the projects and then allows students to choose the specific problem they wish to investigate. Typically, students must follow six steps to complete their projects:

1. Identify a problem to investigate (e.g., Is there a difference between the type of physical activities that girls and boys prefer?).

2. Outline procedures to follow while doing the project (e.g., research the topic, interview a local college professor, develop a survey, conduct the survey, and draw conclusions).

3. Conduct the research (e.g., access the Internet, review books, interview experts, and administer the survey).

4. Revisit the expert to discuss conclusions.

5. Prepare the project (the report and presentation).

6. Present the project to an audience of peers, parents, or community members.

Students, working alone or preferably in groups, complete their projects, including developing all or most of the following: oral presentations, written documentation, visual aids, audio aids, and multimedia presentations. Many schools require students to present their projects to the entire community or at least to outside evaluators. This last step helps add a more realistic dimension to the project. Unfortunately, all too often these projects omit the physical education angle. If your school has eighth grade projects, make sure that the parameters of the project allow students to investigate issues related to physical education. And, of course, projects are not just for eighth graders.

Rubrics

Now that you're using standards-based assessment, it is time to consider using rubrics instead of grades. As mentioned previously, grades have come to mean many different things to different people (i.e., good kids get good grades). When using rubrics, a shift occurs—from simply rewarding kids with grades to documenting the quality of their performance or product. As educational reform has moved forward in the area of alternative assessment, rubrics or scoring guides have emerged as a consistent and fair method that explicitly communicates what you expect students to achieve. If your school is not currently using rubrics, then use the following information to create *criterion-referenced grading* by replacing the numbers with letters. Rubrics were designed to replace grades and not coexist with them, although I realize that many of you are trying to implement rubrics in a system that is still supporting the use of grades. See more about the rubrics and grades later in the section titled "Role of Grading in Assessment."

A rubric (figure 8.9) is similar to a score awarded by a diving or gymnastics judge in that it describes various qualitative levels of performance on a specific performance or product. A well-written rubric presents a picture of what the final performance or product looks like. You can define any number of qualitative levels, such as a range of 1 through 6, with 6 being ideal, or a range of 1 through 4, with 4 being ideal. Typically, teachers consider the score of 4 (on a 6-point rubric) or the score of 3 (on a 4-point rubric) as meeting the minimum standard criteria, with the other levels falling into place as follows:

6-Point Rubric

6: Exceeds the standard substantially

5: Exceeds the standard

4: Meets the standard

3: Does not fully achieve the purposes of the task

2: Omits important purposes of the task

1: Fails to achieve purposes of the task

4-Point Rubric

4: Exceeds the standard

3: Meets the standard

2: Omits important purposes of the task

1: Fails to achieve purposes of the task

Rubrics provide teachers with the criteria for assessment and they tell students, "How good is good enough?"

When creating rubrics, you can either write one rubric that covers all aspects of the performance or product (holistic rubric) or write a separate rubric for each aspect or dimension of the performance or product (analytic rubrics). Either way, creating

---

Sample Rubrics

Grade-level standard: Demonstrates speed, accuracy, and control using the mature form for fundamental movement and manipulative skills. (5th grade)

Unit-level standard: Demonstrates speed, accuracy, and control using the mature form for the overhand throw.

Assessment tool: Structured observation

Criteria for competence:

Performs the overhand throw for speed and accuracy using the mature form (notice the match with the criteria for competence):

_____ *Keeps nonthrowing side and arm toward target.*

_____ *Places weight on back foot.*

_____ *Swings throwing arm backward in preparation.*

_____ *Steps forward with foot on opposite side of body from throwing arm.*

_____ *Makes forward body rotation occur through lower body, then upper body, and then shoulders.*

_____ *Transfers weight to foot on opposite side of body from throwing arm.*

_____ *Leads the way with the elbow for the arm movement, followed by forearm extension, and ending with a wrist snap.*

_____ *Follows through in the direction of the target.*

_____ *Able to throw 75 feet (23 meters) and hit a target (4 feet by 4 feet [1.2 by 1.2 meters]) 60 percent of the time.*

6   Performs the correct technique for an overhand throw with distance and accuracy in game-like situations.

5   Performs the correct technique for an overhand throw with accuracy from a variety of distances (10 to 75 feet [3 to 23 meters]).

4   *Performs the correct technique for the overhand throw (notice the match with the criteria for competence):*

     _____ *Keeps nonthrowing side and arm toward target.*

Figure 8.9   These sample rubrics show both a 6-point rubric and a 4-point rubric.

_____ *Places weight on back foot.*

_____ *Swings throwing arm backward in preparation.*

_____ *Steps forward with foot on opposite side of body from throwing arm.*

_____ *Makes forward body rotation occur through lower body, then upper body, and then shoulders.*

_____ *Transfers weight to foot on opposite side of body from throwing arm.*

_____ *Leads the way with the elbow for the arm movement, followed by forearm extension, and ending with a wrist snap.*

_____ *Follows through in the direction of the target.*

_____ *Able to throw 75 feet (23 meters) and hit a target (4 feet by 4 feet [1.2 by 1.2 meters]) 60 percent of the time.*

3   Is moving toward the correct technique for the overhand throw:

_____ Flexes elbow by swinging throwing arm upward, sideways, and backward.

_____ Rotates trunk and shoulder back.

_____ Steps forward with foot on opposite side of body from throwing arm.

_____ Rotates body forward very little.

_____ Leads way with elbow in the arm movement.

_____ Follows through in the direction of the target very little.

2   Performs an incorrect overhand throw when requested to do so by the teacher:

_____ Stands facing the target.

_____ Generates action mainly from the elbow.

_____ Uses little or no rotation.

_____ Keeps feet stationary.

1   Attempts an overhand throw:

_____ Stands erect, facing the target.

_____ Throws with little or no body rotation.

_____ Throws with very little arm action.

_____ Employs action that resembles a push more than a throw.

Seventh-grade standard: Designs a 1-week personal health-related fitness plan.

Assessment tool: Project

Criteria for minimum competence:

Bases plan on personal assessment of own fitness, includes all five areas of health-related fitness, and correctly applies the FITT concepts to each area of fitness.

4   Bases plan on personal assessment of own fitness, includes all five areas of health-related fitness, and correctly applies the FITT (frequency, intensity, time, type) concepts to each area of fitness. The plan includes muscular strength, endurance, and flexibility exercises for the major muscle groups in the upper and lower body.

3   *Bases plan on personal assessment of own fitness, includes all five areas of health-related fitness, and correctly applies the FITT concepts to each area of fitness.*

2   Does not base plan on personal assessment of own fitness, includes three areas of health-related fitness, and attempts to apply FITT concepts but makes major errors.

1   Does not base plan on personal assessment of own fitness, includes only one or two areas of health-related fitness, and makes major errors in the application of FITT concepts.

Figure 8.9 *(continued)*

rubrics is not an easy task. The following five-step process will assist you when developing your own rubrics for each grade-level standard:

1. Identify the grade-level standard (see chapter 6).

    a. Describe how to absorb force when performing movement and motor skills.

2. Choose the assessment tool that matches the standard and that allows students to demonstrate the standard (see assessment tools in previous sections of this chapter).

    a. Essay question: What are the most effective methods for absorbing the force of a hard-thrown ball?

3. Make a list of the criteria for minimum competence involved in the standard.

    a. Notes that force is absorbed by increasing the surface area.

    b. Notes that force is absorbed by increasing the distance over which force is received.

4. Describe levels of quality starting with a 6, then a 4, then a 3, and then the others—1, 2, and 5 (or 4, then 3, then 1, and then 2 for a 4-point rubric).

    Level 4: Correctly identifies both factors and examples of how they relate to absorbing the force of a hard-thrown ball.

    Level 3: Answer includes the following:

    • Notes that force is absorbed by increasing the surface area.

    • Notes that force is absorbed by increasing the distance over which force is received.

    Level 2: Correctly identifies one of the factors.

    Level 1: Incorrectly identifies the factors.

5. Develop samples of student work illustrating each rubric level.

A number of samples showing the five-step process for creating rubrics (see figure 8.9) have been provided for you. Initially, you'll probably feel more comfortable developing rubrics by yourself. But as your confidence and experience grow, you may wish to include students in the process.

Ideally, once you have created the rubric, you should provide samples of student work (step 5) that illustrate each rubric level. These are known as *anchors*. In physical education, these anchors may be products at each level or video clips that illustrate each level if the rubric relates to the demonstration of a skill. By providing examples, you show students and other stakeholders what you expect.

What score should you assign if a student's performance falls between two levels? Most teachers give the lower score. Perhaps in the future we'll eliminate the actual rating number, and thus this problem, by simply providing a descriptive analysis of the product. The description could list those elements of the critical features that the student can demonstrate, thereby giving a more accurate picture of the student's progress.

Portfolios

How do you keep track of student work? How do you assess the total learning of each student? Assessment reform brings us another new concept: the student portfolio. A portfolio is a permanent collection, similar to an artist's portfolio, of a student's best work, showing her progress toward the grade-level standards. The portfolio can contain a wide range of assessment tools.

To get started, have students create a working portfolio, which will temporarily hold everything the student completes. Then have the students, selecting from their working portfolios, develop a performance portfolio, your ultimate goal. These portfolios are purposeful collections of work that demonstrate student learning, emerging insights, progress, and achievement in physical education over time. Most teachers who use portfolios suggest that each student's performance portfolio include 2 or 3 pieces of work for each standard—some from earlier and some from later in the year. In addition, a portfolio should include a reflective essay in which the student comments on his portfolio.

But what exactly should go into a performance portfolio? Typically, the student does the selecting; however, you may wish to select one particular project that you want included in all student portfolios and then leave the rest of the selecting to the students. A performance portfolio for sixth grade may include the following:

• Rubric scores for several different motor skills as assessed by the teacher

• A copy of a checklist showing feedback given to a peer

• A video of one motor skill accompanied by an oral description of how the application of Newton's third law can help improve performance

- A group project, created out of paper, that illustrates a new cooperative game

- A log showing participation in out-of-school activities

- A chart showing a 1-day fitness development plan for all five areas of health-related fitness

- A reflective essay describing participation in a cooperative activity

- Rubric scores for how well the student, when working in a small group, was able to assess others' strengths and weaknesses based on physical development and was able to use this information to solve a physical challenge

- A report on one game from ancient times that has had an influence on a physical activity engaged in today

- A description of an aesthetically pleasing movement activity accompanied by a description of the qualities of movement in that activity in response to an open-ended question

These items collectively document student progress through all of the sixth grade standards. Therefore, students must be informed about the grade-level standards at the beginning of the school year.

At the end of the year, the portfolio provides the teacher and students with a springboard to discuss student progress and set goals for the next year. During this end-of-the-year conference, ask students to explain the connection between the grade-level standards and the pieces they selected to demonstrate their learning. This process will help students understand how learning occurs. You may also wish to ask students to share their work with their parents during end-of-the-year parent conferences. In many schools, the teacher takes a secondary role during these conferences while the student explains her own progress to her parents. This conference is also an opportunity for students to reflect on their own work. Finally, it presents students with a real-world experience, because they must explain (and perhaps justify and defend) their performances as they will when they are adult employees.

Time and Storage Management

The storage of portfolios for every student in all your classes and the school can become an overwhelming task. Then there's the time students need to create projects and the time you need to assess student projects and performances. If you are currently assessing your students exclusively on motor skills and fitness, you will notice a significant increase in the amount of work you face when you start using portfolios. How can you manage the storage of portfolios? More important, how can you handle the additional workload?

To store portfolios, schools tend to follow one of three paths. The first requires students to take full responsibility for their own portfolios. They keep their portfolio in a locker or at home and bring it to class as requested by the teacher. Naturally, the drawback to this approach is that students may forget their portfolios. The second approach puts the responsibility for the portfolios completely on the teacher, who stores portfolios in large boxes or crates by class period. Then, when the students need their portfolios, the teacher brings the box or crate to class. Still other schools have moved to electronic portfolios (see chapter 12 for more details). In an electronic portfolio, you and your students store everything in a digital format. Electronic portfolios can include text, drawings, pictures, audio recordings, video clips, rubrics, and projects—all available at the click of the mouse. The appropriate choice among these three options depends on your situation and your students' general level of responsibility.

In terms of the time it takes for students to complete some of the projects and reports, we must examine two issues. The first, which I introduced in chapter 1, is the need for depth over breadth; the second issue is the use of homework in physical education. If you believe that students need to develop the ability to investigate problems so that they can understand a few things well, then the amount of time needed to complete projects and reports is justified. Everything related to the projects does not have to be produced during class time. Students can work on these projects and reports as homework.

You also can reduce the time needed for assessment in a number of ways. First, you can ask students to self-assess and then peer-assess, and finally you assess their performances. This alone should reduce the amount of your time spent on assessment. Embedded assessment, which allows for instruction and assessment to occur simultaneously, will also reduce the time you spend on assessment. In chapter 12, we also discuss the use of handheld data collection devices that can reduce the amount of teacher time spent collecting and storing rubric levels. Last, too often when teachers begin to focus on cognitive development in physical education, they hand out one assignment after another and then are frustrated by the amount of paperwork. Instead, choose your assignments carefully, remembering to focus on depth over breadth. A few well-chosen large projects in which students look for connections themselves are better for both you and your students than a large quantity of shorter assignments for which you must create the connections.

Role of Grading in Assessment

Grading requires the selection and display of a final symbol to communicate the results of assessment. But if you base your grading on standards, identify and use alternative assessment tools, and set clear criteria for each letter grade, then you can move toward standards-based assessment—even if you are required to assign a single grade representing student learning.

Take, for example, a student who receives a C in physical education. This particular student excels in motor skill—standard 1 (A); has no understanding of movement concepts—standard 2 (F); participates daily in moderate to vigorous physical activity—standard 3 (A); has limited understanding of creating a fitness plan—standard 4 (D); is very poor at the social skill being addressed—standard 5 (F); and highly values physical activity—standard 5 (A). You average out these abilities and report to the parents that the student's grade is a C. This in reality tells the parents nothing about their child's strengths or weaknesses related to physical education. Hence, the problem with a grading system is that you have to commingle different capabilities into a single symbol. If at all possible, provide parents with one grade per standard.

To make matters worse, some physical educators are still giving grades based on variables other than grade-level standards. These variables, including attendance, tardiness, showering, participation, effort, and dressing out, still account for a major portion of a student's grade in some physical education programs. Although you need to address these issues, you should not consider them when calculating the physical education grade. Some schools and districts do give a "work habits" grade and perhaps a "cooperation" grade, as well as a physical education grade. Use this type of forum to grade issues not directly related to attaining the grade-level standards. Certainly, as you begin to understand the many different methods and tools available for assessment, you'll also begin to recognize the limitations of calculating the physical education grade based on attendance and dressing out.

When basing grades on grade-level standards, you must first decide whether all standards are created equal. If your philosophy holds that all grade-level standards are, in fact, created equal and if there are 10 grade-level standards, then each one contributes 10% to the total grade. If, however, you believe that grade-level standard 1 is significantly more important than the other standards, then perhaps standard 1 contributes 28% and the other nine standards contribute 8% each. This is strictly a philosophical issue, because once you calculate the final grade, it will either equally reflect all the grade-level standards or be biased by one or more standards, depending on the weights given to the standards. Again, this is the inherent weakness in grading: the difficulty of determining an appropriate final grade that represents an individual's wide range of abilities in different areas.

Once you decide whether all standards are created equal, your second major decision is whether to give unit grades. If you decide to, you may wish to assign one grade for each unit standard. Then, at the end of the year, average all unit grades into a final grade (figure 8.10*a*). Another option involves giving one grade for each grade-level

Grading on Dressing?

A friend of mine (who is a college professor) and I were discussing the issue of universities not including the grade from high school physical education in the grade point average used for admissions. As we talked, a number of high school physical educators were sitting nearby and were engaged in their own conversation about grading. As I challenged my colleague about why she didn't approach her dean on this matter, the high school teachers were discussing the number of "non-suits" that should result in an F in physical education. My colleague turned to me and said, "That's why!"

Dressing Policy and Grading

Students are expected to dress out daily in their physical education uniform, which is available for purchase from the teaching staff. If a student's uniform is unavailable, a loan uniform will be issued for that day. Dressing out is not included in the student's grade but instead is an expectation of all students.

—Ball Junior High School, Anaheim, California

standard—perhaps assigning one major project for each standard regardless of the number or type of instructional units you've covered during the year (figure 8.10*b*). Or assign one grade per unit or every other unit related to each standard.

If you give more than one grade for a grade-level standard, then you must average those grades to find the final grade for each standard. Then you calculate the grading period's final grade based on the standard grade (figure 8.10*c*).

Sample Grading Procedures Based on Standards

(a) Grading on units: average standards' grades for each unit (top to bottom) and then average final unit grades (left to right) to determine final grade.

	UNIT				
	1	2	3	4	5
Standard 1.0	A	B	B	C	A
Standard 2.1	A	B	C	B	A
Standard 2.2	A	B	B	C	A
Standard 2.3	A	B	C	B	A
Standard 2.4	A	A	B	B	A
Standard 2.5	A	B	B	B	A
Standard 3.1	B	C	B	A	A
Standard 3.2	A	B	B	C	B
Standard 4.1	A	B	B	C	B
Standard 4.2	B	C	B	A	A
Standard 5.1	B	C	A	A	B
Standard 5.2	B	C	A	A	B
Standard 6.1	A	B	C	B	A
Standard 6.2	A	C	A	B	A
Standard 6.3	A	B	B	B	B
Standard 6.4	A	A	B	B	B
Final unit grade	A	B	B	B	A
Final grade = B					

(b) Grading on standards only: average standards' grades (top to bottom) to determine final grade.

Standard 1.0	A
Standard 2.1	B
Standard 2.2	B
Standard 2.3	B
Standard 2.4	C
Standard 2.5	C
Standard 3.1	A
Standard 3.2	A
Standard 4.1	C
Standard 4.2	C
Standard 5.1	A
Standard 5.2	A
Standard 6.1	B
Standard 6.2	B
Standard 6.3	C
Standard 6.4	A
Final grade = B	

(continued)

Figure 8.10 There are three options for assigning grades: *(a)* averaging all unit grades into a final grade; *(b)* giving one grade for each grade-level standard; or *(c)* assigning one grade per unit or every other unit and then averaging the grade-level standard grade.

(continued)

(c) Grading on a combination of unit and grade standards: average unit grades for each standard (left to right) and then average final grade for each standard (top to bottom) to determine final grade.

	UNIT				STANDARD
	1	2	3	4	FINAL
Standard 1.0	A	A	B	A	A
Standard 2.1	A	B	B	B	B
Standard 2.2	A	B	B	B	B
Standard 2.3	—	—	—	—	C
Standard 2.4	—	—	C	A	C
Standard 2.5	A	—	A	—	A
Standard 3.1	—	—	—	—	C
Standard 3.2	—	A	A	A	A
Standard 4.1	B	A	—	A	A
Standard 4.2	C	C	A	A	B
Standard 5.1	B	B	B	B	B
Standard 5.2	B	B	B	B	B
Standard 6.1	C	—	C	—	C
Standard 6.2	—	—	—	—	B
Standard 6.3	—	—	—	—	B
Standard 6.4	—	—	—	—	A
Final grade = B					

Figure 8.10 *(continued)*

Use one or more assessment tools to collect data on student progress for each standard. For example, when determining the grade for standard 3.1, you may simply require that students turn in logs that chronicle participation in physical activity outside the school day. When determining the grade for standard 1.0, however, you might consider a wide variety of grades (or rubrics) on various motor or sport skills. Of course, one project or other assessment tool may provide data for more than one standard. For example, you might assign students a project for which you assess how well they perform a motor skill (standard 1.0). They, in turn, analyze their own performances and then develop ideas for improvement (standard 2.1) based on biomechanical principles (standard 2.2). To communicate the grading scheme to parents,

prepare a standards-based report card (see figure 8.11) for each student. Notice that the specific grade-level standard is noted along with all assessment tools used to assess student learning relative to that standard. Then, the standards are averaged to determine the student's final grade.

Grading based on the achievement of clearly stated grade-level standards informs parents and students of what you expect and what progress students are making. Furthermore, giving students feedback on their projects and performances as soon as possible motivates students to perform well on the next assessment. Ultimately, use assessment and appropriate grading to prove you're accountable. At a time when accountability in education is at a premium, take this responsibility seriously.

Grade Report

Sue **Brown** **Period** **1**

Final Grade **3.38** **Letter Grade** **B** **Total** **Avg**

				Total	Avg
Demonstrates competency in motor skills				30	3
Volleyball set	2	Volleyball serve			3
Volleyball forearm pass	4	Basketball dribble			2
Basketball layup	3	Basketball set shot			1
Soccer dribble	4	Soccer pass			3
Badminton serve	4	Badminton clear			4
Explains movement concepts related to skill acquisition				7	3.5
Practice plan	4	Quiz on motor learning concepts			3
		Badminton clear			
Participates daily in physical activity				4	4
Daily log	4				
Creates a 1-week fitness plan				7	3.5
Fitness plan	4	Quiz on fitness concepts			3
Demonstrates cooperation when working with others				6	3
Cooperation rubric	3	Journal entries			3

Figure 8.11 Standards-based report card created using Record Book (software) by Bonnie's Fitware, Inc.

Summary

Alternative assessment tools such as structured observations, written tests, logs and journals, role-playing, reports, and projects benefit your students greatly by focusing on their strengths and uncovering their weaknesses in ways that are not demeaning to them. No matter how much or how well you teach, you must demonstrate that the students have learned. Positive and relevant feedback, which flows naturally from a well-planned assessment system, develops skills in young adolescents. Moreover, helpful feedback may motivate students to work hard to successfully complete the task, skill, or exercise. Ultimately, they will apply the techniques they learn in physical education to real-life situations, thereby becoming prepared for the future.

PART III

Travel Toward Your Destination

Now that you know your destination and the checkpoints along the way, let's determine the mode of transportation. In part III, we look at the various factors that influence the instructional process. In **chapter 9**, we examine the learning styles of middle school students. In **chapter 10**, we discuss the behaviors of an effective teacher. In **chapter 11**, we look at a variety of teaching styles and strategies that you can use to reach all your students. In **chapter 12**, we examine effective instructional materials. And in **chapter 13**, we discuss the necessity for change in physical education, steps for change, and how effective staff development can assist with this change as you and your staff continue along on your journey.

Understanding Today's Learner

- Accomplished physical education teachers use their knowledge of students to make every student feel important. They communicate through a humane, sensitive approach that each child, regardless of ability, can succeed and will benefit from a physically active, healthy lifestyle.

  —*National Board for Professional Teaching Standards*

You have just finished teaching what you consider to be one of your finest lessons. You gave great demonstrations, used exciting drills and activities, and equitably distributed effective teaching behaviors throughout the lesson to all your students (see chapter 10). But are you sure that all your students have learned the material? How can you be sure that what you teach is actually being learned by all of your students? In this chapter, we'll examine what motivates students, how students learn, and how students may learn differently from one another.

Motivating Students

I often hear teachers ask, "How can I motivate my students?" or "How can I get the apathetic learner turned on to what I am teaching?" The reality is that you can't motivate students—you can only influence how they motivate themselves. A

Middle schoolers are very self-centered. I decided to use that to their advantage—focusing on personal best scores in fitness testing and asking them to meet or beat their best score. The shift eradicated the "competition" within the fitness testing scenario and changed it to a goal-setting mode, resulting in enthusiasm for reaching an achievable goal as opposed to embarrassment because one couldn't beat the athlete of the class.

—*physical educator Francesca Zavacky, Clark School, Charlottesville, Virginia*

newborn's brain is designed to learn; the newborn is naturally curious and is motivated to learn. Some students continue to remain intrinsically motivated and do not need your influence. These are the self-confident students in your class who are willing to try new and challenging activities. They are also the ones who are the first to volunteer for an extra responsibility (e.g., equipment monitor) or answer a question.

For other students, you need to ensure that certain elements are present in your classes to help motivate them. I have found that five key elements are associated with motivated students. These elements include providing learning experiences that:

- are safe,

- are interesting and meaningful,

- are more cooperative and less competitive in nature,

- allow students to set their own goals and monitor their own progress, and

- promote success for all students.

Interestingly, many of these elements also help prevent discipline problems. Base your units and lessons on student needs, and high motivation and good discipline follow naturally. Let's take a closer look at how you can set up student-centered classes using these five elements.

Safe Learning Experiences

We discussed providing a physically safe environment in chapter 4 and helping students to feel psychologically safe in chapter 5. Certainly, students who feel physically and psychologically safe are also more motivated to learn. Remember, too, that both verbal and nonverbal interactions with you affect the student's feelings and attitudes about learning. Review the concepts in chapters 4 and 5 for more information on providing safe learning experiences.

Interesting and Meaningful Learning Experiences

Students are more motivated to learn when the content and activities you present are interesting and meaningful. When you explain the purpose of the lesson, relate the lesson to the overall outcome of the unit, and connect the material to students' current knowledge, skills, and experiences, the material becomes more meaningful.

For example, in a self-defense unit, you could start the first lesson by asking, "What do you know about protecting yourself?" You could chart the students' responses in one of two categories: preventive measures and protective measures. Then explain that throughout the self-defense unit, students will increase their understanding and skills related to both of these areas; however, the first several lessons will focus on prevention because it can eliminate the need for protective measures.

Teachers can deliver more interesting lessons by

- connecting the material to students' existing interests,

- setting up a variety of drills or activities for practicing the same skill,

- using a variety of teaching styles,

- engaging a variety of intelligences (see multiple intelligences later in this chapter),

- setting up stations or learning centers so that students can review different skills at each station,

- holding students accountable for the completion of the task through the use of worksheets where students must record their participation or success in the activity, and

- introducing topics in a problematic fashion and asking students to resolve the issues.

The last suggestion refers to the involvement you experience when trying to solve a puzzle or riddle. Your challenge is to set up learning situations that elicit from students the same intensity and involvement they feel when trying to solve a mystery. For example, give each group of students a fitness scenario for a fictitious person. Then the group must create a fitness plan for this person so that he can increase his life expectancy by 10 years.

More Cooperative and Less Competitive Learning Experiences

Many teachers share with me how much their classes enjoy a competitive situation. The teachers convey that they see a high level of enthusiasm and motivation whenever they incorporate competitive activities. But when I ask them to take a closer look at their classes and to chart the students who are displaying enthusiasm and motivation, it becomes clear that what was perceived as class-wide enthusiasm is, in fact, the enthusiasm of a few boisterous students. Pitting students against one another can actually significantly lower student motivation and the quality of student work. Remember, peer approval is very important to middle school students, and competition tends to promote conflicts instead of approval.

You may also remember from chapter 1 that businesses want students who can work together cooperatively, because more and more work situations require cooperation rather than competition. The grade-level standards reflect this trend by including cooperation-related skills. Therefore, you need to use instructional time to provide opportunities for students to work together. Furthermore, the social aspect of working and discussing with others motivates many middle school students. So look for more ways to include cooperative learning experiences. For example, instead of a culminating tournament at the end of a unit, have students participate in lead-up activities and scrimmages for which you continually rotate the opponent and don't keep score. For those of you concerned that students learn competitive skills, remember that students experience many situations in society and school in which competition is the norm (e.g., promotions, awards, elections), so students will learn these skills as well.

Opportunities for Students to Set Goals

What else motivates students? Let them assume more responsibility for their own learning. One way is to teach them how to create appropriate personal goals that are concrete and specific and that have a deadline. For example, "By May 1, I will increase the number of curl-ups I can perform by five." Not surprisingly, setting goals also improves performances.

In conjunction with teaching students to set goals, make students accountable for monitoring their own improvements. They can graph fitness scores, chart motor skill performances, or write their reflections on skill technique improvements. Recently, I visited a middle school physical education class in which students brought a steno pad and pencil to class with them. The students put their pads and pencils in a designated area when not using them. As the students began station practice for volleyball, they picked up their pads and pencils and, after completing each sta-

tion, recorded their personal scores. At the end of the class period, after an additional activity, the teacher asked the students to reflect on their growth over the past several weeks. Once again, the students got their pads and quickly made notes regarding their progress.

To properly monitor progress, students require knowledge or information about their performances. Sharing assessment duties and information in the form of self-, peer, and teacher assessment helps students determine how well they are doing so they can periodically readjust unrealistic goals.

Successful Learning Opportunities for All Students

Success leads to success. Students who are successful want to continue to be successful. To help your students be and feel successful, you must first believe that all students can succeed. Otherwise, it'll be nearly impossible to convince students that they have the potential for success. Adopt the philosophy that although not every student will be successful to the same degree on the same day, each student can succeed.

Using an inclusive style of teaching (see chapter 11) can help to ensure that all students experience success. In addition, eliminate certain practices from your program that tend to promote failure: elimination games, choosing sides, and playing sports by adult rules. Finally, putting students in small practice groups with sufficient equipment promotes many practice opportunities, which also leads to success.

Rewarding Students

Often teachers believe that to motivate students they need to offer rewards. Rewards in this context refer to any tangible (pizza, gift certificates, patches, other small gifts) or intangible (praise, compliments, public approval) item. Current research, however, indicates that rewards do not have a lasting effect on learner motivation; instead, they offer quick fixes that disregard the ultimate impact on students (Kohn 1999).

Several research studies have found that incentives have a detrimental effect on performance. In one study among artists, creativity dropped once they had signed a contract to sell their work upon completion (Amabile 1989). The fact that they knew they were going to be paid for their work lessened their artistic expression. Other researchers

124 Teaching Middle School Physical Education

have found that incentives have a detrimental effect on performance when the task meets two conditions: It is already interesting for subjects, and it is open-ended so that the steps leading to a solution are not immediately obvious.

How do students feel about rewards as motivators? First, rewards communicate to students that the information must not be very interesting, because the teacher feels the need to entice them to learn it. Second, students feel manipulated. All in all, rewards are not the answer to motivating students.

For those middle school teachers trying to wean their students off 6 years of rewards received in elementary school, it's often a difficult task. However, as Kohn (1999) explained, "The more difficult it is to wean students off gold stars and candy bars, the more urgent it is to do so" (p. 200). As a middle school physical educator, you have two options. You can work within the current structure while minimizing the use of rewards or you can work with other teachers to change the structure. Regardless of which approach you take, lean away from the use of rewards and focus your efforts on the five key elements that increase motivation: a safe learning environment, interesting and meaningful learning experiences, cooperative learning situations, goal setting, and success.

How Students Learn

Now let's look at the current research on how students learn and at practical ways to apply this research. We can approach the topic of "how students learn" from many perspectives, including behaviorist and constructivist learning theories. Behaviorists believe that students learn best when the teacher breaks down content into small pieces and feeds it to students one piece at a time. Constructivists believe that learning is an interactive process through which students construct personal meaning from information available to them and then integrate that information with their previous learning. Often referred to as *active learning,* this interactive process involves all the students' senses, places emphasis on developing students' learning and problem-solving skills, engages students in activities that require higher-order thinking skills, and allows students to explore their own ideas.

The constructivists believe that holistic problem-solving activities engage student interest the most, making it more likely that students will learn the lower-level requisite information and skills in the process. Let's take, for example, the learning outcome of students creating their own week-long fitness plans. From the constructivist perspective, you ask students to create their own week-long fitness plan, providing them with the materials to accomplish the project. Then, to complete their projects, the students seek out information by asking questions of the teacher and other experts and searching through books and other data sources about the various components of fitness and how to improve fitness. From a behaviorist perspective, you introduce students to each component of fitness one at a time until they have learned all the parts, and then you ask them to complete a related project.

Many researchers and educators question whether these two perspectives can coexist. I believe that they can. Students learn best in certain situations when you break the information down for them as in the behaviorist perspective. Yet, with the increase in the amount of informa-

Taking Away Extrinsic Rewards

I once heard a speaker tell the following story. There once was an elderly man who lived in a rickety house on the corner of two streets. Every day after school the neighborhood children would walk by his house and taunt him. He tried everything to get them to stop. He yelled at them and he tried calling the police, but nothing worked. Finally one day, he walked out to the children and he gave each of them one dollar, explaining that if they came back the next day he would pay them again. The next day, the children were back taunting the man. He came out of his house, thanked them, and handed them each 50 cents. This continued for several days as the old man paid the children less and less for taunting him. One day, the man came out of his house, thanked the children again, and handed them each a nickel. The man explained that if they came back the next day he would pay them each a penny. The children responded that it wasn't worth it, and they never returned.

tion in our communications-oriented society, the constructivist approach is often more appropriate.

What are some specific ideas for how to improve student learning? Let's explore the current brain-based research on how students learn best, in general, and the motor learning research on how students learn motor skills best. This information not only will help you to become a better teacher but also will give you additional evidence for proving to others the importance of a quality physical education program in every middle school. Share the research with your students as well to help them become lifelong learners.

What the Brain-Based Research Says

Over the last decade, we have learned much about how the brain learns. Creating a physically and psychologically safe environment, presenting concepts in an interesting and meaningful way, allowing students to set goals and monitor their own progress, and showing how new information links to previous information or interests all make learning easier. This section covers additional suggestions that have come out of the brain-based research. By using this information to teach more effectively, you can increase your students' understanding.

Organizing Information

Students learn best when they can organize information in a meaningful way. This is why it is so important to link new information to what students already know: It gives them a hook on which to hang new information. I recently observed a teacher who was giving a lesson on the parts of the golf club. Before she labeled the parts, she asked the students for the names of the parts of the tennis racket (the unit they had just completed). She then compared the common labels for the tennis racket's components with the parts of the golf club, giving students a linking place to store and remember the new information.

People remember information best when it is chunked into groups of seven or fewer pieces. Remembering a list of 10 items is very difficult. However, if you break the list into two parts, the students can memorize five items—a more realistic amount to recall. For example, for the parts of fitness, you might separate the list into health-related items (cardiorespiratory endurance, muscular endurance, muscular strength, body composition, and flexibility) and skill-related items (agility, balance, coordination, power, reaction time, and speed). Making an acronym (first letter of each key word forms a new word) out of new information is a good mnemonic (memory) device. The acronym FITT (frequency, intensity, time, and type) has been very effective in helping students to remember the concepts related to health-related fitness development.

Mapping is yet another strategy for helping students to organize and learn information. The mapping concept refers to organizing material into a graphic that clarifies the relationship of the member information bits or concepts. This is especially effective in helping students to visualize abstract ideas.

Ask students to brainstorm about some subject and then chart their ideas in the form of a graphic organizer. Figure 9.1a shows a comparative graphic, also called a Venn diagram, that one teacher created as the students brainstormed the similarities and differences between basketball and team handball. Figure 9.1b shows a web graphic starting with a central theme (health-related fitness) and brainstorming the various components (e.g., flexibility, muscular strength). Figure 9.1c shows an analogy chart: The relationship of softball to field sports is given along with the word *soccer*. The students must then determine the relationship between softball and field sports and apply that relationship to soccer. Softball is an example of a field sport. So, what is soccer an example of? The answer is an invasion sport.

Active Learning Strategies

Actively using information helps students digest concepts and move the information into long-term memory. Have students apply new information as soon as possible: The more realistic the application, the better. For example, teach students how to calculate their target heart rate zones; then for homework, require students to teach their parents how to calculate their target heart rate zones.

Group projects not only encourage students to apply new information but also call for students to discuss and sort out conflicting ideas to solve problems. And we all know how much middle school students like to talk! So give them a productive social outlet: Ask each small group to create a new game so they can apply their

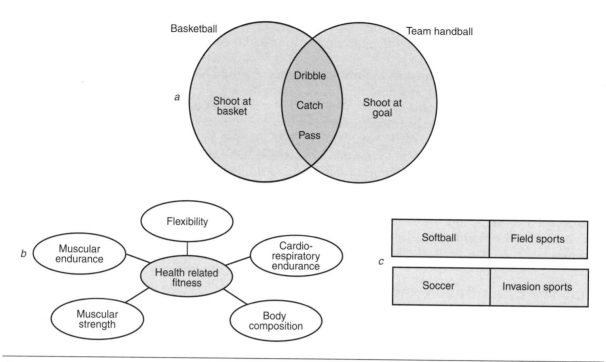

Figure 9.1 Mapping, or graphic organizers, help students to learn new information. *(a)* The Venn diagram shows the skills common and different between basketball and team handball. *(b)* The web graphic illustrates the relationship between the areas of health-related fitness. *(c)* The analogy chart shows that the relationship between softball and field sports is similar to that between soccer and invasion sports.

understanding of game concepts, including the use of equipment, skills, players, rules, and strategies.

Choose from a variety of active learning strategies, including having students create a concrete reminder of information, such as putting the information on large colorful pictures or posters and posting them around the room (figure 9.2); having students act out the information (see simulations in chapter 12); and letting students test new information, by asking, for example, "Does the ball travel farther when released at an angle greater than or less than 45°?" Engage as many of the students' five senses in the learning process as possible.

Use of Music

Many physical educators use music during exercise or other instructional times (see sidebar). When asked why they use music, they often state that the students enjoy music and are motivated by it. Music also increases learning. It helps students (and teachers!) relax, reduces stress, fosters creativity by activating more brain waves, invigorates

Music for Physical Education Class

Baroque Period

Mass in B Minor by Johann Sebastian Bach

Messiah by George Frederik Handel

Classical Period

Minuet from *"Surprise" Symphony* by Josef Hayden

Minuet from *Symphony no. 40* by Wolfgang Amadeus Mozart

Romantic Period

Romeo and Juliet by Peter Tchaikovsky

Traumerei by Robert Schumann

Scherzo from *Midsummer Night's Dream* by Felix Mendelssohn

Lohengrin by Richard Wagner

Figure 9.2 As an active learning strategy, have students create posters showing information they need to remember, and then hang them around the room as reminders.

imagination and higher-order thinking, promotes motor skill development, stimulates speech and vocabulary development, reduces discipline problems, and increases concentration (Halpern 1985). Specifically, Classical music (circa 1750-1825) and Romantic music (circa 1820-1900) are useful while you are introducing new information, and Baroque music (circa 1600-1750) is helpful while you are reviewing information at the end of a lesson (Jensen 1994, 1995, 1998).

Exercise

Of course, as physical educators, we've always been advocates for the physical, psychological, and cognitive benefits of exercise. Finally, research supports our contention that physical exercise has a positive effect on memory and learning (Dwyer et al. 2001; Ethnier et al. 1997; Sibley and Ethnier 2003). The neurons in a child's brain make connections as the child grows and relates to the world around her. Recent studies (Jensen 1994, 1995, 1998; Rhodes and Courneya 2003) have found that exercise activity increases neuronal growth and improves reasoning, short-term memory, reaction time, and creativity. The process of establishing these interconnections is greatest between the ages of 2 and 11. As the child approaches puberty, the connections that the brain finds useful become permanent whereas others are eliminated.

Bihemispheric lateralization involving movements in which limbs on opposite sides of the body move at the same time and cross the midline of the body are especially effective at promoting brain development and improving brain function by engaging both sides of the brain (Clancy 2006). However, simply changing from a sitting to standing position increases the heart rate by 10 extra beats per minute, sending more blood to the brain and thereby telling the central nervous system to increase neural firing (Jensen 1995, 1998). So students really do need quality physical education in schools as well as stand-and-stretch breaks every 20 minutes in other classes (Jensen 1994, 1998).

Proper Nutrition

The foods we consume fall into three categories: carbohydrate, protein, and fat. Carbohydrate tends to have a relaxing effect on the body whereas protein aids alertness, quick thinking, and fast reactions. The best foods to consume for protein are eggs, fish, turkey, tofu, pork, chicken, and yogurt. The best foods for carbohydrate are whole grains, oatmeal, bran, and pinto beans. The best foods for fat are omega-3 or flaxseed oils, olives, olive oil, avocados, cashews, almonds, and peanuts.

Minerals and water help the brain function efficiently as well. Foods high in folic acid (dark leafy greens) and selenium (seafood, whole grain breads, nuts, and meats) reduce depression and boost learning (Jensen 1994, 1995, 1998). Boron (broccoli, apples, pears, peaches, grapes, nuts, and dried beans), zinc (fish, beans, whole grains, and dark turkey meat), and iron are also associated with improved mental activity. Drink 8 to 15 eight-ounce glasses of water per day, depending on the weather and level of physical activity. Don't depend on thirst to dictate when to drink, because the thirst-signaling mechanism lags behind your actual need for fluids. If you find that some of your students are easily bored, listless, or drowsy or that they lack concentration, they may be in a state of dehydration. Suggest that they increase their water intake. If this doesn't help or a student is experiencing other mental deficiencies, such as a reduction in cognitive or physical performance, then review the student's diet to try to determine what she is lacking.

In addition to what you eat, how you eat is important: Your brain prefers a nibbling diet over large meals. Nibblers maintain insulin levels better, have lower cortisol levels, and have better glucose tolerance. This results in better cognitive functioning, fewer discipline problems, and an enhanced sense of well-being. Give students this nutritional information so they can take the first steps toward improving their eating habits and increasing their thinking and learning capacities. Engage the cooperation of your comprehensive school health system committee for even better results (see chapter 3).

Motor Learning Research

Now that their brains are working better, you must help students become more proficient in their motor skills. We have learned much about motor learning over the last decade and can use this information to develop more effective learning experiences. Share this information with your students as well so they can use it throughout their lives. *Concepts and Principles of Physical Education: What Every Student Needs to Know* includes an outstanding chapter on motor learning (Mohnsen 2003).

Stages of Motor Learning

Students progress through three stages to learn a new skill: cognitive, associative, and automatic (Magill 2007). During the cognitive stage, students need an accurate model of the skill. As you provide a demonstration of the skill, identify its most critical features. Cognitive processes are heavily involved at this stage as the learner develops a mental picture of the skill and sequencing pattern. At this stage, however, the learner can't manage small details of the movement or adapt the movement to different environmental conditions. Students in this stage are most in need of direct instruction.

Students usually spend most of their time in the associative stage. Here, students concentrate on refining the mechanics of the skill. As consistency increases during this stage, students begin to adjust to environmental conditions. Students in this stage benefit from partner feedback and guided discovery or divergent styles of teaching (see chapter 11).

At the automatic stage, the learner has mastered the skill and no longer has to concentrate on how to perform the skill. At this point, he shifts his attention from the cognitive aspects of the performance to the environmental. Students at this stage benefit the most from random or variable practice.

Mental Practice

Mental practice is an effective practice strategy. Forming a mental picture of the motor skill before practicing it enhances learning. Continuing mental practice after the initial learning enhances long-term retention. If the student visualizes herself as a noted performer, identifying as completely as possible with that role model, she will develop and improve her performance further. If she gives herself a pep talk while visualizing, she'll enhance her performance even more. So that you don't take away from physical practice time during class, assign or encourage mental practice during rest intervals or as part of a homework assignment.

Improving Speed and Accuracy

When introducing new skills, emphasize generating speed or force without pressuring students to be accurate. In other words, don't emphasize accuracy until students demonstrate that they can generate sufficient force; otherwise, as beginners, they may never develop the force necessary for success in many sport skills. For example, when a student is working on the correct technique for an overhand throw, emphasizing accuracy causes the student to throw with a "dart-throwing" technique. By focusing on force, the student learns to bring the arm back, rotate the body, and transfer body weight to project the ball a greater distance. As the learner progresses to the associative and automatic stages, he can begin to focus more on accuracy. The student will always need to make some trade-off between speed and accuracy but over time can continue to work on improving both.

Practice Schedules

Spacing of practice sessions, often referred to as *distributed practice,* generally leads to more effective (but not necessarily more efficient) learning, especially in the early stages. To apply this finding to physical education classes, consider changing unit plans that focus on one skill each day. You can use instructional time more effectively if you have students practice a number of skills during each class period (Schmidt and Wrisberg 2000).

I've noticed that teachers tend to be behaviorists, breaking each task down into the smallest units possible. Whenever possible, however, introduce new skills in their entirety—especially when breaking down the skill changes it significantly (Magill 2007). For example, breaking the skill of batting into its parts to practice those parts does not teach batting because the parts are significantly different when practiced alone and when applied to the entire skill. But for a very complex skill that has difficult—yet relatively independent—parts, demonstrate the whole skill first, next demonstrate and have students practice the parts, and then as quickly as possible have the students put the parts together and practice the skill as a whole. This approach is often referred to as the "whole–part–whole" approach.

When putting the skill back together, use forward or backward chaining. In the triple jump, for example, forward chaining involves practicing the run, then practicing the run into a hop, then practicing the run into a hop into a skip, and finally practicing the run into a hop into a skip into a jump. In backward chaining, students begin practice with a standing jump and then add the skip, the hop, and finally the run. Backward chaining may be more effective because students see it as more logical and meaningful than forward chaining, or beginning with the first part of the skill (Magill 2007).

Other terms that are used when talking about practice schedules are constant versus variable practice and blocked versus random practice. Although similar, these two concepts are different.

Constant Versus Variable Practice   Constant versus variable practice refers to instruction regarding a single skill and how it is practiced. Constant practice means practicing the same skill in the same way. Variable practice refers to setting up practice with changing conditions. Changing conditions can include speed (fast, slow), distance (far, near), and organization (number of shots per turn) of the practice. Constant practice enhances the learning of open skills (during the cognitive stage of learning only) and closed skills. Variable practice enhances the learning of open skills during the associative and automatic stages of learning, because practicing open skills in unchanging environments after the cognitive stage does little to prepare the learner for the real-life application of the skill to a game setting. Open skills are those that are performed in a changing environment and closed skills are those that are performed in a nonchanging environment. In basketball, dribbling and layups are open skills, whereas the free throw is a closed skill. Therefore, students in the associative and automatic stages of learning should practice the layup by approaching the basket from different angles while defenders try to block their shots. The greatest benefits comes when students practice skills under conditions that match game settings as closely as possible.

Blocked Versus Random Practice   Blocked versus random practice refers to instruction regarding several skills and how they are practiced. In blocked practice, one skill is practiced for say 10 minutes, then a second skill is practiced for 10 minutes, and then a third skill is practiced for 10 minutes. In random practice, the first skill is practiced for a couple of minutes, then the second skill, then the first skill again, then the third skill, then the second skill—in a random fashion. Research (Magill 2007) showed that blocked practice leads to short-term success; however, random practice leads to long-term success. This means that you either need to change activities frequently or use a station approach to instruction.

Feedback

Feedback benefits the learner especially during the associative and automatic stages of learning. The learner needs either corrective (e.g., "Forming a wider triangle with your hands and head gives you a wider base of support, making it easier for you to perform the headstand") or positive specific (e.g., "Good job—you stepped forward on your opposite foot") feedback. In this situation, "Good job!" is used to draw the student's attention to the correct aspect of her performance, which is helpful, as opposed to praise that is used to manipulate students. Delay feedback until about 5 seconds after the student completes the skill so that she has time to process the kinesthetic feelings associated with the performance before hearing external feedback. Teach students to delay feedback when assessing peers as well.

Restrict feedback to commenting on features not readily apparent to the learner. For example, feedback on throwing accuracy does not give the learner any additional information, because he can clearly see the outcome of the throw. But information about the technique of his throw is important because he cannot get that information for himself.

Limit feedback further by concentrating on only one or two critical features at a time. Making too many points at once will overwhelm the learner. Select for feedback only the critical features you highlighted while explaining and demonstrating the skill. If you introduce a skill by only pointing out its main features, you are also less likely to overwhelm the learner. For example, when teaching the basketball dribble, I initially focus on the use of the finger pads and on pushing the ball as opposed to slapping the ball. Therefore, during practice I comment only on these critical features. As we progress through the striking or basketball unit, I highlight other critical features of the basketball dribble so that I can help students refine their skills.

Transfer of Learning

When teaching motor skills, point out the ways in which many skills share similarities with other skills, showing students how to transfer learning appropriately from one situation to another (a positive transfer of learning). For example, we use the underhand movement pattern in the underhand volleyball serve, badminton serve, and softball pitch. Although differences between these patterns can cause negative transfer, whereby the previous learning actually interferes with learning the new skill, highlighting the similarities between skills has a positive effect on learning.

How Students Learn Differently

Throughout this chapter we have looked at enhancing learning for students in general. But students are individuals and what works with one student may not work with another. Over the years, researchers have developed many different methods of and theories for looking at how individual students learn. This disjointed approach reminds me of the story about the blind men and the elephant. Each man held a different part of the elephant (trunk, leg, tail), and when asked to describe what they were holding, they each gave a different description. Likewise, each learning theory looks at learning from a different perspective. Let's discuss two of the more popular theories, Bandler–Grinder and multiple intelligences.

Bandler–Grinder

The Bandler–Grinder (Richard Bandler and John Grinder) approach looks at which modality a student prefers to learn through—auditory, visual, or kinesthetic. A quick method to determine students' preferred learning modality is to ask them a question that they must think about. As the students are pondering their answers, watch their eyes. Visual learners tend to look up; auditory learners, sideways; and kinesthetic learners, down. Teachers tend to teach using their own modality preferences: The majority of educators are visual learners, but the majority of physical educators are kinesthetic learners. The students who often have difficulty in the classroom setting also tend to be kinesthetic learners. They perform well in physical education because they learn best through doing. The challenge in physical education is to engage the visual and auditory learners. By including pictures, graphics, readings, and video clips, you engage the visual learners in the learning situation. Add audio recordings, music, and discussions to engage auditory learners. Provide a wide variety of learning activities so all your students learn. For more information on this topic, read *Mega-Teaching and Learning: Neurolinguistic Programming Applied to Education* (Van Nagel, Siudzinski, and Bandler 1993).

Multiple Intelligences

Another way we are all different is in the area or areas in which we excel. In 1983, Howard Gardner identified seven intelligences (linguistic, logical–mathematical, musical, spatial, bodily–kinesthetic, interpersonal, and intrapersonal) or ways in which we can view intelligence. Since then, he has identified two additional intelligences—the naturalist intelligence and the existential intelligence. Gardner (2000) wrote that each of us has varying levels of ability in each of these intelligences. Typically, however, most people find that they excel in one or two intelligences. Students can usually identify their strongest intelligences themselves. Interestingly, watching how students misbehave will give you insights into those students' most highly developed intelligences as well.

Because most classes are made up of individuals with different primary intelligences, you must use a broad range of teaching strategies in each class (see chapter 11). A station approach (figure 9.3) can address a different intelligence at each station. Although it's not necessary to include every intelligence in every lesson, the greater the number of intelligences addressed in a lesson, the greater the number of students who will be highly engaged in learning. In addition, if you are having particular difficulty with one or two students, you may want to make a special effort to reach them through their primary intelligences.

Linguistic Intelligence

Students whose primary intelligence is linguistic have a capacity to use words effectively. They prefer to learn through lectures, large and small group discussions, reading, storytelling, brainstorming, debate, tape-recording their thoughts, and writing. The types of instructional materials that work best with these students are books, worksheets, manuals, talking books, and word games. When you ask these students to develop a project, they will more than likely develop an oral or written report. When misbehaving, these students tend to talk, interrupt, and argue with the teacher and other students.

Logical–Mathematical Intelligence

Students whose primary intelligence is logical–mathematical have a capacity to use numbers and to reason effectively. They prefer to learn through mathematical problems, scientific demonstrations, logical–sequential presentation of subject matter, classifications and categorizations, critical thinking, and logical problem-solving exercises. They prefer to work with logic puzzles and games, computer programming languages, and mathematical problems on the chalkboard. When you ask these students to develop a project, they will typically include statistics, cause-and-effect charts, and formulas to prove and convey their points of view. When misbehaving, these students tend to daydream or challenge the logic of the teacher.

Spatial Intelligence

Students whose primary intelligence is spatial have the capacity to perceive the visual–spatial world accurately. They prefer to learn through visualizations, picture metaphors, sketching of ideas, charts, graphs, diagrams, maps, slides, photographs, and mind-maps. They prefer to work with building models, hands-on projects, videos, graphics software, visual puzzles and mazes, and microscopes. These students typically develop projects that include maps, flowcharts, sketches, and diagrams. When misbehaving, these students take things apart to see how they work or they doodle on their papers.

Musical Intelligence

Students whose primary intelligence is musical have the capacity to perceive, discriminate, transform, and express musical forms. They prefer to learn through rhythms, songs, raps, chants, memory music, mood music, and musical concepts. They prefer to work with music software, musical instruments, and recorded music. When you ask these students to develop a project, they

---

A Station Approach

Station 1 (spatial). Watch *SyberVision* video to view correct technique.

Station 2 (bodily–kinesthetic). Practice using long iron.

Station 3 (naturalist). Practice golf stroke and record results in a journal.

Station 4 (logical–mathematical). Videotape golf swing and replay for self-assessment. Use Dartfish or other video analysis software.

Station 5 (musical). Practice golf swing to music.

Station 6 (linguistic). Write a description of the correct technique for swinging a golf club.

Station 7 (interpersonal). Practice golf swing with a partner. Provide partner with feedback.

Station 8 (intrapersonal). Perform shadow golf drill to provide self-feedback on own golf swing.

Figure 9.3   Sample station activities for improving golf technique based on the multiple intelligences.

will include music, chants, and raps. I always had one of these students in each of my classes, because whenever I handed out pencils there was a student who insisted on drumming with it. These students also misbehave by humming and by tapping their feet.

Interpersonal Intelligence

Students whose primary intelligence is interpersonal in nature have the capacity to perceive and make distinctions in the moods, intentions, motivations, and feelings of other people. They prefer to learn through cooperative learning, group brainstorming activities, community-based activities, peer sharing, conflict mediation activities, cross-age tutoring, interpersonal interactions, and simulations. They prefer to work with interactive software, simulations, and board games. When you ask these students to develop projects, they will more than likely include their own simulations, demonstrations, and discussions. They tend to misbehave by exerting negative leadership, writing notes, and talking to friends.

Intrapersonal Intelligence

Students whose primary intelligence is intrapersonal have the capacity to understand themselves. They prefer to learn through reflection, personal connections, interest centers, goal setting, self-paced instruction, and self-esteem activities. They prefer to work with programmed instruction materials, individualized projects and games, and journals. When you ask these students to develop a project, they will more than likely include scrapbooks, their own feelings, and their own interpretation of events. They exhibit misbehavior through daydreaming and tuning out the teacher.

Bodily–Kinesthetic Intelligence

Students whose primary intelligence is bodily–kinesthetic have the capacity to use their whole bodies to express ideas and feelings. They prefer to learn through creative movement, physical education activities, mime, crafts, theater, and hands-on activities. They prefer to work with virtual reality software, field trips, hands-on materials, crafts, cooking, and tactile materials. These students typically develop projects that include three-dimensional representations of events, a demonstration, or a performance. Their misbehaviors include being out of their seat in the classroom as well as pushing, shoving, and fighting with others. Similar to the kinesthetic learner

in the Bandler–Grinder model, these students often do well in physical education while getting into trouble in their other classes. You can help these students by sharing strategies for relating to them with their other teachers.

Naturalist Intelligence

Students whose primary intelligence is naturalist are absorbed in things in the natural world. They have the ability to distinguish and categorize objects in nature. They prefer to learn through working in nature, exploring, and learning about plants and natural events. They prefer to work outdoors, participate in field trips, garden, and use hands-on materials. These students typically develop projects that involve making comparisons, distinctions, and categorizing objects. They prefer to keep journals, make drawings, take pictures, and write down their observations. They exhibit misbehavior through daydreaming, wandering off, and focusing on the minute details of an object.

Existential Intelligence

Students whose primary intelligence is existential have the ability to contemplate questions beyond sensory data, such as the infinite. They prefer to learn by tackling deep questions about human existence, such as the meaning of life. The existentially intelligent are more likely to be aware of their personal meaning and thus prefer to keep journals—writing down their thoughts regarding the big questions. They exhibit misbehavior through daydreaming, pondering, and incessantly asking questions.

Summary

For learning to occur in the middle school, you must first motivate students to learn. Next, you must align instruction with what we know about learning—especially motor learning. Finally, you must consider individual learning needs, introducing new information through each student's preferred learning style and then reviewing it through as many other avenues as possible. When you set up a positive and safe learning environment, provide interesting instruction, and ensure success for all, your students will learn. In the next chapter, I look specifically at how you can change your teaching behaviors to ensure success for all your students.

Improving Your Teaching Effectiveness

- Accomplished physical education teachers possess a thorough comprehension of the fundamentals of physical education and broad grasp of relevant principles and theories that give their teaching purpose and guide them as they carry out a flexible, yet effective, instructional program responsive to students' needs and developmental levels.

- Accomplished physical education teachers tenaciously maintain a stimulating, productive setting that encourages participation, discovery, goal setting, and cooperation and that holds all students to the highest expectations.

—National Board for Professional Teaching Standards

My students experience much more quality learning and activity time when I have prepared a well-thought-out and organized lesson. For example, when using a fitness circuit, I set up stations ahead of time with equipment and task cards. The task cards give students clear, concise instructions, along with pictures to illustrate the activity, so I am free to assist students who need me during the lesson.

—physical educator Joan Van Blom, Hill Middle School, Long Beach, California

To a large extent, how much students learn in physical education is directly related to the quality and effectiveness of the physical educator. Teachers who pay little attention to the individual needs of their students and the current research on teaching and learning often see little improvement in their students throughout the school year. However, teachers who are enthusiastic, have high expectations for all students, and use effective teaching behaviors see their students gain motor, cognitive, and affective skills. Have you ever wondered what you can do to improve your teaching? In this chapter, we examine those teaching behaviors that can lead to instructional success in middle school. As you read this chapter, answer the questions I pose at the beginning of each section to see how well you are currently implementing each behavior.

Staying Current

Have you attended a college or university graduate course recently? When was the last time you attended a professional conference? How long has it been since you picked up a professional journal and read all the way through it?

So far in *Teaching Middle School Physical Education,* we have discussed a wealth of information that you need to know to be effective. You may remember helpful information from your college preparation program as well. But have you kept up with the current research? Few of us know everything about what it takes to form a complete physical education program appropriate for middle schoolers. Without up-to-date knowledge and understanding of curriculum development, content, student needs and learning styles, instruction, and assessment, it'll be difficult—if not impossible—to deliver a quality physical education experience. In chapter 13, I provide additional information on professional development opportunities to help you maintain and improve your skills, but first, let's discuss effective teaching behaviors.

Planning

Do you have a unit plan for every unit you teach? Do you always have a lesson plan in hand as you walk into class? Does your lesson plan include written objectives? Have you considered the individual needs of each student in your classes? Are the activities you planned directly related to the objectives?

As a young teacher, I made the decision to never go to class without a lesson plan. I often pretended that the class was full of adults who would otherwise quickly discern that I was unprepared for the lesson. I thought that if I couldn't stand in front of a group of adults without knowing exactly what I was going to do, then why should I try to teach a group of youngsters without being as well prepared?

Unfortunately, many teachers believe that they can walk into class and deliver a lesson on any topic without planning. Many decisions go into a lesson, and not planning simply means that the teacher is unable or unwilling to make those deci-

sions. Teachers who plan for organization, management, and task appropriateness promote learning better, because their students present fewer behavior problems, spend less time waiting, and have more practice time during the lesson (Maryland State Department of Education 1989). By developing unit and lesson plans, you can also see and demonstrate the links among the exit, grade-level, and unit standards and the instruction itself.

Using Time Effectively

Do you spend your instructional time effectively? Do your students spend most of the instructional period engaged in active, hands-on learning? Do you keep the time you spend on management to a minimum?

Typically, state guidelines mandate the number of minutes per day or week allocated to physical education. For example, California's guidelines allocate 200 minutes of physical education every 10 school days to students in fifth and sixth grades and a minimum of 400 minutes to students in seventh and eighth grades every 10 school days. It is important to keep students active during physical education, but students can be active and yet fail to learn. The goal is to use the time that you have to teach students so that they will be physically active for life. How much time do you have to teach? How well do you use it?

Physical educators tend to divide their class time into three categories:

1. Student engagement time: the amount of time in which students are actively involved in physical education content (but not necessarily at the appropriate level for success)

2. Lecture time: the amount of time for which students sit and listen while the teacher provides information

3. Management time: the amount of time spent on noninstructional activities, such as roll call, disciplining students, and handing out equipment

Students should spend at least 70% of class time engaged in active learning and no more than 15% in lectures and 15% in management activities (Batesky 1988), depending on the teacher's style and strategy as well as on the nature of the information. Make it your goal to decrease managerial time and increase engaged learning time whenever possible. How? Some of the most helpful ways to do so are to establish and follow routines, give brief but precise directions and demonstrations followed immediately by practice time, use enough equipment to keep lines short and groups small, and move on to a new activity when interest wanes. To further reduce the time you spend on management, review the management tips in chapter 5 and motivational strategies in chapter 9 as well as the following tips:

- Begin and end class on time.
- Have equipment organized and ready to go.
- Teach your rules.
- Establish routines.
- Reduce the transition time between activities.
- Give brief but precise instructions.
- Use short demonstrations followed by immediate practice.
- Provide students with sufficient equipment so they do not wait in line for a turn.
- Use prompts (verbal cues or task cards) to keep students on task.
- Change practice activities to keep students interested and involved.
- Resolve minor distractions before they become major disturbances.

Once I visited a class that was working on golf putting. Each group of four students was assigned to a carpet square with a tin can as the target. The teacher instructed the students to practice the putting stroke while trying to get the ball into the can. Initially, all the students were actively engaged, taking turns and watching each other try to get the ball into the container. After about 15 minutes, however, the students lost interest in the activity and began to entertain themselves by hitting the ball across the instructional area and, at times, toward me. Sometimes teachers ask, "How do you know when it's time to change an activity?" I respond, "The students will let you know—one way or another."

Using Students' Names

When you address a student, do you use her name? When giving feedback to a student, do you use her name? Do you know the names of all your students?

Everyone likes to hear his own name. More important, a student likes to know that the person teaching him knows his name. Effective teachers take the time to learn their students' names and how to pronounce them correctly. Then they use the students' names during class. One teacher I work with took a picture of each of his students using a digital camera and created a visual seating chart on the computer to help him remember the names of his 250 students.

Knowing students' names promotes not only learning but also class management. As I discussed in chapter 5, calling out a student's name in a respectful manner is a very effective strategy for putting a stop to misbehavior. Several activities, such as the name games, help both students and teachers learn each other's names.

Providing Model Demonstrations and Explanations

Are you able to correctly demonstrate each motor skill that you teach? If there is a skill that you can't demonstrate, do you have a video clip of that skill? When you aren't able to demonstrate a skill, are you willing to use a student as a model? Do you know the critical features for every motor skill that you teach? Do you clearly explain and demonstrate those critical features to your students?

Providing a model performance for the learner during the first stage of learning is critical to the learner's success. Effective models are accurate, highlight the critical features of the skill, provide visual information that students can use to form a mental image of the action, and are performed in their entirety and at normal speed. Effective teachers accompany the demonstration with an explanation that focuses on the same critical features highlighted in the demonstration. The explanations include examples of correct and incorrect form, as well as one or two ideas or cues, and are brief and logically sequenced. For example, cues for bowling are push away, swing back, swing forward, and release, and cues for the overhand volleyball serve are toss, arm back, extend arm, and follow through.

Demonstrate the skill yourself only if you can provide an accurate model. Otherwise, use videos to provide effective demonstrations. Interestingly, students benefit from seeing the demonstration of a task from the performer's viewpoint, which is only possible through the use of video. Or if a video is unavailable, use students who are proficient at the skill as models. Be sure to use student models of both genders and various ethnicities.

Checking for Understanding

Are you sure that your students understand the directions that you have given for an activity? Are you sure that your students understand the critical features of a new skill after your presentation?

When teaching, check for understanding before sending students out to practice the skill. Many teachers are unaware that students do not understand their directions until the students try to demonstrate the skill or implement the activity. Check understanding through a variety of techniques: signaled answers, choral responses, or sampling individual responses. Signaled answers refer to asking students true–false questions and requesting a thumbs-up or thumbs-down response to indicate their understanding. For a choral response, students call out the answer to a question in unison. Questions might include ones like these:

- Where should the weight be when you finish the underhand serve? Why?

- What is the best stance for the tennis ready position? Why?

- Where do you contact the ball for topspin? Why?

Both the signaled answer and choral response are quick ways to check for understanding, saving time and frustration later in the class period.

You can also call on individual students to check understanding of the task and skill and then generalize the understanding of a few students to the entire class (figure 10.1). One alternative to sampling individual responses is a cooperative learning technique in which you ask the question, give partners time to discuss the answer, and then call on a sampling of students to ascertain the level of understanding. This approach gives all students an opportunity to discuss the question and learn from one another.

Follow these effective questioning steps when asking for individual student responses:

1. Ask the question.
2. Wait at least 5 seconds (some students require more time to process).
3. Call on one student.
4. Affirm or correct the student's answer (this indicates to the students that you are interested in the response).
5. Follow up with a second or third question when you receive an incorrect answer to

Figure 10.1   Calling on individual students while in the classroom allows you to check their understanding and, if necessary, lead them to the correct answer before sending them out to practice the skill.

Asking Questions

Mr. Chan: "Today, we are going to see how many curl-ups each of you can perform. Which part of health-related fitness do we test with curl-ups?"

[Teacher waits 5 seconds.]

Mr. Chan: "Temika?"

Temika: "Cardiorespiratory endurance!"

Mr. Chan: "What evidence do you have that the correct answer is cardiorespiratory endurance?"

Temika: "Because my heart beats faster when I do curl-ups."

Mr. Chan: "How long can you do curl-ups?"

Temika: "Three or four minutes."

Mr. Chan: "How long do we need to perform an exercise to work on cardiorespiratory endurance?"

Temika: "Twenty to thirty minutes. Oh, I guess the answer can't be cardiorespiratory endurance—it must be muscular endurance!"

clarify student understanding and to lead students to the correct answer (often a student's incorrect response may indicate a partial understanding of the concept). See the sidebar for an example.

If you immediately call on a student after asking a question, the other students have no reason to even think about the answer. When you wait 5 seconds and then call on a student, the other students also have time to think about their answers. This keeps the entire class involved in the learning process—not just the student answering the question. Then repeat information, if necessary, so all students understand the information.

Providing Effective Practice

Do your students get enough practice opportunities during the class period? Are your students practicing at the appropriate level of difficulty? Are your students using the correct technique when they practice?

Even after you have limited your managerial and lecture time so that most of your class time is left for students to engage in the activity, how do you know that the students are getting enough appropriate practice? Providing effective practice (also known as academic learning time in physical education or ALT-PE) involves engaging students in a maximum amount of practice at the appropriate level of difficulty using the correct technique so that learning can occur. The appropriate level of difficulty is typically defined

as an 80% success rate, although some set the success rate closer to 50% for target activities, especially with beginning learners (Rink 1993a). Unfortunately, research has found that students typically spend less than 15% of their class time in ALT-PE (Lemaster and Lacy 1993).

One day I was observing an in-school bowling class and decided to count the number of opportunities that students had to practice their bowling technique. The class was well organized into practice stations, with four students, one bowling ball, and a set of pins at each station. The students rotated from bowler to pin setter as they practiced their bowling skills. Still, at the end of the practice time (approximately 20 minutes), each student had received only three or four chances to roll the ball.

To increase the amount of ALT-PE, you must first increase student engagement time, thereby making more time for practice as we have already discussed. Second, set up the instructional environment so that students get as many opportunities as possible to practice the skill. Increasing the amount of equipment and limiting the size of practice groups are two of the most effective strategies for increasing the number of practice trials per student. For example, in the previous bowling scenario, I suggested to the teacher that she assign two students to each set of pins and alternate the starting line for the bowling lanes so that students would not have to wait for the ball to be returned. This resulted in three times the number of rolls for each student in the class. Finally, ensure that the tasks and drills are at the appropriate level of difficulty for each student.

The inclusion style of teaching effectively creates the appropriate levels of difficulty for all students through the use of alternative activities (see chapter 11). For example, when students are working on the volleyball serve, let them choose how far from the net they will stand instead of requiring all of them to practice from behind the end line. Other ways to reduce the complexity of a task are to use static objects (i.e., T-ball), reduce the number of players, modify the equipment (shorter striking implement), and reduce the number of defenders.

Actively Supervising

Do you move around the instructional area as your students are practicing? Do you spend an equal amount of time in each quadrant of the instructional area? Do you know where all your students are all the time?

Actively monitoring students during practice helps to keep them on task. Often, misbehavior or off-task behavior (doing something other than the assignment) occurs in the quadrant of the instructional area that the teacher has not visited. Move around the instructional area in an unpredictable pattern, spending an equitable amount of time focusing on each student or group of students while staying aware of the other students in the class. Beginning teachers tend to focus exclusively on the group they are working with, and, as a result, off-task behavior tends to occur in the other groups. This ability to focus on the students you are working with and simultaneously stay aware of the other students is called *overlapping* (Rink 1993a). Awareness and experience improve the skill of overlapping.

Providing Feedback

Do you provide your students with simple, positive, specific feedback as they are practicing their motor skills? Do you provide your students with specific corrective feedback?

Students want to know how they are doing, so effective teachers provide them with feedback on their performances. Base feedback on the critical features you introduced during the demonstration and explanation of the skill so that the student knows what you are looking for in her performance. Comment on only one or two features at a time when correcting a student so as not to

overwhelm her. For example, when introducing the soccer dribble, I initially focus on contacting the ball with the instep of the foot and keeping the ball within 1 to 2 feet (0.3-0.6 meters). Then I limit my feedback to comments related to these two critical features. At this point, I don't comment on other aspects, such as the student's being aware of what is going on around her.

Feedback can be general ("Way to go!") or specific ("Way to bend your knees!"). Specific feedback, however, is much more effective (Siedentop 1991). In fact, effective teachers provide their students with two or three specific feedback comments per minute during practice periods. In addition, feedback can be positive ("Great job!"), negative ("Not that way"), or corrective ("Try bending your knees more"). Effective teachers stay away from negative feedback and focus their energies on positive, specific, and corrective comments, often at a ratio of three or four positive to every corrective comment (Batesky 1988).

Treating Students Equitably

Do you provide all students with the same amount of feedback? Do you have the same expectations for all your students? Do you provide all students with the opportunity to respond to questions and demonstrate activities?

Effective teachers have high expectations of all students, are enthusiastic with all students, and use effective teaching behaviors with all students. Typically, teachers are more likely to call on high achievers than low achievers when asking questions (Kerman 1979). They tend to provide boys with more feedback, but it tends to be more negative in nature. I used to find myself typically asking boys to demonstrate a new skill, even though I had girls who were equally capable of being models. And many teachers tend to give high achievers up to 5 seconds to respond to a question, whereas they give low achievers only 1 or 2 seconds (Kerman 1979).

Students tend to "live up to" or "down to" your expectations (Martinek, Crowe, and Rejeski 1982). When you provide some students with more opportunities to demonstrate, practice, receive feedback, and answer questions, it communicates to the other students that either you don't care as much about them or they are not as good as the other students. Moreover, many students will pick up on your expectations even through nonverbal communication.

What can you do to improve your use of effective teaching behaviors and ensure that all students are on the receiving end? First, become aware of effective teaching behaviors (reading this chapter is a good start). Second, determine to what extent you are currently using these behaviors by doing one of the following:

• Audio recording one of your lessons
• Video recording one of your lessons
• Having a colleague observe one of your lessons

With either of the first two methods, you will collect data (figure 10.2) by listening to or watching the tape of the lesson, whereas with the third method your colleague will collect the data. Regardless of which method you use, list your students' names on a piece of paper, determine which behaviors (e.g., use of names, amount of feedback, types of feedback) you are going to chart and make them column headings, and then simply mark (or have your colleague mark) each time you use the behavior with a student. Sometimes, depending on class size, it's easier to collect data on a few students rather than on the entire class. In addition, when you are collecting data from an audiotape, it's often difficult to determine which student is the recipient of the effective teaching behavior unless you use the student's name. Once you see how you're doing, focus your attention on increasing the use of one or two effective teaching behaviors at a time and equitably distributing the behavior to all students. Collecting data on a regular basis provides you with the feedback you need to continue to increase your use of effective teaching behaviors.

Summary

Effective teachers have high expectations of all students, are enthusiastic with all students, and use effective teaching behaviors with all students. These teachers are constantly looking for ways to improve their effectiveness. You can increase your effectiveness as a physical educator by increasing your knowledge base; spending more time on planning; increasing the time your students spend in active learning; learning students' names; improving your ability to demonstrate and explain new skills, checking for understanding before students practice; actively supervising the instructional area; providing more effective practice; and increasing the amount of positive, specific, and corrective feedback that you give.

Baywater Middle School Teacher Observation Form

Date _____ Class _____

Period _____ Observer _____

STUDENT NAME	USE OF NAME	POSITIVE SPECIFIC FEEDBACK	CORRECTIVE FEEDBACK	POSITIVE FEEDBACK	NEGATIVE FEEDBACK
John Adams					
Sue Brown					
Ann Chen					
Jose Garcia					
Anna Hernandez					
Tony Nguyen					
Juan Ortega					
Tom Smith					
Mary Washington					
Tanya Washington					

Figure 10.2 You can use this form to evaluate yourself from a video- or audio-taped lesson or you can ask a colleague to observe your lesson.

Teaching Styles and Strategies to Meet Learners' Needs

- Accomplished physical education teachers possess a thorough comprehension of the fundamentals of physical education and broad grasp of relevant principles and theories that give their teaching purpose and guide them as they carry out a flexible, yet effective, instructional program responsive to students' needs and developmental levels.

—*National Board for Professional Teaching Standards*

Although Mosston and Ashworth (1994) identified a variety of teaching styles, which they called the "spectrum of teaching styles," in their popular textbook *Teaching Physical Education* (first published in 1968), my own teacher training in the 1970s primarily taught me simply to explain and demonstrate motor skills to students. I learned to follow this by having everyone practice the same skill simultaneously in the same way and giving students feedback afterward. As I visit classes across the United States today, I observe the same strategy in the majority of classes. This style of teaching, often referred to as direct instruction or the behaviorist approach, saves instructional time and

Teaching in southern California makes it crystal clear to me how critical it is to vary my teaching styles and instructional strategies on a weekly basis. Large, heterogeneous classes with the additional challenge of meeting the needs of English learners make it nearly impossible to focus on only one style or strategy. For example, whole-class instruction is not very effective for English learners. Instead, through cooperative learning opportunities, students are able to negotiate meaning with each other, which is especially critical for English learners. I need to meet my students where they are rather than demand that they meet me where I am.

—Brenna Baringer, National Board–certified teacher, 2001, San Diego City Schools

leads to significant learning when the content can be learned in a strictly sequential, progressive manner. Direct instruction, however, is not appropriate for teaching skills requiring higher order. These situations require a more indirect, or constructivist, approach. In this chapter, we look at different ways you can vary your teaching styles and instructional strategies as well as ways you can incorporate specific methods that work well with limited-English-proficient (LEP) students and differently abled students.

Teaching Styles

Mosston and Ashworth's spectrum of teaching styles categorizes instruction according to the types of instructional decisions made by both the teacher and the students, including the decisions made before, during, and immediately after a lesson. In their 1994 edition, the authors identify 11 teaching styles: command, practice, reciprocal, self-check, inclusion, guided discovery, convergent discovery, divergent production, individual program-learner's design, learner initiated, and self-teaching. The styles are on a continuum from the command style, for which the teacher makes all of the decisions, to the self-teaching style, for which the students make virtually all of their own decisions about the learning process.

When the spectrum of teaching styles was introduced, many teachers thought they should move their instruction from the command style to the self-teaching style. In their 1994 edition, however, Mosston and Ashworth clarified their position, explaining that every style has a place, depending on the particular situation, students, teacher, and content. So let's examine each of these styles and identify when each may be appropriate. Although my examples (figure 11.1) are of lessons that focus exclusively on one style, feel free to mix styles as appropriate in any lesson you teach.

Teaching Styles for Sample Lessons

A. Command Style: Grapevine Dance Step

Objective

Students demonstrate the correct technique for the grapevine dance step.

Activities

1. Demonstrate the starting position with your feet together, facing the front of the room with your back to the students.
2. Ask the students to face the front of the room with their feet together and provide them feedback.
3. Say, "Step right," and take one step to the right.
4. Ask the students to step right and provide them with feedback.
5. Say, "Step left behind right," and perform the step.
6. Ask the students to step left behind right and provide them with feedback.
7. Say, "Step right," and perform the step.
8. Ask the students to step right and provide them with feedback.
9. Say, "Close left," and perform the step.
10. Ask the students to close left and provide them with feedback.

Figure 11.1   Sample lessons are shown for the command (A), practice (B), reciprocal (C), self-checking (D), inclusion (E), guided discovery (F), convergent discovery (G), divergent (H), individual program-learner's design (I), and learner-initiated (J) styles.

Sections with asterisks are adapted, by permission, from B. Mohnsen, 2001, *Building a Quality Physical Education Program (Grades 6-12)* (Medina, WA: Institute for Educational Development), 79.

B. Practice Style: Soccer Skills*

Objectives

Students demonstrate the correct technique for dribbling.

Students demonstrate the correct technique for passing.

Students demonstrate the correct technique for trapping.

Students demonstrate the correct technique for dribbling, passing, and trapping while combining the three skills.

Students demonstrate the correct technique for shooting and guarding the goal.

Students demonstrate the correct technique for all skills during a 4-on-4 game.

Activities

After you review each skill, have students rotate through the following stations in groups of four. At each station, place a task card describing that station's activity. I have written the instructions as a model for writing your own task cards so that students can easily follow them. The information in the parentheses is for you only, however. Keep in mind that a lesson can be longer than one instructional period.

1. (Set up two lines of five cones—the distance between the cones depends on how much space is available.) Divide your group of four into two pairs. Each pair of players takes turns dribbling around one line of cones.

2. (Set up two goal areas, marking each area with two cones.) Divide your group of four into two pairs, one pair for each goal area. One partner shoots while the other partner guards the goal area. Switch positions.

3. (Set up the computer.) On the computer, research the history of soccer, noting how the game has changed throughout the years.

4. (Set up four cones to define the area.) In pairs, dribble the ball up and down the field, passing the ball.

5. (Set up four cones to define the playing area.) Play a 4-on-4 mini–soccer game against the group at station 6.

6. Play a 4-on-4 mini–soccer game against the group at station 5.

7. (Mark two areas with four boundary cones for each pair to play in.) Divide your group into two pairs. Each pair plays 1-on-1 keep-away, staying within the marked area. The player without the ball tries to steal the ball away. If the ball goes out of bounds, the ball is given to the player who did not kick it out of bounds.

8. (Mark the area with four boundary cones.) Play a 2-on-2 keep-away game. The team with the ball can dribble and pass anywhere in the marked area. The other team tries to steal the ball. If the ball goes out of bounds, the ball is given to the team that didn't kick it out of bounds.

9. (Provide students with a checklist of critical features for each skill.) Watch the video to review the skills of passing, trapping, dribbling, shooting, and defending the goal, and check the critical elements you observe.

10. Divide your group into two pairs. Each pair passes the ball back and forth, trapping the ball to bring it under control.

11. Divide your group into two pairs. Each pair takes turns shooting the ball at a target on the wall.

12. (Provide appropriate reading and writing materials.) Read about the biomechanical principle of absorption of force and write a paragraph explaining how it relates to soccer.

Circulate from station to station, providing feedback and indicating when students must rotate to the next station.

(continued)

Figure 11.1 *(continued)*

(continued)

C. Reciprocal Style: Front Crawl Stroke*

Objectives

Students identify the critical features of the crawl stroke.

Students demonstrate cooperation by helping partners learn the crawl stroke.

Students demonstrate the correct technique for the crawl stroke.

Students provide accurate feedback to a partner.

Activities

1. Review the crawl stroke.
2. Identify the critical features of the crawl stroke.
3. Demonstrate the crawl stroke incorrectly, requesting feedback from several students.
4. Have students practice the crawl stroke in pairs. Ask one student to perform the stroke while the other student gives feedback. Have the student giving feedback focus first on the arms, then on the breathing, and then on the kick. Have students use the following criteria sheet to guide their feedback. Laminate forms so they stand up to the deck and pool environment and can be used for many years.

Arms

Places hand of one arm in water in line with the shoulder.

Bends elbow slightly as hand pushes water down the center of the body toward the feet.

Stops hand at the thigh and, without hesitating, lifts the arm out of the water with the shoulder and elbow.

While pushing one arm underwater, recovers the other arm over the water.

Breathing and Arms

Turns head to one side, angling the chin slightly up.

Inhales (breathes in) quickly through the mouth.

Turns head back down and exhales (breathes out) from mouth.

Kick

Begins up-and-down flutter kick at hip.

Bends knee downward slightly at the start of the kick.

Straightens knee on the up beat.

Barely breaks the surface of the water with the heel on the up kick.

You give feedback to the student observers.

D. Self-Checking Style: Full Golf Swing

Objectives

Students demonstrate the correct technique for the full golf swing, using an iron club.

Students demonstrate responsibility by assessing their own performances.

Students develop a practice plan for improving their golf swings.

Activities

1. Review the full golf swing.
2. Introduce and demonstrate the concept of shadow golf.

Figure 11.1   (continued)

3. Have students line up with their backs to the sun, each with iron club and five tees in hand.

4. Have students place tees on their own shadows as follows:

   First—top of head

   Second—back hip line

   Third—back knee line

   Fourth—3 inches forward of shadow of front hip line

   Fifth—forward of head toward target

5. Have students practice the three steps of a golf swing, checking their own body positions as follows:

   Stance—shadow line in contact with first through third tees.

   Backswing—shadow line remains in contact with first through third tees.

   Follow-through—maintain shadow line with first tee and move shadow forward to fourth tee and hands to fifth tee.

6. Have students gradually increase the distance of their fourth tees from their shadows to 4, 5, and then 6 inches while maintaining shadow contact with the first tee.

Homework

Have students develop a practice plan for improving their golf swing technique. Encourage students to use their understanding of developing and improving the performance of closed skills, performed in a stable environment (learned in previous lessons), to write their practice plans.

E. Inclusion Style: Clear Stroke Using Badminton Equipment*

Objectives

Students improve the accuracy of the forehand underhand clear, the forehand overhead clear, the backhand underhand clear, and the backhand overhead clear.

Students demonstrate responsibility for selecting the appropriate practice setting.

Activities

1. Set up each court in the gymnasium or outside area for clear stroke practice. Mark one side of the court in three places down the center of the court at different distances from the net. Mark the other side of the court with a large rectangular area and a smaller rectangular area.

2. Have students select one of the three distances from the net to begin practicing. Allow students to make 10 attempts to hit the shuttlecock into the large target area, using one of the four clear strokes. Allow students the choice, based on their success, either to aim for the large target area again or to try for the smaller target area. After they have successfully hit the shuttlecock into the smaller area, allow students to decide whether they want to move farther from the net or try a different clear stroke.

F. Guided Discovery Style: Long Jump*

Objectives

Students demonstrate the correct technique for the long jump.

Students explain how to increase their jumps using the biomechanical principles of projectiles.

Students use higher-order thinking skills to discover the correct technique for the long jump.

(continued)

Figure 11.1 *(continued)*

(continued)

Activities

1. Ask students a series of questions to help them understand the correct technique for the long jump and to increase the distances of their jumps.

   - Is it better to start the long jump from a running or standing position?

     (Anticipated answer: Running.)

   - Is it better to run fast or slow?

     (Anticipated answer: Fast.)

   - Is it better to take off from one or two feet?

     (Anticipated answer: One.)

   - Is it better to land with knees bent or straight?

     (Anticipated answer: Bent.)

   - Is it better to fall forward or backward on landing?

     (Anticipated answer: Forward.)

2. If some students respond incorrectly to a question, ask the students with the correct answer to explain the reason for the correct answer. If most or all students respond incorrectly to the question, ask them to experiment with the skill to determine why the other choice is correct.

Homework

Have students write an essay describing or draw a picture illustrating the correct technique for the running long jump.

G. Convergent Discovery Style: Generating Force

Objectives

Students demonstrate the correct technique for the overhand throw.

Students use higher-order thinking skills to discover the relationships between throwing a ball farther and the size of the ball, the weight of the ball, and the approach before releasing the ball.

Activities

1. Ask students to experiment with throwing several balls of different sizes and weights. Present the students with the following problem: What relationships exist between throwing the ball farther and the size of the ball? Between throwing the ball farther and the weight of the ball? Between throwing the ball farther and the length of the approach before releasing the ball?

2. Have students record their findings on a worksheet or in their notebooks.

Homework

Ask students to draw pictures or create charts depicting the relationships between the size and weight of the ball, length of the approach before releasing the ball, and the distance the ball travels.

H. Divergent Style: Game Design*

Objectives

Students demonstrate their understanding of rules, boundaries, and strategies by developing their own games.

Students use higher-order thinking skills in creating their new games.

Students collaborate to develop their new games.

Figure 11.1 *(continued)*

Activities

1. Explain to students the five important elements of a game, as follows:

    Boundaries—large areas, small areas, specific dimensions

    Equipment—bats, balls, gloves, beanbags

    Players—numbers, positions

    Scoring—how to score, scoring options, point value

    Penalties—illegal events and penalties for those events

2. Have groups of four students each develop a game. Once they have done so, have each group teach their game to another group.

I. Individual Program-Learner's Design Style: Exercise Physiology and Health-Related Fitness*

Objectives

Students improve their personal fitness.

Students develop personalized fitness plans, based on their own fitness levels.

Activities

1. Introduce the exercise physiology and health-related fitness unit to be sure students understand the principles and concepts associated with health-related fitness.

2. Have students select their own questions or problems related to improving their personal fitness (e.g., Do low-carb diets help to reduce body fat?).

3. Have students each research an area of interest and share the information with one other student.

J. Learner-Initiated Style: Motor Learning*

Objectives

Students improve their motor skills in activities of their own choosing.

Students develop personalized learning plans for activities of their own choosing, based on their current performance levels.

Activities

1. Encourage students to approach you with ideas on how to teach themselves a skill or activity.

2. Have students plan the entire learning process as well as the criteria they'll use in the evaluation process (provide feedback by asking probing questions).

3. Have students explain their learning plans while you listen, ask questions, and point out when they have omitted important decisions (provide feedback by asking probing questions).

4. Have students implement their learning plans (provide feedback by asking probing questions).

5. Learners produce final projects, demonstrating their learning.

Figure 11.1   *(continued)*

Command

In the command style of teaching, you make all the decisions. You give step-by-step instructions, for example, demonstrating a dance sequence or skill (see figure 11.1, part A), and the students copy each step. In other words, all students perform the same task at the same time as directed by you (figure 11.2). This style is often appropriate for the initial stage of learning, especially for situations in which safety is a concern, such as for beginning swimming and archery. The command

Figure 11.2   Command-style learning, in which all students are directed by you to perform the same task at the same time, is often appropriate during the initial stage of learning, when instructional time is limited, or when a class routine needs to be very structured.

style is also appropriate when instructional time is limited or student behavior dictates a highly structured class routine.

Practice

The practice style is the most commonly used style in physical education. In the practice style, you determine what you'll teach, introducing the skills and tasks through demonstration or the use of task cards (see chapter 12 for sample task cards). Then the students determine the number of practice trials and often the order in which they will practice the tasks (if there are more than one) within the time you allocate. During the practice time, you circulate throughout class, giving feedback and answering students' questions.

Like the command style, the practice style is also most appropriate for the initial stage of learning and when you don't have much instructional time. Compared with the command style, however, the practice style gives students more time to master motor skills and concepts as well as more responsibility for their own learning (see figure 11.1, part B, for a station approach using the practice style for learning new soccer skills). But if, like most physical educators, you do the majority of your teaching in this style, it may be helpful to reevaluate your lessons and determine which ones you might be able to teach more effectively using another style.

Reciprocal

In the reciprocal style, students give each other feedback. You, however, determine the task they'll practice and identify the critical features for them. Before starting the activity phase of the lesson, check for student understanding by providing a number of demonstrations that include common errors, asking students to identify the errors and give you appropriate feedback. Then have students work in pairs. While one student (the doer) performs the task, the second student (the observer) gives feedback, and the two reverse roles as appropriate. For this style, it is helpful to provide students with a checklist or criteria sheet with pictures (if possible) to remind them of the critical features they are looking for in the performance (see figure 11.1, part C, for an example of a lesson related to reviewing the front crawl stroke in a swimming unit).

You circulate from pair to pair, communicating only with the observer, who is providing the feedback. If the observer correctly identifies the error and gives the appropriate feedback, then you give positive, specific feedback to the observer. If, however, the observer incorrectly identifies the error or provides inappropriate feedback, then you give corrective feedback to the observer. Refrain from speaking directly to the doer so as not to disrupt the student-to-student relationship that this style fosters.

Because the reciprocal style emphasizes social relationships, it can help students learn social as well as motor skills, making it especially effective with middle school students. Limit its use, however, to the review of previously learned skills. The reason is that learning a new skill requires accurate feedback and coverage of safety rules, which often cannot be delivered by someone who is just learning the new skill herself.

Self-Check

In the self-checking style, the feedback comes from the learners themselves. You still determine the task the students will practice and identify its critical features. For this style, however, you must select a task that students can evaluate for themselves. Typically, activities such as throwing and shooting for accuracy are appropriate because students can clearly see for themselves the results of their efforts. However, part D in figure 11.1 shows an unusual self-check lesson that focuses on the technique of golfing using one's own shadow as a source for feedback. On the continuum of teaching styles, this style gives students opportunities to become more self-reliant as they determine how to address their own limitations and how to use their practice time effectively. Unfortunately, however, this style does limit the interaction between you and your students and between students. Therefore, I don't recommend that you use it much in middle school physical education.

Inclusion

Because the inclusion style gives middle school students the feeling of success so important to them, it is especially well suited to the middle school physical education setting. In the inclusion style, you still determine the task your students will practice and identify its critical features, but you also give students a choice of performance levels for the task from which they may select the level of practice they think is right for them (see figure 11.1, part E, for a lesson involving the badminton clear stroke). Factors that alter the performance level of the task include the size and weight of an object; size, distance, and height of a target; body position; and quantity or quality of performance. For example, when students are performing push-ups, let students choose from wall push-ups (the easiest form), chair push-ups, modified push-ups, regular push-ups, and elevated feet push-ups (the hardest form).

In the inclusion style, it is the students' responsibility to determine when they are ready to move to a more difficult performance level. This style is ideal for heterogeneous middle school classes, because it accommodates all learners at their levels of readiness. This style also takes the students one step closer to taking full responsibility for their own learning.

Guided Discovery

In the guided discovery style, you determine the task and then arrange a sequence of problems or questions that, when solved by the students, lead to the one correct response (see part F in figure 11.1 for an example related to the correct technique for the running long jump). The students must give a verbal or motor response to each of your prompts. Thus, the students improve their motor performances by using their higher-order thinking skills to discover the correct technique for a particular skill.

When using the guided discovery style, you must give students sufficient time to think through each question or problem. Be prepared to adjust your questions or problems, depending on the students' responses. If all or most students respond incorrectly to the prompt or question, you will need to present an activity through which students can test their answers.

When you use this style, your role is not simply to ask questions but to logically guide students to the correct solution. Indeed, students' success will depend on your ability to ask the appropriate questions at the right time. The strength of this style is that although it takes more time and you are leading students to the one correct answer, students are more likely to remember the information than if you had simply told them the answer.

Convergent Discovery

Extending the guided discovery style, the convergent discovery style is fairly new to the spectrum of teaching styles. In the convergent discovery style, the learner proceeds through the discovery process without any guiding clues from you. In addition to the benefits of the guided discovery style, this style encourages students to take on even more responsibility for their own learning (see figure 11.1, part G, for a convergent discovery lesson related to increasing force). I recommend using this style after your students have demonstrated success with the guided discovery approach. Both the guided discovery and convergent discovery styles are useful in the middle school setting as long as you select learning activities through which the students are able to discover the correct answer—either through your use of questions or problems or through student trial and error.

Divergent Production

I think of the divergent production style as the problem-solving style. You select the task and design a problem that can be solved in a variety of ways. Then you ask students to discover different solutions to the problem and evaluate the effectiveness of each solution. This style improves student motor performances by showing students the many possibilities for solving movement problems.

Problem-solving conditions are best for learning tasks similar to tasks students have already mastered (see figure 11.1, part H, for an example related to student creation of new games). I have found this style effective in team-building activities in which small groups of students must work together to find a solution to a physical challenge. Indeed, this style is especially effective for developing social skills.

Individual Program-Learner's Design

In this style, the responsibility for designing the task, question, or problem shifts from you to the learner. You still choose the general subject material (see part I in figure 11.1 for a lesson related to fitness), but you allow the learner to choose the specific question and determine possible solutions. This style provides learners with opportunities to develop their own learning programs, based on their capabilities, intelligences, and learning styles. Other than for assigning the development of special projects, middle school physical educators rarely use this style. However, as schools restructure for more individualized learning, we should see this style used more often.

Learner-Initiated

The learner-initiated style is similar to the individual program-learner's design style, except that learners initiate the style for themselves. The students approach you and state their willingness to initiate and conduct learning activities (see part J in figure 11.1 for examples related to students creating their own practice plans). For students who are ready, this style allows them to initiate their own learning projects. As with the individual program-learner's design style, we don't use this style very often at present, yet we should strive to include it more as we encounter students who have special interests.

Self-Teaching

The self-teaching style is at the opposite end of the spectrum from the command style. In this style, learners make virtually all the decisions on their own without any input or assistance from the teacher. If able to implement this style, individuals truly become lifelong learners, capable of creating their own learning experiences. This style does not currently exist in the classroom; however, it does exist in real life. To this end, encourage students to pursue their own educational interests, based on their own capabilities and needs both outside the school setting and, when possible, within the school setting.

Instructional Strategies

Whereas teaching styles address the question of who is making the decisions about instruction, instructional strategies refer to the arrangement of the teacher, learner, and environment. You can choose from many instructional strategies; however, I have found two that are especially effective with middle school students: station teaching and cooperative learning.

Station Teaching

The station teaching strategy, in which students in small groups rotate from learning center to learning center effectively and efficiently, provides students with a variety of drills or tasks (figure 11.3). This strategy works especially well when your equipment or space is limited because many stations require very little or different equipment or space, although some stations may require a great deal of equipment and space. The station approach can also give students opportunities to practice and apply the same skill to different situations—crucial to mastering open skills (skills performed in open environments such as dribbling).

Courtesy of Karen Mendon.

Figure 11.3   Middle school students rotate from one type of equipment to the next in a station approach.

To use the station approach, set up different activities around the gymnasium, room, or outdoor area. Divide the class into an equal number of groups with no more than four students per group and assign each group to a different starting station. To keep students focused at each station, place a task card describing what you want them to perform or accomplish there (see chapter 12 for sample task cards). Make sure that the time required to complete each task is about the same so that students at one station are not waiting for other students to finish their tasks before rotating. Many teachers have found it effective to have students complete a data collection sheet at each station, making students accountable for completing the work (see chapter 12 for sample data sheets).

Planning for the stations requires a great deal of thought. Will the stations focus on a variety of activities (e.g., different gymnastics equipment or track-and-field events), a review of several skills for a given sport (e.g., forearm pass, set, spike, serve, and block for volleyball), or the application of one skill (e.g., overhand movement pattern) in a variety of activities or sports? Whatever your plan, it is best at first to introduce only three or four types of stations, setting up more than one of each type as necessary to keep groups small. In most cases, you'll need to give students some instruction regarding each station before allowing them to try it. So by limiting the number of initial stations, you limit the amount of lecture time. Then, you can gradually add three or four

Teaching Stations

Students learn in a variety of ways. By using teaching stations, I can use a variety of teaching styles in one lesson. I use station teaching in many activities throughout the year to maximize student time on task, to provide a variety of skill practice, and to allow students to become more independent learners.

—Karen Mendon, Montebello Intermediate

more stations every day or two until every station is unique. Later, you can change or alter stations as necessary.

You can use this strategy with a variety of teaching styles, including reciprocal, self-check, and inclusion. Either you, a peer, or the student himself gives feedback, depending on the teaching style you choose. Keep the tasks fairly simple so that students can work independently as you circulate, offering feedback and noting special needs.

Cooperative Learning

Cooperative learning is an effective strategy that promotes the development of social skills while augmenting learning (Johnson and Johnson 1991, 1998; Kagan 1997). Numerous studies have shown that cooperative learning results in greater achievement gains, improved cross-cultural friendships, increased social skills, enhanced self-esteem, greater interdependence (teamwork), increased cognitive and affective abilities, and an improved classroom climate (Johnson and Johnson 1991). Thus, it's an effective strategy for middle school students.

Putting students into groups is not in and of itself cooperative learning. True cooperative learning requires (1) the formation of heterogeneous teams, (2) the establishment of positive interdependence and individual accountability, (3) the opportunity for team members to get acquainted with one another and establish a team identity, (4) the use of an established structure, and (5) the opportunity to debrief the situation. When teachers first started using this strategy, they used extrinsic rewards (including grades) to motivate students to work cooperatively to achieve a common goal. As we discussed in chapter 9, however, extrinsic rewards are not necessary if you make sure that the learning tasks are challenging and meaningful, if you allow students to make some key decisions about what they are doing,

and if you emphasize that students should help one another to learn.

Form Heterogeneous Teams

To get started using cooperative learning, form teams that include a balance of gender, ethnicity, ability, and other aspects. You can randomly assign students to teams and then ensure that each team is heterogeneous, or you can rank students according to ability and then assign students to teams by selecting one student from the top, one from the bottom, and several from the middle. Usually, cooperative groups range in size from four to six; however, partners work well, too.

Establish Positive Interdependence and Individual Accountability

For the second step of cooperative learning, set up one task to be accomplished by each group. Ensure that the task (e.g., report, project, skill development) can be completed only if the students cooperate. This establishes positive interdependence among team members. For example, assign a group the task of developing a report on the modern Olympics or of analyzing the overhand movement pattern. Each group turns in one report or project.

Sometimes, a group may lean on the most able or most committed member, expecting this member to accomplish the task alone. To eliminate this possibility, establish individual accountability, making sure each member has a specific task (e.g., for the overhand movement pattern report, striking with hand, striking with short object, and striking with long object), role (e.g., facilitator, arbitrator, encourager, monitor, reporter, questioner, recorder, timekeeper, group manager), or resource (e.g., textbooks, videos, software), ensuring that each must contribute to the successful completion of the task. In this way, group success will depend on the indi-

Cooperative Learning Activities

I use cooperative learning activities from the first day of school to help my students improve their social skills and learn to work together to provide an emotionally and physically safe environment in which to learn. I constantly use cooperative activities throughout the year and conclude the spring semester with a 3-week Project Adventure unit in which students can apply all the team-building skills they have learned.

—Karen Mendon, Montebello Intermediate

vidual learning of all group members. To create an effective cooperative learning structure, you must address both positive interdependence and individual accountability.

Promote Team Building

Think about the last time you joined a committee or group. Did the group immediately begin to work on the topic, or did the committee members spend some time getting to know each other? Tuckman's team development model (Tuckman 1965) looks at four stages of development: forming, storming, norming, and performing. At the forming stage of team building, members become acquainted by learning each other's names, backgrounds, and interests. At the storming stage of development, the group determines who in the group will have the most power to make the decisions. This is a good time to introduce social initiatives (physical or mental challenges that groups must work together to solve) or physical challenges in which group members must support one another in order to be successful, increasing the level of trust among team members (see Problem Solving unit in chapter 17). At the norming stage, members determine roles and make decisions through consensus. Asking the group members to establish a team name and determine the outcome of their work together is appropriate for this stage. Finally, at the performing stage, group members see the value of working together and are ready for you to tell them (or for the group to select) the specific structure that they will use to complete their task.

Although this model is typically used with adult work groups, the steps are just as important for middle school cooperative learning groups. Indeed, students need time to get to know one another and develop trust before being presented with a task. Therefore, use cooperative games, social initiatives, and physical challenges with middle school students, helping them establish their group or team identities whenever new groups are formed.

Select a Structure

The structure or format determines how students will work together in cooperative learning groups. Although quite a few structures exist, we'll limit our discussion to four of the more popular ones appropriate for middle school physical education: think, pair, share; numbered heads; student team achievement divisions (STAD); and jigsaw (Kagan 1997).

Think, Pair, Share   For think, pair, share, ask students to work in partners. Pose a question and give students time to think about their answers. For example, you might ask, "Which area of health-related fitness is most important?" After students have time to think about their answers, have them share their responses (e.g., cardiorespiratory endurance) with their partners. Then repeat the question and call on one student in a pair to respond.

Numbered Heads   For numbered heads, you again ask students to work in partners. Pose a question, such as "What are the five areas of health-related fitness?" Then ask students to discuss their answers with their partners to ensure that both of them will be able to name the five areas if called on. Then call on one student in one pair to share the answer.

STAD   For STAD, assign the students to four-member groups. Present the lesson and supply instructional materials, such as information sheets and checklists of critical features for motor skills. Then have groups ensure that all team members master the information. You should usually assess students (written test, motor skills test) on an individual basis; however, some teachers on some occasions assess group members together. Your lesson material can be a cognitive concept or a motor skill. For example, team members can work together to master juggling. Using the reciprocal style from the spectrum of teaching styles, have students give each other feedback so that each member learns to juggle.

Jigsaw   For jigsaw, assign students to home teams of four to six members. Then let each member of the home team select a different piece of the material to learn. For example, if students are learning the rules of softball, then the four-member teams divide up the pitching, baserunning, batting, and miscellaneous rules. Next have students from different teams, who have similar pieces of information, form expert groups to discuss their information and to develop a presentation for their home teams. Expert groups should be no larger than six members (four is ideal), so you may need to form double or triple expert groups covering the same material. Finally, have the students return to their home teams to share their information. Require all students to take a quiz or complete an individual or group project to assess their learning of all the softball rules. Another example of a jigsaw strategy, related to outdoor education, is shown in figure 11.4.

Cooperative Learning Style Sample Lesson: Jigsaw

Objective

Students increase knowledge about wilderness survival.

Preparation

1. Assign students to one of eight heterogeneous groups of five (six if necessary). These groups are their home teams.

2. After several preliminary team-building activities (see Problem Solving unit in chapter 17), give a short introduction to wilderness survival and the jigsaw activity.

3. Give each group time to decide who will specialize in each of the following areas: navigating and traveling, setting up camp, obtaining food and water, maintaining health and giving first aid, and dealing with wildlife (in groups with six members, two will specialize in the same area).

4. Once each student has selected a role, form expert groups for each area of specialization. If necessary, form more than one group for each area, keeping expert group size to no more than six members.

Expert Activity

Have each expert group read through the chapter or material on their area, noting important points. Have other resources available so that students who finish early can use the extra time to find additional information. If students have difficulty reading the material, the group can read through it together. Once all group members have read and taken notes on the material, have each group member prepare a presentation for her home group.

Home Group Activity

Have each team member return to her home group to present her findings. At this point, the students will be very dependent on one another for the knowledge their teammates gained in their expert groups.

Concluding Group Activity

After each expert has had a chance to present his information, use the last day of the unit to present each group with a different outdoor education survival scenario that they must resolve using the information they have learned throughout the unit.

Figure 11.4   An example of the jigsaw strategy.

Adapted, by permission, from B. Mohnsen, 2003, *Using Technology in Physical Education* (Cerritos, CA: Bonnie's Fitware).

Be Sure to Debrief

Unfortunately, teachers often omit this last, but not least, step, either because of lack of time or because they are uncomfortable with the facilitator role. Like anything else in teaching, practice and experience can help you feel more comfortable with completing this task. Mercier (1992) suggested several processing questions that you should have students answer to debrief an activity:

- Was the task completed?
- If not, why?
- How did it feel to have someone accept your suggestion?
- How did it feel to have someone compliment you?
- What can you do next time to make your group work more successfully?
- What learning can you take from this experience to use in future experiences?
- What were some encouraging things you saw or heard?

By allowing students time to answer these or similar questions, this step ensures that they practice social skills as well as learn what you planned. In addition, this step allows for reflection (thinking process in which the person carefully examines an action in order to learn from it) and metacognition (thinking about thinking in order to reflect on one's own thinking process). This step is important in all lessons (see the closure section of each lesson in chapters 14-17).

Working With Limited-English-Proficient Students

Working with limited-English-proficient (LEP) students calls for the use of additional teaching methods—often referred to as sheltered instruction or SDAIE (specially designed academic instruction in English)—to help these students to understand the information you're presenting in English. Use the following four methods to ensure the LEP student's success:

1. Create a supportive environment.
2. Use a variety of instructional strategies, including cooperative learning.
3. Make sure information is comprehensible to the students.
4. Include a technique referred to as total physical response (TPR) (described subsequently).

These methods also work well with English-proficient students and should therefore be included in all classes. In this section, let's look closely at each element that contributes to the LEP student's success. The Orange County Department of Education (1998) has created an outstanding video on sheltered instruction in physical education that illustrates each of these methods.

Supportive Environment

We discussed the importance of developing a supportive learning environment in chapters 5 and 9. However, you must ensure that all students benefit equally from the supportive learning environment that you have established. Naturally, if either you or other students target non-English-speaking or limited-English-speaking students for ridicule, these students will feel isolated and rejected, becoming less likely to risk either verbal or motor participation. In contrast, if you model respect for these students by asking them to share their unique experiences for the educational benefit of all students in the class, they will develop stronger

self-esteem and take more responsibility for their own learning, thereby living up to the expectations you communicate to them.

If you become more informed about your students' cultures, you'll be able to acknowledge and incorporate various aspects of these cultures into the learning experiences of all your students. This will also help the non-English-speaking or limited-English-speaking students feel more comfortable in your class. To further help these students, establish consistent patterns and routines so that they will know what is coming next in the lesson.

Moreover, establish an environment in which these students grow not only in terms of physical education but also in terms of English language acquisition. Within the context of a supportive environment, two techniques that you can use to help them learn English work well. First, avoid forcing these students to speak: It often takes non-English-speaking students 6 months to 1 year before they have mastered enough English to communicate. Second, when the students begin to speak English, correct their errors only through verbal mirroring. For example, if a student says, "My clothes home," you should respond, "I see. You left your clothes at home."

Variety of Strategies, Including Cooperative Learning

The English-speaking students in your class represent various levels of motor skill ability, divergent learning styles, and different primary intelligences. So too do the limited-English-speaking and non-English-speaking students in your classes. Therefore, both groups need a variety of interactive strategies and teaching styles to be successful. You may even be asked to assist in the teaching of reading, writing, and vocabulary skills using physical education content. The use of technology (see chapter 12) and cooperative learning strategies has proven especially effective with non-English-speaking or limited-English-speaking students. If possible, when setting up cooperative learning groups, place a bilingual student (who speaks the same language) in every group that has a limited-English-speaking or non-English-speaking student. In this way, the limited-English-speaking or non-English-speaking student will have someone to share ideas and information with in her dominant language.

Comprehensible Input

During a sheltered-English workshop that I attended, the instructor gave a lesson in German. She stood in one place and without using any facial expressions whatsoever rambled on in German for 20 minutes. Not one person in the room had any idea what she was saying. Then, she began the lesson again. This time she began to hold up prompts, such as toy people, small balls, and plastic horses. She pointed to pictures and ran around the room acting out various parts of her presentation. Although we still did not understand a word of German, this time we understood that she was reenacting a polo match.

How can we communicate more effectively with our non-English-speaking students? Here are some strategies that will facilitate communication and help your students to understand the content of the lesson:

- Use simple terms.
- Reinforce key concepts over and over.
- Check often for student understanding.
- Slow down your speech pattern.
- Pause frequently.
- Enunciate clearly.
- Emphasize key words of phrases.
- Use visual aids, gestures, organizers, and other real objects.
- Demonstrate concepts.
- Simplify information.
- Expand on a student's ideas by asking additional questions.
- Provide definitions.

- Make comparisons.
- Provide lots of examples.
- Avoid idioms.
- Summarize often.
- Increase wait time.

Figure 11.5 provides additional strategies for introducing students to written material.

Providing information to students in both languages simultaneously only causes confusion to the learner (Echevarria and Graves 1997; Echevarria et al. 1999; Wong-Fillmore 1980). Therefore, if you have classes that include both English and limited-English-speaking students, convey the information in English and use a number of sheltered strategies to ensure that the information is comprehensible to the limited-English-speaking students. Deliver the information within the appropriate context, because isolated pieces of information lack relevance and connection, making it even more difficult for limited-English-speaking students to understand new words. Finally, if at all possible, use a translator when conveying new information to non-English-speaking students.

Total Physical Response

Asher (1977), the developer of total physical response (TPR), was a pioneer in second language learning. He maintained that learning on the immediate, physical, and gut levels actually speeds language acquisition dramatically. Total physical response is actually an English language development (ELD) method used with non–English speakers; however, because physical education classes contain both non-English-speaking

---

Reading and Vocabulary Teaching Strategies

Reading Strategies

Anticipation Guide

Identify the major concepts of the reading material.

Develop statements to challenge students' thinking about the topic.

Arrange statements in a format that requires students to respond yes or no to each statement.

Distribute statements (anticipation guide) to students prior to reading.

Students complete the guide individually and then discuss responses in small groups.

Figure 11.5 You can use these strategies to help your students with reading and vocabulary.

Students read the material.

Students again respond to the statements (anticipation guide) to determine whether their beliefs have changed.

Graphic Outlining

Students skim the reading material, examining the titles and headings and looking for an organizational pattern.

Students make predictions about the material's basic structure.

Students make a graphic representation of the pattern.

Students read material and update their graphic representation as necessary.

Students use their graphic representations to write a summary of the material.

KWL (Know, Want to Know, What Is Learned)

Students brainstorm what they know about the topic of the reading material.

Students generate questions they want answered about the topic.

After reading, students check for answers to their questions.

Students note what they have learned from the reading.

Vocabulary Teaching Strategies

Analogy Graphic Organizer

Provide students with an explanation of an analogy.

Provide students with an example of an analogy.

Students identify the commonalties between the concepts in the analogy.

Students identify the differences between the concepts in the analogy.

Students discuss the categories that form the basis for the relationship between the concepts.

Students use the analogy to write a summary describing the similarities and differences between the two concepts.

LINK

The teacher identifies the concept or term to be learned.

List: Students brainstorm words associated with the concept or term.

Inquire: Students question one another about the words they brainstormed.

Note: Students write down everything they have learned from the class discussion.

Know: Students read the material.

Contextual Redefinition

Present a list of the key terminology from the reading material.

Students brainstorm meanings of the words.

Students support their choices and, as a group, determine the best meaning.

Present key terminology in a sentence.

Students offer suggestions for the meaning of each word and defend their definitions.

Students consult a dictionary to verify their choices.

Figure 11.5 *(continued)*

and limited-English-proficient students, this method is appropriate for physical education.

All physical educators and second-language acquisition teachers must recognize the link between physical activity and language acquisition. The teaching of new vocabulary words in English, English as a second language (ESL), and physical education classes must include physical involvement. For example, the best way to teach words such as *over, under, behind, walk, skip, jump, fast,* and *slow* is through a physical demonstration by you, followed by a physical response from the student. Certainly, some words may require you to be creative to convey their meanings to students. For example, the term *cardiorespiratory* does not easily translate into the physical. Creative teachers, however, have developed heart–lung models that students physically move through to better understand the cardiorespiratory system and its function, a boon to all students—not only those who are struggling with English. Fortunately, in physical education you can communicate most of the motor skill vocabulary to students by demonstrating the skill, repeating the appropriate vocabulary, and having the students practice the skill.

Working With Differently Abled Students

Physical education classes consist of students with many different ability levels. Some of your students may have an individualized education program (IEP), whereas others may simply be poorly skilled. The inclusion style of teaching, along with cooperative learning and station strategies, works well with these students. In addition, depending on the student's specific weakness (see figure 11.6), specific modifications can be used to assist the student. Martin Block wrote an excellent book on this topic titled *A Teacher's Guide to Including Students With Disabilities in General Physical Education, Second Edition* (2000). The book provides a wealth of strategies for modifying different activities to meet the needs of your students.

Summary

As a physical educator, you'll often work with 20 to 60 different learning styles during one instruc-

Working With Students Who Are Differently Abled

Lack of Visual Acuity

Increase size of object.

Attach a sound to the object.

Lack of Balance

Increase width of object on which students are balancing.

Allow students to lower their center of gravity.

Allow students to increase their base of support.

Lack of Strength

Reduce the weight of the object.

Reduce the size of the object.

Allow students to get closer to the goal.

Lower the height of the goal.

Shorten striking implement.

Reduce the weight of striking implements.

Poor Coordination

Increase size of goal.

Start with stationary objects for hitting (hang ball from a string or use a batting tee).

Lack of Accuracy

Enlarge the size of the goal.

Allow students to get closer to the goal.

Slow Reaction Time

Use balls with less air.

Reduce weight of the object.

Slow down the tempo of the activity.

Figure 11.6 Modifications to assist students with disabilities.

tional period. Taking into consideration recent research on "brain-based" learning, you must ensure that learning is hands-on, relevant, and student centered. You must base your selection of the specific teaching style or strategy on both the content and the learning styles of the students. By using a wide variety of instructional styles and strategies, you will engage and promote learning for all. In the next chapter, we examine various types of instructional materials that can help you teach even better.

12

Selecting Instructional Materials and Management Tools

> • Accomplished physical education teachers possess a thorough comprehension of the fundamentals of physical education and broad grasp of relevant principles and theories that give their teaching purpose and guide them as they carry out a flexible, yet effective, instructional program responsive to students' needs and developmental levels.
>
> —*National Board for Professional Teaching Standards*

We know that some of our students are kinesthetic learners, some are visual learners, and some are auditory learners. And they come to us with strengths in one or more of the multiple intelligences as well. Because we emphasize movement in physical education, we tend to do an excellent job of engaging bodily–kinesthetic learners. Even the auditory learner may fare well through oral communication. But what about your visual learners and those with strengths in the other intelligences? Are we reaching all of our students through movement and oral communication, or do we need to provide them with other avenues to the information we're trying to teach?

By using a wide variety of visual and auditory aids, task cards, worksheets, textbooks, simulations, videos, technological devices, Internet

I like to be on the cutting edge of innovation. I want my students to be one step ahead of the rest of the world; I want them to be the leaders when they get to high school and know what it's all about. I want to talk to them in their language of high-tech and computerized understanding. Creating learning scenarios in their realm of life makes the learning real and meaningful. When we speak and work within the world of today's youth, the learning curve goes up and the retention is real.

—Jeanne Fifer, Corner Lake Middle School, Orlando, Florida

161

access, instructional software, and virtual reality hardware and software, you can increase the involvement of all your students in the instructional process. Perhaps as important, you'll be preparing them to use the tools of the 21st century. In this chapter, I describe many types of instructional materials and provide samples of appropriate materials for a middle school program. In addition, I conclude this chapter with tools that you can use to make your teaching life easier, including the Internet, electronic record books, fitness reports, and electronic portfolios.

Visual and Auditory Aids

Visual aids (see CD for examples) can provide visual learners with the information they need to understand the concepts you're explaining. Pictures (e.g., still images of sport skill techniques), charts (e.g., calendar showing frequency, intensity, time, and type of exercise over a week), graphs (e.g., showing average heart rate before, during, and after aerobic exercise), and diagrams (e.g., of offensive basketball plays) are fairly common in physical education, but have you ever used models? Models (e.g., of soccer players demonstrating offensive and defensive situations) are three-dimensional representations of real-life events. They can be made of boards that depict playing fields and toy people for you to demonstrate how players move during a real game. Soon these models may be replaced with holographic images. A hologram is a collection of all possible views of a scene combined into a single plane of light-modulating patterns. In the future, you will actually experience a sensation when you come in contact with the holographic image, and the image will be capable of reacting to such stimuli.

Naturally, auditory aids are especially effective with auditory learners. These aids include classical music for relaxation, a variety of music to accompany different movement experiences (e.g., exercising, tumbling routines, dances), or recordings that explain specific concepts. When using auditory aids, you must have a good stereo system. Purchase or select one with a compact disc player (or an MP3 player), amplifier, mixer, and good speakers (minimum of 200 watts for indoor use and higher for outdoor use) so all students can hear clearly. In addition, a remote microphone can save your voice when you must give oral instructions to large groups or over music.

Task Cards

Task cards are typically used in station teaching. You can either purchase preprinted cards (see CD for examples of a complete set of task cards

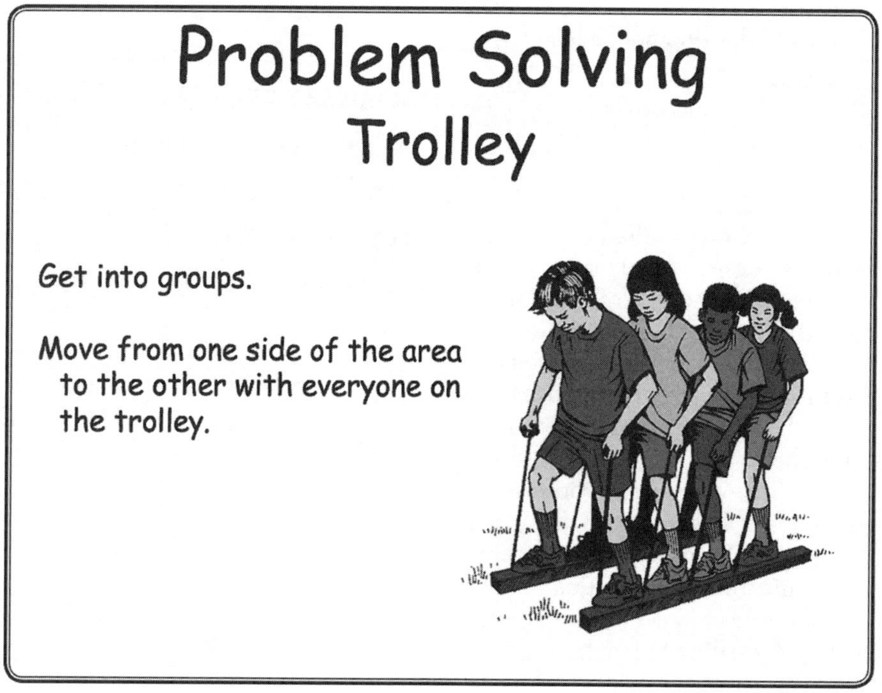

Figure 12.1   Sample task card for problem solving.

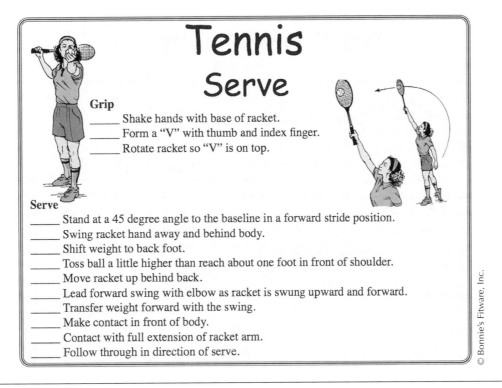

Tennis Serve

Grip
_____ Shake hands with base of racket.
_____ Form a "V" with thumb and index finger.
_____ Rotate racket so "V" is on top.

Serve
_____ Stand at a 45 degree angle to the baseline in a forward stride position.
_____ Swing racket hand away and behind body.
_____ Shift weight to back foot.
_____ Toss ball a little higher than reach about one foot in front of shoulder.
_____ Move racket up behind back.
_____ Lead forward swing with elbow as racket is swung upward and forward.
_____ Transfer weight forward with the swing.
_____ Make contact in front of body.
_____ Contact with full extension of racket arm.
_____ Follow through in direction of serve.

© Bonnie's Fitware, Inc.

Figure 12.2 Sample task card with critical features.

published by Bonnie's Fitware, Inc. to accompany this book) or create your own by hand or on a computer. Print each task on a separate card and post one card per station. Then have students, in groups of four, follow the directions on the task cards (figure 12.1) as they rotate through the stations. Encourage students to compete against the task or their own scores—not against each other.

Make your task cards do double duty by incorporating the option of a reciprocal lesson. To do this, list the critical elements for each skill on its card (figure 12.2) so students can check a partner's performance. When making your own task cards, include color and graphics and laminate the cards or put them into a clear sleeve so that they withstand the tests of time and of middle school students. You can also encourage your students to make task cards for you. Kids can create wonderful and effective task cards.

Worksheets

Worksheets (see CD for additional examples) give students directions and a set format for written responses. For example, students fill in their own data and follow the directions to calculate their own personal target heart rate range (figure 12.3). Another worksheet is a data collection sheet (figure 12.4) on which a student records quantitative information (e.g., distance, time, accuracy, heart rate). Later have students transfer data to a computer spreadsheet or analyze their own data. Or during a weight training unit exercise, ask students to identify the muscle that they worked (figure 12.5).

As with task cards, many teachers have found that worksheets help keep students on task. But don't let your students become dependent on worksheets; use them as one option, along with open-ended questions and logs.

Textbooks

Textbooks are still relatively new to physical education. Currently, three types are available: sport activity textbooks, fitness-specific textbooks, and conceptually based textbooks. The *Australian Physical Education* books by Blackall and Davis contain information (playing area, skills, rules) on a variety of traditional activities (e.g., basketball, volleyball) separated into one activity per chapter. Two fitness books, *Fitness for Life—Middle School* (Corbin, Le Masurier, and Lambdin 2007) and *Personal Fitness and You* (Stokes, Moore, and Schultz 2002), provide students with comprehensive information on the topic of fitness. You can purchase *Fitness for Life—Middle School* with

Target Heart Rate Range Worksheet

Name _____ Date _____ Class _____

Purpose: To identify a target heart rate zone, which is the safe and comfortable level of overload that you should maintain to achieve a training effect.

Procedure:

1. Calculate your maximum heart rate according to your age. 208 – 0.7(age) = maximum heart rate (MHR). The example is for a 13-year-old: 13 x 0.7 = 9.1.

Do for both Upper and Lower columns.

2. Determine your resting heart rate (RHR) by counting your pulse for 15 seconds before you get out of bed in the morning, and then multiply the number by 4. Subtract RHR from MHR.

3. Multiply this number by percent overload (e.g., 60% for the lower limit and 85% for the upper limit).

EXAMPLE	LOWER	UPPER
208	208	208
– 9	–	–
199 MHR	MHR	MHR
– 70 RHR	– RHR	– RHR
129		
× 0.60	× 0.60	× 0.85
77.4		

Figure 12.3   Worksheet for computing target heart rate range.

From *Teaching Middle School Physical Education: A Standards-Based Approach for Grades 5–8, Third Edition,* by Bonnie S. Mohnsen, 2008, Champaign, IL: Human Kinetics.

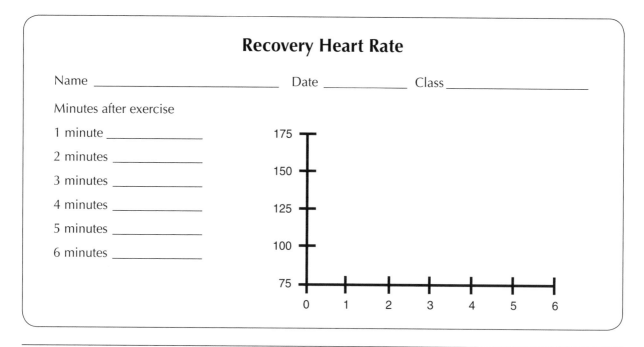

Figure 12.4   Data worksheet to determine recovery heart rate.

From *Teaching Middle School Physical Education: A Standards-Based Approach for Grades 5–8, Third Edition,* by Bonnie S. Mohnsen, 2008, Champaign, IL: Human Kinetics.

Muscles and Exercises Worksheet

As you rotate through each exercise, match the exercise with the muscle or muscle group that it works.

Wings	Deltoid
Butterfly	Pectoralis major
Rowing machine	Biceps brachii
Knee lifts	Rectus abdominis
Leg press	Quadriceps femoris
Military press	Trapezius
Lateral pulls	Latissimus dorsi
Lunges	Gluteus maximus
Toe press	Gastrocnemius
Bar dips	Triceps
Leg curls (flexion)	Hamstrings

Figure 12.5 Worksheet for matching exercises with muscles. Note: In this example, the correct muscle is lined up with its corresponding exercise.

From *Teaching Middle School Physical Education: A Standards-Based Approach for Grades 5–8, Third Edition* by Bonnie S. Mohnsen, 2008, Champaign, IL: Human Kinetics.

a teacher resource book that gives you instructional ideas for the teaching of fitness. Finally, the three books by Spindt, Monti, and Hennessy (2002a, 2002c, 2002e) are the first comprehensive textbook series for middle school students. The sixth grade book is titled *Moving With Confidence,* the seventh grade book is *Moving With Skill,* and the eighth grade book is *Moving as a Team.* This series, in its second edition, covers motor skills, fitness, social skills, self-esteem concepts, pursuit of lifelong movement activities, and promotion of individual excellence. You can purchase the series with hard-copy portfolios and a teacher resource book containing instructional suggestions and ideas for each grade level.

Although textbooks are an excellent resource for students, be careful how you use them in physical education. Using limited instructional time to sit students down to read a chapter in their books is not consistent with physical education goals. You can, however, instruct students to read a section of a textbook as homework to prepare them for a physical activity they'll do during class time. Another approach to using textbooks

is to create a reading station in a circuit of more physically active activities. Here, you can have students read a section of a book. If, like many physical educators, you have limited equipment for practice, a reading station can provide a valuable learning experience for students who might otherwise be waiting to use a piece of equipment. Another advantage of using textbooks in the station approach is that you may need only four to eight copies of the textbook, thereby saving your limited funds. Finally, you can make a variety of textbooks available to students who are working on projects to use as a resource.

Simulations

Simulations are lifelike events that allow students to experience situations they typically cannot experience otherwise because of risk of injury, lack of real-life equipment, or lack of access to the real situation. Figure 12.6 shows an example of a simulation that gives students the opportunity to travel through the cardiorespiratory system. Using different pieces of physical education apparatus and equipment, you create a route approximating the path that blood takes through the heart and lungs. Students then follow the route, disposing of blue balls and collecting red balls to simulate the exchange of carbon monoxide for oxygen in the lungs. The second time they go through the course, they encounter stress factors that cause heart attacks, strokes, and blood clots. You can simulate the stress factors by raising the temperature in the gym and altering the course by clogging an artery. This simulation is available from U.S. Games (see appendix C), or you can create your own.

You can also simulate—either in the gymnasium or on the playground—a self-defense scenario; swimming, gymnastics, or track-and-field meets; a medieval festival; an orienteering event; and an Olympic festival. An easier vehicle for simulations, however, is the computer. I discuss several examples of computer simulations in the Instructional Software and Virtual Reality sections later in this chapter.

Video Clips

Earlier we discussed single still images as a form of visual aids. Still images can show your students key positions for different phases of a motor skill, but only moving images (video clips) can provide

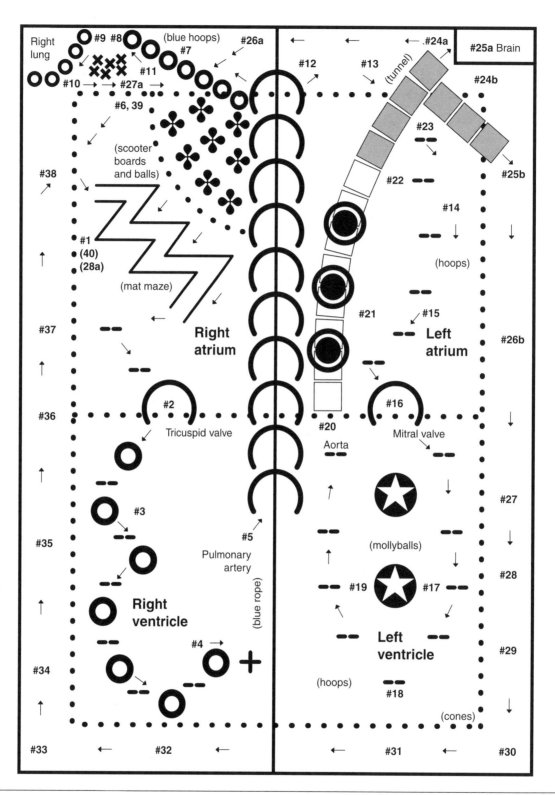

Figure 12.6 Gymnasium design for Heart Adventures Challenge Course.

This diagram is reprinted with permission from *Journal of Physical Education, Recreation and Dance*, February 1995, 19. *JOPERD* is a publication of the American Alliance for Health, Physical Education, Recreation and Dance, 1900 Association Drive, Reston VA 22091.

students with a complete demonstration of the skill or strategic play.

As physical educators, many of us are not able to demonstrate a perfect model of every motor skill. To fill your skill gaps, use recorded model performances from video, the Internet, or broadcasts. In addition, you can use video images to illustrate strategic plays or at the beginning of a unit to create excitement (anticipatory set) about the upcoming sport or activity.

The main difference between videotapes and CD-ROM/DVD discs is that you can access any image on the CD-ROM/DVD disc within a few seconds; in contrast, accessing a particular clip on video requires a linear search and risks going past the desired image. In addition, CD-ROMs/DVDs are more durable and produce much higher quality images (digital video). For both videotapes and CD-ROM/DVD discs, you will need a monitor or projection system to display the images and will need cables or wireless capabilities to connect the display to the appropriate player. In the instructional software section later in this chapter, I will explain that there are some programs that come with video clips that can be shown on a handheld computer, making it very convenient for the teacher.

Budget limited? You can record a broadcast (check state and federal guidelines) and show it to your students without having to purchase a video—if what you want is being broadcast in your area. Sporting events, instructional television shows, and the Olympics are excellent types of shows to record. Shows with messages about self-esteem or the demonstration of prosocial skills are also appropriate in physical education (e.g., *The Wonder Years* or *After School Specials*). After you have shown clips of such broadcasts, have students describe their feelings about the incident you showed, or stop the program before the issue is resolved and have students write their own endings to the stories. But don't misuse this technology, giving in to the temptation of showing an entire video or broadcast. Preview the program before showing it to your students, selecting only those clips that depict the concept or skill you are teaching. Then show the clips to the entire class or use them at a station.

Camcorders are especially effective devices in helping students master skills and analyze strategy. You can train students to record each other performing motor skills or participating in a scrimmage so that they can immediately view their performances. The video cameras that have a 3- or 4-inch viewfinder are ideal for physical education because students can replay the video in the camera and still see the images clearly. For cameras with a 1-inch viewfinder, students will need to hook the camera up to a monitor, remove the videotape and play it through a video cassette recorder or video cassette player, or try to view the video through the eyepiece.

Provide students with a form that lists the critical features of the motor skill or the main concepts of the strategy they are observing, so that they analyze their own performances as they observe them. To make this learning process most effective, allow students to stop and start the video at their own discretion. You should act as a facilitator, questioning the students regarding the significance of particular movements, actions, or behaviors at a station while keeping an eye on the rest of the stations.

Technological Devices

Devices such as electronic blood pressure machines, heart monitors, and pedometers help students learn more about the scientific side of fitness (see appendix C for vendors). Granted, often the school versions of these devices don't compare with the more sophisticated—and expensive—models available to professionals, but they do motivate students, increasing their understanding of exercise physiology concepts while introducing them to the use of technology in physical activity. Many commercial fitness centers already use these technologies, so you also will be preparing students for healthy lifestyles, including participation at fitness centers.

Electronic blood pressure devices (approximately $60-100) allow students to take each other's blood pressure. If a student's blood pressure reading is abnormal, you should refer the student to a nurse or physician. Some of these machines take readings on the index finger, but I recommend that you use a cuff model with automatic inflation. A cuff model works by inflating until the screen display reads 180. The machine then deflates the cuff as it reads the systolic and diastolic blood pressure as well as the pulse rate, displaying all three on the screen for viewing.

When teaching students to reach and maintain a pulse in the target heart rate training zone, consider using heart rate monitors to make tracking easier. Although heart rate monitors come in various forms such as ear clips and index finger connections, I recommend the heart rate monitors that have a wireless transmitter attached to a chest strap and a receiver on a wrist strap. Also, purchase heart monitors that allow you to change the battery in the transmitter, so you won't have to purchase a new transmitter when the battery dies. See the CD for appropriate heart monitor packages.

For heart rate monitors to be used in physical education, I recommend either the bottom or the top of the line (see appendix C). The models in between don't seem to meet the needs of most physical educators. The heart rate monitor at the bottom of the line (approximately $70) simply displays the student's heart rate. The top of the line (approximately $300) can store heart rate data and transfer the data from the heart monitor to a computer. The software, which comes with the transfer interface, displays each student's heart rate as a data table, line graph, or bar graph that you can print out.

Although you may not be able to purchase a heart rate monitor for each student, you can have students share these devices so that each student wears one once every week or month. Use heart rate monitors to collect data during aerobic workouts, to compare heart rates for different activities (e.g., football and jump rope), and to determine fitness levels by analyzing the recovery heart rates (how long it takes to return the heart rate to normal after a workout).

Pedometers accurately measure the number of steps that an individual takes. Several research studies have shown the Walk4Life (specifically, model LS2525) and the Yamax pedometers (Digi-Walker) to be most accurate (Bassett et al. 1996; Crouter et al. 2003; Schneider et al. 2003; Welk & Wood 2000). The industry standard for accuracy is within 3%. See the CD for appropriate pedometer packages.

Pedometers are worn on the waistband, positioned directly above the midline of the thigh on either side of the body (Bassett et al. 1996). However, this is not the best location for 20% to 30% of the users. Have each student walk 100 steps and if the device is not within 3% (97-103), then have the student move the device laterally and try again. Repeat the process until there is no more than a 3% error. If you can't get the pedometer within a 3% error, either the batteries need to be replaced or you are using an inaccurate model.

I recommend the purchase of the steps-only pedometer, because that is what pedometers were designed to do. You will need to replace the batteries every year or two. In one study of 6- to 12-year-olds, Vincent and Pangrazi (2002) found that boys who walked 13,000 steps and girls who walked 11,000 steps met the recommended daily requirement for physical activity. Students can record the number of steps taken during physical education, during a specified time period, during a specified activity, outside of school, or during an entire day. The data recorded also can be graphed for comparison. For students who fall short of the suggested number of steps per day, a 10% increase every day or two is recommended. If you can't afford to purchase a pedometer for each student, then have the students share pedometers.

Internet

Web technology can bring resources into the classroom to facilitate active, problem-based collaborative learning and can provide information that otherwise would be unavailable or prohibitively expensive. You no longer need to rely exclusively on the resources available within your district. When you are searching the Internet, find high-quality sites that contain accurate information. If you plan on having your students search the Internet, provide them with criteria for evaluating Web sites so that they can distinguish between accurate and inaccurate information.

Students can use the Internet to conduct research, participate in electronic field trips, solve problems, complete tutorials, and perform simulations. See the CD for sample pages from Web booklets. Students can access the Internet as a homework assignment or you can set up one or more computers for use in a station approach. This will also work for the instructional software discussed in the next section.

Instructional Software

Instructional software can enhance the learning process as students interact with computers. Several different types of instructional software have been developed: comprehensive physical education software, simulation, reference, authoring, and portfolios. The comprehensive physical education software includes tutorials and interactive activities as well as a quiz and portfolio. Examples of comprehensive physical education software include Short Jump Rope Complete, Volleyball Complete, and Health-Related Fitness. See the CD for access to trial versions.

• **Short Jump Rope Complete (Bonnie's Fitware, Inc.).** This program (see figure 12.7) provides a comprehensive (exercise physiology, motor learning, biomechanics, psychology, motor development, aesthetics, sociology, and historical information) perspective to the teaching of jumping short ropes. Teachers and students can access and interact with the information to increase their understanding of jumping short ropes on their desktop or notebook computer. In addition, they can access video clips from this program on their handheld computer. Finally, assignments are provided for students that can be added to their electronic portfolio. The information in the Short Jump Rope Complete portfolio may be exported to the Middle School Physical Education Portfolio (see the section on electronic portfolios later in this chapter) or the Physical Education Record Book program (see the section on grading programs later in this chapter).

• **Volleyball Complete (Bonnie's Fitware, Inc.).** This program (see figure 12.8) relates each of the eight subdisciplines of physical education (exercise physiology, motor learning, biomechanics, psychology, motor development, aesthetics, sociology, and historical perspectives) to the teaching of volleyball. Teachers and students can access and interact with the information to increase their understanding of volleyball skills, techniques, strategies, training, and teamwork. Video clips and animations are provided to illustrate model performances. These visual images may be viewed via a projection system, a desktop computer monitor, a notebook or tablet monitor, or even the screen of a handheld computer. Information from the portfolio can be exported to the Middle School Physical Education Portfolio and the Physical Education Record Book.

• **Health-Related Fitness (Bonnie's Fitware, Inc.).** This program (see figure 12.9) covers the five components of health-related fitness and the FITT concepts. It also includes the principles of fitness, safe versus dangerous exercises, and warm-up and cool-down procedures. Students create their own portfolios that contain fitness scores, journal entries, selected exercises, caloric input and output, and video clips. Information from the portfolio can be exported to the Middle School Physical Education Portfolio and the Physical Education Record Book.

Figure 12.7 A screen from Short Jump Rope Complete (Bonnie's Fitware, Inc.). Students can access information on short jump roping (Tinikling and long jump rope also are available), take quizzes, and maintain their own electronic short jump rope portfolio.

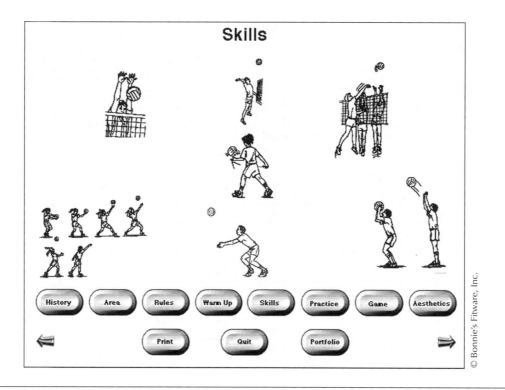

Figure 12.8 A screen from Volleyball Complete (Bonnie's Fitware, Inc.). Students can access information on volleyball and maintain their own electronic volleyball portfolio.

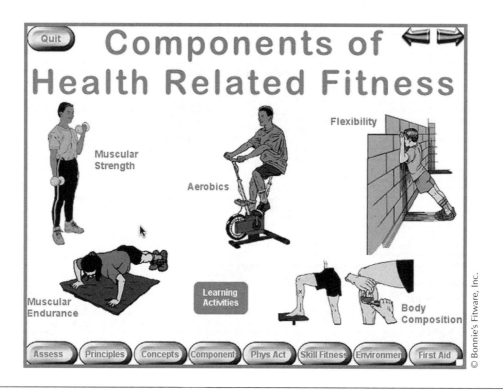

Figure 12.9 A screen from Health-Related Fitness: Tutorial and Portfolio (Bonnie's Fitware, Inc.). Students can access information on health-related fitness and maintain their own electronic fitness portfolios.

Simulation software, much like its nondigital format, provides students with situations that require them to use higher-order thinking skills. Students are presented with scenarios that they must analyze and respond to. Then the software evaluates their response. Examples of this type of software include SimAthlete and Biomechanics Made Easy (Bonnie's Fitware, Inc.). See the CD for access to trial versions.

• **SimAthlete (Bonnie's Fitware, Inc.).** This program (see figure 12.10) teaches students how to develop their own motor learning practice plan. SimAthlete provides a reference section on each of the motor learning principles. It also has a simulation section where students can assume the role of a coach and develop a practice plan for an athlete. If they create an effective practice plan, their athlete performs well. If their plan is ineffective, then their athlete performs poorly. The scores for the simulation are recorded so teachers can monitor student progress.

• **BioMechanics Made Easy (Bonnie's Fitware, Inc.).** This program (see figure 12.11) instructs students on analysis of movement. It provides a reference section on each of the biomechanical principles (e.g., stability, projection, levers). In addition, there is a lab section where students

analyze movement scenarios and a quiz section in which students demonstrate their knowledge of biomechanics.

Reference software, such as encyclopedias and Middle Muscle Flash (Bonnie's Fitware, Inc.), offers detailed reference information, including pictures, graphs, and short video clips (figure 12.12). Students can search for the information they seek by typing the name of the topic in the "Find" box, or they can click on related information until they find the appropriate information. The Middle Muscle Flash software also includes a quiz so that you can monitor students' learning of the names and functions of the muscles as well as exercises used to strengthen the muscles.

Software authoring programs, such as Hyper-Studio (Knowledge Adventure), offer students an open-ended program with which to create any project they want. These programs give students the tools to add text, pictures, video, sound, and animation to their electronic projects. There is no limit to what students can create! Authoring programs are like Lego sets with which students can build whatever they want. In some physical education classes, students have even created their own computer programs for various sports, such as tennis, basketball, and softball. See the

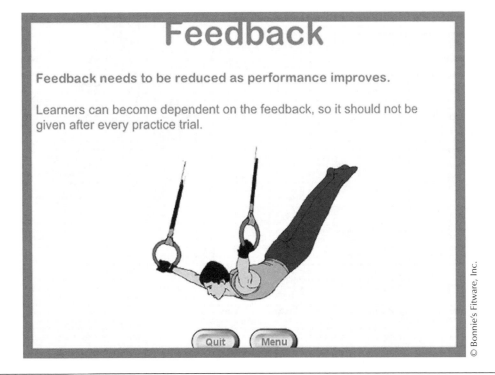

© Bonnie's Fitware, Inc.

Figure 12.10 A screen from SimAthlete (Bonnie's Fitware, Inc.). The software contains information on motor learning concepts and gives students an opportunity to apply their understanding of these concepts by coaching an athlete.

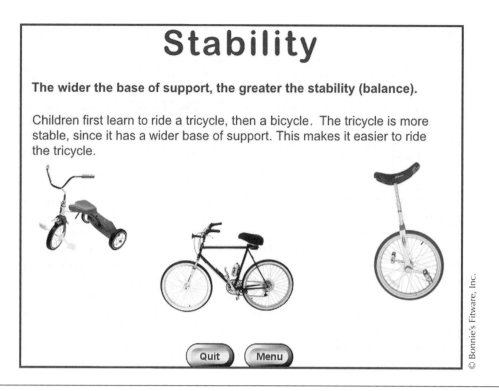

Figure 12.11 A screen from Biomechanics Made Easy (Bonnie's Fitware, Inc.). The software contains information on biomechanics concepts and gives students an opportunity to apply their understanding of these concepts.

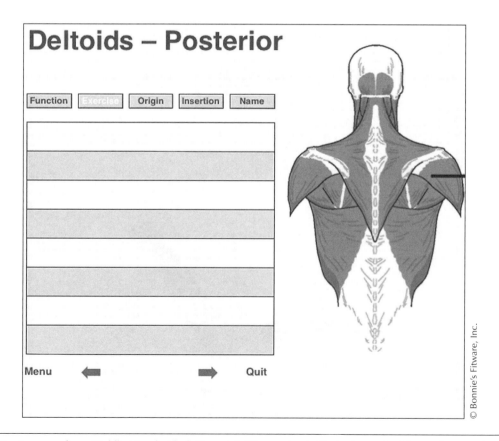

Figure 12.12 A screen from Middle Muscle Flash (Bonnie's Fitware, Inc.). Students can test themselves on the names of muscles, locations, and exercises.

Using Technology

We offer a 9-week course titled *Personal Sport and Technology* in which eighth grade students select their own personal sport for an in-depth study and investigate through technology the benefits of fitness and the development of sport skills. Technology is used with heart rate analysis (heart monitors and spreadsheets), skill analysis (HyperStudio, video, and laser discs), and research efforts (on-line services). The course culminates with a multimedia presentation by every student that highlights their learning experiences from their studies.

—Physical educator Carol Chestnut, Simmons Middle School, Birmingham, Alabama

sidebar for more ideas about incorporating technology into physical education.

Students can also use HyperStudio to design their own electronic portfolios (see also chapter 8). Or they can use a preset generic electronic portfolio, such as Grady Profile (Aurbach and Associates), into which students simply add their own pictures, writings, and video clips. Finally, there are preset electronic portfolios tailored to physical education needs, into which students can add video clips of their motor skills, rate their performances based on preset rubrics, and analyze their own fitness scores—among other things.

• **Middle School Physical Education Portfolio.** The Middle School Physical Education Portfolio (see figure 12.13) is formatted around the six national content standards for physical education. Students enter their own information related to the learning of the physical education standards (e.g., fitness scores, journal entries, and video clips). The portfolio also contains predesigned rubrics for basic movement (run, hop, skip) and motor (throw, catch, kick) skills. Teachers can assess students or students can self-assess or peer assess. There are also elementary and high school versions. Information can be imported from the sport and fitness specific

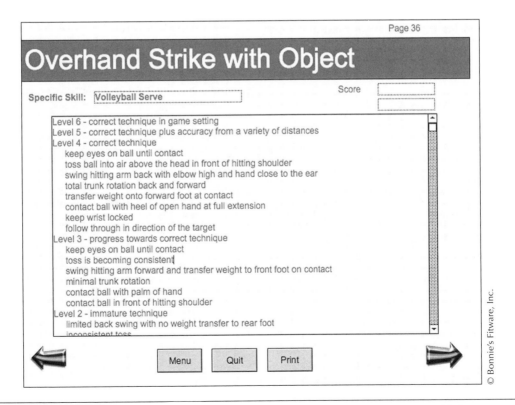

Figure 12.13 A sample screen from the Middle School Electronic Portfolio (Bonnie's Fitware, Inc.). This is a comprehensive program for students in physical education to maintain their own electronic portfolio throughout middle school.

portfolio. With this portfolio, the teacher can open the file and see all of the students' work on one assignment or one entire student portfolio with the click of a button. While looking at an assignment, the teacher can grade it and then have the grade automatically transferred into the Physical Education Record Book, which works on both a desktop or notebook computer (Macintosh or PC) and a handheld computer (Palm OS/Pocket PC). See the CD for access to trial versions.

Physical education classes across the United States range from 20 to 80 students per class. Physical educators who wish to use electronic portfolios often face time constraints and limited access to computers. For individualized portfolios to be successful, a physical educator must have access to at least one computer for every eight students or access to a computer lab. In the former case, students form eight groups and rotate through a circuit. The circuit's computer station contains a computer for each student. Typically, each student is given (or purchases) a CD-RW, DVD-RW, flash memory drive, or folder on a server or the Internet that contains his or her portfolio. Physical education teachers with access to a computer lab send their students to the lab on a rotating basis. In the lab, students enter data into their personal portfolios. At the end of the year, the electronic portfolio provides the teacher and student with concrete information to use in discussing progress and setting goals for the following year.

Virtual Reality

Virtual reality is the ultimate when it comes to interactive computer hardware and software. The purpose of virtual reality is to give the user the sensory illusion of being in a different environment. Components of a virtual reality system include some form of a computer (Windows®, Macintosh, PlayStation, xBox, Wii), special user interfaces (fitness equipment, sport equipment, gloves, and a monitor, which is sometimes built into a head-mounted device but typically is a separate device), and a sound system. The interface, monitor, and sound system are connected to the computer; and software controls the visual images on the monitors, the audio from the sound system, and even the pressure exerted on the tactile stimulators in the glove. The user interacts with the virtual environment by gesturing with the gloves, manipulating the fitness or sport equipment, or moving the helmeted head.

Virtual reality is appealing to most learners because of its novelty; however, it is especially effective with students whose primary intelligence is bodily–kinesthetic. Although few schools currently use virtual reality, it is an emerging technology that will have a significant impact on the future of physical education. Here are a few current systems that we are seeing in middle schools.

Dance Dance Revolution (DDR) functions as an aerobic activity as well as an interactive videogame. It includes a dance pad (including very inexpensive home versions, foam pads, and metal pads costing more than $1,500 each) that connects to a PlayStation or Xbox, which, in turn, connects to a monitor. The software (the actual game) is placed in the PlayStation or Xbox. On screen there are arrows that the user is to follow. Correct movement on the part of the user results in positive feedback, whereas incorrect movement results in negative feedback. Several pieces of software are available for DDR, with numerous songs on each piece of software. In addition, there are tutorials and lessons to help students learn to use DDR.

GameBike (CatEye) is an interactive exercise bike for the Sony Playstation. The bike acts as a game controller whereby pedal speed and left and right handlebar movement accurately control the game vehicle's speed and direction. Any of the many types of racing games available on the market may be used with the bicycling interface.

Although DDR and GameBike allow the user to control the video-based games, they do not allow for the player to actually become part of the game. This is where EyeToy comes into play. Attaching an inexpensive camera to the Sony PlayStation, the user actually becomes a part of the game by using video overlay technology. The software (games specifically designed for use with the EyeToy) actually interprets the player's movement and uses the motion as the interface with the game. This technology will continue to develop in the next several years. It is ideal for schools, because you don't need to purchase hardware such as DDR pads or GameBike.

Other Resources

Many sport organizations provide free or inexpensive instructional materials just for the asking. For example, the United States Tennis Association has developed an instructional manual that it provides free to teachers who attend one free training session. Other associations listed in appendix C can assist you with instructional manuals, orienteering maps, and other materials that may be of benefit to your students. Simply request a list of their complimentary or inexpensive resources.

Resources and Management Tools for Teachers

Instructional materials are designed to help students learn, whereas management tools are designed to help teachers be more efficient. Next we explore uses of the Internet so that you can easily find information and stay connected with colleagues. We also discuss the use of software programs specifically designed to help you manage the ever-increasing amount of paperwork that you must address daily.

Internet

We discussed earlier in this chapter the use of the Internet as an instructional device. In addition, with access to the World Wide Web (WWW), you can use e-mail to share information about instructional techniques, lesson plans, and student worksheets with teachers at other schools and around the world. You can access tons of information using a Web browser. And you can have instantaneous conversations with friends and colleagues through messaging software.

One extension of e-mail is a listserv, which works much like a mailing list. You can send one message to the listserv distribution address, and a copy of the message goes to everyone on the list. The most popular listserv for physical education is the NASPE-L listserv (sign-up is available at the Web site for this book: www.pesoftware.com/Middle/resources.html).

Web browsers (e.g., Netscape Navigator, Internet Explorer) provide an easy way to search the Internet for information. Once you open a browser, type in an address such as www.HumanKinetics.com and press the return key to gather information that could be from halfway around the world. The address I listed will bring you information from a computer that contains news from Human Kinetics. Everywhere you look today, you see these addresses, known as URLs (uniform resource locators). To move from one page to the next, you simply click on the hyperlink (special text embedded with a URL, often in a different-color text that turns your cursor into a pointing finger).

You can also access information by using a search engine. Popular search engines include yahoo.com (www.yahoo.com), altavista.com (www.altavista.com), and google.com (www.google.com). Once at the Web site of the search engine, you will see a rectangular area where you can type in a topic (i.e., Pickleball, ancient Olympics). You then click on the word *search*, and the software shows you a list of locations where related information is stored. When you click on one of those locations, the information from that site appears on your screen. The same query will yield different results from different search engines.

No matter which search engine you use, a focused search will produce more exact results. You need to be as specific as possible to conduct a successful search. If you type in something general like *sports*, you may end up with more than a million sites. It is better to perform many narrow searches that result in fewer matches than to make your search too broad and spend valuable time looking at information that doesn't interest you. To perform a narrow search, you use limiting words such as *AND (+), OR,* or *PHRASE.* If you enter the words *teaching adolescents volleyball* separated by spaces, some search engines will perform an OR search and return all the pages that have the word *teaching,* all the pages that have the word *adolescents,* and all the pages that have the word *volleyball.* This isn't exactly what you wanted. Some engines require you to specify a phrase search, put your phrase in quotes, put the word *AND* between your search words, or use a plus sign in front of each word. The search page of each search engine contains directions for use of that search engine.

As you visit various sites, you will no doubt run across information that you want to either save or print. The browser allows you to do both easily. For example, using Netscape Navigator, you would go to the Web page that is of interest to you. Select "File" from the menu bar, and then select "Save" to save the information from the Web page to your hard drive. Or, select "File" from the menu bar and then select "Print" to generate a hard copy of the information. Be careful when printing Web sites with frames. You must first click the mouse on the information you wish to print and then select "File" and "Print." You also can save images and some videos from the Internet onto your computer:

1. Macintosh: Click and hold the mouse over the image or

Windows: Right click and hold the mouse over the image.

2. When the pop-up menu appears, choose "Save this image as."

3. Type in a name for the image.

4. Select the location on your hard drive where you would like the image to be saved.

The images and information printed or saved can then be shared with your students or used in the development of lesson plans.

Software for Teaching Efficiency

Computer software can help you perform many of your daily tasks more efficiently and effectively, including creating instructional materials. Integrated software programs such as Microsoft Office include word processing, a database, and a spreadsheet and can help you create newsletters, worksheets, task cards, visual aids, locker systems, budgets, and inventories. Using specialty software, you also can create fitness reports and grade reports to keep parents up to date with student progress.

Fitness Reporting Software

Fitness reporting programs analyze raw fitness scores, print summaries, and store data for pretest–posttest comparisons. Fitness reporting programs can follow a student from kindergarten through 12th grade, providing year-to-year comparisons. Raw scores can be analyzed quickly to provide information on student improvement. In addition, class averages for each test item allow you to ascertain whether the instructional program is producing the intended learning outcomes. And, of course, you can easily print a variety of reports. However, entering data can be very time consuming unless you use some type of scanner or handheld computer. Some of the more popular programs include Fitnessgram (Human Kinetics), Fitness Report for Palm OS/Pocket PC (Bonnie's Fitware, Inc.), and PE Manager (Polar/HealthFirst). Each program offers unique features. Choose the one that best fits your needs, your computer, and the test items to be administered.

For example, Fitness Report for Palm OS/Pocket PC is available for Macintosh, Windows, Palm OS, and Pocket PC. It includes several test batteries, including one that focuses on health-related fitness, providing users with the option of pacer, walk or target heart rate, or 1-mile run for cardiorespiratory endurance; push-ups, pull-ups, modified pull-ups, or flexed-arm hang for upper-body strength and endurance; curl-ups for abdominal strength and endurance; trunk lift for low back strength and flexibility; back-saver sit-and-reach or shoulder stretch for flexibility; and body mass index (calculated from height and weight data) or skinfold measurements (triceps and medial calves) for body composition. A President's Challenge version also is included as well as test batteries for individual states, including Missouri, California, Connecticut, and Virginia.

Input is by keyboard or through a handheld computer (Palm operating system or Pocket PC). The fitness pretest printout shows the pretest score, minimum standards, whether the student met the minimum standards, and the recommended improvement. It provides space for students to write their own goals for improvement. There is also space for the collection of fitness scores four times throughout the school year. The fitness posttest printout includes the pre and post fitness scores, pre and post scores met or not met, and the minimum competency scores. The statistics program includes averages for each test item and the number of students meeting minimum standards on six of six, five of six, four of six, three of six, two of six, one of six, and zero of six test areas. A master file is included so that scores can be maintained for 13 years. Additional reports and graphs (see figure 12.14) are included. Finally, the Fitness Report interfaces with the Physical Education Portfolio (Bonnie's Fitware, Inc.) and Health-Related Fitness: Tutorial and Portfolio (Bonnie's Fitware, Inc.). Each of these portfolios provides space to record physical activity.

Record Book

A wide variety of grading programs are on the market for teachers in all areas of the curriculum. Popular desktop grading programs that work for physical education include Making the Grade (Jay Klein Productions) and Grade Machine (Misty City Software). Popular handheld grading programs designed for physical education include Record Book for Palm OS/Pocket PC (Bonnie's Fitware, Inc.) and PE Manager (Polar/Health First). It is always prudent to try out demo or trial versions before purchasing, because software typically cannot be returned. As with the fitness report software, base your selection on the specific features and report formats you need.

For example, Record Book for Palm OS/Pocket PC (Bonnie's Fitware, Inc.) allows for the collection of attendance, behavior, and grading information using the Palm OS/Pocket PC (see figure 12.15). The program allows you to enter assign-

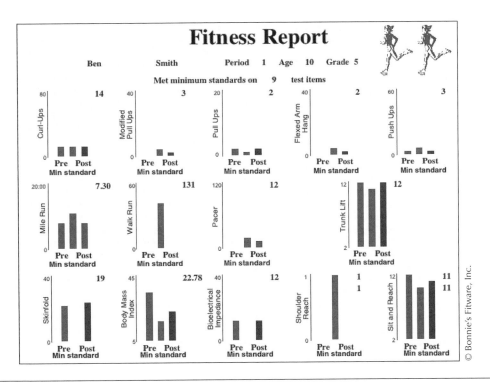

Figure 12.14 A sample report from Fitness Report Software (Bonnie's Fitware, Inc.).

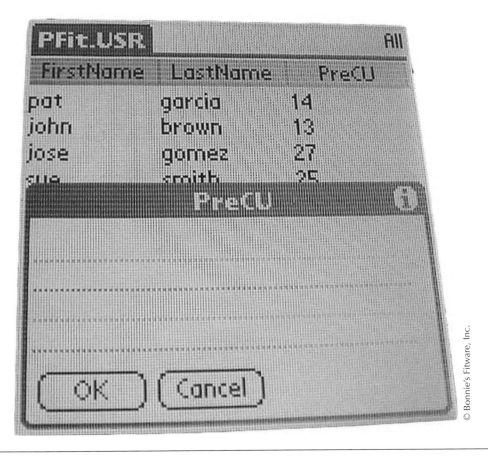

Figure 12.15 A handheld computer displaying Fitness Report software (Bonnie's Fitware, Inc.).

ments, categorize assignments according to the standard assessed, weight assignments and standards, record grades, note absences and tardies along with behavior issues, and transfer the data to the computer where the final grade is calculated and a variety of reports can be printed.

Summary

Technological devices, camcorders, videos, the Internet, instructional software, and virtual reality systems offer students exciting ways to learn physical education concepts. In the future these tools will become commonplace, and our students need to know how to use them. Use the information in this chapter to get you started. In the next chapter, we look at ways you can stay current in physical education theory and practice.

Continuing to Grow as a Professional

> • Accomplished physical education teachers participate in a wide range of reflective practices that foster their creativity, stimulate personal growth, contribute to content knowledge and classroom skill, and enhance professionalism.
>
> —*National Board for Professional Teaching Standards*

With knowledge doubling every year, change is coming so quickly that we can barely adjust to one change before another is on our doorstep. Thus, we must learn to accept and adjust effectively to constant change. This affects the teaching of physical education because as information increases, we gain a better understanding of the world around us, which, in turn, requires us to adjust our programs to reflect the most recent information and research. The three terms that most accurately describe education in the 21st century are *learn*, *unlearn*, and *relearn*.

If you are ready to apply the concepts addressed in this book, you have already accepted the challenge of change. This makes you one of the "paradigm pioneers." Remember, however, that the pioneers often take the arrows as they clear the way for the next group of settlers. As a pioneer, or teacher–leader, you must not only learn to deal effectively with change personally but also learn to help your colleagues see the benefits of and accept change. For if we have learned nothing else, we

Are you familiar with the game of Midnight (aka What Time Is It, Mr. Fox?)? When I was first out of college 30 years ago, I played it with the kids because I didn't know any better. They played that game for a few minutes each day, and I just watched them and refereed. They all loved the game, and they followed the rules, but I knew they weren't learning anything, and it drove me crazy. It didn't take me long to realize that I couldn't spend my life being a referee: I had to teach them something. So I started by changing the games they seemed to like.

—*Vinnie Minotti*

From S. Petersen, V.L. Allen, and V.L. Minotti, 1994, "Teacher knowledge and reflection," *Journal of Physical Education, Recreation and Dance* 65(7):32.

have learned that change must be systemic (system-wide) and not piecemeal (single-person) to be effective. In this chapter, I share methods and strategies to help you and your colleagues prepare for and implement the many changes that lie ahead.

Change

You can't mandate change—it is a journey that takes time. It helps to view change in the 21st century as a process and not an event. This process is highly personal because it gives each of us an opportunity to reinvent ourselves as well as the world around us. Change takes a different length of time for each individual, and during the process, life can seem chaotic. It is important, however, that throughout what appears to be chaos and uncertainty you stay focused on your values and ultimate purpose, so that the decisions you make during these times of confusion are aligned with your ultimate goal.

Requisites for Change

Change requires vision, skills, resources, and an action plan. Vision is a clearly defined, yet flexible, view of what your program will look like after the change occurs. To get on track, list the positive benefits that the change will create. Although the vision is often articulated by the leader, it must include everyone's view and everyone must buy into it.

Skills refer to both knowledge and processing skills. Knowledge provides the information necessary to create the vision. For example, you—whether you're a teacher or an administrator—need to understand standards-based assessment in order to put it into practice. In addition, process skills are necessary to help a department or committee go through the process of change. Teacher–leaders who possess process skills can form groups, help those groups make decisions, and facilitate effective communication between group members. *The New Leadership Paradigm for Physical Education: What We Need to Lead* (Mohnsen 1999) will assist you with both knowledge and processing skills.

Resources are the equipment, supplies, and other financial requirements needed to facilitate the change. For example, to implement a swimming program, you need either a pool or access and transportation to a pool. To train teachers in a new instructional strategy, you need money for either stipends or substitutes.

Finally, an action plan requires a well-defined step-by-step blueprint that identifies the activities necessary to implement change and defines a clear pathway to the vision. Your action plan, however, must be open-ended, allowing for changes along the way. The open-ended structure has always been an important feature of any action plan, but as rapidly as change is occurring today, this structure becomes essential to an effective plan.

Model for Change

Change is much more effective when a group, such as the physical education department, embraces the change collectively, such as deciding to try a new program together. Still, if you have successfully implemented the changes in your classes, it will be easier to sell those changes to your colleagues. Taking time to share with your colleagues and provide them with resources is a great way to ensure that everyone agrees with and adopts the change.

It may appear at times that everyone has different concerns about implementing the new program. Everyone will move toward the changes at his own pace. In fact, according to the Concerns-Based Adoption Model (CBAM), developed at the Center for R & D in Teaching at the University of Texas, Austin, everyone will progress through a seven-step process on her way to adopting any new program (Hall, Wallace, and Dossett 1973). These seven steps were designed to explain the lack of teacher buy-in and to propose ways to monitor and increase implementation of educational innovations. By becoming aware of the seven steps (figure 13.1), you can appropriately assist an individual who is having difficulty with the changes.

Practical Ideas for Change

You, as a teacher–leader, must also consider strategies that have proven effective for other teacher–leaders. If you have several new ideas that you wish to implement in your program and you encounter resistance either from the administration or from other teachers, pick one new idea at a time on which to focus your attention. Once you are successful with that idea, then progress to the next.

Here are 12 steps to take as you work with your colleagues to accept and adapt to change:

Stage 1: Secure as much information as possible about the change from in-services, videotapes, audiotapes, discussions, and observations.

Seven Stages of the Concerns-Based Adoption Model

Stage 1: Awareness—Little Concern About or Involvement With the Innovation

Involve individuals in discussions and decisions about the innovation and its implementation.

Share enough information to arouse interest but not so much that it overwhelms.

Minimize gossip and inaccurate sharing of information about the innovation.

Stage 2: Informational—General Awareness of the Innovation and Interest in Learning More Detail

Use a variety of ways to share information: oral, written, and through any other available media.

Have individuals who have used the innovation in other settings talk with your teachers.

Help individuals see how the innovation relates to their current practices.

Stage 3: Personal—Uncertainty About the Demands of the Innovation

Legitimize the existence and expression of personal concerns.

Connect these individuals with others whose concerns have diminished.

Do not push innovation; rather, encourage and support it.

Stage 4: Management—Focus on the Processes and Tasks of Using the Innovation

Provide answers that address the small specific how-to issues.

Demonstrate exact and practical solutions to the logistical problems.

Stage 5: Consequence—Focus on the Impact of the Innovation on Students

Provide individuals with opportunities to visit other settings where the innovation is in use.

Provide positive feedback and necessary support.

Find opportunities for these persons to share their skills with others.

Stage 6: Collaboration—Focus on Coordination and Cooperation With Others

Provide these individuals with opportunities to develop those skills necessary for working collaboratively.

Use these individuals to provide technical assistance to others who need assistance.

Encourage the collaborators, but don't attempt to force collaboration on those who are not interested.

Stage 7: Refocusing—Focus on Exploration of More Universal Benefits From the Innovation

Help these individuals access the resources they may need to refine their ideas and put them into practice.

Be aware of and willing to accept the fact that these persons may replace or significantly modify the existing innovations.

Figure 13.1 Suggestions are provided to help others with the seven steps to change.

Adapted from G.E. Hall, R.C. Wallace, and W.A. Dossett, 1973, *A developmental conceptualization of the adoption process within educational institutions* (Washington, DC: ERIC).

Stage 2: Set written goals for implementing the change.

Stage 3: Experiment with one class.

Stage 4: Visit other teachers who are also attempting to implement the change.

Stage 5: Share information, successes, and failures with other teachers who are attempting to implement the change.

Stage 6: Modify the new approach if it seems necessary.

Stage 7: Implement the change in all your classes.

Stage 8: Adapt the change as necessary.

Stage 9: Document your success.

Stage 10: Invite administrators to visit your classes.

Stage 11: Take advantage of opportunities to share new strategies with your colleagues.

Stage 12: Offer to support a colleague through the change process.

Professional Development

Professional development is a process through which you'll learn about new ideas and begin the process of transferring these new ideas to your classes. NASPE (2006a) reports that 43 states require professional development or continuing education to maintain or renew physical education teacher certification or licensing and 18 states provide funding to support the training. This is, no doubt, attributable to the research (Tucker and Stronge 2005) showing that formal teacher preparation in physical education has a positive impact on student achievement. This includes content knowledge and pedagogy skills.

Unfortunately, many physical educators believe that professional development is useless. This opinion is based on their many experiences with school-wide in-services that did not relate directly to their jobs. The typical problem with these school-wide professional development seminars is not the content per se (cooperative learning, restructuring, technology) but rather the inability of the presenter to relate the content to physical education. Physical educators can benefit from understanding cooperative learning strategies, instructional technology, and the issues related to educational reform. Still, when the presenter discusses cooperative learning only in the context of classroom situations with a small number of students, it is difficult for the physical educators to apply the suggestions. You can address this problem by educating the presenter on how to relate his topic to physical educators, by allowing time after the presentation for each department to discuss implementing the new ideas, or by encouraging the administration to schedule separate presentations for each department on the same topic.

Effective professional development programs require sustained, ongoing efforts through which teachers have time to learn and try new ideas in a safe, controlled situation. In addition, such programs must address one or more of the skills necessary to teach physical education. You should be able to see a direct relationship between the professional development program and what goes on in your classes. Although professional development can take on many different forms, several principles should be incorporated into all professional development opportunities. Effective, ongoing professional development

- is based on the school's strategic long-term professional development plan;
- is built on providing time for teachers to network;
- presents theory and practical applications;
- allows for teacher input on content;
- commits to a long-term financial investment;
- focuses on teachers' questions, needs, and concerns;
- encourages initial practice in the workshop; and
- provides for adequate follow-up, including prompt feedback from a coach in the classroom.

Now let's examine a few professional development models.

In-Services

In-services are learning experiences that are planned and organized for teachers within a fairly local geographic area (county, district, or school). These in-services can take the form of a single meeting on one topic or a series of meetings on one or more topics. Suggested topics include

- understanding middle school students,
- setting up a positive environment,
- developing an effective curriculum,
- examining the content of physical education,
- exploring student learning styles,
- increasing effective teaching behaviors,
- exploring teaching styles,
- examining how the brain learns,
- expanding your teaching strategies,
- selecting instructional materials,
- using technology in physical education,

- selecting assessment tools,
- implementing standards-based assessment, and
- grading in physical education.

In-services can be times for teachers to share with others or times for teachers to learn new information from visiting experts. Some districts and schools set up a number of in-service days or times per year for specific subject area issues. In this way, the physical educators are not excluded from school-wide in-services, as is too often the case; instead, all departments are able to benefit from some in-service time devoted to their specific content field. A new direction for in-services is Internet-based professional development.

In-service training is typically conducted by local colleges or universities, professional associations, or regional educational institutions (district offices, local educational agencies). These agencies award college credits or salary points for teachers. However, physical educators (especially those with coaching responsibilities) often have found it difficult to attend professional development workshops. Today, training can take place via the Internet, allowing educators to learn at their convenience. The number of virtual colleges and training centers on the Internet is growing by leaps and bounds. Emporia State University (Emporia, Kansas), for example, offers a master's degree program in physical education delivered exclusively via the Internet.

In another example, Bonnie's Fitware, Inc. provides a number of online learning experiences each year that are designed specifically for physical educators:

- PowerPoint® for physical education courses
- Fitness reporting software
- Record book
- Web design
- Instructional software
- Technology devices

- Electronic portfolios
- Spreadsheets for physical educators

Information about the courses is distributed nationally through flyers and journal articles. Each course consists of six learning modules (one college credit) that can be completed any time one of three semesters during the year (fall, winter–spring, and summer). Class sizes have ranged from 5 to 50 students per course.

Each course starts with an e-mail message to the participants. The message welcomes students to the course and provides an Internet address that they can click on to access the course syllabus. The syllabus includes the objectives, a list of the six modules, course assessments, and textbook references. The participants are asked to read the syllabus and then click on module 1 to begin. Participants are informed that at any time throughout the course they can interact with the instructor or other students for assistance or additional information.

Online courses appear to meet the lifelong learning, lifestyle, and sharing and social needs of the participants. Research comparing distance education to traditional face-to-face instruction indicates that teaching and studying at a distance can be as effective as traditional instruction when the method and technologies used are appropriate to the instructional tasks, student-to-student interaction occurs, and there is timely teacher-to-student feedback (Moore et al. 1990; Verduin and Clark 1991). Additional studies have found that the teacher was the most significant contributor to students' perceptions of their learning experience online (Fredericksen et al. 2000). However, to truly understand a professional development experience via the Internet, you must experience one for yourself.

Conferences and Workshops

Compared with in-services, conferences and workshops provide opportunities for teachers

Physical Education Clinics

I have encouraged clinics that are conducted by the physical education teachers. Teachers who are experts in a particular activity would conduct a training session for the rest of the physical education staff. We would get together at 7:00 p.m. for two hours. This really helped our program. These evening clinics, for example, contributed to making our gymnastics units an outstanding feature in this district.

From L.F. Butler and G. Mergardt, 1994, "The many forms of administrative support," *Journal of Physical Education, Recreation and Dance* 65(7): 45.

from a wider geographic area to share ideas and activities on a wide variety of topics. For example, the American Alliance for Health, Physical Education, Recreation and Dance (AAHPERD) holds a national convention each year as well as a number of specialty conferences and workshops. Most of the state AHPERD organizations (depending on the size of the state) offer yearly conferences as well, in addition to a number of local workshops.

An especially effective workshop presented by AAHPERD is the Physical Best Health–Fitness Specialist Certification workshop. This 7-hour workshop covers the concepts of health-related fitness and effective teaching using the Physical Best program. Participants learn ready-to-use activities for teaching the concepts through movement. The workshop also addresses effective use of assessment and reporting via the Fitnessgram test battery. Certification is awarded pending successful completion of a postworkshop self-study examination.

Reflections

Opportunities to attend conferences, workshops, and in-services are only three pieces of the learning puzzle. Time to reflect on those learning endeavors and your teaching experiences extends your thinking and learning. As Petersen, Allen, and Minotti (1994) stated, "It was through experience that thoughtful teachers gained much of their professional knowledge, but it was through reflection that they effectively used that knowledge to build outstanding programs and maintain their motivation to continue to gain knowledge" (p. 31). The quote at the beginning of this chapter is one example of a teacher's reflection regarding his own teaching and what he learned from it.

Peer Coaching

Many new teachers feel isolated because they have no one with whom to share successes or concerns. At the other end of the spectrum is the teacher who suffers from burnout. Having done the same job day in and day out for 20 years with the daily stresses inherent to teaching, many experienced teachers experience the burnout syndrome. These teachers tend to plan less, become inflexible in their views, and expect less both from themselves and from their students. Teachers on both ends of this continuum can benefit from peer coaching, which gives teachers someone to share ideas and

concerns with. The peer coach can also help the teacher implement new ideas. For peer coaching to work, however, it must take place in a safe environment in which the teacher being observed invites the peer into her class—not the other way around. Training on how to observe and give feedback to peers also facilitates the process.

> There is evidence that peer coaching, a system of collegial support and feedback, can greatly facilitate transfer of learning. Peer coaching provides companionship, provides technical feedback, extends executive control, helps teachers adapt to students, and provides personal facilitation. The end result is that teachers achieve a higher level of mastery and are better able to adapt innovations to unique demands. (Randall, 1992b, p. 210)

Visitations

The common saying "A picture is worth a thousand words" certainly holds true for implementing a new teaching idea or strategy. Teachers who can see the actual technique in action with adolescents are more likely to believe the technique is valuable and therefore are more likely to try the technique. These visits can be to schools whose teachers have mastered the new technique or to schools whose teachers are in the beginning stages of implementing the new technique. Beyond the actual observation, the visiting teachers can benefit from discussions with other practicing teachers.

Visitations, whenever possible, should be done in teams or at least with a colleague. The dialogue that results between two or more participants can be much more valuable than the thoughts of a single person. It is also important to determine ahead of time the specific questions to ask and points to observe, so that you are ready to benefit from the experience.

Even teachers who are not ready to try a specific new technique may benefit from visiting other programs. The reason is that such visits tend to give us a wealth of new ideas and confirm for us what we are already doing well. As with visits made by more enthusiastic teachers, a visit by reluctant teachers should be a two-way exchange of information, covering successes, concerns, and failures. Indeed, you may find that reluctant teachers have their fears allayed and join your reform efforts after all.

Your state's Association for Health, Physical Education, Recreation and Dance and your state's department of education are great places to start looking for schools to visit. Many states have program or exemplary status awards, granted to physical education programs that are implementing new and exciting ideas. Ask for a list of award winners. You can also ask colleagues from other schools in your district where they have visited.

Video Learning

Often you hear of schools you would like to visit but are unable to travel to them. In these instances, ask whether the school has a video of its program to share. For example, one demonstration school, Montebello Intermediate in the Montebello (California) Unified School District, has developed a video that it will send for the cost of the video and shipping to any other school interested in the program. In addition, the Educational Telecommunications Network (ETN) has produced more than a dozen videos on quality physical education designed to be used as part of in-service programs. Each ETN video includes a discussion on a specific topic and footage of actual classes implementing the concept. The Orange County Department of Education has also created professional development videos on a wide variety of topics from teaching standards-based self-defense to teaching standards-based circus skills. (See appendix C for addresses and phone numbers.) Here are some additional suggestions for professional development audiotapes and videotapes:

Building a Quality Physical Education Program (Bureau of Education and Research)

Sheltered Instruction for Physical Education (Orange County Department of Education

Using Technology in Physical Education Video Series (Bonnie's Fitware, Inc.)

Reading, Listening, or Discussing: Do It Your Way

In chapter 9, we discussed how students learn in different ways. Of course, this is also true for teachers. Some teachers like to belong to discussion groups, some like to listen to audiotapes, and others like to read. Whatever is your preferred learning style, find a way to keep abreast of current research and its application to your instructional program. If you like to read, avail yourself of books, journals, and the Internet; if you like to listen, make use of the many excellent audiotapes on the market, such as *Building a Quality Physical Education Program* (Bureau of Education and Research), *Brain Compatible Learning* (The Brain Store), and *Super Teaching* (The Brain Store).

Professional Reading

Educational Leadership. Available from Association for Supervision and Curriculum Development, 1703 N. Beauregard St., Alexandria, VA 22311-1714; 800-933-2723.

Journal of Physical Education, Recreation and Dance. Available from American Alliance for Health, Physical Education, Recreation and Dance, 1900 Association Dr., Reston, VA 20191-1598; 800-213-7193.

Journal of Teaching in Physical Education. Available from Human Kinetics, P.O. Box 5076, Champaign, IL 61825-5076; 800-747-4457.

The Physical Educator. Available from Phi Epsilon Kappa Fraternity, 901 W. New York St., Indianapolis, IN 46202.

Research Quarterly for Exercise and Sport. Available from American Alliance for Health, Physical Education, Recreation and Dance, 1900 Association Dr., Reston, VA 20191-1598; 800-213-7193.

Strategies: A Journal for Sport and Physical Education. Available from American Alliance for Health, Physical Education, Recreation and Dance, 1900 Association Dr., Reston, VA 20191-1598; 800-213-7193.

Update. Available from American Alliance for Health, Physical Education, Recreation and Dance, 1900 Association Dr., Reston, VA 20191-1598; 800-213-7193.

Graduate School

A great way to stay on top of current information and move up the pay scale at the same time is to attend graduate school. Many colleges and universities offer degree programs in physical education pedagogy, making their programs relevant to your teaching situation. If you are interested in obtaining an administrative position, graduate programs can help you pursue a master's degree in educational administration while fulfilling the credentialing requirements.

National Board Certification

National Board Certification is for those physical educators who would like to demonstrate their expertise as physical educators. Currently, 30 states actively support the National Board Certification process (NASPE 2006a). Becoming certified requires demonstration of proficiency related to each of the National Board for Professional Teaching Standards (figure 13.2). Teachers demonstrate this proficiency through a professional portfolio that addresses instruction, setting a positive learning environment, assessment, and professional contributions. Proficiency is further demonstrated through a 3-hour examination that addresses six major areas, held at a local Sylvan Learning Center.

Interested individuals can read more about the standards and process at www.nbpts.org.

Contributing to the Profession

Contributing to the profession is one way to give something back to the profession as you extend the change process beyond your own school. In addition, many professionals have found that contributing to the profession renews their own excitement about the role they play in the lives of their students. Finally, the contact with other professionals can make you feel that your own ideas and feelings are valid.

Committee Work

Become involved in your professional association, if not as an officer then as a committee member, working on an area of interest to you. The time to pitch in has never been better, because more professional associations are establishing committees through which most of their work is done. They do this because they find that their members like the idea of working on one project that interests them rather than taking on the role of an officer.

Physical Education Standards Adopted by the National Board for Professional Teaching Standards

I. Knowledge of Students

Accomplished physical education teachers use their knowledge of students to make every student feel important. They communicate through a humane, sensitive approach that each child, regardless of ability, can succeed and will benefit from a physically active, healthy lifestyle.

II. Knowledge of Subject Matter

Accomplished physical education teachers have a deep and broad understanding of the content and principles of physical education, which enables them to devise sound and developmentally appropriate instructional activities.

III. Sound Teaching Practices

Accomplished physical education teachers possess a thorough comprehension of the fundamentals of physical education and a broad grasp of relevant principles and theories that give their teaching purpose and guide them as they carry out a flexible, yet effective instructional program responsive to students' needs and developmental levels.

Figure 13.2   To achieve certification, you must show proficiency in each of the teaching standards.

IV. Student Engagement in Learning

Through their own passion for teaching and their personal example, accomplished physical education teachers inspire their students to learn and to participate in and appreciate physical education.

V. High Expectations for Learners

Accomplished physical education teachers tenaciously maintain a stimulating, productive setting that encourages participation, discovery, goal setting, and cooperation and that holds all students to the highest expectations.

VI. Learning Environment

Accomplished teachers of physical education create and sustain a welcoming, safe, and challenging environment in which students engage in and enjoy physical activity. They establish an orderly atmosphere with established protocols and expectations conducive to providing maximum learning for all students.

VII. Curricular Choices

Accomplished physical education teachers select, plan, and evaluate curriculum in a continuous process meant to ensure a sensible, properly structured, positive physical education program that meets students' needs and results in student learning.

VIII. Assessment

Accomplished physical education teachers design assessment strategies appropriate to the curriculum and to the learner. They use assessment results to provide feedback to the learner, to report student progress, and to shape instruction.

IX. Equity, Fairness, and Diversity

Accomplished physical education teachers model and promote behavior appropriate in a diverse society by showing respect for and valuing all members of their communities and by having high expectations that their students will treat one another fairly and with dignity.

X. Reflective Practice and Professional Growth

Accomplished physical education teachers participate in a wide range of reflective practices that foster their creativity, stimulate personal growth, contribute to content knowledge and classroom skill, and enhance professionalism.

XI. Promoting an Active Lifestyle

Accomplished physical education teachers recognize the multiple benefits of a physically active lifestyle and promote purposeful daily activities for all students that will encourage them to become lifelong adherents of physical activity.

XII. Collaboration and Colleagues

Accomplished physical education teachers do not work in isolation but function as members of a large learning community. Recognizing that their responsibilities extend beyond their own classrooms, they contribute purposefully to enhancing instructional programs and improving the professional culture of their field.

XIII. Family and Community Partnerships

Accomplished physical education teachers create advocates for physical education by providing opportunities for family involvement and the involvement of the broader community in the physical education program.

Figure 13.2 *(continued)*

Of course, you can also become involved in committee work at your local school. All too often, physical educators remain in their isolated offices, never interacting with the rest of the staff. This often leads to feelings of isolation as well as the perception on the part of the other staff members that the physical education department is outside the educational realm. Don't let this happen to you and your department! By becoming involved in school committees, you can participate in an area that may be of interest to you as well as educate the other committee members about the role and importance of physical education. Perhaps most important, however, your inclusion on the committee also ensures that physical education will be represented and included in the committee's project.

Supervise a Student Teacher

Another way that you as an experienced teacher can give something back to the profession is through supervising a student teacher. Although having a student teacher is often thought of as a one-way process through which the master teacher passes on to the student teacher the wisdom he has gained over the years, many master teachers often learn as much from student teachers. Frequently student teachers have recently completed their physical education classes (exercise physiology, motor learning, biomechanics) and can share this information with you and the rest of the department. Be certain, however, if you are interested in taking on a student teacher, that you truly are an outstanding teacher who has kept up with the times and that you are willing to spend the extra time necessary to work directly with the student teacher. Then you must prove to the university in question that you're qualified to supervise.

Make Presentations

When you teach a middle school physical education class, you reach 20, 30, 40, or more students. But by making a presentation to other teachers, you can reach 100 to 300 students multiplied by the number of the teachers in the audience. Indeed, many experienced teachers have wonderful ideas that other teachers are interested in learning. State AHPERD conferences, district or county in-services, and school-based in-services are all excellent places to offer your services as a speaker. If you are new to making presentations,

pick your best lesson or unit and build your presentation around that. As you shape your presentation, remember what we have discussed about student learning in terms of learning styles, multiple intelligences, and learning modalities, because these concepts also apply to teachers. Finally, make sure, as with adolescent students, that the information you provide is relevant to your audience.

The physical educators at one middle school decided that they wanted their entire school staff to understand how they were working with students on social skills. The physical educators asked for and were given one of the school-wide in-service days. The physical educators divided the staff into four groups and rotated them through four stations:

1. Low ropes course elements
2. Physical challenges
3. In-class social initiatives
4. Debriefing activities

The physical education staff assumed the leadership role at each station. At the conclusion of the day, the school staff decided that the school's focus the following year should be on social skill development. They decided that this would entail all subject areas addressing one social skill each month. The physical education department was asked to provide monthly in-service training on how to address each new social skill.

You can also use and hone your speaking skills at the local parent and teacher association, community service organizations, and boards of education. Naturally, the topic of your speech should be different from what you presented to other teachers because these groups will not be as interested in how to teach physical education. Rather, they'll be interested in the benefits of physical education, how they can help their youngsters or the youngsters in their community perform well in physical education, and other important issues associated with physical education.

Summary

We've come to the end of our journey. Or is it the beginning? At any rate, it's time for you to chart your own course and follow your own path. To help you further, in the next four chapters I outline fifth, sixth, seventh, and eighth grade programs, complete with lesson plan outlines, appropriate tasks, and standards-based assessment tools. Before you read chapters 14 through 17, look at the scenario I asked you to write in chapter 2. Now that you have read through the book, would you change that scenario? Go ahead: Make those changes and spell out the steps you will take next year, the year after that, and the third year. I trust that the path you have chosen to follow leads you toward quality physical education. Now let's take a look at our destination: a quality middle school physical education program.

PART IV

Discover Your Destination

Physical education textbooks that address curriculum, instruction, and assessment are common. These books are filled with dos and don'ts and conclude with well wishes for you, the reader, to translate the information into a useful day-to-day program. In contrast, I want to share real-life scenarios as well as concrete examples of the ideas we've discussed throughout this book, which is why this part contains a sample middle school program. Please don't view my sample program as the only program! Instead, use my ideas as springboards for your own ideas. Adopt, adapt, and discard what you will because only you know how you want your program to look.

I have organized chapters 14 to 17 based on the standards and instructional units I identified in chapters 6 and 7. For each unit of instruction, I briefly discuss the reason for using the particular unit; I list equipment, facilities, and instructional materials you'll need to implement the unit; I suggest interdisciplinary and community ideas for making the unit more like real life; and I alert you to class environment issues associated with the unit. After each introduction, I list the unit standards (see CD for a database containing the grade-level and unit standards) that are linked directly to the grade-level standards. This is followed by a unit plan, which contains a day-by-day outline for what you should teach, explaining how the information and activities connect to the unit standards (any agenda item without a standards reference number is included for class management). Look for the motivational, learning, assessment, teaching style, and strategy ideas I have embedded in these daily plans. But don't confuse these unit outlines with detailed lesson plans (see CD for sample lesson plans), which would elaborate on each of the daily agendas, providing detailed drills, activities, and learning experiences. Also, please keep in mind that depending on the initial general ability level and progress of your students, you may need to teach preliminary concepts as well as review new concepts frequently throughout

a unit. Ongoing monitoring of progress can be a big help to you in this regard.

As we discussed in chapter 8, some teachers provide an assessment tool for each unit standard, whereas others only provide assessment tools for each grade-level standard. You can choose to follow one of these two strategies or combine the two in the way that works best for you. To guide you, I provide the numbers of the grade-level standards through the unit standards, activities, and assessment ideas. Assessments that can be completed in 1 day are noted as assessment opportunities, whereas those being assigned and collected later are noted as assessment assignment opportunities. Many assessment assignment opportunities are noted as homework and are collected the next day, unless otherwise indicated. The closure unit ties all of the assessments together. As you read through part IV, think about how you can apply the concepts we discussed in the first 13 chapters to these model units as well as to your own program.

A Fifth Grade Program: Manipulating Objects Efficiently and Effectively

Traditionally, the middle school physical education curriculum has been activity centered. The activity was viewed as the end. However, a skills theme curriculum reverses the means–ends relationship. The curriculum is organized around specific skills or groups of skills. The focus is on student performance outcomes. The activities now become the means through which the student can practice, refine, and develop competence in the skills. The end is students who are able to use skills in a variety of contexts and situations.

—*Palm Beach County Middle School Physical Education Curriculum Focus, Florida*

Fifth Grade Standards

By the end of fifth grade, each student

1.0—Demonstrates speed, accuracy, and control using the mature form for fundamental movement and manipulative skills.

2.1—Explains the types of practice that improve motor skill performance for speed and accuracy.

2.2—Describes how to generate and absorb force when performing movement and motor skills.

2.3—Describes how the qualities of movement (e.g., space, time, force) are used in basic game tactics.

2.4—Describes changes from birth through puberty along with their impact on physical performance.

2.5—Describes critical elements of fundamental movement and manipulative skills.

3.1—Engages in moderate physical activity for 60 minutes 5 days each week.

3.2—Describes opportunities in the school setting for regular participation in physical activity.

4.1—Works toward a health-enhancing level of physical fitness.

4.2—Designs a cardiorespiratory and body composition fitness plan, including a warm-up and cool-down, for 1 day.

5.1—Works with an individual who is differently abled in a physical activity.

5.2—Accepts responsibility for personal safety during physical activity.

6.1—Describes the development and role of movement-related activities in the United States during the 17th and 18th centuries.

6.2—Expresses personal feelings through a movement-based routine.

6.3—Chooses to engage in skill competencies at a level that leads to personal satisfaction, success, and enjoyment.

6.4—Describes the physical benefits of regular participation in physical activity.

In this chapter, I have selected Manipulating Objects Efficiently and Effectively as the theme for my sample fifth grade program. As I mentioned in chapter 7, my fifth graders are coming to me from a less than ideal elementary experience, so I want to ensure that they are competent in the basic motor and movement skills before moving on to sport-specific skills. In addition, I want to set the tone for both the physical education and school environments by focusing on social skill development during the students' first year in middle school.

As we discussed in chapter 7, I have used the skills theme approach to guide my selection of most fifth grade units of instruction because my emphasis is on refining manipulative skills. I do, however, conclude the year with an opportunity for students to apply these skills in early American cultural games (a link to their social science curriculum) and in the creation of their own games. Specifically, the following are the units for fifth grade:

1. Introduction (3 weeks)
2. Cooperative Activities (3 weeks)
3. Body Management (3 weeks)
4. Locomotor Skills (3 weeks)
5. Throwing and Catching (3 weeks)
6. Throwing and Catching With Implements (3 weeks)
7. Striking With Hands (3 weeks)
8. Striking With Feet (3 weeks)
9. Striking With Implements (3 weeks)
10. Early American Dances (3 weeks)
11. Early American Games (3 weeks)
12. Closure and Fitness Assessment (3 weeks)

Notice that I move from simple to complex units throughout the year: from body management to locomotor skills, to throwing and catching, to throwing and catching using implements, to striking with hands, then feet, and then implements. Such sequencing is important so students can develop their skills progressively. I conclude the year with units on dances and games from early American history—the time period my students are studying in history and social science. Your sequence in this grade level and the others may be different because of your teaching situation and the facilities at your school.

In addition, within each of the skills themes in fifth grade, I move students from simple to complex learning tasks through informing, extending, refining, and finally applying each skill. In the informing stage, I present the new skill. In the extending stage, I increase the complexity or difficulty of the skill, for example by decreasing the size of the target or increasing the distance to the target. In the refining stage, I focus more on the critical elements of the skill performance, improving the technique aspects of the skill performance.

Finally, I encourage the most complex learning to occur by having students apply the skill in an activity. Your own unit plans should incorporate each of these stages as well.

You will notice that throughout each unit, opportunities for assessment and assessment assignments are noted. An assessment assignment refers to the giving of an assignment, whereas assignment refers to either the collection of an assessment or the actual lesson in which an assessment occurs. Assessment can be done using paper and pencil or the Middle School Physical Education Portfolio (Bonnie's Fitware, Inc.), which has been listed as a resource for each unit.

Introduction — Unit 1

This unit is an introductory unit for fifth grade students. For my students, this is the first year they don't stay together as a class for every subject, including physical education. Therefore, I emphasize their getting to know each other so they can start feeling comfortable with new classmates in a new school under new circumstances—a very important issue to young adolescents. This introductory unit also gives me the opportunity to set my expectations as I teach the class rules to the students. Finally, in this unit, I assess the students' fitness levels, setting the stage for goal setting in the next unit.

You can conduct this particular unit in just about any facility. If you must have students perform exercises on the ground or grass, however, provide students with carpet squares or some other material so that they don't get dirty. The equipment necessary to implement the unit depends on the type of introductory games you choose and the fitness assessments you plan to administer. I administer the Fitnessgram health-related fitness assessment battery, including the back-saver sit-and-reach, curl-ups, skinfold measurements, push-ups, trunk lift, and 1-mile run. You can order the Fitnessgram test administration procedures from Human Kinetics (see appendix C). You will see from the sample daily agendas that my students prepare for the fitness assessment through different aerobic activities. In addition, the students enter their fitness scores into their own electronic portfolios using the Health-Related Fitness: Tutorial and Portfolio (Bonnie's Fitware, Inc.).

This introductory unit is especially effective when the other fifth grade teachers also help students learn each other's names, get to know one another, learn class and school rules, and connect to their new school. Certainly, the most important aspect of this introductory unit is that it creates a psychologically safe environment, setting the stage for learning throughout the year. It is especially important for you to model acceptance of all students regardless of skill or fitness level during this unit. If you focus on including everyone from the start, you will set the stage for students to accept each other's strengths and weaknesses. Furthermore, if you protect the privacy of students during fitness assessments, this approach will show students that you have respect for them as individuals. In turn, students will be more likely to respect you as well as each other.

Unit 1 Standards

1.0—Demonstrates accuracy and speed using the mature form for the underhand toss and catch.

2.1—Defines *practice*.

2.2—Defines *force*.

2.3—Defines a game.

2.4—Describes the changes related to physical performance that occur in the human body from birth through prepuberty.

2.5—Describes the critical elements for the underhand toss and catch.

3.1—Engages in moderate physical activity for 15 minutes 3 days each week.

3.2—Lists extracurricular physical activities available during the school day.

4.1—Participates in fitness pre-assessment.

4.2—Describes the elements of a warm-up.

5.1—Demonstrates supportive skills.

5.2—Follows class rules.

6.1—Describes the development of fitness training in the United States during the 17th and 18th centuries.

6.2—Demonstrates qualities of movement.

6.3—Chooses to engage in skill competencies at a level that leads to personal satisfaction, success, and enjoyment.

6.4—Identifies physical activity.

Unit 1 Assessments

1.0—Structured observation (days 2-5)

2.1—Quiz (days 14-15)

2.2—Quiz (days 14-15)

2.3—Quiz (days 14-15)

2.4—Essay (assigned on day 13; collected on day 14)

2.5—Quiz (days 14-15)

3.1—Log (assigned on day 8; collected on day 15)

3.2—List (assigned on day 9; collected on day 11)

4.1—Fitness assessment (days 9-15) and food log (days 11-15)

4.2—Quiz (days 14-15)

5.1—Structured observation (days 2-8)

5.2—Structured observation (days 2-8)

6.1—Report (assigned on day 4; collected on day 15)

6.2—Structured observation (days 4-8)

6.3—Structured observation (days 2-8)

6.4—Quiz (days 14-15)

Resources

Fitnessgram testing materials (Human Kinetics)

Fit Kids' Classroom Workout DVD (Human Kinetics and Bonnie's Fitware, Inc.)

Health-Related Fitness: Tutorial and Portfolio (Bonnie's Fitware, Inc.)

Middle School Physical Education Portfolio (Bonnie's Fitware, Inc.)

Fifth grade introductory task cards (Bonnie's Fitware, Inc.)

Fitness task cards (Bonnie's Fitware, Inc.)

Fifth grade unit 1 posters (Bonnie's Fitware, Inc.—included in the Middle School Detailed Lesson Plans)

Fitness posters (Bonnie's Fitware, Inc.—included in the Middle School Detailed Lesson Plans)

Qualities of Movement chart (Bonnie's Fitware, Inc.—included in the Middle School Detailed Lesson Plans)

Equipment

Fleece balls

Fitness assessment materials (sit-and-reach box; curl-up test strip and recording materials; gymnastics mat for curl-ups and trunk lift; ruler for trunk lift; stopwatch for mile run; skinfold calipers; push-up recording materials)

Games

Toss-a-Name Game

Toss-and-Catch-a-Name Game

Introducer

Interest Circle

Sit in Circle

Unit 1 Outline

DAY 1	Display posters.
	Establish a roll call procedure.
	Introduce class rules. 5.2
	Have students record the class rules in their notebooks. 5.2
	Discuss routines and procedures specific to your class. 5.2
	Have students record the routines and procedures in their notebooks. 5.2
	Have students brainstorm what it means to be supportive. 5.1
	Have students record the definition of *supportive* in their notebooks. 5.1
	Have students brainstorm the definition of *practice*. 2.1
	Have students record the definition of *practice* in their notebooks. 2.1
	Let students know that you have high expectations for them to follow the rules, to be supportive, and to practice this semester. 2.1, 5.1, 5.2
DAY 2	Review class rules. 5.2
	Review what it means to be supportive. 5.1
	Review what it means to practice. 2.1
	Demonstrate and review (from grades K to 4) the mature form for the underhand toss. 1.0, 2.5
	Demonstrate and review (from grades K to 4) the mature form for catching. 1.0, 2.5
	Have students record the critical elements for the underhand toss and catch in their notebooks. 2.5
	Have students practice the underhand toss and catch with a partner. 1.0
	Demonstrate and describe how to play Toss-a-Name Game (see figure 14.1) using the Toss-a-Name Game task cards. 1.0
	Have students play Toss-a-Name Game. (Assessment opportunity: structured observation 1.0, 5.1, 5.2, 6.3)
	Ask the students if they enjoyed the game and, if so, why. 6.3
	Ask the students if they found the game to be satisfying and, if so, why. 6.3
	Explain how to open lockers.
	Ask students if anyone can name all of the class rules. 5.2

(continued)

Figure 14.1　Toss-a-Name Game.

Unit 1 Outline *(continued)*

DAY 3

Review class rules. 5.2

Review what it means to be supportive. 5.1

Review what it means to practice. 2.1

Review the mature form for the underhand toss. 1.0, 2.5

Review the mature form for catching. 1.0, 2.5

Have students practice the underhand toss and catch with a partner. 1.0

Demonstrate how to play Toss-and-Catch-a-Name Game using the Toss-and-Catch-a-Name Game task card. 1.0

Have students play Toss-and-Catch-a-Name Game. (Assessment opportunity: structured observation 1.0, 5.1, 5.2, 6.3)

Ask the students what they enjoyed about the game. 6.3

Ask the students what they found satisfying about the game. 6.3

Assign lockers.

Review how to open a locker.

Have students practice opening lockers.

DAY 4

Have students dress for physical education.

Review class rules. 5.2

Review what it means to be supportive. 5.1

Review what it means to practice. 2.1

Discuss the elements of a warm-up. 4.2

Have students record the elements of a warm-up in their notebooks. 4.2

DAY 4 (continued)

Have students perform a warm-up along with muscular strength and muscular endurance exercises. 4.1, 4.2

Provide each student with a Qualities of Movement handout. 6.2

Review (from grades K to 4) movement qualities and discuss their application to tossing a ball. 6.2

Provide students with feedback on their use of different movement qualities (i.e., throw the ball high, throw the ball fast, throw ball) as they play Toss-and-Catch-a-Name Game. (Assessment opportunity: structured observation 1.0, 5.1, 5.2, 6.2, 6.3)

Lead students through a cool-down and flexibility exercises appropriate to the physical activity level of the lesson. 4.1

Discuss the types of fitness training that occurred in the United States during the 17th and 18th centuries. 6.1

Assign students the task of completing a report on the fitness training that went on in the United States during the 17th and 18th centuries. This assignment is due the last day of this unit. (Assessment assignment opportunity: report 6.1)

DAY 5

Review class rules. 5.2

Review what it means to be supportive. 5.1

Review what it means to practice. 2.1

Review the elements of a warm-up. 4.2

Have students perform a warm-up along with a cardiorespiratory workout. 4.1, 4.2

Have students play Toss-and-Catch-a-Name Game while focusing on the accuracy of their throws. (Assessment opportunity: structured observation 1.0, 5.1, 5.2, 6.2, 6.3)

Define force. 2.2

Have students record the definition of *force* in their notebooks. 2.2

Have students play Toss-and-Catch-a-Name Game while focusing on the speed of their throws. (Assessment opportunity: structured observation—underhand toss 1.0)

Lead students through a cool-down and flexibility exercises appropriate to the physical activity level of the lesson. 4.1

Ask the students what they enjoyed about the game. 6.3

Ask the students what they found satisfying about the game. 6.3

DAY 6

Review class rules. 5.2

Review the definition of *force*. 2.2

Review what it means to be supportive. 5.1

Review what it means to practice. 2.1

Review the qualities of movement. 6.2

Review the elements of a warm-up. 4.2

Have students perform a warm-up along with a cardiorespiratory workout. 4.1, 4.2

Demonstrate Introducer using the Introducer task card. 5.1, 6.2, 6.3

Have students play Introducer. (Assessment opportunity: structured observation 5.1, 5.2, 6.2, 6.3)

Lead students through a cool-down and flexibility exercises appropriate to the physical activity level of the lesson. 4.1

Ask the students what they enjoyed about the game. 6.3

Ask the students what they found satisfying about the game. 6.3

(continued)

Unit 1 Outline   *(continued)*

DAY 7	Use the words *warm-up, supportive, force,* and *practice* during this lesson. 2.1, 2.2, 5.1
	Have students perform a warm-up along with muscular strength and muscular endurance exercises. 4.1, 4.2
	Demonstrate how to play Interest Circle using the Interest Circle task card. 5.1, 6.2, 6.3
	Have students play Interest Circle. (Assessment opportunity: structured observation 5.1, 5.2, 6.2, 6.3)
	Lead students through a cool-down and flexibility exercises appropriate to the physical activity level of the lesson. 4.1
	Ask the students what they enjoyed about the game. 6.3
	Ask the students what they found satisfying about the game. 6.3
DAY 8	Use the words *warm-up, supportive, force,* and *practice* during this lesson. 2.1, 2.2, 5.1
	Have students perform a warm-up along with a cardiorespiratory workout. 4.1, 4.2
	Demonstrate Sit in Circle using the Sit in Circle task card. 5.1, 6.3
	Have students play Sit in Circle. (Assessment opportunity: structured observation 5.1, 5.2, 6.3)
	Lead students through a cool-down and flexibility exercises appropriate to the physical activity level of the lesson. 4.1
	Have students identify what constitutes physical activity. 6.4
	Have students write a definition of *physical activity* in their notebooks along with several examples. 6.4
	Tell students that they are expected to engage in moderate physical activity for 15 minutes 3 days each week. 3.1
	Assign students to keep a log of daily activity. (Assessment assignment opportunity: log 3.1)
DAY 9	Use the words *supportive, force, physical activity,* and *practice* during this lesson. 2.1, 2.2, 5.1, 6.4
	Have students perform warm-up exercises for the back-saver sit-and-reach assessment. 4.1
	Assign students randomly to groups of four.
	Explain the back-saver sit-and-reach assessment (see figure 14.2) and why it is being administered. 4.1
	Have students brainstorm the definition of a game as well as the differences between a game and physical activity. 2.3
	Administer the back-saver sit-and-reach assessment to one group at a time while students work on their definition of a game. (Assessment opportunity: fitness assessment 4.1) 2.3
	Have students input fitness scores into their Health-Related Fitness Portfolio. 4.1
	Lead students through a cool-down and flexibility exercises appropriate to the physical activity level of the lesson. 4.1
	Have students record the definition of a game in their notebooks. 2.3
	Assign students the task of creating a list of extracurricular physical activities available during the school day. (Assessment assignment opportunity: list 3.2)

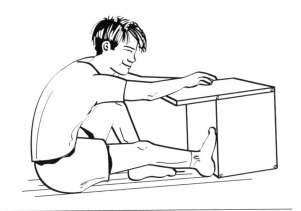

Figure 14.2 Back-saver sit-and-reach assessment.

DAY 10

Use the words *warm-up, supportive, force, physical activity, game,* and *practice* during this lesson. 2.1, 2.2, 2.3, 5.1, 6.4

Have students perform warm-up exercises for the curl-up assessment. 4.1

Explain the curl-up assessment and the reasons for administering the assessment (see figure 14.3). 4.1

Have students participate in a flexibility circuit (using fitness task cards) while administering the curl-up assessment at one station in the circuit. (Assessment opportunity: fitness assessment 4.1)

Have students input fitness scores into their Health-Related Fitness Portfolio. 4.1

Lead students through a cool-down and flexibility exercises appropriate to the physical activity level of the lesson. 4.1

(continued)

Figure 14.3 Curl-up assessment.

Unit 1 Outline *(continued)*

DAY 11

Use the words *warm-up, supportive, force, physical activity, game,* and *practice* during this lesson. 2.1, 2.2, 2.3, 5.1, 6.2

Explain the skinfold measurement and the reasons for administering the assessment. 4.1

Administer the skinfold measurement (see figure 14.4) to students one at a time in private while the others participate with Fit Kids' Classroom Workout DVD. (Assessment opportunity: fitness assessment 4.1)

Have students input fitness scores into their Health-Related Fitness Portfolio. 4.1

Lead students through a cool-down and flexibility exercises appropriate to the physical activity level of the lesson. 4.1

Collect lists of extracurricular physical activities. (Assessment opportunity: list 3.2)

Assign students the task of collecting data on their food intake for the next 3 days. (Assessment assignment opportunity: log 4.1)

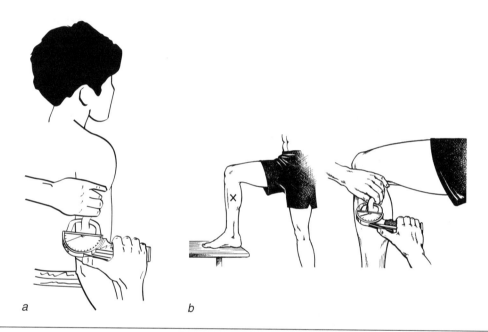

a　　　　　　　　　　　b

Figure 14.4　(*a*) Triceps skinfold and (*b*) medial calf skinfold measurements.

DAY 12

Use the words *supportive, force, physical activity, game,* and *practice* during this lesson. 2.1, 2.2, 2.3, 5.1, 6.4

Have students perform warm-up exercises for the push-up assessment. 4.1

Explain the push-up assessment and the reasons for administering the assessment. 4.1

Have students participate in a flexibility circuit (using fitness task cards) while administering the push-up assessment at one station in the circuit. (Assessment opportunity: fitness assessment 4.1)

Have students input fitness scores into their Health-Related Fitness Portfolio. 4.1

Lead students through a cool-down and flexibility exercises appropriate to the physical activity level of the lesson. 4.1

Explain to the students the changes relating to physical performance that occur in the human body from birth through prepuberty. 2.4

Have students record the information in their notebooks. 2.4

DAY 13

Use the words *warm-up, supportive, force, physical activity, game,* and *practice* during this lesson. 2.1, 2.2, 2.3, 5.1, 6.4

Review changes related to physical performance that occur from birth through prepuberty. 2.4

Have students perform warm-up exercises for the trunk-lift assessment. 4.1

Explain the trunk-lift assessment and the purpose for administering it (see figure 14.5). 4.1

Have students participate in an aerobic circuit (using the fitness task cards) while administering the trunk-lift assessment at one station in the circuit. (Assessment opportunity: fitness assessment 4.1)

Have students input fitness scores into their Health-Related Fitness Portfolio. 4.1

Lead students through a cool-down and flexibility exercises appropriate to the physical activity level of the lesson. 4.1

Play word games with students as a review for their quiz on day 15. 2.1, 2.2, 2.3, 2.5, 6.4, 4.2

For homework, ask students to write a description of the changes that occur from birth through prepuberty related to physical performance. (Assessment assignment opportunity: essay 2.4)

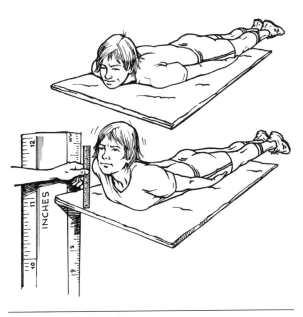

Figure 14.5   Trunk-lift assessment.

DAY 14

Explain the 1-mile run assessment and the reasons for administering the assessment. 4.1

Have students perform warm-up exercises for the 1-mile run prior to the assessment. 4.1

Administer the 1-mile run assessment to half the class. (Assessment opportunity: fitness assessment 4.1)

Administer the written quiz to the other half of the class. (Assessment opportunity: quiz 2.1, 2.2, 2.3, 2.5, 4.2, 6.4)

Have students input fitness scores into their Health-Related Fitness Portfolio. 4.1

Lead students through a cool-down and flexibility exercises appropriate to the physical activity level of the lesson. 4.1

Collect descriptions of changes from birth through prepuberty. (Assessment opportunity: essay 2.4)

(continued)

Unit 1 Outline *(continued)*

DAY 15

Review the 1-mile run assessment and the reasons for administering the assessment. 4.1

Have students perform warm-up exercises for the 1-mile run and any other makeup assessments that they need. 4.1

Administer the 1-mile run assessment to half the class. (Assessment opportunity: fitness assessment 4.1)

Administer the written quiz to the other half of the class. (Assessment opportunity: quiz 2.1, 2.2, 2.3, 2.5, 4.2, 6.4)

Administer makeup assessments. (Assessment opportunity: fitness assessment 4.1)

Have students input fitness scores into their Health-Related Fitness Portfolio. 4.1

Lead students through a cool-down and flexibility exercises appropriate to the physical activity level of the lesson. 4.1

Collect students' reports on fitness training. (Assessment opportunity: report 6.1)

Collect students' physical activity logs. (Assessment opportunity: log 3.1)

Collect students' food intake logs. (Assessment opportunity: log 4.1)

Cooperative Activities

~ Unit 2 ~

This unit provides students with an opportunity to extend, refine, and apply their personal responsibility and social skills. To accomplish this, rotate group members frequently. The Cooperative and Problem Solving Activities CD as well as the fifth grade cooperative activities task cards can be used to introduce and review each cooperative activity or problem-solving activity. As with the first unit, you can conduct this instructional unit in a variety of locations, and the equipment you need depends on the types of challenges or cooperative activities you choose.

This unit is also an extension of the last unit in terms of developing a supportive and psychologically safe environment through which students can feel comfortable with their physical abilities. It is an opportunity for students to continue to get to know one another and extend their relationships through cooperation and trust building. After conducting an activity that requires cooperation and trust, ask your students a number of debriefing questions, including these:

- "Did you cooperate to solve the challenge?"
- "Did you share your ideas?"
- "Did you listen to others?"
- "What will you do differently next time?"

Ideally, the other fifth grade teachers at your school will also use this time to continue to help students develop their social and cooperative skills, so that by the end of this unit you and your colleagues will have set the stage for a supportive school environment in which the students can learn during their next 4 years of middle school.

Unit 2 Standards

1.0—Demonstrates control using the mature form for jumping and running.

2.1—Explains that whole–part, accuracy–speed, mass–distributed, and mental–physical are four different ways to organize motor skill practice.

2.2—States Newton's first law.

2.3—Describes game tactics in a cooperative game setting.

2.4—Describes the changes related to physical performance that occur in the human body from pre-puberty through puberty.

2.5—Describes the critical elements for jumping and running.

3.1—Engages in moderate physical activity for 20 minutes 3 days each week.

3.2—Lists extracurricular physical activities available before the school day. (Assessment opportunity: structured observation)

4.1—Works toward a health-enhancing level of physical fitness.

4.2—Describes the elements of a cool-down.

5.1—Contributes ideas and listens with empathy to the ideas of everyone in cooperative activities.

5.2—Follows rules for cooperative activities.

6.1—Describes the development of physical education in the United States during the 17th and 18th centuries.

6.2—Expresses personal feelings during cooperative activities.

6.3—Chooses to engage in skill competencies found in cooperative activities at a level that leads to personal satisfaction, success, and enjoyment.

6.4—Describes the short-term muscular strength benefits derived from participation in physical activity.

Unit 2 Assessments

1.0—Structured observation (days 6 and 7)

2.1—Quiz (day 15)

2.2—Quiz (day 15)

2.3—Essay (assigned on day 9; collected on day 11)

2.4—Quiz (day 15)

2.5—Quiz (day 15)

3.1—Log (assigned on day 2; collected on day 15)

3.2—List (assigned on day 2; collected on day 15)

4.1—List of goals (day 1); structured observation (days 2-14)

4.2—Quiz (day 15)

5.1—Structured observation (days 1-14)

5.2—Structured observation (days 1-14)

6.1—Report (assigned on day 3; collected on day 15)

6.2—Journal entry (days 5, 6, 10, 14)

6.3—Structured observation (days 1-14)

6.4—Quiz (day 15)

Resources

Middle School Physical Education Portfolio (Bonnie's Fitware, Inc.)

Fifth grade cooperative task cards (Bonnie's Fitware, Inc.)

Cooperative and Problem Solving Activities CD (Bonnie's Fitware, Inc.)

Fifth grade unit 2 posters (Bonnie's Fitware, Inc.—included in the Middle School Detailed Lesson Plans)

Fitness posters (Bonnie's Fitware, Inc.—included in the Middle School Detailed Lesson Plans)

Qualities of Movement chart (Bonnie's Fitware, Inc.—included in the Middle School Detailed Lesson Plans)

Equipment

Flag-a-tag rings   Hula hoops   Empty soda bottle
Rope   Scarves and blindfolds   Tarp or newspaper
Twine   Poly spots   Tennis ball
Balloons   Bucket

Games

Name Line-Up   Icebreaker   Bull Ring
Birthday Line-Up   Blob Tag   Everyone In
Introducer   Courtesy Tag   Tarps
Bottoms Up   Stump Jump   Nitro Crossing
Inchworm   Carry Me   Blind Carry
Balloon Trolley   Tree of Knots   Circle the Circle

Unit 2 Outline

DAY 1

Display the posters.

Instruct students to examine the results of their fitness assessment and food and activity logs. 4.1

Instruct students to set three long-term goals and three short-term goals for improvement. Have students record their goals in the Health-Related Fitness Portfolio. (Assessment opportunity: goal setting 4.1)

Introduce the Cooperative Activities unit.

Discuss rules for safe participation in cooperative activities. 5.2

Discuss the reasons for rules in cooperative activities. 5.2

Have students brainstorm what it means to contribute ideas and listen with empathy to the ideas of others. 5.1

Tell students that you expect them to follow the rules for cooperative activities, demonstrate active listening, share ideas, and engage in the skill competencies found in the cooperative activities at a level that leads to personal satisfaction, success, and enjoyment. 5.1, 5.2, 6.1

Have students perform a warm-up along with a cardiorespiratory workout. (Assessment opportunity: structured observation 4.1)

Explain Name Line-Up. 5.1, 5.2

Have students participate in Name Line-Up. (Assessment opportunity: structured observation 5.1, 5.2, 6.3)

Explain Birthday Line-Up. 5.1, 5.2

Have students participate in Birthday Line-Up. (Assessment opportunity: structured observation 5.1, 5.2, 6.3)

Lead students through a cool-down and flexibility exercises appropriate to the physical activity level of the lesson. (Assessment opportunity: structured observation 4.1) 4.2

Debrief activities. 5.1

DAY 2

Describe the short-term muscular strength and muscular endurance benefits derived from participation in physical activity. 6.4

Have students record the short-term muscular strength and muscular endurance benefits derived from participation in physical activity. 6.4

DAY 2 (continued)

Have students keep a log of daily activity, noting date, activity, and length of time. (Assessment assignment opportunity: log 3.1)

Have students create a list of extracurricular physical activities available before the school day. (Assessment assignment opportunity: list 3.2)

Have students perform a warm-up along with muscular strength and muscular endurance exercises. (Assessment opportunity: structured observation 4.1)

Demonstrate Introducer (also known as Greeter) and show students the task card. 5.1, 5.2

Have students participate in Introducer. (Assessment opportunity: structured observation 5.1, 5.2, 6.3)

Review Birthday Line-Up and Name Line-Up. 5.1, 5.2

Describe the elements of a cool-down. 4.2

Have students record the elements of a cool-down in their notebooks. 4.2

Lead students through a cool-down and flexibility exercises appropriate to the physical activity level of the lesson. (Assessment opportunity: structured observation 4.1) 4.2

Review with students the short-term muscular strength and endurance benefits derived from participation in physical activity and the elements of a cool-down. 6.4, 4.2

DAY 3

State Newton's first law. 2.2

Have students write Newton's first law in their notebooks. 2.2

Review rules and procedures for cooperative activities. 5.2

Have students perform a warm-up along with a cardiorespiratory workout. (Assessment opportunity: structured observation 4.1)

Explain Bottoms Up and show students the task card. 5.1, 2.2, 5.2

Explain how Newton's first law relates to Bottoms Up. 2.2

Have students participate in Bottoms Up. (Assessment opportunity: structured observation 5.1, 5.2, 6.3) 2.2

Explain Inchworm and show students the task card. 5.1, 2.2, 5.2

Explain how Newton's first law relates to Inchworm. 2.2

Have students participate in Inchworm. (Assessment opportunity: structured observation 5.1, 5.2, 6.3) 2.2

Lead students through a cool-down and flexibility exercises appropriate to the physical activity level of the lesson. (Assessment opportunity: structured observation 4.1)

Debrief each activity. 5.1

Introduce physical education during the 17th and 18th centuries in the United States. 6.1

Have students research and write a comparison between physical education during the 17th and 18th centuries and today. (Assessment assignment opportunity: report 6.1)

DAY 4

Review Newton's first law. 2.2

Have students perform a warm-up along with muscular strength and muscular endurance exercises. (Assessment opportunity: structured observation 4.1)

Explain Balloon Trolley and show students the task cards. 5.1, 2.2, 5.2

Have students participate in Balloon Trolley. (Assessment opportunity: structured observation 5.1, 5.2, 6.3) 2.2

(continued)

Unit 2 Outline *(continued)*

DAY 4 *(continued)*

Explain how Newton's first law relates to Balloon Trolley. 2.2

Explain Icebreaker and show students the task cards. 5.1, 2.2, 5.2

Have students participate in Icebreaker. (Assessment opportunity: structured observation 5.1, 5.2, 6.3) 2.2

Explain how Newton's first law relates to Icebreaker. 2.2

Lead students through a cool-down and flexibility exercises appropriate to the physical activity level of the lesson. (Assessment opportunity: structured observation 4.1)

Debrief each activity, including a question related to whether the students were successful. 5.1

Review with students the short-term muscular strength and endurance benefits derived from participation in physical activity and the elements of a cool-down. 6.4, 4.2

DAY 5

Explain how the qualities of movement relate to expression of feelings. 6.2

Ask students what the different qualities of movement mean to them, using the Qualities of Movement handout. 6.2

Have students record the explanation of qualities of movement and expression of feelings in their notebooks. 6.2

Review Bottoms Up, Inchworm, Balloon Trolley, and Icebreaker in a station approach using the task cards. 5.1, 5.2

Have students perform a warm-up along with a cardiorespiratory workout. (Assessment opportunity: structured observation 4.1)

Have students participate in Bottoms Up, Inchworm, Balloon Trolley, and Icebreaker in a station approach using task cards. (Assessment opportunity: structured observation 5.1, 5.2, 6.3)

Lead students through a cool-down and flexibility exercises appropriate to the physical activity level of the lesson. (Assessment opportunity: structured observation 4.1)

Debrief each activity. 5.1

Have students respond to the journal prompt: How did you express personal feelings during the cooperative activities today? (Assessment opportunity: journal entry 6.2)

DAY 6

Review (from grades K to 4) the correct technique for running. 1.0, 2.5

Have students write in their notebooks the critical elements for running. 2.5

Explain the four different ways to organize motor skill practice. 2.1

Have students write in their notebooks the four different ways to organize motor skill practice. 2.1

Have students perform a warm-up. (Assessment opportunity: structured observation 4.1)

Explain Blob Tag and show students the task cards. 1.0, 5.1, 5.2, 2.2

Have students participate in Blob Tag. (Assessment opportunity: structured observation 1.0, 5.1, 5.2, 6.3) 2.2

Explain how Newton's first law relates to Blob Tag. 2.2

Explain Courtesy Tag and show students the task card. 5.1, 5.2

Explain how Newton's first law relates to Courtesy Tag. 2.2

DAY 6 (continued)

Lead students through a cool-down and flexibility exercises appropriate to the physical activity level of the lesson. (Assessment opportunity: structured observation 4.1)

Debrief Blob Tag and Courtesy Tag, including questions related to whether the students were successful and how students used different qualities of movement to express different feelings. 5.1, 6.2, 6.3

Have students respond to the journal prompt: How did you use different qualities of movement to express personal feelings during Blob Tag? (Assessment opportunity: journal entry 6.2)

DAY 7

Review (from grade 4) the correct technique for jumping. 1.0, 2.5

Have students write in their notebooks the critical elements for jumping. 1.0, 2.5

Review the four different ways to organize motor skill practice. 2.1

Have students perform a warm-up along with muscular strength and muscular endurance exercises. (Assessment opportunity: structured observation 4.1)

Explain Stump Jump (see figure 14.6) and show students the task card. 1.0, 5.1, 2.2, 5.2

Have students participate in Stump Jump. (Assessment opportunity: structured observation 1.0, 5.1, 5.2, 6.3) 2.2

Explain how Newton's first law relates to Stump Jump. 2.2

Review Blob Tag and Courtesy Tag as time permits. 5.1, 5.2

Lead students through a cool-down and flexibility exercises appropriate to the physical activity level of the lesson. (Assessment opportunity: structured observation 4.1)

Debrief Stump Jump, including questions related to whether the students were successful and how students used different qualities of movement to express different feelings. 5.1, 6.2

(continued)

Figure 14.6 Stump Jump.

Unit 2 Outline *(continued)*

DAY 8

Describe the use of game tactics in cooperative games. 2.3

Have students write in their notebooks a description of using game tactics in cooperative games. 2.3

Have students perform a warm-up along with a cardiorespiratory workout. (Assessment opportunity: structured observation 4.1)

Explain Carry Me and show students the task card. 5.1, 5.2

Have students participate in Carry Me. (Assessment opportunity: structured observation 5.1, 5.2, 6.3)

Explain Tree of Knots and show students the task card. 5.1, 5.2

Have students participate in Tree of Knots. (Assessment opportunity: structured observation 5.1, 5.2, 6.3)

Lead students through a cool-down and flexibility exercises appropriate to the physical activity level of the lesson. (Assessment opportunity: structured observation 4.1)

Debrief Carry Me and Tree of Knots, including questions related to whether the students were successful and how students used different qualities of movement to express different feelings. 5.1, 6.2

DAY 9

Review game tactics. 2.3

Describe changes that relate to physical performance that occur in the human body from prepuberty through puberty. 2.4

Have students record in their notebooks the changes that occur between prepuberty and puberty. 2.4

Have students perform a warm-up along with muscular strength and muscular endurance exercises. (Assessment opportunity: structured observation 4.1)

Explain Bull Ring (see figure 14.7) and show students the task card. 5.1, 5.2

Have students participate in Bull Ring. (Assessment opportunity: structured observation 5.1, 5.2, 6.3)

Review Carry Me and Tree of Knots as time permits. 5.1, 5.2

Lead students through a cool-down and flexibility exercises appropriate to the physical activity level of the lesson. (Assessment opportunity: structured observation 4.1)

Debrief Bull Ring, including questions related to whether the students were successful, how students used different qualities of movement to express different feelings, and how game tactics were used in the cooperative challenge. 5.1, 6.2, 2.3

For homework, have students write an essay on the use of game tactics in cooperative game settings. (Assessment assignment opportunity: essay 2.3)

Figure 14.7 Bull Ring.

DAY 10

Have students perform a warm-up along with a cardiorespiratory workout. (Assessment opportunity: structured observation 4.1)

Have students participate in Stump Jump, Tree of Knots, Carry Me, and Bull Ring in a station approach using the task cards. (Assessment opportunity: structured observation 5.1, 5.2, 6.3)

Lead students through a cool-down and flexibility exercises appropriate to the physical activity level of the lesson. (Assessment opportunity: structured observation 4.1)

Debrief each activity, including questions regarding how game tactics were used in the cooperative challenge. 2.3

Have students respond to the journal prompt: How did you express personal feelings during the cooperative activities today? (Assessment opportunity: journal entry 6.2)

DAY 11

Have students perform a warm-up along with a cardiorespiratory workout. (Assessment opportunity: structured observation 4.1)

Explain Everyone In and show students the task card. 5.1, 5.2

Have students participate in Everyone In. (Assessment opportunity: structured observation 5.1, 5.2, 6.3)

Explain Tarps (see figure 14.8) and show students the task card. 5.1, 5.2

Have students participate in Tarps. (Assessment opportunity: structured observation 5.1, 5.2, 6.3)

Debrief activities, including questions related to whether the students were successful, how students used different qualities of movement to express different feelings, and how game tactics were used in the cooperative challenge. 5.1, 6.2, 2.3

Lead students through a cool-down and flexibility exercises appropriate to the physical activity level of the lesson. (Assessment opportunity: structured observation 4.1)

Review the changes that occur in the human body from prepuberty through puberty. 2.4

Collect essays on the use of game tactics in cooperative activities. (Assessment opportunity: essay 2.3)

(continued)

Figure 14.8   Tarps.

Unit 2 Outline *(continued)*

DAY 12

Have students perform a warm-up along with muscular strength and muscular endurance exercises. (Assessment opportunity: structured observation 4.1)

Demonstrate swinging on a rope. 5.1, 5.2

Have students practice swinging on a rope. 5.1, 5.2

Explain Nitro Crossing (see figure 14.9) and show students the task card. 5.1, 5.2

Have students participate in Nitro Crossing. (Assessment opportunity: structured observation 5.1, 5.2, 6.3)

Review Tarps and Everyone In as time permits. 5.1, 5.2

Lead students through a cool-down and flexibility exercises appropriate to the physical activity level of the lesson. (Assessment opportunity: structured observation 4.1)

Debrief Nitro Crossing, including questions related to whether the students were successful, how students used different qualities of movement to express different feelings, and how game tactics were used in the cooperative challenge. 5.1, 6.2, 2.3

Figure 14.9   Nitro Crossing.

DAY 13

Have students perform a warm-up along with a cardiorespiratory workout. (Assessment opportunity: structured observation 4.1)

Explain Blind Carry (see figure 14.10) and show students the task card. 5.1, 5.2

Have students participate in Blind Carry. (Assessment opportunity: structured observation 5.1, 5.2, 6.3)

Explain Circle the Circle and show students the task card. 5.1, 5.2

Have students participate in Circle the Circle. (Assessment opportunity: structured observation 5.1, 5.2, 6.3)

Lead students through a cool-down and flexibility exercises appropriate to the physical activity level of the lesson. (Assessment opportunity: structured observation 4.1)

Debrief Blind Carry and Circle The Circle, including questions related to whether the students were successful, how students used different qualities of movement to express different feelings, and how game tactics were used in the cooperative challenge. 5.1, 6.2, 2.3

Figure 14.10   Blind Carry.

DAY 14

Have students perform a warm-up along with muscular strength and muscular endurance exercises. (Assessment opportunity: structured observation 4.1)

Have students participate in Blind Carry, Circle the Circle, Nitro Crossing, and Tarps in a station approach using the task cards. (Assessment opportunity: structured observation 5.1, 5.2, 6.3)

Lead students through a cool-down and flexibility exercises appropriate to the physical activity level of the lesson. (Assessment opportunity: structured observation 4.1)

Debrief each activity, including questions regarding how game tactics were used in the cooperative challenge. 2.3

Review material for tomorrow's quiz. 2.1, 2.2, 2.4, 2.5, 4.2, 6.4

Have students respond to the journal prompt: How did you express personal feelings during the cooperative activities today? (Assessment opportunity: journal entry 6.2)

(continued)

Unit 2 Outline *(continued)*

DAY 15

Instruct students to take the quiz. (Assessment opportunity: quiz 2.1, 2.2, 2.4, 2.5, 4.2, 6.4)

Collect comparisons between physical education during the 17th and 18th centuries and today. (Assessment opportunity: report 6.1)

Collect students' physical activity logs. (Assessment opportunity: log 3.1)

Collect list of extracurricular physical activities. (Assessment opportunity: list 3.2)

Body Management

 — Unit 3

This unit begins our focus on the skills theme units, starting with how our bodies can assume different shapes in either stationary or moving situations. Building on the trust developed between students throughout the last unit, begin to have students spot one another as they attempt to perform activities in this body management unit. The Body Management CD as well as the fifth grade body management task cards can be used to introduce each new stunt. The task cards can also be placed at each station as students practice the stunts.

During the body management unit and subsequent stunts, tumbling, and gymnastics units in higher grades, train your students to be effective and safe spotters:

- Instruct your students on the correct spotting technique.
- Test your students on the correct spotting technique.
- Provide your students with lots of practice opportunities.
- Match students of comparable height and weight.
- Never use student spotters for difficult skills.
- Continuously monitor your student spotters.

It is best if you conduct this unit inside a gymnasium or closed area. You can, however, conduct the unit outside in an open area, but only if you can bring mats or some other protective material outside.

Unit 3 Standards

1.0—Demonstrates control using the mature form for front scale, knee scale, squat forward roll, back squat roll, tip up, and tripod.

2.1—Explains the characteristics of physical practice and mental practice.

2.2—Describes internal forces.

2.3—Identifies the qualities of movement in body management activities.

2.4—Describes the similarities and differences between boys and girls from birth through puberty.

2.5—Describes the critical elements of front scale, knee scale, squat forward roll, back squat roll, tip up, and tripod.

3.1—Engages in moderate physical activity for 25 minutes 4 days each week.

3.2—Lists extracurricular physical activities available after the school day.

4.1—Works toward a health-enhancing level of physical fitness.

4.2—Describes overload, specificity, regularity, individual differences, and progression and how they relate to each area of health-related fitness.

5.1—Acknowledges orally the contributions and strengths of others.

5.2—Follows class procedures.

6.1—Describes the development of gymnastics in the United States during the 17th and 18th centuries.

6.2—Expresses personal feelings through a movement-based routine that involves stunts.

6.3—Chooses to engage in skill competencies found in body management activities at a level that leads to personal satisfaction, success, and enjoyment.

6.4—Describes the short-term flexibility benefits derived from participation in physical activity.

Unit 3 Assessments

1.0—Structured observation (days 3-14)

2.1—Quiz (day 15)

2.2—Quiz (day 15)

2.3—Quiz (day 15)

2.4—Quiz (day 15)

2.5—Quiz (day 15)

3.1—Log (assigned on day 1; collected on day 15)

3.2—List (assigned on day 10; collected on day 15)

4.1—Structured observation (days 1-14)

4.2—Quiz (day 15)

5.1—Structured observation (days 3-14)

5.2—Structured observation (days 3-14)

6.1—Report (assigned on day 1; collected on day 15)

6.2—Project (assigned day 12; collected day 14)

6.3—Structured observation (days 3-14)

6.4—Quiz (day 15)

Resources

Health-Related Fitness: Tutorial and Portfolio (Bonnie's Fitware, Inc.)

Middle School Physical Education Portfolio (Bonnie's Fitware, Inc.)

Body Management CD (Bonnie's Fitware, Inc.)

Fifth grade body management task cards (Bonnie's Fitware, Inc.)

Fifth grade unit 3 posters (Bonnie's Fitware, Inc.—included in the Middle School Detailed Lesson Plans)

Fitness posters (Bonnie's Fitware, Inc.—included in the Middle School Detailed Lesson Plans)

Qualities of Movement chart (Bonnie's Fitware, Inc.—included in the Middle School Detailed Lesson Plans)

Equipment

Tumbling mats

Stunts

Log rolls	Front scale	Flip-flop
Back shoulder roll	Knee scale	Jackknife
Front shoulder roll	Squat forward roll	Tripod
Walrus walk	L-support	Walk-through
Cross leg stand	Circular jump rope	Tip-up
Balancing on body parts	Squat backward roll	Seat circles

Unit 3 Outline

DAY 1

Introduce the body management unit.

Assign students to working groups of four for the unit.

Describe class procedures for body management activities and the reason for the procedures. 5.2

Have students record in their notebooks the class procedures for body management activities and the reasons for the procedures. 5.2

Discuss what it means to engage in skill competencies at levels that lead to personal satisfaction, success, and enjoyment. 6.3

Have students perform a warm-up along with a cardiorespiratory workout. (Assessment opportunity: structured observation 4.1)

Demonstrate and explain log rolls. 1.0, 2.5

Have students practice log rolls (this should provide students with an initial success). 1.0

Lead students through a cool-down and flexibility exercises appropriate to the physical activity level of the lesson. (Assessment opportunity: structured observation 4.1)

Assign unit-long homework:

- Have students research and write a description about the development of gymnastics in the United States during the 17th and 18th centuries. (Assessment assignment opportunity: report 6.1)

- Have students keep a log of daily activity. (Assessment assignment opportunity: log 3.1)

DAY 2

Review the class procedures for body management activities and the reason for the procedures. 5.2

Explain the features of physical practice and mental practice. 2.1

Have students perform a warm-up along with muscular strength and muscular endurance exercises. 4.1

Review log rolls. 1.0, 2.5

Have students perform log rolls. 1.0, 5.1

Demonstrate and describe back shoulder rolls. 1.0, 2.5

Have students mentally practice back shoulder rolls. 2.1, 1.0

Have students perform back shoulder rolls. 1.0, 5.1

Have students mentally practice back shoulder rolls. 2.1, 1.0

Have students discuss whether it was more effective to do the mental practice or the physical practice first. 2.1

Demonstrate and describe front shoulder rolls. 1.0, 2.5

Have students perform front shoulder rolls. 1.0, 5.1

Have students mentally practice front shoulder rolls. 1.0, 5.1

Lead students through a cool-down and flexibility exercises appropriate to the physical activity level of the lesson. 4.1

Have students discuss the effectiveness of mental practice. 2.1

DAY 3

Describe the short-term flexibility benefits derived from participation in physical activity. 6.4

Have students record in their notebooks the short-term flexibility benefits derived from participating in physical activity. 6.4

Have students perform a warm-up along with a cardiorespiratory workout. (Assessment opportunity: structured observation 4.1)

DAY 3 *(continued)*	Review log rolls, back shoulder rolls, and front shoulder rolls. 1.0
	Have students perform log rolls, back shoulder rolls, and front shoulder rolls. (Assessment opportunity: structured observation 1.0, 5.1, 5.2, 6.3)
	Have students mentally practice log rolls, back shoulder rolls, and forward shoulder rolls.
	Demonstrate and describe the walrus walk. 1.0, 2.5
	Have students practice the walrus walk. (Assessment opportunity: structured observation 1.0, 5.1, 5.2, 6.3)
	Have students mentally practice the walrus walk. 2.1
	Demonstrate and describe the cross leg stand. 1.0, 2.5
	Have students practice the cross leg stand. (Assessment opportunity: structured observation 1.0, 5.1, 5.2, 6.3)
	Have students mentally practice the cross leg stand. 2.1
	Lead students through a cool-down and flexibility exercises appropriate to the physical activity level of the lesson. (Assessment opportunity: structured observation 4.1)
	Remind students that they can practice these stunts at home physically or mentally. 2.1
DAY 4	Explain the station approach and hand out a checklist on which students may record their progress in the skills. 1.0
	Explain the importance of orally acknowledging the contributions and strengths of others. 5.1
	Have students perform a warm-up along with muscular strength and muscular endurance exercises. (Assessment opportunity: structured observation 4.1)
	Demonstrate and describe balancing on three body parts, a front scale, and a knee scale. 1.0, 2.5
	Have students practice balancing on three body parts, a front scale, and a knee scale. 1.0
	Have students rotate through the following stations: log roll, back shoulder roll, front shoulder roll, walrus walk, cross leg stand, balancing on three body parts, front scale, knee scale, and Health-Related Fitness: Tutorial and Portfolio computer station, at which they look up the definitions of *overload, specificity, regularity, individual differences,* and *progression* and how each relates to each area of health-related fitness. (Assessment opportunity: structured observation 1.0, 5.1, 5.2, 6.3) 4.2
	Lead students through a cool-down and flexibility exercises appropriate to the physical activity level of the lesson. (Assessment opportunity: structured observation 4.1)
	Have students record in their notebooks the information they learned about overload, specificity, regularity, individual differences, and progression. 4.2
DAY 5	Discuss the application of each fitness principle to the five areas of health-related fitness. 4.2
	Discuss frequency, intensity, time, and type variables related to muscular strength, muscular endurance, and flexibility. 4.2
	Have students perform a warm-up along with a cardiorespiratory workout. (Assessment opportunity: structured observation 4.1)
	Have students rotate through the following stations: log roll, back shoulder roll, front shoulder roll, walrus walk, cross leg stand, balancing on three body parts, front scale, and knee scale. (Assessment opportunity: structured observation 1.0, 5.1, 5.2, 6.3)
	Lead students through a cool-down and flexibility exercises appropriate to the physical activity level of the lesson. (Assessment opportunity: structured observation 4.1)
	Review the definitions of *overload, specificity, regularity, individual differences,* and *progression.* 4.2

(continued)

Unit 3 Outline *(continued)*

DAY 6

Describe internal forces. 2.2

Have students write in their notebooks the description of internal forces. 2.2

Have students perform a warm-up along with a cardiorespiratory workout. (Assessment opportunity: structured observation 4.1)

Demonstrate squat forward roll, L-support, and circular jump rope. 1.0, 2.5

Discuss the role of internal force when performing the squat forward roll, L-support, and circular jump rope. 2.2

Have students perform squat forward roll, L-support, and circular jump rope. 1.0

Have students rotate through the following stations: cross leg stand, walrus walk, squat forward roll, back shoulder roll, front shoulder roll, L-support, circular jump rope, balancing on three body parts, front scale, and knee scale. (Assessment opportunity: structured observation 1.0, 5.1, 5.2, 6.3)

Lead students through a cool-down and flexibility exercises appropriate to the physical activity level of the lesson. (Assessment opportunity: structured observation 4.1)

Review the application of overload, specificity, regularity, individual differences, and progression to muscular strength and endurance. 4.2

DAY 7

Review internal forces. 2.2

Have students perform a warm-up along with muscular strength and muscular endurance exercises. (Assessment opportunity: structured observation 4.1)

Have students rotate through the following stations: cross leg stand, walrus walk, squat forward roll, back shoulder roll, front shoulder roll, L-support, circular jump rope, balancing on three body parts, front scale, and knee scale. (Assessment opportunity: structured observation 1.0, 5.1, 5.2, 6.3)

Lead students through a cool-down and flexibility exercises appropriate to the physical activity level of the lesson. 4.1

Review the role of internal force when performing the squat forward roll, L-support, and circular jump rope. 2.2

DAY 8

Describe the similarities and differences between boys and girls from birth through puberty. 2.4

Have students record the description in their notebooks. 2.4

Have students perform a warm-up along with a cardiorespiratory workout. (Assessment opportunity: structured observation 4.1)

Demonstrate squat backward roll, flip-flop, and jackknife. 1.0, 2.5

Discuss the role of internal force when performing the squat backward roll, flip-flop, and jackknife. 2.2

Have students rotate through the following stations: back shoulder roll, cross leg stand, walrus walk, squat forward roll and front shoulder roll, squat backward roll, L-support, circular jump rope, flip-flop, front and knee scales, and jackknife. (Assessment opportunity: structured observation 1.0, 5.1, 5.2, 6.3)

Lead students through a cool-down and flexibility exercises appropriate to the physical activity level of the lesson. (Assessment opportunity: structured observation 4.1)

Have students discuss the similarities and differences that they have observed between boys and girls during the body management unit. 2.4

Review the application of overload, specificity, regularity, individual differences, and progression to the five areas of health-related fitness. 4.2

DAY 9

Review the similarities and differences between boys and girls from birth through puberty. 2.4

Have students perform a warm-up along with muscular strength and muscular endurance exercises. (Assessment opportunity: structured observation 4.1)

Have students rotate through the following stations: back shoulder roll, cross leg stand, walrus walk, squat forward roll and front shoulder roll, squat backward roll, L-support, circular jump rope, flip-flop, front and knee scales, and jackknife. (Assessment opportunity: structured observation 1.0, 5.1, 5.2, 6.3)

Lead students through a cool-down and flexibility exercises appropriate to the physical activity level of the lesson. (Assessment opportunity: structured observation 4.1)

Have students discuss the similarities and differences that they have observed between boys and girls during the body management unit. 2.4

DAY 10

Review the similarities and differences between boys and girls from birth through puberty. 2.4

Have students perform a warm-up along with a cardiorespiratory workout. (Assessment opportunity: structured observation 4.1)

Demonstrate tripod, walk-through, tip-up (see figure 14.11), and seat circles. 1.0. 2.5

Have students rotate through the following stations: squat forward roll; squat backward roll; tripod; walk-through; L-support, front scale, and knee scale; flip-flop; seat circles; jackknife; circular jump rope; and tip-up. (Assessment opportunity: structured observation 1.0, 5.1, 5.2, 6.3)

Lead students through a cool-down and flexibility exercises appropriate to the physical activity level of the lesson. (Assessment opportunity: structured observation 4.1)

Review the role of internal force when performing the squat backward roll, flip-flop, and jackknife. 2.2

Have students create a list of extracurricular physical activities available after the school day. (Assessment assignment opportunity: list 3.2)

(continued)

Figure 14.11   Tip-up.

Unit 3 Outline *(continued)*

DAY 11	Have students perform a warm-up along with a cardiorespiratory workout. (Assessment opportunity: structured observation 4.1)
	Have students rotate through the following stations: squat forward roll; squat backward roll; tripod; walk-through; L-support, front scale, and knee scale; flip-flop; seat circles; jackknife; circular jump rope; and tip-up. (Assessment opportunity: structured observation 1.0, 5.1, 5.2, 6.3)
	Lead students through a cool-down and flexibility exercises appropriate to the physical activity level of the lesson. (Assessment opportunity: structured observation 4.1)
	Review the application of overload, specificity, regularity, individual differences, and progression to the five areas of health-related fitness. 4.2
DAY 12	Review qualities of movement. 2.3
	Discuss the use of qualities of movement in body management activities. 2.3
	Have students perform a warm-up along with muscular strength and muscular endurance exercises. (Assessment opportunity: structured observation 4.1)
	Have students, in groups of four, create a stunts routine that uses qualities of movement to express personal feelings. (Assessment assignment opportunity: project 6.2)
	Have groups practice their stunts routine. 1.0, 6.2, 5.1
	Lead students through a cool-down and flexibility exercises appropriate to the physical activity level of the lesson. (Assessment opportunity: structured observation 4.1)
DAY 13	Have students perform a warm-up along with a cardiorespiratory workout. (Assessment opportunity: structured observation 4.1)
	Have groups practice their stunts routines. 1.0, 6.2, 5.1
	Lead students through a cool-down and flexibility exercises appropriate to the physical activity level of the lesson. (Assessment opportunity: structured observation 4.1)
DAY 14	Have students perform a warm-up along with muscular strength and muscular endurance exercises. (Assessment opportunity: structured observation 4.1)
	Have students demonstrate their routines to several other groups. 1.0, 6.2
	Lead students through a cool-down and flexibility exercises appropriate to the physical activity level of the lesson. (Assessment opportunity: structured observation 4.1)
	Collect projects. (Assessment opportunity: project 6.2)
	Review material for tomorrow's quiz (or hand out quiz if you would like for it to be a take-home quiz). 2.1, 2.2, 2.3, 2.4, 2.5, 4.2, 6.4
DAY 15	Have students take the quiz. (Assessment opportunity: quiz 2.1, 2.2, 2.3, 2.4, 2.5, 4.2, 6.4)
	Collect student activity logs. (Assessment opportunity: log 3.1)
	Collect reports on the development of gymnastics in the United States during the 17th and 18th centuries. (Assessment opportunity: report 6.1)
	Collect lists of the extracurricular physical activities available after school. (Assessment opportunity: lists 3.2)

Locomotor Skills

In this unit, the second with the skills theme approach, I expand on body management by reviewing the basic locomotor skills with students (walking, running, hopping, skipping, jumping, leaping, galloping, sliding). Then, I apply these skills to rhythm activities such as Tinikling and jump rope. For those unfamiliar with Tinikling, it originated in the Republic of the Philippines and involves dance steps performed to music over two moving parallel poles. This unit works best in a closed area or gymnasium, but you can present it outside. If you must conduct the unit outside, choose a secluded area so that students do not feel self-conscious about performing to music in front of other classes.

Throughout the unit, I have students wear heart rate monitors to determine whether they are in their target heart rate zones long enough to improve their cardiorespiratory endurance. On different days, I have different students download the data from their heart rate monitors into the computer; then I have them place the computer-generated graphs into their Health-Related Fitness: Tutorial and Portfolio (Bonnie's Fitware, Inc.).

Unit 4 Standards

1.0—Demonstrates control using the mature form for walk, run, hop, skip, jump for distance, jump for height, leap, gallop, and slide.

2.1—Explains the features of whole and part practice.

2.2—Describes how internal force is generated.

2.3—Describes the qualities of movement of locomotor activities.

2.4—Describes potential injuries related to physical activity from prepuberty through puberty.

2.5—Describes the critical elements for walk, run, hop, skip, jump for distance, jump for height, leap, gallop, and slide.

3.1—Engages in moderate physical activity for 30 minutes 4 days each week.

3.2—Lists extracurricular physical activities available at school on the weekends.

4.1—Works toward a health-enhancing level of physical fitness.

4.2—Describes the FITT concepts related to cardiorespiratory endurance.

5.1—Demonstrates inclusive skills.

5.2—Acts responsibly when confronted by negative peer pressure.

6.1—Describes the development of games using locomotor skills in the United States during the 17th and 18th centuries.

6.2—Expresses personal feelings through a movement-based routine that involves locomotor skills.

6.3—Chooses to engage in skill competencies found in locomotor activities at a level that leads to personal satisfaction, success, and enjoyment.

6.4—Describes the short-term cardiorespiratory benefits derived from participation in physical activity.

Unit 4 Assessments

1.0—Structured observation (days 1-12, 14-15)

2.1—Quiz (day 13)

2.2—Quiz (day 13)

2.3—Quiz (day 13)

2.4—Quiz (day 13)

2.5—Quiz (day 13)

3.1—Log (assigned on day 1; collected on day 15)

3.2—List (assigned on day 1; collected on day 15)

4.1—Structured observation (days 1-12, 14-15)

4.2—Quiz (day 13)

5.1—Structured observation (days 4-12, 14-15)

5.2—Structured observation (days 8-12, 14-15)

6.1—Project (assigned on day 1; collected on day 15)

6.2—Project (assigned on day 14; collected on day 15)

6.3—Structured observation (days 3-12, 14-15)

6.4—Quiz (day 13)

Resources

Tinikling music

Music for jumping rope and locomotor movements

Fit Kids' Classroom Workout DVD (Human Kinetics)

Health-Related Fitness: Tutorial and Portfolio (Bonnie's Fitware, Inc.)

Middle School Physical Education Portfolio (Bonnie's Fitware, Inc.)

Fifth grade locomotor task cards

Tinikling CD (Bonnie's Fitware, Inc.)

Short Jump Ropes CD (Bonnie's Fitware, Inc.)

Long Jump Ropes CD (Bonnie's Fitware, Inc.)

Fifth grade unit 4 posters (Bonnie's Fitware, Inc.—included in the Middle School Detailed Lesson Plans)

Fitness posters (Bonnie's Fitware, Inc.—included in the Middle School Detailed Lesson Plans)

Qualities of Movement chart (Bonnie's Fitware, Inc.—included in the Middle School Detailed Lesson Plans)

Equipment

Heart monitors

Tinikling poles or jump bands (elastic bands)

Short jump ropes

Long jump ropes

Locomotor Skills

Sliding	Galloping	Running
Skipping	Horizontal jumping	Walking
Hopping	Leaping	Vertical jumping

Tinikling Skills

Striker skills	Crossover step	Side jump
Basic step	Circle poles	Cross step
Rocker step	Fast trot	Straddle step

Long Jump Rope Skills

Basic jump	Toss and catch ball	Double dutch
Front entry	Dribble ball	Short/long rope
Back entry	Eggbeater	

Short Jump Rope Skills

Basic jump forward	Chorus	Continuous front cross
Basic jump backward	Cross country	Caboose and engine
Jogging step	Skier	Engine and caboose
Straddle step	Continuous side-swing	

Unit 4 Outline

DAY 1

Introduce unit.

Randomly assign students to working groups of four.

Describe how internal force is generated. 2.2

Have students hold a muscle (e.g., biceps) and feel how the muscles moves when bending and extending the arm. 2.2

Have students record in their notebooks how internal force is generated. 2.2

Review (from grades K to 4) four of the locomotor skills (hopping, skipping, galloping, sliding—see figure 4.12). 1.0, 2.5

Have students record in their notebooks the critical elements for the four locomotor skills or provide students with a handout. 2.5

Review (from grades K to 4) the qualities of movement related to locomotor activities. 2.3

Have students record in their notebooks the qualities of movement related to locomotor activities. 2.3

Have students perform a warm-up. (Assessment opportunity: structured observation 4.1)

Have students perform the four locomotor skills while you play music. (Assessment opportunity: structured observation 1.0)

(continued)

a   *b*

c

Figure 14.12   *(a)* Galloping, *(b)* leaping, and *(c)* sliding.

Unit 4 Outline *(continued)*

DAY 1 *(continued)*

Have students perform the four locomotor skills, demonstrating different qualities of movement while you play music. (Assessment opportunity: structured observation 1.0) 2.3

Lead students through a cool-down and flexibility exercises appropriate to the physical activity level of the lesson. (Assessment opportunity: structured observation 4.1)

Have students discuss the qualities of movement they observed while performing locomotor movements. 2.3

Debrief with students the critical elements for the four locomotor skills. 2.5

Assign unit-long homework:

- Have students research and write a report on games that were developed in the United States during the 17th and 18th centuries that used only locomotor skills. (Assessment assignment opportunity: report 6.1)
- Have students keep a log of daily activity. (Assessment assignment opportunity: log 3.1)
- Have students create a list of extracurricular physical activities available at school on the weekends. (Assessment assignment opportunity: list 3.2)

DAY 2

Describe the concepts of frequency, intensity, time, and type (FITT) as they relate to cardiorespiratory endurance. 4.2

Have students create a chart in their notebooks showing the concepts of frequency, intensity, time, and type as they relate to cardiorespiratory endurance. 4.2

Describe short-term cardiorespiratory benefits derived from participation in physical activity. 6.4

Have student record in their notebooks the short-term cardiorespiratory benefits derived from participation in physical activity. 6.4

Have students perform a warm-up along with muscular strength and muscular endurance exercises. (Assessment opportunity: structured observation 4.1)

Review (from grades K to 4) four of the locomotor skills (walking, running, jumping, leaping). 1.0, 2.5

Have students record the critical elements for the four locomotor skills in their notebooks or provide them with a handout (reproduce task cards). 2.5

Review the qualities of movement related to locomotor activities. 2.3

Have students perform the four locomotor skills while you play music. (Assessment opportunity: structured observation 1.0)

Have students perform the four locomotor skills demonstrating different qualities of movement while you play music. (Assessment opportunity: structured observation 1.0) 2.3

Have students participate in Fit Kids' Classroom Workout DVD. (Assessment opportunity: structured observation 4.1)

Lead students through a cool-down and flexibility exercises appropriate to the physical activity level of the lesson. (Assessment opportunity: structured observation 4.1)

Have students discuss the qualities of movement they observed during the workout. 2.3

DAY 3

Display posters.

Discuss what it means to engage in skill competencies at all levels that lead to personal satisfaction, success, and enjoyment. 6.3

Have students record the information in their notebooks. 6.3

Review FITT concepts related to cardiorespiratory endurance. 4.2

Review cardiorespiratory benefits. 6.4

DAY 3 (continued)

Have students perform a warm-up. (Assessment opportunity: structured observation 4.1)

Review the vertical jump. 1.0

Have students practice the vertical jump. 1.0

Demonstrate the basic jump forward and the basic jump backward for short ropes using the Short Jump Rope CD. 1.0, 2.5

Have pairs practice the basic jump forward and the basic jump backward using short ropes. (Assessment opportunity: structured observation 1.0, 6.3)

Lead students through a cool-down and flexibility exercises appropriate to the physical activity level of the lesson. (Assessment opportunity: structured observation 4.1)

Have students discuss how internal force is generated when jumping rope. 2.2

DAY 4

Identify behaviors that are supportive and inclusive of others. 5.1

Have student record in their notebooks the behaviors that are supportive and inclusive of others. 5.1

Demonstrate the basic jump and the front and back entries for long ropes using the Long Jump Rope CD. 1.0, 2.5

Have students brainstorm ways to make long jump roping inclusive of others. 5.1

Have students perform a warm-up along with muscular strength and muscular endurance exercises. (Assessment opportunity: structured observation 4.1)

Have students, in groups of four, practice the basic jump and the front and back entries for long ropes. (Assessment opportunity: structured observation 1.0, 5.1, 6.3)

Lead students through a cool-down and flexibility exercises appropriate to the physical activity level of the lesson. (Assessment opportunity: structured observation 4.1)

Have students discuss how internal force is generated when jumping rope. 2.2

Have students discuss the qualities of movement they observed while jumping rope. 2.3

DAY 5

Explain the features of whole and part practice. 2.1

Have students record the features of whole and part practice in their notebooks. 2.1

Introduce Tinikling and its origin using the Tinikling CD. 1.0

Have students perform a warm-up. (Assessment opportunity: structured observation 4.1)

Demonstrate striker skills for Tinikling or ender skills for jump bands. 1.0, 2.5

Have students practice striker skills. (Assessment opportunity: structured observation 1.0, 5.1, 6.3)

Demonstrate the basic step for Tinikling using the Tinikling CD. 1.0, 2.5

Have students brainstorm ways to make Tinikling activities inclusive of others. 5.1

Have students practice striker skills and the basic jump for Tinikling. (Assessment opportunity: structured observation 1.0, 5.1, 6.3)

Lead students through a cool-down and flexibility exercises appropriate to the physical activity level of the lesson. (Assessment opportunity: structured observation 4.1)

Have students discuss the qualities of movement they observed while Tinikling. 2.3

Have students discuss whether whole or part practice is best when learning or improving Tinikling skills. 2.1

(continued)

Unit 4 Outline (continued)

DAY 6

Describe the potential injuries related to physical activity from prepuberty through puberty. 2.4

Have students record in their notebooks the potential injuries related to physical activity. 2.4

Introduce new short jump rope skills (jogging step and straddle step) using the Short Jump Rope CD. 1.0, 2.5

Introduce new Tinikling skills (rocker step and crossover step) using the Tinikling CD. 1.0, 2.5

Have students brainstorm ways to make short jump roping inclusive of others. 5.1

Have students perform a warm-up. (Assessment opportunity: structured observation 4.1)

Have students rotate through the following stations (use task cards at each station):

- Tinikling: rocker step and crossover step
- Short ropes: jogging step and straddle step
- Long ropes: basic jump (Assessment opportunity: structured observation 1.0, 5.1, 6.3)

Lead students through a cool-down and flexibility exercises appropriate to the physical activity level of the lesson. (Assessment opportunity: structured observation 4.1)

Have students discuss potential injuries related to short rope jumping. 2.4

DAY 7

Review the potential injuries related to physical activity from prepuberty through puberty. 2.4

Have students perform a warm-up along with muscular strength and muscular endurance exercises. (Assessment opportunity: structured observation 4.1)

Introduce new long jump rope skills (toss and catch ball) using the Long Jump Rope CD. 1.0, 2.5

Introduce new short jump rope skills (chorus and cross country) using the Short Jump Rope CD. 1.0, 2.5

Have students rotate through the following stations (use task cards at each station):

- Tinikling: rocker step and crossover step
- Short ropes: jogging step, straddle step, chorus, and cross country
- Long ropes: basic jump and toss and catch ball (Assessment opportunity: structured observation 1.0, 5.1, 6.3)

Lead students through a cool-down and flexibility exercises appropriate to the physical activity level of the lesson. (Assessment opportunity: structured observation 4.1)

Have students discuss potential injuries related to long rope jumping. 2.4

DAY 8

Define peer pressure. 5.2

Have students record the definition of peer pressure in their notebooks. 5.2

Introduce new short jump rope skills (skier and continuous side-swing open) using the Short Jump Rope CD. 1.0, 2.5

Introduce new Tinikling skills (circle poles and fast trot step) using the Tinikling CD. 1.0, 2.5

Have students perform a warm-up. (Assessment opportunity: structured observation 4.1)

Have students rotate through stations (use task cards at each station):

- Tinikling: circle poles step and fast trot step
- Short ropes: skier, continuous side-swing open, chorus, and cross country
- Long ropes: toss and catch ball and basic jump (Assessment opportunity: structured observation 1.0, 5.1, 5.2, 6.3)

Lead students through a cool-down and flexibility exercises appropriate to the physical activity level of the lesson. (Assessment opportunity: structured observation 4.1)

Have students discuss potential injuries related to Tinikling. 2.4

DAY 9

Review peer pressure. 5.2

Introduce new short jump rope skills (continuous front cross) using the Short Jump Rope CD. 1.0, 2.5

Introduce new long jump rope skills (dribble ball) using the Long Jump Rope CD. 1.0, 2.5

Have students perform a warm-up along with muscular strength and muscular endurance exercises. (Assessment opportunity: structured observation 4.1)

Have students rotate through stations (use task cards at each station):

- Tinikling: circle poles, rocker, cross over, and fast trot step
- Short ropes: skier, continuous side-swing open, continuous front cross, and cross country
- Long ropes: toss and catch ball and dribble ball (Assessment opportunity: structured observation 1.0, 5.1, 5.2, 6.3)

Lead students through a cool-down and flexibility exercises appropriate to the physical activity level of the lesson. (Assessment opportunity: structured observation 4.1)

DAY 10

Describe the negative effect that peer pressure can have on someone's behavior. 5.2

Have students record in their notebooks the negative effect that peer pressure can have on someone's behavior. 5.2

Introduce new long jump rope skills (eggbeater) using the Long Jump Rope CD. 1.0, 2.5

Introduce new Tinikling skills (side jump, cross step, and straddle step) using the Tinikling CD. 1.0, 2.5

Have students perform a warm-up. (Assessment opportunity: structured observation 4.1)

Have students rotate through stations (use task cards at each station):

- Tinikling: side jump, cross step, circle poles step, and straddle step.
- Short ropes: skier, continuous side-swing open, continuous front cross, and cross country
- Long ropes: dribble ball and eggbeater (Assessment opportunity: structured observation 1.0, 5.1, 5.2, 6.3)

Lead students through a cool-down and flexibility exercises appropriate to the physical activity level of the lesson. (Assessment opportunity: structured observation 4.1)

DAY 11

Review the negative effect that peer pressure can have on someone's behavior. 5.2

Review long jump rope skills (eggbeater) using the Long Jump Rope CD. 1.0, 2.5

Introduce new short jump rope skills (caboose and engine, engine and caboose) using the Short Jump Rope CD. 1.0, 2.5

Have students perform a warm-up. (Assessment opportunity: structured observation 4.1)

Have students rotate through stations (use task cards at each station):

- Tinikling: side jump, cross step, circle poles step, and straddle step
- Short ropes: caboose and engine, engine and caboose, continuous front cross, and skier
- Long ropes: dribble ball and eggbeater (Assessment opportunity: structured observation 1.0, 5.1, 5.2, 6.3)

Lead students through a cool-down and flexibility exercises appropriate to the physical activity level of the lesson. (Assessment opportunity: structured observation 4.1)

(continued)

Unit 4 Outline *(continued)*

DAY 12

Introduce new long jump rope skills (double dutch and short/long rope) using the Long Jump Rope CD. 1.0, 2.5

Have students perform a warm-up along with muscular strength and muscular endurance exercises. (Assessment opportunity: structured observation 4.1)

Have students rotate through stations (use task cards at each station):

- Tinikling: cross step, circle poles step, straddle step, and fast trot
- Short ropes: caboose and engine, engine and caboose, continuous front cross, and cross country
- Long ropes: double dutch and short/long rope (Assessment opportunity: structured observation 1.0, 5.1, 5.2, 6.3)

Lead students through a cool-down and flexibility exercises appropriate to the physical activity level of the lesson. (Assessment opportunity: structured observation 4.1)

Review material for tomorrow's quiz (or handout quiz if you would like for it to be a take-home quiz). 2.1, 2.2, 2.3, 2.4, 2.5, 4.2, 6.4

DAY 13

Have students take the quiz. (Assessment opportunity: quiz 2.1, 2.2, 2.3, 2.4, 2.5, 4.2, 6.4)

Figure 14.13   Jump rope routine.

DAY 14

Have students perform a warm-up along with muscular strength and muscular endurance exercises. (Assessment opportunity: structured observation 4.1)

Have students, in groups of four, design a creative jump rope or Tinikling routine (figures 14.13 and 14. 14) that includes changes in speed and direction to express feelings. (Assessment assignment opportunity: project 6.2)

Have the students view their routine using the Short Jump Rope CD, Long Jump Rope CD, or Tinikling CD. 6.2

Have students practice their routine. 6.2

Lead students through a cool-down and flexibility exercises appropriate to the physical activity level of the lesson. (Assessment opportunity: structured observation 4.1)

(continued)

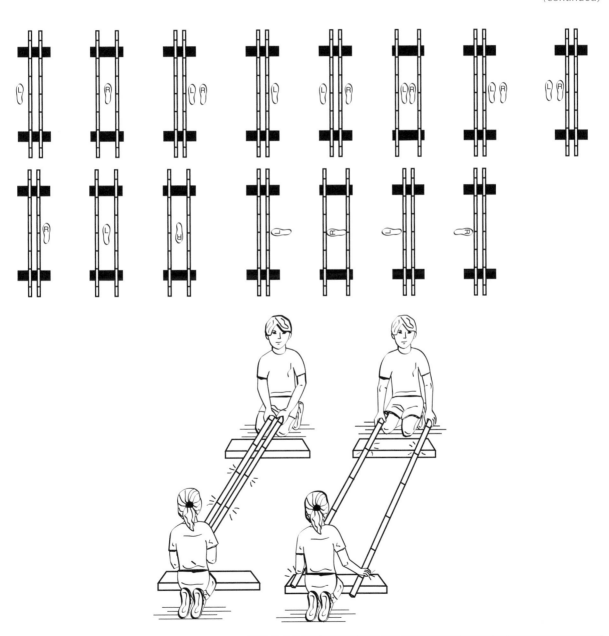

Figure 14.14   Tinikling routine.

Unit 4 Outline *(continued)*

DAY 15

Have students perform a warm-up. (Assessment opportunity: structured observation 4.1)

Have students, in groups of four, demonstrate their locomotor routines. (Assessment opportunity: structured observation 1.0, 5.1, 5.2, 6.3)

Lead students through a cool-down and flexibility exercises appropriate to the physical activity level of the lesson. (Assessment opportunity: structured observation 4.1)

Collect written routines. (Assessment opportunity: project 6.2)

Collect history reports. (Assessment opportunity: report 6.1)

Collect activity logs. (Assessment opportunity: log 3.1)

Collect lists of extracurricular activities available at school on the weekends. (Assessment opportunity: list 3.2)

Throwing and Catching — Unit 5

In this, our third skills theme unit, we move to the manipulation of objects. The overhand throw is one of the most common skills used in sport. I teach this unit to ensure that the students have the correct throwing and catching technique; then I extend that skill to both throwing for distance and throwing for accuracy. Once the students have acquired some distance and accuracy, I have them throw at moving objects and finally throw while they are moving. We then apply the skill to a variety of movement activities, including a modified team handball game. Finally, I have the students create their own ball-handling routines to Globetrotter music. You can conduct this unit on grass, on blacktop, or in a gymnasium.

Unit 5 Standards

1.0—Demonstrates speed and accuracy using the mature form for a throw, catch, chest pass, jump stop, two-step stop, and pivot.

2.1—Explains the appropriate situations for whole practice and for part practice.

2.2—Describes external forces.

2.3—Describes game tactics in a competitive game setting.

2.4—Describes the positive impact of physical changes on physical performance from prepuberty through puberty.

2.5—Describes the critical elements for a throw, catch, chest pass, jump stop, two-step stop, and pivot.

3.1—Engages in moderate physical activity for 30 minutes 5 days each week.

3.2—Describes the extracurricular physical activities available in the school setting related to throwing and catching.

4.1—Works toward a health-enhancing level of physical fitness.

4.2—Describes the FITT concepts for body composition.

5.1—Modifies throwing and catching tasks to fit the needs of a differently abled student.

5.2—Accepts responsibility for personal safety during throwing and catching activities.

6.1—Describes the development of games using throwing and catching in the United States during the 17th and 18th centuries.

6.2—Expresses personal feelings through a ball-handling routine.

6.3—Chooses to engage in throwing and catching skill competencies at a level that leads to personal satisfaction, success, and enjoyment.

6.4—Describes the short-term body composition benefits derived from participation in physical activity.

Unit 5 Assessments

1.0—Structured observation (days 1-14)

2.1—Quiz (day 15)

2.2—Quiz (day 15)

2.3—Quiz (day 15)

2.4—Quiz (day 15)

2.5—Quiz (day 15)

3.1—Log (assigned on day 1; collected on day 15)

3.2—Essay (assigned on day 1; collected on day 15)

4.1—Structured observation (days 1-14)

4.2—Quiz (day 15)

5.1—Structured observation (days 1-14)

5.2—Structured observation (days 1-14)

6.1—Report (assigned on day 1; collected on day 15)

6.2—Project (assigned on day 12; collected on day 14)

6.3—Structured observation (days 1-14)

6.4—Quiz (day 15)

Resources

Harlem Globetrotters music for routine (Bonnie's Fitware, Inc.)

Health-Related Fitness: Tutorial and Portfolio (Bonnie's Fitware, Inc.)

Middle School Physical Education Portfolio (Bonnie's Fitware, Inc.)

Fifth grade overhand throwing task cards (Bonnie's Fitware, Inc.)

Fifth grade unit 5 posters (Bonnie's Fitware, Inc.—included in the Middle School Detailed Lesson Plans)

Fitness posters (Bonnie's Fitware, Inc.—included in the Middle School Detailed Lesson Plans)

Qualities of Movement chart (Bonnie's Fitware, Inc.—included in the Middle School Detailed Lesson Plans)

Equipment

Variety of throwing objects (playground balls, footballs, fleece balls, tennis balls, beanbags)

Variety of targets

Games

Goalie Ball

4-on-4 team handball

Pickle

Unit 5 Outline

DAY 1

Introduce unit.

Explain the safety procedures for throwing and catching activities. 5.2

Have students record in their notebooks the safety procedures for throwing and catching activities. 5.2

Explain that engaging in throwing and catching skill practice can lead to personal satisfaction, success, and enjoyment. 6.3

Have students brainstorm ways to modify throwing and catching tasks to fit the needs of a differently abled student. 5.1

Assign students to heterogeneous working groups of four.

Have students perform a warm-up along with a cardiorespiratory workout. (Assessment opportunity: structured observation 4.1)

Demonstrate the one-handed overhand throw and catch. 1.0, 2.5

Have students practice the overhand throw and catch with a partner while counting the number of successful throws and catches (see figure 14.15 to see the differences between an overhand throw, underhand throw, and sidearm throw). (Assessment opportunity: structured observation 1.0, 5.1, 5.2, 6.3)

Review qualities of movement using the qualities of movement poster. 6.2

Have students throw and catch with a partner, using various qualities of movement (e.g., throwing the ball fast, low, high). (Assessment opportunity: structured observation 1.0, 5.1, 5.2, 6.3)

Lead students through a cool-down and flexibility exercises appropriate to the physical activity level of the lesson. (Assessment opportunity: structured observation 4.1)

Assign unit-long homework:

- Have students research and write a description of dancing in the United States during the 17th and 18th centuries. (Assessment assignment opportunity: report 6.1)

- Have students determine a goal for physical activity and keep a log of daily activity. (Assessment assignment opportunity: log 3.1)
- Have students write a description about the extracurricular physical activities available in the school setting related to throwing and catching. (Assessment assignment opportunity: essay 3.2)

a

Figure 14.15 *(a)* Underhand throw; *(b)* sidearm throw; *(c)* overhand throw.

Figure 14.15   *(continued)*

Display posters.

Review the safety procedures for throwing and catching activities. 5.2

Review the overhand throw and catch. 1.0

Explain the appropriate situations for whole practice and for part practice. 2.1

Have students record in their notebooks the appropriate situations for whole practice and for part practice. 2.1

Have students perform a warm-up along with muscular strength and muscular endurance exercises. (Assessment opportunity: structured observation 4.1)

Review the overhand throw and catch. 1.0

Have students practice the overhand throw and catch with a partner while counting the number of successful throws and catches. (Assessment opportunity: structured observation 1.0, 5.1, 5.2, 6.3)

Demonstrate the underhand toss and fielding a ground ball. 1.0

Have students throw (overhand and underhand) and catch (or field) with a partner, using various qualities of movement (e.g., throwing the ball fast, low, high). (Assessment opportunity: structured observation 1.0, 5.1, 5.2, 6.3)

Put students into groups of three and have two of the students throw (overhand and underhand) and catch while the third provides feedback (rotate positions). (Assessment opportunity: structured observation 1.0, 5.1, 5.2, 6.3)

Lead students through a cool-down and flexibility exercises appropriate to the physical activity level of the lesson. (Assessment opportunity: structured observation 4.1)

(continued)

Unit 5 Outline *(continued)*

DAY 3

Describe the short-term body composition benefits derived from participation in physical activity. 6.4

Have students record in their notebooks the short-term body composition benefits derived from participation in physical activity. 6.4

Discuss the concepts of frequency, intensity, time, and type as they relate to body composition (use Health-Related Fitness: Tutorial and Portfolio). 4.2

Have students record in their notebooks the FITT concepts related to body composition. 4.2

Discuss the relationship between intake and output of calories and the role of fluid intake during physical activity. 4.2

Have students record in their notebooks the relationship between intake and output of calories and the role of fluid intake during physical activity. 4.2

Have students perform a warm-up along with a cardiorespiratory workout. (Assessment opportunity: structured observation 4.1)

Review overhand and underhand throw and catch. 1.0, 2.5

Have students throw (overhand and underhand) and catch (or field) with a partner, using various qualities of movement (e.g., throwing the ball fast, low, high). (Assessment opportunity: structured observation 1.0, 5.1, 5.2, 6.3)

Demonstrate and describe the two-handed overhead pass. 1.0, 2.5

Have students practice the two-handed overhead pass and catch while counting the number of successful passes and catches. (Assessment opportunity: structured observation 1.0, 5.1, 5.2, 6.3)

Demonstrate and describe the football pass. 1.0, 2.5

Have students practice passing and catching the football. (Assessment opportunity: structured observation 1.0, 5.1, 5.2, 6.3)

Lead students through a cool-down and flexibility exercises appropriate to the physical activity level of the lesson. (Assessment opportunity: structured observation 4.1)

DAY 4

Describe external forces. 2.2

Have students record in their notebooks the information on external forces. 2.2

Review the appropriate situations for whole practice. 2.1

Review the appropriate situations for part practice. 2.1

Have students perform a warm-up along with muscular strength and muscular endurance exercises. (Assessment opportunity: structured observation 4.1)

Demonstrate the chest pass. 1.0

Have students practice the chest pass and catch. 1.0

Demonstrate throwing at a moving target or player. 1.0, 2.5

Have students practice throwing at a moving target. (Assessment opportunity: structured observation 1.0, 5.1, 5.2, 6.3)

Demonstrate the jump-stop and pivot. 1.0, 2.5

Have students practice throwing overhand at moving players who catch the ball, perform a jump-stop, and then pivot. (Assessment opportunity: structured observation 1.0, 5.1, 5.2, 6.3)

Lead students through a cool-down and flexibility exercises appropriate to the physical activity level of the lesson. (Assessment opportunity: structured observation 4.1)

DAY 5	Review external forces. 2.2 Describe the positive impact of physical changes on physical performance from prepuberty through puberty. 2.4 Have students record in their notebooks the positive impact of physical changes on physical performance from prepuberty through puberty. 2.4 Have students perform a warm-up along with a cardiorespiratory workout. (Assessment opportunity: structured observation 4.1) Demonstrate the two-step stop and pivot. 1.0, 2.5 Have students practice passing to moving players who catch the ball, then perform a two-step stop and pivot. (Assessment opportunity: structured observation 1.0, 5.1, 5.2, 6.3) Put students in groups of three and have two play Goalie Ball using overhand throws while the third retrieves the ball. (Assessment opportunity: structured observation 1.0, 5.1, 5.2, 6.3) Lead students through a cool-down and flexibility exercises appropriate to the physical activity level of the lesson. (Assessment opportunity: structured observation 4.1)
DAY 6	Review the short-term body composition benefits derived from participation in physical activity. 6.4 Review the frequency, intensity, time, and type concepts related to body composition (use Health-Related Fitness: Tutorial and Portfolio). 4.2 Review the relationship between intake and output of calories and the role of water during physical activity. 4.2 Have students perform a warm-up along with a cardiorespiratory workout. (Assessment opportunity: structured observation 4.1) Demonstrate throwing overhand (one handed) at a stationary target while moving. 1.0, 2.5 Have students practice throwing overhand (one handed) at a stationary target. (Assessment opportunity: structured observation 1.0, 5.1, 5.2, 6.3) Have students play Pickle. (Assessment opportunity: structured observation 1.0, 5.1, 5.2, 6.3) Demonstrate throwing overhand (one handed) at a moving target while moving. (Assessment opportunity: structured observation 1.0, 5.1, 5.2, 6.3) Have students in pairs practice throwing (one handed) and catching while both are moving. (Assessment opportunity: structured observation 1.0, 5.1, 5.2, 6.3) Demonstrate throwing overhand (two handed) at a moving target while moving. (Assessment opportunity: structured observation 1.0, 5.1, 5.2, 6.3) Have students in pairs perform an overhand throw (one or two hands) and catch using a 6-inch playground ball while moving up and down the field. (Assessment opportunity: structured observation 1.0, 5.1, 5.2, 6.3) Lead students through a cool-down and flexibility exercises appropriate to the physical activity level of the lesson. (Assessment opportunity: structured observation 4.1)
DAY 7	Have students perform a warm-up along with muscular strength and muscular endurance exercises. (Assessment opportunity: structured observation 4.1) Review throwing and catching. 1.0, 2.5 Have students rotate through a variety of stations: throwing overhand (one handed) at stationary targets (fleece ball); Goalie Ball with two-hand overhand throw (8.5-inch playground ball); passing the football at stationary targets (football); throwing underhand and fielding with a partner (tennis ball); Pickle (fleece ball); the sequence of chest pass, catch, stop (jump stop or two step), and pivot (8.5-inch playground ball); throwing overhand with one or two hands at moving targets (6-inch playground ball); throwing overhand with one or two hands while moving (6-inch playground ball); throwing overhand with one or two hands at a moving target while moving (6-inch playground ball). (Assessment opportunity: structured observation 1.0, 5.1, 5.2, 6.3) Lead students through a cool-down and flexibility exercises appropriate to the physical activity level of the lesson. (Assessment opportunity: structured observation 4.1)

(continued)

Unit 5 Outline *(continued)*

DAY 8

Have students perform a warm-up along with a cardiorespiratory workout. (Assessment opportunity: structured observation 4.1)

Review the overhand throw and catch. 1.0, 2.5

Have students rotate through a variety of stations: throwing overhand (one handed) at stationary targets (fleece ball); throwing overhand (two hands) at stationary targets (8.5-inch playground ball); passing the football at stationary targets (football); throwing underhand and fielding with a partner (tennis ball); Pickle (fleece ball); the sequence of chest pass, catch, stop (jump stop or two step), and pivot (8.5-inch playground ball); throwing overhand with one or two hands at moving targets (6-inch playground ball); throwing overhand with one or two hands while moving (6-inch playground ball); throwing overhand with one or two hands at a moving target while moving (6-inch playground ball). (Assessment opportunity: structured observation 1.0, 5.1, 5.2, 6.3)

Lead students through a cool-down and flexibility exercises appropriate to the physical activity level of the lesson. (Assessment opportunity: structured observation 4.1)

DAY 9

Describe game tactics in a competitive game setting. 2.3

Have students record information about game tactics in their notebooks. 2.3

Have students perform a warm-up along with muscular strength and muscular endurance exercises. (Assessment opportunity: structured observation 4.1)

Introduce modified 4-on-4 team handball (no dribbling). 2.3

Have students play modified 4-on-4 team handball, scoring by throwing the ball into the goal area. (Assessment opportunity: structured observation 1.0, 5.1, 5.2, 6.3)

Lead students through a cool-down and flexibility exercises appropriate to the physical activity level of the lesson. (Assessment opportunity: structured observation 4.1)

DAY 10

Review game tactics in a competitive game setting. 2.3

Have students perform a warm-up along with a cardiorespiratory workout. (Assessment opportunity: structured observation 4.1)

Review modified 4-on-4 team handball (no dribbling). 2.3

Have students play modified 4-on-4 team handball, scoring by throwing the ball into the goal area. (Assessment opportunity: structured observation 1.0, 5.1, 5.2, 6.3)

Lead students through a cool-down and flexibility exercises appropriate to the physical activity level of the lesson. (Assessment opportunity: structured observation 4.1)

DAY 11

Review game tactics in a competitive game setting. 2.3

Have students perform a warm-up along with a cardiorespiratory workout. (Assessment opportunity: structured observation 4.1)

Review modified 4-on-4 team handball (no dribbling). 2.3

Have students play modified 4-on-4 team handball, scoring by throwing the ball into the goal area. (Assessment opportunity: structured observation 1.0, 5.1, 5.2, 6.3)

Lead students through a cool-down and flexibility exercises appropriate to the physical activity level of the lesson. (Assessment opportunity: structured observation 4.1)

DAY 12

Have students perform a warm-up along with muscular strength and muscular endurance exercises. (Assessment opportunity: structured observation 4.1)

Demonstrate circle waist, circle both knees, circle head, and circle knee. 6.2

Have students practice ball-handling activities. (Assessment opportunity: structured observation 1.0, 5.1, 5.2, 6.3)

Have students in pairs create a ball-handling routine to go along with the Harlem Globetrotters music that expresses their personal feelings. (Assessment assignment opportunity: project 6.2)

Lead students through a cool-down and flexibility exercises appropriate to the physical activity level of the lesson. (Assessment opportunity: structured observation 4.1)

DAY 13

Have students perform a warm-up along with a cardiorespiratory workout. (Assessment opportunity: structured observation 4.1)

Demonstrate circle lifted leg, speed switch, figure eight one bounce, and two-hand control. 6.2

Have students in pairs work on their routines. 1.0, 5.1, 5.2, 6.2

Lead students through a cool-down and flexibility exercises appropriate to the physical activity level of the lesson. (Assessment opportunity: structured observation 4.1)

DAY 14

Have students perform a warm-up along with muscular strength and muscular endurance exercises. (Assessment opportunity: structured observation 4.1)

Have students in pairs work on their routines. 1.0, 5.1, 5.2, 6.2

Have each pair teach their ball-handling routine to another pair, including an explanation about how the routine expresses their feelings. (Assessment opportunity: project 6.2)

Lead students through a cool-down and flexibility exercises appropriate to the physical activity level of the lesson. (Assessment opportunity: structured observation 4.1)

Review material for tomorrow's quiz (or hand out quiz if you would like for it to be a take-home quiz). 2.1, 2.2, 2.3, 2.4, 2.5, 4.2, 6.4

DAY 15

Have students take the quiz. (Assessment opportunity: quiz 2.1, 2.2, 2.3, 2.4, 2.5, 4.2, 6.4)

Collect student activity logs. (Assessment opportunity: log 3.1)

Collect reports on the development of games using throwing and catching in the United States during the 17th and 18th centuries. (Assessment opportunity: report 6.1)

Collect essays about the extracurricular physical activities available in the school setting related to throwing and catching. (Assessment opportunity: essay 3.2)

Throwing and Catching With Implements

~ Unit 6

In this, our fourth skills theme unit, we move on to the manipulation of objects using an implement. The implement can be a bleach bottle, a scoop, or a lacrosse stick. I teach this unit to ensure that the students have the correct overhand throw technique using an implement; then I extend that skill to both throwing for distance and throwing for accuracy. Once the students have acquired some distance and accuracy, I have them explore throwing at moving objects and, finally, throwing while they are moving. We then apply the skill in a variety of games including modified lacrosse. You can conduct this unit on grass, on blacktop, or in a gymnasium.

Unit 6 Standards

1.0—Demonstrates speed and accuracy using the mature form for throwing and catching objects using an implement.

2.1—Explains the features of mass and distributed practice.

2.2—Describes how external force affects object manipulation.

2.3—Describes how space is used as a basic game tactic.

2.4—Describes the negative impact of physical changes on physical performance from prepuberty through puberty.

2.5—Describes the critical elements for throwing and catching objects using an implement.

3.1—Engages in moderate physical activity for 35 minutes 5 days each week.

3.2—Describes the extracurricular physical activities available in the school setting related to throwing and catching with an implement.

4.1—Works toward a health-enhancing level of physical fitness.

4.2—Creates a 1-day cardiorespiratory endurance improvement plan.

5.1—Modifies throwing and catching with an implement tasks to fit the needs of a differently abled student.

5.2—Accepts responsibility for personal safety during throwing and catching with implement activities.

6.1—Describes the development of games using throwing and catching with an implement in the United States during the 17th and 18th centuries.

6.2—Expresses personal feelings through a movement-based routine that involves throwing and catching with an implement.

6.3—Chooses to engage in throwing and catching with an implement skill competencies at a level that leads to personal satisfaction, success, and enjoyment.

6.4—Describes the short-term muscular endurance benefits derived from participation in physical activity.

Unit 6 Assessments

1.0—Structured observation (days 1-14)

2.1—Quiz (day 15)

2.2—Quiz (day 15)

2.3—Quiz (day 15)

2.4—Quiz (day 15)

2.5—Quiz (day 15)

3.1—Log (assigned on day 1; collected on day 15)

3.2—Essay (assigned on day 1; collected on day 15)

4.1—Structured observation (days 1-14)

4.2—Project (assigned on day 3; collected on day 15)

5.1—Structured observation (days 1-14)

5.2—Structured observation (days 1-14)

6.1—Report (assigned on day 1; collected on day 15)

6.2—Project (assigned on day 12; collected on day 15)

6.3—Structured observation (days 1-14)

6.4—Quiz (day 15)

Resources

Globetrotters music for routines (Bonnie's Fitware, Inc.)

Health-Related Fitness: Tutorial and Portfolio (Bonnie's Fitware, Inc.)

Middle School Physical Education Portfolio (Bonnie's Fitware, Inc.)

Fifth grade throwing and catching with an implement task cards (Bonnie's Fitware, Inc.)

Fifth grade unit 6 posters (Bonnie's Fitware, Inc.—included in the Middle School Detailed Lesson Plans)

Fitness posters (Bonnie's Fitware, Inc.—included in the Middle School Detailed Lesson Plans)

Qualities of Movement chart (Bonnie's Fitware, Inc.—included in the Middle School Detailed Lesson Plans)

Equipment

Variety of objects (e.g., team handballs, fleece balls, beanbags, softballs, footballs, and basketballs)

Variety of throwing implements (bleach bottles, lacrosse sticks, scoops)

Variety of targets or goals to throw the objects at

Games

Goalie Ball

Keep Away

Modified 4-on-4 lacrosse

Unit 6 Outline

DAY 1

Introduce unit.

Explain the rules, procedures, and etiquette for safely participating in throwing activities that involve an implement. 5.2

Have students record the rules, procedures, and etiquette for safely participating in throwing activities that involve an implement. 5.2

Have students brainstorm modifying throwing and catching using an implement to fit the needs of a differently abled student. 5.1

Explain that skill competency in throwing and catching can lead to personal satisfaction, success, and enjoyment. 6.3

Assign students to heterogeneous working groups of four.

Have students perform a warm-up along with a cardiorespiratory workout. (Assessment opportunity: structured observation 4.1)

Have students experiment with throwing to and catching by themselves using scoops and a beanbag (see figure 14.16). (Assessment opportunity: structured observation 1.0, 5.1, 5.2, 6.3)

Demonstrate the underhand throw and catch using a scoop. 1.0, 2.5

Have students practice the underhand throw and catch using a scoop with a partner while counting the number of successful throws and catches in a row. (Assessment opportunity: structured observation 1.0, 5.1, 5.2, 6.3)

Review qualities of movement. 6.2

Have students throw and catch using a scoop with a partner, using various qualities of movement (e.g., throwing the ball fast, low, high). (Assessment opportunity: structured observation 1.0, 5.1, 5.2, 6.2, 6.3)

Lead students through a cool-down and flexibility exercises appropriate to the physical activity level of the lesson. (Assessment opportunity: structured observation 4.1)

Assign unit-long homework:

- Have students research and write a description of the development of games using throwing and catching with an implement in the United States during the 17th and 18th centuries. (Assessment assignment opportunity: report 6.1)

- Have students keep a log of daily activity. (Assessment assignment opportunity: log 3.1)

- Have students write a description of the extracurricular physical activities available in the school setting related to throwing and catching with an implement. (Assessment assignment opportunity: essay 3.2)

Figure 14.16   Scoop to self.

Figure 14.17   Overhand throw and catch using a lacrosse stick.

Unit 6 Outline *(continued)*

DAY 2

Display the posters.

Review the rules, procedures, and etiquette for safely participating in throwing activities that involve an implement. 5.2

Review modifying throwing-and-catching-with-an-implement tasks to fit the needs of a differently abled student. 5.1

Have students perform a warm-up along with muscular strength and muscular endurance exercises. (Assessment opportunity: structured observation 4.1)

Review the underhand throw and catch using a scoop. 1.0, 2.5

Have students practice the underhand throw and catch using a scoop with a partner while counting the number of successful throws and catches in a row. (Assessment opportunity: structured observation 1.0, 5.1, 5.2, 6.3)

Demonstrate and describe the overhand throw and catch using a lacrosse stick (see figure 14.17). 1.0, 2.5

DAY 2 (continued)

Have students practice the overhand throw and catch using a lacrosse stick with a partner while counting the number of successful throws and catches in a row. (Assessment opportunity: structured observation 1.0, 5.1, 5.2, 6.3)

Have students experiment with different release angles, forces, and mechanics to determine the most effective way to throw for distance with a scoop and lacrosse stick. (Assessment opportunity: structured observation 1.0, 5.1, 5.2, 6.3) 2.2

Lead students through a cool-down and flexibility exercises appropriate to the physical activity level of the lesson. (Assessment opportunity: structured observation 4.1)

Explain the features of mass and distributed practice. 2.1

Have students record the features of mass and distributed practice in their notebooks. 2.1

DAY 3

Discuss the frequency, intensity, time, and type concepts related to cardiorespiratory endurance (using the Health-Related Fitness: Tutorial and Portfolio). 4.2

Have students record the concepts of frequency, intensity, time, and type as they relate to cardiorespiratory endurance. 4.2

Describe the short-term muscular endurance benefits derived from participation in physical activity. 6.4

Have students record the short-term muscular endurance benefits derived from participation in physical activity. 6.4

Have students create a 1-day cardiorespiratory endurance improvement plan. (Assessment assignment opportunity: project 4.2)

Have students perform a warm-up along with a cardiorespiratory workout. (Assessment opportunity: structured observation 4.1)

Have students rotate through several stations, throwing overhand using a lacrosse stick for distance, throwing underhand using a scoop for distance, throwing overhand using a lacrosse stick with a partner, throwing underhand using a scoop with a partner, throwing overhand using a lacrosse stick at targets, throwing underhand using a scoop at targets. (Assessment opportunity: structured observation 1.0, 5.1, 5.2, 6.3)

Lead students through a cool-down and flexibility exercises appropriate to the physical activity level of the lesson. (Assessment opportunity: structured observation 4.1)

Review the features of mass and distributed practice. 2.1

DAY 4

Describe how external forces affect object manipulation. 2.2

Have students record the information on external forces in their notebooks. 2.2

Have students perform a warm-up along with muscular strength and muscular endurance exercises. (Assessment opportunity: structured observation 4.1)

Demonstrate overhand throwing using an implement at a moving target or player. 1.0, 2.5

Have students practice throwing overhand at a moving target using an implement. (Assessment opportunity: structured observation 1.0, 5.1, 5.2, 6.3)

Review the jump-stop and pivot. 1.0, 2.5

Have students practice overhand throwing using an implement at moving players who catch the ball, perform a jump-stop, and then pivot. (Assessment opportunity: structured observation 1.0, 5.1, 5.2, 6.3)

Lead students through a cool-down and flexibility exercises appropriate to the physical activity level of the lesson. (Assessment opportunity: structured observation 4.1)

Review the features of mass and distributed practice. 2.1

(continued)

Unit 6 Outline *(continued)*

DAY 5

Describe the negative impact of physical changes on physical performance from prepuberty through puberty. 2.4

Have students record in their notebooks the negative impact of physical changes on physical performance from prepuberty through puberty. 2.4

Have students perform a warm-up along with a cardiorespiratory workout. (Assessment opportunity: structured observation 4.1)

Review overhand throwing using a lacrosse stick at a moving target. 1.0, 2.5

Have students, in pairs, practice overhand throwing using a lacrosse stick at a moving target. (Assessment opportunity: structured observation 1.0, 5.1, 5.2, 6.3)

Review underhand throwing using a scoop at a moving target. 1.0, 2.5

Review the two-step stop and pivot. 1.0, 2.5

Have students practice throwing underhand at moving players who catch the ball, then perform a two-step stop and pivot. (Assessment opportunity: structured observation 1.0, 5.1, 5.2, 6.3)

Have students play Goalie Ball while throwing with an implement. (Assessment opportunity: structured observation 1.0, 5.1, 5.2, 6.3)

Lead students through a cool-down and flexibility exercises appropriate to the physical activity level of the lesson. (Assessment opportunity: structured observation 4.1)

Review how external forces affect object manipulation. 2.2

DAY 6

Have students perform a warm-up along with a cardiorespiratory workout. (Assessment opportunity: structured observation 4.1)

Demonstrate underhand throwing using a scoop at a moving target. 1.0, 2.5

Have students practice underhand throwing using a scoop at a moving target. (Assessment opportunity: structured observation 1.0, 5.1, 5.2, 6.3)

Demonstrate overhand throwing using a lacrosse stick at a moving target. 1.0, 2.5

Have students practice overhand throwing using a lacrosse stick at a moving target. (Assessment opportunity: structured observation 1.0, 5.1, 5.2, 6.3)

Demonstrate underhand throwing using a scoop at a moving target while moving. 1.0, 2.5

Have students, in pairs, perform an underhand throw and catch using a scoop while moving up and down the field. (Assessment opportunity: structured observation 1.0, 5.1, 5.2, 6.3)

Demonstrate overhand throwing using a lacrosse stick at a moving target while moving. 1.0, 2.5

Have students, in pairs, perform an overhand throw and catch using a lacrosse stick while moving up and down the field. (Assessment opportunity: structured observation 1.0, 5.1, 5.2, 6.3)

In groups of three, have students play Keep Away using a scoop to throw and catch the ball. (Assessment opportunity: structured observation 1.0, 5.1, 5.2, 6.3)

In groups of three, have students play Keep Away using a lacrosse stick to throw and catch the ball. (Assessment opportunity: structured observation 1.0, 5.1, 5.2, 6.3)

Lead students through a cool-down and flexibility exercises appropriate to the physical activity level of the lesson. (Assessment opportunity: structured observation 4.1)

Review the short-term muscular endurance benefits derived from participation in physical activity. 6.4

DAY 7

Have students perform a warm-up along with muscular strength and muscular endurance exercises. (Assessment opportunity: structured observation 4.1)

Review the overhand throw and catch using an implement. 1.0, 2.5

Have students rotate through a variety of stations: throwing overhand using a lacrosse stick at stationary targets; throwing underhand using a scoop at stationary targets; throwing overhand using a lacrosse stick with a partner; the sequence of throwing underhand using scoops, catching, stopping, and pivoting (review from unit 5); throwing overhand using a lacrosse stick at moving targets; throwing underhand using a scoop at moving targets; throwing overhand using a lacrosse stick while moving; throwing underhand using a scoop while moving; throwing underhand using a scoop at a moving target while moving; throwing overhand using a lacrosse stick at a moving target while moving. (Assessment opportunity: structured observation 1.0, 5.1, 5.2, 6.3)

Lead students through a cool-down and flexibility exercises appropriate to the physical activity level of the lesson. (Assessment opportunity: structured observation 4.1)

Review the negative impact of physical changes on physical performance from prepuberty through puberty. 2.4

DAY 8

Have students perform a warm-up along with a cardiorespiratory workout. (Assessment opportunity: structured observation 4.1)

Review the overhand throw and catch using an implement. 1.0, 2.5

Have students rotate through a variety of stations: throwing overhand using a lacrosse stick at stationary targets; throwing underhand using a scoop at stationary targets; throwing overhand using a lacrosse stick with a partner; the sequence of throwing underhand using scoops, catching, stopping, and pivoting (review from unit 5); throwing overhand using a lacrosse stick at moving targets; throwing underhand using a scoop at moving targets; throwing overhand using a lacrosse stick while moving; throwing underhand using a scoop while moving; throwing underhand using a scoop at a moving target while moving; throwing overhand using a lacrosse stick at a moving target while moving. (Assessment opportunity: structured observation 1.0, 5.1, 5.2, 6.3)

Lead students through a cool-down and flexibility exercises appropriate to the physical activity level of the lesson. (Assessment opportunity: structured observation 4.1)

DAY 9

Have students perform a warm-up along with muscular strength and muscular endurance exercises. (Assessment opportunity: structured observation 4.1)

Review the overhand throw and catch using an implement. 1.0, 2.5

Have students rotate through a variety of stations: throwing overhand using a lacrosse stick at stationary targets; throwing underhand using a scoop at stationary targets; throwing overhand using a lacrosse stick with a partner; the sequence of throwing underhand using scoops, catching, stopping, and pivoting (review from unit 5); throwing overhand using a lacrosse stick at moving targets; throwing underhand using a scoop at moving targets; throwing overhand using a lacrosse stick while moving; throwing underhand using a scoop while moving; throwing underhand using a scoop at a moving target while moving; throwing overhand using a lacrosse stick at a moving target while moving. (Assessment opportunity: structured observation 1.0, 5.1, 5.2, 6.3)

Lead students through a cool-down and flexibility exercises appropriate to the physical activity level of the lesson. (Assessment opportunity: structured observation 4.1)

(continued)

Unit 6 Outline *(continued)*

DAY 10

Introduce modified 4-on-4 lacrosse. 1.0

Describe how space is used as a basic game tactic. 2.3

Have students perform a warm-up along with a cardiorespiratory workout. (Assessment opportunity: structured observation 4.1)

Have students play modified 4-on-4 lacrosse, scoring by throwing the ball using an implement into the goal area. (Assessment opportunity: structured observation 1.0, 5.1, 5.2, 6.3) 5.1, 2.3

Lead students through a cool-down and flexibility exercises appropriate to the physical activity level of the lesson. (Assessment opportunity: structured observation 4.1)

DAY 11

Review modified 4-on-4 lacrosse. 1.0

Review how space is used as a basic game tactic. 2.3

Have students perform a warm-up along with a cardiorespiratory workout. (Assessment opportunity: structured observation 4.1)

Have students play modified 4-on-4 lacrosse, scoring by throwing the ball using an implement into the goal area. (Assessment opportunity: structured observation 1.0, 5.1, 5.2, 6.3) 5.1, 2.3

Lead students through a cool-down and flexibility exercises appropriate to the physical activity level of the lesson. (Assessment opportunity: structured observation 4.1)

DAY 12

Have students perform a warm-up along with muscular strength and muscular endurance exercises. (Assessment opportunity: structured observation 4.1)

Have students, in pairs, create a ball-handling routine (using an implement) to go along with the Harlem Globetrotters music. (Assessment assignment opportunity: project 6.2)

Lead students through a cool-down and flexibility exercises appropriate to the physical activity level of the lesson. (Assessment opportunity: structured observation 4.1)

DAY 13

Have students perform a warm-up along with a cardiorespiratory workout. (Assessment opportunity: structured observation 4.1)

Have students practice their ball-handling routine. (Assessment opportunity: structured observation 1.0, 5.1, 5.2, 6.2, 6.3)

Lead students through a cool-down and flexibility exercises appropriate to the physical activity level of the lesson. (Assessment opportunity: structured observation 4.1)

DAY 14

Have students perform a warm-up along with muscular strength and muscular endurance exercises. (Assessment opportunity: structured observation 4.1)

Have each pair teach their ball-handling routine to another pair. (Assessment opportunity: project 6.2)

Lead students through a cool-down and flexibility exercises appropriate to the physical activity level of the lesson. (Assessment opportunity: structured observation 4.1)

Review material for tomorrow's quiz (or hand out quiz if you would like for it to be a take-home quiz). 2.1, 2.2, 2.3, 2.4, 2.5, 6.4

For homework, have students write a description about how the manipulation of an object routine to music expresses personal feelings. (Assessment assignment opportunity: project 6.2)

DAY 15

Have students take the quiz. (Assessment opportunity: quiz 2.1, 2.2, 2.3, 2.4, 2.5, 6.4)

Collect activity log. (Assessment opportunity: log 3.1)

Collect history report. (Assessment opportunity: report 6.1)

Collect essay on extracurricular activities. (Assessment opportunity: essay 3.2)

Collect 1-day cardiorespiratory endurance improvement plan. (Assessment opportunity: project 4.2)

Collect description regarding routine to music. (Assessment opportunity: project 6.2)

Striking With Hands   — Unit 7

In this, our fifth skills theme unit, we look at the skill of striking with hands. I teach this unit to ensure that my students have the correct technique for the many skills that involve striking with hands. Then, I extend the skill by having students strike while they are moving. Finally, I have students apply the skills to gamelike settings, such as basketball and volleyball. You can conduct this unit in any open area; however, a net is ideal for the modified volleyball activities.

Unit 7 Standards

1.0—Demonstrates speed and accuracy using the mature form for underhand and overhand striking with hand(s) and hand dribbling.

2.1—Explains the appropriate situations for mass practice and for distributed practice.

2.2—Describes ways to absorb force.

2.3—Describes how time is used as a basic game tactic.

2.4—Describes the positive impact of cognitive changes on physical performance from prepuberty through puberty.

2.5—Describes the critical elements for underhand and overhand striking with hand(s) and hand dribbling.

3.1—Engages in moderate physical activity for 40 minutes 5 days each week.

3.2—Describes the extracurricular physical activities available in the school setting related to striking objects with hand(s).

4.1—Works toward a health-enhancing level of physical fitness.

4.2—Creates a 1-day body composition improvement plan.

5.1—Modifies striking with hand(s) tasks to fit the needs of a differently abled student.

5.2—Accepts responsibility for personal safety during striking with hand(s) activities.

6.1—Describes the development of games using striking with hand(s) in the United States during the 17th and 18th centuries.

6.2—Expresses personal feelings through a movement-based routine that involves striking with hand(s).

6.3—Chooses to engage in striking with hand(s) skill competencies at a level that leads to personal satisfaction, success, and enjoyment.

6.4—Describes the long-term body composition benefits derived from participation in physical activity.

Unit 7 Assessments

1.0—Structured observation (days 1-14)

2.1—Quiz (day 15)

2.2—Quiz (day 15)

2.3—Quiz (day 15)

2.4—Quiz (day 15)

2.5—Quiz (day 15)

3.1—Log (assigned on day 1; collected on day 15)

3.2—Essay (assigned on day 1; collected on day 15)

4.1—Structured observation (days 1-14)

4.2—Project (assigned on day 2; collected on day 15)

5.1—Structured observation (days 1-14)

5.2—Structured observation (days 1-14)

6.1—Report (assigned on day 1; collected on day 15)

6.2—Project (assigned on day 12; collected on day 15)

6.3—Structured observation (days 1-14)

6.4—Quiz (day 15)

Resources

Globetrotters music for routine (Bonnie's Fitware, Inc.)

Health-Related Fitness: Tutorial and Portfolio (Bonnie's Fitware, Inc.)

Middle School Physical Education Portfolio (Bonnie's Fitware, Inc.)

Fifth grade striking with hands task cards (Bonnie's Fitware, Inc.)

Fifth grade unit 7 posters (Bonnie's Fitware, Inc.—included in the Middle School Detailed Lesson Plans)

Fitness posters (Bonnie's Fitware, Inc.—included in the Middle School Detailed Lesson Plans)

Qualities of Movement chart (Bonnie's Fitware, Inc.—included in the Middle School Detailed Lesson Plans)

Equipment

Variety of objects (e.g., volleyballs, rubber playground balls, beach balls)

Variety of targets

Games

Dribble tag

Keep It Up

Unit 7 Outline

DAY 1

Display the poster.

Introduce the striking with hands unit.

Explain the rules, procedures, and etiquette for safely participating in activities that involve striking an object with hands. 5.2

Explain that skill competency in striking with hands can lead to personal satisfaction, success, and enjoyment. 6.3

Assign students to heterogeneous working groups of four.

Have students perform a warm-up along with a cardiorespiratory workout. (Assessment opportunity: structured observation 4.1)

Demonstrate hand dribbling while standing still. 1.0, 2.5

Have students brainstorm ways to modify striking with hand(s) tasks for students who are differently abled. 5.1

Have students practice hand dribbling alone while standing still. (Assessment opportunity: structured observation 1.0, 5.1, 5.2, 6.3)

Demonstrate dribbling while moving. 1.0, 2.5

Have students practice dribbling while moving. (Assessment opportunity: structured observation 1.0, 5.1, 5.2, 6.3)

Lead students through a cool-down and flexibility exercises appropriate to the physical activity level of the lesson. (Assessment opportunity: structured observation 4.1)

DAY 1 *(continued)*	Assign unit-long homework: • Have students research and write a description of the development of games using striking with hand(s) in the United States during the 17th and 18th centuries. (Assessment assignment opportunity: report 6.1) • Have students keep a log of daily activity. (Assessment assignment opportunity: log 3.1) • Have students write a description of the extracurricular physical activities available in the school setting related to striking objects with hand(s). (Assessment assignment opportunity: essay 3.2)
DAY 2	Discuss the long-term body composition benefits derived from participation in physical activity. 6.4 Have students record in their notebooks the long-term body composition benefits derived from participation in physical activity. 6.4 Discuss concepts of frequency, intensity, time, and type as they relate to body composition. 4.2 Have students create a 1-day body composition maintenance and improvement plan. (Assessment assignment opportunity: project 4.2) Have students perform a warm-up along with muscular strength and muscular endurance exercises. (Assessment opportunity: structured observation 4.1) Review dribbling while moving. 1.0, 2.5 Have students practice dribbling while moving. (Assessment opportunity: structured observation 1.0, 5.1, 5.2, 6.3) Have students practice dribbling around an obstacle course. (Assessment opportunity: structured observation 1.0, 5.1, 5.2, 6.3) Lead students through a cool-down and flexibility exercises appropriate to the physical activity level of the lesson. (Assessment opportunity: structured observation 4.1) Review the rules, procedures, and etiquette for safely participating in activities that involve striking an object with hand(s). 5.2
DAY 3	Explain the appropriate situations for mass practice and for distributed practice. 2.1 Have students record the appropriate situations for mass practice and for distributed practice in their notebooks. 2.1 Have students perform a warm-up along with a cardiorespiratory workout. (Assessment opportunity: structured observation 4.1) Review hand dribbling. 1.0, 2.5 Explain dribble tag. 1.0 Have students play dribble tag. (Assessment opportunity: structured observation 1.0, 5.1, 5.2, 6.3) Lead students through a cool-down and flexibility exercises appropriate to the physical activity level of the lesson. (Assessment opportunity: structured observation 4.1) Review the long-term body composition benefits derived from participation in physical activity. 6.4

(continued)

Unit 7 Outline *(continued)*

DAY 4

Describe ways to absorb force. 2.2

Have students record the information on reducing forces in their notebooks. 2.2

Have students perform a warm-up along with muscular strength and muscular endurance exercises. (Assessment opportunity: structured observation 4.1)

Demonstrate one-hand underhand serving of a ball (see figure 14.18). 1.0, 2.5

Have students practice one-hand underhand serving of a ball with a partner. (Assessment opportunity: structured observation 1.0, 5.1, 5.2, 6.3)

Have students strike the ball back and forth over a net with a partner, allowing them to choose how far from the net they wish to stand. (Assessment opportunity: structured observation 1.0, 5.1, 5.2, 6.3)

Have students practice striking the ball over a net with a partner, aiming for a spot on the other side. Allow students to choose how far from the net they wish to stand. (Assessment opportunity: structured observation 1.0, 5.1, 5.2, 6.3)

Lead students through a cool-down and flexibility exercises appropriate to the physical activity level of the lesson. (Assessment opportunity: structured observation 4.1)

Review the appropriate situations for mass practice and for distributed practice. 2.1

Figure 14.18 Underhand serve.

DAY 5

Describe the positive impact of cognitive changes on physical performance from prepuberty through puberty. 2.4

Have students record in their notebooks the positive impact of cognitive changes on physical performance from prepuberty through puberty. 2.4

Review ways to absorb force. 2.2

DAY 5 *(continued)*

Have students perform a warm-up along with a cardiorespiratory workout. (Assessment opportunity: structured observation 4.1)

Demonstrate two-hand underhand striking of a ball (see figure 14.19). 1.0, 2.5

Demonstrate catching a ball using and not using appropriate reduction of force techniques. 1.0, 2.2

Have students practice the two-handed underhand striking of a ball with a partner who catches the ball, using and not using appropriate reduction of force techniques. 1.0, 2.2, 2.5

In groups of four, have two students practice two-handed underhand striking of a ball while the other two provide feedback. (Assessment opportunity: structured observation 1.0, 5.1, 5.2, 6.3)

Have students, in pairs, practice two-handed underhand striking of a ball while aiming at a target. (Assessment opportunity: structured observation 1.0, 5.1, 5.2, 6.3)

Lead students through a cool-down and flexibility exercises appropriate to the physical activity level of the lesson. (Assessment opportunity: structured observation 4.1)

Figure 14.19 Two-hand underhand strike.

DAY 6

Have students perform a warm-up along with a cardiorespiratory workout. (Assessment opportunity: structured observation 4.1)

Review the appropriate situations for mass practice and for distributed practice. 2.1

In groups of two, have students practice forearm pass with partner. (Assessment opportunity: structured observation 1.0, 5.1, 5.2, 6.3)

Lead students through a cool-down and flexibility exercises appropriate to the physical activity level of the lesson. (Assessment opportunity: structured observation 4.1)

(continued)

Unit 7 Outline (continued)

DAY 7

Have students perform a warm-up along with muscular strength and muscular endurance exercises. (Assessment opportunity: structured observation 4.1)

Demonstrate one-hand overhand striking of a ball. 1.0, 2.5

Have students practice one-hand overhand striking of a ball with a partner. (Assessment opportunity: structured observation 1.0, 5.1, 5.2, 6.3)

Have students strike the ball back and forth over a net with a partner, allowing them to choose how far from the net they wish to stand. (Assessment opportunity: structured observation 1.0, 5.1, 5.2, 6.3)

Have students strike the ball back and forth over a net with a partner while aiming for a spot on the other side. Allow students to choose how far from the net they wish to stand. (Assessment opportunity: structured observation 1.0, 5.1, 5.2, 6.3)

Lead students through a cool-down and flexibility exercises appropriate to the physical activity level of the lesson. (Assessment opportunity: structured observation 4.1)

DAY 8

Have students perform a warm-up along with a cardiorespiratory workout. (Assessment opportunity: structured observation 4.1)

Demonstrate two-hand overhand striking of a ball. 1.0, 2.5

Have students, in pairs, practice tossing and two-hand overhand striking of a ball. (Assessment opportunity: structured observation 1.0, 5.1, 5.2, 6.3)

Have students, in pairs, practice two-hand overhand striking of a ball while aiming at a target. (Assessment opportunity: structured observation 1.0, 5.1, 5.2, 6.3)

In pairs, have students practice two-hand overhand striking back and forth, when ready. (Assessment opportunity: structured observation 1.0, 5.1, 5.2, 6.3)

Lead students through a cool-down and flexibility exercises appropriate to the physical activity level of the lesson. (Assessment opportunity: structured observation 4.1)

DAY 9

Have students perform a warm-up along with muscular strength and muscular endurance exercises. (Assessment opportunity: structured observation 4.1)

Review two-hand overhand striking of a ball. 1.0, 2.5

Have students rotate through stations: dribble tag, two-hand underhand striking with partner, two-hand overhand striking with partner, one-hand underhand striking with partner, and one-hand overhand striking with partner. (Assessment opportunity: structured observation 1.0, 5.1, 5.2, 6.3)

Lead students through a cool-down and flexibility exercises appropriate to the physical activity level of the lesson. (Assessment opportunity: structured observation 4.1)

DAY 10

Review striking with hand skills. 1.0, 2.5

Describe how time is used as a basic game tactic. 2.3

Have students record in their notebooks how time is used as a basic game tactic. 2.3

Have students perform a warm-up along with a cardiorespiratory workout. (Assessment opportunity: structured observation 4.1)

Teach students to play Keep It Up. (Assessment opportunity: structured observation 1.0, 5.1, 5.2, 6.3)

Have students rotate through stations, practicing the skills and receiving feedback: dribble tag, two-hand underhand striking with partner, two-hand overhand striking with partner, one-hand underhand striking with partner, one-hand overhand striking with with partner, Keep It Up. (Assessment opportunity: structured observation 1.0, 5.1, 5.2, 6.3)

Lead students through a cool-down and flexibility exercises appropriate to the physical activity level of the lesson. (Assessment opportunity: structured observation 4.1)

Have students debrief on how time was used as a game tactic for Keep it Up. 2.3

DAY 11	Have students perform a warm-up along with a cardiorespiratory workout. (Assessment opportunity: structured observation 4.1)
	Review striking with hand(s) skills (dribbling, overhand, underhand). 1.0, 2.5
	Review how time is used as a basic game tactic. 2.3
	Have students rotate through stations, practicing the skills and receiving feedback: dribble tag, two-hand underhand striking with partner, two-hand overhand striking with partner, one-hand underhand striking with partner, one-hand overhand striking with partner, Keep It Up. (Assessment opportunity: structured observation 1.0, 5.1, 5.2, 6.3)
	Lead students through a cool-down and flexibility exercises appropriate to the physical activity level of the lesson. (Assessment opportunity: structured observation 4.1)
DAY 12	Have students perform a warm-up along with muscular strength and muscular endurance exercises. (Assessment opportunity: structured observation 4.1)
	Demonstrate one-hand ball control dribble, change hands–control dribble, figure eight one bounce, and figure eight two bounces ball-handling skills. 1.0
	Have students practice one-hand ball control dribble, change hands–control dribble, figure eight one bounce, and figure eight two bounces ball-handling skills. 1.0
	Have students, in pairs, create a ball-handling routine that involves throwing and striking with hands to go along with the Harlem Globetrotters music. (Assessment assignment opportunity: project 6.2)
	Lead students through a cool-down and flexibility exercises appropriate to the physical activity level of the lesson. (Assessment opportunity: structured observation 4.1)
DAY 13	Have students perform a warm-up along with a cardiorespiratory workout. (Assessment opportunity: structured observation 4.1)
	Have students practice their ball-handling routine. 1.0. 5.1, 5.2, 6.2, 6.3
	Lead students through a cool-down and flexibility exercises appropriate to the physical activity level of the lesson. (Assessment opportunity: structured observation 4.1)
DAY 14	Have students perform a warm-up along with muscular strength and muscular endurance exercises. (Assessment opportunity: structured observation 4.1)
	Have each pair teach their ball-handling routine to another pair. (Assessment opportunity: project 6.2)
	Lead students through a cool-down and flexibility exercises appropriate to the physical activity level of the lesson. (Assessment opportunity: structured observation 4.1)
	Review material for tomorrow's quiz (or hand out quiz if you would like for it to be a take-home quiz). 2.1, 2.2, 2.3, 2.4, 2.5, 6.4
	Instruct students to write a description of their ball-handling routine and how they expressed their personal feelings through the routine. (Assessment opportunity: project 6.2)
DAY 15	Have students take the quiz. (Assessment opportunity: quiz 2.1, 2.2, 2.3, 2.4, 2.5, 6.4)
	Collect activity log. (Assessment opportunity: log 3.1)
	Collect history report. (Assessment opportunity: report 6.1)
	Collect essay on extracurricular activities. (Assessment opportunity: essay 3.2)
	Collect 1-day body composition maintenance/improvement plan. (Assessment opportunity: project 4.2)
	Collect description regarding routine to music. (Assessment opportunity: project 6.2)

(continued)

Striking With Feet   ~ Unit 8 ⌇

In this, our sixth skills theme unit, we look at the skill of striking with feet. I teach this unit to ensure that my students have the correct technique for striking using lower-body limbs. Then, I extend the skill by having students dribble with feet, kick at moving targets, and kick while they are moving. Finally, I have the students apply these skills in soccerlike settings. You can conduct this unit in any open area; however, a grassy area is best.

Unit 8 Standards

1.0—Demonstrates speed and accuracy using the mature form for instep kick, sole-of-foot trap, instep trap, outside-of-foot kick, punting, and dribbling.

2.1—Explains the features of practicing for speed and practicing for accuracy.

2.2—Describes ways to generate and absorb force using the feet.

2.3—Describes how force is used in basic game tactics.

2.4—Describes the negative impact of cognitive changes on physical performance from prepuberty through puberty.

2.5—Describes the critical elements for instep kick, sole-of-foot trap, instep trap, punting, outside-of-foot kick, and dribbling.

3.1—Engages in moderate physical activity for 45 minutes 5 days each week.

3.2—Describes the extracurricular physical activities available in the school setting related to striking objects with feet.

4.1—Works toward a health-enhancing level of physical fitness.

4.2—Refines 1-day body composition plan.

5.1—Modifies striking with feet tasks to fit the needs of a differently abled student.

5.2—Accepts responsibility for personal safety during striking with feet activities.

6.1—Describes the development of games using striking with feet in the United States during the 17th and 18th centuries.

6.2—Expresses personal feelings through a movement-based routine that involves striking with feet.

6.3—Chooses to engage in striking with feet skill competencies at a level that leads to personal satisfaction, success, and enjoyment.

6.4—Describes the long-term flexibility benefits derived from participation in physical activity.

Unit 8 Assessments

1.0—Structured observation (days 1-14)

2.1—Quiz (day 15)

2.2—Quiz (day 15)

2.3—Quiz (day 15)

2.4—Quiz (day 15)

2.5—Quiz (day 15)

3.1—Log (assigned on day 1; collected on day 15)

3.2—Essay (assigned on day 1; collected on day 15)

4.1—Structured observation (days 1-14)

4.2—Project (assigned on day 3; collected on day 15)

5.1—Structured observation (days 1-14)

5.2—Structured observation (days 1-14)

6.1—Report (assigned on day 1; collected on day 15)

6.2—Project (assigned on day 12; collected on day 15)

6.3—Structured observation (days 1-14)

6.4—Quiz (day 15)

Resources

Health-Related Fitness: Tutorial and Portfolio (Bonnie's Fitware, Inc.)

Middle School Physical Education Portfolio (Bonnie's Fitware, Inc.)

Globetrotters music for routine (Bonnie's Fitware, Inc.)

Fifth grade striking with feet task cards (Bonnie's Fitware, Inc.)

Fifth grade unit 8 posters (Bonnie's Fitware, Inc.—included in the Middle School Detailed Lesson Plans)

Fitness posters (Bonnie's Fitware, Inc.—included in the Middle School Detailed Lesson Plans)

Equipment

Variety of objects (e.g., soccer balls, kick balks, rubber playground balls)

Variety of targets and goals

Scarves or flags for dribble tag

Games

Goalie Ball

Dribble tag

2-on-2 soccer

Unit 8 Outline

DAY 1

Display posters.

Introduce the unit on striking with feet.

Describe rules that are safe and effective for activities that involve striking with feet. 5.2

Have students record in their notebooks the safety rules for striking with feet. 5.2

Explain that skill competency in striking with feet can lead to personal satisfaction, success, and enjoyment. 6.3

Demonstrate and describe instep kick and sole-of-foot trap. 1.0, 2.5

Describe ways to modify striking with feet tasks for students who are differently abled. 5.1

Have students record modification for striking with feet for students who are differently abled. 5.1

Assign students to heterogeneous groups of four.

Have students perform a warm-up along with a cardiorespiratory workout. (Assessment opportunity: structured observation 4.1)

Have students practice instep kick and sole-of-foot trap with a partner. (Assessment opportunity: structured observation 1.0, 5.1, 5.2, 6.3)

Lead students through a cool-down and flexibility exercises appropriate to the physical activity level of the lesson. (Assessment opportunity: structured observation 4.1)

Assign unit-long homework:

- Have students research and write a description of the development of games using striking with feet in the United States during the 17th and 18th centuries. (Assessment assignment opportunity: report 6.1)

- Have students keep a log of daily activity. (Assessment assignment opportunity: log 3.1)

- Have students write a description of the extracurricular physical activities available in the school setting related to striking with feet. (Assessment assignment opportunity: essay 3.2)

(continued)

Unit 8 Outline *(continued)*

DAY 2

Describe the long-term flexibility benefits derived from participation in physical activity. 6.4

Have students record in their notebooks the long-term flexibility benefits derived from participation in physical activity. 3.1

Have students perform a warm-up along with muscular strength and muscular endurance exercises. (Assessment opportunity: structured observation 4.1)

Review instep kick and the sole-of-foot trap. 1.0, 2.5

Have students practice instep kick and sole-of-foot trap with a partner. (Assessment opportunity: structured observation 1.0, 5.1, 5.2, 6.3)

Demonstrate and describe outside-of-foot kick. 1.0, 2.5

Have students practice outside-of-foot kick and sole-of-foot trap with a partner. (Assessment opportunity: structured observation 1.0, 5.1, 5.2, 6.3)

Lead students through a cool-down and flexibility exercises appropriate to the physical activity level of the lesson. (Assessment opportunity: structured observation 4.1)

Review rules that are safe and effective for activities that involve striking with feet. 5.2

DAY 3

Explain the features of practicing for speed and/or accuracy. 2.1

Have students record in their notebooks the features of practicing for speed and/or accuracy. 2.1

Discuss frequency, intensity, time, and type as they relate to body composition, using Health-Related Fitness: Tutorial and Portfolio. 4.2

Have students refine 1-day body composition plan. (Assessment assignment opportunity: project 4.2)

Have students perform a warm-up along with a cardiorespiratory workout. (Assessment opportunity: structured observation 4.1)

Demonstrate and describe instep trap. 1.0, 2.5

Have students practice instep trapping. 1.0

Demonstrate and describe kicking to a partner who is moving. 1.0, 2.5

Have students practice kicking to a partner who is moving; have the partner use the sole-of-foot trap. (Assessment opportunity: structured observation 1.0, 5.1, 5.2, 6.3)

Demonstrate and describe kicking on the run to a partner who is moving. 1.0, 2.5

Have students practice kicking back and forth to a partner while both are moving. (Assessment opportunity: structured observation 1.0, 5.1, 5.2, 6.3)

Lead students through a cool-down and flexibility exercises appropriate to the physical activity level of the lesson. (Assessment opportunity: structured observation 4.1)

Review the long-term flexibility benefits derived from participation in physical activity. 6.4

DAY 4

Describe ways to generate and absorb force using feet. 2.2

Have students record in their notebooks the information on generating and absorbing force. 2.2

Review instep kick, outside-of-foot kick, and sole-of-foot trap. 1.0, 2.5

Describe how force is used in basic game tactics. 2.3

Have students record how force is used in basic game tactics in their notebooks. 2.3

Have students perform a warm-up along with muscular strength and muscular endurance exercises. (Assessment opportunity: structured observation 4.1)

Teach students Goalie Ball. 1.0

DAY 4 (continued)

Have students participate in the following stations: instep pass and sole-of-foot trap with partner, outside-of-foot pass and sole-of-foot trap with partner, passing to a moving partner, passing while on the move, Goalie Ball, passing back and forth while both are moving. (Assessment opportunity: structured observation 1.0, 5.1, 5.2, 6.3)

Lead students through a cool-down and flexibility exercises appropriate to the physical activity level of the lesson. (Assessment opportunity: structured observation 4.1)

Review the features of practicing for speed and/or accuracy. 2.1

DAY 5

Describe the negative impact of cognitive changes on physical performance from prepuberty through puberty. 2.4

Have students record in their notebooks the negative impact of cognitive changes on physical performance from prepuberty through puberty. 2.4

Have students perform a warm-up along with a cardiorespiratory workout. (Assessment opportunity: structured observation 4.1)

Have students participate in the following stations: instep pass and sole-of-foot trap with partner, outside-of-foot pass and sole-of-foot trap with partner, passing to a moving partner, passing while on the move, Goalie Ball, passing back and forth while both are moving. (Assessment opportunity: structured observation 1.0, 5.1, 5.2, 6.3)

Lead students through a cool-down and flexibility exercises appropriate to the physical activity level of the lesson. (Assessment opportunity: structured observation 4.1)

Review ways to generate and absorb force using feet. 2.2

DAY 6

Have students perform a warm-up along with a cardiorespiratory workout. (Assessment opportunity: structured observation 4.1)

Demonstrate and describe foot dribbling. 1.0, 2.5

Have students practice foot dribbling alone. (Assessment opportunity: structured observation 1.0, 5.1, 5.2, 6.3)

Have students practice foot dribbling around cones. (Assessment opportunity: structured observation 1.0, 5.1, 5.2, 6.3)

Lead students through a cool-down and flexibility exercises appropriate to the physical activity level of the lesson. (Assessment opportunity: structured observation 4.1)

DAY 7

Have students perform a warm-up along with muscular strength and muscular endurance exercises. (Assessment opportunity: structured observation 4.1)

Review foot dribbling. 1.0, 2.5

Have students practice foot dribbling around an obstacle course. (Assessment opportunity: structured observation 1.0, 5.1, 5.2, 6.3)

Have students play foot dribble tag. (Assessment opportunity: structured observation 1.0, 5.1, 5.2, 6.3)

Demonstrate and describe foot dribbling and instep kick to a partner. 1.0, 2.5

Have students practice foot dribbling and instep kick to a stationary partner. (Assessment opportunity: structured observation 1.0, 5.1, 5.2, 6.3)

Have students practice foot dribbling and instep kick to a target. (Assessment opportunity: structured observation 1.0, 5.1, 5.2, 6.3)

Have students practice foot dribbling and instep kick to a moving partner. (Assessment opportunity: structured observation 1.0, 5.1, 5.2, 6.3)

Lead students through a cool-down and flexibility exercises appropriate to the physical activity level of the lesson. (Assessment opportunity: structured observation 4.1)

Review the negative impact of cognitive changes on physical performance from prepuberty through puberty. 2.4

(continued)

Unit 8 Outline *(continued)*

DAY 8

Have students perform a warm-up along with a cardiorespiratory workout. (Assessment opportunity: structured observation 4.1)

Review foot dribbling. 1.0, 2.5

Have students practice foot dribbling around an obstacle course. (Assessment opportunity: structured observation 1.0, 5.1, 5.2, 6.3)

Have students play foot dribble tag. (Assessment opportunity: structured observation 1.0, 5.1, 5.2, 6.3)

Review foot dribbling and instep kick to a partner (see figure 14.20). 1.0, 2.5

Have students practice foot dribbling and instep kick to a stationary partner. (Assessment opportunity: structured observation 1.0, 5.1, 5.2, 6.3)

Have students practice foot dribbling and instep kick to a target. (Assessment opportunity: structured observation 1.0, 5.1, 5.2, 6.3)

Have students practice foot dribbling and instep kick to a moving partner. (Assessment opportunity: structured observation 1.0, 5.1, 5.2, 6.3)

Lead students through a cool-down and flexibility exercises appropriate to the physical activity level of the lesson. (Assessment opportunity: structured observation 4.1)

Figure 14.20   Dribbling and instep kick combination.

DAY 9

Review how force is used in basic game tactics. 2.3

Have students perform a warm-up along with muscular strength and muscular endurance exercises. (Assessment opportunity: structured observation 4.1)

Demonstrate and describe punting. 1.0, 2.5

Have students practice punting. (Assessment opportunity: structured observation 1.0)

Teach 2-on-2 soccer. 1.0, 2.3

Have students play 2-on-2 soccer. (Assessment opportunity: structured observation 1.0. 5.1, 5.2, 6.3)

Lead students through a cool-down and flexibility exercises appropriate to the physical activity level of the lesson. (Assessment opportunity: structured observation 4.1)

DAY 10	Review how force is used in basic game tactics. 2.3
	Have students perform a warm-up along with a cardiorespiratory workout. (Assessment opportunity: structured observation 4.1)
	Review punting. 1.0, 2.5
	Have students practice punting. (Assessment opportunity: structured observation 1.0)
	Review 2-on-2 soccer. 1.0, 2.3
	Have students play 2-on-2 soccer. (Assessment opportunity: structured observation 1.0, 5.1, 5.2, 6.3)
	Lead students through a cool-down and flexibility exercises appropriate to the physical activity level of the lesson. (Assessment opportunity: structured observation 4.1)
DAY 11	Review how force is used in basic game tactics. 2.3
	Have students perform a warm-up along with a cardiorespiratory workout. (Assessment opportunity: structured observation 4.1)
	Review 2-on-2 soccer. 1.0, 2.3
	Have students play 2-on-2 soccer. (Assessment opportunity: structured observation 1.0, 5.1, 5.2, 6.3)
	Lead students through a cool-down and flexibility exercises appropriate to the physical activity level of the lesson. (Assessment opportunity: structured observation 4.1)
DAY 12	Have students perform a warm-up along with muscular strength and muscular endurance exercises. (Assessment opportunity: structured observation 4.1)
	Have students, in pairs, create a ball routine using just the feet that expresses feelings. (Assessment assignment opportunity: project 6.2)
	Lead students through a cool-down and flexibility exercises appropriate to the physical activity level of the lesson. (Assessment opportunity: structured observation 4.1)
DAY 13	Have students perform a warm-up along with a cardiorespiratory workout. (Assessment opportunity: structured observation 4.1)
	Have students practice their ball routines. 1.0, 5.1, 5.2, 6.3
	Lead students through a cool-down and flexibility exercises appropriate to the physical activity level of the lesson. (Assessment opportunity: structured observation 4.1)
DAY 14	Have students perform a warm-up along with muscular strength and muscular endurance exercises. (Assessment opportunity: structured observation 4.1)
	Have each pair teach their ball routine to another pair. (Assessment opportunity: project 6.2)
	Lead students through a cool-down and flexibility exercises appropriate to the physical activity level of the lesson. (Assessment opportunity: structured observation 4.1)
	Review material for tomorrow's quiz (or hand out quiz if you would like for it to be a take-home quiz). 2.1, 2.2, 2.3, 2.4, 2.5, 6.4
	For homework, have students write a description about how the manipulation of an object routine to music expresses personal feelings. (Assessment assignment opportunity: project 6.2)
DAY 15	Have students take the quiz. (Assessment opportunity: quiz 2.1, 2.2, 2.3, 2.4, 2.5, 6.4)
	Collect activity log. (Assessment opportunity: log 3.1)
	Collect history report. (Assessment opportunity: report 6.1)
	Collect essay on extracurricular activities. (Assessment opportunity: essay 3.2)
	Collect 1-day body composition improvement plan. (Assessment opportunity: project 4.2)
	Collect description regarding routine to music. (Assessment opportunity: project 6.2)

(continued)

Striking With Implements   — Unit 9

In this, our seventh skills theme unit, we look at the skill of striking with an implement. I teach this unit to ensure that students can demonstrate the correct technique for striking a variety of objects using a variety of implements; then I extend their skill performance for both distance and accuracy. Once students have acquired some distance and accuracy, I have them explore aiming at moving objects and aiming while moving. Finally, I have the students apply the skill of striking to gamelike settings, such as softball, tennis, and hockey. This unit can be conducted in any open area; however, a blacktop area is best for racket and hockey skills (street hockey), and grass is best for batting skills. If you choose to teach field hockey instead of street hockey, then conduct the hockey skill lessons on the grass as well.

Unit 9 Standards

1.0—Demonstrates speed and accuracy using the mature form for striking with a bat, hockey stick, and racket or paddle (backhand and forehand).

2.1—Explains the type of situations in which practice should focus on speed and the type of situations in which practice should focus on accuracy.

2.2—Describes ways to generate and absorb force using an implement.

2.3—Describes how space, time, and force are used together to create basic game tactics.

2.4—Describes the positive impact of social changes on physical performance from prepuberty through puberty.

2.5—Describes the critical elements for striking with a bat, hockey stick, and racket or paddle (backhand and forehand).

3.1—Engages in moderate physical activity for 50 minutes 5 days each week.

3.2—Describes the extracurricular physical activities available in the school setting related to striking objects with an implement.

4.1—Works toward a health-enhancing level of physical fitness.

4.2—Refines 1-day cardiorespiratory endurance plan.

5.1—Modifies striking with an implement tasks to fit the needs of a differently abled student.

5.2—Accepts responsibility for personal safety during striking with implement activities.

6.1—Describes the development of games using implements in the United States during the 17th and 18th centuries.

6.2—Expresses personal feelings through a movement-based routine that involves striking with an implement.

6.3—Chooses to engage in striking with an implement skill competencies at a level that leads to personal satisfaction, success, and enjoyment.

6.4—Describes the long-term cardiorespiratory benefits derived from participation in physical activity.

Unit 9 Assessments

1.0—Structured observation (days 1-14)

2.1—Quiz (day 15)

2.2—Quiz (day 15)

2.3—Quiz (day 15)

2.4—Quiz (day 15)

2.5—Quiz (day 15)

3.1—Log (assigned on day 1; collected on day 15)

3.2—Essay (assigned on day 1; collected on day 15)

4.1—Structured observation (days 1-14)

4.2—Project (assigned on day 2; collected on day 15)

5.1—Structured observation (days 1-14)

5.2—Structured observation (days 1-14)

6.1—Report (assigned on day 1; collected on day 15)

6.2—Project (assigned on day 11; collected on day 14)

6.3—Structured observation (days 1-14)

6.4—Quiz (day 15)

Resources

Health-Related Fitness: Tutorial and Portfolio (Bonnie's Fitware, Inc.)

Middle School Physical Education Portfolio (Bonnie's Fitware, Inc.)

Fifth grade striking with implements task cards (Bonnie's Fitware, Inc.)

Globetrotters music for routine (Bonnie's Fitware, Inc.)

Fifth grade unit 9 posters (Bonnie's Fitware, Inc.—included in the Middle School Detailed Lesson Plans)

Fitness posters (Bonnie's Fitware, Inc.—included in the Middle School Detailed Lesson Plans)

Equipment

Variety of objects (e.g., rubber balls, softballs, tennis balls, hockey pucks)

Variety of striking implements (e.g., bats, rackets or paddles, hockey sticks)

Variety of targets, nets, and goals

Batting tees

Games

No-serve Pickleball

2-on-2 hockey

Unit 9 Outline

DAY 1	Display posters.
	Introduce the unit on striking with an implement.
	Explain procedures that are safe and effective for activities involving striking with an implement. 5.2
	Have students record the safety tips in their notebooks. 5.2
	Explain that skill competency in striking can lead to personal satisfaction, success, and enjoyment. 6.3
	Discuss ways to modify activities for differently abled students. 5.1
	Assign students to heterogeneous working groups of four.
	Have students perform a warm-up along with a cardiorespiratory workout. (Assessment opportunity: structured observation 4.1)
	Demonstrate striking a stationary object, using a variety of implements (see figure 14.21). 1.0, 2.5
	Have students brainstorm ways to modify striking with implement activities for differently abled students. 5.1
	Have students practice striking a stationary object, using a variety of implements (e.g., bat, paddle, hockey stick). (Assessment opportunity: structured observation 1.0, 5.1, 5.2, 6.3)
	Lead students through a cool-down and flexibility exercises appropriate to the physical activity level of the lesson. (Assessment opportunity: structured observation 4.1)

(continued)

Unit 9 Outline *(continued)*

DAY 1 *(continued)*

Assign unit-long homework:

- Have students research and write a description of the development of games using striking implements in the United States during the 17th and 18th centuries. (Assessment assignment opportunity: report 6.1)

- Have students keep a log of daily activity. (Assessment assignment opportunity: log 3.1)

- Have students describe the extracurricular physical activities available in the school setting related to striking with an implement. (Assessment assignment opportunity: essay 3.2)

a   b

Figure 14.21   *(a)* Striking with a racket and *(b)* grip.

DAY 2

Discuss the long-term cardiorespiratory benefits derived from participation in physical activity. 6.4

Have students record in their notebooks the long-term cardiorespiratory benefits derived from participation in physical activity. 6.4

Review the cardiorespiratory frequency, intensity, time, and type concepts using the Health-Related Fitness: Tutorial and Portfolio. 4.2

Have students refine their 1-day cardiorespiratory endurance improvement plans. (Assessment assignment opportunity: project 4.2)

Have students perform a warm-up along with muscular strength and muscular endurance exercises. (Assessment opportunity: structured observation 4.1)

Review striking a stationary object. 1.0, 2.5

Have students practice striking a stationary object, using a variety of implements (e.g., bat, paddle, hockey stick). (Assessment opportunity: structured observation 1.0, 5.1, 5.2, 6.3)

Demonstrate striking an object tossed by the striker. 1.0, 2.5

DAY 2 (continued)

Have students practice striking an object they toss for themselves, using a variety of implements (e.g., bat, paddle, racket). (Assessment opportunity: structured observation 1.0, 5.1, 5.2, 6.3)

Lead students through a cool-down and flexibility exercises appropriate to the physical activity level of the lesson. (Assessment opportunity: structured observation 4.1)

Review procedures that are safe and effective for activities that involve striking with an implement. 5.2

DAY 3

Explain the type of situations in which practice should focus on speed and the type of situations in which practice should focus on accuracy. 2.1

Have students record in their notebooks the type of situations in which practice should focus on speed and the type of situations in which practice should focus on accuracy. 2.1

Have students perform a warm-up along with a cardiorespiratory workout. (Assessment opportunity: structured observation 4.1)

Review striking a self-tossed object. 1.0, 2.5

Have students practice striking a self-tossed object, using a variety of implements (e.g., bat, paddle, racket). (Assessment opportunity: structured observation 1.0, 5.1, 5.2, 6.3)

Demonstrate and describe striking an object tossed by a partner. 1.0, 2.5

Have students practice striking an object tossed or rolled by their partners, using a variety of implements, while their partners give feedback. (Assessment opportunity: structured observation 1.0, 5.1, 5.2, 6.3)

Lead students through a cool-down and flexibility exercises appropriate to the physical activity level of the lesson. (Assessment opportunity: structured observation 4.1)

Review the long-term cardiorespiratory benefits derived from participation in physical activity. 6.4

DAY 4

Describe ways to generate and absorb force when using an implement. 2.2

Have students describe in their notebooks ways to generate and absorb force when using an implement. 2.2

Have students perform a warm-up along with muscular strength and muscular endurance exercises. (Assessment opportunity: structured observation 4.1)

Demonstrate striking an object that has rebounded off a wall. 1.0, 2.5

Have students pick either striking a self-tossed object, striking an object tossed by a partner, or striking an object that has rebounded off a wall, using a variety of implements (e.g., bat, paddle, hockey stick). Insist that students make all strikes forehanded, aiming for a target. (Assessment opportunity: structured observation 1.0, 5.1, 5.2, 6.3)

Lead students through a cool-down and flexibility exercises appropriate to the physical activity level of the lesson. (Assessment opportunity: structured observation 4.1)

Review the type of situations in which practice should focus on speed and the type of situations in which practice should focus on accuracy. 2.1

DAY 5

Describe how space, time, and force are used together to create basic game tactics. 2.3

Have students record in their notebooks how space, time, and force are used together to create basic game tactics. 2.3

Have students perform a warm-up along with a cardiorespiratory workout. (Assessment opportunity: structured observation 4.1)

Demonstrate no-serve Pickleball. 1.0, 2.3

Have students choose from tennis rackets and paddles to play no-serve Pickleball, using only forehand strokes. (Assessment opportunity: structured observation 1.0, 5.1, 5.2, 6.3)

Lead students through a cool-down and flexibility exercises appropriate to the physical activity level of the lesson. (Assessment opportunity: structured observation 4.1)

Review ways to generate and absorb force when using an implement. 2.2

(continued)

Unit 9 Outline *(continued)*

DAY 6

Describe the positive impact of social changes on physical performance from prepuberty through puberty. 2.4

Have students record the positive impact of social changes on physical performance from prepuberty through puberty in their notebooks. 2.4

Have students perform a warm-up along with a cardiorespiratory workout. (Assessment opportunity: structured observation 4.1)

Demonstrate and describe using a backhand stroke to strike an object, using a variety of implements (e.g., paddle, racket). 1.0, 2.5

Have students practice the backhand stroke striking a self-tossed object, using a variety of implements (e.g., paddle, racket). (Assessment opportunity: structured observation 1.0, 5.1, 5.2, 6.3)

Demonstrate and describe using a backhand stroke to strike an object tossed by a partner. 1.0, 2.5

Have students practice using the backhand stroke to strike an object tossed by a partner, using a variety of implements. (Assessment opportunity: structured observation 1.0, 5.1, 5.2, 6.3)

Lead students through a cool-down and flexibility exercises appropriate to the physical activity level of the lesson. (Assessment opportunity: structured observation 4.1)

Review the type of situations when practice should focus on speed and the type of situations when practice should focus on accuracy. 2.1

DAY 7

Have students perform a warm-up along with muscular strength and muscular endurance exercises. (Assessment opportunity: structured observation 4.1)

Review using a backhand stroke to strike an object that has rebounded off a wall. 1.0, 2.5

Have students pick either striking a self-tossed object, striking an object tossed by a partner, or striking an object that has rebounded off a wall, using a variety of implements (e.g., paddle, racket). (Assessment opportunity: structured observation 1.0, 5.1, 5.2, 6.3)

Lead students through a cool-down and flexibility exercises appropriate to the physical activity level of the lesson. (Assessment opportunity: structured observation 4.1)

Review ways to generate and absorb force when using an implement. 2.2

DAY 8

Have students perform a warm-up along with a cardiorespiratory workout. (Assessment opportunity: structured observation 4.1)

Have students play no-serve Pickleball using both the forehand and backhand strokes. (Assessment opportunity: structured observation 1.0, 5.1, 5.2, 6.3)

Lead students through a cool-down and flexibility exercises appropriate to the physical activity level of the lesson. (Assessment opportunity: structured observation 4.1)

Have students brainstorm a list of various sports and sport skills that use the skill of striking with an implement. 1.0, 2.3, 2.5

DAY 9

Have students perform a warm-up along with muscular strength and muscular endurance exercises. (Assessment opportunity: structured observation 4.1)

Demonstrate the underhand striking motion, using a hockey stick. 1.0, 2.5

Have students practice the underhand striking motion, using a hockey stick, at a stationary object. (Assessment opportunity: structured observation 1.0, 5.1, 5.2, 6.3)

Have students practice the underhand striking motion, using a hockey stick, at a stationary object and aiming at a target. (Assessment opportunity: structured observation 1.0, 5.1, 5.2, 6.3)

Lead students through a cool-down and flexibility exercises appropriate to the physical activity level of the lesson. (Assessment opportunity: structured observation 4.1)

DAY 10

Have students perform a warm-up along with a cardiorespiratory workout. (Assessment opportunity: structured observation 4.1)

Review underhand striking of a stationary object using a hockey stick. 1.0, 2.5

Have students practice underhand striking of a stationary object using a hockey stick while aiming at a variety of targets. (Assessment opportunity: structured observation 1.0, 5.1, 5.2, 6.3)

Demonstrate and describe underhand striking back and forth with a partner while moving, using a hockey stick (see figure 14.22). 1.0, 2.5

Have pairs practice underhand striking back and forth while moving, using a hockey stick. (Assessment opportunity: structured observation 1.0, 5.1, 5.2, 6.3)

Lead students through a cool-down and flexibility exercises appropriate to the physical activity level of the lesson. (Assessment opportunity: structured observation 4.1)

(continued)

Figure 14.22   Dribbling and passing an object with a partner.

Unit 9 Outline *(continued)*

DAY 11	Review ways to generate and absorb force when using an implement. 2.2
	Have students perform a warm-up along with a cardiorespiratory workout. (Assessment opportunity: structured observation 4.1)
	Demonstrate and describe dribbling using a hockey stick. 1.0, 2.5
	Have students practice dribbling. (Assessment opportunity: structured observation 1.0, 5.1, 5.2, 6.3)
	Have students practice dribbling, using various movement qualities (e.g., dribbling fast, slow, in a straight line, in a curved line). (Assessment opportunity: structured observation 1.0, 5.1, 5.2, 6.3)
	Have students dribble around obstacles. (Assessment opportunity: structured observation 1.0, 5.1, 5.2, 6.3)
	Have students create a routine that involves using a hockey stick and object to music that expresses personal feelings. (Assessment assignment opportunity: structured observation 6.2)
	Lead students through a cool-down and flexibility exercises appropriate to the physical activity level of the lesson. (Assessment opportunity: structured observation 4.1)
DAY 12	Have students perform a warm-up along with muscular strength and muscular endurance exercises. (Assessment opportunity: structured observation 4.1)
	Review hockey dribbling. 1.0, 2.5
	Review how space, time, and force are used together to create basic game tactics. 2.3
	Teach 2-on-2 hockey. 1.0, 2.3
	Have students play 2-on-2 hockey. (Assessment opportunity: structured observation 1.0, 5.1, 5.2, 6.3)
	Have students work on their routines. 1.0, 6.2
	Lead students through a cool-down and flexibility exercises appropriate to the physical activity level of the lesson. (Assessment opportunity: structured observation 4.1)
DAY 13	Have students perform a warm-up along with a cardiorespiratory workout. (Assessment opportunity: structured observation 4.1)
	Have students work on their routines. 1.0, 6.2
	Lead students through a cool-down and flexibility exercises appropriate to the physical activity level of the lesson. (Assessment opportunity: structured observation 4.1)
DAY 14	Have students perform a warm-up along with muscular strength and muscular endurance exercises. (Assessment opportunity: structured observation 4.1)
	Have students demonstrate their routines. (Assessment opportunity: project 6.2)
	Lead students through a cool-down and flexibility exercises appropriate to the physical activity level of the lesson. (Assessment opportunity: structured observation 4.1)
DAY 15	Have students take the quiz. (Assessment opportunity: quiz 2.1, 2.2, 2.3, 2.4, 2.5, 6.4)
	Collect activity log. (Assessment opportunity: log 3.1)
	Collect history report. (Assessment opportunity: report 6.1)
	Collect essay on extracurricular activities. (Assessment opportunity: essay 3.2)
	Refine 1-day cardiorespiratory endurance improvement plan. (Assessment opportunity: project 4.2)

Early American Dances  ~Unit 10

The dances selected for this unit align with the area of study in history and social science for my students—early America, 17th and 18th centuries. The dances in this sample unit are sequenced so that the locomotor skills presented in the first dance are repeated in subsequent dances. You won't see cardiorespiratory exercises in this unit because dancing satisfies the need for cardiorespiratory training.

This unit works best in a closed area or gymnasium, but you can present it outside. If you must conduct the unit outside, choose a secluded area so that students do not feel self-conscious about performing to music in front of other classes. For equipment, you'll need a stereo and music to accompany the dances. I have students wear heart rate monitors to determine whether they are in their target heart rate zones long enough to improve their cardiorespiratory endurance. On different days, I have different students download the data from their heart rate monitors into the computer; then I have them place the computer-generated graphs into their electronic portfolios.

Unit 10 Standards

1.0—Demonstrates control using the mature form for dance steps (forearm swing, right-hand star, do-si-do, two-step, heel–toe, grapevine, chug steps, cross kick, stomp, knee lift, slide, and polka).

2.1—Explains the appropriate types of practice for improving one's dance performance.

2.2—Describes ways to generate and absorb force when dancing.

2.3—Describes how the qualities of movement are combined to create dances.

2.4—Describes the negative impact of social changes on physical performance from prepuberty through puberty.

2.5—Diagrams the dance steps (grapevine step, polka step, forearm swing, do-si-do, two-step, right-hand star).

3.1—Engages in moderate physical activity for 55 minutes 5 days each week.

3.2—Describes the extracurricular physical activities available in the school setting related to dance.

4.1—Works toward a health-enhancing level of physical fitness.

4.2—Refines 1-day cardiorespiratory endurance and body composition plan.

5.1—Modifies dance activities to fit the needs of a differently abled student.

5.2—Accepts responsibility for personal safety during dancing activities.

6.1—Describes the development of dance in the United States during the 17th and 18th centuries.

6.2—Expresses personal feelings through the creation of a creative dance.

6.3—Chooses to engage in skill competencies found in early American dances at a level that leads to personal satisfaction, success, and enjoyment.

6.4—Describes the long-term muscular strength benefits derived from participation in physical activity.

Unit 10 Assessments

1.0—Structured observation (days 1-15)

2.1—Quiz (day 11)

2.2—Quiz (day 11)

2.3—Project (assigned on day 13; collected on day 14)

2.4—Quiz (day 11)

2.5—Quiz (day 11)

3.1—Log (assigned on day 1; collected on day 15)

3.2—Essay (assigned on day 1; collected on day 15)

4.1—Structured observation (days 1-15)

4.2—Project (assigned on day 2; collected on day 15)

5.1—Structured observation (days 1-15)

5.2—Structured observation (days 1-15)

6.1—Project (assigned on day 1; collected on day 15)

6.2—Project (assigned on day 12; collected on day 15)

6.3—Structured observation (days 1-15)

6.4—Quiz (day 11)

Resources (Music and Dance Steps Included)

Health-Related Fitness: Tutorial and Portfolio (Bonnie's Fitware, Inc.)

Middle School Physical Education Portfolio (Bonnie's Fitware, Inc.)

Dance Instructional CD (Bonnie's Fitware, Inc.)

Fifth grade American dance task cards (Bonnie's Fitware, Inc.)

Fifth grade unit 10 posters (Bonnie's Fitware, Inc.—included in the Middle School Detailed Lesson Plans)

Fitness posters (Bonnie's Fitware, Inc.—included in the Middle School Detailed Lesson Plans)

Qualities of Movement chart (Bonnie's Fitware, Inc.—included in the Middle School Detailed Lesson Plans)

Alley Cat music (Bonnie's Fitware, Inc.)

Cotton Eye Joe music (Bonnie's Fitware, Inc.)

Jiffy Mixer music (Bonnie's Fitware, Inc.)

Patty Cake Polka music (Bonnie's Fitware, Inc.)

Red River Valley music (Bonnie's Fitware, Inc.)

Shoo Fly music (Bonnie's Fitware, Inc.)

Teton Mountain Stomp music (Bonnie's Fitware, Inc.)

Equipment

Sound system

American dance music

Heart monitors

Tambourine

Dances

Shoo Fly: walking

Teton Mountain Stomp: two-step, dance stomp, slide

Alley Cat: grapevine, touch step, knee lifts

Cotton Eye Joe: heel–toe, two-step, cross kick

Jiffy Mixer: heel–toe, chug step

Patty Cake Polka: polka step, elbow swing

Red River Valley: do-si-do, star right, shuffle

Dance Steps

Grapevine	Polka step	Stomp
Touch step	Two-step	Do-si-do
Knee lifts	Chug step	Star right
Heel–toe	Cross kick	Shuffle
Elbow swing	Slide	Forearm swing
Walking	Side step	

Unit 10 Outline

DAY 1

Display the posters.

Introduce the unit.

Describe safety issues related to dancing. 5.2

Have students record in their notebooks safety issues related to dancing. 5.2

Have students brainstorm ways to modify dances for students who are differently abled. 5.1

Explain that skill competency in dancing can lead to personal satisfaction, success, and enjoyment. 6.3

Have students perform a warm-up. (Assessment opportunity: structured observation 4.1)

Have students move around in the defined area, using locomotor movements to the sound of the teacher beating a tambourine, without bumping into others. 1.0

Explain that dances have a starting point (no movement) and stopping point (when the dance finishes and the music or beat stops). 1.0

Have students perform four-direction four-count walking pattern to the sound of teacher beating a tambourine. 1.0

Lead students through a cool-down and flexibility exercises appropriate to the physical activity level of the lesson. (Assessment opportunity: structured observation 4.1)

Assign unit-long homework:

- Have students research and write a description on the development of dance in the United States during the 17th and 18th centuries. (Assessment assignment opportunity: report 6.1)

- Have students keep a log of daily activity. (Assessment assignment opportunity: log 3.1)

- Have students write a description of the extracurricular physical activities available in the school setting related to dance. (Assessment assignment opportunity: essay 3.2)

DAY 2

Describe to students the long-term muscular strength benefits derived from participation in physical activity. 6.4

Have students write in their notebooks the long-term muscular strength benefits derived from participation in physical activity. 6.4

Review frequency, intensity, time, and type for cardiorespiratory endurance and body composition using the Health-Related Fitness: Tutorial and Portfolio. 4.2

Have students perform a warm-up along with muscular strength and muscular endurance exercises. (Assessment opportunity: structured observation 4.1)

Demonstrate and describe forearm swing. 1.0, 2.5

Have students practice forearm swing. 1.0

Demonstrate and describe forming arch. 1.0, 2.5

Have students practice forming arch. 1.0

Describe and demonstrate Shoo Fly. 1.0, 2.5

Walk students through Shoo Fly. 1.0, 2.5

Lead students through a cool-down and flexibility exercises appropriate to the physical activity level of the lesson. (Assessment opportunity: structured observation 4.1)

For homework, have students refine their 1-day cardiorespiratory endurance and body composition plan. (Assessment assignment opportunity: project 4.2)

(continued)

Unit 10 Outline (continued)

DAY 3

Discuss with students ways to generate and absorb force when dancing. 2.2

Have students write in their notebooks ways to generate and absorb force when dancing. 2.2

Have students perform a warm-up. (Assessment opportunity: structured observation 4.1)

Have students dance to Shoo Fly. (Assessment opportunity: structured observation 1.0, 5.1, 5.2, 6.3)

Demonstrate and describe shuffle step. 1.0, 2.5

Have students practice shuffle step. 1.0

Demonstrate and describe star right. 1.0, 2.5

Have students practice star right. 1.0

Demonstrate and describe do-si-do. 1.0, 2.5

Have students practice do-si-do. 1.0

Describe and demonstrate Red River Valley. 1.0, 2.5

Walk students through Red River Valley. (Assessment opportunity: structured observation 1.0, 5.1, 5.2, 6.3)

Have students dance to Red River Valley. (Assessment opportunity: structured observation 1.0, 5.1, 5.2, 6.3)

Lead students through a cool-down and flexibility exercises appropriate to the physical activity level of the lesson. (Assessment opportunity: structured observation 4.1)

Have students discuss the ways to generate and absorb force when dancing. 2.2

DAY 4

Explain the appropriate type (mass or distributed, whole or part, focus on speed or accuracy, mental or physical) of practice for improving one's dance performance. 2.1

Have students record in their notebooks the appropriate type of practice for improving one's dance performance. 2.1

Have students perform a warm-up along with muscular strength and muscular endurance exercises. (Assessment opportunity: structured observation 4.1)

Have students dance to Red River Valley. (Assessment opportunity: structured observation 1.0, 5.1, 5.2, 6.3)

Demonstrate and describe slide. 1.0, 2.5

Have students practice slide. 1.0

Demonstrate and describe stomp. 1.0, 2.5

Have students practice stomp. 1.0

Describe and demonstrate Teton Mountain Stomp. 1.0, 2.5

Walk students through Teton Mountain Stomp. (Assessment opportunity: structured observation 1.0, 5.1, 5.2, 6.3)

Have students dance to Teton Mountain Stomp. (Assessment opportunity: structured observation 1.0, 5.1, 5.2, 6.3)

Lead students through a cool-down and flexibility exercises appropriate to the physical activity level of the lesson. (Assessment opportunity: structured observation 4.1)

Have students brainstorm ways to modify today's dances for students with special needs. 5.1

DAY 5	Describe the negative impact of social changes on physical performance from prepuberty through puberty. 2.4
	Have students record in their notebooks the negative impact of social changes on physical performance from prepuberty through puberty. 2.4
	Have students perform a warm-up. (Assessment opportunity: structured observation 4.1)
	Have students dance to Shoo Fly. (Assessment opportunity: structured observation 1.0, 5.1, 5.2, 6.3)
	Have students dance to Red River Valley. (Assessment opportunity: structured observation 1.0, 5.1, 5.2, 6.3)
	Have student dance to Teton Mountain Stomp. (Assessment opportunity: structured observation 1.0, 5.1, 5.2, 6.3)
	Lead students through a cool-down and flexibility exercises appropriate to the physical activity level of the lesson. (Assessment opportunity: structured observation 4.1)
	Have students discuss how they can practice on their own to get better at dancing. 2.1
DAY 6	Have students perform a warm-up. (Assessment opportunity: structured observation 4.1)
	Demonstrate and describe cross kick. 1.0, 2.5
	Have students practice cross kick. 1.0
	Demonstrate and describe two-step. 1.0, 2.5
	Have students practice two-step. 1.0
	Describe and demonstrate Cotton Eye Joe. 1.0, 2.5
	Walk students through Cotton Eye Joe. (Assessment opportunity: structured observation 1.0, 5.1, 5.2, 6.3)
	Have students dance to Cotton Eye Joe. (Assessment opportunity: structured observation 1.0, 5.1, 5.2, 6.3)
	Lead students through a cool-down and flexibility exercises appropriate to the physical activity level of the lesson. (Assessment opportunity: structured observation 4.1)
	Have students discuss whether they feel vulnerable to the negative impact of social changes. 2.4
DAY 7	Have students perform a warm-up along with muscular strength and muscular endurance exercises. (Assessment opportunity: structured observation 4.1)
	Have students dance to Cotton Eye Joe. (Assessment opportunity: structured observation 1.0, 5.1, 5.2, 6.3)
	Demonstrate and describe side step. 1.0, 2.5
	Have students practice side step. 1.0
	Demonstrate and describe heel–toe. 1.0, 2.5
	Have students practice heel–toe. 1.0
	Demonstrate and describe chug step. 1.0, 2.5
	Have students practice chug step. 1.0
	Describe and demonstrate Jiffy Mixer. 1.0, 2.5
	Walk students through Jiffy Mixer. (Assessment opportunity: structured observation 1.0, 5.1, 5.2, 6.3)
	Have students dance to Jiffy Mixer. (Assessment opportunity: structured observation 1.0, 5.1, 5.2, 6.3)
	Lead students through a cool-down and flexibility exercises appropriate to the physical activity level of the lesson. (Assessment opportunity: structured observation 4.1)
	Have students brainstorm ways to modify today's dances for students who are differently abled. 5.1

(continued)

Unit 10 Outline *(continued)*

DAY 8

Have students perform a warm-up. (Assessment opportunity: structured observation 4.1)

Have students dance to Jiffy Mixer. (Assessment opportunity: structured observation 1.0, 5.1, 5.2, 6.3)

Have students dance to Cotton Eye Joe. (Assessment opportunity: structured observation 1.0, 5.1, 5.2, 6.3)

Repeat dances as time allows. (Assessment opportunity: structured observation 1.0, 5.1, 5.2, 6.3)

Lead students through a cool-down and flexibility exercises appropriate to the physical activity level of the lesson. (Assessment opportunity: structured observation 4.1)

DAY 9

Have students perform a warm-up along with muscular strength and muscular endurance exercises. (Assessment opportunity: structured observation 4.1)

Demonstrate and describe grapevine. 1.0, 2.5

Have students practice grapevine. 1.0

Demonstrate and describe knee lift. 1.0, 2.5

Have students practice knee lift. 1.0

Demonstrate and describe touch step (back). 1.0, 2.5

Have students practice touch step (back). 1.0

Demonstrate and describe Alley Cat. 1.0, 2.5

Walk students through Alley Cat. (Assessment opportunity: structured observation 1.0, 5.1, 5.2, 6.3)

Have students dance to Alley Cat. (Assessment opportunity: structured observation 1.0, 5.1, 5.2, 6.3)

Lead students through a cool-down and flexibility exercises appropriate to the physical activity level of the lesson. (Assessment opportunity: structured observation 4.1)

DAY 10

Have students perform a warm-up. (Assessment opportunity: structured observation 4.1)

Have students dance to Alley Cat. (Assessment opportunity: structured observation 1.0, 5.1, 5.2, 6.3)

Review heel–toe. 1.0, 2.5

Have students practice heel–toe. 1.0

Demonstrate and describe polka step. 1.0, 2.5

Have students practice polka step. 1.0

Demonstrate and describe right elbow swing. 1.0, 2.5

Have students practice right elbow swing. 1.0

Demonstrate and describe Patty Cake Polka. 1.0, 2.5

Walk students through Patty Cake Polka. (Assessment opportunity: structured observation 1.0, 5.1, 5.2, 6.3)

Have students dance to Patty Cake Polka. (Assessment opportunity: structured observation 1.0, 5.1, 5.2, 6.3)

Lead students through a cool-down and flexibility exercises appropriate to the physical activity level of the lesson. (Assessment opportunity: structured observation 4.1)

Review material for tomorrow's quiz (or hand out quiz if you would like for it to be a take-home quiz). 2.1, 2.2, 2.4, 2.5, 6.4

DAY 11	Have students take the quiz. (Assessment opportunity: quiz 2.1, 2.2, 2.4, 2.5, 6.4) Have students perform a warm-up. (Assessment opportunity: structured observation 4.1) Have students dance to Alley Cat as time permits. (Assessment opportunity: structured observation 1.0, 5.1, 5.2, 6.3) Have students dance to Patty Cake Polka as time permits. (Assessment opportunity: structured observation 1.0, 5.1, 5.2, 6.3) Lead students through a cool-down and flexibility exercises appropriate to the physical activity level of the lesson. (Assessment opportunity: structured observation 4.1)
DAY 12	Describe how the qualities of movement are combined to create dances. 2.3 Have students write in their notebooks how qualities of movement are combined to create dances. 2.3 Have students perform a warm-up along with muscular strength and muscular endurance exercises. (Assessment opportunity: structured observation 4.1) Have students, in groups of four, create their own dance that expresses personal feelings using a combination of the steps practiced over the last 2 weeks while considering the abilities and needs of all students in their group. (Assessment assignment opportunity: project 6.2) Lead students through a cool-down and flexibility exercises appropriate to the physical activity level of the lesson. (Assessment opportunity: structured observation 4.1) Ask students to discuss how they are using qualities of movement in their new dances. 2.3
DAY 13	Have students perform a warm-up. (Assessment opportunity: structured observation 4.1) Have students continue to work on their own dances. (Assessment opportunity: structured observation: 1.0, 5.1, 5.2, 6.3) 6.2 Lead students through a cool-down and flexibility exercises appropriate to the physical activity level of the lesson. (Assessment opportunity: structured observation 4.1) For homework, have students write a description of how they used qualities of movement in their dance. (Assessment assignment opportunity: project 2.3)
DAY 14	Have students perform a warm-up along with muscular strength and muscular endurance exercises. (Assessment opportunity: structured observation 4.1) Have students, in their groups, teach another group their new dance. (Assessment opportunity: project 6.2) Lead students through a cool-down and flexibility exercises appropriate to the physical activity level of the lesson. (Assessment opportunity: structured observation 4.1) Collect descriptions of use of movement qualities in dance. (Assessment opportunity: project 2.3)
DAY 15	Have students perform a warm-up. (Assessment opportunity: structured observation 4.1) Have students, in their groups, teach another group their new dance. (Assessment opportunity: project 6.2) Lead students through a cool-down and flexibility exercises appropriate to the physical activity level of the lesson. (Assessment opportunity: structured observation 4.1) Collect physical activity log. (Assessment opportunity: log 3.1) Collect history project. (Assessment opportunity: report 6.1) Collect list of extracurricular activities. (Assessment opportunity: essay 3.2) Collect 1-day cardiorespiratory endurance and body composition plan. (Assessment opportunity: project 4.2)

Early American Games

~ Unit 11 ~

Several times throughout my sample curriculum I have had the fifth graders participate in game activities, using the specific skills addressed in each unit. In this unit, however, we take a more comprehensive look at games and how they have been played throughout American history, and we elaborate on the various elements of a game. In the 21st century, the knowledge of fair play is far more important than remembering the official rules for every sport. Moreover, students need to see how they can adapt games, depending on the situation. For example, individuals may enjoy playing football; but they are not often in situations in which they have 11 players on a team, so they must know how to modify football or any other game. I continue during this unit to review the cognitive concepts associated with cardiorespiratory endurance, body composition, warm-up, and cool-down so that students can create their 1-day fitness plan relative to those areas.

You can teach this unit in any open area, keeping in mind the specific requirements of each game. As I introduce each game, I explain the history of that game. I've saved this unit until the end of the school year for two reasons: First, it applies the various skills the students have learned and practiced throughout the year, and second, it includes games from early America as the fifth graders conclude their U.S. history course in their history or social science class.

Unit 11 Standards

1.0—Demonstrates speed and accuracy using the mature form for sidearm throw.

2.1—Explains the types of practice that improve motor skill performance for speed and accuracy.

2.2—Describes ways to generate and absorb force when performing movement and motor skills.

2.3—Describes basic game tactics for early American games and the use of space, time, and force.

2.4—Describes changes from birth through puberty along with their impact on physical performance.

2.5—Describes critical elements for the sidearm throw.

3.1—Engages in moderate physical activity for 60 minutes 5 days each week.

3.2—Describes opportunities in the school setting for regular participation in physical activity.

4.1—Works toward a health-enhancing level of physical fitness.

4.2—Designs a cardiorespiratory and body composition fitness plan including a warm-up and cool-down for 1 day.

5.1—Modifies game activities to fit the needs of a differently abled student.

5.2—Accepts responsibility for personal safety during game play.

6.1—Describes the development of games in the United States during the 17th and 18th centuries.

6.2—Expresses personal feelings through a movement-based routine that involves manipulatives.

6.3—Chooses to engage in skill competencies found in early American games at a level that leads to personal satisfaction, success, and enjoyment.

6.4—Describes the long-term muscular endurance benefits derived from participation in physical activity.

Unit 11 Assessments

1.0—Structured observation (days 1-14)

2.1—Quiz (day 15)

2.2—Quiz (day 15)

2.3—Quiz (day 15)

2.4—Quiz (day 15)

2.5—Quiz (day 15)

3.1—Log (assigned on day 1; collected on day 15)

3.2—Essay (assigned on day 1; collected on day 15)

4.1—Structured observation (days 1-14)

4.2—Project (assigned on day 2; collected on day 15)

5.1—Structured observation (days 1-14)

5.2—Structured observation (days 1-14)

6.1—Report (assigned on day 1; collected on day 15)

6.2—Essay (assigned on day 1; collected on day 5)

6.3—Structured observation (days 1-14)

6.4—Quiz (day 15)

Resources

Health-Related Fitness: Tutorial and Portfolio (Bonnie's Fitware, Inc.)

Middle School Physical Education Portfolio (Bonnie's Fitware, Inc.)

Multicultural Games and Activities CD (Bonnie's Fitware, Inc.)

Fifth grade American games task cards (Bonnie's Fitware, Inc.)

Fifth grade unit 11 posters (Bonnie's Fitware, Inc.—included in the Middle School Detailed Lesson Plans)

Fitness posters (Bonnie's Fitware, Inc.—included in the Middle School Detailed Lesson Plans)

Equipment

Popsicle sticks	Paddles	Deck rings
Playground balls	Hula hoops	Foam noodles
Walnuts	Ruler or stick	Variety of items available for students to create their own games
Pegs	Twelve-inch cones	
Beanbags	Badminton shuttlecocks	

Games

Battledore and Shuttlecock	Choctaw Sticks Game	Rolling Target Relay
Turn-Around Game	Bas Quoits	Gegoudge
Toss Ball	Kinxe	Ha-Goo
Stone Throwing		

Unit 11 Outline

DAY 1

Display the posters.

Remind students about the dances they created in the last unit. 6.2

Review the role of movement qualities in dance performances. 6.2

For homework, have students write an essay describing how the dance that they created expresses personal feelings. (Assessment assignment opportunity: essay) 6.2

Introduce early American games unit. 6.1

Describe safety and etiquette for playing early American games. 5.2

Remind students that skill competency in games can lead to personal satisfaction, success, and enjoyment. 6.3

Have students brainstorm accommodating individual differences in game settings. 5.1

Have students perform a warm-up along with a cardiorespiratory workout. (Assessment opportunity: structured observation 4.1)

Review striking with a paddle. 1.0, 2.5

(continued)

Unit 11 Outline *(continued)*

DAY 1 *(continued)*

Describe Battledore and Shuttlecock (North American Native Americans). 2.3

Describe basic game tactics for early American games and the use of space, time, and force. 2.3

Have students record in their notebooks how space, time, and force are used in basic game tactics. 2.3

Have students play Battledore and Shuttlecock. (Assessment opportunity: structured observation 1.0, 5.1, 5.2, 6.3)

Lead students through a cool-down and flexibility exercises appropriate to the physical activity level of the lesson. (Assessment opportunity: structured observation 4.1)

Debrief the game. 2.3

Assign unit-long homework:

- Have students research and write a description of the development of games in the United States during the 17th and 18th centuries. (Assessment assignment opportunity: report 6.1)

- Have students keep a log of daily activity. (Assessment assignment opportunity: log 3.1)

- Have students write a description of the opportunities in the school setting for regular participation in physical activity. (Assessment assignment opportunity: essay 3.2)

DAY 2

Review safety and etiquette for playing early American games. 5.2

Describe the long-term muscular endurance benefits derived from participation in physical activity. 6.4

Have the students record the long-term muscular endurance benefits derived from participation in physical activity in their notebooks. 6.4

Review frequency, intensity, time, and type for cardiorespiratory endurance and body composition using the Health-Related Fitness: Tutorial and Portfolio. 4.2

Review concepts related to warm-up and cool-down using the Health-Related Fitness: Tutorial and Portfolio. 4.2

Have students perform a warm-up along with muscular strength and muscular endurance exercises. (Assessment opportunity: structured observation 4.1)

Review tossing and catching. 1.0, 2.5

Describe Turn-Around Game (North American Native Americans). 2.3

Have students brainstorm ways to include individuals who may be differently abled in the game. 5.1

Have students play Turn-Around Game. (Assessment opportunity: structured observation 1.0, 5.1, 5.2, 6.3)

Lead students through a cool-down and flexibility exercises appropriate to the physical activity level of the lesson. (Assessment opportunity: structured observation 4.1)

Debrief the game. 2.3

Have students design a cardiorespiratory and body composition fitness plan including a warm-up and cool-down for 1 day. (Assessment assignment opportunity: project 4.2)

DAY 3	Describe ways to generate and absorb force when performing movement and motor skills. 2.2

Have students record in their notebooks ways to generate and absorb force when performing movement and motor skills. 2.2

Have students perform a warm-up along with a cardiorespiratory workout. (Assessment opportunity: structured observation 4.1)

Review forearm pass and volley. 1.0, 2.5

Describe Toss Ball (North American Native Americans). 2.3

Have students brainstorm ways to include individuals who may be differently abled in the game. 5.1

Have students play Toss Ball. (Assessment opportunity: structured observation 1.0, 5.1, 5.2, 6.3)

Lead students through a cool-down and flexibility exercises appropriate to the physical activity level of the lesson. (Assessment opportunity: structured observation 4.1)

Debrief the game. 2.3 |
| **DAY 4** | Have students perform a warm-up along with muscular strength and muscular endurance exercises. (Assessment opportunity: structured observation 4.1)

Review underhand toss. 1.0, 2.5

Describe Stone Throwing (North American Native Americans). 2.3

Have students brainstorm ways to include individuals who may be differently abled in the game. 5.1

Have students play Stone Throwing. (Assessment opportunity: structured observation 1.0, 5.1, 5.2, 6.3)

Lead students through a cool-down and flexibility exercises appropriate to the physical activity level of the lesson. (Assessment opportunity: structured observation 4.1)

Debrief the game. 2.3

Review generating and absorbing force. 2.2 |
| **DAY 5** | Have students perform a warm-up along with a cardiorespiratory workout. (Assessment opportunity: structured observation 4.1)

Review running. 1.0, 2.5

Describe Choctaw Sticks Game (Choctaw Indians). 2.3

Have students brainstorm ways to include individuals who may be differently abled in the game. 5.1

Have students play Choctaw Sticks Game. (Assessment opportunity: structured observation 1.0, 5.1, 5.2, 6.3)

Lead students through a cool-down and flexibility exercises appropriate to the physical activity level of the lesson. (Assessment opportunity: structured observation 4.1)

Debrief the game. 2.3

Collect students' essays on how their dances expressed personal feelings. (Assessment opportunity: essay 6.2) |
| **DAY 6** | Explain the appropriate type of practice (mass or distributed, whole or part, focus on speed or accuracy, mental or physical) for improving one's performance of a motor skill. 2.1

Have students perform a warm-up along with a cardiorespiratory workout. (Assessment opportunity: structured observation 4.1)

Review tossing rings. 1.0, 2.5

Have students brainstorm the appropriate type of practice for practicing tossing rings. 2.1 |

(continued)

Unit 11 Outline *(continued)*

DAY 6 (continued)

Describe Bas Quoits (North American Native Americans). 2.3

Have students brainstorm ways to include individuals who may be differently abled in the game. 5.1

Have students play Bas Quoits. (Assessment opportunity: structured observation 1.0, 5.1, 5.2, 6.3)

Lead students through a cool-down and flexibility exercises appropriate to the physical activity level of the lesson. (Assessment opportunity: structured observation 4.1)

Debrief the game. 2.3

DAY 7

Describe the changes from birth through puberty along with their impact on physical performance. 2.4

Have students summarize the description for their notebooks. 2.4

Have students perform a warm-up along with muscular strength and muscular endurance exercises. (Assessment opportunity: structured observation 4.1)

Describe Kinxe (North American Native Americans). 2.3

Have students play Kinxe. (Assessment opportunity: structured observation 1.0, 5.1, 5.2, 6.3)

Lead students through a cool-down and flexibility exercises appropriate to the physical activity level of the lesson. (Assessment opportunity: structured observation 4.1)

Debrief the game. 2.3

Have students brainstorm the impact of changes from birth through puberty on physical performance. 2.4

DAY 8

Have students perform a warm-up along with a cardiorespiratory workout. (Assessment opportunity: structured observation 4.1)

Review the sidearm throw. 1.0, 2.5

Have students brainstorm the appropriate type of practice for practicing the sidearm throw. 2.1

Review the overhand throw. 1.0, 2.5

Have students brainstorm the appropriate type of practice for practicing the overhand throw. 2.1

Describe Rolling Target Relay (North American Native Americans). 2.3

Have students play Rolling Target Relay. (Assessment opportunity: structured observation 1.0, 5.1, 5.2, 6.3)

Lead students through a cool-down and flexibility exercises appropriate to the physical activity level of the lesson. (Assessment opportunity: structured observation 4.1)

Debrief the game. 2.3

Review the changes from birth through puberty. 2.4

Review the impact of these changes on physical performance. 2.4

DAY 9

Have students perform a warm-up along with muscular strength and muscular endurance exercises. (Assessment opportunity: structured observation 4.1)

Describe Gegoudge (Alaskan Native Americans). 2.3

Have students play Gegoudge. (Assessment opportunity: structured observation 1.0, 5.1, 5.2, 6.3)

Lead students through a cool-down and flexibility exercises appropriate to the physical activity level of the lesson. (Assessment opportunity: structured observation 4.1)

Debrief the game. 2.3

Review the appropriate type of practice (mass or distributed, whole or part, focus on speed or accuracy, mental or physical) for improving one's performance of a motor skill. 2.1

DAY 10	Have students perform a warm-up along with a cardiorespiratory workout. (Assessment opportunity: structured observation 4.1) Describe Ha-Goo (Southeastern Alaskan Native Americans—Thlinger tribe). 2.3 Have students play Ha-Goo. (Assessment opportunity: structured observation 1.0, 5.1, 5.2, 6.3) Lead students through a cool-down and flexibility exercises appropriate to the physical activity level of the lesson. (Assessment opportunity: structured observation 4.1) Debrief the game. 2.3
DAY 11	Have students perform a warm-up along with a cardiorespiratory workout. (Assessment opportunity: structured observation 4.1) Have students create their own game (including rules, skills, strategies, and etiquette) participants with and without special needs. (Assessment opportunity: structured observation 1.0, 5.1, 5.2, 6.3) 2.3 Lead students through a cool-down and flexibility exercises appropriate to the physical activity level of the lesson. (Assessment opportunity: structured observation 4.1)
DAY 12	Have students perform a warm-up along with muscular strength and muscular endurance exercises. (Assessment opportunity: structured observation 4.1) Have students work on their own games (including rules, skills, strategies, and etiquette) for participants with and without special needs. 1.0, 2.3, 5.1, 5.2, 6.3 Lead students through a cool-down and flexibility exercises appropriate to the physical activity level of the lesson. (Assessment opportunity: structured observation 4.1)
DAY 13	Have students perform a warm-up along with a cardiorespiratory workout. (Assessment opportunity: structured observation 4.1) Have students teach their game (including rules, skills, strategies, and etiquette) to the rest of the class. (Assessment opportunity: structured observation 1.0, 5.1, 5.2, 6.3) Lead students through a cool-down and flexibility exercises appropriate to the physical activity level of the lesson. (Assessment opportunity: structured observation 4.1)
DAY 14	Have students perform a warm-up along with muscular strength and muscular endurance exercises. (Assessment opportunity: structured observation 4.1) Have students teach their games (including rules, skills, strategies, and etiquette) to the rest of the class. (Assessment opportunity: structured observation 1.0, 5.1, 5.2, 6.3) Lead students through a cool-down and flexibility exercises appropriate to the physical activity level of the lesson. (Assessment opportunity: structured observation 4.1) Review material for tomorrow's quiz (or hand out quiz if you would like for it to be a take-home quiz). 2.1, 2.2, 2.3, 2.4, 2.5, 6.4
DAY 15	Have students take the quiz. (Assessment opportunity: quiz 2.1, 2.2, 2.3, 2.4, 2.5, 6.4) Collect student activity logs. (Assessment opportunity: log 3.1) Collect reports on the development of games in the United States during the 17th and 18th centuries. (Assessment opportunity: report 6.1) Collect essay about the opportunities in the school setting for regular participation in physical activity. (Assessment opportunity: essay 3.2) Collect cardiorespiratory and body composition fitness plan. (Assessment opportunity: project 4.2)

Closure and Fitness Assessment

Unit 12

This unit provides for the closure for your school year, including the chance to ensure that the students are able to demonstrate all grade-level standards. Although students have been working on projects throughout the year, this unit provides an opportunity for them to focus on depth over breadth. Moreover, while your students focus on completing their demonstrations of their learning and creating and collecting work for their portfolios, you are free to administer the fitness post-assessments and to act as a resource for student projects.

For this unit, I present students with the 16 standards for fifth grade and ask them to present evidence of their learning related to each standard. For some of the standards, students will be able to demonstrate their learning by looking through their working portfolios and pulling from work that they have already accomplished during the year. For other standards, students will be able to pull from interdisciplinary projects that they have completed throughout the year. For still other standards, students will need to create new projects during this closure unit to demonstrate their learning.

Once the students have collected their evidence, it goes into their performance portfolios. Then I ask students to write a reflection paper (a one-page essay) on their cumulative learning throughout fifth grade physical education. Ideally, the students then present their portfolios not only to their peers but also to their parents. In this case, during a parent, teacher, and student conference, the student is in charge of the conference as she presents the evidence that she has accumulated during the year and explains how the evidence demonstrates her learning of the various standards. This conference can focus exclusively on physical education or can be a comprehensive conference in which the student explains her learning in all subject areas.

As with the introduction unit, you can conduct this unit in just about any facility. I recommend, however, that if you are having your students perform exercises on the ground or on grass you provide them with carpet squares or some other material so they won't get dirty. An indoor facility is also helpful for the project development phase of this unit. In addition, many teachers reserve the library or arrange for some of their students to do research in the library. Of course, the equipment necessary to implement the unit depends on the type of fitness assessments you plan to administer. I administer the same Fitnessgram tests that I gave at the beginning of the school year. After the post-assessments, the students enter their fitness post-assessment scores into their own electronic portfolios so that you and they can compare these scores to pre-assessment scores, health standards, and goals. Students will also need access to reference books, CD-ROMs, DVDs, computers, videotape/DVD players, monitors, video recorders, and other materials to assist project development.

Sample Assessment for Fifth Grade Standards

1.0—Demonstrates speed, accuracy, and control using the mature form for fundamental movement and manipulative skills.

Teacher assessment during each instructional unit based on a rubric determines whether a student has reached this standard. The following is a sample rubric for underhand throwing:

    6: Performs a mature underhand throwing pattern using speed and accuracy in a game or activity situation.

        _____ Demonstrates 50% accuracy at a variety of distances using a mature underhand throwing pattern during a game or activity situation.

    5: Performs a mature underhand throwing pattern using greater speed and accuracy.

        _____ Demonstrates 70% accuracy at a variety of distances using a mature underhand throwing pattern.

    4: Performs a mature underhand throwing pattern using speed and accuracy.

        _____ Demonstrates 50% accuracy at a variety of distances using a mature underhand throwing pattern.

3: Performs a mature underhand throwing pattern.

_____ Faces the direction of the throw.

_____ Keeps shoulders perpendicular to the line of throw.

_____ Swings arm in pendulum action on preferred side of body.

_____ Steps forward on opposite foot.

_____ Transfers weight to forward foot.

_____ Follows through in direction of throw.

2: Performs an immature underhand throwing pattern.

1: Randomly attempts an immature underhand throwing pattern.

2.1—Explains the types of practice that improve motor skill performance for speed and accuracy.

Student writes an essay explaining when and how the following strategies should be used to improve performance for speed and accuracy: whole–part practice, mass–distributed practice, physical–mental practice, and speed–accuracy practice.

2.2—Describes how to generate and absorb force when performing movement and motor skills.

Student writes an essay describing ways to generate and absorb force when performing movement and motor skills.

2.3—Describes how the qualities of movement (e.g., space, time, force) are used in basic game tactics.

Student writes an essay describing how the qualities of movement (space, time, force) are used in basic offensive and defensive strategies.

2.4—Describes changes from birth through puberty along with their impact on physical performance.

Student writes an essay describing the changes that occur during puberty along with their impact on physical performance.

2.5—Describes critical elements of fundamental movement and manipulative skills.

Teacher assessment during each instructional unit based on responses to quiz questions for each motor or movement skill taught.

3.1—Engages in moderate physical activity for 60 minutes 5 days each week.

Student maintains a log of participation in physical activity throughout the school year.

3.2—Describes opportunities in the school setting for regular participation in physical activity.

Student writes a description of the opportunities in the school setting for regular participation in physical activity.

4.1—Works toward a health-enhancing level of physical fitness.

Student submits prefitness assessment data, goals, monitoring logs, and postfitness assessment data.

4.2—Designs a cardiorespiratory and body composition fitness plan including a warm-up and cool-down for 1 day.

Student creates a chart, essay, video, or computer program that shows her 1-day cardiorespiratory/body composition plans.

5.1—Works with an individual who is differently abled in a physical activity.

Teacher assessment throughout the year based on a rubric determines whether a student has reached this standard.

5.2—Accepts responsibility for personal safety during physical activity.

Teacher assessment throughout the year based on a rubric determines whether a student has reached this standard.

6.1—Describes the development and role of movement-related activities in the United States during the 17th and 18th centuries.

Student selects his best research report on the history of an activity that originated during the 17th and 18th centuries in the United States.

6.2—Expresses personal feelings through a movement-based routine.

Student selects her best movement-based routine developed during the school year and writes a reflection on how this routine best expresses her personal feelings for inclusion in the portfolios.

6.3—Chooses to engage in skill competencies at a level that leads to personal satisfaction, success, and enjoyment.

Teacher assessment throughout the year based on a rubric determines whether a student has reached this standard.

6.4—Describes the physical benefits of regular participation in physical activity.

Student writes an essay describing the physical benefits derived from participation in physical activity.

Resources

Health-Related Fitness: Tutorial and Portfolio (Bonnie's Fitware, Inc.)

Middle School Physical Education Electronic Portfolios (Bonnie's Fitware, Inc.)

Equipment

Fitness assessment equipment

Games

None

Unit 12 Outline

DAY 1	Assign students to working groups of four. Remind students why you administer fitness assessments twice a year.
	Remind students how and why you administer the 1-mile run assessment. 4.1
	Have students perform warm-up exercises for the 1-mile run assessment. 4.1
	Administer the 1-mile run assessment to half the class at a time, while the other half helps to count laps for the runners. (Assessment opportunity: fitness assessment 4.1)
	Have students input fitness scores into their Health-Related Fitness Portfolios. 4.1
	Lead students through a cool-down and flexibility exercises appropriate to the physical activity level of the lesson. 4.1
DAY 2	Describe the projects and portfolios you expect students to complete in this unit. All
	Describe the project and portfolio design steps. All
	Remind students why you administer the curl-up assessment. 4.1
	Have students perform warm-up exercises for the curl-up assessment. 4.1
	Have students begin to work on their projects and Middle School Physical Education Portfolios. (Assessment opportunity: all)
	Administer the curl-up assessment to one group at a time. (Assessment opportunity: fitness assessment 4.1)
	Have students input fitness scores into their Health-Related Fitness Portfolios. 4.1
	Lead students through a cool-down and flexibility exercises appropriate to the physical activity level of the lesson. 4.1

DAY 3	Remind students why you administer the skinfold measurement. 4.1

Have students work on their projects and Middle School Physical Education Portfolios. (Assessment opportunity: all)

Administer the skinfold measurement privately to one student at a time. (Assessment opportunity: fitness assessment 4.1)

Have students input fitness scores into their Health-Related Fitness Portfolios. 4.1 |
| **DAY 4** | Remind students why you administer the back-saver sit-and-reach and trunk-lift assessments. 4.1

Have students perform warm-up exercises for the back-saver sit-and-reach and trunk-lift assessments. 4.1

Have students work on their projects and Middle School Physical Education Portfolios. (Assessment opportunity: all)

Administer the back-saver sit-and-reach and trunk-lift assessments to one group at a time. (Assessment opportunity: fitness assessment 4.1)

Have students input fitness scores into their Health-Related Fitness Portfolios. 4.1

Lead students through a cool-down and flexibility exercises appropriate to the physical activity level of the lesson. 4.1 |
| **DAY 5** | Remind students why you administer the push-up assessment. 4.1

Have students perform warm-up exercises for the push-up assessment. 4.1

Have students work on their projects and Middle School Physical Education Portfolios. (Assessment opportunity: all)

Administer the push-up assessment to one group at a time. (Assessment opportunity: fitness assessment 4.1)

Have students input fitness scores into their Health-Related Fitness Portfolios. 4.1

Lead students through a cool-down and flexibility exercises appropriate to the physical activity level of the lesson. 4.1 |
| **DAY 6** | Have students perform warm-up exercises for the makeup assessments. 4.1

Have students work on their projects and Middle School Physical Education Portfolios. (Assessment opportunity: all)

Administer makeup fitness assessments to one group at a time. (Assessment opportunity: fitness assessment 4.1)

Have students input fitness scores into their Health-Related Fitness Portfolios. 4.1

Lead students through a cool-down and flexibility exercises appropriate to the physical activity level of the lesson. 4.1 |
| **DAYS 7-12** | Have students work on their projects and Middle School Physical Education Portfolios. (Assessment opportunity: all) |
| **DAY 13** | Have each group share their projects and Middle School Physical Education Portfolios with another group. (Assessment opportunity: all) |

(continued)

Unit 12 Outline *(continued)*

DAY 14 Have other groups share their projects and Middle School Physical Education Portfolios. (Assessment opportunity: all)

DAY 15 Debrief Middle School Physical Education Portfolios. (Assessment opportunity: all)

15

A Sixth Grade Program: Learning Skills Through Cooperation

I asked my students why they liked the circus unit and I got the following responses: "I thought the circus unit was a lot of fun. It gave us a chance to act like clowns." "I felt like a clown when I learned to juggle. One of the coolest things I've done!" "I liked the circus unit because it was challenging and something new." "It allowed us to learn and try new things we hadn't done before."

—*physical educator Carol Bell, Los Alamitos Unified School District, California*

Sixth Grade Standards

By the end of sixth grade, each student

1.0—Demonstrates the mature form for specialized skills and combinations during cooperative activities; lead-up or simple target, invasion, field, and net activities; stunts and tumbling; and dance activities.

2.1—Explains how to provide appropriate feedback to a partner who is developing or improving specialized skills.

2.2—Explains ways to use force to increase speed or distance of a body or propelled object.

2.3—Describes offensive strategies for cooperative and bowling activities and offensive and defensive strategies for simple invasion, field, and net activities.

2.4—Describes the characteristics of physical activities appropriate for early adolescents.

2.5 —Describes the critical elements of specialized skills and combinations in cooperative activities; lead-up or simple target, invasion, field, and net activities; stunts and tumbling; and dance activities.

3.1—Engages in moderate and vigorous physical activity for 60 minutes 5 days each week.

3.2—Describes opportunities in the local community for regular participation in physical activity.

4.1—Works toward a health-enhancing level of physical fitness.

4.2—Designs a 1-day personal health-related fitness plan.

5.1—Works cooperatively with a small group in physical activity settings.

5.2—Accepts responsibility for safely completing assigned role when working with a small group during physical activity.

6.1—Describes the development and role of movement-related activities in the ancient world and their influences on physical activities today.

6.2—Expresses personal feelings through a manipulative or movement-based routine.

6.3—Chooses to engage in new activities.

6.4—Describes the health benefits of regular participation in physical activity.

In this chapter, I describe a sample sixth grade program, having selected Learning Skills Through Cooperation as the theme. At this level, the students begin to apply the motor skills that they refined in fifth grade to a variety of lead-up games. In addition, I continue to set the tone for both the physical education and the school environments by focusing on the development of cooperation in partners, small groups, and small teams.

I have based my program on my sample standards. Review your grade-level standards for sixth grade before planning your own program. As I discussed in chapter 7, I have used the lead-up activity approach for selecting the sixth grade units of instruction. The following are the units for sixth grade:

1. Introduction (3 weeks)
2. Cooperative Activities (3 weeks)
3. Stunts and Tumbling (3 weeks)
4. Folk Dance (3 weeks)
5. Target Sport: Bowling (3 weeks)
6. Target and Invasion Sport: Flying Disc (3 weeks)
7. Invasion Sport: 3-on-3 Basketball (3 weeks)
8. Net Sport: Pickleball (3 weeks)
9. Field Sport: Three-Team Softball (3 weeks)
10. Ancient Games (3 weeks)
11. Circus Skills (3 weeks)
12. Closure and Fitness Assessment (3 weeks)

Notice that I move from simple to complex units throughout the year: from body management (stunts) to locomotor skills (folk dance). Then, I move from simple target sports (bowling and flying disc golf) to invasion sports (flying disc and 3-on-3 basketball) to net sports (Pickleball) and finally to field sports (three-team softball). Another sequence embedded in the selection of activities is locomotor to underhand pattern to sidearm pattern to overhand pattern and catching, or striking with a body part (hand for dribbling) to striking with a short object (Pickleball) to striking with a longer object (batting in softball). Also, by keeping the number of players on each team small, I can encourage the development of cooperation skills and provide for more practice opportunities. I conclude the year with ancient times and circus skills units, so that the students can apply their motor skills to fun, new, and challenging games and activities.

Introduction

Unit 1

This unit is an introductory unit for sixth grade students. It gives students time to get reacquainted and to meet new members of the class. I also use this introductory unit to set my expectations, to teach the class rules, to assess the students' fitness levels, and to guide them as they set their yearlong goals for fitness development.

You can conduct this particular unit in just about any facility. It does help, however, if you are performing exercises on the ground or grass to provide students with carpet squares or some other material so they don't get dirty. The equipment necessary to implement the unit depends on the type of introductory games you choose and the fitness assessments you administer. I administer the Fitnessgram health-related fitness assessment battery, including the back-saver sit-and-reach, curl-ups, skinfold measurements, push-ups, trunk lift, and 1-mile run. You can order the Fitnessgram test administration procedures from Human Kinetics (see appendix C). You will see in the daily agendas that my students prepare for the fitness assessment through various aerobic activities. In addition, the students enter their fitness scores into their own electronic portfolios using Health-Related Fitness: Tutorial and Portfolio (Bonnie's Fitware, Inc.).

Unit 1 Standards

1.0—Demonstrates the mature form for the forearm pass.

2.1—Defines feedback.

2.2—Defines force.

2.3—Describes the differences between a cooperative game and a competitive game.

2.4—Describes that the selection of equipment, games, and activities should be based on the developmental level of the participants.

2.5—Describes the critical elements for the forearm pass.

3.1—Engages in moderate physical activity for 60 minutes 5 days each week.

3.2 —Defines physical activity and local community.

4.1—Participates in fitness preassessment.

4.2—Describes the elements of an appropriate warm-up.

5.1—Demonstrates cooperative skills with a partner.

5.2—Follows the class rules for safe participation.

6.1—Describes fitness activities in the ancient world.

6.2—Demonstrates qualities of movement during introductory activities.

6.3—Chooses to engage in new fitness and cooperative activities.

6.4—Defines physical activity.

Unit 1 Assessments

1.0—Structured observation (days 4, 5)

2.1—Quiz (days 14-15)

2.2—Quiz (days 14-15)

2.3—Essay (assigned on day 6; collected on day 7)

2.4—Quiz (days 14-15)

2.5—Quiz (days 14-15)

3.1—Log (assigned on day 7; collected on day 15)

3.2—Quiz (days 14-15)

4.1—Fitness assessment (days 9-15), food log (days 10-15), caloric output log (days 10-15)

4.2—Quiz (days 14-15)

5.1—Structured observation (days 1-7)

5.2—Structured observation (days 1-8)

6.1—Report (assigned on day 5; collected on day 15)

6.2—Structured observation (days 3-8)

6.3—Structured observation (days 1-8)

6.4—Quiz (days 14-15)

Resources

Health-Related Fitness: Tutorial and Portfolio (Bonnie's Fitware, Inc.)

Middle School Physical Education Portfolio (Bonnie's Fitware, Inc.)

Fitnessgram assessment materials (Human Kinetics)

Fit Kids Classroom Workout DVD (Human Kinetics)

Sixth grade introduction task cards (Bonnie's Fitware, Inc.)

Fitness task cards (Bonnie's Fitware, Inc.)

Sixth grade unit 1 posters (Bonnie's Fitware, Inc.—included in the Middle School Detailed Lesson Plans)

Fitness posters (Bonnie's Fitware, Inc.—included in the Middle School Detailed Lesson Plans)

Qualities of Movement chart (Bonnie's Fitware, Inc.—included in the Middle School Detailed Lesson Plans)

Equipment

Fleece balls

Fitness assessment materials

Strings

Games

Toss-a-Name Game using the forearm pass

Toss-and-Catch-a-Name game using the forearm pass

Group Juggle

Partner Strings

Unit 1 Outline

DAY 1	Display the posters.
	Establish a roll call order.
	Introduce class rules. 5.2
	Have students record the rules in their notebooks, along with the safety reasons for the rules. 5.2
	Discuss routines and procedures specific to your class.
	Discuss the definition of feedback. 2.1
	Have students write the definition of feedback in their notebooks. 2.1
	Discuss cooperation. 5.1

DAY 1 (continued)

Review (from grade 5) Toss-a-Name Game using task card. 5.1

Give students feedback on their use of cooperative skills as they play Toss-a-Name Game. (Assessment opportunity: structured observation 5.1, 5.2, 6.3)

Ask students to define feedback. 2.1

Ask students to define cooperation. 5.1

DAY 2

Review class rules. 5.2

Review the definition of feedback. 2.1

Review cooperation. 5.1

Give students feedback as they play Toss-a-Name Game. 2.1, 5.1

Review (from grade 5) Toss-and-Catch-a-Name Game using task card. 5.1

Give students feedback on their use of cooperative skills as they play Toss-and-Catch-a-Name Game. (Assessment opportunity: structured observation 5.1, 5.2, 6.3)

Ask students to define feedback. 2.1

Ask students to define cooperation. 2.1

DAY 3

Review class rules. 5.2

Review (from grades K to 4) movement qualities and discuss their application to tossing a ball. 6.2

Provide students with feedback on their use of different movement qualities (i.e., throw the ball high, throw the ball fast, throw the ball low) as they play Toss-and-Catch-a-Name Game. (Assessment opportunity: structured observation 5.1, 5.2, 6.2, 6.3)

Assign lockers.

Explain how to open lockers.

Have students practice opening lockers.

Ask students to define feedback. 2.1

DAY 4

Have students dress for physical education.

Review class rules. 5.2

Review (from grade 5) what constitutes an appropriate warm-up. 4.2

Have students write in their notebooks what constitutes an appropriate warm-up. 4.2

Have students perform a warm-up along with muscular strength and muscular endurance exercises. 4.1, 4.2

Demonstrate and describe the mature form for the forearm pass. 1.0, 2.5

Have students record in their notebooks the critical elements for the forearm pass. 2.5

Have students practice the forearm pass with a partner. (Assessment opportunity: structured observation 1.0, 5.1, 5.2, 6.2, 6.3)

Lead students through a cool-down and flexibility exercises appropriate to the physical activity level of the lesson. 4.1

Ask students to describe an appropriate warm-up. 4.2

Ask students to list the critical elements for the forearm pass. 2.5

(continued)

Unit 1 Outline *(continued)*

DAY 5	Review class rules. 5.2
	Review (from grade 5) the definition of force. 2.2
	Review (from grade 5) force absorption. 2.2
	Have students record in their notebooks the definition of force and how it can be absorbed. 2.2
	Have students perform a warm-up along with a cardiorespiratory workout. 4.1, 4.2
	Have students play Toss-a-Name Game using a forearm pass. (Assessment opportunity: structured observation 1.0, 5.1, 5.2, 6.2, 6.3)
	Lead students through a cool-down and flexibility exercises appropriate to the physical activity level of the lesson. 4.1
	As a project, have students research the fitness activities that occurred during ancient times. (Assessment opportunity: report 6.1)
DAY 6	Review class rules. 5.2
	Define physical activity and local community. 3.2, 6.4
	Have students record in their notebooks the definitions for physical activity and local community. 3.2, 6.4
	Have students perform a warm-up along with a cardiorespiratory workout. 4.1, 4.2
	Have students play Toss-a-Name Game using a forearm pass. (Assessment opportunity: structured observation 1.0, 5.1, 5.2, 6.2, 6.3)
	Teach students how to play Group Juggle using task card. 5.2
	Discuss with students safe participation during Group Juggle. 5.2
	Have students play Group Juggle. (Assessment opportunity: structured observation 5.2, 6.2, 6.3)
	Lead students through a cool-down and flexibility exercises appropriate to the physical activity level of the lesson. 4.1
	Discuss the differences between a cooperative game and a competitive game. 2.3
	For homework, have students write an essay describing the differences between a cooperative game and a competitive game. (Assessment assignment opportunity: essay 2.3)
DAY 7	Discuss with students that the selection of equipment, games, and activities should be based on the mental, social, and cognitive development of the individuals. 2.4
	Have students record in their notebooks that the selection of equipment, games, and activities should be based on a person's developmental level. 2.4
	Review the definitions of physical activity and local community. 6.4, 3.2
	Assign students to keep a log of daily activity. (Assessment assignment opportunity: log 3.1)
	Have students perform a warm-up along with muscular strength and muscular endurance exercises. 4.1, 4.2
	Teach students how to play Partner Strings using task card. 6.3
	Have students play Partner Strings. (Assessment opportunity: structured observation 5.1, 5.2, 6.2, 6.3)
	Lead students through a cool-down and flexibility exercises appropriate to the physical activity level of the lesson. 4.1
	Collect essay on differences between cooperative games and competitive games. (Assessment opportunity: essay 2.3)

DAY 8	Review with students that the selection of equipment, games, and activities should be based on the mental, social, and cognitive development of the individuals. 2.4
	Review the definition of force. 2.2
	Have students perform a warm-up along with a cardiorespiratory workout. 4.1, 4.2
	Have students participate with Fit Kids Classroom Workout DVD. (Assessment opportunity: structured observation 5.2, 6.2, 6.3) 4.1
	Lead students through a cool-down and flexibility exercises appropriate to the physical activity level of the lesson. 4.1
DAY 9	Have students perform warm-up exercises for the back-saver sit-and-reach assessment. 4.1
	Explain the back-saver sit-and-reach test and the reasons for administering the assessment. 4.1
	Assign students randomly to groups of four.
	Administer the back-saver sit-and-reach assessment to one group at a time while the rest of the students participate in a flexibility circuit using the fitness task cards. (Assessment opportunity: fitness assessment 4.1)
	Have students input fitness scores into their Health-Related Fitness Portfolio. 4.1
	Lead students through a cool-down and flexibility exercises appropriate to the physical activity level of the lesson. 4.1
	Have students record the definition of a game in their notebooks. 2.3
DAY 10	Have students perform warm-up exercises for the curl-up assessment. 4.1
	Explain the curl-up test and the reasons for administering the assessment. 4.1
	Administer the curl up assessment to one group at a time while the rest of the students participate in a flexibility circuit using the fitness task cards. (Assessment opportunity: fitness assessment 4.1)
	Have students input fitness scores into their Health-Related Fitness Portfolio. 4.1
	Lead students through a cool-down and flexibility exercises appropriate to the physical activity level of the lesson. 4.1
	Assign students the task of collecting data on their food intake and caloric output for 3 days. (Assessment assignment opportunity: log 4.1)
DAY 11	Explain the skinfold measurement and the reasons for administering the assessment. 4.1
	Have students perform warm-up exercises. 4.1
	Have students participate with Fit Kids Classroom Workout DVD. 4.1
	Administer the skinfold measurement to students one at a time in private, while the others participate with the Fit Kids Classroom Workout DVD. (Assessment opportunity: fitness assessment 4.1)
	Have students input fitness scores into their Health-Related Fitness Portfolio. 4.1
	Lead students through a cool-down and flexibility exercises appropriate to the physical activity level of the lesson. 4.1
	Review the definitions of physical activity and local community. 6.4, 3.2

(continued)

Unit 1 Outline *(continued)*

DAY 12

Have students perform warm-up exercises for the push-up assessment. 4.1

Explain the push-up assessment and the reasons for administering the assessment. 4.1

Administer the push-up assessment to one group at a time while the rest of the students participate in a flexibility circuit using the fitness task cards. (Assessment opportunity: fitness assessment 4.1)

Have students input fitness scores into their Health-Related Fitness Portfolio. 4.1

Lead students through a cool-down and flexibility exercises appropriate to the physical activity level of the lesson. 4.1

DAY 13

Have students perform warm-up exercises for the trunk-lift assessment. 4.1

Explain the trunk-lift assessment and the reasons for administering the assessment. 4.1

Administer the trunk-lift assessment to one group at a time while the rest of the students participate in a flexibility circuit using the fitness task cards. (Assessment opportunity: fitness assessment 4.1)

Have students input fitness scores into their Health-Related Fitness Portfolio. 4.1

Lead students through a cool-down and flexibility exercises appropriate to the physical activity level of the lesson. 4.1

Review material for tomorrow's quiz (or hand out quiz if you would like for it to be a take home quiz). 2.1, 2.2, 2.4, 2.5, 3.2, 4.2, 6.4

DAY 14

Have students perform warm-up exercises for the 1-mile run assessment. 4.1

Explain the 1-mile run assessment and the reasons for administering the assessment. 4.1

Administer the 1-mile run assessment to half the class. (Assessment opportunity: fitness assessment 4.1)

Administer the written quiz to the other half of the class. (Assessment opportunity: quiz 2.1, 2.2, 2.4, 2.5, 3.2, 4.2, 6.4)

Have students input fitness scores into their Health-Related Fitness Portfolio. 4.1

Lead students through a cool-down and flexibility exercises appropriate to the physical activity level of the lesson. 4.1

DAY 15

Have students perform warm-up exercises, depending on the fitness assessments they need to make up because of absences. 4.1

Administer makeup tests. (Assessment opportunity: fitness assessment 4.1)

Have students perform warm-up exercises for the 1-mile run. 4.1

Administer the 1-mile run test to half the class. (Assessment opportunity: fitness assessment 4.1)

Administer the written quiz to the other half of the class. (Assessment opportunity: quiz 2.1, 2.2, 2.4, 2.5, 3.2, 4.2, 6.4)

Have students input fitness scores into their Health-Related Fitness Portfolio. 4.1

Lead students through a cool-down and flexibility exercises appropriate to the physical activity level of the lesson. 4.1

Collect students' reports on fitness training. (Assessment opportunity: report 6.1)

Collect students' physical activity logs. (Assessment opportunity: log 3.1)

Collect students' food intake and caloric output logs. (Assessment opportunity: log 4.1)

Cooperative Activities  ~ Unit 2

This unit provides students with an opportunity to extend, refine, and apply their social skills, especially those we associate with cooperation, during many different types of physical challenges. I use the teaching strategies that help develop cooperation and social skills during this unit. I also show you how to give students opportunities to learn different ways of working together to accomplish a specific goal.

After students have participated in an activity that requires cooperation and trust, ask them a number of debriefing questions, including these:

- "Did you cooperate to solve the challenge?"
- "Did you support one another?"
- "Did you believe that you could trust your partner?"
- "What will you do differently next time?"
- "How else might you have solved the challenge?

As with the first unit, you can conduct this instructional unit in a variety of locations, and the equipment you need depends on the type of challenges or cooperative activities you choose.

This unit is also an extension of the previous one in terms of developing a supportive and psychologically safe environment through which students can feel comfortable with their physical abilities. It is an opportunity for students to continue to get to know one another and extend their relationships through cooperation and trust building. Students will also have the opportunity to extend their learning into the community as they research opportunities for physical activities in the community. Ideally, the other sixth grade teachers at your school will also use this time to help students develop their social and cooperative skills, so that by the end of this unit you and your colleagues will have set the stage for a supportive school environment in which the students can learn during their next 3 years of school.

Unit 2 Standards

1.0—Demonstrates the mature form for static and dynamic balance, running and changing directions, and jumping in coordination with others.

2.1—Explains the purpose of feedback.

2.2—States Newton's third law.

2.3—Designs a cooperative movement game that requires locomotor skills and object manipulation.

2.4—Describes the importance of early adolescents' participating in cooperative activities.

2.5—Not applicable.

3.1—Engages in moderate and vigorous physical activity for 60 minutes (at least 5 minutes of vigorous activity) 5 days each week.

3.2—Lists physical activity opportunities in the local community.

4.1—Works toward a health-enhancing level of physical fitness.

4.2—Describes an effective cool-down.

5.1—Demonstrates cooperative skills with a partner.

5.2—Follows procedures for safe participation when working with a small group in cooperative activities.

6.1—Describes physical education in the ancient world.

6.2—Not applicable.

6.3—Chooses to engage in new cooperative activities.

6.4—Defines health benefits.

Unit 2 Assessments

1.0—Structured observation (days 1-14)

2.1—Quiz (day 15)

2.2—Quiz (day 15)

2.3—Project (assigned day 13; presented on day 14)

2.4—Quiz (day 15)

2.5—Not applicable.

3.1—Log (assigned on day 2; collected on day 15)

3.2—List (assigned on day 2; collected on day 15)

4.1—Goal setting (day 1); structured observation (days 2-14)

4.2—Quiz (day 15)

5.1—Structured observation (days 3-12)

5.2—Structured observation (days 5, 10, 14)

6.1—Report (assigned on day 2, collected on day 15)

6.2—Not applicable.

6.3—Structured observation (days 2-12)

6.4—Quiz (day 15)

Resources

Health-Related Fitness: Tutorial and Portfolio (Bonnie's Fitware, Inc.)

Middle School Physical Education Portfolio (Bonnie's Fitware, Inc.)

Sixth grade cooperative activities task cards

Cooperative and Problem Solving Activities CD

Sixth grade unit 2 posters (Bonnie's Fitware, Inc.—included in the Middle School Detailed Lesson Plans)

Fitness posters (Bonnie's Fitware, Inc.—included in the Middle School Detailed Lesson Plans)

Equipment

Hula hoops	Balloons or playground balls	Poly spots
Scarves or blindfolds	Fleece balls	Rope
Long jump ropes		

Games

Interest Circle	Two-Person Trust Fall	Turnstile
Switch	Across the Great Divide	Four Points
Back-to-Back Get Up	Warp Speed	Traffic Jam
Everyone Up in Pairs	Rope Pull-Up	Maze
Human Spring	Blind Polygon	Minefield
Trust Walk	Shark Attack	Trust Circle
Car	Wall Knots	Levitation

Unit 2 Outline

DAY 1

Display the posters.

Instruct students to examine the results of their fitness assessment and food and activity logs and to set goals for improvement for each of the five areas of health-related fitness. Students should record their goals in the Health-Related Fitness Portfolio. (Assessment opportunity: goal setting 4.1)

Introduce the unit.

Explain that students will be experiencing new activities daily. 6.3

DAY 1 (continued)

Discuss safety during cooperative activities. 5.2

Describe what is needed (e.g., cooperation) to be successful at these activities. 5.1

Have students perform a warm-up along with a cardiorespiratory workout. (Assessment opportunity: structured observation 4.1)

Teach students the rules for Interest Circle. 2.3, 6.3

Have students play Interest Circle, instructing them to focus only on physical activity interests. (Assessment opportunity: structured observation 5.1, 5.2, 6.3)

Describe an appropriate cool-down. 4.2

Have students record the elements of an appropriate cool-down in their notebooks. 4.2

Lead students through a cool-down and flexibility exercises appropriate to the physical activity level of the lesson. (Assessment opportunity: structured observation 4.1)

Debrief the activity, including a discussion on the role of cooperation in being successful at cooperative activities. 5.1

DAY 2

Explain the purpose of feedback. 2.1

Have students record in their notebooks the purpose of feedback. 2.1

Describe the mature form for static and dynamic balance. 1.0

Have students perform a warm-up along with muscular strength and muscular endurance exercises. (Assessment opportunity: structured observation 4.1)

Explain Switch, Back-to-Back Get Up, and Everyone Up in Pairs. 2.3

Give students feedback as they participate and encourage one another in Switch, Stand Up, and Everyone Up in Pairs. (Assessment opportunity: structured observation 1.0, 5.1, 5.2, 6.3)

Lead students through a cool-down and flexibility exercises appropriate to the physical activity level of the lesson. (Assessment opportunity: structured observation 4.1)

Debrief each activity. 5.1

Assign unit-long homework:

- Have students research and write a summary describing physical education in the ancient world. (Assessment assignment opportunity: report 6.1)

- Have students keep a log of daily activity. (Assessment assignment opportunity: log 3.1)

- Have students create a list of physical activity opportunities in the local community. (Assessment assignment opportunity: list 3.2)

DAY 3

State Newton's third law. 2.2

Demonstrate examples of Newton's third law. 2.2

Have student write Newton's third law in their notebooks. 2.2

Have students perform a warm-up along with a cardiorespiratory workout. (Assessment opportunity: structured observation 4.1)

Teach students the rules for Human Spring. 2.3

Have students participate in Human Spring (see figure 15.1). (Assessment opportunity: structured observation 5.1, 5.2, 6.3) 2.2

Lead students through a cool-down and flexibility exercises appropriate to the physical activity level of the lesson. (Assessment opportunity: structured observation 4.1)

Review Newton's third law and discuss how it is used in Human Spring. 2.2

(continued)

Figure 15.1   Human Spring.

Unit 2 Outline   *(continued)*

DAY 4

Describe the importance of early adolescents' participating in cooperative activities. 2.4

Have students write in their notebooks the importance of early adolescents' participating in cooperative activities. 2.4

Have students perform a warm-up along with muscular strength and muscular endurance exercises. (Assessment opportunity: structured observation 4.1)

Teach students the rules for Trust Walk. 2.3

Have students participate in Trust Walk. (Assessment opportunity: structured observation 5.1, 5.2, 6.3)

Teach students the rules for Car. 2.3

Have students participate in Car. (Assessment opportunity: structured observation 1.0, 5.1, 5.2, 6.3)

Lead students through a cool-down and flexibility exercises appropriate to the physical activity level of the lesson. (Assessment opportunity: structured observation 4.1)

Have students brainstorm how participation in Trust Walk and Car develops social skills. 2.4

DAY 5

Define health benefits. 6.4

Have students write in their notebooks the health benefits derived from participation in physical activity. 6.4

Have students perform a warm-up along with a cardiorespiratory workout. (Assessment opportunity: structured observation 4.1)

Review the rules for Trust Walk. 2.3

Have students participate in Trust Walk. (Assessment opportunity: structured observation 1.0, 5.1, 5.2, 6.3)

Review the rules for Car. 2.3

Have students participate in Car. (Assessment opportunity: structured observation 1.0, 5.1, 5.2, 6.3)

Teach the rules for Two-Person Trust Fall (see figure 15.2). 2.3

Have students participate in Two-Person Trust Fall. (Assessment opportunity: structured observation 1.0, 5.1, 5.2, 6.3)

Lead students through a cool-down and flexibility exercises appropriate to the physical activity level of the lesson. (Assessment opportunity: structured observation 4.1)

Debrief each activity. 5.1

Figure 15.2   Trust Fall.

Figure 15.3   Across the Great Divide.

DAY 6

Have students perform a warm-up along with a cardiorespiratory workout. (Assessment opportunity: structured observation 4.1)

Teach students the rules for Across the Great Divide (see figure 15.3). 2.3

Have students participate in Switch, Human Spring, Back-to-Back Get Up, Everyone Up in Pairs, Two-Person Trust Fall, Across the Great Divide, Trust Walk, and Car by rotating through stations. Have half the students rotate clockwise and the other half rotate counterclockwise so that each person has a new partner for each activity. (Assessment opportunity: structured observation 1.0, 5.1, 5.2, 6.3)

Debrief each activity before students rotate to the next station. 5.1

Lead students through a cool-down and flexibility exercises appropriate to the physical activity level of the lesson. (Assessment opportunity: structured observation 4.1)

Ask students to brainstorm examples of cooperation. 5.1

DAY 7

Assign students randomly to groups of four.

Have students perform a warm-up along with muscular strength and muscular endurance exercises. (Assessment opportunity: structured observation 4.1)

Teach students the rules for Warp Speed. 2.3

Have students play Warp Speed. (Assessment opportunity: structured observation 1.0, 5.1, 5.2, 6.3)

Teach students the rules for Rope Pull-Up. 2.3

Have students play Rope Pull-Up. (Assessment opportunity: structured observation 1.0, 5.1, 5.2, 6.3)

Lead students through a cool-down and flexibility exercises appropriate to the physical activity level of the lesson. (Assessment opportunity: structured observation 4.1)

Debrief each activity. 5.1

(continued)

Unit 2 Outline *(continued)*

DAY 8

Review mature form for running and changing directions quickly. 1.0

Have students perform a warm-up along with a cardiorespiratory workout. (Assessment opportunity: structured observation 4.1)

Teach students the rules for Blind Polygon. 2.3

Have students play Blind Polygon (see figure 15.4). (Assessment opportunity: structured observation 1.0, 5.2, 6.3)

Teach students the rules for Shark Attack. 2.3

Have students play Shark Attack. (Assessment opportunity: structured observation 1.0, 5.2, 6.3)

Lead students through a cool-down and flexibility exercises appropriate to the physical activity level of the lesson. (Assessment opportunity: structured observation 4.1)

Debrief each activity. 5.1

Figure 15.4   Blind Polygon.

DAY 9

Have students perform a warm-up along with muscular strength and muscular endurance exercises. (Assessment opportunity: structured observation 4.1)

Teach students the rules for Wall Knots. 2.3

Have students play Wall Knots (see figure 15.5). (Assessment opportunity: structured observation 1.0, 5.2, 6.3)

Review the mature form for jumping in coordination with others. 1.0

Teach students the rules for Turnstile. 2.3

Have students play Turnstile. (Assessment opportunity: structured observation 1.0, 5.2, 6.3)

Lead students through a cool-down and flexibility exercises appropriate to the physical activity level of the lesson. (Assessment opportunity: structured observation 4.1)

Debrief each activity. 5.1

Figure 15.5   Wall Knots.

DAY 10	Have students perform a warm-up along with a cardiorespiratory workout. (Assessment opportunity: structured observation 4.1)
	Teach students the rules for Four Points. 2.3
	Have students play Four Points. (Assessment opportunity: structured observation 1.0, 5.1, 5.2, 6.3)
	Debrief the activity. 5.1
	Teach students the rules for Traffic Jam. 2.3
	Have students play Traffic Jam. (Assessment opportunity: structured observation 1.0, 5.2, 6.3)
	Debrief the activity. 5.1
	Lead students through a cool-down and flexibility exercises appropriate to the physical activity level of the lesson. (Assessment opportunity: structured observation 4.1)
DAY 11	Have students perform a warm-up along with a cardiorespiratory workout. (Assessment opportunity: structured observation 4.1)
	Teach students the rules for Maze. 2.3
	Have students play Maze. (Assessment opportunity: structured observation 5.1, 5.2, 6.3)
	Debrief the activity. 5.1
	Teach students the rules for Minefield (see figure 15.6). 2.3
	Have students play Minefield. (Assessment opportunity: structured observation 5.1, 5.2, 6.3)
	Lead students through a cool-down and flexibility exercises appropriate to the physical activity level of the lesson. (Assessment opportunity: structured observation 4.1)
	Debrief the activity. 5.1

(continued)

Figure 15.6 Minefield.

Unit 2 Outline *(continued)*

DAY 12

Have students perform a warm-up along with muscular strength and muscular endurance exercises. (Assessment opportunity: structured observation 4.1)

Teach students the rules for Trust Circle. 2.3

Have students play Trust Circle. (Assessment opportunity: structured observation 1.0, 5.2, 6.3)

Debrief the activity. 5.1

Teach students the rules for Levitation. 2.3

Have students play Levitation. (Assessment opportunity: structured observation 5.2, 6.3)

Lead students through a cool-down and flexibility exercises appropriate to the physical activity level of the lesson. (Assessment opportunity: structured observation 4.1)

Debrief the activity. 5.1

DAY 13

Have students perform a warm-up along with a cardiorespiratory workout. (Assessment opportunity: structured observation 4.1)

Have groups design a cooperative movement game that requires locomotor skills and object manipulation. (Assessment assignment opportunity: project 2.3)

Lead students through a cool-down and flexibility exercises appropriate to the physical activity level of the lesson. (Assessment opportunity: structured observation 4.1)

DAY 14

Have students perform a warm-up along with muscular strength and muscular endurance exercises. (Assessment opportunity: structured observation 4.1)

Have each group present their cooperative movement game to another group, asking the other group to solve the challenge. (Assessment opportunity: project 2.3)

Lead students through a cool-down and flexibility exercises appropriate to the physical activity level of the lesson. (Assessment opportunity: structured observation 4.1)

DAY 15

Instruct students to take the quiz. (Assessment opportunity: quiz 2.1, 2.2, 2.4, 4.2, 6.4)

Collect descriptions of physical education during ancient times. (Assessment opportunity: report 6.1)

Collect students' physical activity logs. (Assessment opportunity: log 3.1)

Collect lists of community physical activities. (Assessment opportunity: list 3.2)

Stunts and Tumbling

Unit 3

This unit continues the work from the fifth grade body management unit. Specifically, this unit focuses on balance, weight transfer, flight, and rolling. Building on the trust developed between students throughout the last unit, you can begin to have students spot one another as they attempt to perform activities in this stunts and tumbling unit. From days 3 through 11, I have the students rotate from station to station, performing activities in five or more categories. As students demonstrate competency in the first skill in each category, I have them document their performances on their progress cards that list all the skills and then practice the next skill in that category.

Depending on the number of students in each class, you can double each of the stations and add a video or computer station. In lieu of having students perform the exercises at the beginning of the instructional period, you can add abdominal strength, upper-body strength, and cardiorespiratory stations.

It is best if you conduct this unit inside a gymnasium or closed area. You can, however, conduct the unit outside in an open area if you can bring mats or some other protective material outside. Although I make several references to a balance beam, you can have students use a line on the gym floor if a balance beam is unavailable. Students can perform the flight skills without the springboard, but the springboard gives students an additional challenge. Instructional material for this unit includes an instructional Body Management CD that includes information on circus skills, stunts, tumbling, and gymnastics, as well as task cards. The visual images on the task cards and in the CD provide students with model performances for the many movements they will attempt during the unit.

Unit 3 Standards

1.0—Demonstrates the mature form for headstand, handstand, handstand roll out, cartwheel, walk on beam with dip, squat turn on beam, pike forward roll, and straddle roll.

2.1—Explains that feedback is based on the critical elements for each skill.

2.2—Explains that the stronger the action, the greater the reaction and provides examples.

2.3—Defines offensive strategy.

2.4—Describes the importance of early adolescents' participating in challenging activities.

2.5—Describes the critical elements for headstand, handstand, handstand roll out, cartwheel, walk on beam with dip, squat turn on beam, pike forward roll, and straddle roll.

3.1—Engages in moderate and vigorous physical activity for 60 minutes (at least 5 minutes of vigorous activity) 5 days each week.

3.2—Searches the Internet for physical activity opportunities in the local community.

4.1—Works toward a health-enhancing level of physical fitness.

4.2—Refines 1-day body composition plan.

5.1—Works cooperatively with a small group during stunts and tumbling activities.

5.2—Follows procedures for safe participation when working with a small group in stunts activities.

6.1—Describes movement-related activities in ancient Babylon.

6.2—Expresses personal feelings through the creation of a stunts routine.

6.3—Chooses to engage in new stunt and tumbling activities.

6.4—Describes the respiratory benefits of regular participation in physical activity.

Unit 3 Assessments

1.0—Structured observation (days 1-14)

2.1—Quiz (day 15)

2.2—Quiz (day 15)

2.3—Quiz (day 15)

2.4—Quiz (day 15)

2.5—Quiz (day 15)

3.1—Log (assigned on day 1; collected on day 15)

3.2—Project (assigned on day 1; collected on day 15)

4.1—Structured observation (days 1-14)

4.2—Project (assigned on day 3; collected on day 15)

5.1—Structured observation (days 1-14)

5.2—Structured observation (days 1-14)

6.1—Report (assigned on day 1; collected on day 15)

6.2—Project (assigned on day 12; collected on day 14)

6.3—Structured observation (days 1-14)

6.4—Quiz (day 15)

Resources

Health-Related Fitness: Tutorial and Portfolio (Bonnie's Fitware, Inc.)

Middle School Physical Education Portfolio (Bonnie's Fitware, Inc.)

Body Management CD (Bonnie's Fitware, Inc.)

Sixth grade stunts and tumbling task cards (Bonnie's Fitware, Inc.)

Sixth grade unit 3 posters (Bonnie's Fitware, Inc.—included in the Middle School Detailed Lesson Plans)

Fitness posters (Bonnie's Fitware, Inc.—included in the Middle School Detailed Lesson Plans)

Equipment

Mats

Skills

Rolling (see figure 15.7)

- Log roll (review)
- Front shoulder roll (review)
- Triple roll
- Back shoulder roll (review)
- Squat forward roll (review)
- Squat backward roll (review)
- Pike forward roll
- Straddle roll

Static Balance

- Balancing on different body parts (review)
- Front scale (review)
- Knee scale (review)
- Tripod (review)
- Three-point tip-up (review)
- Headstand (see figure 15.8)
- Teeter-Totter (see figure 15.9a) (lead up for handstand)
- Switcheroo (see figure 15.9b) (lead up for handstand)
- Handstand (see figure 15.9c)

Dynamic Balance

- Thread the Needle
- Jump-through
- Walking on a balance beam
- Walking on a balance beam with a dip

Figure 15.7   Tumbling routine.

Weight Transfer

- Pivoting in place
- Pivoting on a balance beam
- Squat turning on the balance beam
- Cartwheel (see figure 15.10)
- Handstand roll-out (see figure 15.9d)

Flight

- Heel click
- Running and leaping (review)
- Running and leaping for distance (review)
- Running, hopping, and jumping on a springboard (review)
- Running, hopping, and jumping on a springboard for height (review)
- Running, hopping, and jumping on a springboard for height and distance (review)

Figure 15.8   Headstand.

Figure 15.9   Types of handstands. *(a)* teeter-totter, *(b)* switcheroo, *(c)* handstand, and *(d)* handstand rollout.

Figure 15.9 *(continued)*

Figure 15.10   Cartwheel.

Unit 3 Outline

DAY 1

Display the posters.

Have students brainstorm what it looks like to work cooperatively with a small group. 5.1

Have students record in their notebooks what it looks like to work cooperatively with a small group. 5.1

Describe the safe participation guidelines for participating in stunts and tumbling. 5.2

Have students record the safe participation guidelines in their notebooks. 5.2

Discuss the importance of choosing to engage in new stunt and tumbling activities. 6.3

Introduce unit.

Assign students to working groups of four.

Have students perform a warm-up along with a cardiorespiratory workout. (Assessment opportunity: structured observation 4.1)

Review log rolls. 1.0, 2.5

Have students practice log rolls. (Assessment opportunity: structured observation 1.0, 5.1, 5.2, 6.3)

Lead students through a cool-down and flexibility exercises appropriate to the physical activity level of the lesson. (Assessment opportunity: structured observation 4.1)

Assign unit-long homework:

- Have students research and write a description about the movement-related activities in ancient Babylon. (Assessment assignment opportunity: report 6.1)

- Have students keep a log of daily activity. (Assessment assignment opportunity: log 3.1)

- Have students search the Internet for opportunities in the local community for participation in physical activity. (Assessment assignment opportunity: project 3.2)

DAY 2

Explain that feedback is based on the critical elements for each skill. 2.1

Have students record in their notebooks that feedback is based on the critical elements for each skill. 2.1

Have students perform a warm-up along with muscular strength and muscular endurance exercises. (Assessment opportunity: structured observation 4.1)

Demonstrate the following skills: 1.0, 2.5

- Static balance: balancing on different body parts
- Dynamic balance: Thread the Needle
- Rolling: log roll
- Weight transfer: pivoting in place
- Flight: heel click

Have students perform the first skill in each category with partner feedback. (Assessment opportunity: structured observation 1.0, 5.1, 5.2, 6.3)

Lead students through a cool-down and flexibility exercises appropriate to the physical activity level of the lesson. (Assessment opportunity: structured observation 4.1)

Review the safety precautions for the activities in this unit. 5.2

DAY 3

Review with students the frequency, intensity, time, and type concepts related to body composition using the Health-Related Fitness: Tutorial and Portfolio. 4.2

Have students record in their notebooks the concepts of frequency, intensity, time, and type as they relate to body composition. 4.2

Describe the respiratory benefits derived from participation in physical activity. 6.4

Have students record in their notebooks the respiratory benefits derived from participation in physical activity. 6.4

Have students perform a warm-up along with a cardiorespiratory workout. (Assessment opportunity: structured observation 4.1)

Explain station approach and hand out a checklist on which students may record their progress in the skills in each category (see posters or list at the beginning of this unit).

Demonstrate new skills. 1.0, 2.5

- Static balance: front scale
- Rolling: front shoulder roll
- Weight transfer: pivoting in place on the balance beam
- Flight: run and jump for height

Have pairs practice the skills, giving feedback to each other as they rotate through the stations in groups of four. (Note: Students perform the first skill in each category. Once they can perform a skill they may move on to the next skill in the sequence.) (Assessment opportunity: structured observation 1.0, 5.1, 5.2, 6.3)

Lead students through a cool-down and flexibility exercises appropriate to the physical activity level of the lesson. (Assessment opportunity: structured observation 4.1)

Have students refine their 1-day body composition plan. (Assessment assignment opportunity: project 4.2)

(continued)

Unit 3 Outline (continued)

DAY 4

Discuss the importance of early adolescents' participating in challenging activities. 2.4

Have students record the information in their notebooks. 2.4

Have students perform a warm-up along with muscular strength and muscular endurance exercises. (Assessment opportunity: structured observation 4.1)

Demonstrate new skills. 1.0, 2.5

- Static balance: knee scale
- Rolling: triple roll
- Weight transfer: squat turn on beam
- Flight: run and jump for height

Explain that the stronger the action, the greater the reaction. 2.2

Have students record in their notebook that the stronger the action, the greater the reaction. 2.2

Have pairs practice the skills, giving feedback to each other as they rotate through the stations in groups of four. (Assessment opportunity: structured observation 1.0, 5.1, 5.2, 6.3)

Have students discuss how the concept "the stronger the action, the greater the reaction" was used in the skills practiced today. 2.2

Lead students through a cool-down and flexibility exercises appropriate to the physical activity level of the lesson. (Assessment opportunity: structured observation 4.1)

DAY 5

Have students perform a warm-up along with a cardiorespiratory workout. (Assessment opportunity: structured observation 4.1)

Demonstrate new skills. 1.0, 2.5

- Static balance: tripod
- Rolling: back shoulder roll
- Weight transfer: cartwheel
- Dynamic balance: jump through

Review that the stronger the action, the greater the reaction. 2.2

Have pairs practice the skills, giving feedback to each other as they rotate through the stations in groups of four. (Assessment opportunity: structured observation 1.0, 5.1, 5.2, 6.3)

Have students discuss how the concept "the stronger the action, the greater the reaction" was used in the skills practiced today. 2.2

Lead students through a cool-down and flexibility exercises appropriate to the physical activity level of the lesson. (Assessment opportunity: structured observation 4.1)

DAY 6

Have students perform a warm-up along with a cardiorespiratory workout. (Assessment opportunity: structured observation 4.1)

Demonstrate new skills. 1.0, 2.5

- Static balance: three point tip-up
- Rolling: squat forward roll
- Weight transfer: run, hop, and jump for distance

Have pairs practice the skills, giving each other feedback as they rotate through the stations in groups of four. (Assessment opportunity: structured observation 1.0, 5.1, 5.2, 6.3)

Lead students through a cool-down and flexibility exercises appropriate to the physical activity level of the lesson. (Assessment opportunity: structured observation 4.1)

Have students discuss how the concept "the stronger the action, the greater the reaction" was used in the skills practiced today. 2.2

DAY 7

Have students perform a warm-up along with muscular strength and muscular endurance exercises. (Assessment opportunity: structured observation 4.1)

Demonstrate new skills. 1.0, 2.5

- Static balance: headstand
- Rolling: squat backward roll
- Flight: run and leap
- Dynamic balance: walk on beam

Have pairs practice the skills, giving each other feedback as they rotate through the stations in groups of four. (Assessment opportunity: structured observation 1.0, 5.1, 5.2, 6.3)

Lead students through a cool-down and flexibility exercises appropriate to the physical activity level of the lesson. (Assessment opportunity: structured observation 4.1)

Have students discuss how the concept "the stronger the action, the greater the reaction" was used in the skills practiced today. 2.2

DAY 8

Have students perform a warm-up along with a cardiorespiratory workout. (Assessment opportunity: structured observation 4.1)

Demonstrate new skills. 1.0, 2.5

- Static balance: switcheroo
- Rolling: pike forward roll
- Flight: run and leap for distance

Have pairs practice the skills, giving each other feedback as they rotate through the stations in groups of four. (Assessment opportunity: structured observation 1.0, 5.1, 5.2, 6.3)

Lead students through a cool-down and flexibility exercises appropriate to the physical activity level of the lesson. (Assessment opportunity: structured observation 4.1)

Have students discuss how the concept "the stronger the action, the greater the reaction" was used in the skills practiced today. 2.2

DAY 9

Have students perform a warm-up along with muscular strength and muscular endurance exercises. (Assessment opportunity: structured observation 4.1)

Demonstrate new skills. 1.0, 2.5

- Static balance: teeter-totter
- Rolling: straddle roll
- Flight: run, hop, jump
- Dynamic balance: walk on beam with dip

Have pairs practice the skills, giving each other feedback as they rotate through the stations in groups of four. (Assessment opportunity: structured observation 1.0, 5.1, 5.2, 6.3)

Lead students through a cool-down and flexibility exercises appropriate to the physical activity level of the lesson. (Assessment opportunity: structured observation 4.1)

Have students discuss how the concept "the stronger the action, the greater the reaction" was used in the skills practiced today. 2.2

(continued)

Unit 3 Outline (continued)

DAY 10

Have students perform a warm-up along with a cardiorespiratory workout. (Assessment opportunity: structured observation 4.1)

Demonstrate new skills. 1.0, 2.5

- Static balance: handstand
- Flight: run, hop, jump for height

Have pairs practice the skills, giving each other feedback as they rotate through the stations in groups of four. (Assessment opportunity: structured observation 1.0, 5.1, 5.2, 6.3)

Lead students through a cool-down and flexibility exercises appropriate to the physical activity level of the lesson. (Assessment opportunity: structured observation 4.1)

DAY 11

Have students perform a warm-up along with a cardiorespiratory workout. (Assessment opportunity: structured observation 4.1)

Demonstrate new skills. 1.0, 2.5

- Weight transfer: handstand roll out
- Flight: run-hop-jump for height and distance

Have pairs practice the skills, giving each other feedback as they rotate through the stations in groups of four. (Assessment opportunity: structured observation 1.0, 5.1, 5.2, 6.3)

Lead students through a cool-down and flexibility exercises appropriate to the physical activity level of the lesson. (Assessment opportunity: structured observation 4.1)

DAY 12

Define offensive strategy. 2.3

Have students record in their notebooks the definition for offensive strategy. 2.3

Describe the components of a routine. 6.2

Have students record in their notebooks the components of a routine. 6.2

Have students perform a warm-up along with muscular strength and muscular endurance exercises. (Assessment opportunity: structured observation 4.1)

Place students in groups of four and have them create their own tumbling routines that express their feelings. (Assessment assignment opportunity: project 6.2)

Lead students through a cool-down and flexibility exercises appropriate to the physical activity level of the lesson. (Assessment opportunity: structured observation 4.1)

DAY 13

Have students perform a warm-up along with a cardiorespiratory workout. (Assessment opportunity: structured observation 4.1)

Have groups work on their routines. (Assessment opportunity: structured observation 1.0, 5.1, 5.2, 6.2, 6.3)

Lead students through a cool-down and flexibility exercises appropriate to the physical activity level of the lesson. (Assessment opportunity: structured observation 4.1)

DAY 14

Have students perform a warm-up along with muscular strength and muscular endurance exercises. (Assessment opportunity: structured observation 4.1)

Have each group demonstrate its routine to several other groups. (Assessment opportunity: project 6.2)

Lead students through a cool-down and flexibility exercises appropriate to the physical activity level of the lesson. (Assessment opportunity: structured observation 4.1)

Review material for tomorrow's quiz (or hand out quiz if you would like for it to be a take home quiz). 2.1, 2.2, 2.3, 2.4, 2.5, 6.4

DAY 15

Have students take the quiz. (Assessment opportunity: quiz 2.1, 2.2, 2.3, 2.4, 2.5, 6.4)

Collect student activity logs. (Assessment opportunity: log 3.1)

Collect reports on movement-related activities in ancient Babylon. (Assessment opportunity: report 6.1)

Collect computer printouts on opportunities in the local community for participation in physical activity. (Assessment opportunity: project 3.2)

Collect 1-day body composition plans. (Assessment assignment opportunity: project 4.2)

Folk Dance

– Unit 4

The dances selected for this unit align with the various countries studied in sixth grade history and social science, but you can use different dances from other countries, depending on the history and social science units taught at your school. I have sequenced the dances in this unit so that the locomotor skills presented in the first dance are repeated in subsequent dances. The dance steps for each dance are shown from the Dance Instruction CD to introduce each dance.

This unit works best in a closed area or gymnasium, but you can present it outside. If you must conduct the unit outside, choose a secluded area so that students do not feel self-conscious about performing to music in front of other classes. You'll need a variety of music to match the dances you plan to teach. I also use the Health-Related Fitness: Tutorial and Portfolio (Bonnie's Fitware, Inc.) to convey the cognitive concepts associated with health-related fitness. Throughout the unit, I have students wear heart rate monitors to determine whether they are in their target heart rate zones long enough to improve their cardiorespiratory endurance. On different days, I have different students download the data from their heart rate monitors into the computer; then I have them place the computer-generated graphs into their own portfolios using the Health-Related Fitness: Tutorial and Portfolio.

Unit 4 Standards

1.0—Demonstrates the mature form for dance steps used in folk and line dances: step hop; elbow swing; toes out, heels out, heels in, toes in; 1/4 pivot; turn under; step swing; schottische; and Bleking.

2.1—Explains that feedback should be corrective or positive.

2.2—States Newton's second law.

2.3—Defines defensive strategy.

2.4—Describes the importance of early adolescents' trying new activities.

2.5—Describes the critical elements for dance steps used in folk and line dances: elbow swing; toes out, heels out, heels in, toes in; 1/4 pivot; schottische; and Bleking.

3.1—Engages in moderate and vigorous physical activity for 60 minutes (at least 10 minutes of vigorous activity) 5 days each week.

3.2—Describes dance activities available in the local community.

4.1—Works toward a health-enhancing level of physical fitness.

4.2—Refines 1-day cardiorespiratory endurance plan.

5.1—Works cooperatively with a small group during folk dancing.

5.2—Follows procedures for safe participation when working with others in dance activities.

6.1—Describes dance in the ancient world.

6.2—Expresses personal feelings through the creation of a dance routine.

6.3—Chooses to engage in new folk dance activities.

6.4—Describes the heart benefits of regular participation in physical activity.

Unit 4 Assessments

1.0—Structured observation (days 1-14)

2.1—Quiz (day 15)

2.2—Quiz (day 15)

2.3—Quiz (day 15)

2.4—Quiz (day 15)

2.5—Quiz (day 15)

3.1—Log (assigned on day 1; collected on day 15)

3.2—Essay (assigned on day 1; collected on day 15)

4.1—Structured observation (days 1-14)

4.2—Project (assigned on day 6; collected on day 15)

5.1—Structured observation (days 1-14)

5.2—Structured observation (days 1-14)

6.1—Essay (assigned on day 1; collected on day 15)

6.2—Project (assigned on day 10; graded on day 14)

6.3—Structured observation (days 1-14)

6.4—Quiz (day 15)

Resources (Music Included)

Apat Apat music (Bonnie's Fitware, Inc.)

Doudlebska Polka music (Bonnie's Fitware, Inc.)

Hora music (Bonnie's Fitware, Inc.)

Korobushka music (Bonnie's Fitware, Inc.)

La Raspa music (Bonnie's Fitware, Inc.)

Miserlou music (Bonnie's Fitware, Inc.)

Pata Pata music (Bonnie's Fitware, Inc.)

Seven Jumps music (Bonnie's Fitware, Inc.)

Troika music (Bonnie's Fitware, Inc.)

Health-Related Fitness: Tutorial and Portfolio (Bonnie's Fitware, Inc.)

Middle School Physical Education Portfolio (Bonnie's Fitware, Inc.)

Dance Instruction CD (Bonnie's Fitware, Inc)

Sixth grade dance task cards (Bonnie's Fitware, Inc.)

Heart monitors

Sixth grade unit 4 posters (Bonnie's Fitware, Inc.—included in the Middle School Detailed Lesson Plans)

Fitness posters (Bonnie's Fitware, Inc.—included in the Middle School Detailed Lesson Plans)

Qualities of Movement chart (Bonnie's Fitware, Inc.—included in the Middle School Detailed Lesson Plans)

Equipment

Heart monitors

Sound system

Dances

Apat Apat—walk forward and reverse, back away, walk in opposite directions; elbow swing. Philippines

Doudlebska Polka—polka, walk, clap. Czech Republic

Hora—step sideward, step-swing. Israel

Korobushka—schottische step, balance step, cross-out-together step, walking step. Russia

La Raspa—Bleking step, running, shuffle, skipping, elbow swing. Mexico

Miserlou—two-step; grapevine. Greece

Pata Pata—toe touches, knee lift, quarter turns. Africa

Seven Jumps—hop, stomp, clap hands. Denmark

Troika—running step, turning under. Russia

Unit 4 Outline

DAY 1

Display the posters.

Introduce dance unit.

Discuss with students the importance of early adolescents' trying new activities. 2.4, 6.3

Have students write in their notebooks the importance of early adolescents' trying new activities. 2.4, 6.3

Randomly assign students to groups of four.

Describe safety procedures related to dance activities. 5.2

Have students write in their notebooks safety procedures related to dance to activities. 5.2

Have students perform a warm-up. (Assessment opportunity: structured observation 4.1)

Review (from grade 5) hopping, walking, skipping, and sliding. 1.0

Have students review the four locomotor skills while you play music. (Assessment opportunity: structured observation 1.0, 5.2, 6.3)

Review (from grade 5) qualities of movement. 1.0

Have students perform the four locomotor skills while you play music, using various qualities of movement as you call them out. (Assessment opportunity: structured observation 1.0, 5.2, 6.3)

Have students perform the four locomotor skills while you play music at a speed fast enough to raise their heart rates into their target heart rate zones. (Assessment opportunity: structured observation 1.0, 5.2, 6.3)

Lead students through a cool-down and flexibility exercises appropriate to the physical activity level of the lesson. (Assessment opportunity: structured observation 4.1)

Have students discuss whether performing locomotor skills to music is an aerobic activity. 4.2

Assign unit-long homework:

- Have students research and describe dances from the ancient world. (Assessment assignment opportunity: report 6.1)

- Have students keep a log of daily activity. (Assessment assignment opportunity: log 3.1)

- Have students write a description of dance activities available in the local community. (Assessment assignment opportunity: essay 3.2)

(continued)

Unit 4 Outline *(continued)*

DAY 2

Discuss giving feedback to a partner when working on dance skills. 2.1

Have students record in their notebooks that feedback should be corrective or positive. 2.1

Have students perform a warm-up along with muscular strength and muscular endurance exercises. (Assessment opportunity: structured observation 4.1)

Demonstrate and describe dance stomp. 1.0, 2.5

Have students practice stomp. 1.0

Demonstrate and describe step hop. 1.0, 2.5

Have students practice step hop. 1.0

Demonstrate and describe knee lift. 1.0, 2.5

Have students practice knee lift. 1.0

Teach the Seven Jumps dance (Denmark). 1.0

Have students practice the Seven Jumps dance. (Assessment opportunity: structured observation 1.0, 5.2, 6.3)

Lead students through a cool-down and flexibility exercises appropriate to the physical activity level of the lesson. (Assessment opportunity: structured observation 4.1)

Review that trying new activities is important for students. 2.4

DAY 3

Discuss working cooperatively with a small group during folk dancing. 5.1

Have students brainstorm what cooperation looks like, sounds like, and feels like. 5.1

Have students record in their notebooks what cooperation looks like, sounds like, and feels like. 5.1

Have students perform a warm-up. (Assessment opportunity: structured observation 4.1)

Demonstrate and describe elbow swing. 1.0, 2.5

Have students practice elbow swing. 1.0

Teach the Apat Apat (Philippines). 1.0

Have students practice the Apat Apat. (Assessment opportunity: structured observation 1.0, 5.1, 5.2, 6.3)

Introduce walking and bending movements. 1.0, 2.5

Review the Seven Jumps dance. 1.0

Have students practice the Seven Jumps dance. (Assessment opportunity: structured observation 1.0, 5.1, 5.2, 6.3)

Lead students through a cool-down and flexibility exercises appropriate to the physical activity level of the lesson. (Assessment opportunity: structured observation 4.1)

Review that feedback should be corrective or positive. 2.1

DAY 4

State Newton's second law. 2.2

Have students record Newton's second law in their notebooks. 2.2

Demonstrate the application of Newton's second law. 2.2

Have students perform a warm-up along with muscular strength and muscular endurance exercises. (Assessment opportunity: structured observation 4.1)

Demonstrate and describe toes out, heels out, heels in, toes in. 1.0, 2.5

Have students practice toes out, heels out, heels in, toes in. 1.0

DAY 4 (continued)

Demonstrate and describe cross kick. 1.0, 2.5

Have students practice cross kick. 1.0

Demonstrate and describe 1/4 pivot. 1.0, 2.5

Have students practice 1/4 pivot. 1.0

Teach the Pata Pata (Africa). 1.0

Have students practice the Pata Pata. (Assessment opportunity: structured observation 1.0, 5.1, 5.2, 6.3)

Have students practice the Apat Apat. (Assessment opportunity: structured observation 1.0, 5.1, 5.2, 6.3)

Lead students through a cool-down and flexibility exercises appropriate to the physical activity level of the lesson. (Assessment opportunity: structured observation 4.1)

Review cooperation. 5.1

For homework, have students memorize Newton's second law. 2.2

DAY 5

Define defensive strategy. 2.3

Have students record the definition of defensive strategy in their notebooks. 2.3

Have students perform a warm-up. (Assessment opportunity: structured observation 4.1)

Introduce running steps and turning under. 1.0, 2.5

Demonstrate and describe running steps. 1.0, 2.5

Have students practice running steps. 1.0

Demonstrate and describe turning under. 1.0, 2.5

Have students practice turning under. 1.0

Teach the Troika (Russia). 1.0

Have students practice the Troika. (Assessment opportunity: structured observation 1.0, 5.1, 5.2, 6.3)

Have students practice the Pata Pata. (Assessment opportunity: structured observation 1.0, 5.1, 5.2, 6.3)

Lead students through a cool-down and flexibility exercises appropriate to the physical activity level of the lesson. (Assessment opportunity: structured observation 4.1)

Review Newton's second law. 2.2

Review how to increase force.

DAY 6

Have students view the Cardiorespiratory Fitness segment from the Health-Related Fitness: Tutorial and Portfolio (Bonnie's Fitware, Inc.). 4.2

Have students write in their notebooks about the concepts of frequency, intensity, time, and type (FITT) as they relate to cardiorespiratory endurance. 4.2

Have students discuss the difference between aerobic and anaerobic activities, methods for monitoring heart rate intensity, and how to calculate target heart rate. 4.2

Have students record the information in their notebooks. 4.2

Have students discuss the heart benefits derived from participation in physical activities. 6.4

Have students record in their notebooks the heart benefits derived from participation in physical activity. 6.4

(continued)

Unit 4 Outline *(continued)*

DAY 6 *(continued)*

Have students refine their 1-day cardiorespiratory endurance plan. (Assessment assignment opportunity: plan 4.2)

Have students perform a warm-up. (Assessment opportunity: structured observation 4.1)

Demonstrate and describe step swing. 1.0, 2.5

Have students practice step swing. 1.0

Teach the Hora (Israel). 1.0

Have students practice the Hora. (Assessment opportunity: structured observation 1.0, 5.1, 5.2, 6.3)

Have students practice the Troika. (Assessment opportunity: structured observation 1.0, 5.1, 5.2, 6.3)

Lead students through a cool-down and flexibility exercises appropriate to the physical activity level of the lesson. (Assessment opportunity: structured observation 4.1)

DAY 7

Have students perform a warm-up along with muscular strength and muscular endurance exercises. (Assessment opportunity: structured observation 4.1)

Demonstrate and describe two-step. 1.0, 2.5

Have students practice two-step. 1.0

Demonstrate and describe grapevine. 1.0, 2.5

Have students practice grapevine. 1.0

Teach the Miserlou (Greece). 1.0

Have students practice the Miserlou. (Assessment opportunity: structured observation 1.0, 5.1, 5.2, 6.3)

Have students practice the Hora. (Assessment opportunity: structured observation 1.0, 5.1, 5.2, 6.3)

Lead students through a cool-down and flexibility exercises appropriate to the physical activity level of the lesson. (Assessment opportunity: structured observation 4.1)

DAY 8

Have students perform a warm-up. (Assessment opportunity: structured observation 4.1)

Demonstrate and describe polka step. 1.0, 2.5

Have students practice polka step. 1.0

Teach the Doudlebska Polka (Czech Republic). 1.0

Have students practice the Doudlebska Polka. (Assessment opportunity: structured observation 1.0, 5.1, 5.2, 6.3)

Have students practice the Miserlou. (Assessment opportunity: structured observation 1.0, 5.1, 5.2, 6.3)

Lead students through a cool-down and flexibility exercises appropriate to the physical activity level of the lesson. (Assessment opportunity: structured observation 4.1)

DAY 9

Have students perform a warm-up along with muscular strength and muscular endurance exercises. (Assessment opportunity: structured observation 4.1)

Demonstrate and describe schottische. 1.0, 2.5

Have students practice schottische. 1.0

Teach the Korobushka (Russia). 1.0

Have students practice the Korobushka. (Assessment opportunity: structured observation 1.0, 5.1, 5.2, 6.3)

Have students practice the Doudlebska Polka. (Assessment opportunity: structured observation 1.0, 5.1, 5.2, 6.3)

Lead students through a cool-down and flexibility exercises appropriate to the physical activity level of the lesson. (Assessment opportunity: structured observation 4.1)

DAY 10

Have students perform a warm-up. (Assessment opportunity: structured observation 4.1)

Demonstrate and describe shuffle. 1.0, 2.5

Have students practice shuffle. 1.0

Demonstrate and describe Bleking. 1.0, 2.5

Have students practice Bleking. 1.0

Demonstrate and describe skip. 1.0, 2.5

Have students practice skip. 1.0

Teach La Raspa (Mexico). 1.0

Have students practice La Raspa. (Assessment opportunity: structured observation 1.0, 5.1, 5.2, 6.3)

Have students practice the Korobushka. (Assessment opportunity: structured observation 1.0, 5.1, 5.2, 6.3)

Lead students through a cool-down and flexibility exercises appropriate to the physical activity level of the lesson. (Assessment opportunity: structured observation 4.1)

Assign students the project of designing a dance that expresses personal feelings. (Assessment assignment opportunity: project 6.2)

DAY 11

Have students perform a warm-up. (Assessment opportunity: structured observation 4.1)

Have students practice all the dances learned in this unit. (Assessment opportunity: structured observation 1.0, 5.1, 5.2, 6.3)

Have students work on rhythmic patterns project. (Assessment opportunity: structured observation 1.0, 5.1, 5.2, 6.3)

Lead students through a cool-down and flexibility exercises appropriate to the physical activity level of the lesson. (Assessment opportunity: structured observation 4.1)

DAY 12

Have students perform a warm-up along with muscular strength and muscular endurance exercises. (Assessment opportunity: structured observation 4.1)

Have students work on rhythmic patterns project. (Assessment opportunity: structured observation 1.0, 5.1, 5.2, 6.3)

Lead students through a cool-down and flexibility exercises appropriate to the physical activity level of the lesson. (Assessment opportunity: structured observation 4.1)

DAY 13

Have students perform a warm-up. (Assessment opportunity: structured observation 4.1)

Have students work on rhythmic patterns project. (Assessment opportunity: structured observation 1.0, 5.1, 5.2, 6.3)

Lead students through a cool-down and flexibility exercises appropriate to the physical activity level of the lesson. (Assessment opportunity: structured observation 4.1)

DAY 14

Have students perform a warm-up along with muscular strength and muscular endurance exercises. (Assessment opportunity: structured observation 4.1)

Have groups present their rhythmic patterns to the class. (Assessment opportunity: project 6.2)

Lead students through a cool-down and flexibility exercises appropriate to the physical activity level of the lesson. (Assessment opportunity: structured observation 4.1)

For homework, have students write an evaluation of the other group's performance of rhythmic patterns. (Assessment opportunity: project 6.2)

(continued)

Unit 4 Outline *(continued)*

DAY 15

Have students take quiz. (Assessment opportunity: quiz 2.1, 2.2, 2.3, 2.4, 2.5, 6.4)

Collect physical activity log. (Assessment opportunity: log 3.1)

Collect history report. (Assessment opportunity: report 6.1)

Collect description of dance activities in the local community. (Assessment opportunity: essay 3.2)

Collect 1-day cardiorespiratory endurance plan. (Assessment opportunity: plan 4.2)

Target Sport: Bowling  — Unit 5

In this unit, we move on to the manipulation of objects. The underhand throw and catch are used in many of our traditional sports, and in this unit we apply the skills to bowling.

You can conduct the bowling skills activities on any blacktop or gym area. You will need bowling balls and pins or something similar for the activity. You can use plastic liter bottles and student-made targets or contact your local bowling center. Bowling centers often have the Learn in School program whereby they rent plastic or rubber bowling balls and pins to schools.

This unit and the next four lend themselves especially well to interdisciplinary links with the science curriculum and math curriculum. As students strive to improve and apply their manipulative skills to lead-up activities, the scientific principles of how these occur come into play. Specifically in this unit, I have students focus on ways to use force to increase the speed of the bowling ball.

Unit 5 Standards

1.0—Demonstrates the mature form for bowling.

2.1—Explains that feedback is most helpful when it is specific and meaningful.

2.2—Explains that speed affects the amount of force developed.

2.3—Describes basic offensive strategies for bowling.

2.4—Describes the importance of early adolescents' participating in games using lighter equipment.

2.5—Describes the critical elements for bowling.

3.1—Engages in moderate and vigorous physical activity for 60 minutes (at least 10 minutes of vigorous activity) 5 days each week.

3.2—Describes bowling activities available in the local community.

4.1—Works toward a health-enhancing level of physical fitness.

4.2—Explains the FITT concepts related to muscular endurance.

5.1—Works cooperatively with a small group during bowling activities.

5.2—Follows procedures for safe participation when working with a small group in bowling activities.

6.1—Describes movement-related activities in ancient Egypt.

6.2—Not applicable.

6.3—Chooses to engage in new bowling activities.

6.4—Describes the skeletal benefits derived from participation in physical activity.

Unit 5 Assessments

1.0—Structured observation (days 1-14)

2.1—Quiz (day 15)

2.2—Quiz (day 15)

2.3—Essay (assigned on day 12; collected on day 14)

2.4—Quiz (day 15)

2.5—Quiz (day 15)

3.1—Log (assigned on day 1; collected on day 15)

3.2—Essay (assigned on day 1; collected on day 15)

4.1—Structured observation (days 1-15)

4.2—Quiz (day 15)

5.1—Structured observation (days 1-14)

5.2—Structured observation (days 1-14)

6.1—Report (assigned on day 1; collected on day 15)

6.2—Not applicable

6.3—Structured observation (days 1-14)

6.4—Quiz (day 15)

Resources

Target Sports CD (Bonnie's Fitware, Inc.)

Health-Related Fitness: Tutorial and Portfolio (Bonnie's Fitware, Inc.)

Middle School Physical Education Portfolio (Bonnie's Fitware, Inc.)

Sixth grade bowling task cards (Bonnie's Fitware, Inc.)

Sixth grade unit 5 posters (Bonnie's Fitware, Inc.—included in the Middle School Detailed Lesson Plans)

Fitness posters (Bonnie's Fitware, Inc.—included in the Middle School Detailed Lesson Plans)

Equipment

Bowling set (1 ball and 10 pins)

Game

Bowling

Unit 5 Outline

DAY 1	Display the posters.
	Introduce bowling unit.
	Discuss working cooperatively with a small group during bowling. 5.1
	Discuss the importance of choosing to engage in new bowling activities. 6.3
	Describe the safety guidelines for participating in bowling activities. 5.2
	Have students write in their notebooks the safety guidelines for participating in bowling activities. 5.2
	Discuss the importance of early adolescents' participating in games using lighter equipment. 2.4
	Have students record in their notebooks the importance of early adolescents' participating in games using lighter equipment. 2.4
	Assign students to heterogeneous working groups of four.
	Have students perform a warm-up along with a cardiorespiratory workout. (Assessment opportunity: structured observation 4.1)
	Demonstrate rolling and catching a ball. 1.0, 2.5

(continued)

Unit 5 Outline *(continued)*

DAY 1 *(continued)*	Have students roll and catch with their partners while focusing on accuracy. (Assessment opportunity: structured observation 1.0, 5.1, 5.2, 6.3) Lead students through a cool-down and flexibility exercises appropriate to the physical activity level of the lesson. (Assessment opportunity: structured observation 4.1) Assign unit-long homework: • Have students research and write a description of the movement-related activities in ancient Egypt. (Assessment assignment opportunity: report 6.1) • Have students keep a log of daily activity. (Assessment assignment opportunity: log 3.1) • Have students describe the bowling activities available in the local community. (Assessment assignment opportunity: essay 3.2)
DAY 2	Explain that feedback is most helpful when it is specific and meaningful. 2.1 Have students summarize in their notebooks the explanation of helpful feedback. 2.1 Have students perform a warm-up along with muscular strength and muscular endurance exercises. (Assessment opportunity: structured observation 4.1) Review rolling skill. 1.0, 2.5 Have students rotate through several stations, rolling different-sized balls (including bowling balls) at a variety of stationary targets from different distances with feedback from their partners. (Assessment opportunity: structured observation 1.0, 5.1, 5.2, 6.3) Lead students through a cool-down and flexibility exercises appropriate to the physical activity level of the lesson. (Assessment opportunity: structured observation 4.1) Review the importance of early adolescents' participating in games using lighter equipment. 2.4
DAY 3	Have students view the Muscular Endurance section on the Health-Related Fitness: Tutorial and Portfolio (Bonnie's Fitware, Inc.) and discuss what they learned. 4.2 Review the concepts of frequency, intensity, time, and type (FITT) as they relate to muscular endurance. 4.2 Have students record in their notebooks the concepts of frequency, intensity, time, and type as they relate to muscular endurance. 4.2 Describe the skeletal benefits derived from participating in physical activity. 6.4 Have students record the skeletal benefits in their notebook. 6.4 Have students watch the bowling technique on the Target Sports CD. 1.0, 2.5 Have students perform a warm-up along with a cardiorespiratory workout. (Assessment opportunity: structured observation 4.1) Demonstrate and describe the proper bowling ball grip. 1.0, 2.5 Have students practice gripping a ball with feedback from their partners. (Assessment opportunity: structured observation 1.0, 5.1, 5.2, 6.3) Demonstrate and describe the bowling four-step approach (see figure 15.11). 1.0, 2.5 Have students practice the four-step approach with and without a ball, with feedback from their partners. (Assessment opportunity: structured observation 1.0, 5.1, 5.2, 6.3) Lead students through a cool-down and flexibility exercises appropriate to the physical activity level of the lesson. (Assessment opportunity: structured observation 4.1) Review the fact that feedback is most important when it is specific and meaningful. 2.1

Figure 15.11 Bowling four-step approach.

DAY 4

Review the bowling four-step approach. 1.0, 2.5

Explain that speed affects the amount of force developed. 2.2

Have students record in their notebooks that speed affects the amount of force developed. 2.2

Have students perform a warm-up along with muscular strength and muscular endurance exercises. (Assessment opportunity: structured observation 4.1)

Have students practice the four-step approach without a ball, with feedback from their partners. (Assessment opportunity: structured observation 1.0, 5.1, 5.2, 6.3)

Explain spot bowling. 1.0, 2.5

Have students practice spot bowling. (Assessment opportunity: structured observation 1.0, 5.1, 5.2, 6.3)

Review the importance of early adolescents' participating in games using lighter equipment. 2.4

Lead students through a cool-down and flexibility exercises appropriate to the physical activity level of the lesson. (Assessment opportunity: structured observation 4.1)

Review concepts of frequency, intensity, time, and type (FITT) as they relate to muscular endurance. 4.2

DAY 5

Teach students how to score in bowling. 2.3

Discuss offensive strategies that are used in bowling. 2.3

Demonstrate the scoring part of the Target Sports CD and how students will use it to practice scoring. 2.3

Review spot bowling. 1.0

Have students perform a warm-up along with a cardiorespiratory workout. (Assessment opportunity: structured observation 4.1)

Have students practice the four-step approach using a ball, with feedback from their partners. (Assessment opportunity: structured observation 1.0, 5.1, 5.2, 6.3)

Lead students through a cool-down and flexibility exercises appropriate to the physical activity level of the lesson. (Assessment opportunity: structured observation 4.1)

Have students brainstorm how the concept "speed affects the amount of force developed" applies to bowling. 2.2

(continued)

Unit 5 Outline *(continued)*

DAY 6	Have students perform a warm-up along with a cardiorespiratory workout. (Assessment opportunity: structured observation 4.1)
	Review the bowling grip, the four-step approach, and spot bowling. 1.0, 2.5
	Have students rotate through three stations: the bowling four-step approach using a ball with feedback from their partners, scoring in bowling, and bowling at pins. (Assessment opportunity: structured observation 1.0, 5.1, 5.2, 6.3) 2.3
	Lead students through a cool-down and flexibility exercises appropriate to the physical activity level of the lesson. (Assessment opportunity: structured observation 4.1)
	Review scoring in bowling along with offensive strategies. 2.3
DAY 7	Have students perform a warm-up along with muscular strength and muscular endurance exercises. (Assessment opportunity: structured observation 4.1)
	Review the bowling grip, the four-step approach, and spot bowling. 1.0, 2.5
	Have students rotate through three stations: the bowling four-step approach using a ball with feedback from their partners, scoring in bowling, and bowling at pins. (Assessment opportunity: structured observation 1.0, 5.1, 5.2, 6.3) 2.3
	Lead students through a cool-down and flexibility exercises appropriate to the physical activity level of the lesson. (Assessment opportunity: structured observation 4.1)
DAY 8	Have students perform a warm-up along with a cardiorespiratory workout. (Assessment opportunity: structured observation 4.1)
	Review the bowling grip, the four-step approach, and spot bowling. 1.0, 2.5
	Have students rotate through three stations: the bowling four-step approach using a ball with feedback from their partners, scoring in bowling, and bowling at pins. (Assessment opportunity: structured observation 1.0, 5.1, 5.2, 6.3) 2.3
	Lead students through a cool-down and flexibility exercises appropriate to the physical activity level of the lesson. (Assessment opportunity: structured observation 4.1)
DAY 9	Have students perform a warm-up along with muscular strength and muscular endurance exercises. (Assessment opportunity: structured observation 4.1)
	Have students participate in bowling including scorekeeping. (Assessment opportunity: structured observation 1.0, 5.1, 5.2, 6.3) 2.3
	Lead students through a cool-down and flexibility exercises appropriate to the physical activity level of the lesson. (Assessment opportunity: structured observation 4.1)
DAY 10	Have students perform a warm-up along with a cardiorespiratory workout. (Assessment opportunity: structured observation 4.1)
	Have students participate in bowling including scorekeeping. (Assessment opportunity: structured observation 1.0, 5.1, 5.2, 6.3) 2.3
	Lead students through a cool-down and flexibility exercises appropriate to the physical activity level of the lesson. (Assessment opportunity: structured observation 4.1)
DAY 11	Have students perform a warm-up along with a cardiorespiratory workout. (Assessment opportunity: structured observation 4.1)
	Have students participate in bowling including scorekeeping. (Assessment opportunity: structured observation 1.0, 5.1, 5.2, 6.3) 2.3
	Lead students through a cool-down and flexibility exercises appropriate to the physical activity level of the lesson. (Assessment opportunity: structured observation 4.1)

DAY 12

Have students perform a warm-up along with muscular strength and muscular endurance exercises. (Assessment opportunity: structured observation 4.1)

Have students participate in bowling including scorekeeping. (Assessment opportunity: structured observation 1.0, 5.1, 5.2, 6.3) 2.3

Lead students through a cool-down and flexibility exercises appropriate to the physical activity level of the lesson. (Assessment opportunity: structured observation 4.1)

Assign students the writing of an essay that describes the offensive strategies used in bowling. (Assessment opportunity: essay 2.3)

DAY 13

Have students perform a warm-up along with a cardiorespiratory workout. (Assessment opportunity: structured observation 4.1)

Have students participate in bowling including scorekeeping. (Assessment opportunity: structured observation 1.0, 5.1, 5.2, 6.3) 2.3

Lead students through a cool-down and flexibility exercises appropriate to the physical activity level of the lesson. (Assessment opportunity: structured observation 4.1)

DAY 14

Have students perform a warm-up along with muscular strength and muscular endurance exercises. (Assessment opportunity: structured observation 4.1)

Have students participate in bowling including scorekeeping. (Assessment opportunity: structured observation 1.0, 5.1, 5.2, 6.3) 2.3

Lead students through a cool-down and flexibility exercises appropriate to the physical activity level of the lesson. (Assessment opportunity: structured observation 4.1)

Review material for tomorrow's quiz (or hand out quiz if you would like for it to be a take home quiz). 2.1, 2.2, 2.4, 2.5, 4.2, 6.4

Collect essays that describe the offensive strategies used in bowling. (Assessment opportunity: essay 2.3)

DAY 15

Have students take the quiz. (Assessment opportunity: quiz 2.1, 2.2, 2.4, 2.5, 4.2, 6.4)

Collect student activity logs. (Assessment opportunity: log 3.1)

Collect reports on movement-related activities in ancient Egypt. (Assessment opportunity: report 6.1)

Collect descriptions of bowling activities available in the local community. (Assessment opportunity: essay 3.2)

Target and Invasion Sport: Flying Disc — Unit 6

Flying disc activities provide students with an opportunity to refine their throwing and catching skill using a unique object. Specifically, flying disc golf presents students with a new target game and prepares them for the seventh grade golf unit. In addition, Ultimate introduces students to a simple invasion sport, thus preparing them for the eighth grade invasion unit.

You can conduct flying disc activities on any blacktop area, although a grassy area is much nicer. You will need one flying disc for every two students and targets for flying disc golf. Appropriate instructional materials include the Invasion Sports CD and Target Sports CD, which give students visual images of model flying disc players.

Unit 6 Standards

1.0—Demonstrates the mature pattern for the flying disc backhand throw and pancake, thumb-up, and thumb-down catching.

2.1—Explains that only one or two corrections should be identified when providing feedback.

2.2—Explains that the distance an object travels is affected by the number and strength of the muscles available for the task.

2.3—Describes the opportunities that allow a player to pass the flying disc while being guarded.

2.4—Describes the importance of early adolescents' participating in games on smaller fields.

2.5—Describes the critical elements for the flying disc backhand throw and pancake, thumb-up, and thumb-down catching.

3.1—Engages in moderate and vigorous physical activity for 60 minutes (at least 15 minutes of vigorous activity) 5 days each week.

3.2—Describes flying disc activities available in the local community.

4.1—Works toward a health-enhancing level of physical fitness.

4.2—Identifies contraindicated exercises and their adverse effects on the body.

5.1—Works cooperatively with a small group during flying disc activities.

5.2—Follows procedures for safe participation in flying disc activities when working in a small group.

6.1—Describes movement-related activities in ancient Rome.

6.2—Not applicable.

6.3—Chooses to engage in new flying disc activities.

6.4—Describes the muscular benefits of regulation participation in physical activity.

Unit 6 Assessments

1.0—Structured observation (days 1-14)

2.1—Quiz (day 15)

2.2—Quiz (day 15)

2.3—Quiz (day 15)

2.4—Quiz (day 15)

2.5—Quiz (day 15)

3.1—Log (assigned on day 1; collected on day 15)

3.2—Essay (assigned on day 1; collected on day 15)

4.1—Structured observation (days 1-14)

4.2—Quiz (day 15)

5.1—Structured observation (days 1-14)

5.2—Structured observation (days 1-14)

6.1—Report (assigned on day 1; collected on day 15)

6.2—Not applicable

6.3—Structured observation (days 1-14)

6.4—Quiz (day 15)

Resources

Health-Related Fitness: Tutorial and Portfolio (Bonnie's Fitware, Inc.)

Middle School Physical Education Portfolio (Bonnie's Fitware, Inc.)

Invasion Sports CD (Bonnie's Fitware, Inc.)

Target Sports CD (Bonnie's Fitware, Inc.)

Sixth grade flying disc task cards (Bonnie's Fitware, Inc.)

Dangerous task cards

Fitness task cards

Sixth grade unit 6 posters (Bonnie's Fitware, Inc.—included in the Middle School Detailed Lesson Plans)

Fitness posters (Bonnie's Fitware, Inc.—included in the Middle School Detailed Lesson Plans)

Qualities of Movement chart (Bonnie's Fitware, Inc.—included in the Middle School Detailed Lesson Plans)

Equipment

Flying discs

Games

Flying disc golf

Ultimate 4-on-4

2-on-2 Keep-Away

Unit 6 Outline

DAY 1

Display the posters.

Introduce flying disc unit.

Explain what it means to choose to engage in new flying disc activities. 6.3

Explain the procedures for safe participation in flying disc activities when working in small groups. 5.2

Have students record safety procedures in their notebook. 5.2

Assign students to heterogeneous working groups of four.

Describe working cooperatively in small groups during flying disc activities and the role of each participant. 5.1

Have students perform a warm-up along with a cardiorespiratory workout. (Assessment opportunity: structured observation 4.1)

Demonstrate and describe grasping a flying disc. 1.0, 2.5

Have students practice grasping a flying disc. (Assessment opportunity: structured observation 1.0, 5.1, 5.2, 6.3)

Have students experiment with throwing a flying disc. (Assessment opportunity: structured observation 1.0, 5.1, 5.2, 6.3)

Lead students through a cool-down and flexibility exercises appropriate to the physical activity level of the lesson. (Assessment opportunity: structured observation 4.1)

Assign unit-long homework:

- Have students research and write a description of movement-related activities in ancient Rome. (Assessment assignment opportunity: report 6.1)

- Have students keep a log of daily activity. (Assessment assignment opportunity: log 3.1)

- Have students write a description about flying disc activities available in the local community. (Assessment assignment opportunity: essay 3.2)

DAY 2

Review safety procedures. 5.2

Describe the muscular benefits derived from participation in physical activity. 6.4

Have students record the muscular benefits in their notebook. 6.4

Have students view the section on bad exercise in the Health-Related Fitness: Tutorial and Portfolio (Bonnie's Fitware, Inc.) and then discuss what they learned. 4.2

Have students perform a warm-up along with muscular strength and muscular endurance exercises. (Assessment opportunity: structured observation 4.1)

Review safety procedures. 5.2

Show the backhand flying disc throw on the Invasion Sports or Target Sports CD. 1.0, 2.5

(continued)

Unit 6 Outline *(continued)*

DAY 2 *(continued)*

Demonstrate and describe the correct technique for the backhand throw (see figure 15.12). 1.0, 2.5

Demonstrate and describe the correct technique for the pancake catch (catching the flying disc between the two palms). 1.0, 2.5

Have students, in pairs, practice throwing and catching the flying disc. (Assessment opportunity: structured observation 1.0, 5.1, 5.2, 6.3)

Lead students through a cool-down and flexibility exercises appropriate to the physical activity level of the lesson. (Assessment opportunity: structured observation 4.1)

Figure 15.12   Backhand throw and thumb-down catch.

DAY 3

Explain that only one or two corrections should be identified when providing feedback. 2.1

Have students record in their notebooks that only one or two corrections should be identified when providing feedback. 2.1

Have students brainstorm why only one or two corrections should be identified when providing feedback. 2.1

Have students perform a warm-up along with a cardiorespiratory workout. (Assessment opportunity: structured observation 4.1)

Demonstrate and describe the correct technique for the thumb-up catch and thumb-down catch (see figure 15.11). 1.0, 2.5

Explain when to use the thumb-up catch and thumb-down catch (low catches and high catches). 1.0, 2.5

Have students, in pairs, practice throwing and catching the flying disc while giving feedback to their partners. (Assessment opportunity: structured observation 1.0, 5.1, 5.2, 6.3)

Lead students through a cool-down and flexibility exercises appropriate to the physical activity level of the lesson. (Assessment opportunity: structured observation 4.1)

DAY 4

Have students perform a warm-up along with muscular strength and muscular endurance exercises. (Assessment opportunity: structured observation 4.1)

Demonstrate and describe throwing and catching the flying disc while moving. 1.0, 2.5

Have students, in pairs, practice throwing and catching the flying disc while on the run (while providing feedback to their partners). (Assessment opportunity: structured observation 1.0, 5.1, 5.2, 6.3)

Lead students through a cool-down and flexibility exercises appropriate to the physical activity level of the lesson. (Assessment opportunity: structured observation 4.1)

DAY 5	Have students perform a warm-up along with a cardiorespiratory workout. (Assessment opportunity: structured observation 4.1) Have students, in groups of four, participate in the following eight stations: throwing a flying disc into a trash can, throwing a flying disc through a hula hoop, throwing and catching a flying disc with a partner, playing 2-on-2 Keep-Away using the flying disc, throwing a flying disc at a pole, throwing and catching a flying disc, playing 2-on-2 Keep-Away using the flying disc, and throwing a flying disc at a target on the wall while providing feedback to their partners. (Assessment opportunity: structured observation 1.0, 5.1, 5.2, 6.3) Lead students through a cool-down and flexibility exercises appropriate to the physical activity level of the lesson. (Assessment opportunity: structured observation 4.1)
DAY 6	Have students perform a warm-up along with a cardiorespiratory workout. (Assessment opportunity: structured observation 4.1) Have students, in groups of four, participate in the following eight stations: throwing a flying disc into a trash can, throwing a flying disc through a hula hoop, throwing and catching a flying disc with a partner, playing 2-on-2 Keep-Away using the flying disc, throwing a flying disc at a pole, throwing and catching a flying disc, playing 2-on-2 Keep-Away using the flying disc, and throwing a flying disc at a target on the wall while providing feedback to their partners. (Assessment opportunity: structured observation 1.0, 5.1, 5.2, 6.3) Lead students through a cool-down and flexibility exercises appropriate to the physical activity level of the lesson. (Assessment opportunity: structured observation 4.1)
DAY 7	Explain that the distance an object travels is affected by the number and strength of the muscles available for the task. 2.2 Have students record in their notebooks that the distance an object travels is affected by the number and strength of the muscles available for the task. 2.2 Have students perform a warm-up along with muscular strength and muscular endurance exercises. (Assessment opportunity: structured observation 4.1) Demonstrate flying disc golf. 1.0 Have students participate in flying disc golf as they keep track of their scores. (Assessment opportunity: structured observation 1.0, 5.1, 5.2, 6.3) Lead students through a cool-down and flexibility exercises appropriate to the physical activity level of the lesson. (Assessment opportunity: structured observation 4.1)
DAY 8	Have students perform a warm-up along with a cardiorespiratory workout. (Assessment opportunity: structured observation 4.1) Have students, in pairs, participate in flying disc golf as they keep track of their scores. (Assessment opportunity: structured observation 1.0, 5.1, 5.2, 6.3) Lead students through a cool-down and flexibility exercises appropriate to the physical activity level of the lesson. (Assessment opportunity: structured observation 4.1) Review that the distance an object travels is affected by the number and strength of the muscles available for the task. 2.2
DAY 9	Have students perform a warm-up along with muscular strength and muscular endurance exercises. (Assessment opportunity: structured observation 4.1) Have students participate in matching bad exercises to safer alternative exercises. 4.2 Have students, in pairs, participate in flying disc golf as they keep track of their scores. (Assessment opportunity: structured observation 1.0, 5.1, 5.2, 6.3) Lead students through a cool-down and flexibility exercises appropriate to the physical activity level of the lesson. (Assessment opportunity: structured observation 4.1)

(continued)

Unit 6 Outline *(continued)*

DAY 10

Teach students how to play Ultimate 4-on-4. 1.0

Describe the importance of early adolescents' participating in games on smaller fields. 2.4

Have students record in their notebooks the reasons why early adolescents should participate in games on smaller fields. 2.4

Have students perform a warm-up along with a cardiorespiratory workout. (Assessment opportunity: structured observation 4.1)

Have students play Ultimate 4-on-4. (Assessment opportunity: structured observation 1.0, 5.1, 5.2, 6.3)

Lead students through a cool-down and flexibility exercises appropriate to the physical activity level of the lesson. (Assessment opportunity: structured observation 4.1)

DAY 11

Describe the opportunities that allow a player to pass the flying disc while being guarded. 2.3

Have student record in their notebooks the opportunities that allow a player to pass the flying disc while being guarded. 2.3

Have students perform a warm-up along with a cardiorespiratory workout. (Assessment opportunity: structured observation 4.1)

Have students play Ultimate 4-on-4. (Assessment opportunity: structured observation 1.0, 5.1, 5.2, 6.3)

Lead students through a cool-down and flexibility exercises appropriate to the physical activity level of the lesson. (Assessment opportunity: structured observation 4.1)

DAY 12

Have students perform a warm-up along with muscular strength and muscular endurance exercises. (Assessment opportunity: structured observation 4.1)

Have students play Ultimate 4-on-4. (Assessment opportunity: structured observation 1.0, 5.1, 5.2, 6.3)

Lead students through a cool-down and flexibility exercises appropriate to the physical activity level of the lesson. (Assessment opportunity: structured observation 4.1)

DAY 13

Have students perform a warm-up along with a cardiorespiratory workout. (Assessment opportunity: structured observation 4.1)

Teach students a variety of trick flying disc catches (between-the-legs catch, behind-the-back catch). 1.0, 2.5

Have students practice throwing and using the trick catches. (Assessment opportunity: structured observation 1.0, 5.1, 5.2, 6.3)

Have students play 2-on-2 Keep-Away using the trick catches. (Assessment opportunity: structured observation 1.0, 5.1, 5.2, 6.3)

Lead students through a cool-down and flexibility exercises appropriate to the physical activity level of the lesson. (Assessment opportunity: structured observation 4.1)

DAY 14

Have students perform a warm-up along with muscular strength and muscular endurance exercises. (Assessment opportunity: structured observation 4.1)

Review a variety of trick flying disc catches (between-the-legs catch, behind-the-back catch). 1.0, 2.5

Have students practice throwing and using the trick catches. (Assessment opportunity: structured observation 1.0, 5.1, 5.2, 6.3)

Have students play 2-on-2 Keep-Away using the trick catches. (Assessment opportunity: structured observation 1.0, 5.1, 5.2, 6.3)

Lead students through a cool-down and flexibility exercises appropriate to the physical activity level of the lesson. (Assessment opportunity: structured observation 4.1)

DAY 15

Have students take the quiz. (Assessment opportunity: quiz 2.1, 2.2, 2.3, 2.4, 2.5, 4.2, 6.4)

Collect student activity logs. (Assessment opportunity: log 3.1)

Collect reports on the movement-related activities in ancient Rome. (Assessment opportunity: report 6.1)

Collect essays on flying disc activities available in the local community. (Assessment opportunity: essay 3.2)

Invasion Sport: 3-on-3 Basketball  ~ Unit 7 ~

Basketball skills provide students with an opportunity to refine their throwing, catching, and striking skills in the context of a game. Specifically, basketball provides the students with an invasion sport—building on the strategies they learned during the flying disc unit. At the sixth grade level, I have my students play half-court 3-on-3 basketball, followed in eighth grade with full court basketball. You can conduct this unit on blacktop or in a gymnasium. You will need one basketball or rubber ball for every two students.

Unit 7 Standards

1.0—Demonstrates the mature form for basketball dribbling, passing, and shooting.

2.1—Explains that feedback should be given when the performer cannot see the results of his or her performance.

2.2—Explains that the distance an object travels is increased by moving the muscles in order.

2.3—Describes basic offensive and defensive strategies for invasion sports.

2.4—Describes the importance of early adolescents' participating in games with a smaller number of players.

2.5—Describes the critical elements for basketball dribbling, passing, and shooting.

3.1—Engages in moderate and vigorous physical activity for 60 minutes (at least 15 minutes of vigorous activity) 5 days each week.

3.2—Describes basketball activities available in the local community.

4.1—Works toward a health-enhancing level of physical fitness.

4.2—Explains the FITT concepts related to muscular strength.

5.1—Works cooperatively with a small group during 3-on-3 basketball activities.

5.2—Follows procedures for safe participation when working with a small group in basketball activities.

6.1—Describes movement-related activities in ancient China.

6.2—Expresses personal feelings through a ball-handling routine.

6.3—Chooses to engage in new basketball activities.

6.4—Describes the nervous system benefits derived from participation in physical activity.

Unit 7 Assessments

1.0—Structured observation (days 1-14)

2.1—Quiz (day 15)

2.2—Quiz (day 15)

2.3—Quiz (day 15)

2.4—Quiz (day 15)

2.5—Quiz (day 15)

3.1—Log (assigned on day 1; collected on day 15)

3.2—Essay (assigned on day 1; collected on day 15)

4.1—Structured observation (days 1-14)

4.2—Quiz (day 15)

5.1—Structured observation (days 1-14)

5.2—Structured observation (days 1-14)

6.1—Report (assigned on day 1; collected on day 15)

6.2—Project (assigned on day 13; collected on day 14)

6.3—Structured observation (days 1-14)

6.4—Quiz (day 15)

Resources

Health-Related Fitness: Tutorial and Portfolio (Bonnie's Fitware, Inc.)

Middle School Physical Education Portfolio (Bonnie's Fitware, Inc.)

Invasion Sports CD (Bonnie's Fitware, Inc.)

Globetrotters music (Bonnie's Fitware, Inc.)

Sixth grade basketball task cards (Bonnie's Fitware, Inc.)

Sixth grade unit 7 posters (Bonnie's Fitware, Inc.—included in the Middle School Detailed Lesson Plans)

Fitness posters (Bonnie's Fitware, Inc.—included in the Middle School Detailed Lesson Plans)

Equipment

Basketballs

Football flags

Games

2-on-2 Keep-Away

3-on-3 basketball

Dribble tag

Unit 7 Outline

DAY 1	Display the posters.
	Assign students to heterogeneous working groups of four.
	Introduce basketball unit.
	Discuss the importance of choosing to engage in new basketball activities. 6.3
	Describe the safety tips for participation in basketball activities. 5.2
	Have students record the safety tips in their notebooks. 5.2
	Describe working cooperative during basketball activities. 5.1
	Have students perform a warm-up along with a cardiorespiratory workout. (Assessment opportunity: structured observation 4.1)
	Demonstrate and describe basketball chest pass and catch using the Invasion Sports CD. 1.0, 2.5
	Have students practice basketball chest pass and catch with a partner, counting the number of successful passes and catches. (Assessment opportunity: structured observation 1.0, 5.1, 5.2, 6.3)
	Demonstrate and describe the basketball bounce pass and catch using the Invasion Sports CD. 1.0, 2.5

DAY 1 (continued)

Have students practice the basketball bounce pass and catch with a partner, counting the number of successful passes and catches. (Assessment opportunity: structured observation 1.0, 5.1, 5.2, 6.3)

Have students brainstorm how they applied the safety tips to basketball practice today. 5.2

Lead students through a cool-down and flexibility exercises appropriate to the physical activity level of the lesson. (Assessment opportunity: structured observation 4.1)

Assign unit-long homework:

- Have students research and write a description of movement-related activities in ancient China. (Assessment assignment opportunity: report 6.1)

- Have students keep a log of daily activity. (Assessment assignment opportunity: log 3.1)

- Have students write a description of the basketball activities available in the community. (Assessment assignment opportunity: essay 3.2)

DAY 2

Review safety tips for basketball. 5.2

Have students perform a warm-up along with muscular strength and muscular endurance exercises. (Assessment opportunity: structured observation 4.1)

Review basketball chest pass and catch. 1.0, 2.5

Have students practice basketball chest pass and catch with a partner, counting the number of successful passes and catches. (Assessment opportunity: structured observation 1.0, 5.1, 5.2, 6.3)

Review basketball bounce pass and catch. 1.0, 2.5

Have students practice basketball bounce pass and catch with a partner, counting the number of successful passes and catches. (Assessment opportunity: structured observation 1.0, 5.1, 5.2, 6.3)

Demonstrate and describe basketball overhead pass and catch using the Invasion Sports CD. 1.0, 2.5

Have students practice basketball overhead pass and catch with a partner, counting the number of successful passes and catches. (Assessment opportunity: structured observation 1.0, 5.1, 5.2, 6.3)

Have students practice the basketball bounce pass, chest pass, and overhead pass and catch with a partner on command from the teacher. (Assessment opportunity: structured observation 1.0, 5.1, 5.2, 6.3)

Demonstrate 2-on-2 Keep-Away. 1.0

Have students participate in 2-on-2 Keep-Away. (Assessment opportunity: structured observation 1.0, 5.1, 5.2, 6.3)

Lead students through a cool-down and flexibility exercises appropriate to the physical activity level of the lesson. (Assessment opportunity: structured observation 4.1)

Review working cooperative with others during basketball activities. 5.1

DAY 3

Explain that feedback should be given when the performer cannot see the results of his or her performance (technique). 2.1

Have students record in their notebooks that feedback should only be given when the performer cannot see the results of his or her performance. 2.1

Have students perform a warm-up along with a cardiorespiratory workout. (Assessment opportunity: structured observation 4.1)

Review ball-handling skills from fifth grade: circle leg lift, circle two knees, bounce between legs, and figure eights (see figure 15.13). 1.0, 2.5

Have students practice the four ball-handling skills. 1.0

(continued)

Unit 7 Outline *(continued)*

Have students, in small groups, rotate through the following stations and provide feedback to their partners: chest pass and catch, circle both legs, circle lifted leg, bounce pass and catch, figure eight, overhead pass and catch, two knees circle. (Assessment opportunity: structured observation 1.0, 5.1, 5.2, 6.3)

Lead students through a cool-down and flexibility exercises appropriate to the physical activity level of the lesson. (Assessment opportunity: structured observation 4.1)

Review the importance of choosing to engage in new basketball activities. 6.3

Figure 15.13   Ball-handling skills: circle head, circle two knees, bounce between legs, circle leg lift, circle one knee, circle waist.

DAY 4

Have students perform a warm-up along with muscular strength and muscular endurance exercises. (Assessment opportunity: structured observation 4.1)

Demonstrate and describe pivoting using the Invasion Sports CD. 1.0, 2.5

Have students practice pivoting while receiving feedback from their partners. (Assessment opportunity: structured observation 1.0, 5.1, 5.2, 6.3)

Demonstrate and describe the jump-stop using the Invasion Sports CD. 1.0, 2.5

Have students practice jump-stops while receiving feedback from their partners. (Assessment opportunity: structured observation 1.0, 5.1, 5.2, 6.3)

Demonstrate and describe the two-step stop using the Invasion Sports CD. 1.0, 2.5

Have students practice two-step stops while receiving feedback from their partners. (Assessment opportunity: structured observation 1.0, 5.1, 5.2, 6.3)

Have students, in pairs, practice passing the basketball to a moving player, who performs a jump-stop, pivots, and returns the ball. (Assessment opportunity: structured observation 1.0, 5.1, 5.2, 6.3)

Have students, in pairs, practice passing the basketball to a moving player, who performs a two-step stop, pivots, and returns the ball. (Assessment opportunity: structured observation 1.0, 5.1, 5.2, 6.3)

Lead students through a cool-down and flexibility exercises appropriate to the physical activity level of the lesson. (Assessment opportunity: structured observation 4.1)

Review that feedback should be given when the performer cannot see the results of his or her performance. 2.1

DAY 5

Explain the frequency, intensity, time, and type (FITT) concepts related to muscular strength using the Health-Related Fitness: Tutorial and Portfolio. 4.2

Have students create a chart in their notebooks that shows the FITT concepts related to muscular strength. 4.2

Describe the nervous system benefits derived from participation in physical activity. 6.4

Have students record in their notebooks the nervous system benefits derived from participation in physical activity. 6.4

Have students perform a warm-up along with a cardiorespiratory workout. (Assessment opportunity: structured observation 4.1)

Have students, in pairs, practice passing the basketball to a moving player, who performs a jump-stop, pivots, and returns the ball (see figure 15.14). (Assessment opportunity: structured observation 1.0, 5.1, 5.2, 6.3)

Have students, in pairs, practice passing the basketball to a moving player, who performs a two-step stop, pivots, and returns the ball (see figure 15.15). (Assessment opportunity: structured observation 1.0, 5.1, 5.2, 6.3)

Lead students through a cool-down and flexibility exercises appropriate to the physical activity level of the lesson. (Assessment opportunity: structured observation 4.1)

Have students quiz one another on the FITT concepts related to muscular strength and the nervous system benefits derived from participation in physical activity. 4.2, 6.4

(continued)

Figure 15.14   Overhead pass, catch, jump-stop.

Figure 15.15   Bounce pass, catch, two-step stop.

Unit 7 Outline (continued)

DAY 6

Explain that the distance an object travels is increased by moving the muscles in sequential order. 2.2

Have students record the explanation in their notebooks. 2.2

Have students perform a warm-up along with a cardiorespiratory workout. (Assessment opportunity: structured observation 4.1)

Demonstrate and describe the set shot (see figure 15.16) using the Invasion Sports CD, stressing the sequential movement of the muscles during the shot. 1.0, 2.5

Have students practice set shots in groups of three (one shoots, one retrieves, and one provides feedback to the shooter). (Assessment opportunity: structured observation 1.0, 5.1, 5.2, 6.3)

Lead students through a cool-down and flexibility exercises appropriate to the physical activity level of the lesson. (Assessment opportunity: structured observation 4.1)

Figure 15.16 Set shot.

DAY 7

Have students perform a warm-up along with muscular strength and muscular endurance exercises. (Assessment opportunity: structured observation 4.1)

Review the set shot. 1.0, 2.5

Have students practice set shots in groups of three (one shoots, one retrieves, and one provides feedback to the shooter). (Assessment opportunity: structured observation 1.0, 5.1, 5.2, 6.3)

Have students practice passing and set shots in groups of four (one passes, one shoots, one retrieves, and one provides feedback). (Assessment opportunity: structured observation 1.0, 5.1, 5.2, 6.3)

Lead students through a cool-down and flexibility exercises appropriate to the physical activity level of the lesson. (Assessment opportunity: structured observation 4.1)

Review that the distance an object travels is increased by moving the muscles in sequential order. 2.2

(continued)

Unit 7 Outline *(continued)*

DAY 8

Have students perform a warm-up along with a cardiorespiratory workout. (Assessment opportunity: structured observation 4.1)

Demonstrate and describe the offensive and defensive stance using the Invasion Sports CD. 1.0, 2.5

Have students demonstrate the offensive and defensive stances. (Assessment opportunity: structured observation 1.0, 5.1, 5.2, 6.3)

Demonstrate and describe 3-on-3 basketball with no dribbling. 1.0, 2.3

Have students participate in 3-on-3 basketball with no dribbling. (Assessment opportunity: structured observation 1.0, 5.1, 5.2, 6.3)

Lead students through a cool-down and flexibility exercises appropriate to the physical activity level of the lesson. (Assessment opportunity: structured observation 4.1)

DAY 9

Have students perform a warm-up along with muscular strength and muscular endurance exercises. (Assessment opportunity: structured observation 4.1)

Demonstrate and describe the basketball dribble using the Invasion Sports CD. 1.0, 2.5

Have students practice the basketball dribble while receiving feedback from their partners. (Assessment opportunity: structured observation 1.0, 5.1, 5.2, 6.3)

Demonstrate dribble tag. 1.0, 2.3

Have students play dribble tag. (Assessment opportunity: structured observation 1.0, 5.1, 5.2, 6.3)

Lead students through a cool-down and flexibility exercises appropriate to the physical activity level of the lesson. (Assessment opportunity: structured observation 4.1)

DAY 10

Describe why it is important for early adolescents to participate in games with a smaller number of players. 2.4

Have students record a summary of the description in their notebooks. 2.4

Demonstrate 3-on-3 basketball. 1.0, 2.3

Have students play 3-on-3 basketball. (Assessment opportunity: structured observation 1.0, 5.1, 5.2, 6.3)

Lead students through a cool-down and flexibility exercises appropriate to the physical activity level of the lesson. (Assessment opportunity: structured observation 4.1)

DAY 11

Describes basic offensive and defensive strategies for invasion sports. 2.3

Describe the application of the basic offensive and defensive strategies for invasion sports to basketball. 2.3

Have students perform a warm-up along with a cardiorespiratory workout. (Assessment opportunity: structured observation 4.1)

Have students play 3-on-3 basketball. (Assessment opportunity: structured observation 1.0, 5.1, 5.2, 6.3)

Lead students through a cool-down and flexibility exercises appropriate to the physical activity level of the lesson. (Assessment opportunity: structured observation 4.1)

Review the reasons why it is important for early adolescents to participate in games with a smaller number of players. 2.4

DAY 12

Have students perform a warm-up along with muscular strength and muscular endurance exercises. (Assessment opportunity: structured observation 4.1)

Review basic offensive and defensive strategies for invasion sports. 2.3

Review the application of basic offensive and defensive strategies for invasion sports to basketball. 2.3

Have students play 3-on-3 basketball. (Assessment opportunity: structured observation 1.0, 5.1, 5.2, 6.3)

Review the elements of a routine. 6.2

Tell students that tomorrow they will be creating a ball-handling routine to music that expresses feelings in small groups. (Assessment assignment opportunity: project 6.2)

Lead students through a cool-down and flexibility exercises appropriate to the physical activity level of the lesson. (Assessment opportunity: structured observation 4.1)

DAY 13

Have students perform a warm-up along with a cardiorespiratory workout. (Assessment opportunity: structured observation 4.1)

Demonstrate ball-handling skills: speed switch, change hands–control dribble, two-hand control drill, and exchange ball. 6.2

Have students practice their ball-handling routine to music. (Assessment opportunity: structured observation 1.0, 5.1, 5.2, 6.2, 6.3)

Lead students through a cool-down and flexibility exercises appropriate to the physical activity level of the lesson. (Assessment opportunity: structured observation 4.1)

DAY 14

Have students perform a warm-up along with muscular strength and muscular endurance exercises. (Assessment opportunity: structured observation 4.1)

Review (from grade 5) ball-handling skills: circle waist, circle head, circle one knee, and two-hand control drill. 6.2

Have students practice their ball-handling routines to music. (Assessment opportunity: structured observation 1.0, 5.1, 5.2, 6.2, 6.3)

Have each group demonstrate their ball-handling routine to music. (Assessment opportunity: project 6.2)

Lead students through a cool-down and flexibility exercises appropriate to the physical activity level of the lesson. (Assessment opportunity: structured observation 4.1)

Review material for tomorrow's quiz (or hand out quiz if you would like for it to be a take home quiz). 2.1, 2.2, 2.3, 2.4, 2.5, 4.2, 6.4

DAY 15

Have students take the quiz. (Assessment opportunity: quiz 2.1, 2.2, 2.3, 2.4, 2.5, 4.2, 6.4)

Collect student activity logs. (Assessment opportunity: log 3.1)

Collect reports on movement-related activities in ancient China. (Assessment opportunity: report 6.1)

Collect essays about the basketball activities available in the community. (Assessment opportunity: essay 3.2)

Net Sport: Pickleball

– Unit 8

Pickleball provides students with an opportunity to refine their skills at striking with an implement in the context of a game. Pickleball gives the students an introduction to net sports—which prepares them for the tennis unit in seventh grade and the net team sport unit in eighth grade. The assignment to research physical activity and physical education during the times of the ancient Athenians is interdisciplinary. Your students' history or social science teacher should assess the assignment from a historical perspective; their language arts teacher should assess the assignment from a writing perspective; and you should assess the assignment from the perspective of physical activity and physical education. I have assumed that students will have research time during their history or social science class and language arts class.

You can conduct this unit on blacktop or in a gymnasium. It is helpful if you have Pickleball courts; however, you can complete the unit in an open area with a string to divide the courts. You will need one paddle per student and one ball for every two students. Wiffle balls are preferred, because they help to slow down the game so more students are successful.

Unit 8 Standards

1.0—Demonstrates the mature form for the Pickleball serve, forehand, and backhand strokes.

2.1—Explains that feedback is not given when the performer can see the results of his or her performance.

2.2—Explains that the distance an object travels is affected by increasing the distance through which force is applied.

2.3—Describes offensive and defensive strategies for simple net sports.

2.4—Describes the importance of early adolescents' participating in games with concrete rules and directions.

2.5—Describes the critical elements for the Pickleball serve and forehand and backhand strokes.

3.1—Engages in moderate and vigorous physical activity for 60 minutes (at least 20 minutes of vigorous activity) 5 days each week.

3.2—Describes Pickleball activities available in the local community.

4.1—Works toward a health-enhancing level of physical fitness.

4.2—Creates a 1-day muscular strength and endurance plan.

5.1—Works cooperatively with a small group during Pickleball activities.

5.2—Follows procedures for safe participation when working with a small group in Pickleball activities.

6.1—Describes movement-related activities in which the Athenians participated.

6.2—Not applicable.

6.3—Chooses to engage in new Pickleball activities.

6.4—Describes the diabetes prevention benefits derived from participation in physical activity.

Unit 8 Assessments

1.0—Structured observation (days 1-14)

2.1—Quiz (day 15)

2.2—Quiz (day 15)

2.3—Quiz (day 15)

2.4—Quiz (day 15)

2.5—Quiz (day 15)

3.1—Log (assigned on day 1; collected on day 15)

3.2—Essay (assigned on day 1; collected on day 15)

4.1—Structured observation (days 1-15)

4.2—Project (assigned on day 4; collected on day 15)

5.1—Structured observation (days 1-14)

5.2—Structured observation (days 1-14)

6.1—Report (assigned on day 1; collected on day 15)

6.2—not applicable

6.3—Structured observation (days 3-14)

6.4—Quiz (day 15)

Resources

Health-Related Fitness: Tutorial and Portfolio (Bonnie's Fitware, Inc.)

Middle School Physical Education Portfolio (Bonnie's Fitware, Inc.)

Racket Sports CD (Bonnie's Fitware, Inc.)

Sixth grade Pickleball task cards (Bonnie's Fitware, Inc.)

Sixth grade unit 8 posters (Bonnie's Fitware, Inc.—included in the Middle School Detailed Lesson Plans)

Fitness posters (Bonnie's Fitware, Inc.—included in the Middle School Detailed Lesson Plans)

Equipment

Pickleball paddles

Wiffle balls

Games

Modified Pickleball

Unit 8 Outline

DAY 1

Display the posters.

Introduce Pickleball unit.

Discuss the importance of choosing to engage in new Pickleball activities. 6.3

Discuss safe participation procedures for participation in Pickleball. 5.2

Have students record in their notebooks safe participation procedures for Pickleball. 5.2

Discuss working cooperatively with a small group during Pickleball activities. 5.1

Assign students to heterogeneous working groups of four.

Have students perform a warm-up along with a cardiorespiratory workout. (Assessment opportunity: structured observation 4.1)

Demonstrate and describe the forehand grip using the Racket Sports CD. 1.0, 2.5

Have students demonstrate the forehand grip while their partners provide appropriate feedback. (Assessment opportunity: structured observation 1.0, 5.1, 5.2, 6.3)

Demonstrate paddle to self using the Racket Sports CD. 1.0, 2.5

Have students paddle to self while their partners provide appropriate feedback. (Assessment opportunity: structured observation 1.0, 5.1, 5.2, 6.3)

Lead students through a cool-down and flexibility exercises appropriate to the physical activity level of the lesson. (Assessment opportunity: structured observation 4.1)

Assign unit-long homework:

- Have students research and write a description of movement-related activities in which the Athenians participated. (Assessment assignment opportunity: report 6.1)
- Have students keep a log of daily activity. (Assessment assignment opportunity: log 3.1)
- Have students write a description of the Pickleball activities available in the local community. (Assessment assignment opportunity: essay 3.2)

(continued)

Unit 8 Outline *(continued)*

DAY 2

Explain that feedback is not given when the performer can see the results of his or her performance. 2.1

Have students record the information about feedback in their notebooks. 2.1

Have students perform a warm-up along with muscular strength and muscular endurance exercises. (Assessment opportunity: structured observation 4.1)

Review the forehand grip. 1.0, 2.5

Have students demonstrate the forehand grip while their partners provide appropriate feedback. (Assessment opportunity: structured observation 1.0, 5.1, 5.2, 6.3)

Review paddling to self. 1.0, 2.5

Have students paddle to self while their partners provide appropriate feedback. (Assessment opportunity: structured observation 1.0, 5.1, 5.2, 6.3)

Demonstrate and describe the forehand drive using the Racket Sports CD. 1.0, 2.5

Have students practice the forehand drive off a ball toss from their partners. (Assessment opportunity: structured observation 1.0, 5.1, 5.2, 6.3)

Lead students through a cool-down and flexibility exercises appropriate to the physical activity level of the lesson. (Assessment opportunity: structured observation 4.1)

DAY 3

Explain that the distance an object travels is affected by increasing the distance through which the force is applied. 2.2

Have students record in their notebooks that the distance an object travels is affected by increasing the distance through which the force is applied. 2.2

Have students perform a warm-up along with a cardiorespiratory workout. (Assessment opportunity: structured observation 4.1)

Review forehand grip and forehand drive. 1.0, 2.5

Have students practice forehand drive off a toss from their partner, who provides feedback. (Assessment opportunity: structured observation 1.0, 5.1, 5.2, 6.3)

Lead students through a cool-down and flexibility exercises appropriate to the physical activity level of the lesson. (Assessment opportunity: structured observation 4.1)

Review the concept that feedback is not given when the performer can see the results of his or her performance. 2.1

DAY 4

Post fitness posters.

Discuss the diabetes prevention benefits derived from participation in physical activity. 6.4

Have students record the diabetes prevention benefits derived from participation in physical activity. 6.4

Review frequency, intensity, time, and type concepts related to muscular strength and endurance using the Health-Related Fitness: Tutorial and Portfolio program. 4.2

Have students record in their notebooks the frequency, intensity, time, and type concepts related to muscular strength and endurance. 4.2

Have students create a 1-day muscular strength and endurance plan. (Assessment assignment opportunity: project 4.2)

Have students perform a warm-up along with muscular strength and muscular endurance exercises. (Assessment opportunity: structured observation 4.1)

Demonstrate the ready position using the Racket Sports CD. 1.0, 2.5

Have students, in pairs, practice the ready position while their partners provide feedback. (Assessment opportunity: structured observation 1.0, 5.1, 5.2, 6.3)

DAY 4 (continued)

Review the forehand grip and forehand drive. 1.0, 2.5

Explain practical ways to increase the distance through which force is applied in the forehand drive. 2.2

Have students, in pairs, practice striking the ball back and forth using the forehand drive, counting the number of correct contacts. (Assessment opportunity: structured observation 1.0, 5.1, 5.2, 6.3)

Lead students through a cool-down and flexibility exercises appropriate to the physical activity level of the lesson. (Assessment opportunity: structured observation 4.1)

DAY 5

Have students perform a warm-up along with a cardiorespiratory workout. (Assessment opportunity: structured observation 4.1)

Demonstrate and describe the backhand grip using the Racket Sports CD. 1.0, 2.5

Have students demonstrate the backhand grip while their partners provide appropriate feedback. (Assessment opportunity: structured observation 1.0, 5.1, 5.2, 6.3)

Demonstrate and describe the backhand drive using the Racket Sports CD. 1.0, 2.5

Explain practical ways to increase the distance through which force is applied in the backhand drive. 2.2

Have students practice the backhand drive off a ball toss from their partners. (Assessment opportunity: structured observation 1.0, 5.1, 5.2, 6.3)

Lead students through a cool-down and flexibility exercises appropriate to the physical activity level of the lesson. (Assessment opportunity: structured observation 4.1)

DAY 6

Have students perform a warm-up along with a cardiorespiratory workout. (Assessment opportunity: structured observation 4.1)

Review backhand grip and backhand drive. 1.0, 2.5

Have students practice backhand drive off a toss from their partner, who provides feedback. 1.0, 2.1, 5.2, 6.3

Lead students through a cool-down and flexibility exercises appropriate to the physical activity level of the lesson. (Assessment opportunity: structured observation 4.1)

DAY 7

Have students perform a warm-up along with muscular strength and muscular endurance exercises. (Assessment opportunity: structured observation 4.1)

Review forehand grip, forehand drive, backhand grip, and backhand drive. 1.0, 2.5

Have students, in pairs, strike the ball back and forth using both the forehand drive and backhand drive, counting the number of correct contacts. (Assessment opportunity: structured observation 1.0, 5.1, 5.2, 6.3)

Lead students through a cool-down and flexibility exercises appropriate to the physical activity level of the lesson. (Assessment opportunity: structured observation 4.1)

DAY 8

Have students perform a warm-up along with a cardiorespiratory workout. (Assessment opportunity: structured observation 4.1)

Review forehand grip, forehand drive, backhand grip, and backhand drive. 1.0, 2.5

Have students, in groups of four, rotate through the following eight stations practicing their Pickleball skills: perform forehand drives while partner provides feedback, perform backhand drives while partner provides feedback, rally back and forth (2 vs. 2), rally with a partner using only forehand drives, rally with a partner using only backhand drives, paddle to self, practice going from forehand grip to backhand grip while partner provides feedback, practice forehand drives that express a seriousness about the game. (Assessment opportunity: structured observation 1.0, 5.1, 5.2, 6.3)

Lead students through a cool-down and flexibility exercises appropriate to the physical activity level of the lesson. (Assessment opportunity: structured observation 4.1)

(continued)

Unit 8 Outline *(continued)*

DAY 9

Have students perform a warm-up along with muscular strength and muscular endurance exercises. (Assessment opportunity: structured observation 4.1)

Review forehand grip, forehand drive, backhand grip, and backhand drive. 1.0, 2.5

Have students, in groups of four, rotate through the following eight stations practicing their Pickleball skills: perform forehand drives while partner provides feedback, perform backhand drives while partner provides feedback, rally back and forth (2 vs. 2), rally with a partner using only forehand drives, rally with a partner using only backhand drives, paddle to self, practice going from forehand grip to backhand grip while partner provides feedback, practice forehand drives that express a seriousness about the game. (Assessment opportunity: structured observation 1.0, 5.1, 5.2, 6.3)

Lead students through a cool-down and flexibility exercises appropriate to the physical activity level of the lesson. (Assessment opportunity: structured observation 4.1)

DAY 10

Describe the importance of early adolescents' participating in games with concrete rules and directions, given their level of cognitive development. 2.4

Have students record in their notebooks that early adolescents need concrete rules and directions. 2.4

Have students perform a warm-up along with a cardiorespiratory workout. (Assessment opportunity: structured observation 4.1)

Review forehand grip, forehand drive, backhand grip, and backhand drive. 1.0, 2.5

Demonstrate serving using a dropped ball and forehand drive. 1.0, 2.5

Have students practice the serve while their partners provide feedback. (Assessment opportunity: structured observation 1.0, 5.1, 5.2, 6.3)

Explain the game Pickleball (see figure 15.17). 1.0, 2.3

Have students play Pickleball. (Assessment opportunity: structured observation 1.0, 5.1, 5.2, 6.3)

Lead students through a cool-down and flexibility exercises appropriate to the physical activity level of the lesson. (Assessment opportunity: structured observation 4.1)

Figure 15.17   Pickleball.

DAY 11	Have students perform a warm-up along with a cardiorespiratory workout. (Assessment opportunity: structured observation 4.1)
	Describe basic offensive and defensive strategies for net sports. 2.3
	Have students record basic offensive and defensive strategies for net sports. 2.3
	Have students play Pickleball. (Assessment opportunity: structured observation 1.0, 5.1, 5.2, 6.3)
	Lead students through a cool-down and flexibility exercises appropriate to the physical activity level of the lesson. (Assessment opportunity: structured observation 4.1)
	Review the importance of early adolescents' participating in games with concrete rules and directions. 2.4
DAY 12	Review basic offensive and defensive strategies for net sports. 2.3
	Have students perform a warm-up along with muscular strength and muscular endurance exercises. (Assessment opportunity: structured observation 4.1)
	Have students play Pickleball. (Assessment opportunity: structured observation 1.0, 5.1, 5.2, 6.3)
	Lead students through a cool-down and flexibility exercises appropriate to the physical activity level of the lesson. (Assessment opportunity: structured observation 4.1)
DAY 13	Have students perform a warm-up along with a cardiorespiratory workout. (Assessment opportunity: structured observation 4.1)
	Review basic offensive and defensive strategies for net sports. 2.3
	Have students play Pickleball. (Assessment opportunity: structured observation 1.0, 5.1, 5.2, 6.3)
	Lead students through a cool-down and flexibility exercises appropriate to the physical activity level of the lesson. (Assessment opportunity: structured observation 4.1)
DAY 14	Have students perform a warm-up along with muscular strength and muscular endurance exercises. (Assessment opportunity: structured observation 4.1)
	Review basic offensive and defensive strategies for net sports. 2.3
	Have students play Pickleball. (Assessment opportunity: structured observation 1.0, 5.1, 5.2, 6.3)
	Lead students through a cool-down and flexibility exercises appropriate to the physical activity level of the lesson. (Assessment opportunity: structured observation 4.1)
	Review material for tomorrow's quiz (or hand out quiz if you would like for it to be a take home quiz). 2.1, 2.2, 2.3, 2.4, 2.5, 6.4
DAY 15	Have students take the quiz. (Assessment opportunity: quiz 2.1, 2.2, 2.3, 2.4, 2.5, 6.4)
	Collect student activity logs. (Assessment opportunity: log 3.1)
	Collect reports on the movement-related activities in which the Athenians participated. (Assessment opportunity: report 6.1)
	Collect essays on the Pickleball activities available in the local community. (Assessment opportunity: essay 3.2)
	Collect 1-day muscular strength and endurance plans with notes on changes that need to be made to the plan. (Assessment opportunity: project 4.2)

Field Sport: Three-Team Softball ~ Unit 9

Softball provides students with an opportunity to refine their throwing, catching, and striking skills in the context of a game. Specifically, softball offers students an introduction to a field sport. This unit prepares students for the field sport unit in eighth grade. You can conduct this unit on blacktop, but grass is preferred. You will need one bat and one ball for every two students. In addition, gloves are recommended for all students. Anyone playing a catcher position must wear protective equipment and anyone batting must wear a batting helmet. Finally, a batting tee is required for every four students.

Unit 9 Standards

1.0—Demonstrates the mature forms for softball catching, fielding, overhand throw, and batting.

2.1—Explains that feedback should be delayed for a few seconds after the performance to give the performer an opportunity to reflect on the performance.

2.2—Explains that the distance an object travels is affected by the weight of the striking implement.

2.3—Describes basic offensive and defensive strategies for simple field sports.

2.4—Describes the importance of early adolescents' participating in games that avoid repetitive motions.

2.5—Describes the critical elements for softball catching, fielding, overhand throw, pitching, and batting.

3.1—Engages in moderate and vigorous physical activity for 60 minutes (at least 20 minutes of vigorous activity) 5 days each week.

3.2—Describes softball activities available in the local community.

4.1—Works toward a health-enhancing level of physical fitness.

4.2—Explains the FITT concepts related to flexibility.

5.1—Works cooperatively with a small group during three-team softball activities.

5.2—Follows procedures for safe participation when working with a small group in softball activities.

6.1—Describes movement-related activities in which the Spartans participated.

6.2—Not applicable.

6.3—Chooses to engage in new softball activities.

6.4—Describes the decrease in cholesterol level derived from participation in physical activity.

Unit 9 Assessments

1.0—Structured observation (days 1-14)

2.1—Quiz (day 15)

2.2—Quiz (day 15)

2.3—Quiz (day 15)

2.4—Quiz (day 15)

2.5—Quiz (day 15)

3.1—Log (assigned on day 1; collected on day 15)

3.2—Essay (assigned on day 1; collected on day 15)

4.1—Structured observation (days 1-14)

4.2—Quiz (day 15)

5.1—Structured observation (days 1-14)

5.2—Structured observation (days 1-14)

6.1—Report (assigned on day 1; collected on day 15)

6.2—Not applicable

6.3—Structured observation (days 1-14)

6.4—Quiz (day 15)

Resources

Field Sports CD (Bonnie's Fitware, Inc.)

Health-Related Fitness: Tutorial and Portfolio (Bonnie's Fitware, Inc.)

Middle School Physical Education Portfolio (Bonnie's Fitware, Inc.)

Sixth grade softball task cards (Bonnie's Fitware, Inc.)

Sixth grade unit nine posters (Bonnie's Fitware, Inc.—included in the Middle School Detailed Lesson Plans)

Fitness posters (Bonnie's Fitware, Inc.—included in the Middle School Detailed Lesson Plans)

Equipment

Catcher equipment (chest protector, leg protector, mask)	Bases
Batting helmets	Gloves
Bats	Batting tees
Softballs	Hula hoops

Games

Beat the Ball

Three-team softball

Unit 9 Outline

DAY 1

Display the posters.

Introduce students to the three-team softball game unit.

Discuss the importance of choosing to engage in new softball activities. 6.3

Discuss following procedures for safe participation when working with a small group in softball activities. 5.2

Assign students to heterogeneous working groups of four.

Discuss working cooperatively with a small group during three-team softball activities. 5.1

Have students perform a warm-up along with a cardiorespiratory workout. (Assessment opportunity: structured observation 4.1)

Demonstrate and describe the correct technique for the overhand throw using the Field Sports CD. 1.0, 2.5

Have students practice the overhand throw against a backboard. (Assessment opportunity: 1.0, 5.1, 5.2, 6.3)

Lead students through a cool-down and flexibility exercises appropriate to the physical activity level of the lesson. (Assessment opportunity: structured observation 4.1)

Assign unit-long homework:

- Have students research and write a description about movement-related activities in which the Spartans participated. (Assessment assignment opportunity: report 6.1)

- Have students keep a log of daily activity. (Assessment assignment opportunity: log 3.1)

- Have students write a description about softball activities available in the local community. (Assessment assignment opportunity: essay 3.2)

(continued)

Unit 9 Outline (continued)

DAY 2

Explain that feedback should be delayed for a few seconds after the performance to give the performer an opportunity to reflect on his or her own performance. 2.1

Have students perform a warm-up along with muscular strength and muscular endurance exercises. (Assessment opportunity: structured observation 4.1)

Review the correct technique for the overhand throw. 1.0, 2.5

Have students practice the overhand throw against a backboard while their partners provide feedback. (Assessment opportunity: 1.0, 5.1, 5.2, 6.3)

Demonstrate and describe the correct technique for fielding ground balls with a glove using the Field Sports CD. 1.0, 2.5

Have students, in pairs, practice throwing and fielding ground balls, counting the number of good throws and catches. (Assessment opportunity: 1.0, 5.1, 5.2, 6.3)

Lead students through a cool-down and flexibility exercises appropriate to the physical activity level of the lesson. (Assessment opportunity: structured observation 4.1)

DAY 3

Set up fitness posters.

Describe the decrease in cholesterol level derived from participation in physical activity. 6.4

Have students record the benefits of the decrease in cholesterol level in their notebooks. 6.4

Explain the frequency, intensity, time, and type (FITT) concepts related to muscular flexibility using the Health-Related Fitness: Tutorial and Portfolio. 4.2

Have students record the FITT concepts related to muscular flexibility. 4.2

Have students perform a warm-up along with a cardiorespiratory workout. (Assessment opportunity: structured observation 4.1)

Demonstrate the correct technique for fielding fly balls with a glove using the Field Sports CD. 1.0, 2.5

Have students, in pairs, practice throwing and fielding fly balls while counting the number of good throws and catches. (Assessment opportunity: 1.0, 5.1, 5.2, 6.3)

Have students, in pairs, practice throwing and fielding fly balls and grounders while counting the number of good throws and catches. (Assessment opportunity: 1.0, 5.1, 5.2, 6.3)

Lead students through a cool-down and flexibility exercises appropriate to the physical activity level of the lesson. (Assessment opportunity: structured observation 4.1)

Remind students that feedback needs to be delayed a few seconds. 2.1

DAY 4

Describe the importance of early adolescents' participating in games that avoid repetitive motions so as not to cause repetitive stress injuries. 2.4

Have student summarize and record the description in their notebooks. 2.4

Have students perform a warm-up along with muscular strength and muscular endurance exercises. (Assessment opportunity: structured observation 4.1)

Demonstrate and describe the correct technique for baserunning using the Field Sports CD. 1.0, 2.5

Have students practice baserunning. 1.0

Have students participate in the following seven stations: throw softball at a target on the wall, throw and field fly balls with a partner, throw and field grounders with a partner, throw and catch with a partner, throw against a wall while partner provides feedback, practice baserunning, and throw at a hula hoop for accuracy. (Assessment opportunity: 1.0, 5.1, 5.2, 6.3)

Lead students through a cool-down and flexibility exercises appropriate to the physical activity level of the lesson. (Assessment opportunity: structured observation 4.1)

Review the importance of early adolescents participating in games that avoid repetitive motions so as not to cause repetitive stress injuries. 2.4

DAY 5	Remind students that feedback needs to be delayed a few seconds. 2.1
	Have students perform a warm-up along with a cardiorespiratory workout. (Assessment opportunity: structured observation 4.1)
	Students participate in the following seven stations: throw softball at a target on the wall, throw and field fly balls with a partner, throw and field grounders with a partner, throw and catch with a partner, throw against a wall while partner provides feedback, practice baserunning, and throw at a hula hoop for accuracy. (Assessment opportunity: 1.0, 5.1, 5.2, 6.3)
	Lead students through a cool-down and flexibility exercises appropriate to the physical activity level of the lesson. (Assessment opportunity: structured observation 4.1)
DAY 6	Have students perform a warm-up along with a cardiorespiratory workout. (Assessment opportunity: structured observation 4.1)
	Describe the basic offensive and defensive strategies for field sports. 2.3
	Have students record in their notebooks the basic offensive and defensive strategies for field sports. 2.3
	Demonstrate three-team Beat the Ball. 1.0, 2.3
	Have students participate in three-team Beat the Ball. (Assessment opportunity: 1.0, 5.1, 5.2, 6.3)
	Lead students through a cool-down and flexibility exercises appropriate to the physical activity level of the lesson. (Assessment opportunity: structured observation 4.1)
DAY 7	Explain that the distance an object travels is affected by the weight of the striking implement. 2.2
	Have students summarize and record the explanation in their notebooks. 2.2
	Have students perform a warm-up along with muscular strength and muscular endurance exercises. (Assessment opportunity: structured observation 4.1)
	Demonstrate batting off a tee using the Field Sports CD. 1.0, 2.5
	Have students practice batting off a tee in groups of four. One bats, one provides feedback, and two retrieve; then rotate positions. (Assessment opportunity: 1.0, 5.2, 6.3)
	Lead students through a cool-down and flexibility exercises appropriate to the physical activity level of the lesson. (Assessment opportunity: structured observation 4.1)
	Have students brainstorm the optimal weight of the bat they should use. 2.2
DAY 8	Review the basic offensive and defensive strategies for field sports. 2.3
	Have students perform a warm-up along with a cardiorespiratory workout. (Assessment opportunity: structured observation 4.1)
	Have students play three-team Beat the Ball—but instead of throwing the ball, have them bat the ball off a tee. (Assessment opportunity: 1.0, 5.1, 5.2, 6.3)
	Have students select the bat that will provide them with optimal distance. 2.2
	Lead students through a cool-down and flexibility exercises appropriate to the physical activity level of the lesson. (Assessment opportunity: structured observation 4.1)
	Review that the distance an object travels is affected by the weight of the striking implement. 2.2
DAY 9	Have students perform a warm-up along with muscular strength and muscular endurance exercises. (Assessment opportunity: structured observation 4.1)
	Demonstrate and describe pitching using the Field Sports CD. 1.0, 2.5
	Have students practice pitching with a partner, counting the number of strikes. (Assessment opportunity: 1.0, 5.1, 5.2, 6.3)
	Lead students through a cool-down and flexibility exercises appropriate to the physical activity level of the lesson. (Assessment opportunity: structured observation 4.1)

(continued)

Unit 9 Outline *(continued)*

DAY 10

Have students perform a warm-up along with a cardiorespiratory workout. (Assessment opportunity: structured observation 4.1)

Demonstrate and describe batting off a pitch (see figure 15.18) using the Field Sports CD. 1.0, 2.5, 2.2

Have students practice batting off a pitch in groups of four. One pitches, one bats, one catches, and one retrieves. (Assessment opportunity: 1.0, 5.2, 6.3)

Lead students through a cool-down and flexibility exercises appropriate to the physical activity level of the lesson. (Assessment opportunity: structured observation 4.1)

Figure 15.18 Pitching and batting. Put catcher's equipment on the student who is catching the ball behind the batter.

DAY 11

Have students perform a warm-up along with a cardiorespiratory workout. (Assessment opportunity: structured observation 4.1)

Review batting off a pitch (see figure 15.18) using the Field Sports CD. 1.0, 2.5

Have students practice batting off a pitch in groups of four. One pitches, one bats, one catches, and one retrieves. (Assessment opportunity: 1.0, 5.2, 6.3)

Lead students through a cool-down and flexibility exercises appropriate to the physical activity level of the lesson. (Assessment opportunity: structured observation 4.1)

DAY 12

Have students perform a warm-up along with muscular strength and muscular endurance exercises. (Assessment opportunity: structured observation 4.1)

Review the basic offensive and defensive strategies for field sports. 2.3

Explain how to play three-team softball (four players are up to bat, four are in the infield, and four are in the outfield). 1.0, 2.3

Play three-team softball. (Assessment opportunity: 1.0, 5.1, 5.2, 6.3)

Lead students through a cool-down and flexibility exercises appropriate to the physical activity level of the lesson. (Assessment opportunity: structured observation 4.1)

DAY 13

Have students perform a warm-up along with a cardiorespiratory workout. (Assessment opportunity: structured observation 4.1)

Review the basic offensive and defensive strategies for field sports. 2.3

Review three-team softball. 1.0, 2.3

Have students play three-team softball. (Assessment opportunity: 1.0, 5.1, 5.2, 6.3)

Lead students through a cool-down and flexibility exercises appropriate to the physical activity level of the lesson. (Assessment opportunity: structured observation 4.1)

DAY 14

Have students perform a warm-up along with muscular strength and muscular endurance exercises. (Assessment opportunity: structured observation 4.1)

Review the basic offensive and defensive strategies for field sports. 2.3

Review three-team softball.

Have students play three-team softball. (Assessment opportunity: 1.0, 5.1, 5.2, 6.3)

Lead students through a cool-down and flexibility exercises appropriate to the physical activity level of the lesson. (Assessment opportunity: structured observation 4.1)

Review material for tomorrow's quiz (or hand out quiz if you would like for it to be a take home quiz). 2.1, 2.2, 2.3, 2.4, 2.5, 4.2, 6.4

DAY 15

Have students take the quiz. (Assessment opportunity: quiz 2.1, 2.2, 2.3, 2.4, 2.5, 4.2, 6.4)

Collect student activity logs. (Assessment opportunity: log 3.1)

Collect reports on the movement-related activities in which the Spartans participated. (Assessment opportunity: report 6.1)

Collect essays about the extracurricular physical activities available in the school setting related to throwing and catching. (Assessment opportunity: essay 3.2)

Ancient Games

This unit focuses on sport activities from ancient civilizations—specifically the ancient Olympics and the contests held during that era. This is an excellent topic for an interdisciplinary unit with the history or social science teachers. We also look at games from around the world. In the 21st century, the knowledge of fair play is far more important than remembering the official rules for every sport. Moreover, students need to see how they can adapt games, depending on the situation. For example, individuals may enjoy playing football but are not often in situations in which they have 11 players on a team, so they must know how to modify football or any other game.

You can teach this unit in any open area, keeping in mind the specific requirements of each game. The specific pieces of equipment will also depend on the game; make a wide variety of items available as your students start to create their final new games for the year. For track-and-field events, you will need some type of weight for long jumping, javelins (use the insulation material that keeps pipes from freezing), discs (tape two flying discs together), and shot puts (softballs). Finally, encyclopedias, either on CD-ROM, on DVD, or in print, along with the students' history books and access to either the Internet or library will provide resources for the research study in this unit.

I've saved this unit until the end of the school year for two reasons. First, it applies the various skills the students have learned and practiced throughout the year; second, it includes games from various countries around the world as the sixth graders conclude their ancient civilizations course in history class and begin to compare and contrast the cultures they have studied throughout the year. Because of this physical education unit, students can include the area of games and the ancient Olympics in their comparisons.

Unit 10 Standards

1.0—Demonstrates the mature form for sprinting, long jump, javelin throw, shot put, and discus throw.

2.1—Explains that feedback should be given frequently in the early stages of learning and then tapered off.

2.2—Explains that the distance an object travels is affected by the height and angle of the release.

2.3—Describes basic offensive and defensive strategies in the games from other cultures.

2.4—Describes the importance of early adolescents' not lifting very heavy objects.

2.5—Describes the critical elements for sprinting, long jump, javelin throw, shot put, and discus throw.

3.1—Engages in moderate and vigorous physical activity for 60 minutes (at least 20 minutes of vigorous activity) 5 days each week.

3.2—Describes track-and-field activities available in the local community.

4.1—Works toward a health-enhancing level of physical fitness

4.2—Creates a 1-day flexibility plan.

5.1—Works cooperatively with a small group during ancient games activities.

5.2—Follows procedures for safe participation when working with a small group in ancient games activities.

6.1—Describes the origin and activities of the ancient Olympics.

6.2—Not applicable.

6.3—Chooses to engage in new cultural games and ancient activities.

6.4—Describes the long-term stress reduction benefits derived from participation in physical activity.

Unit 10 Assessments

1.0—Structured observation (days 6-14)

2.1—Quiz (day 15)

2.2—Quiz (day 15)

2.3—Quiz (day 15)

2.4—Quiz (day 15)

2.5—Quiz (day 15)

3.1—Log (assigned on day 1; collected on day 15)

3.2—Essay (assigned on day 1; collected on day 15)

4.1—Structured observation (days 1-14)

4.2—Project (assigned on day 3; collected on day 15

5.1—Structured observation (days 1-14)

5.2—Structured observation (days 1-14)

6.1—Report (assigned on day 1; collected on day 15)

6.2—Not applicable

6.3—Structured observation (days 1-14)

6.4—Quiz (day 15)

Resources

Health-Related Fitness: Tutorial and Portfolio (Bonnie's Fitware, Inc.)

Middle School Physical Education Portfolio (Bonnie's Fitware, Inc.)

Multicultural Games and Activities CD (Bonnie's Fitware, Inc.)

Sixth grade ancient games task cards (Bonnie's Fitware, Inc.)

Sixth grade unit 10 posters (Bonnie's Fitware, Inc.—included in the Middle School Detailed Lesson Plans)

Fitness posters (Bonnie's Fitware, Inc.—included in the Middle School Detailed Lesson Plans)

Equipment

Foam noodles (javelins)	Beanbags	Hula hoops
Rubber discus	Paper hat	Cans and other targets
Shot put	Rope	Carpet square

Games

Catch the Dragon's Tail (China)	Bli Yadayim (Israel)	Dolichos race
Hop–Sing Game (Liberia)	Ver Ver Aras Lama (New Guinea)	Chariot races
Hunter and Gazelle (Africa)	Gutera Uriziga (Rwanda)	Long jump
Don-Don Ba Ji (Sudan)	Kukla (Turkey)	Beginning javelin
Ichi-Ni-San (Japan)	Stade race	Modified shot put
Tug-of-Rope (Egypt)	Diauos race	Beginning discus

Unit 10 Outline

DAY 1

Display the posters.

Introduce games unit.

Assign students to heterogeneous working groups of four.

Discuss the importance of choosing to engage in new cultural games and ancient activities. 6.3

Explain safe participation guidelines for cultural games and ancient track-and-field events. 5.2

Have students record the safe participation guidelines in their notebooks. 5.2

Discuss working cooperatively with a small group during ancient games activities. 5.1

Review games and their components, including basic strategies. 2.3

Have students perform a warm-up along with a cardiorespiratory workout. (Assessment opportunity: structured observation 4.1)

Teach the rules of Catch the Dragon's Tail (China). 2.3

Have students play Catch the Dragon's Tail. (Assessment assignment: structured observation 5.1, 5.2, 6.3)

Teach the rules of Hop–Sing Game (Liberia). 2.3

Have students play Hop–Sing Game. (Assessment assignment: structured observation 5.1, 5.2, 6.3)

Lead students through a cool-down and flexibility exercises appropriate to the physical activity level of the lesson. (Assessment opportunity: structured observation 4.1)

Have students analyze these two games, looking for common traits and strategies. 2.3

Assign unit-long homework:

- Have students research and write a description of the origin and activities of the ancient Olympics. (Assessment assignment opportunity: report 6.1)

- Have students keep a log of daily activity. (Assessment assignment opportunity: log 3.1)

- Have students write a description about the track-and-field activities available in the local community. (Assessment assignment opportunity: essay 3.2)

(continued)

Unit 10 Outline *(continued)*

DAY 2

Explain that feedback should be given frequently in the early stages of learning and then tapered off. 2.1

Review that feedback should be given on technique but not on the outcome of the performance. 2.1

Have students record the information in their notebooks. 2.1

Have students perform a warm-up along with muscular strength and muscular endurance exercises. (Assessment opportunity: structured observation 4.1)

Teach the rules of Hunter and Gazelle (Africa). 2.3

Have students play Hunter and Gazelle. (Assessment assignment: structured observation 5.1, 5.2, 6.3)

Teach the rules of Don-Don Ba Ji (Sudan). 2.3

Have students play Don-Don Ba Ji. (Assessment assignment: structured observation 5.1, 5.2, 6.3)

Lead students through a cool-down and flexibility exercises appropriate to the physical activity level of the lesson. (Assessment opportunity: structured observation 4.1)

Have students analyze these two games, looking for common traits and strategies. 2.3

DAY 3

Describe the long-term stress reduction benefits derived from participation in physical activity. 6.4

Have students record the long-term stress reduction benefits derived from participation in physical activity. 6.4

Review the concepts of frequency, intensity, time, and type (FITT) as they relate to flexibility. 3.1

Have students record in their notebooks the FITT concepts related to flexibility. 3.1

Have students create a 1-day flexibility plan. (Assessment assignment opportunity: project 4.2)

Have students perform a warm-up along with a cardiorespiratory workout. (Assessment opportunity: structured observation 4.1)

Teach the rules of Ichi-Ni-San (Japan). 2.3

Have students play Ichi-Ni-San. (Assessment assignment: structured observation 5.1, 5.2, 6.3)

Teach the rules of Tug-of-Rope (Egypt). 2.3

Have students play Tug-of-Rope. (Assessment assignment: structured observation 5.1, 5.2, 6.3)

Lead students through a cool-down and flexibility exercises appropriate to the physical activity level of the lesson. (Assessment opportunity: structured observation 4.1)

Have students analyze these two games, looking for common traits and strategies. 2.3

Review the information that feedback should be given frequently in the early stages of learning and then tapered off. 2.1

DAY 4

Have students perform a warm-up along with muscular strength and muscular endurance exercises. (Assessment opportunity: structured observation 4.1)

Teach the rules of Bli Yadayim (Israel). 2.3

Have students play Bli Yadayim. (Assessment assignment: structured observation 5.1, 5.2, 6.3)

Teach the rules of Ver Ver Aras Lama (New Guinea). 2.3

Have students play Ver Ver Aras Lama. (Assessment assignment: structured observation 5.1, 5.2, 6.3)

Lead students through a cool-down and flexibility exercises appropriate to the physical activity level of the lesson. (Assessment opportunity: structured observation 4.1)

Have students analyze these two games, looking for common traits and strategies. 2.3

DAY 5

Teach the rules of Gutera Uriziga (Rwanda). 2.

Have students perform a warm-up along with a cardiorespiratory workout. (Assessment opportunity: structured observation 4.1)

Have students play Gutera Uriziga. (Assessment assignment: structured observation 5.1, 5.2, 6.3)

Teach the rules of Kukla (Turkey). 2.3

Have students play Kukla. (Assessment assignment: structured observation 5.1, 5.2, 6.3)

Lead students through a cool-down and flexibility exercises appropriate to the physical activity level of the lesson. (Assessment opportunity: structured observation 4.1)

Have students analyze these two games, looking for common traits and strategies. 2.3

DAY 6

Describe the importance of early adolescents' not lifting very heavy objects. 2.4

Have students summarize the description and record it in their notebooks. 2.4

Demonstrate and describe the correct technique for sprinting. 1.0, 2.5

Have students perform a warm-up along with a cardiorespiratory workout. (Assessment opportunity: structured observation 4.1)

Have students practice the correct technique for sprinting. (Assessment assignment: structured observation 1.0, 5.1, 5.2, 6.3)

Describe the Stade race, Diauos race, and Dolichos race from ancient times. 1.0, 2.5, 6.1

Describe chariot races from ancient times. 6.1

Demonstrate a simulated chariot race event (see figure 15.19). 6.1

Set up four stations (Stade race, Diauos race, Dolichos race, and chariot race) and have students rotate from station to station participating in each event. (Assessment assignment: structured observation 1.0, 5.1, 5.2, 6.3)

Lead students through a cool-down and flexibility exercises appropriate to the physical activity level of the lesson. (Assessment opportunity: structured observation 4.1)

(continued)

Figure 15.19 Chariot races.

Unit 10 Outline *(continued)*

DAY 7

Explain that the distance an object travels is affected by the height and angle of release. 2.2

Have students perform a warm-up along with muscular strength and muscular endurance exercises. (Assessment opportunity: structured observation 4.1)

Demonstrate and describe the long jump (the way it was performed during ancient times, with very light hand weights). 1.0 2.5, 6.1

Demonstrate and describe the long jump (the way it is performed today, without the hand weights). 1.0, 2.5

Have students participate in the long jump (old and new method) while receiving feedback from a partner. (Assessment assignment: structured observation 1.0, 5.1, 5.2, 6.3)

Lead students through a cool-down and flexibility exercises appropriate to the physical activity level of the lesson. (Assessment opportunity: structured observation 4.1)

Have students discuss why very light weights were used in today's activity. 2.4

Have students compare the two types of jumping. 6.1

DAY 8

Demonstrate the beginning javelin throw. 1.0, 2.5

Have students perform a warm-up along with a cardiorespiratory workout. (Assessment opportunity: structured observation 4.1)

Have students practice the beginning javelin throw (foam noodle) with a partner. (Assessment assignment: structured observation 1.0, 5.1, 5.2, 6.3)

Lead students through a cool-down and flexibility exercises appropriate to the physical activity level of the lesson. (Assessment opportunity: structured observation 4.1)

Review that the distance an object travels is affected by the height and angle of release. 2.2

DAY 9

Have students perform a warm-up along with muscular strength and muscular endurance exercises. (Assessment opportunity: structured observation 4.1)

Demonstrate the modified shot put (see figure 15.20). 1.0, 2.5

Have students practice the modified shot put in groups of four, rotating from shot putter to providing feedback, and then to retriever. (Assessment assignment: structured observation 1.0, 5.1, 5.2, 6.3)

Lead students through a cool-down and flexibility exercises appropriate to the physical activity level of the lesson. (Assessment opportunity: structured observation 4.1)

Figure 15.20 Shot put.

DAY 10

Explain the history of the discus throw. 6.1

Demonstrate the beginning discus throw (see figure 15.21). 1.0, 2.5

Have students perform a warm-up along with a cardiorespiratory workout. (Assessment opportunity: structured observation 4.1)

Have students practice the beginning discus throw in groups of four, rotating from discus thrower to providing feedback, and then to retriever. (Assessment assignment: structured observation 1.0, 5.1, 5.2, 6.3)

Lead students through a cool-down and flexibility exercises appropriate to the physical activity level of the lesson. (Assessment opportunity: structured observation 4.1)

Figure 15.21 Beginning discus throw.

DAY 11

Have students perform a warm-up along with a cardiorespiratory workout. (Assessment opportunity: structured observation 4.1)

Set up seven stations (javelin throw, modified shot put, discus, short races, long jump, races, chariot races) and have students rotate from station to station practicing each event. (Assessment assignment: structured observation 1.0, 5.1, 5.2, 6.3)

Lead students through a cool-down and flexibility exercises appropriate to the physical activity level of the lesson. (Assessment opportunity: structured observation 4.1)

(continued)

Unit 10 Outline *(continued)*

DAY 12

Have students perform a warm-up along with muscular strength and muscular endurance exercises. (Assessment opportunity: structured observation 4.1)

Set up seven stations (javelin throw, modified shot put, discus, long jump, short races, long races, chariot races) and have students practice at the event in which they are going to participate. (Assessment assignment: structured observation 1.0, 5.1, 5.2, 6.3)

Lead students through a cool-down and flexibility exercises appropriate to the physical activity level of the lesson. (Assessment opportunity: structured observation 4.1)

DAY 13

Have students perform a warm-up along with a cardiorespiratory workout. (Assessment opportunity: structured observation 4.1)

Have students participate in the ancient Olympics event. (Assessment assignment: structured observation 1.0, 5.1, 5.2, 6.3)

Lead students through a cool-down and flexibility exercises appropriate to the physical activity level of the lesson. (Assessment opportunity: structured observation 4.1)

DAY 14

Have students perform a warm-up along with muscular strength and muscular endurance exercises. (Assessment opportunity: structured observation 4.1)

Have students participate in the ancient Olympics event. (Assessment assignment: structured observation 1.0, 5.1, 5.2, 6.3)

Lead students through a cool-down and flexibility exercises appropriate to the physical activity level of the lesson. (Assessment opportunity: structured observation 4.1)

Review material for tomorrow's quiz (or hand out quiz if you would like for it to be a take home quiz). 2.1, 2.2, 2.3, 2.4, 2.5, 6.4

DAY 15

Have students take the quiz. (Assessment opportunity: quiz 2.1, 2.2, 2.3, 2.4, 2.5, 6.4)

Collect student activity logs. (Assessment opportunity: log 3.1)

Collect reports on the ancient Olympics. (Assessment opportunity: report 6.1)

Collect essays about the track-and-field activities available in the local community. (Assessment opportunity: essay 3.2)

Collect 1-day flexibility plans. (Assessment opportunity: project 4.2)

Circus Skills  — Unit 11 ‿

Now that we have provided students with instruction in the major skills theme areas (body management, locomotor skills, underhand and sidearm throw and catch, striking with body parts, and striking with objects), let's give them an opportunity to review these fundamental skills and apply them to a circus skills unit. Because not all students will have mastered the techniques for all the fundamental skills or will be ready to apply the skills to some of the more challenging circus skills, I return to the inclusion style of teaching after the first 2 days. To this end, I use a station approach for instruction so that students may select the skill they wish to work on while their partners give feedback.

This unit can take place in any open area; however, it is best to unicycle on a blacktop area and to use stilts over a protective ground covering. This unit requires some unique equipment, but you can substitute as noted: juggling scarves (plastic bags), juggling balls (beanbags or paper balls with masking tape around them), Hacky Sacks (beanbags or paper balls with masking tape around them), unicycles and helmets, peacock feathers, diabolos, spinning balls (volleyballs), and stilts. There are other circus events (i.e., plate spinning, balance sticks) that you may want to include in your unit. I use the station approach throughout this unit, so you have to purchase only a few of each item of equipment because only a few students will be using one type of equipment at a time.

If you wish, have students use the skills they gain in this unit by performing at an open house, during National Physical Education Week events, or in shopping center demonstrations. One way to approach this unit is to let students select one circus skill event (e.g., juggling, footbag, stilts) in which to specialize and create a routine. The other option, which I present in detail, is to give students instruction in each area and then let them specialize and create a group routine. Either way, the demonstration of the skills or routines in front of a live audience is definitely an authentic assessment.

Unit 11 Standards

1.0—Demonstrates the mature form for the circus skills of foot volleying (inside, knee, outside kick, heel kick), ball spinning, juggling (one-hand juggle, basic cascade), stilt walking, and unicycle mounts and riding.

2.1—Compares situations when feedback should and should not be given.

2.2—Explains ways to use force to increase speed or distance of a body and/or propelled object.

2.3—Not applicable.

2.4—Describes the characteristics of physical activities appropriate for early adolescents.

2.5—Describes the critical elements for circus skills including foot volleying (inside, knee, outside kick, heel kick), ball spinning, juggling (one-hand juggle, basic cascade), stilt walking, and unicycle mounts and riding.

3.1—Engages in moderate and vigorous physical activity for 60 minutes 5 days each week.

3.2—Describes opportunities in the local community for regular participation in physical activity.

4.1—Works toward a health-enhancing level of physical fitness.

4.2—Designs a 1-day personal health-related fitness plan.

5.1—Works cooperatively with a small group during circus activities.

5.2—Follows procedures for safe participation when working with a small group in circus activities.

6.1—Describes the development and role of movement-related activities in the ancient world and their influences on physical activities today.

6.2—Expresses personal feelings through a circus-based routine.

6.3—Chooses to engage in new circus activities.

6.4—Describes the health benefits of regular participation in physical activity.

Unit 11 Assessments

1.0—Structured observation (days 1-14)

2.1—Venn diagram (assigned on day 4; collected on day 6)

2.2—Quiz (day 15)

2.3—Not applicable

2.4—Quiz (day 15)

2.5—Quiz (day 15)

3.1—Log (assigned on day 1; collected on day 15)

3.2—Essay (assigned on day 1; collected on day 15)

4.1—Structured observation (days 1-14)

4.2—Project (assigned on day 2; collected on day 15)

5.1—Structured observation (days 1-14)

5.2—Structured observation (days 1-14)

6.1—Report (assigned on day 1; collected on day 15)

6.2—Routine (assigned on day 12; collected on day 14)

6.3—Structured observation (days 1-14)

6.4—Quiz (day 15)

Resources

Body Management CD (Bonnie's Fitware, Inc.), which includes circus skills, stunts, tumbling, and gymnastics

Globetrotters music (Bonnie's Fitware, Inc.)

Health-Related Fitness: Tutorial and Portfolio (Bonnie's Fitware, Inc.)

Middle School Physical Education Portfolio (Bonnie's Fitware, Inc.)

Sixth grade circus task cards (Bonnie's Fitware, Inc.)

Sixth grade unit 11 posters (Bonnie's Fitware, Inc.—included in the Middle School Detailed Lesson Plans)

Fitness posters (Bonnie's Fitware, Inc.—included in the Middle School Detailed Lesson Plans)

Equipment

Stilts	Footbags	Bicycle helmets
Playground balls	Juggling balls	Pogo stick
Juggle scarves	Juggling clubs	Peacock feathers
Juggle beanbags	Unicycle	Diabolos

Games

Juggling	Stilt walking	Balancing peacock feathers
Footbag	Unicycle riding	Diabolo activities
Ball spinning	Pogo stick	

Unit 11 Outline

DAY 1

Display the posters.

Introduce circus skills unit.

Discuss safety procedures related to participating in circus skills in small groups. 5.2

Have students record in their notebooks the safety procedures related to participating in circus skills. 5.2

Discuss what it means to choose to engage in new circus activities. 6.3

Assign students to heterogeneous groups of four.

Discuss working cooperatively with a small group during circus activities. 5.1

Have students perform a warm-up along with a cardiorespiratory workout. (Assessment opportunity: structured observation 4.1)

Demonstrate a one-scarf cascade. 1.0, 2.5

Have students practice the one-scarf cascade. (Assessment opportunity: 1.0, 5.1, 5.2, 6.3)

Demonstrate the two-scarf cascade. 1.0, 2.5

Have students practice the two-scarf cascade. (Assessment opportunity: 1.0, 5.1, 5.2, 6.3)

Demonstrate the three-scarf cascade. 1.0, 2.5

Have students practice the three-scarf cascade. (Assessment opportunity: 1.0, 5.1, 5.2, 6.3)

Lead students through a cool-down and flexibility exercises appropriate to the physical activity level of the lesson. (Assessment opportunity: structured observation 4.1)

Assign unit-long homework:

- Have students research and write a description about the development and role of movement-related activities in the ancient world and their influences on physical activities today. (Assessment assignment opportunity: report 6.1)
- Have students keep a log of daily activity. (Assessment assignment opportunity: log 3.1)
- Have students write a description about the opportunities in the local community for regular participation in physical activities. (Assessment assignment opportunity: essay 3.2)

DAY 2

Describe the health benefits of regular participation in physical activity. 6.4

Have students record in their notebooks the health benefits of regular participation in physical activity. 6.4

Review frequency, intensity, time, and type (FITT) for all areas of health-related fitness using the Health-Related Fitness: Tutorial and Portfolio. 4.2

Have students design a 1-day personal health-related fitness plan. (Assessment assignment opportunity: project 4.2)

Have students perform a warm-up along with muscular strength and muscular endurance exercises. (Assessment opportunity: structured observation 4.1)

Review the three-scarf cascade. 1.0, 2.5

Have students practice the three-scarf cascade. 1.0

Show one-ball juggling on the Body Management CD. 1.0, 2.5

Have students practice one-ball juggling. (Assessment opportunity: 1.0, 5.1, 5.2, 6.3)

Show two-ball juggling on the Body Management CD. 1.0, 2.5

Have students practice two-ball juggling. (Assessment opportunity: 1.0, 5.1, 5.2, 6.3)

Show three-ball juggling on the Body Management CD. 1.0, 2.5

Review situations when feedback should and should not be given. 2.1

Have students practice three-ball juggling while receiving appropriate feedback from partners. (Assessment opportunity: 1.0, 5.1, 5.2, 6.3)

Lead students through a cool-down and flexibility exercises appropriate to the physical activity level of the lesson. (Assessment opportunity: structured observation 4.1)

Have students brainstorm with one another the health benefits derived from participation in physical activity. 6.4

DAY 3

Compare situations when feedback should and should not be given. 2.1

Have students perform a warm-up along with a cardiorespiratory workout. (Assessment opportunity: structured observation 4.1)

Show balancing peacock feathers on the nose, hand, and finger on the Body Management CD. 1.0, 2.5

Have students practice balancing peacock feathers. 1.0

Show diabolo activities on the Body Management CD. 1.0, 2.5

Have students practice diabolo activities. 1.0

Show the footbag inside kick on the Body Management CD (see figure 15.22). 1.0, 2.5

Have students rotate through the following stations: inside footbag kick; one-scarf cascade juggle, two-scarf cascade juggle, or three-scarf cascade juggle; peacock feather balancing; one-ball juggle; basic ball-juggling cascade; inside footbag kick; lower- and upper-body strength and endurance; and diabolo activities. (Assessment opportunity: 1.0, 5.1, 5.2, 6.3)

Lead students through a cool-down and flexibility exercises appropriate to the physical activity level of the lesson. (Assessment opportunity: structured observation 4.1)

Review the health benefits of regular participation in physical activity. 6.4

(continued)

Figure 15.22   Footbag *(a)* inside, *(b)* back, *(c)* outside, and *(d)* knee kicks.

Unit 11 Outline *(continued)*

DAY 4

Explain ways to increase the speed and/or distance that an object travels. 2.2

Have students write in their notebooks the ways to use force to increase speed and/or distance of a body or propelled object. 2.2

Have students perform a warm-up along with muscular strength and muscular endurance exercises. (Assessment opportunity: structured observation 4.1)

Show inside and outside spins from the Body Management CD. 1.0, 2.5

Have students practice inside and outside spins. 1.0

Have students rotate through stations while receiving feedback from their partners: inside kick; one-scarf, two-scarf, or three-scarf juggle; ball spinning (outside); one-ball juggling; basic ball-juggling cascade; ball spinning (inside); and cardiorespiratory endurance. (Assessment opportunity: 1.0, 5.1, 5.2, 6.3)

Lead students through a cool-down and flexibility exercises appropriate to the physical activity level of the lesson. (Assessment opportunity: structured observation 4.1)

Have students, for homework, design a Venn diagram that shows when feedback should and should not be given. (Assessment assignment opportunity: Venn diagram 2.1)

DAY 5

Have students perform a warm-up along with a cardiorespiratory workout. (Assessment opportunity: structured observation 4.1)

Have students determine their stilt sizes. 1.0

Demonstrate and describe falling safely from stilts. 1.0, 2.5

Have students practice falling safely from stilts. 1.0

Demonstrate and describe stilt mounting with a spotter. 1.0, 2.5

Have students practice stilt mounting with a spotter. 1.0

Demonstrate and describe stilt mounting. 1.0, 2.5

Have students practice stilt mounting. 1.0

Demonstrate and describe taking the first step with stilt walking. 1.0, 2.5

Have students practice taking their first step stilt walking (see figure 15.23). 1.0

Lead students through a cool-down and flexibility exercises appropriate to the physical activity level of the lesson. (Assessment opportunity: structured observation 4.1)

Review ways to use force to increase speed or distance of a body or propelled object. 2.2

(continued)

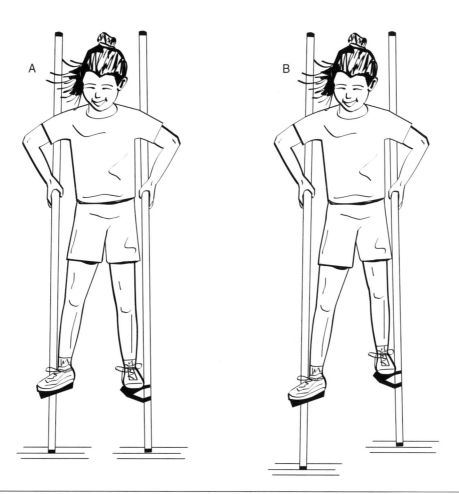

Figure 15.23 Stilt walking.

Unit 11 Outline *(continued)*

DAY 6

Have students perform a warm-up along with a cardiorespiratory workout. (Assessment opportunity: structured observation 4.1)

Demonstrate stilt walking and spotting from the Body Management CD. 1.0, 2.5

Demonstrate standard unicycle mount (see figure 15.24) from the Body Management CD. 1.0, 2.5

Demonstrate pogo stick jump from the Body Management CD. 1.0, 2.5

Demonstrate the knee kick (see figure 15.22) for footbag skills from the Body Management CD. 1.0, 2.5

Have students rotate through stations while receiving feedback from their partners: inside kick; knee kick; one-scarf, two-scarf, three-scarf, or reverse cascade; ball spinning; basic ball-juggling cascade; reverse cascade scarf juggling; stilt walking; and unicycle mounts and pogo stick. (Assessment opportunity: 1.0, 5.1, 5.2, 6.3)

Lead students through a cool-down and flexibility exercises appropriate to the physical activity level of the lesson. (Assessment opportunity: structured observation 4.1)

Collect Venn diagrams. (Assessment opportunity: Venn diagram 2.1)

A   B

Figure 15.24   Unicycle mount and riding.

DAY 7

Have students perform a warm-up along with muscular strength and muscular endurance exercises. (Assessment opportunity: structured observation 4.1)

Show unicycle riding (see figure 15.24) on the Body Management CD. 1.0, 2.5

Show outside kick (see figure 5.22) for footbag skills on the Body Management CD. 1.0, 2.5

Show column juggling with scarves on the Body Management CD. 1.0, 2.5

Have students rotate through stations while receiving feedback from their partners: outside kick; one-scarf, two-scarf, three-scarf, or reverse cascade; ball spinning; basic ball-juggling cascade or overhand throw juggle; stilt walking; unicycle riding and pogo stick; column juggling with scarves; and lower- and and upper-body strength and endurance. (Assessment opportunity: 1.0, 5.1, 5.2, 6.3)

Lead students through a cool-down and flexibility exercises appropriate to the physical activity level of the lesson. (Assessment opportunity: structured observation 4.1)

DAY 8

Have students perform a warm-up along with a cardiorespiratory workout. (Assessment opportunity: structured observation 4.1)

Show the back kick from the Body Management CD. 1.0, 2.5

Show the catch-ball-on-finger skill for ball spinning from the Body Management CD. 1.0, 2.5

Have students rotate through stations while receiving feedback from their partners: heel kick; back kick; cascade, reverse cascade, or column skill for scarf juggling; ball spinning and catch-ball-on-finger skill; basic ball-juggling cascade or overhand throw juggle; stilt walking; unicycle riding with standard mount and pogo stick; and cardiorespiratory endurance. (Assessment opportunity: 1.0, 5.1, 5.2, 6.3)

Lead students through a cool-down and flexibility exercises appropriate to the physical activity level of the lesson. (Assessment opportunity: structured observation 4.1)

DAY 9

Have students perform a warm-up along with muscular strength and muscular endurance exercises. (Assessment opportunity: structured observation 4.1)

Demonstrate stilt twirling from the Body Management CD. 1.0, 2.5

Demonstrate the unicycle side mount from the Body Management CD. 1.0, 2.5

Demonstrate clawing (use the Body Management CD if you like) for ball juggling. 1.0, 2.5

Have students rotate through stations while receiving feedback from their partners: inside, knee, back, or outside kick; cascade, reverse cascade, or column skill for scarf juggling; ball spinning with catch; basic ball-juggling cascade, overhand throw juggle, or one-handed juggling; stilt walking with reverse pivot; unicycle riding with side mount and pogo stick; shower skill for scarf juggling; and clawing for ball juggling. (Assessment opportunity: structured observation 1.0, 5.1, 5.2, 6.3)

Lead students through a cool-down and flexibility exercises appropriate to the physical activity level of the lesson. (Assessment opportunity: structured observation 4.1)

DAY 10

Describe the characteristics of physical activities appropriate and inappropriate for early adolescents. 2.4

Have students record in their notebooks the characteristics of physical activities appropriate and inappropriate for early adolescents. 2.4

Have students perform a warm-up along with a cardiorespiratory workout. (Assessment opportunity: structured observation 4.1)

Demonstrate the reverse mount for unicycle riding or show from the Body Management CD. 1.0, 2.5

Have students rotate through stations while receiving feedback from their partners: inside, knee, back, or outside kick; cascade or column skill for scarf juggling; ball spinning with catch on finger; basic ball-juggling cascade, overhand throw for juggling or one-handed juggling; stilt walking; unicycle riding with reverse mount and pogo stick; clawing for ball juggling; and cardiorespiratory endurance. (Assessment opportunity: structured observation 1.0, 5.1, 5.2, 6.3)

Lead students through a cool-down and flexibility exercises appropriate to the physical activity level of the lesson. (Assessment opportunity: structured observation 4.1)

(continued)

Unit 11 Outline (continued)

DAY 11	Have students perform a warm-up along with a cardiorespiratory workout. (Assessment opportunity: structured observation 4.1)
	Show column juggling for balls from the Body Management CD. 1.0, 2.5
	Demonstrate ball-on-ball spinning from the Body Management CD. 1.0, 2.5
	Have students rotate through stations while receiving feedback from their partners: inside, knee, back, or outside kick; cascade or column skill for scarf juggling; ball spinning with catch on finger; basic ball-juggling cascade, overhand throw for juggling or one-handed juggling; stilt walking; unicycle riding with reverse mount and pogo stick; clawing for ball juggling; and cardiorespiratory endurance. (Assessment opportunity: structured observation 1.0, 5.1, 5.2, 6.3)
	Lead students through a cool-down and flexibility exercises appropriate to the physical activity level of the lesson. (Assessment opportunity: structured observation 4.1)
	Review the characteristics of physical activities appropriate and inappropriate for early adolescents. 2.4
DAY 12	Have students perform a warm-up along with muscular strength and muscular endurance exercises. (Assessment opportunity: structured observation 4.1)
	Discuss using qualities of movement to express feelings when performing a routine. 6.2
	Have students, in groups of four, create a circus routine that uses the movement qualities to express feelings. (Assessment assignment opportunity: project 6.2)
	Lead students through a cool-down and flexibility exercises appropriate to the physical activity level of the lesson. (Assessment opportunity: structured observation 4.1)
DAY 13	Have students perform a warm-up along with a cardiorespiratory workout. (Assessment opportunity: structured observation 4.1)
	Have each group work on its routine. (Assessment opportunity: 1.0, 5.1, 5.2, 6.3) 6.2
	Lead students through a cool-down and flexibility exercises appropriate to the physical activity level of the lesson. (Assessment opportunity: structured observation 4.1)
DAY 14	Have students perform a warm-up along with muscular strength and muscular endurance exercises. (Assessment opportunity: structured observation 4.1)
	Have groups demonstrate their circus skills routines. (Assessment opportunity: project 6.2)
	Collect the circus skills routines. (Assessment opportunity: project 6.2)
	Lead students through a cool-down and flexibility exercises appropriate to the physical activity level of the lesson. (Assessment opportunity: structured observation 4.1)
	Review material for tomorrow's quiz (or hand out quiz if you would like for it to be a take home quiz). 2.2, 2.4, 2.5, 6.4
DAY 15	Have students take the quiz. (Assessment opportunity: quiz 2.2, 2.4, 2.5, 6.4)
	Collect student activity logs. (Assessment opportunity: log 3.1)
	Collect reports on purpose of games, dance, and sport in the ancient world. (Assessment opportunity: report 6.1
	Collect essays about the opportunities in the local community for regular participation in physical activities. (Assessment opportunity: essay 3.2)
	Collect 1-day personal health-related fitness plan projects. (Assessment opportunity: project 4.2)

Closure and Fitness Assessment   ~Unit 12 ~

This unit creates appropriate closure for your school year, including the chance to ensure that the students are able to demonstrate the grade-level standards. Although students have been working on projects throughout the year, this unit provides an opportunity for them to focus on depth over breadth. Moreover, while your students focus on completing their demonstrations of their learning and creating and collecting work for their portfolios, you are free to administer the fitness postassessments and to act as a resource for student projects.

For this unit, I present students with the 16 standards for the sixth grade and ask them to present evidence of their learning related to each standard. For some of the standards, students will be able to demonstrate their learning by looking through their working portfolios and pulling from work that they have already accomplished during the year. For other standards, students will be able to pull from interdisciplinary projects that they have accomplished throughout the year. For still other standards, students will need to create new projects during this closure unit to demonstrate their learning.

Once the students have collected their evidence, it goes into their performance portfolios. Then I ask students to write a reflection paper (a one-page essay) on their cumulative learning throughout sixth grade physical education. Ideally, the students then present their portfolios not only to their peers but also to their parents. In this case, during a parent, teacher, and student conference, the student is in charge of the conference as she presents the evidence that she has accumulated during the year and explains how the evidence demonstrates her learning of the various standards. This conference can focus exclusively on physical education or can be a comprehensive conference in which the student explains her learning in all subject areas.

As with the introduction unit, you can conduct this unit in just about any facility. However, if you are having your students perform exercises on the ground or grass, provide carpet squares or some other material so they won't get dirty. An indoor facility is also helpful for the project development phase of this unit. In addition, many teachers reserve the library or arrange for some of their students to do research in the library. Of course, the equipment necessary to implement the unit depends on the type of fitness assessments you plan to administer. I administer the same Fitnessgram assessments that I gave at the beginning of the school year. After the postassessments, the students will be able to enter their fitness postassessment scores into their own electronic portfolios so that you and they can compare these scores to preassessments, standards, and goals. Students will also need access to reference books, CD-ROMs, DVDs, computers, videotape or DVD players, monitors, camcorders, and other materials to assist project development.

Assessment for Each Sixth Grade Standard

1.0—Demonstrates the mature form for specialized skills and combinations during cooperative activities; lead-up or simple target activities; invasion, field, and net activities; stunts and tumbling; and dance activities.

Teacher assessment during each instructional unit based on a rubric determines whether a student has reached this standard. The following is a sample rubric for the overhand softball throw:

6: Performs a mature overhand throwing pattern in a game or activity situation.

5: Performs a mature overhand throwing pattern when throwing for accuracy and distance.

4: Performs a mature overhand throwing pattern.

_____ Arm is swung backward in preparation.

_____ Trunk rotates to throwing side.

_____ Weight transfers to opposite foot.

_____ Body rotation occurs through lower body, then upper body, and then shoulders.

_____ Elbow leads the way in the arm movement, followed by forearm extension and ending with a wrist snap.

_____ Follows through in the direction of the target.

3: Is moving toward a mature overhand throwing pattern.

2: Performs an immature overhand throwing pattern.

1: Randomly attempts an immature overhand throwing pattern.

2.1—Explains how to provide appropriate feedback to a partner who is developing or improving specialized skills.

Student writes an essay explaining how to provide appropriate feedback to a partner who is developing or improving specialized skills.

2.2—Explains ways to use force to increase speed or distance of a body or propelled object.

Student writes an essay explaining ways to use force to increase speed or distance of a body or propelled object.

2.3—Describes offensive strategies for cooperative and bowling activities and offensive and defensive strategies for simple invasion, field, and net activities.

Student writes an essay describing basic offensive strategies for cooperative and bowling activities and offensive and defensive strategies for simple invasion, field, and net activities.

2.4—Describes the characteristics of physical activities appropriate for early adolescents.

Student writes an essay describing the characteristics of physical activities appropriate for early adolescents.

2.5—Describes the critical elements of specialized skills and combinations in cooperative activities; lead-up or simple target activities; invasion, field, and net activities; stunts and tumbling; and dance activities.

Teacher assessment during each instructional unit based on responses to quiz questions for each motor or movement skill taught.

3.1—Engages in moderate and vigorous physical activity for 60 minutes 5 days each week.

Student maintains a log of participation in physical activity throughout the school year.

3.2—Describes opportunities in the local community for regular participation in physical activity.

Student writes a description of the opportunities in the local community for regular participation in physical activity.

4.1—Works toward a health-enhancing level of physical fitness.

Student submits prefitness assessment data, goals, monitoring logs, and postfitness assessment data.

4.2—Designs a 1-day personal health-related fitness plan.

Student designs a chart, essay, video, or computer program that shows his 1-day personal health-related fitness plan.

5.1—Works cooperatively with a small group in physical activity settings.

Teacher assessment during each instructional unit based on a rubric determines whether a student has reached this standard. The following is a rubric for use during this assessment:

6: Consistently exhibits cooperative skills with all during physical activity, class time, nutrition, and lunch.

5: Consistently exhibits cooperative skills with all during physical activity in the school setting.

4: Consistently works cooperatively with team members during physical activity during class time.

3: Inconsistently works cooperatively with team members during physical activity during class time.

2: Rarely works cooperatively with team members during physical activity during class time.

1: Does not cooperate with others.

5.2—Accepts responsibility for safely completing assigned role when working with a small group during physical activity.

Teacher assessment throughout the year based on a rubric determines whether a student has reached this standard.

6.1 —Describes the development and role of movement-related activities in the ancient world and their influences on physical activities today.

Student conducts research and reports on the history of one activity that originated in the ancient world and comments on its influence on physical activities today.

6.2—Expresses personal feelings through a manipulative or movement-based routine.

Student selects her best manipulative or movement-based routine developed during the school year and writes a reflection on how this routine best expresses her personal feelings for inclusion in the portfolio.

6.3—Chooses to engage in new activities.

Teacher assessment throughout the year based on a rubric determines whether a student has reached this standard.

6.4—Describes the health benefits of regular participation in physical activity.

Student writes a description of the health benefits of regular participation in physical activity.

Resources

  Health-Related Fitness: Tutorial and Portfolio (Bonnie's Fitware, Inc.)

  Middle School Physical Education Electronic Portfolio (Bonnie's Fitware, Inc.)

Equipment

  Fitness assessment equipment

Games

  None

Unit 12 Outline

DAY 1	Assign students to working groups of four.
	Remind students why you administer fitness assessments twice a year.
	Remind students how and why you administer the 1-mile run assessment. 4.1
	Have students perform warm-up exercises for the 1-mile run assessment. 4.1
	Administer the 1-mile run assessment. (Assessment opportunity: fitness assessment 4.1)
	Have students input fitness scores into their Health-Related Fitness Portfolios. 4.1
	Lead students through a cool-down and flexibility exercises appropriate to the physical activity level of the lesson. 4.1
DAY 2	Describe the projects and portfolios you expect students to complete in this unit. All
	Describe the project and portfolios design steps. All
	Remind students how and why you administer the curl-up assessment. 4.1
	Have students perform warm-up exercises for the curl-up assessment. 4.1
	Have students begin to work on their projects and Middle School Physical Education Portfolios. (Assessment opportunity: all)
	Administer the curl-up assessment to one group at a time. (Assessment opportunity: fitness assessment 4.1)
	Have students input curl-up scores into their Health-Related Fitness Portfolios. 4.1
	Lead students through a cool-down and flexibility exercises appropriate to the physical activity level of the lesson. 4.1

(continued)

Unit 12 Outline (continued)

DAY 3	Remind students how and why you administer the skinfold measurement. 4.1
	Have students work on their projects and Middle School Physical Education Portfolios. (Assessment opportunity: all)
	Administer the skinfold measurement privately to one student at a time. (Assessment opportunity: fitness assessment 4.1)
	Have students input fitness scores into their Health-Related Fitness Portfolios. 4.1
DAY 4	Remind students how and why you administer the back-saver sit-and-reach and trunk-lift assessments. 4.1
	Have students perform warm-up exercises for the back-saver sit-and-reach and trunk-lift assessments. 4.1
	Have students work on their projects and Middle School Physical Education Portfolios. (Assessment opportunity: all)
	Administer the back-saver sit-and-reach and trunk-lift assessments to one group at a time. (Assessment opportunity: fitness assessment 4.1)
	Have students input fitness scores into their Health-Related Fitness Portfolios. 4.1
	Lead students through a cool-down and flexibility exercises appropriate to the physical activity level of the lesson. 4.1
DAY 5	Remind students how and why you administer the push-up assessment. 4.1
	Have students perform warm-up exercises for the push-up assessment. 4.1
	Have students work on their projects and Middle School Physical Education Portfolios. (Assessment opportunity: all)
	Administer the push-up assessment to one group at a time. (Assessment opportunity: fitness assessment 4.1)
	Have students input fitness scores into their Health-Related Fitness Portfolios. 4.1
	Lead students through a cool-down and flexibility exercises appropriate to the physical activity level of the lesson. 4.1
DAY 6	Have students perform warm-up exercises for makeup assessments. 4.1
	Administer makeup fitness assessments to one group at a time. (Assessment opportunity: fitness assessment 4.1)
	Have students input fitness scores into their Health-Related Fitness Portfolios. 4.1
	Lead students through a cool-down and flexibility exercises appropriate to the physical activity level of the lesson. 4.1
	Have students work on their projects and Middle School Physical Education Portfolios. (Assessment opportunity: all)
DAYS 7-12	Have students work on their projects and Middle School Physical Education Portfolios. (Assessment opportunity: all)
DAY 13	Have each group share their projects and Middle School Physical Education Portfolios with another group. (Assessment opportunity: all)

DAY 14

Have other groups share their projects and Middle School Physical Education Portfolios. (Assessment opportunity: all)

DAY 15

Debrief Middle School Physical Education Portfolios. (Assessment opportunity: all)

16

A Seventh Grade Program: Taking Acceptable Risks Through Problem Solving

An innovative teaching idea is not so much reinventing the wheel but a spark of potential energy mounting in your head that your kids inspired. It is the students who stretch our thinking and constantly call on us to get them thinking and creating new ideas. In their processing and coming up with unique ways to respond, they continually take us to new levels, helping us to go beyond what we know and expect. These moments make teaching personal, real, and exciting.

—*physical educator Anne Fontaine, Florida*

Seventh Grade Standards

By the end of seventh grade, each student

1.0—Demonstrates the mature form for specialized skills and combinations during individual and dual activities.

2.1—Explains the process of setting appropriate goals, conducting appropriate practice, and monitoring changes in the development of specialized skills.

2.2—Explains how force can be used to make an object spin.

2.3—Explains offensive and defensive strategies for individual net and target sports.

2.4—Explains individual differences and how these differences affect performance in physical activities.

2.5—Explains the critical elements of specialized skills and combinations in individual and dual sports.

3.1—Engages in moderate and vigorous physical activity for 60 minutes 6 days each week.

3.2—Describes opportunities in the larger community for participation in individual and dual physical activities.

4.1—Works toward a health-enhancing level of physical fitness.

4.2—Designs a 1-week personal health-related fitness plan.

5.1—Applies problem-solving techniques when working with another person in physical activity settings.

5.2—Accepts responsibility for individual improvement during challenging physical activity.

6.1—Describes the development and role of movement-related activities in medieval times and their influences on physical activities today.

6.2—Appreciates one's own stylistic approach to creating a routine.

6.3—Chooses to engage in activities at the appropriate level of personal challenge.

6.4—Describes the social benefits of regular participation in physical activity.

In this chapter, I describe a sample seventh grade program with the theme Accepting Appropriate Challenges Through Problem Solving. Seventh graders are passing through a critical stage in their development in which they find personal identity and establish self-worth and confidence. Students in this age group like to experiment with new challenges, and unless the school provides opportunities for appropriate personal challenges, these students are likely to experiment with inappropriate activities, such as trying illegal drugs, joining gangs, drinking and driving, and engaging in unsafe sexual activity. In physical education, we can encourage students to engage in appropriate challenges by providing students with exciting new activities that require creative thinking and problem solving in a controlled, safe environment.

I have based my program on my sample standards. Review your grade-level standards for seventh grade before planning your own program. As I discussed in chapter 7, I have used the activity approach for selecting the seventh grade units

of instruction. The following are the units for seventh grade:

1. Introduction (3 weeks)
2. Tumbling and Gymnastics (5 weeks)
3. Orienteering (4 weeks)
4. Net Sport: Tennis (4 weeks)
5. Aquatics (4 weeks)
6. Target Sport: Golf (4 weeks)
7. Self-Defense (5 weeks)
8. Medieval Times Activities (4 weeks)
9. Closure and Fitness Assessment (3 weeks)

Each of these units challenges my students. In activities such as tumbling and gymnastics, outdoor education, aquatics, and self-defense, students face the challenge of what I call "physical fear" as they strive to overcome ingrained fear for their own safety by accepting the challenges presented. In addition, because golf and racket sports are new to my students, they experience the physical challenges of mastering new sports. The medieval times unit extends the history and social science content my seventh graders are studying. In addition, many of the activities participated in during medieval times, such as sword fighting, hand-to-hand combat, Melee, and jousting, both challenge students and help them understand history.

Throughout each unit, opportunities are noted for assessment and assessment assignments. An assessment assignment refers to the giving of an assignment, whereas assignment refers to either the collection of an assessment or the actual lesson in which an assessment occurs. Assessment can be done using paper and pencil or the Middle School Physical Education Portfolio (Bonnie's Fitware, Inc.), which is listed as a resource for each unit.

Introduction — Unit 1

This unit is an introductory unit for seventh grade students. It gives students time to get reacquainted and to meet new members of the class. I also use this introductory unit to set my expectations, teach the class rules, assess the students' fitness levels, and guide students as they prepare to set their yearlong goals for fitness development.

You can conduct this unit in just about any facility. It does help, however, if you are performing exercises on the ground or grass to provide students with carpet squares or some other material so they don't get dirty. The equipment necessary to implement the unit depends on the type of introductory games you choose and the fitness assessments you administer. I administer the Fitnessgram health-related fitness assessment battery, including the back-saver sit-and-reach, curl-ups, skinfold measurements, push-ups, trunk lift, and 1-mile run. You can order the Fitnessgram test administration procedures from Human Kinetics. You will see in the daily agendas that my students prepare for the fitness assessments through various aerobic activities. In addition, the students enter their fitness scores into their own electronic portfolios using Health-Related Fitness: Tutorial and Portfolio (Bonnie's Fitware, Inc.).

Unit 1 Standards

1.0—Demonstrates the mature form for the underhand toss, catch, foot pass, and trap.

2.1—Defines goal setting.

2.2—Compares internal and external force.

2.3—Explains the elements of a dual sport.

2.4—Explains body types and their impact on physical performance.

2.5—Explains the critical elements of underhand toss, catch, foot pass, and trap.

3.1—Engages in moderate and vigorous physical activity for 60 minutes 5 days each week.

3.2—Defines individual and dual activities.

4.1—Participates in fitness preassessment.

4.2—Define the terms warm-up, cool-down, progression, overload, and specificity.

5.1—Applies problem-solving techniques when working with another person in cooperative activities.

5.2—Accepts responsibility for individual improvement in fitness.

6.1—Describes fitness activities during medieval times.

6.2—Appreciates one's own stylistic approach to movement.

6.3—Chooses to engage in fitness and cooperative activities.

6.4—Defines physical activity and sociology.

Unit 1 Assessments

1.0—Structured observation (days 1-5)

2.1—Quiz (days 14-15)

2.2—Quiz (days 14-15)

2.3—Quiz (days 14-15)

2.4—Quiz (days 14-15)

2.5—Quiz (days 14-15)

3.1—Log (assigned on day 6; collected on day 15)

3.2—Quiz (days 14-15)

4.1—Fitness assessment (days 9-15); food intake and caloric output analysis log (assigned on day 10; collected on day 15)

4.2—Quiz (days 14-15)

5.1—Structured observation (day 7)

5.2—Journal entry (days 10-15)

6.1—Report (assigned on day 7; collected on day 15)

6.2—Journal entry (days 8-9)

6.3—Structured observation (days 1-15)

6.4—Quiz (days 14-15)

Resources

Fitnessgram testing materials (Human Kinetics)

Health-Related Fitness: Tutorial and Portfolio (Bonnie's Fitware, Inc.)

Middle School Physical Education Portfolio (Bonnie's Fitware, Inc.)

Seventh grade introduction task cards (Bonnie's Fitware, Inc.)

Fitness task cards (Bonnie's Fitware, Inc.)

Short jump task cards (Bonnie's Fitware, Inc.)

Macarena music

Seventh grade unit 1 posters (Bonnie's Fitware, Inc.—included in the Middle School Detailed Lesson Plans)

Fitness posters (Bonnie's Fitware, Inc.—included in the Middle School Detailed Lesson Plans)

Qualities of Movement chart (Bonnie's Fitware, Inc.—included in the Middle School Detailed Lesson Plans)

Equipment

Fleece balls	Sound system
Hula hoops	Macarena music
Playground balls or balloons	Fitness assessment equipment
Flags	Short jump ropes
Rope	

Games

Toss-a-Name Game	Circle the Circle
Toss-and-Catch-a-Name Game	Dribble tag
Booop	Soccer dribble tag

Unit 1 Outline

DAY 1	Display the posters.
	Establish a roll call order.
	Introduce the class rules.
	Have students record the rules in their notebooks.
	Discuss routines and procedures specific for your class.
	Explain to students that the theme for this year is Accepting Appropriate Challenges Through Problem Solving.
	Explain to students that many of the instructional units this year will focus on individual and dual sports. Define individual and dual sports and describe the elements of a dual sport. 2.3, 3.2
	Review (from grades 5 and 6) underhand throwing. 1.0, 2.5
	Review (from grades 5 and 6) catching. 1.0, 2.5
	Have students write the critical elements of the underhand throw and catching. 2.5
	Have students throw and catch with a partner, counting the number of times they can throw and catch without dropping the ball. (Assessment opportunity: structured observation 1.0, 6.3)
	Review (from grades 5 to 6) Toss-a-Name Game using the task card. 1.0
	Have students participate in Toss-a-Name Game. Rotate students so they get to know many of the other students. (Assessment opportunity: structured observation 1.0, 6.3)
DAY 2	Review class rules.
	Have students participate in Toss-a-Name game. Rotate students so they get to know many of the other students. (Assessment opportunity: structured observation 1.0, 6.3)
	Review (from grades 5 and 6) Toss-and-Catch-a-Name Game using the task card. 1.0
	Have students participate in Toss-and-Catch-a-Name Game. Rotate students so that they get to know many of the other students. (Assessment opportunity: structured observation 1.0, 6.3)
	Review (from grades 5 and 6) how to open lockers.
	Assign lockers to students.
	Instruct students to check that their locker combination is working.
DAY 3	Have students dress for physical education.
	Explain the following terms: warm-up, cool-down, progression, overload, and specificity. 4.2
	Instruct students to write the terms and their definitions in their notebooks. 4.2
	Review class rules.
	Have students perform a warm-up along with a cardiorespiratory workout. 4.1, 4.2
	Have students participate in Toss-and-Catch-a-Name Game. Rotate students so that they get to know many of the other students. (Assessment opportunity: structured observation 1.0, 6.3)
	Review punting (from grade 5). 1.0, 2.5
	Have students practice punting with a partner. (Assessment opportunity: structured observation 1.0)
	Lead students through a cool-down and flexibility exercises appropriate to the physical activity level of the lesson. 4.1, 4.2

(continued)

Unit 1 Outline *(continued)*

DAY 4

Review class rules.

Review the following terms: warm-up, cool-down, progression, overload, and specificity. 4.2

Have students perform a warm-up along with muscular strength and muscular endurance exercises. 4.1, 4.2

Review punting. 1.0, 2.5

Have students practice punting with a partner. (Assessment opportunity: structured observation 1.0)

Review (from grades 5 and 6) foot passing. 1.0, 2.5

Review (from grades 5 and 6) foot trapping. 1.0, 2.5

Have students pass and trap with a partner. (Assessment opportunity: structured observation 1.0, 6.3)

Have students participate in Toss-and-Catch-a-Name Game using foot passing and trapping. Rotate students so that they get to know many of the other students. (Assessment opportunity: structured observation 1.0, 6.3)

Review (from grades 5-6) hand dribbling. 1.0, 2.5

Review dribble tag. 1.0

Have students play dribble tag. (Assessment opportunity: structured observation 1.0, 6.3)

Review (from grades 5-6) foot dribbling. 1.0, 2.5

Have students play dribble tag with feet. (Assessment opportunity: structured observation 1.0, 6.3)

Lead students through a cool-down and flexibility exercises appropriate to the physical activity level of the lesson. 4.1, 4.2

Have students write in their notebooks the critical elements for foot passing and foot trapping. 1.0, 2.5

DAY 5

Review the following terms: warm-up, cool-down, progression, overload, and specificity. 4.2

Review class rules.

Have students perform a warm-up along with a cardiorespiratory workout. 4.1, 4.2

Have students participate in Toss-and-Catch-a-Name Game using foot passing and trapping. Rotate students so that they get to know many of the other students. (Assessment opportunity: structured observation 1.0, 6.3)

Review (from grades 5-6) hand dribbling. 1.0, 2.5

Have students practice dribble tag. (Assessment opportunity: structured observation 1.0, 6.3)

Review (from grades 5-6) foot dribbling. 1.0, 2.5

Have students practice dribble tag with feet. (Assessment opportunity: structured observation 1.0, 6.3)

Have students practice punting with a partner. (Assessment opportunity: structured observation 1.0, 6.3)

Lead students through a cool-down and flexibility exercises appropriate to the physical activity level of the lesson. 4.1, 4.2

DAY 6

Describe the differences between internal and external force. 2.2

Have students record the differences between internal and external force in their notebooks. 2.2

Have students perform a warm-up along with a cardiorespiratory workout. 4.1, 4.2

Describe the problem-solving technique. 5.1

Teach students how to play Booop using the task card. 6.3

Have students, in pairs, discuss Booop using the problem-solving technique. (Assessment opportunity: structured observation 6.3, 5.1)

Have students participate in Booop, calling out the name of the person who is contacting the beach ball. (Assessment opportunity: structured observation 6.3)

Teach students to play Circle the Circle (see figure 16.1) using the task card. 6.3

Have students, in pairs, discuss Circle the Circle using the problem-solving technique. (Assessment opportunity: structured observation 5.1)

Have students participate in Circle the Circle. (Assessment opportunity: structured observation 6.3)

Have students practice dribble tag. (Assessment opportunity: structured observation 1.0, 6.3)

Have students practice dribble tag with feet. (Assessment opportunity: structured observation 1.0, 6.3)

Have students practice punting with a partner. (Assessment opportunity: structured observation 1.0, 6.3)

Lead students through a cool-down and flexibility exercises appropriate to the physical activity level of the lesson. 4.1, 4.2

Define physical activity and sociology. 6.4

Have students record in their notebooks the definition of physical activity and sociology. 6.4

Assign students to keep a log of daily activity (Assessment assignment opportunity: log 3.1)

(continued)

Figure 16.1   Circle the Circle.

Unit 1 Outline *(continued)*

DAY 7	Review the differences between internal and external force. 2.2
	Review (from grades 5-6) the qualities of movement. 6.2
	Have students record the qualities of movement in their notebooks. 6.2
	Have students perform a warm-up along with muscular strength and muscular endurance exercises. 4.1, 4.2
	Teach students the Macarena. 4.1, 6.2, 6.3
	Have students perform the Macarena. 4.1, 6.2, 6.3
	Lead students through a cool-down and flexibility exercises appropriate to the physical activity level of the lesson. 4.1, 4.2
	Assign students a report to compare the fitness training that occurred during medieval times and fitness training today. (Assessment assignment opportunity: report 6.1)
DAY 8	Review class rules.
	Have students perform a warm-up. 4.1, 4.2
	Discuss the aerobic impact of the dances. 4.1
	Review the Macarena. 4.1, 6.2, 6.3
	Have students perform the Macarena. 4.1, 6.2, 6.3
	Lead students through a cool-down and flexibility exercises appropriate to the physical activity level of the lesson. 4.1, 4.2
	Discuss how different students used different qualities of movement to show their stylistic differences. 6.2
	Have students respond to the following journal prompt: How did you feel about your dance performance today? What was unique about your performance? (Assessment opportunity: journal entry 6.2)
DAY 9	Have students perform warm-up exercises for the back-saver sit-and-reach assessment. 4.1, 4.2
	Assign students to working groups of four for the introduction unit.
	Describe the different body types and the impact of these types on performance. 2.4
	Explain the back-saver sit-and-reach assessment, why you give it, and the influence of body type on performance. 4.1, 2.4
	Administer the back-saver sit-and-reach test to one group at a time while the other groups practice the Macarena. (Assessment opportunity: fitness assessment 4.1, structured observation 6.3)
	Have students input fitness scores into their Health-Related Fitness Portfolio. 4.1
	Lead students through a cool-down and flexibility exercises appropriate to the physical activity level of the lesson. 4.1, 4.2
	Have students respond to the following journal prompt: How did you feel about your dance performance today? What was unique about your performance? (Assessment opportunity: journal entry 6.2)

DAY 10

Have students perform warm-up exercises for the curl-up assessment. 4.1, 4.2

Explain the curl-up assessment, why you give it, and the influence of body type on performance. 4.1, 2.4

Administer the curl-up assessment to two groups at a time while the other groups practice the Macarena. (Assessment opportunity: fitness assessment 4.1, structured observation 6.3)

Have students input fitness scores into their Health-Related Fitness Portfolios. 4.1

Lead students through a cool-down and flexibility exercises appropriate to the physical activity level of the lesson. 4.1, 4.2

Have students respond to the following prompt in their journals: Has your curl-up score or back-saver sit-and-reach score improved since last year? Why has that occurred? (Assessment opportunity: journal entry 5.2)

Assign students the task of collecting data on their food intake and caloric output for 3 days. (Assessment assignment opportunity: log 4.1)

DAY 11

Explain the skinfold measurement, why you give it, and the influence of body types on performance. 4.1, 2.4

Have students perform warm-up exercises. 4.1

Have students participate in a jump rope circuit using short jump rope task cards. 4.1, 6.3

Administer the skinfold measurement to students one at a time in private. (Assessment opportunity: fitness assessment 4.1)

Have students input fitness scores in their Health-Related Fitness Portfolios. 4.1

Lead students through a cool-down and flexibility exercises appropriate to the physical activity level of the lesson. 4.1

Have students respond to the following prompt in their journals: Has your body composition improved since last year? Why has that occurred? (Assessment opportunity: journal entry 5.2)

DAY 12

Have students perform warm-up exercises for the push-up assessment. 4.1

Explain the push-up assessment, why you give it, and the effects of body types on performance. 4.1, 2.4

Have students participate in a flexibility circuit using fitness task cards. 4.1, 6.3

Administer the push-up assessment at one station in the circuit. (Assessment opportunity: fitness assessment 4.1)

Have students input fitness scores in their Health-Related Fitness Portfolios. 4.1

Lead students through a cool-down and flexibility exercises appropriate to the physical activity level of the lesson. 4.1

Have students respond to the following prompt in their journals: Has your push up score improved since last year? Why has that occurred? (Assessment opportunity: journal entry 5.2)

(continued)

Unit 1 Outline *(continued)*

DAY 13

Have students perform warm-up exercises for the trunk-lift assessment. 4.1, 4.2

Explain the trunk-lift assessment and the reasons for administering the assessment. 4.1

Define goal setting and explain that students will set goals once they have completed all of the pre-assessment. 2.1

Have student write the definition of goal setting in their notebooks. 2.1

Administer the trunk-lift assessment to two groups at a time while the other groups study for their quiz. (Assessment opportunity: fitness assessment 4.1, structured observation 6.3)

Have students input fitness scores in their Health-Related Fitness Portfolio. 4.1

Lead students through a cool-down and flexibility exercises appropriate to the physical activity level of the lesson. 4.1, 4.2

Have students respond to the following prompt in their journals: Has your trunk lift score improved since last year? Why has that occurred? (Assessment opportunity: journal entry 5.2)

DAY 14

Have students perform warm-up exercises for the 1-mile run. 4.1, 4.2

Explain the 1-mile run assessment, why you give it, and the influences of body types on performance (students with longer legs have an advantage attributable to a longer stride length). 4.1, 2.4

Administer the 1-mile run assessment to half the class. (Assessment opportunity: fitness assessment 4.1, structured observation 6.3)

Administer the written quiz to the other half of the class. (Assessment opportunity: quiz 2.1, 2.2, 2.3, 2.4, 2.5, 3.2, 4.2, 6.4)

Administer makeup assessments as needed. (Assessment opportunity: fitness assessment 4.1)

Have students input fitness scores in their Health-Related Fitness Portfolios. 4.1, 4.2

Lead students through a cool-down and flexibility exercises appropriate to the physical activity level of the lesson. 4.1, 4.2

Have students respond to the following prompt in their journals: Has your mile run time improved since last year? Why has that occurred? (Assessment opportunity: journal entry 5.2)

DAY 15

Have students perform warm-up exercises for the 1-mile run. 4.1, 4.2

Administer the 1-mile run assessment to half the class. (Assessment opportunity: fitness assessment 4.1, structured observation 6.3)

Administer the written quiz to the other half of the class. (Assessment opportunity: quiz 2.1, 2.2, 2.3, 2.4, 2.5, 3.2, 4.2, 6.4)

Administer makeup assessments as needed. (Assessment opportunity: fitness assessment 4.1)

Have students input fitness scores in their Health-Related Fitness Portfolios. 4.1

Lead students through a cool-down and flexibility exercises appropriate to the physical activity level of the lesson. 4.1, 4.2

Have students respond to the following prompt in their journals: Has your mile run time improved since last year? Why has that occurred? (Assessment opportunity: journal entry 5.2)

Collect students' reports on fitness training. (Assessment opportunity: report 6.1)

Collect students' physical activity logs. (Assessment opportunity: log 3.1)

Collect students' food intake and caloric output logs. (Assessment opportunity: log 4.1)

Tumbling and Gymnastics   — Unit 2

In this unit, we begin to focus on accepting challenges by having the students challenge themselves to participate in body management activities relating to tumbling and gymnastics. Because many tumbling and gymnastics moves involve rotation, this unit is ideal for teaching students how the scientific principles associated with rotation relate to movement. From days 5 through 22, I have students move through 10 stations. Initially, I repeat some of the stations; however, as the unit progresses, I make the activities more specific and distinctive. As students demonstrate competency in the first skill in each category, I have them document their performances on their progress cards and then practice the next skill in the category. This inclusion style of teaching works well throughout the entire unit.

You can also include stations for cardiorespiratory endurance, muscular strength, and muscular endurance in the rotation so that the class can move into the station approach immediately after warm-up and flexibility exercises. Depending on the number of students in each class, you can double each of the stations. If you have a camcorder available, use it to take video clips of the students as they perform various activities, giving them immediate feedback.

If at all possible, teach this unit in a gymnasium or other indoor facility. Tumbling mats or other floor padding is a must. Additional gymnastics equipment, such as a beam, low beam, pommel horse, side horse, long horse, horizontal bar, and parallel bars, adds to the effectiveness of this unit. In lieu of balance beams, draw a line on the floor for your students to use. In addition, if you only have one horse, either focus on one use of the horse or use the horse as a pommel horse one day, a side horse the next day, and a long horse on the third day. For instructional materials, use the Body Management CD, which includes information on tumbling and gymnastics, to demonstrate each skill.

Tumbling and gymnastics provide an excellent opportunity to integrate physical science with physical education. Students can learn a variety of physics principles during their science classes, including those principles associated with rotation, and then apply the concepts while participating in the tumbling and gymnastics stunts. As a final project for science, have your students take one gymnastics stunt and apply the various physics concepts to performing the stunt correctly.

Unit 2 Standards

1.0—Demonstrates the mature form for long horse vaulting (straddle dismount from croup, straddle vault); vaulting (squat vault); pommels (jump front support, hand walk, leg cut); floor exercises (back extension [see figure 16.2], front walkover); balance beam (straddle support mount, walk with dip, squat turn, jump dismount); horizontal bar (wide arm chinning, knee hang, front pullover, penny drop, forward hip circle); and parallel bars (forward hand walk, half-turn, back hand walk, forward hand jump, swing with straight-arm support, series of straddle seats, front dismount from straight-arm support).

2.1—Describes what needs to be considered when setting effective goals.

2.2—Explains how force can be used to make the body rotate in tumbling and gymnastics.

2.3—Explains the elements of an individual sport.

2.4—Defines individual differences in terms of physical performance.

2.5—Explains the critical elements of long horse vaulting (straddle dismount from croup, straddle vault); vaulting (squat vault); pommels (jump front support, hand walk, leg cut); floor exercises (front walkover, back extension); balance beam (straddle support mount, walk with dip, squat turn, jump dismount); horizontal bar (knee hang, front pullover, penny drop, forward hip circle); and parallel bars (forward hand walk, half-turn, back hand walk, forward hand jump, swing with straight-arm support, series of straddle seats, front dismount from straight-arm support).

3.1—Engages in moderate and vigorous physical activity for 60 minutes 5 days each week.

3.2—Describes opportunities in the larger community for participation in tumbling and gymnastics activities.

4.1—Works toward a health-enhancing level of physical fitness.

4.2—Creates a 1-week flexibility plan.

5.1—Applies problem-solving techniques when working with another person in tumbling activities.

5.2—Accepts responsibility for individual improvement during tumbling and gymnastics activities.

6.1—Describes recreational activities during medieval times.

6.2—Appreciates one's own stylistic approach to creating a tumbling or gymnastics routine.

6.3—Chooses to engage in tumbling and gymnastics activities at the appropriate level of personal challenge.

6.4—Explains that in many societies physical activity is a shared intergenerational experience.

Figure 16.2   Back extension.

Unit 2 Assessments

1.0—Structured observation (days 1-24)

2.1—Quiz (day 25)

2.2—Quiz (day 25)

2.3—Quiz (day 25)

2.4—Quiz (day 25)

2.5—Report (assigned on day 1; collected on day 25)

3.1—Log (assigned on day 1; collected on day 25)

3.2—Essay (assigned on day 1; collected on day 25)

4.1—Goal setting (day 2); structured observation (days 2-22)

4.2—Project (assigned on day 2; collected on day 25)

5.1—Structured observation (days 1-24)

5.2—Structured observation (days 4-24)

6.1—Report (assigned on day 1; collected on day 25)

6.2—Project (assigned on day 21; collected on day 24)

6.3—Structured observation (days 1-24)

6.4—Quiz (day 25)

Resources

Biomechanics Made Easy (Bonnie's Fitware, Inc.)

Body Management CD (Bonnie's Fitware, Inc.)

Health-Related Fitness: Tutorial and Portfolio (Bonnie's Fitware, Inc.)

Middle School Physical Education Portfolio (Bonnie's Fitware, Inc.)

Seventh grade tumbling and gymnastics task cards (Bonnie's Fitware, Inc.)

Seventh grade unit 2 posters (Bonnie's Fitware, Inc.—included in the Middle School Detailed Lesson Plans)

Fitness posters (Bonnie's Fitware, Inc.—included in the Middle School Detailed Lesson Plans)

Qualities of Movement chart (Bonnie's Fitware, Inc.—included in the Middle School Detailed Lesson Plans)

Equipment

Mats	Side horse	Horizontal bar
Balance beam	Long horse	Parallel bar
Pommel horse		

Skills

Floor Exercise, Transitions

- V-sit*
- L-support

Floor Exercise, Forward Sequence

- Log roll
- Front shoulder roll
- Forward squat roll*
- Forward squat roll walk-out*
- Pike forward roll*
- Forward roll combinations

Floor Exercise, Backward Sequence

- Log roll
- Back shoulder roll
- Backward roll
- Back roll to standing*
- Backward roll combinations
- Back extension*

Floor Exercise, Headstand Sequence

- Trust Fall
- Tripod
- Headstand*

Floor Exercise, Handstand Sequence

- Switcheroo
- Teeter-Totter
- Handstand*
- Front walkover*

Floor Exercise, Lateral Sequence

- Cartwheel*
- Round-Off

Balance Beam

- Walk*
- Walk with dip*

- Arabesque
- Straddle support mount*
- Squat turn*
- Jump dismount*
- Backward roll

Horizontal Bar

- Wide-arm chinning
- Knee hang*
- Front pullover*
- Swing turn*
- Penny Drop*
- Forward hip circle*
- Forward hip circle dismount

Parallel Bars

- Forward hand walk*
- Half-turn*
- Back hand walk*
- Forward hand jump*
- Swing with straight-arm support*
- Series of straddle seats*
- Shoulder stand
- Shoulder roll
- Front dismount from straight-arm support*

Pommels

- Jump front support*
- Hand walk*
- Flank mount to rear support*
- Rear mount to rear support
- Single-leg cut*
- Single-leg circle

Vaulting

- Knee spring dismount*
- Squat vault*
- Flank vault
- Straddle vault

Long Horse Vaulting

- Straddle dismount from croup*
- Straddle vault*
- Squat dismount from croup

*Skills for which form is assessed

Unit 2 Outline

DAY 1

Set up posters.

Introduce the tumbling and gymnastics unit and discuss safety.

Explain the elements of an individual sport. 2.3

Have students record in their notebooks the elements of an individual sport. 2.3

Discuss what is needed when setting effective goals. 2.1

Have students record in their notebooks what is needed when setting effective goals. 2.1

Have students set goals for the tumbling and gymnastics unit. 2.1

Discuss problem-solving techniques when working with a partner. 5.1

Have students record the information in their notebooks. 5.1

Introduce tumbling and gymnastics and discuss safety.

Assign students to new working groups of four.

Have students perform a warm-up along with a cardiorespiratory workout. (Assessment opportunity: structured observation 4.1)

Describe the importance of engaging in tumbling and gymnastics activities at the appropriate level of personal challenge. 6.3

Demonstrate Trust Fall. 1.0, 2.5

Have students perform Trust Fall. (Assessment opportunity: structured observation 1.0, 5.1, 6.3)

Demonstrate the log roll. 1.0, 2.5

Have students perform the log roll. (Assessment opportunity: structured observation 1.0, 5.1, 6.3)

Lead students through a cool-down and flexibility exercises appropriate to the physical activity level of the lesson. (Assessment opportunity: structured observation 4.1)

Assign unit-long homework:

- Have students research and write a description about recreational activities during medieval times. (Assessment assignment opportunity: report 6.1)

- Have students keep a log of daily activity. (Assessment assignment opportunity: log 3.1)

- Have students write a description of the opportunities in the larger community for participation in tumbling and gymnastics activities. (Assessment assignment opportunity: essay 3.2)

- Have students record the critical features for each skill introduced and present it to the teacher as a report. (Assessment assignment opportunity: report 2.5)

DAY 2

Set up fitness posters.

Have students review the results of their fitness assessment and food intake and caloric output analysis. 4.1

Have students set goals for each area of fitness. 4.1

Review the frequency, intensity, time, and type (FITT) concepts for flexibility using the Health-Related Fitness: Tutorial and Portfolio. 4.2

Have students summarize in their notebooks the FITT concepts for flexibility. 4.2

Assign students the creation and implementation of a 1-week flexibility plan. (Assessment assignment opportunity: project 4.2)

Describe that in many societies physical activity is a shared intergenerational experience. 6.4

Have students record in their notebooks that physical activity is a shared intergenerational experience in many societies. 6.4

Introduce exercises for all five areas of health-related fitness specific to tumbling and gymnastics. 4.1

Have students perform a warm-up along with muscular strength and muscular endurance exercises. (Assessment opportunity: structured observation 4.1)

Demonstrate Trust Fall. 1.0, 2.5

Have students perform Trust Fall. (Assessment opportunity: structured observation 1.0, 5.1, 6.3)

Demonstrate the log roll. 1.0, 2.5

Have students perform the log roll. (Assessment opportunity: structured observation 1.0, 5.1, 6.3)

Demonstrate the V-sit. 1.0, 2.5

Have students perform the V-sit. (Assessment opportunity: structured observation 1.0, 5.1, 6.3)

Demonstrate the L-support. 1.0, 2.5

Have students perform the L-support. (Assessment opportunity: structured observation 1.0, 5.1, 6.3)

Review Trust Falls. 1.0, 2.5

Have students perform Trust Fall. (Assessment opportunity: structured observation 1.0, 5.1, 6.3)

Lead students through a cool-down and flexibility exercises appropriate to the physical activity level of the lesson. (Assessment opportunity: structured observation 4.1)

DAY 3

Define individual differences. 2.4

Have students summarize individual differences in their notebooks. 2.4

Have students perform a warm-up along with a cardiorespiratory workout. (Assessment opportunity: structured observation 4.1)

Review the log roll, V-sit, L-support, and Trust Fall. 1.0, 2.5

Have students perform log roll, V-sit, L-support, and Trust Fall. (Assessment opportunity: structured observation 1.0, 5.1, 6.3)

Demonstrate the front shoulder roll. 1.0, 2.5

Have students perform front shoulder roll. (Assessment opportunity: structured observation 1.0, 5.1, 6.3)

Lead students through a cool-down and flexibility exercises appropriate to the physical activity level of the lesson. (Assessment opportunity: structured observation 4.1)

Review that in many societies physical activity is a shared intergenerational experience. 6.4

(continued)

Unit 2 Outline *(continued)*

DAY 4

Explain to students the station approach to tumbling and gymnastics and provide students with forms on which to keep track of their progress.

Explain to students that they will need to be responsible for their own progress in tumbling and gymnastics. 5.2

Have students perform a warm-up along with muscular strength and muscular endurance exercises. (Assessment opportunity: structured observation 4.1)

Demonstrate the new stunts (tripod, back shoulder roll, walk on beam, and switcheroo) using the Body Management CD. 1.0, 2.5

Have students rotate through these stations: floor exercise, transitions (V-sit); floor exercise, transitions (L-support); floor exercise, forward sequence (log roll); floor exercise, forward sequence (front shoulder roll); floor exercise, backward sequence (back shoulder roll); floor exercise, headstand sequence (Trust Fall); floor exercise, headstand sequence (tripod); floor exercise, handstand sequence (switcheroo); beam (walking); and computer (Biomechanics Made Easy CD). (Assessment opportunity: structured observation 1.0, 5.1, 5.2, 6.3) 2.2

Lead students through a cool-down and flexibility exercises appropriate to the physical activity level of the lesson. (Assessment opportunity: structured observation 4.1)

DAY 5

Define individual differences in terms of physical performance. 2.4

Have students record the information in their notebooks. 2.4

Have students perform a warm-up along with a cardiorespiratory workout. (Assessment opportunity: structured observation 4.1)

Review the new stunts (tripod, back shoulder roll, walk on beam, and switcheroo) using the Body Management CD. 1.0, 2.5

Have students rotate through these stations: floor exercise, transitions (V-sit); floor exercise, transitions (L-support); floor exercise, forward sequence (log roll); floor exercise, forward sequence (front shoulder roll); floor exercise, backward sequence (back shoulder roll); floor exercise, headstand sequence (Trust Fall); floor exercise, headstand sequence (tripod); floor exercise, handstand sequence (switcheroo); beam (walking); and computer (Biomechanics Made Easy CD). (Assessment opportunity: structured observation 1.0, 5.1, 5.2, 6.3) 2.2

Lead students through a cool-down and flexibility exercises appropriate to the physical activity level of the lesson. (Assessment opportunity: structured observation 4.1)

DAY 6

Have students perform a warm-up along with a cardiorespiratory workout. (Assessment opportunity: structured observation 4.1)

Demonstrate the new stunts (Teeter-Totter, squat back roll, squat forward roll, walk on beam with dip) using the Body Management CD. 1.0, 2.5

Have students rotate through stations (I have listed the skills that are new; students can work on the new skill or any previous skill in that category): floor exercise, transitions (V-sit); floor exercise, transitions (L-support); floor exercise, forward sequence (forward roll); floor exercise, backward sequence (backward roll); floor exercise, headstand sequence (tripod); floor exercise, handstand sequence (Teeter-Totter); beam (walk with dip); horizontal bar (wide-arm chinning); parallel bars (forward hand walk); and computer (Biomechanics Made Easy CD). (Assessment opportunity: structured observation 1.0, 5.1, 5.2, 6.3) 2.2

Lead students through a cool-down and flexibility exercises appropriate to the physical activity level of the lesson. (Assessment opportunity: structured observation 4.1)

DAY 7

Have students perform a warm-up along with muscular strength and muscular endurance exercises. (Assessment opportunity: structured observation 4.1)

Demonstrate the new stunts (wide arm chinning, forward hand walk) using the Body Management CD. 1.0, 2.5

DAY 7 (continued)	Have students rotate through stations (I have listed the skills that are new; students can work on the new skill or any previous skill in that category): floor exercise, transitions (L-support); floor exercise, forward sequence (forward roll); floor exercise, backward sequence (backward roll); floor exercise, headstand sequence (tripod); floor exercise, handstand sequence (Teeter-Totter); beam (walk with dip); horizontal bar (wide-arm chinning); parallel bars (forward hand walk); vaulting (squat mount, jump dismount); and computer (Biomechanics Made Easy CD). (Assessment opportunity: structured observation 1.0, 5.1, 5.2, 6.3) 2.2
	Lead students through a cool-down and flexibility exercises appropriate to the physical activity level of the lesson. (Assessment opportunity: structured observation 4.1)
DAY 8	Have students perform a warm-up along with a cardiorespiratory workout. (Assessment opportunity: structured observation 4.1)
	Demonstrate the new stunts (arabesque, half-turn, back hand walk, jump front support) using the Body Management CD. 1.0, 2.5
	Have students rotate through stations: floor exercise, forward sequence (forward roll); floor exercise, backward sequence (backward roll); floor exercise, headstand sequence (tripod); floor exercise, handstand sequence (Teeter-Totter); beam (arabesque); horizontal bar (wide-arm chinning); parallel bars (half-turn, back hand walk); pommels (jump front support); vaulting (squat mount, jump dismount); and computer (Biomechanics Made Easy CD). (Assessment opportunity: structured observation 1.0, 5.1, 5.2, 6.3) 2.2
	Lead students through a cool-down and flexibility exercises appropriate to the physical activity level of the lesson. (Assessment opportunity: structured observation 4.1)
DAY 9	Have students perform a warm-up along with muscular strength and muscular endurance exercises. (Assessment opportunity: structured observation 4.1)
	Demonstrate the new stunt (pommel hand walk). 1.0, 2.5
	Have students rotate through stations: floor exercise, forward sequence (forward roll); floor exercise, backward sequence (backward roll); floor exercise, headstand sequence (tripod); floor exercise, handstand sequence (Teeter-Totter); beam (arabesque); horizontal bar (wide-arm chinning); parallel bars (half-turn, back hand walk); pommels (jump front support, hand walk); vaulting (squat mount, jump dismount); and computer (Biomechanics Made Easy CD). (Assessment opportunity: structured observation 1.0, 5.1, 5.2, 6.3) 2.2
	Lead students through a cool-down and flexibility exercises appropriate to the physical activity level of the lesson. (Assessment opportunity: structured observation 4.1)
	Ask students to discuss the relationships between the scientific principles associated with rotation and the stunts they performed today. 2.2
DAY 10	Have students perform a warm-up along with a cardiorespiratory workout. (Assessment opportunity: structured observation 4.1)
	Demonstrate the new stunts (forward roll walk-out, back roll to stand, handstand, straddle support mount) using the Body Management CD. 1.0, 2.5
	Have students rotate through stations: floor exercise, forward sequence (forward roll walk-out); floor exercise, backward sequence (back roll to standing); floor exercise, headstand sequence (tripod); floor exercise, handstand sequence (handstand); beam (straddle support mount); horizontal bar (wide arm chinning); parallel bars (half turn, back walk); pommels (jump support, hand walk); vaulting (squat mount, jump dismount); and computer (Biomechanics Made Easy CD). (Assessment opportunity: structured observation 1.0, 5.1, 5.2, 6.3) 2.2
	Lead students through a cool-down and flexibility exercises appropriate to the physical activity level of the lesson. (Assessment opportunity: structured observation 4.1)

(continued)

Unit 2 Outline *(continued)*

DAY 11

Have students perform a warm-up along with a cardiorespiratory workout. (Assessment opportunity: structured observation 4.1)

Demonstrate the new stunts (knee hang, forward hand jump, flank mount to rear support, knee spring dismount) using Body Management CD. 1.0, 2.5

Have students rotate through stations: floor exercise, forward sequence (forward roll walk-out); floor exercise, backward sequence (back roll to standing); floor exercise, headstand sequence (tripod); floor exercise, handstand sequence (handstand); beam (straddle support mount; horizontal bar (knee hang); parallel bars (forward hand jump); pommels (flank mount to rear support); vaulting (knee spring dismount); and computer (Biomechanics Made Easy CD). (Assessment opportunity: structured observation 1.0, 5.1, 5.2, 6.3) 2.2

Lead students through a cool-down and flexibility exercises appropriate to the physical activity level of the lesson. (Assessment opportunity: structured observation 4.1)

Ask students to discuss the relationships between the scientific principles associated with rotation and the stunts they performed today. 2.2

DAY 12

Have students perform a warm-up along with muscular strength and muscular endurance exercises. (Assessment opportunity: structured observation 4.1)

Demonstrate the new stunts (headstand, swing in a straight-arm support, rear mount to rear support, and front pullover) using the Body Management CD. 1.0, 2.5

Have students rotate through stations: floor exercise, forward sequence (forward roll walk-out); floor exercise, backward sequence (back roll to standing); floor exercise, headstand sequence (headstand); floor exercise, handstand sequence (handstand); beam (straddle support mount); horizontal bar (front pullover); parallel bars (swing with straight-arm support); pommels (rear mount to rear support); side horse (knee spring dismount); and computer (Biomechancs Made Easy, rotation section). (Assessment opportunity: structured observation 1.0, 5.1, 5.2, 6.3) 2.2

Lead students through a cool-down and flexibility exercises appropriate to the physical activity level of the lesson. (Assessment opportunity: structured observation 4.1)

DAY 13

Have students perform a warm-up along with muscular strength and muscular endurance exercises. (Assessment opportunity: structured observation 4.1)

Demonstrate the new stunts (squat vault, croup straddle dismount) using Body Management CD. 1.0, 2.5

Have students rotate through stations: floor exercise, forward sequence (forward roll walk-out); floor exercise, backward sequence (back roll to standing); floor exercise, headstand sequence (headstand); floor exercise, handstand sequence (handstand); beam (straddle support mount); horizontal bar (front pullover); parallel bars (swing with straight-arm support); pommels (rear mount to rear support); side horse (squat vault—see figure 16.3); and long horse (straddle dismount from croup). (Assessment opportunity: structured observation 1.0, 5.1, 5.2, 6.3)

Lead students through a cool-down and flexibility exercises appropriate to the physical activity level of the lesson. (Assessment opportunity: structured observation 4.1)

Ask students to discuss the relationships between the scientific principles associated with rotation and the stunts they performed today. 2.2

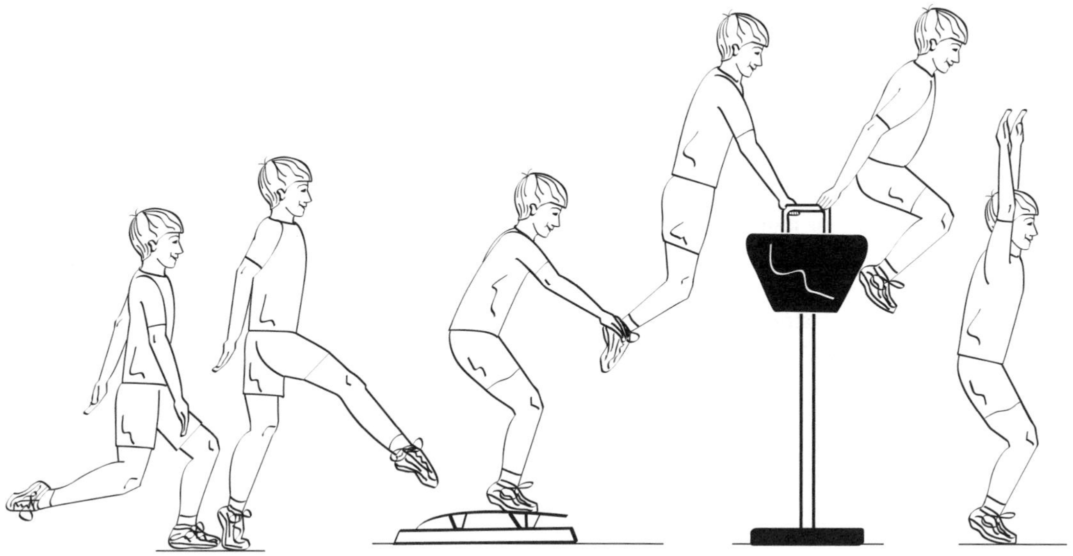

Figure 16.3 Approach and squat vault.

DAY 14

Have students perform a warm-up along with muscular strength and muscular endurance exercises. (Assessment opportunity: structured observation 4.1)

Demonstrate the new stunts using the Stunts, Tumbling, and Gymnastics CD. 1.0, 2.5

Explain the impact of radius of rotation on speed for new stunts. 2.2

Have students rotate through stations: floor exercise, forward sequence (pike forward roll); floor exercise, backward sequence (backward roll combinations); floor exercise, headstand sequence (headstand); floor exercise, lateral sequence (cartwheel); beam (squat turn); horizontal bar (front pullover); parallel bars (series of straddle seats); pommels (single-leg cut); vaulting (squat vault); and long horse (straddle dismount from croup). (Assessment opportunity: structured observation 1.0, 5.1, 5.2, 6.3)

Lead students through a cool-down and flexibility exercises appropriate to the physical activity level of the lesson. (Assessment opportunity: structured observation 4.1)

DAY 15

Have students perform a warm-up along with a cardiorespiratory workout. (Assessment opportunity: structured observation 4.1)

Demonstrate the new stunts (series of straddle seats, single-leg cut) using Body Management CD. 1.0, 2.5

Have students rotate through stations: floor exercise, forward sequence (pike forward roll); floor exercise, backward sequence (backward roll combinations); floor exercise, headstand sequence (headstand); floor exercise, lateral sequence (cartwheel); beam (squat turn); horizontal bar (front pullover); parallel bars (series of straddle seats); pommels (single-leg cut); vaulting (squat vault); and long horse (straddle dismount from croup). (Assessment opportunity: structured observation 1.0, 5.1, 5.2, 6.3)

Lead students through a cool-down and flexibility exercises appropriate to the physical activity level of the lesson. (Assessment opportunity: structured observation 4.1)

Ask students to discuss the relationships between the scientific principles associated with rotation and the stunts they performed today. 2.2

(continued)

Unit 2 Outline *(continued)*

DAY 16

Have students perform a warm-up along with a cardiorespiratory workout. (Assessment opportunity: structured observation 4.1)

Demonstrate the new stunts (swing turn, shoulder stand, flank vault, straddle vault on long horse) using Body Management CD. 1.0, 2.5

Have students rotate through stations: floor exercise, forward sequence (pike forward roll); floor exercise, backward sequence (backward roll combinations); floor exercise, headstand sequence (headstand); floor exercise, lateral sequence (cartwheel); beam (jump dismount); horizontal bar (swing turn); parallel bars (shoulder stand); pommels (single-leg cut); vaulting (flank vault—see figure 16.4); and long horse (straddle vault). (Assessment opportunity: structured observation 1.0, 5.1, 5.2, 6.3)

Lead students through a cool-down and flexibility exercises appropriate to the physical activity level of the lesson. (Assessment opportunity: structured observation 4.1)

Figure 16.4   Flank vault.

DAY 17

Have students perform a warm-up along with muscular strength and muscular endurance exercises. (Assessment opportunity: structured observation 4.1)

Demonstrate the new stunt (jump dismount off beam) using Body Management CD. 1.0, 2.5

Have students rotate through stations: floor exercise, forward sequence (pike forward roll); floor exercise, backward sequence (backward roll combinations); floor exercise, headstand sequence (headstand); floor exercise, lateral sequence (cartwheel); beam (jump dismount); horizontal bar (swing turn); parallel bars (shoulder stand); pommels (one-leg cut); vaulting (flank vault—see figure 16.4); and long horse (straddle vault). (Assessment opportunity: structured observation 1.0, 5.1, 5.2, 6.3)

Lead students through a cool-down and flexibility exercises appropriate to the physical activity level of the lesson. (Assessment opportunity: structured observation 4.1)

Ask students to discuss the relationships between the scientific principles associated with rotation and the stunts they performed today. 2.2

DAY 18

Have students perform a warm-up along with a cardiorespiratory workout. (Assessment opportunity: structured observation 4.1)

Demonstrate the new stunts (forward roll combinations, Penny Drop, shoulder roll on parallel bar, front dismount from straight-arm support) using Body Management CD. 1.0, 2.5

Have students rotate through stations: floor exercise, forward sequence (forward roll combinations); floor exercise, backward sequence (backward roll combinations); floor exercise, headstand sequence (headstand); floor exercise, lateral sequence (cartwheel); beam (jump dismount); horizontal bar (Penny Drop); parallel bars (shoulder roll, front dismount from straight-arm support); pommels (single-leg cut); vaulting horse (flank vault); and long horse (straddle vault). (Assessment opportunity: structured observation 1.0, 5.1, 5.2, 6.3)

Lead students through a cool-down and flexibility exercises appropriate to the physical activity level of the lesson. (Assessment opportunity: structured observation 4.1)

DAY 19

Have students perform a warm-up along with muscular strength and muscular endurance exercises. (Assessment opportunity: structured observation 4.1)

Demonstrate the new stunts (round off, single-leg circle, back extension) from Body Management CD. 1.0, 2.5

Have students rotate through stations: floor exercise, forward sequence (forward roll combinations); floor exercise, backward sequence (back extension); floor exercise, headstand sequence (headstand); floor exercise, lateral sequence (round-off); beam (jump dismount); horizontal bar (Penny Drop); parallel bars (shoulder roll); pommels (single-leg circle); vaulting horse (flank vault); and long horse (straddle vault). (Assessment opportunity: structured observation 1.0, 5.1, 5.2, 6.3)

Lead students through a cool-down and flexibility exercises appropriate to the physical activity level of the lesson. (Assessment opportunity: structured observation 4.1)

Ask students to discuss the relationships between the scientific principles associated with rotation and the stunts they performed today. 2.2

DAY 20

Have students perform a warm-up along with a cardiorespiratory workout. (Assessment opportunity: structured observation 4.1)

Demonstrate the new stunts (backward roll on beam, front walkover, squat dismount from croup, forward hip circle) using Body Management CD. 1.0, 2.5

Have students rotate through stations: floor exercise, backward sequence (back extension); floor exercise, headstand sequence (headstand); floor exercise, handstand sequence (front walkover); floor exercise, lateral sequence (round-off); beam (backward roll); horizontal bar (forward hip circle); parallel bars (front dismount from straight-arm support); pommels (single-leg circle); vaulting horse (straddle vault—see figure 16.6); and long horse (squat dismount from croup). (Assessment opportunity: structured observation 1.0, 5.1, 5.2, 6.3)

Lead students through a cool-down and flexibility exercises appropriate to the physical activity level of the lesson. (Assessment opportunity: structured observation 4.1)

Review qualities of movement. 6.2

Have students summarize the review in their notebooks. 6.2

DAY 21

Assign students homework to create a tumbling and gymnastics routine (see figures 16.6-16.9) that includes the qualities of movement and a description of the routine along with a description of what they appreciated about their own stylistic approach to the routine. (Assessment assignment opportunity: project 6.2)

Have students work on their routines as they rotate through the stations. 6.2

Have students perform a warm-up along with a cardiorespiratory workout. (Assessment opportunity: structured observation 4.1)

(continued)

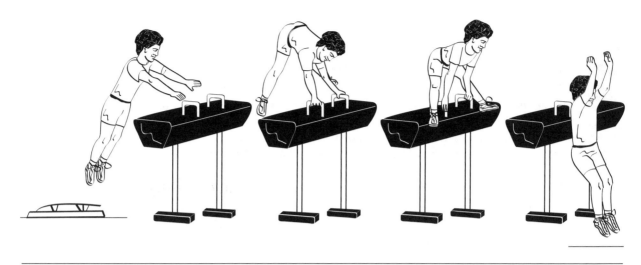

Figure 16.5   Straddle vault.

Unit 2 Outline   *(continued)*

DAY 21 *(continued)*	Demonstrate the new stunts (forward hip circle dismount, straddle vault). 1.0, 2.5
	Have students rotate through stations: floor exercise, backward sequence (back extension); floor exercise, headstand sequence (headstand); floor exercise, handstand sequence (front walkover); floor exercise, lateral sequence (round-off); beam (backward roll); horizontal bar (forward hip circle, forward hip circle dismount); parallel bars (front dismount from straight-arm support); pommels (single-leg circle); vaulting horse (straddle vault—see figure 16.5); and long horse (squat dismount from croup). (Assessment opportunity: structured observation 1.0, 5.1, 5.2, 6.3)
	Lead students through a cool-down and flexibility exercises appropriate to the physical activity level of the lesson. (Assessment opportunity: structured observation 4.1)
	Ask students to discuss the relationships between the scientific principles associated with rotation and the stunts they performed today. 2.2
DAY 22	Have students perform a warm-up along with muscular strength and muscular endurance exercises. (Assessment opportunity: structured observation 4.1)
	Have students work on their routines. (Assessment opportunity: structured observation 1.0, 5.1, 5.2, 6.3) 6.2
	Lead students through a cool-down and flexibility exercises appropriate to the physical activity level of the lesson. (Assessment opportunity: structured observation 4.1)
DAY 23	Have students perform a warm-up along with a cardiorespiratory workout. (Assessment opportunity: structured observation 4.1)
	Have students work on their routines. (Assessment opportunity: structured observation 1.0, 5.1, 5.2, 6.3) 6.2
	Lead students through a cool-down and flexibility exercises appropriate to the physical activity level of the lesson. (Assessment opportunity: structured observation 4.1)

(continued)

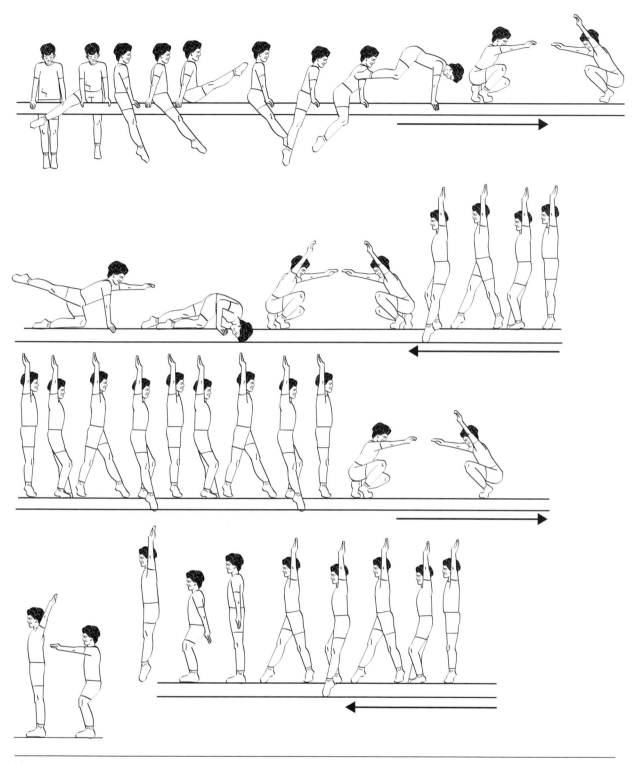

Figure 16.6 Beam routine.

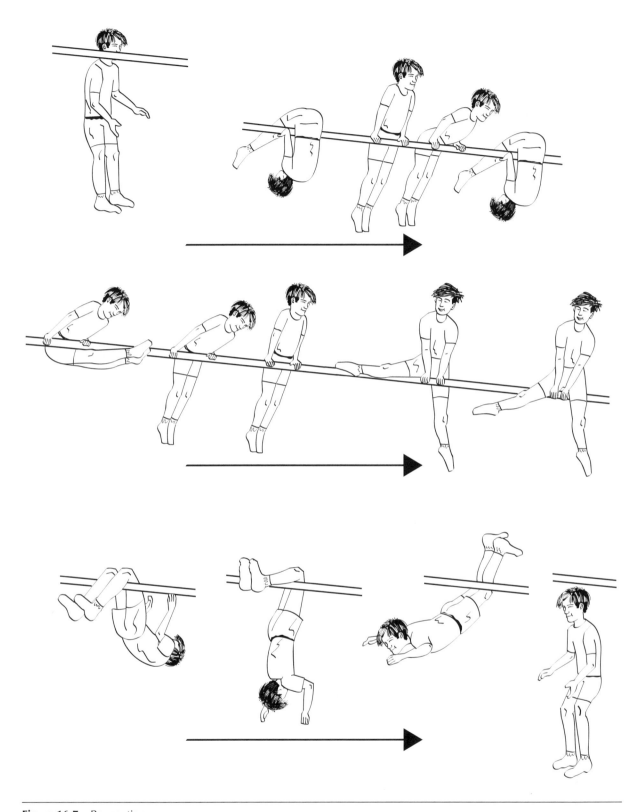

Figure 16.7 Bar routine.

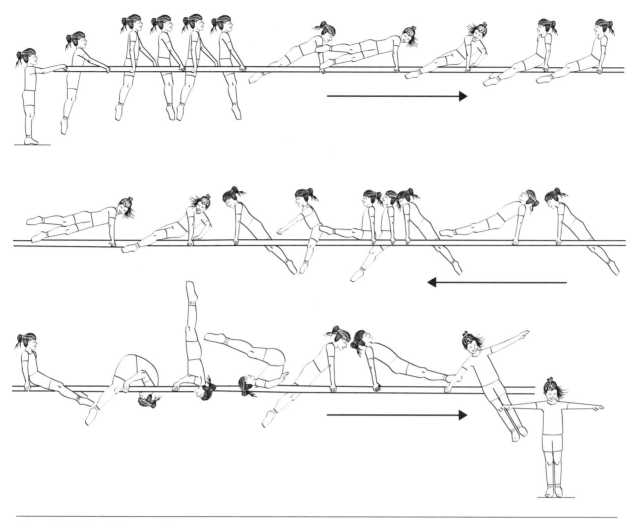

Figure 16.8   Parallel bars routine.

Unit 2 Outline   *(continued)*

DAY 24

Have students perform a warm-up along with muscular strength and muscular endurance exercises. (Assessment opportunity: structured observation 4.1)

Have students perform their routines for their groups. (Assessment opportunity: project 6.2)

Lead students through a cool-down and flexibility exercises appropriate to the physical activity level of the lesson. (Assessment opportunity: structured observation 4.1)

Collect the routines and descriptions of what students appreciated about their stylistic approach to the routine. (Assessment opportunity: project 6.2)

(continued)

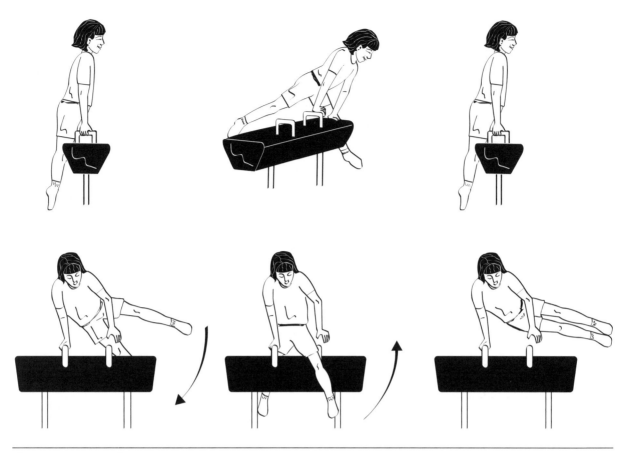

Figure 16.9   Pommel routine.

Unit 2 Outline   *(continued)*

DAY 25

Have students take the quiz. (Assessment opportunity: quiz 2.1, 2.2, 2.3, 2.4, 6.4)

Collect student activity logs. (Assessment opportunity: log 3.1)

Collect reports on the description of recreational activities during medieval times. (Assessment opportunity: report 6.1)

Collect essays about the opportunities in the larger community for participation in tumbling and gymnastics. (Assessment opportunity: essay 3.2)

Collect 1-week flexibility plans with notes on changes needed to be made to plan. (Assessment opportunity: project 4.2)

Collect reports on critical features of tumbling and gymnastics skills. (Assessment opportunity: report 2.5)

Orienteering   — Unit 3

This unit continues our focus on accepting challenges by having the students challenge themselves to participate in orienteering. You may elect to have your students participate in other outdoor education activities, such as hiking, bicycling, in-line skating, climbing, or camping, depending on your situation. Because of the physical nature of life in the inner city where my school is located, I focus on orienteering.

Ideally, you should conduct this unit on open terrain so students can actually perform real-life orienteering events; however, any open outdoor area will do. Even in an inner-city setting, students can experience orienteering through simulated events held on the school campus. To culminate simulated events, you can take students on a field trip for their final orienteering challenge. In this unit, students must learn to use a compass and a topographic map; you can order the maps from the National Cartographic Information Center.

Orienteering is an excellent activity with which to integrate physical education with history and social science. Reading maps, understanding map symbols, and following route directions help students in physical education, in the regular classroom, and—most important—in real life. Ideally, you should have your students' history or social science teacher cover the types of maps, reading of maps, and meaning of map symbols just before the start of your orienteering unit.

Unit 3 Standards

1.0—Demonstrates the correct technique for holding a compass, reading a compass, taking a bearing, following a bearing, and reading topographic maps.

2.1—Explains the role of monitoring improvement in goal setting.

2.2—Not applicable.

2.3—Explains the use of strategy in orienteering.

2.4—Explains that individuals proceed through similar stages on their way to learning skills, but each progresses at a different rate.

2.5—Explains the technique for holding a compass, reading a compass, taking a bearing, and following a bearing.

3.1—Engages in moderate and vigorous physical activity for 60 minutes 5 days each week.

3.2—Describes opportunities in the larger community for participation in outdoor education activities.

4.1—Works toward a health-enhancing level of physical fitness.

4.2—Creates a 1-week nutrition plan.

5.1—Applies problem-solving techniques when working with another person in orienteering activities.

5.2—Accepts responsibility for individual improvement during orienteering activities.

6.1—Describes outdoor activities during medieval times.

6.2—Not applicable.

6.3—Chooses to engage in orienteering activities at the appropriate level of personal challenge.

6.4—Describes the social benefits of regular participation in orienteering.

Unit 3 Assessments

1.0—Structured observation (days 3-19)

2.1—Quiz (day 20)

2.2—Not applicable

2.3—Quiz (day 20)

2.4—Quiz (day 20)

2.5—Quiz (day 20)

3.1—Log (assigned on day 1; collected on day 20)

3.2—Essay (assigned on day 1; collected on day 20)

4.1—Structured observation (days 1-19)

4.2—Project (assigned on day 3; collected on day 20)

5.1—Structured observation (days 3-19)

5.2—Structure observation (days 3-19)

6.1—Report (assigned on day 1; collected on day 20)

6.2—Not applicable

6.3—Structured observation (days 3-19)

6.4—Quiz (day 20)

Resources

Orienteering and Outdoor Education CD (Bonnie's Fitware, Inc.)

Health-Related Fitness: Tutorial and Portfolio (Bonnie's Fitware, Inc.)

Middle School Physical Education Portfolio (Bonnie's Fitware, Inc.)

Seventh grade orienteering task cards (Bonnie's Fitware, Inc.)

Seventh grade unit 3 posters (Bonnie's Fitware, Inc.—included in the Middle School Detailed Lesson Plans)

Fitness posters (Bonnie's Fitware, Inc.—included in the Middle School Detailed Lesson Plans)

Equipment

Compasses	Cones	Control points
Maps (school and topographic)	Paper plates or poly spots	

Games

Contour map matching

Orienteering (line, point-to-point, score)

Unit 3 Outline

DAY 1	Put up posters.
	Assign students to new working groups of four.
	Introduce orienteering.
	Describe the social benefits of regular participation in orienteering. 6.4
	Have students record the social benefits of regular participation in orienteering in their notebooks. 6.4
	Describe the importance of engaging in orienteering activities at the appropriate level of personal challenge. 6.3
	Explain the importance of accepting responsibility for individual improvement during orienteering activities. 5.2
	Have students perform a warm-up. (Assessment opportunity: structured observation 4.1)
	Have students participate in a cardiorespiratory activity that involves following a school map with control points drawn on it. 1.0
	Lead students through a cool-down and flexibility exercises appropriate to the physical activity level of the lesson. (Assessment opportunity: structured observation 4.1)

DAY 1 *(continued)*

Assign unit-long homework:

- Have students research and describe outdoor activities during medieval times. (Assessment assignment opportunity: report 6.1)

- Have students keep a log of daily activity. (Assessment assignment opportunity: log 3.1)

- Have students describe the opportunities in the larger community for participation in orienteering activities. (Assessment assignment opportunity: essay 3.2)

DAY 2

Have students perform a warm-up along with muscular strength and muscular endurance exercises. (Assessment opportunity: structured observation 4.1)

Have students participate in a cardiorespiratory activity that involves following a school map with control points drawn on it. 1.0, 4.1

Explain the parts of a compass (see figure 16.10) and orienting a compass. 1.0, 2.5

Lead students through a cool-down and flexibility exercises appropriate to the physical activity level of the lesson. (Assessment opportunity: structured observation 4.1)

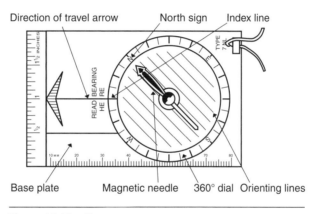

Figure 16.10 Compass.

DAY 3

Post fitness posters.

Describe the new food pyramid. 4.2

Have students read the information on the food pyramid chart in the Health-Related Fitness CD. 4.2

Have students use the Health-Related Fitness CD to determine their individual nutrition requirements. 4.2

Assign students a 1-week nutrition plan. (Assessment assignment opportunity: project 4.2)

Have students perform a warm-up. (Assessment opportunity: structured observation 4.1)

Review parts of a compass and orienting a compass. 1.0, 2.5

Explain how to read a compass. 1.0, 2.5

Explain how to take a bearing. 1.0, 2.5

Have students take a bearing on a physical feature (e.g., a point in the gym). (Assessment opportunity: structured observation 1.0, 5.1, 5.2, 6.3)

Lead students through a cool-down and flexibility exercises appropriate to the physical activity level of the lesson. (Assessment opportunity: structured observation 4.1)

(continued)

Unit 3 Outline (continued)

DAY 4

Have students perform a warm-up along with muscular strength and muscular endurance exercises. (Assessment opportunity: structured observation 4.1)

Have students participate in a cardiorespiratory activity that involves following a school map with control points drawn on it. 1.0

Review how to take a bearing. 1.0, 2.5

Have students take a bearing on a physical feature (e.g., a point in the gym). (Assessment opportunity: structured observation 1.0, 5.1, 5.2, 6.3)

Explain following a bearing. 1.0, 2.5

Have students participate in an activity in which they walk 20 steps and turn 90°, repeating four times to end up in the original location. Repeat using other degrees. (Assessment opportunity: structured observation 1.0, 5.1, 5.2, 6.3)

Lead students through a cool-down and flexibility exercises appropriate to the physical activity level of the lesson. (Assessment opportunity: structured observation 4.1)

Review the social benefits of regular participation in orienteering. 6.4

DAY 5

Explain that individuals proceed through similar stages on their way to learning skills, but each progresses at a different rate. 2.4

Have students summarize the explanation in their notebooks. 2.4

Have students perform a warm-up along with muscular strength and muscular endurance exercises. (Assessment opportunity: structured observation 4.1)

Have students participate in a cardiorespiratory activity that involves following a school map with control points drawn on it. 1.0, 4.1

Review parts of a compass, orienting a compas taking a bearing, and following a bearing. 1.0, 2.5

Have students walk 10 steps at a 30° bearing, 15 steps at a 40° bearing, and 20 steps at a 60° bearing. Repeat using other degrees. (Assessment opportunity: structured observation 1.0, 5.1, 5.2, 6.3)

Have students create a bearing route with a partner, lay out paper plates or poly spots, and note the bearing between the plates. (Assessment opportunity: structured observation 1.0, 5.1, 5.2, 6.3)

Have partners participate in the bearing route activity created by the other two members of their group. (Assessment opportunity: structured observation 1.0, 5.1, 5.2, 6.3)

Lead students through a cool-down and flexibility exercises appropriate to the physical activity level of the lesson. (Assessment opportunity: structured observation 4.1)

Review the food pyramid chart. 4.2

DAY 6

Have students perform a warm-up. (Assessment opportunity: structured observation 4.1)

Have students participate in a cardiorespiratory activity that involves following a school map with control points drawn on it. 1.0

Lead students through a cool-down and flexibility exercises appropriate to the physical activity level of the lesson. (Assessment opportunity: structured observation 4.1)

Discuss topographic maps. 1.0

Discuss the key points related to topographic maps: opening, folding, and protecting the map; the four cardinal directions; symbols; contour lines; scale; and orienting a map. 1.0

Have students identify different types of mountains and hills on a topographic map. 1.0

Have students identify the meanings of the symbols on a topographic map. 1.0

Have students find the distance between several points marked on a map. 1.0

DAY 7	Have students perform a warm-up along with muscular strength and muscular endurance exercises. (Assessment opportunity: structured observation 4.1)

Have students participate in a cardiorespiratory activity that involves following a school map with control points drawn on it. 1.0, 4.1

Lead students through a cool-down and flexibility exercises appropriate to the physical activity level of the lesson. (Assessment opportunity: structured observation 4.1)

Review topographic maps. 1.0

Review key points related to topographic maps: opening, folding, and protecting the map; the four cardinal directions; symbols; contour lines; scale; and orienting a map. 1.0

Have students participate in the contour map matching activity. 1.0

Have students identify different types of mountains and hills on a topographic map. 1.0

Have students identify the meanings of the symbols on a topographic map. 1.0

Have students find the distance between several points marked on a map. 1.0

Have students create a topographic map of the school. 1.0 |
| **DAY 8** | Have students perform a warm-up.

Have students participate in a cardiorespiratory activity that involves following a school map with control points drawn on it. 1.0, 4.1

Lead students through a cool-down and flexibility exercises appropriate to the physical activity level of the lesson. (Assessment opportunity: structured observation 4.1)

Discuss declination (the difference between true north and magnetic north). 1.0, 2.5

Have students take a map bearing (bearing between two points on a map) and then convert it to a real bearing based on the declination. (Assessment opportunity: structured observation 1.0, 5.1, 5.2, 6.3)

Discuss reading an isogenic chart. 1.0, 2.5

Have students take a map bearing on an isogenic chart, determining the real bearing. (Assessment opportunity: structured observation 1.0, 5.1, 5.2, 6.3)

Show how to adjust a compass for declination. 1.0, 2.5 |
| **DAY 9** | Have students perform a warm-up along with muscular strength and muscular endurance exercises. (Assessment opportunity: structured observation 4.1)

Have students participate in a cardiorespiratory activity that involves following a school map with control points drawn on it. 1.0, 4.1

Lead students through a cool-down and flexibility exercises appropriate to the physical activity level of the lesson. (Assessment opportunity: structured observation 4.1)

Review problem-solving techniques when working with another person during orienteering activities. 5.1

Discuss pace and route choice. 1.0, 2.5

Have students determine the most effective route between two points on a map. (Assessment opportunity: structured observation 1.0, 5.1, 5.2, 6.3)

Have students determine the number of steps they must take to go between the two points on the map. (Assessment opportunity: structured observation 1.0, 5.1, 5.2, 6.3) |

(continued)

Unit 3 Outline *(continued)*

DAY 10

Have students perform a warm-up. (Assessment opportunity: structured observation 4.1)

Have students participate in a cardiorespiratory activity that involves following a school map with control points drawn on it. 1.0, 4.1

Explain control marker, control code, control description, and control feature. 1.0, 2.5

Describe orienteering. 1.0

Have students travel to one control point. (Assessment opportunity: structured observation 1.0, 5.1, 5.2, 6.3)

Lead students through a cool-down and flexibility exercises appropriate to the physical activity level of the lesson. (Assessment opportunity: structured observation 4.1)

DAY 11

Have students perform a warm-up. (Assessment opportunity: structured observation 4.1)

Have students participate in a cardiorespiratory activity that involves following a school map with control points drawn on it. 1.0, 4.1

Review control marker, control code, control description, and control feature. 1.0, 2.5

Review orienteering. 1.0

Have students travel to one control point. (Assessment opportunity: structured observation 1.0, 5.1, 5.2, 6.3)

Lead students through a cool-down and flexibility exercises appropriate to the physical activity level of the lesson. (Assessment opportunity: structured observation 4.1)

Explain the use of strategy in an orienteering experience. 2.3

For the first orienteering activity, give students the map to study overnight. 1.0

Explain the role of monitoring improvement in the goal-setting process. 2.1

Have students set goals for their orienteering experiences and determine how they are going to monitor their progress. 2.1

DAY 12

Have students perform a warm-up along with muscular strength and muscular endurance exercises. (Assessment opportunity: structured observation 4.1)

Teach line orienteering. 1.0

Have students in pairs participate in a line orienteering activity. (Assessment opportunity: structured observation 1.0, 5.1, 5.2, 6.3)

Lead students through a cool-down and flexibility exercises appropriate to the physical activity level of the lesson. (Assessment opportunity: structured observation 4.1)

DAY 13

Have students perform a warm-up along with a cardiorespiratory workout. (Assessment opportunity: structured observation 4.1)

Review line orienteering. 1.0

Have students, working in pairs, participate in a line orienteering activity. (Assessment opportunity: structured observation 1.0, 5.1, 5.2, 6.3)

Lead students through a cool-down and flexibility exercises appropriate to the physical activity level of the lesson. (Assessment opportunity: structured observation 4.1)

DAY 14

Have students perform a warm-up along with muscular strength and muscular endurance exercises. (Assessment opportunity: structured observation 4.1)

Teach students point-to-point orienteering. 1.0

Have pairs participate in a point-to-point orienteering activity. (Assessment opportunity: structured observation 1.0, 5.1, 5.2, 6.3)

Lead students through a cool-down and flexibility exercises appropriate to the physical activity level of the lesson. (Assessment opportunity: structured observation 4.1)

DAY 15	Have students perform a warm-up. (Assessment opportunity: structured observation 4.1)
	Review point-to-point orienteering. 1.0
	Have pairs participate in a point-to-point orienteering activity. (Assessment opportunity: structured observation 1.0, 5.1, 5.2, 6.3)
	Lead students through a cool-down and flexibility exercises appropriate to the physical activity level of the lesson. (Assessment opportunity: structured observation 4.1)
DAY 16	Have students perform a warm-up. (Assessment opportunity: structured observation 4.1)
	Teach students score orienteering. 1.0
	Have pairs participate in a score orienteering activity. (Assessment opportunity: structured observation 1.0, 5.1, 5.2, 6.3)
	Lead students through a cool-down and flexibility exercises appropriate to the physical activity level of the lesson. (Assessment opportunity: structured observation 4.1)
DAY 17	Have students perform a warm-up along with muscular strength and muscular endurance exercises. (Assessment opportunity: structured observation 4.1)
	Review score orienteering. 1.0
	Have pairs participate in a score orienteering activity. (Assessment opportunity: structured observation 1.0, 5.1, 5.2, 6.3)
	Lead students through a cool-down and flexibility exercises appropriate to the physical activity level of the lesson. (Assessment opportunity: structured observation 4.1)
DAY 18	Have students perform a warm-up along with a cardiorespiratory workout. (Assessment opportunity: structured observation 4.1)
	Have each group create their own orienteering-like game including strategic ideas for performing well in the game. (Assessment opportunity: structured observation 1.0, 5.1, 5.2, 6.3) 2.3
	Lead students through a cool-down and flexibility exercises appropriate to the physical activity level of the lesson. (Assessment opportunity: structured observation 4.1)
DAY 19	Have students perform a warm-up along with muscular strength and muscular endurance exercises. (Assessment opportunity: structured observation 4.1)
	Have each group work on their own outdoor education or orienteering-like game including strategic ideas for performing well in the game. (Assessment opportunity: structured observation 1.0, 5.1, 5.2, 6.3) 2.3
	Have each group teach their game to another group. 2.3
	Lead students through a cool-down and flexibility exercises appropriate to the physical activity level of the lesson. (Assessment opportunity: structured observation 4.1)
	Review material for tomorrow's quiz (or hand out quiz if you would like for it to be a take home quiz). 2.1, 2.3, 2.4, 2.5, 6.4
DAY 20	Have students take the quiz. (Assessment opportunity: quiz 2.1, 2.3, 2.4, 2.5, 6.4)
	Collect student activity logs. (Assessment opportunity: log 3.1)
	Collect reports on the description of outdoor activities during medieval times. (Assessment opportunity: report 6.1)
	Collect essays about the orienteering activities in the larger community and social opportunities in outdoor education activities. (Assessment opportunity: essay 3.2)
	Collect 1-week nutrition plans. (Assessment opportunity: project 4.2)

Note: Other activities appropriate for the outdoor education unit include in-line skating (see figures 16.11 and 16.12) and rock or wall climbing (see figure 16.13).

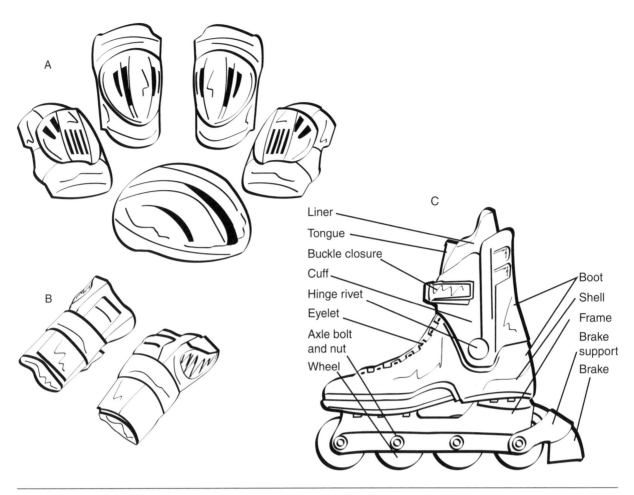

Figure 16.11   In-line skating equipment.

Figure 16.12   In-line skating.

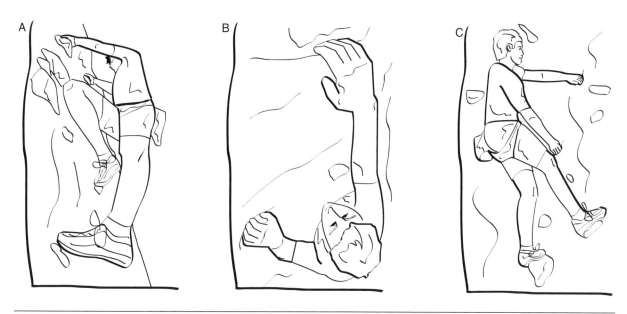

Figure 16.13 Climbing.

Net Sport: Tennis   – Unit 4

Because tennis is a new sport for my students, this unit continues the focus on accepting challenges. You can conduct this unit in any open outdoor area, but naturally it's helpful if you have access to a tennis court. Check with your local racket club or park district to see if you can gain free or low-cost access to appropriate facilities—at least to culminate the unit. Although you can do without proper courts, tennis rackets are essential to this unit. If you are unfamiliar with teaching tennis or lack equipment or facilities, contact the United States Tennis Association (USTA), which provides free training, curriculum materials, rackets, and balls. The USTA curriculum guide is based on teaching tennis in an open area without regular tennis courts. Simply call the United States Tennis Association and ask for an office near you.

Unit 4 Standards

1.0—Demonstrates the mature form for the tennis forehand, backhand, serve, and volley strokes.

2.1—Explains whole/part, mass/distributed, constant/variable, and blocked/random practice.

2.2—Describes the relationship between point of application and spin.

2.3—Explains offensive and defensive strategies for tennis.

2.4—Explains individual differences and how these differences impact tennis performance.

2.5—Explains the critical elements of the tennis forehand, backhand, serve, serve, and volley strokes.

3.1—Engages in moderate and vigorous physical activity for 60 minutes 6 days each week.

3.2—Describes opportunities in the larger community for participation in tennis activities.

4.1—Works toward a health-enhancing level of physical fitness.

4.2—Creates a 1-week body composition plan.

5.1—Applies problem-solving techniques when working with another person in tennis activities.

5.2—Accepts responsibility for individual improvement during tennis activities.

6.1—Describes ball games during medieval times.

6.2—Not applicable.

6.3—Chooses to engage in tennis activities at the appropriate level of personal challenge.

6.4—Describes the social benefits of regular participation in tennis.

Unit 4 Assessments

1.0—Structured observation (days 1-19)

2.1—Quiz (day 20)

2.2—Quiz (day 20)

2.3—Quiz (day 20)

2.4—Quiz (day 20)

2.5—Quiz (day 20)

3.1—Log (assigned on day 1; collected on day 20)

3.2—Essay (assigned on day 1; collected on day 20)

4.1—Structured observation (days 1-19)

4.2—Project (assigned on day 2; collected on day 20)

5.1—Structured observation (days 1-19)

5.2—Structure observation (days 1-19)

6.1—Report (assigned on day 1; collected on day 20)

6.2—Not applicable

6.3—Structured observation (days 1-19)

6.4—Quiz (day 20)

Resources

SimAthlete (Bonnie's Fitware Inc)

Health-Related Fitness: Tutorial and Portfolio (Bonnie's Fitware, Inc.)

Middle School Physical Education Portfolio (Bonnie's Fitware, Inc.)

Racket Sports CD (Bonnie's Fitware, Inc.)

Seventh grade tennis task cards (Bonnie's Fitware, Inc.)

Seventh grade unit 4 posters (Bonnie's Fitware, Inc.—included in the Middle School Detailed Lesson Plans)

Fitness posters (Bonnie's Fitware, Inc.—included in the Middle School Detailed Lesson Plans)

Equipment

Tennis rackets

Tennis balls

Games

Modified racket sport

Unit 4 Outline

DAY 1	Put up posters.
	Introduce tennis, including discussion of safety, equipment, and unit overview.
	Discuss the importance of engaging in tennis at the appropriate level of personal challenge. 6.3
	Have students summarize the discussion in their notebooks. 6.3
	Discuss the importance of accepting responsibility for individual improvement. 5.2
	Have students summarize the discussion in their notebooks. 5.2

DAY 1 (continued)

Discuss problem-solving techniques when working with another person in tennis. 5.1

Have students record the information in their notebooks. 5.1

Assign students to working groups of four.

Have students perform a warm-up along with a cardiorespiratory workout. (Assessment opportunity: structured observation 4.1)

Introduce the ready position and grip using the Racket Sports CD. 1.0, 2.5

Have students practice the ready position and grip. (Assessment opportunity: structured observation 1.0, 5.1, 5.2, 6.3)

Lead students through a cool-down and flexibility exercises appropriate to the physical activity level of the lesson. (Assessment opportunity: structured observation 4.1)

Assign unit-long homework:

- Have students research and write a description of ball games during medieval times. (Assessment assignment opportunity: report 6.1)

- Have students keep a log of daily activity. (Assessment assignment opportunity: log 3.1)

- Have students describe the opportunities in the larger community for participation in tennis. (Assessment assignment opportunity: essay 3.2)

DAY 2

Review frequency, intensity, time, and type related to body composition using Health-Related Fitness: Tutorial and Portfolio. 4.2

Describe the role of physical activity and nutrition in achieving fitness. 4.2

Have students record the information in their notebooks. 4.2

Assign 1-week body composition plan. (Assessment assignment opportunity: project 4.2)

Have students perform a warm-up along with muscular strength and muscular endurance exercises. (Assessment opportunity: structured observation 4.1)

Review the ready position and grip. 1.0, 2.5

Have students demonstrate the ready position and grip to you so you can provide feedback. (Assessment opportunity: structured observation 1.0, 5.1, 5.2, 6.3)

Demonstrate and describe the forehand drive using the Racket Sports CD. 1.0, 2.5

Have students, in pairs, practice dropping the ball and executing the forehand drive. (Assessment opportunity: structured observation 1.0, 5.1, 5.2, 6.3)

Lead students through a cool-down and flexibility exercises appropriate to the physical activity level of the lesson. (Assessment opportunity: structured observation 4.1)

DAY 3

Explain individual differences and how these differences impact tennis performance. 2.4

Have students summarize the explanation in their notebooks. 2.4

Have students perform a warm-up along with a cardiorespiratory workout. (Assessment opportunity: structured observation 4.1)

Review the ready position, grip, and forehand drive. 1.0, 2.5

Have students, in pairs, practice dropping the ball and executing the forehand drive. (Assessment opportunity: structured observation 1.0, 5.1, 5.2, 6.3)

Have pairs who are ready practice tossing the ball to each other and executing the forehand drive. (Assessment opportunity: structured observation 1.0, 5.1, 5.2, 6.3)

Lead students through a cool-down and flexibility exercises appropriate to the physical activity level of the lesson. (Assessment opportunity: structured observation 4.1)

(continued)

Unit 4 Outline *(continued)*

DAY 4

Have students perform a warm-up along with muscular strength and muscular endurance exercises. (Assessment opportunity: structured observation 4.1)

Demonstrate the footwork necessary to move to the ball to execute a forehand drive using the Racket Sports CD. 1.0, 2.5

Have students demonstrate the necessary footwork as you model it. (Assessment opportunity: structured observation 1.0, 5.1, 5.2, 6.3)

Have students, in pairs, practice dropping the ball and executing the forehand drive. (Assessment opportunity: structured observation 1.0, 5.1, 5.2, 6.3)

Have pairs who are ready practice tossing the ball to each other and executing the forehand drive. (Assessment opportunity: structured observation 1.0, 5.1, 5.2, 6.3)

Have pairs who are ready begin hitting back and forth to each other with forehand drives. (Assessment opportunity: structured observation 1.0, 5.1, 5.2, 6.3)

Have pairs who are ready hit the ball back and forth with forehand drives, counting the number of hits they can make without missing. (Assessment opportunity: structured observation 1.0, 5.1, 5.2, 6.3)

Lead students through a cool-down and flexibility exercises appropriate to the physical activity level of the lesson. (Assessment opportunity: structured observation 4.1)

Review individual differences and how these differences impact tennis performance. 2.4

DAY 5

Describe the social benefits of regular participation in racket sports. 6.4

Have students record the information in their notebooks. 6.4

Have students perform a warm-up along with a cardiorespiratory workout. (Assessment opportunity: structured observation 4.1)

Demonstrate and describe the backhand grip and backhand drive (see figure 16.14) on the Racket Sports CD. 1.0, 2.5

Have students, in pairs, practice dropping the ball and executing the backhand drive. (Assessment opportunity: structured observation 1.0, 5.1, 5.2, 6.3)

Lead students through a cool-down and flexibility exercises appropriate to the physical activity level of the lesson. (Assessment opportunity: structured observation 4.1)

Figure 16.14 Backhand *(a)* drive and *(b)* grip.

DAY 6

Have students perform a warm-up along with a cardiorespiratory workout. (Assessment opportunity: structured observation 4.1)

Review the ready position, backhand grip, and backhand drive. (Assessment opportunity: structured observation 1.0, 5.1, 5.2, 6.3)

Have students, in pairs, practice dropping the ball and executing the backhand drive. (Assessment opportunity: structured observation 1.0, 5.1, 5.2, 6.3)

Lead students through a cool-down and flexibility exercises appropriate to the physical activity level of the lesson. (Assessment opportunity: structured observation 4.1)

DAY 7

Explain effective types of practice using SimAthlete. 2.1

Have students record the explanation in their notebooks. 2.1

Have students perform a warm-up along with muscular strength and muscular endurance exercises. (Assessment opportunity: structured observation 4.1)

Demonstrate and describe the footwork necessary to move to the ball to execute a backhand drive using the Racket Sports CD. 1.0, 2.5

Have students demonstrate the necessary footwork as you model it. (Assessment opportunity: structured observation 1.0, 5.1, 5.2, 6.3)

Have students, in pairs, practice dropping the ball and executing the backhand drive. (Assessment opportunity: structured observation 1.0, 5.1, 5.2, 6.3)

Have pairs who are ready practice tossing the ball to each other and executing the backhand drive. (Assessment opportunity: structured observation 1.0, 5.1, 5.2, 6.3)

Have pairs who are ready begin hitting back and forth to each other with backhand drives. (Assessment opportunity: structured observation 1.0, 5.1, 5.2, 6.3)

Have pairs who are ready hit the ball back and forth with backhand drives, counting the number of hits they can make without missing. (Assessment opportunity: structured observation 1.0, 5.1, 5.2, 6.3)

Lead students through a cool-down and flexibility exercises appropriate to the physical activity level of the lesson. (Assessment opportunity: structured observation 4.1)

DAY 8

Have students perform a warm-up along with a cardiorespiratory workout. (Assessment opportunity: structured observation 4.1)

Demonstrate and describe the serve (see figure 16.15) using the Racket Sports CD. 1.0, 2.5

Have students, in pairs, practice the serve. (Assessment opportunity: structured observation 1.0, 5.1, 5.2, 6.3)

Lead students through a cool-down and flexibility exercises appropriate to the physical activity level of the lesson. (Assessment opportunity: structured observation 4.1)

Have students discuss the effective types of practice for tennis. 2.1

DAY 9

Explain the relationship between point of application and spin. 2.2

Have students record the explanation in their notebooks. 2.2

Have students perform a warm-up along with muscular strength and muscular endurance exercises. (Assessment opportunity: structured observation 4.1)

Have students, in pairs, practice the serve. (Assessment opportunity: structured observation 1.0, 5.1, 5.2, 6.3)

Have pairs practice the serve while applying topspin, backspin, and sidespin while observing the results. (Assessment opportunity: structured observation 1.0, 5.1, 5.2, 6.3)

Lead students through a cool-down and flexibility exercises appropriate to the physical activity level of the lesson. (Assessment opportunity: structured observation 4.1)

(continued)

Figure 16.15   Tennis serve.

Unit 4 Outline   *(continued)*

DAY 10

Have students perform a warm-up along with a cardiorespiratory workout. (Assessment opportunity: structured observation 4.1)

Teach modified tennis rules. 2.3

Have pairs of students play modified tennis sports. (Assessment opportunity: structured observation 1.0, 5.1, 5.2, 6.3)

Lead students through a cool-down and flexibility exercises appropriate to the physical activity level of the lesson. (Assessment opportunity: structured observation 4.1)

Review the relationship between the point of application and spin. 2.2

DAY 11

Have students perform a warm-up along with a cardiorespiratory workout. (Assessment opportunity: structured observation 4.1)

Demonstrate and describe the volley using the Racket Sports CD 1.0, 2.5

Have students, in pairs, practice tossing the ball and executing a volley. (Assessment opportunity: structured observation 1.0, 5.1, 5.2, 6.3)

Lead students through a cool-down and flexibility exercises appropriate to the physical activity level of the lesson. (Assessment opportunity: structured observation 4.1)

DAY 12

Have students perform a warm-up along with muscular strength and muscular endurance exercises. (Assessment opportunity: structured observation 4.1)

Review the volley. 1.0, 2.5

Have pairs practice tossing the ball and executing the volley. (Assessment opportunity: structured observation 1.0, 5.1, 5.2, 6.3)

Have pairs who are ready practice tossing the ball to each other and executing the volley. (Assessment opportunity: structured observation 1.0, 5.1, 5.2, 6.3)

Lead students through a cool-down and flexibility exercises appropriate to the physical activity level of the lesson. (Assessment opportunity: structured observation 4.1)

DAY 13

Explain offensive and defensive strategies for tennis. 2.3

Have students record in their notebooks offensive and defensive strategies for tennis. 2.3

Have students perform a warm-up along with a cardiorespiratory workout. (Assessment opportunity: structured observation 4.1)

Have students, in pairs, play modified tennis. (Assessment opportunity: structured observation 1.0, 5.1, 5.2, 6.3) 2.3

Lead students through a cool-down and flexibility exercises appropriate to the physical activity level of the lesson. (Assessment opportunity: structured observation 4.1)

Have students, in pairs, discuss problem-solving techniques regarding strategic situations that occur during games. 2.3, 5.1

DAY 14

Introduce students to the concept of using stations to practice tennis skills.

Have students perform a warm-up along with muscular strength and muscular endurance exercises. (Assessment opportunity: structured observation 4.1)

Have students participate in the following tennis stations: volley practice, modified tennis game, serving practice, modified tennis game, backhand drive practice, modified tennis game, forehand drive practice, and modified tennis game (Assessment opportunity: structured observation 1.0, 5.1, 5.2, 6.3)

Lead students through a cool-down and flexibility exercises appropriate to the physical activity level of the lesson. (Assessment opportunity: structured observation 4.1)

DAY 15

Have students perform a warm-up along with a cardiorespiratory workout. (Assessment opportunity: structured observation 4.1)

Have students participate in the following tennis stations: volley practice, modified tennis game, serving practice, modified tennis game, backhand drive practice, modified tennis game, forehand drive practice, modified tennis game. (Assessment opportunity: structured observation 1.0, 5.1, 5.2, 6.3)

Lead students through a cool-down and flexibility exercises appropriate to the physical activity level of the lesson. (Assessment opportunity: structured observation 4.1)

DAY 16

Have students perform a warm-up along with a cardiorespiratory workout. (Assessment opportunity: structured observation 4.1)

Have students participate in the following tennis stations: volley practice, modified tennis game, serving practice, modified tennis game, backhand drive practice, modified tennis game, forehand drive practice, and modified tennis game. (Assessment opportunity: structured observation 1.0, 5.1, 5.2, 6.3)

Lead students through a cool-down and flexibility exercises appropriate to the physical activity level of the lesson. (Assessment opportunity: structured observation 4.1)

(continued)

Unit 4 Outline   *(continued)*

DAY 17	Have students perform a warm-up along with muscular strength and muscular endurance exercises. (Assessment opportunity: structured observation 4.1)
	Have students participate in the following tennis stations: volley practice, modified tennis game, serving practice, modified tennis game, backhand drive practice, modified tennis game, forehand drive practice, and modified tennis game. (Assessment opportunity: structured observation 1.0, 5.1, 5.2, 6.3)
	Lead students through a cool-down and flexibility exercises appropriate to the physical activity level of the lesson. (Assessment opportunity: structured observation 4.1)
DAY 18	Have students perform a warm-up along with a cardiorespiratory workout. (Assessment opportunity: structured observation 4.1)
	Have students play modified tennis. (Assessment opportunity: structured observation 1.0, 5.1, 5.2, 6.3)
	Lead students through a cool-down and flexibility exercises appropriate to the physical activity level of the lesson. (Assessment opportunity: structured observation 4.1)
DAY 19	Have students perform a warm-up along with muscular strength, muscular endurance exercises. (Assessment opportunity: structured observation 4.1)
	Have students play modified tennis. (Assessment opportunity: structured observation 1.0, 5.1, 5.2, 6.3)
	Lead students through a cool-down and flexibility exercises appropriate to the physical activity level of the lesson. (Assessment opportunity: structured observation 4.1)
	Review material for tomorrow's quiz (or hand out quiz if you would like for it to be a take home quiz). 2.1, 2.2, 2.3, 2.4, 2.5, 6.4
DAY 20	Have students take the quiz. (Assessment opportunity: quiz 2.1, 2.2, 2.3, 2.4, 2.5, 6.4)
	Collect student activity logs. (Assessment opportunity: log 3.1)
	Collect reports on ball games during medieval times. (Assessment opportunity: report 6.1)
	Collect essays regarding opportunities in the larger community for participation in tennis. (Assessment opportunity: essay 3.2)
	Collect 1-week body composition plans. (Assessment opportunity: project 4.2)

Aquatics   — Unit 5

This unit continues our focus on taking appropriate risks by having students challenge themselves in a water setting. Because this unit is directly related to student safety, it is one of the most important units that physical education can offer. Most of my students are beginning swimmers, although a few have more advanced skills. Before I allow my students in the water, they must pass a water safety test in their native language to demonstrate that they understand the safety principles associated with swimming.

I have organized the swimming skills into three levels (beginning, intermediate, and advanced). Students are tested at the beginning of the unit to determine the level at which they will start. Then students work through the skills in their level, attempting new skills only after demonstrating proficiency on prerequisite skills.

Naturally, this unit requires a swimming pool or other aquatic facility. If a pool is unavailable, you can still teach water safety concepts to your students; however, this approach makes for a much shorter unit. *Longfellow's Whales Tales* (video and workbook), available from the American Red Cross, provides you with the instructional materials you need to put together a no-water aquatics unit.

Unit 5 Standards

1.0—Demonstrates the mature form for the survival float, prone glide with flutter kick, beginning crawl with breathing, back glide with sculling, back glide with kick, reverse directions, jump into deep water, tread water with scissor kick, and feet-first surface dive.

2.1—Explains the process of setting appropriate goals, conducting appropriate practice, and monitoring changes in the development of aquatic skills.

2.2—Explains how force can be used to make the body rotate when performing a turn in swimming.

2.3—Creates a new aquatics game that uses a manipulative device.

2.4—Explains individual differences and how these differences affect aquatic performance.

2.5—Explains the critical elements of the survival float, prone glide with flutter kick, beginning crawl with breathing, back glide with sculling, back glide with kick, reverse directions, jump into deep water, tread water with scissor kick, and feet-first surface dive.

3.1—Engages in moderate and vigorous physical activity for 60 minutes 6 days each week.

3.2—Describes opportunities in the larger community for participation in aquatic activities.

4.1—Works toward a health-enhancing level of physical fitness.

4.2—Creates a 1-week cardiorespiratory plan.

5.1—Applies problem-solving techniques when working with another person in aquatic activities.

5.2—Accepts responsibility for individual improvement during aquatic activities.

6.1—Describes swimming activities during medieval times.

6.2—Not applicable.

6.3—Chooses to engage in aquatic activities at the appropriate level of personal challenge.

6.4—Describes the social benefits of regular participation in aquatic activities.

Unit 5 Assessments

1.0—Structured observation (days 4-16)

2.1—Quiz (day 20)

2.2—Quiz (day 20)

2.3—Project (assigned on day 17; collected on day 19)

2.4—Quiz (day 20)

2.5—Quiz (day 20)

3.1—Log (assigned on day 1; collected on day 20)

3.2—Essay (assigned on day 1; collected on day 20)

4.1—Structured observation (days 2-19)

4.2—Project (assigned on day 2; collected on day 20)

5.1—Structured observation (days 17-19)

5.2—Structure observation (days 4-16)

6.1—Report (assigned on day 1; collected on day 20)

6.2—Not applicable

6.3—Structured observation (days 4-16)

6.4—Quiz (day 20)

Resources

Health-Related Fitness: Tutorial and Portfolio (Bonnie's Fitware, Inc.)

Middle School Physical Education Portfolio (Bonnie's Fitware, Inc.)

Swimming CD (Bonnie's Fitware, Inc.)

Seventh grade swimming task cards (Bonnie's Fitware, Inc.)

SimAthlete (Bonnie's Fitware, Inc.)

Seventh grade unit 5 posters (Bonnie's Fitware, Inc.—included in the Middle School Detailed Lesson Plans)

Fitness posters (Bonnie's Fitware, Inc.—included in the Middle School Detailed Lesson Plans)

Equipment

Swimming pool

Variety of equipment for creating own games

Games

None

Skills

Beginner

- Face in water
- Whole head underwater
- Blowing bubbles
- Jellyfish float
- Prone float
- Jellyfish to prone float
- Back float
- Survival float*
- Prone glide
- Flutter kick
- Prone glide with flutter kick*
- Back glide
- Back glide with kick*
- Back glide with finning
- Back glide with sculling*
- Beginning pull
- Combined stroke on front
- Reverse direction on front
- Breathing on side
- Beginning crawl with breathing* (figure 16.16)
- Jump into deep water*
- Tread water with scissor kick*
- Feet-first surface dive*
- Swim under water

Intermediate

- Prone glide
- Flutter kick
- Prone glide with flutter kick*
- Back glide
- Back glide with kick*
- Back glide with finning
- Back glide with sculling*
- Beginning pull
- Combined stroke on front
- Reverse direction on front
- Breathing on side
- Beginning crawl with breathing* (see figure 16.16)
- Swim under water
- Jump into deep water*
- Tread water with scissor kick*
- Feet-first surface dive*
- Turnover (front-to-back)
- Turnover (back-to-front)
- Kneeling dive
- One-foot dive
- Crawl stroke
- Back crawl (see figure 16.17)
- Standing front dive
- Sidestroke (see figure 16.18)

_____
*Assessed skill.

Figure 16.16 Correct technique for the front crawl.

Figure 16.17 Correct technique for the back crawl.

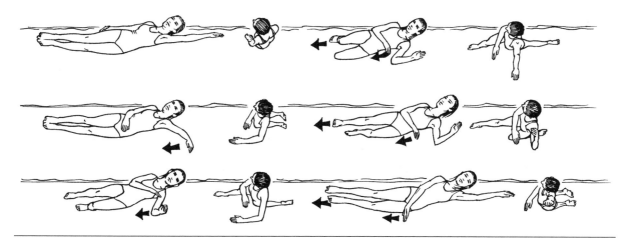

Figure 16.18 Correct technique for the sidestroke.

Unit 5 Outline

DAY 1	Set up posters.
	Introduce the aquatics unit.
	Explain the safety rules for swimming.
	Have students watch the water safety section on the Swimming CD.
	Administer a written water safety test (for liability purposes).
	Assign unit-long homework:
	• Have students research and write about swimming activities during medieval times. (Assessment assignment opportunity: report 6.1)
	• Have students keep a log of daily activity. (Assessment assignment opportunity: log 3.1)
	• Have students describe opportunities in the larger community for participation in aquatic activities. (Assessment assignment opportunity: essay 3.2)
DAY 2	Set up fitness posters.
	Describe the social benefits of participating in swimming. 6.4
	Have students summarize in their notebooks the description of social benefits. 6.4
	Review frequency, intensity, time, and type for cardiorespiratory endurance using the Health-Related Fitness: Tutorial and Portfolio. 4.2
	Have students summarize the information in their notebooks. 4.2
	Assign the creation of a 1-week cardiorespiratory plan. (Assessment assignment opportunity: project 4.2)
	Have students perform a warm-up along with muscular strength and muscular endurance exercises. (Assessment opportunity: structured observation 4.1)
	Have all students get into the water. 1.0
	Have all students submerge their faces in the water. 1.0
	Demonstrate bobbing. 1.0, 2.5
	Have all students practice bobbing. 1.0
	Lead students through a cool-down and flexibility exercises appropriate to the physical activity level of the lesson. (Assessment opportunity: structured observation 4.1)
DAY 3	Discuss the importance of engaging in aquatic activities at the appropriate level of personal challenge. 6.3
	Discuss the importance of accepting responsibility for individual improvement during aquatic activities. 5.2
	Explain individual differences and how these differences affect aquatic performance. 2.4
	Have students record in their notebooks the explanation of individual differences and their impact on aquatic performance. 2.4
	Have students perform a warm-up. (Assessment opportunity: structured observation 4.1)
	Assess students' current skill levels in swimming and assign them to a starting ability group. 1.0
	Lead students through a cool-down and flexibility exercises appropriate to the physical activity level of the lesson. (Assessment opportunity: structured observation 4.1)

DAY 4

Explain the process of setting appropriate goals, conducting appropriate practice, and monitoring changes in the development of aquatic skills. 2.1

Have students record the information in their notebooks. 2.1

Have students set goals for swimming. 2.1

Review appropriate practice using SimAthlete. 2.1

Hand out a skill sheet so that students can monitor their own progress. 2.1

Review the importance of engaging in aquatic activities at the appropriate level of personal challenge. 6.3

Review the importance of accepting responsibility for individual improvement during aquatic activities. 5.2

Have students perform a warm-up along with muscular strength and muscular endurance exercises. (Assessment opportunity: structured observation 4.1)

Demonstrate new skills to each group using the Swimming CD. 1.0, 2.5

- Beginners—jellyfish float
- Intermediate—prone glide and flutter kick

Have students practice swimming skills based on their current ability levels. (Assessment opportunity: structured observation 1.0, 5.2, 6.3)

Work with one group at a time while assigning practice tasks to other groups. Note to students when whole practice is used and when part practice is used. 1.0, 2.1, 2.5

Lead students through a cool-down and flexibility exercises appropriate to the physical activity level of the lesson. (Assessment opportunity: structured observation 4.1)

DAY 5

Explain how force can be used to make the body rotate when performing a turn in swimming. 2.2

Have students perform a warm-up. (Assessment opportunity: structured observation 4.1)

Demonstrate new skills to each group using the Swimming CD. 1.0, 2.5

- Beginner—prone float and jellyfish to prone float
- Intermediate—prone glide with flutter kick

Have students practice swimming skills based on their current ability levels. (Assessment opportunity: structured observation 1.0, 5.2, 6.3)

Work with one group at a time while assigning practice tasks to other groups. Note to students when whole practice is used and when part practice is used. 1.0, 2.1, 2.5

Lead students through a cool-down and flexibility exercises appropriate to the physical activity level of the lesson. (Assessment opportunity: structured observation 4.1)

DAY 6

Have students perform a warm-up. (Assessment opportunity: structured observation 4.1)

Demonstrate new skills to each group using Swimming CD. 1.0, 2.5

- Beginner—back float and survival float
- Intermediate—back glide and back glide with kick

Have students practice swimming skills based on their current ability levels. (Assessment opportunity: structured observation 1.0, 5.2, 6.3)

Work with one group at a time while assigning practice tasks to other groups. Note to students when whole practice is used and when part practice is used. 1.0, 2.1, 2.5

Lead students through a cool-down and flexibility exercises appropriate to the physical activity level of the lesson. (Assessment opportunity: structured observation 4.1)

Review how force can be used to make the body rotate when performing a turn in swimming. 2.2

(continued)

Unit 5 Outline *(continued)*

DAY 7

Have students perform a warm-up along with muscular strength and muscular endurance exercises. (Assessment opportunity: structured observation 4.1)

Demonstrate new skills to each group using Swimming CD. 1.0, 2.5

- Beginner—prone glide
- Intermediate—back glide with kick, back glide with finning, back glide with sculling

Have students practice swimming skills based on their current ability levels. (Assessment opportunity: structured observation 1.0, 5.2, 6.3)

Work with one group at a time while assigning practice tasks to other groups. Note to students when whole practice is used and when part practice is used. 1.0, 2.1, 2.5

Lead students through a cool-down and flexibility exercises appropriate to the physical activity level of the lesson. (Assessment opportunity: structured observation 4.1)

DAY 8

Have students perform a warm-up. (Assessment opportunity: structured observation 4.1)

Demonstrate new skills to each group using Swimming CD. 1.0, 2.5

- Beginner—flutter kick, prone glide with flutter kick
- Intermediate—beginning pull, combined stroke on front

Have students practice swimming skills based on their current ability levels. (Assessment opportunity: structured observation 1.0, 5.2, 6.3)

Work with one group at a time while assigning practice tasks to other groups. Note to students when whole practice is used and when part practice is used. 1.0, 2.1, 2.5

Lead students through a cool-down and flexibility exercises appropriate to the physical activity level of the lesson. (Assessment opportunity: structured observation 4.1)

DAY 9

Have students perform a warm-up along with muscular strength and muscular endurance exercises. (Assessment opportunity: structured observation 4.1)

Demonstrate new skills to each group using Swimming CD. 1.0, 2.5

- Beginner—back glide and back glide with kick
- Intermediate—reverse direction on front, breathing on side

Have students practice swimming skills based on their current ability levels. (Assessment opportunity: structured observation 1.0, 5.2, 6.3)

Work with one group at a time while assigning practice tasks to other groups. Note to students when whole practice is used and when part practice is used. 1.0, 2.1, 2.5

Lead students through a cool-down and flexibility exercises appropriate to the physical activity level of the lesson. (Assessment opportunity: structured observation 4.1)

DAY 10

Have students perform a warm-up. (Assessment opportunity: structured observation 4.1)

Demonstrate new skills to each group using Swimming CD. 1.0, 2.5

- Beginner—back glide with finning, back glide with sculling
- Intermediate—beginning crawl with breathing, swimming under water

Have students practice swimming skills based on their current ability levels. (Assessment opportunity: structured observation 1.0, 5.2, 6.3)

Work with one group at a time while assigning practice tasks to other groups. Note to students when whole practice is used and when part practice is used. 1.0, 2.1, 2.5

Lead students through a cool-down and flexibility exercises appropriate to the physical activity level of the lesson. (Assessment opportunity: structured observation 4.1)

DAY 11

Have students perform a warm-up. (Assessment opportunity: structured observation 4.1)

Demonstrate new skills to each group using Swimming CD. 1.0, 2.5

- Beginner—beginning pull, combined stroke on front
- Intermediate—jump into deep water, tread water with scissor kick (same kick used for side-stroke)

Have students practice swimming skills based on their current ability levels. (Assessment opportunity: structured observation 1.0, 5.2, 6.3)

Work with one group at a time while assigning practice tasks to other groups. Note to students when whole practice is used and when part practice is used. 1.0, 2.1, 2.5

Lead students through a cool-down and flexibility exercises appropriate to the physical activity level of the lesson. (Assessment opportunity: structured observation 4.1)

DAY 12

Have students perform a warm-up. (Assessment opportunity: structured observation 4.1)

Demonstrate new skills to each group using Swimming CD. 1.0, 2.5

- Beginner—reverse on front, breathing on side
- Intermediate—feet-first surface dive, turn front to back

Have students practice swimming skills based on their current ability levels. (Assessment opportunity: structured observation 1.0, 5.2, 6.3)

Work with one group at a time while assigning practice tasks to other groups. Note to students when whole practice is used and when part practice is used. 1.0, 2.1, 2.5

Lead students through a cool-down and flexibility exercises appropriate to the physical activity level of the lesson. (Assessment opportunity: structured observation 4.1)

DAY 13

Have students perform a warm-up. (Assessment opportunity: structured observation 4.1)

Demonstrate new skills to each group using Swimming CD. 1.0, 2.5

- Beginner—beginning crawl with breathing
- Intermediate—turn back to front, kneeling dive, one-foot dive

Have students practice swimming skills based on their current ability levels. (Assessment opportunity: structured observation 1.0, 5.2, 6.3)

Work with one group at a time while assigning practice tasks to other groups. Note to students when whole practice is used and when part practice is used. 1.0, 2.1, 2.5

Lead students through a cool-down and flexibility exercises appropriate to the physical activity level of the lesson. (Assessment opportunity: structured observation 4.1)

DAY 14

Have students perform a warm-up along with muscular strength and muscular endurance exercises. (Assessment opportunity: structured observation 4.1)

Demonstrate new skills to each group using Swimming CD. 1.0, 2.5

- Beginner—jump into deep water, tread water with scissor kick
- Intermediate—crawl stroke, one-foot dive

Have students practice swimming skills based on their current ability levels. (Assessment opportunity: structured observation 1.0, 5.2, 6.3)

Work with one group at a time while assigning practice tasks to other groups. Note to students when whole practice is used and when part practice is used. 1.0, 2.1, 2.5

Lead students through a cool-down and flexibility exercises appropriate to the physical activity level of the lesson. (Assessment opportunity: structured observation 4.1)

(continued)

Unit 5 Outline *(continued)*

DAY 15	Have students perform a warm-up. (Assessment opportunity: structured observation 4.1) Demonstrate new skills to each group using Swimming CD. 1.0, 2.5 • Beginner—feet-first surface dive, swimming underwater • Intermediate—back crawl, front dive Have students practice swimming skills based on their current ability levels. (Assessment opportunity: structured observation 1.0, 5.2, 6.3) Work with one group at a time while assigning practice tasks to other groups. Note to students when whole practice is used and when part practice is used. 1.0, 2.1, 2.5 Lead students through a cool-down and flexibility exercises appropriate to the physical activity level of the lesson. (Assessment opportunity: structured observation 4.1)
DAY 16	Have students perform a warm-up. (Assessment opportunity: structured observation 4.1) Demonstrate new skills to each group using Swimming CD. 1.0, 2.5 • Beginner—continue with the same skill • Intermediate—sidestroke Have students practice swimming skills based on their current ability levels. (Assessment opportunity: structured observation 1.0, 5.2, 6.3) Work with one group at a time while assigning practice tasks to other groups. Note to students when whole practice is used and when part practice is used. 1.0, 2.1, 2.5 Lead students through a cool-down and flexibility exercises appropriate to the physical activity level of the lesson. (Assessment opportunity: structured observation 4.1)
DAY 17	Have students perform a warm-up along with muscular strength and muscular endurance exercises. (Assessment opportunity: structured observation 4.1) Have students, in groups, continue with skill practice. 1.0 Discuss how to use problem-solving techniques in a small group. 5.1 Review components of a game. 2.3 Have students, in small groups, use problem-solving techniques to create an aquatic game with scoring options. (Assessment assignment opportunity: project 2.3) Have students, in small groups, work on their aquatic game with scoring options. (Assessment opportunity: structured observation 5.1) 2.3 Lead students through a cool-down and flexibility exercises appropriate to the physical activity level of the lesson. (Assessment opportunity: structured observation 4.1)
DAY 18	Review how to use problem-solving techniques in a small group. 5.1 Review components of a game. 2.3 Have students perform a warm-up. (Assessment opportunity: structured observation 4.1) Have students, in small groups, continue with skill practice. 1.0 Have students, in small groups, work on their aquatic game with scoring options. (Assessment opportunity: structured observation 5.1) 2.3 Lead students through a cool-down and flexibility exercises appropriate to the physical activity level of the lesson. (Assessment opportunity: structured observation 4.1)

DAY 19

Have students perform a warm-up along with muscular strength and muscular endurance exercises. (Assessment opportunity: structured observation 4.1)

Have students, in small groups, continue with skill practice. 1.0

Have groups teach their aquatic game to another group and then allow the groups to play each other's games (Assessment opportunity: project 2.3, structured observation 5.1).

Review material for tomorrow's quiz (or hand out quiz if you would like for it to be a take home quiz). 2.1, 2.2, 2.4, 2.5, 6.4

Lead students through a cool-down and flexibility exercises appropriate to the physical activity level of the lesson. (Assessment opportunity: structured observation 4.1)

DAY 20

Have students take the quiz. (Assessment opportunity: quiz 2.1, 2.2, 2.4, 2.5, 6.4)

Collect student activity logs. (Assessment opportunity: log 3.1)

Collect reports on swimming during medieval times. (Assessment opportunity: report 6.1)

Collect essays describing opportunities in the larger community for participation in aquatics. (Assessment opportunity: essay 3.2)

Collect 1-week cardiorespiratory endurance plans based on personal preferences. (Assessment opportunity: project 4.2)

Target Sport: Golf
~ Unit 6 ~

This unit continues our focus on taking appropriate risks by having students challenge themselves in an activity that very few of them have ever tried: golf. I teach golf and tennis to students not only to challenge them but also to introduce them to two lifetime sports. Most students at my school are not introduced to these activities in a community or park setting; however, golf and tennis are the types of sports that adults are more likely to play as they get older.

As you might expect, this unit requires a grass facility or at least carpet squares to hit off of. In addition, you'll need golf clubs (irons and putters), golf balls, and cones. If you do not have access to golf equipment, contact your local driving range or golf association. These organizations often have surplus equipment to donate to schools. The type of ball you use will depend on the amount of space you have available for the golf unit. You can use regular golf balls, Wiffle golf balls, or special golf balls for limited spaces.

Unit 6 Standards

1.0—Demonstrates the mature form for the iron and putter strokes.

2.1—Explains the process of setting appropriate goals, conducting appropriate practice, and monitoring changes in the development of golf skills.

2.2—Explains how force causes a golf ball to spin.

2.3—Explains offensive strategies for golf.

2.4—Explains individual differences and how these differences impact golf performance.

2.5—Explains the critical elements of iron and putter strokes.

3.1—Engages in moderate and vigorous physical activity for 60 minutes 6 days each week.

3.2—Describes opportunities in the larger community for participation in golf activities.

4.1—Works toward a health-enhancing level of physical fitness.

4.2—Creates a 1-week muscular endurance plan.

5.1—Applies problem-solving techniques when working with another person in golf activities.

5.2—Accepts responsibility for individual improvement during golf activities.

6.1—Describes golf during medieval times and the Renaissance.

6.2—Not applicable.

6.3—Chooses to engage in golf activities at the appropriate level of personal challenge.

6.4—Describes the social benefits of regular participation in golf.

Unit 6 Assessments

1.0—Structured observation (days 1-18)

2.1—Quiz (day 20)

2.2—Quiz (day 20)

2.3—Quiz (day 20)

2.4—Quiz (day 20)

2.5—Quiz (day 20)

3.1—Log (assigned on day 1 and collected on day 20)

3.2—Essay (assigned on day 1; collected on day 20)

4.1—Structured observation (days 1-18)

4.2—Project (assigned on day 3; collected on day 20)

5.1—Structured observation (day 19)

5.2—Structure observation (days 1-18)

6.1—Report (assigned on day 1; collected on day 20)

6.2—Not applicable

6.3—Structured observation (days 1-18)

6.4—Quiz (day 20)

Resources

Health-Related Fitness: Tutorial and Portfolio (Bonnie's Fitware, Inc.)

Middle School Physical Education Portfolio (Bonnie's Fitware, Inc.)

Target Sports CD (Bonnie's Fitware, Inc.)

Seventh grade golf task cards (Bonnie's Fitware, Inc.)

SimAthlete (Bonnie's Fitware, Inc.)

Seventh grade unit 6 posters (Bonnie's Fitware, Inc.—included in the Middle School Detailed Lesson Plans)

Fitness posters (Bonnie's Fitware, Inc.—included in the Middle School Detailed Lesson Plans)

Equipment

Iron clubs

Putters

Golf balls

Tees

Targets

Games

Miniature golf

Simulated golf

Unit 6 Outline

DAY 1	Set up posters.
	Introduce golf unit, safety, and equipment.
	Assign students to working groups of four.
	Describe the importance of engaging in golf activities at the appropriate level of personal challenge. 6.3
	Describe the importance of accepting responsibility for individual improvement during golf activities. 5.2
	Demonstrate and describe the golf grip (see figure 16.19*b)* on the Target Sports CD. 1.0, 2.5
	Check each student's golf grip. (Assessment opportunity: structured observation 1.0, 5.2, 6.3)
	Demonstrate and describe the golf stance and address on the Target Sports CD. 1.0, 2.5
	Check each student's stance and address. (Assessment opportunity: structured observation 1.0, 5.2, 6.3)
	Demonstrate and describe the swing (see figure 16.19*a)* using the Target Sports CD. 1.0, 2.5
	Check each student's swing. (Assessment opportunity: structured observation 1.0, 5.2, 6.3)
	Lead students through a cool-down and flexibility exercises appropriate to the physical activity level of the lesson. (Assessment opportunity: structured observation 4.1)
	Assign unit-long homework:
	• Have students research and write a description of golf during medieval times and the Renaissance. (Assessment assignment opportunity: report 6.1)
	• Have students keep a log of daily activity. (Assessment assignment opportunity: log 3.1).
	• Have students write a description of golf activities in the larger community. (Assessment assignment opportunity: essay 3.2)
DAY 2	Explain the process of setting appropriate goals, conducting appropriate practice, and monitoring changes in the development of golf skills. 2.1
	Have students set goals for the golf unit. 2.1
	Review appropriate practice using SimAthlete. 2.1
	Remind students to monitor changes in their own development of golf skills. 2.1
	Have students perform a warm-up along with muscular strength and muscular endurance exercises. (Assessment opportunity: structured observation 4.1)
	Review student grip, stance, and address. 1.0, 2.5
	Have students practice the grip, stance, and address. (Assessment opportunity: structured observation 1.0, 5.2, 6.3)
	Demonstrate and describe the golf swing using the Target Sports CD. 1.0, 2.5
	Have students practice the golf swing. (Assessment opportunity: structured observation 1.0, 5.2, 6.3)
	Lead students through a cool-down and flexibility exercises appropriate to the physical activity level of the lesson. (Assessment opportunity: structured observation 4.1)
DAY 3	Set up fitness posters.
	Describe the social benefits of participating in golf. 6.4
	Have students record the information in their notebooks. 6.4
	Have students look at the Muscular Endurance section of the Health-Related Fitness program. 4.2

(continued)

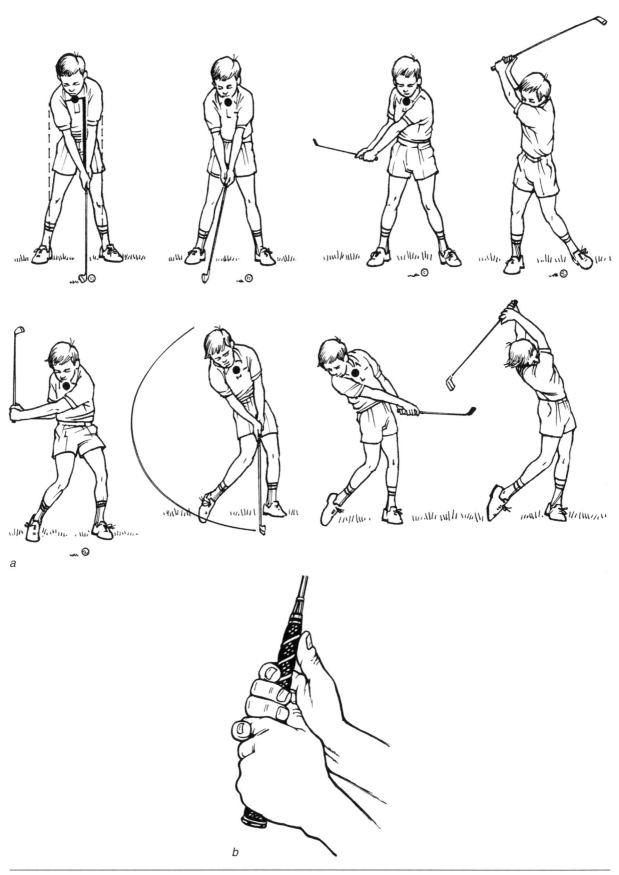

Figure 16.19 Golf *(a)* swing and *(b)* grip.

Unit 6 Outline *(continued)*

DAY 3 *(continued)*	Have students record in their notebooks the concepts of frequency, intensity, time, and type as they relate to muscular endurance. 4.2
	Have students create a 1-week muscular endurance plan. (Assessment assignment opportunity: project 4.2)
	Have students perform a warm-up along with a cardiorespiratory workout. (Assessment opportunity: structured observation 4.1)
	Review grip, stance, address, and swing. 1.0, 2.5
	Have students practice the iron stroke. (Assessment opportunity: structured observation 1.0, 5.2, 6.3)
	Lead students through a cool-down and flexibility exercises appropriate to the physical activity level of the lesson. (Assessment opportunity: structured observation 4.1)
DAY 4	Explain how force causes a golf ball to spin. 2.2
	Have students perform a warm-up along with muscular strength and muscular endurance exercises. (Assessment opportunity: structured observation 4.1)
	Review grip, stance, address, and swing. 1.0
	Have students practice the iron stroke. (Assessment opportunity: structured observation 1.0, 5.2, 6.3)
	Lead students through a cool-down and flexibility exercises appropriate to the physical activity level of the lesson. (Assessment opportunity: structured observation 4.1)
DAY 5	Explain individual differences and how these differences generally affect golf performance. 2.4
	Have students record the explanation in their notebooks. 2.4
	Have students perform a warm-up along with a cardiorespiratory workout. (Assessment opportunity: structured observation 4.1)
	Demonstrate and describe the pitching stroke using the Target Sports CD. 1.0, 2.5
	Have students practice the pitching stroke. (Assessment opportunity: structured observation 1.0, 5.2, 6.3)
	Lead students through a cool-down and flexibility exercises appropriate to the physical activity level of the lesson. (Assessment opportunity: structured observation 4.1)
	Have students discuss individual differences and their impact on the golf stroke practiced today. 2.4
DAY 6	Have students perform a warm-up along with a cardiorespiratory workout. (Assessment opportunity: structured observation 4.1)
	Review the pitching stroke. 1.0, 2.5
	Have students practice the pitching stroke. (Assessment opportunity: structured observation 1.0, 5.2, 6.3)
	Lead students through a cool-down and flexibility exercises appropriate to the physical activity level of the lesson. (Assessment opportunity: structured observation 4.1)
	Review how force causes a golf ball to spin. 2.2
DAY 7	Have students perform a warm-up along with muscular strength and muscular endurance exercises. (Assessment opportunity: structured observation 4.1)
	Demonstrate and describe the chipping stroke using the Target Sports CD. 1.0, 2.5
	Have students practice the chipping stroke. (Assessment opportunity: structured observation 1.0, 5.2, 6.3)
	Lead students through a cool-down and flexibility exercises appropriate to the physical activity level of the lesson. (Assessment opportunity: structured observation 4.1)
	Have students discuss individual differences and their impact on the golf stroke practiced today. 2.4

(continued)

Unit 6 Outline (continued)

DAY 8

Have students perform a warm-up along with a cardiorespiratory workout. (Assessment opportunity: structured observation 4.1)

Review the chipping stroke. 1.0, 2.5

Have students practice the chipping stroke. (Assessment opportunity: structured observation 1.0, 5.2, 6.3)

Lead students through a cool-down and flexibility exercises appropriate to the physical activity level of the lesson. (Assessment opportunity: structured observation 4.1)

Review how force causes a golf ball to spin. 2.2

DAY 9

Have students perform a warm-up along with muscular strength and muscular endurance exercises. (Assessment opportunity: structured observation 4.1)

Review pitching and chipping. 1.0, 2.5

Have students practice pitching and chipping. (Assessment opportunity: structured observation 1.0, 5.2, 6.3)

Lead students through a cool-down and flexibility exercises appropriate to the physical activity level of the lesson. (Assessment opportunity: structured observation 4.1)

DAY 10

Have students perform a warm-up along with a cardiorespiratory workout. (Assessment opportunity: structured observation 4.1)

Review pitching and chipping. 1.0, 2.5

Have students practice pitching and chipping. (Assessment opportunity: structured observation 1.0, 5.2, 6.3)

Lead students through a cool-down and flexibility exercises appropriate to the physical activity level of the lesson. (Assessment opportunity: structured observation 4.1)

Have students discuss the differences between pitching and chipping. 1.0, 2.5

DAY 11

Have students perform a warm-up along with a cardiorespiratory workout. (Assessment opportunity: structured observation 4.1)

Demonstrate and describe the putting stroke (see figure 16.21) using the Target Sports CD. 1.0, 2.5

Have students practice the putting stroke. (Assessment opportunity: structured observation 1.0, 5.2, 6.3)

Lead students through a cool-down and flexibility exercises appropriate to the physical activity level of the lesson. (Assessment opportunity: structured observation 4.1)

Have students discuss individual differences and their impact on the golf stroke practiced today. 2.4

DAY 12

Have students perform a warm-up along with muscular strength and muscular endurance exercises. (Assessment opportunity: structured observation 4.1)

Review the putting stroke (see figure 16.20). 1.0, 2.5

Have students practice the putting stroke. (Assessment opportunity: structured observation 1.0, 5.2, 6.3)

Explain miniature golf. 2.3

Have students play miniature golf. (Assessment opportunity: structured observation 1.0, 5.2, 6.3)

Lead students through a cool-down and flexibility exercises appropriate to the physical activity level of the lesson. (Assessment opportunity: structured observation 4.1)

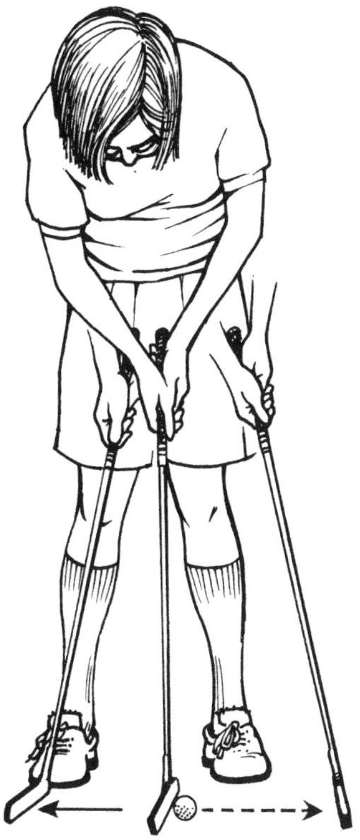

Figure 16.20 Putting stroke.

DAY 13	Have students perform a warm-up along with a cardiorespiratory workout. (Assessment opportunity: structured observation 4.1)
	Explain the golf stations to students.
	Have students rotate through the stations, aiming at targets to practice their strokes: iron swing, putting, chipping, and pitching. (Assessment opportunity: structured observation 1.0, 5.2, 6.3)
	Lead students through a cool-down and flexibility exercises appropriate to the physical activity level of the lesson. (Assessment opportunity: structured observation 4.1)
DAY 14	Have students perform a warm-up along with muscular strength and muscular endurance exercises. (Assessment opportunity: structured observation 4.1)
	Have students rotate through the stations, aiming at targets to practice their strokes: iron swing, putting, chipping, and pitching. (Assessment opportunity: structured observation 1.0, 5.2, 6.3)
	Lead students through a cool-down and flexibility exercises appropriate to the physical activity level of the lesson. (Assessment opportunity: structured observation 4.1)
DAY 15	Have students perform a warm-up along with a cardiorespiratory workout. (Assessment opportunity: structured observation 4.1)
	Have students rotate through the stations, aiming at targets to practice their strokes: iron swing, putting, chipping, and pitching. (Assessment opportunity: structured observation 1.0, 5.2, 6.3)
	Lead students through a cool-down and flexibility exercises appropriate to the physical activity level of the lesson. (Assessment opportunity: structured observation 4.1)

(continued)

Unit 6 Outline *(continued)*

DAY 16

Have students perform a warm-up along with a cardiorespiratory workout. (Assessment opportunity: structured observation 4.1)

Have students rotate through the stations, aiming at targets to practice their strokes: iron swing, putting, chipping, and pitching. (Assessment opportunity: structured observation 1.0, 5.2, 6.3)

Lead students through a cool-down and flexibility exercises appropriate to the physical activity level of the lesson. (Assessment opportunity: structured observation 4.1)

DAY 17

Teach the rules of golf as well as how to be courteous when playing golf. 1.0

Introduce golf strategies. 2.3

Have students perform a warm-up along with muscular strength and muscular endurance exercises. (Assessment opportunity: structured observation 4.1)

Have students play on a simulated golf course. (Assessment opportunity: structured observation 1.0, 5.2, 6.3)

Lead students through a cool-down and flexibility exercises appropriate to the physical activity level of the lesson. (Assessment opportunity: structured observation 4.1)

DAY 18

Have students perform a warm-up along with a cardiorespiratory workout. (Assessment opportunity: structured observation 4.1)

Review the rules of golf as well as how to be courteous when playing golf. 1.0

Discuss golf strategy. 2.3

Have students play on a simulated golf course. (Assessment opportunity: structured observation 1.0, 5.2, 6.3)

Lead students through a cool-down and flexibility exercises appropriate to the physical activity level of the lesson. (Assessment opportunity: structured observation 4.1)

DAY 19

Discuss solving problems using the problem-solving process. 5.1

Have students record the problem-solving process in their notebooks. 5.1

Review golf strategy. 2.3

Have students analyze different holes using the problem-solving process. (Assessment opportunity: structured observation 5.1)

Review material for tomorrow's quiz (or hand out quiz if you would like for it to be a take home quiz). 2.1, 2.2, 2.3, 2.4, 2.5, 6.4

DAY 20

Have students take a quiz. (Assessment opportunity: quiz 2.1, 2.2, 2.3, 2.4, 2.5, 6.4)

Collect student activity logs. (Assessment opportunity: log 3.1)

Collect reports on the description of golf during medieval times and the Renaissance. (Assessment opportunity: report 6.1)

Collect muscular endurance plans. (Assessment opportunity: project 4.2)

Collect descriptions of golf activities in the larger community. (Assessment opportunity: essay 3.2)

Self-Defense   – Unit 7

This unit continues our focus on challenge by challenging students in the area of self-defense. Like outdoor education, this area is especially important because it is directly related to student safety in our increasingly violent society. Be careful, however, to emphasize defense—not fighting. I start the unit by teaching students to be more aware of potentially unsafe situations and how to avoid them. Discussing survival skills, such as staying alert, walking assertively with purse or bag under an arm and keys in hand, staying in lighted areas, staying away from suspicious-looking strangers, installing dead bolts, and not hitchhiking, sets the tone for the unit. Then, and only then, do I instruct students on how to protect themselves if they are attacked.

You can teach this unit in any open area; however, I prefer to teach it inside. In addition, combatives (bags) allow students the opportunity to kick and hit full force without hurting someone else. Some teachers also like to use foam "heads" on PVC pipe, football equipment, soccer shin guards, or bleach bottles with faces painted on them as additional targets. Finally, I often bring in a guest speaker for this unit, usually someone connected with a law enforcement agency. I have the guest either assist with the demonstrations or teach additional information on self-defense.

Unit 7 Standards

1.0—Demonstrates the mature form for stance, stomp, knee kick, front snap kick, side kick, rear kick, elbow strike, palm–heel strike, side fall, wrist release, front choke release, rear choke release, and hair release.

2.1—Explains the process of setting appropriate goals, conducting appropriate practice, and monitoring changes in the development of self-defense skills.

2.2—Explains how magnitude affects spin and rotation of the body or an object.

2.3—Explains the use of strategy in self-defense.

2.4—Explains individual differences and how these differences affect self-defense performance.

2.5—Explains the critical elements of stance, stomp, knee kick, front snap kick, side kick, rear kick, elbow strike, palm–heel strike, side fall, wrist release, front choke release, rear choke release, and hair release.

3.1—Engages in moderate and vigorous physical activity for 60 minutes 6 days each week.

3.2—Describes opportunities in the larger community for participation in self-defense activities.

4.1—Works toward a health-enhancing level of physical fitness.

4.2—Creates a 1-week muscular strength plan.

5.1—Applies problem-solving techniques when working with another person in self-defense activities.

5.2—Accepts responsibility for individual improvement during self-defense activities.

6.1—Describes combative activities during medieval times.

6.2—Not applicable.

6.3—Chooses to engage in self-defense activities at the appropriate level of personal challenge.

6.4—Describes the social benefits of regular participation in self-defense.

Unit 7 Assessments

1.0—Structured observation (days 4-24)

2.1—Quiz (day 25)

2.2—Quiz (day 25)

2.3—Quiz (day 25)

2.4—Quiz (day 25)

2.5—Report (assigned on day 1; collected on day 25)

3.1—Log (assigned on day 1; collected on day 25)

3.2—Essay (assigned on day 1; collected on day 25)

4.1—Structured observation (days 3-24)

4.2—Project (assigned on day 2; collected on day 25)

5.1—Structured observation (days 2-24)

5.2—Structure observation (days 1-24)

6.1—Report (assigned on day 1; collected on day 25)

6.2—Not applicable

6.3—Structured observation (days 1-24)

6.4—Quiz (day 25)

Resources

Self-Defense CD (Bonnie's Fitware, Inc.)

Health-Related Fitness: Tutorial and Portfolio (Bonnie's Fitware, Inc.)

Middle School Physical Education Portfolio (Bonnie's Fitware, Inc.)

Seventh grade self-defense task cards (Bonnie's Fitware, Inc.)

SimAthlete (Bonnie's Fitware, Inc.)

Seventh grade unit 7 posters (Bonnie's Fitware, Inc.—included in the Middle School Detailed Lesson Plans)

Fitness posters (Bonnie's Fitware, Inc.—included in the Middle School Detailed Lesson Plans)

Equipment

Combatives

Games

None

Unit 7 Outline

DAY 1

Display the posters.

Introduce self-defense and its safety rules.

Assign students to groups of four.

Explain the importance of engaging in self-defense activities at the appropriate level of personal challenge. 6.3

Explain the importance of accepting responsibility for individual improvement during self-defense activities. 5.2

Discuss ways to eliminate danger in daily lives. 2.3

Have students record in their notebooks ways to eliminate danger in their daily lives. (Assessment opportunity: structured observation 5.2, 6.3) 2.3

Introduce personal weapons (voice, elbows and hands, legs and feet, fingers and thumbs, and knees—see figure 16.21a). 2.3

Have students draw a picture in their notebooks and label personal weapons. (Assessment opportunity: structured observation 5.2, 6.3) 2.3

Introduce vulnerable areas (knees and shins, nose, groin, eyes, throat or neck, and ears—see figure 16.21b). 2.3

Have students draw a picture in their notebooks and label vulnerable areas. (Assessment opportunity: structured observation 5.2, 6.3) 2.3

Assign unit-long homework:

- Have students research and describe combative activities during medieval times and the Renaissance. (Assessment assignment opportunity: report 6.1)

- Have students keep a log of daily activity. (Assessment assignment opportunity: log 3.1)

- Have students describe the opportunities in the larger community for participation in self-defense activities. (Assessment assignment opportunity: essay 3.2)

- Have students record the critical features for each skill introduced and present it to the teacher as a report. (Assessment assignment opportunity: report 2.5)

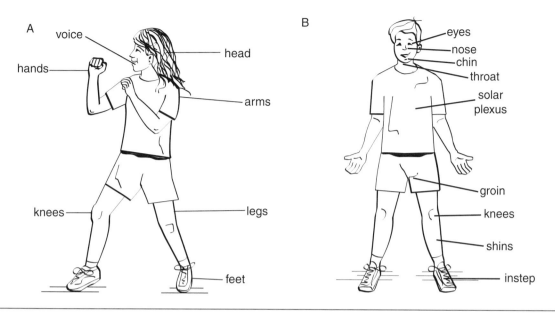

Figure 16.21 *(a)* Personal weapons and *(b)* vulnerable areas.

DAY 2	Display fitness posters.
	Describes the social benefits of regular participation in self-defense. 6.4
	Have students summarize the benefits in their notebooks. 6.4
	Review frequency, intensity, time, and type (FITT) concepts for muscular strength using the Health-Related Fitness: Tutorial and Portfolio. 4.2
	Have students record in their notebooks the FITT concepts for muscular strength. 4.2
	Assign students the creation of a 1-week muscular strength plan. (Assessment assignment opportunity: project 4.2)
	Review ways to reduce danger. 2.3
	Discuss problem-solving techniques related to self-defense. 5.1
	Explain the use of strategy in self-defense. 2.3
	Give students several scenarios in which they must determine ways to eliminate danger. (Assessment opportunity: structured observation 5.1, 5.2, 6.3) 2.3
DAY 3	Review ways to reduce danger. 1.0
	Review problem-solving techniques related to self-defense. 5.1
	Review the use of strategy in self-defense. 2.3
	Give students several scenarios in which they must determine ways to eliminate danger. (Assessment opportunity: structured observation 5.1, 5.2, 6.3) 2.3
DAY 4	Have students perform a warm-up along with muscular strength and muscular endurance exercises. (Assessment opportunity: structured observation 4.1)
	Explain the process for improving self-defense skills. 2.1
	Have students summarize the information in their notebooks. 2.1
	Have students set goals for self-defense. 2.1
	Review appropriate practice using SimAthlete. 2.1

(continued)

Unit 7 Outline *(continued)*

DAY 4 *(continued)*

Remind students to monitor their progress throughout the unit. 2.1

Demonstrate and describe the self-defense stance and correct breathing using the Self-Defense CD. 1.0, 2.5

Give students feedback as they assume the self-defense stance and practice correct breathing. (Assessment opportunity: structured observation 1.0, 5.1, 5.2, 6.3)

Lead students through a cool-down and flexibility exercises appropriate to the physical activity level of the lesson. (Assessment opportunity: structured observation 4.1)

Review personal weapons (voice, elbows and hands, legs and feet, fingers and thumbs, and knees). 2.3

Review vulnerable areas (knees and shins, nose, groin, eyes, throat or neck, and ears). 2.3

Have students discuss personal weapons and vulnerable areas with their partners. 2.3

DAY 5

Have students perform a warm-up along with a cardiorespiratory workout. (Assessment opportunity: structured observation 4.1)

Lead students through a cool-down and flexibility exercises appropriate to the physical activity level of the lesson. (Assessment opportunity: structured observation 4.1)

Have a guest speaker. 1.0

DAY 6

Explain how magnitude affects spin and rotation of the body or an object. 2.2

Have students summarize the information in their notebooks. 2.2

Have students perform a warm-up along with a cardiorespiratory workout. (Assessment opportunity: structured observation 4.1)

Demonstrate and describe the stomp using the Self-Defense CD. 1.0, 2.5

Have students, in groups of four, perform stomps giving feedback to each other. (Assessment opportunity: structured observation 1.0, 5.1, 5.2, 6.3)

Demonstrate and describe knee kicks using the Self-Defense CD. 1.0, 2.5

Have students, in groups of four, perform knee kicks, giving feedback to each other. (Assessment opportunity: structured observation 1.0, 5.1, 5.2, 6.3)

Lead students through a cool-down and flexibility exercises appropriate to the physical activity level of the lesson. (Assessment opportunity: structured observation 4.1)

Have students brainstorm the use of force for effectively executing the skills they learned today. 2.2

DAY 7

Explain individual differences and how these differences impact self-defense performance. 2.4

Have students perform a warm-up along with muscular strength and muscular endurance exercises. (Assessment opportunity: structured observation 4.1)

Demonstrate and describe the correct technique for the front snap kick using the Self-Defense CD. 1.0, 2.5

Have students, in groups of four, perform the front snap kick, giving feedback to each other. (Assessment opportunity: structured observation 1.0, 5.1, 5.2, 6.3)

Demonstrate and describe the correct technique for the side kick using the Self-Defense CD. 1.0, 2.5

Have students, in groups of four, perform front side kick, giving feedback to each other. (Assessment opportunity: structured observation 1.0, 5.1, 5.2, 6.3)

Lead students through a cool-down and flexibility exercises appropriate to the physical activity level of the lesson. (Assessment opportunity: structured observation 4.1)

Have students discuss how individual differences affect self-defense performance. 2.4

DAY 8

Review individual differences and how these differences affect self-defense performance. 2.4

Have students perform a warm-up along with a cardiorespiratory workout. (Assessment opportunity: structured observation 4.1)

Review the correct technique for the front snap kick. 1.0, 2.5

Have students, in groups of four, perform the front snap kick, giving feedback to each other. (Assessment opportunity: structured observation 1.0, 5.1, 5.2, 6.3)

Review the correct technique for the side kick. 1.0, 2.5

Have students, in groups of four, perform the side kick, giving feedback to each other. (Assessment opportunity: structured observation 1.0, 5.1, 5.2, 6.3)

Lead students through a cool-down and flexibility exercises appropriate to the physical activity level of the lesson. (Assessment opportunity: structured observation 4.1)

Have students brainstorm how magnitude affects spin and rotation of the body or an object. 2.2

DAY 9

Have students perform a warm-up along with muscular strength and muscular endurance exercises. (Assessment opportunity: structured observation 4.1)

Demonstrate and describe the correct technique for the rear kick using the Self-Defense CD. 1.0, 2.5

Have students, in groups of four, perform the rear kick, giving each other feedback. (Assessment opportunity: structured observation 1.0, 5.1, 5.2, 6.3)

Have students, in groups of four, perform the front snap kick, giving feedback to each other. (Assessment opportunity: structured observation 1.0, 5.1, 5.2, 6.3)

Have students, in groups of four, perform the side kick, giving feedback to each other. (Assessment opportunity: structured observation 1.0, 5.1, 5.2, 6.3)

Lead students through a cool-down and flexibility exercises appropriate to the physical activity level of the lesson. (Assessment opportunity: structured observation 4.1)

Have students discuss how individual differences affect self-defense performance. 2.4

DAY 10

Have students perform a warm-up along with a cardiorespiratory workout. (Assessment opportunity: structured observation 4.1)

Review how to participate in a circuit.

Have students, in groups of four, rotate through kicking stations (stomp, knee kick, front snap kick, side kick, and rear kick). (Assessment opportunity: structured observation 1.0, 5.1, 5.2, 6.3)

Lead students through a cool-down and flexibility exercises appropriate to the physical activity level of the lesson. (Assessment opportunity: structured observation 4.1)

DAY 11

Have students perform a warm-up along with a cardiorespiratory workout. (Assessment opportunity: structured observation 4.1)

Review how to participate in a circuit.

Have students, in groups of four, rotate through kicking stations (stomp, knee kick, front snap kick, side kick, and rear kick). (Assessment opportunity: structured observation 1.0, 5.1, 5.2, 6.3)

Lead students through a cool-down and flexibility exercises appropriate to the physical activity level of the lesson. (Assessment opportunity: structured observation 4.1)

DAY 12

Have students perform a warm-up along with muscular strength and muscular endurance exercises. (Assessment opportunity: structured observation 4.1)

Demonstrate and describe the correct technique for the elbow strike using the Self-Defense CD. 1.0, 2.5

Have students, in groups of four, perform the elbow strikes, giving each other feedback. (Assessment opportunity: structured observation 1.0, 5.1, 5.2, 6.3)

(continued)

Unit 7 Outline *(continued)*

DAY 12 *(continued)*	Demonstrate and describe the correct technique for the palm–heel strike using the Self-Defense CD. 1.0, 2.5
	Have students, in groups of four, perform the palm–heel strike, giving each other feedback. (Assessment opportunity: structured observation 1.0, 5.1, 5.2, 6.3)
	Review previously introduced skills. (Assessment opportunity: structured observation 1.0, 5.1, 5.2, 6.3)
	Lead students through a cool-down and flexibility exercises appropriate to the physical activity level of the lesson. (Assessment opportunity: structured observation 4.1)
	Have students discuss how individual differences impact self-defense performance. 2.4
DAY 13	Have students perform a warm-up along with a cardiorespiratory workout. (Assessment opportunity: structured observation 4.1)
	Review the correct technique for the elbow strike. 1.0, 2.5
	Have students, in groups of four, perform the elbow strike, giving each other feedback. (Assessment opportunity: structured observation 1.0, 5.1, 5.2, 6.3)
	Review the correct technique for the palm–heel strike. 1.0, 2.5
	Have students, in groups of four, perform the palm–heel strike, giving each other feedback. (Assessment opportunity: structured observation 1.0, 5.1, 5.2, 6.3)
	Review previously introduced skills. (Assessment opportunity: structured observation 1.0, 5.1, 5.2, 6.3)
	Lead students through a cool-down and flexibility exercises appropriate to the physical activity level of the lesson. (Assessment opportunity: structured observation 4.1)
	Have students brainstorm how magnitude affects spin and rotation of the body or an object. 2.2
DAY 14	Have students perform a warm-up along with muscular strength and muscular endurance exercises. (Assessment opportunity: structured observation 4.1)
	Have students, in groups of four, rotate through striking and kicking stations (elbow strike, stomp, knee kick, front snap kick, side kick, rear kick, and palm–heel strike). (Assessment opportunity: structured observation 1.0, 5.1, 5.2, 6.3)
	Lead students through a cool-down and flexibility exercises appropriate to the physical activity level of the lesson. (Assessment opportunity: structured observation 4.1)
DAY 15	Have students perform a warm-up along with a cardiorespiratory workout. (Assessment opportunity: structured observation 4.1)
	Demonstrate and describe the correct technique for the side fall (see figure 16.22) using the Self-Defense CD. 1.0, 2.5
	Have students, in groups of four, perform the side fall, giving each other feedback. (Assessment opportunity: structured observation 1.0, 5.1, 5.2, 6.3)
	Have students, in groups of four, rotate through striking and kicking stations (elbow strike, stomp, knee kick, front snap kick, side kick, rear kick, and palm–heel strike). (Assessment opportunity: structured observation 1.0, 5.1, 5.2, 6.3)
	Lead students through a cool-down and flexibility exercises appropriate to the physical activity level of the lesson. (Assessment opportunity: structured observation 4.1)
	Have students discuss how individual differences affect self-defense performance. 2.4

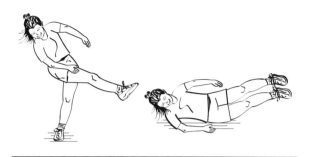

Figure 16.22 Side fall.

DAY 16

Have students perform a warm-up along with a cardiorespiratory workout. (Assessment opportunity: structured observation 4.1)

Demonstrate and describe the correct technique for the wrist release using Self-Defense CD. 1.0, 2.5

Have students, in groups of four, perform the wrist release, giving feedback to each other. (Assessment opportunity: structured observation 1.0, 5.1, 5.2, 6.3)

Have students, in groups of four, rotate through striking and kicking stations (elbow strike, stomp, knee kick, side fall, front snap kick, side kick, rear kick, and palm–heel strike). (Assessment opportunity: structured observation 1.0, 5.1, 5.2, 6.3)

Lead students through a cool-down and flexibility exercises appropriate to the physical activity level of the lesson. (Assessment opportunity: structured observation 4.1)

DAY 17

Have students perform a warm-up along with muscular strength and muscular endurance exercises. (Assessment opportunity: structured observation 4.1)

Demonstrate and describe the correct technique for the front choke release using the Self-Defense CD. 1.0, 2.5

Have students, in groups of four, perform the front choke release, giving each other feedback. (Assessment opportunity: structured observation 1.0, 5.1, 5.2, 6.3)

Have students, in groups of four, rotate through striking and kicking stations (elbow strike, stomp, knee kick, wrist release, side fall, front snap kick, side kick, rear kick, and palm–heel strike). (Assessment opportunity: structured observation 1.0, 5.1, 5.2, 6.3)

Lead students through a cool-down and flexibility exercises appropriate to the physical activity level of the lesson. (Assessment opportunity: structured observation 4.1)

Have students brainstorm how magnitude affects spin and rotation of the body or an object. 2.2

DAY 18

Have students perform a warm-up along with a cardiorespiratory workout. (Assessment opportunity: structured observation 4.1)

Demonstrate and describe the correct technique for the rear choke release using the Self-Defense CD. 1.0, 2.5

Have students, in groups of four, perform the rear choke release, giving each other feedback. (Assessment opportunity: structured observation 1.0, 5.1, 5.2, 6.3)

Have students, in groups of four, rotate through striking and kicking stations (elbow strike, stomp, front choke release, knee kick, wrist release, side fall, front snap kick, side kick, rear kick, and palm–heel strike). (Assessment opportunity: structured observation 1.0, 5.1, 5.2, 6.3)

Lead students through a cool-down and flexibility exercises appropriate to the physical activity level of the lesson. (Assessment opportunity: structured observation 4.1)

(continued)

Unit 7 Outline *(continued)*

DAY 19

Have students perform a warm-up along with muscular strength and muscular endurance exercises. (Assessment opportunity: structured observation 4.1)

Demonstrate the correct technique for the hair release (hold one hand near scalp) using the Self-Defense CD. 1.0, 2.5

Have students simulate practicing the hair release. 1.0

Have students, in groups of four, perform the front choke release and rear choke release giving each other feedback. (Assessment opportunity: structured observation 1.0, 5.1, 5.2, 6.3)

Lead students through a cool-down and flexibility exercises appropriate to the physical activity level of the lesson. (Assessment opportunity: structured observation 4.1)

Have students discuss how magnitude affects spin and rotation of the body or an object. 2.2

DAY 20

Have students perform a warm-up along with a cardiorespiratory workout. (Assessment opportunity: structured observation 4.1)

Have students, in groups of four, rotate through striking, kicking, and release stations (elbow strike, stomp, front choke release, rear choke release, knee kick, wrist release, side fall, front snap kick, side kick, rear kick, and palm–heel strike) (see figures 16.23-16.26). (Assessment opportunity: structured observation 1.0, 5.1, 5.2, 6.3)

Lead students through a cool-down and flexibility exercises appropriate to the physical activity level of the lesson. (Assessment opportunity: structured observation 4.1)

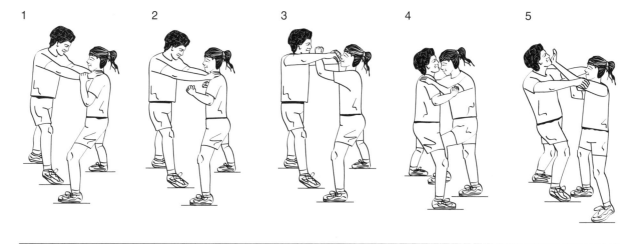

1   **2**   **3**   **4**   **5**

Figure 16.23   Front choke release, knee kick, and palm–heel strike combination.

DAY 21

Have students perform a warm-up along with a cardiorespiratory workout. (Assessment opportunity: structured observation 4.1)

Have students, in groups of four, rotate through striking, kicking, and release stations (elbow strike, stomp, front choke release, rear choke release, knee kick, wrist release, side fall, front snap kick, side kick, rear kick, and palm–heel strike) (see figures 16.23-16.26). (Assessment opportunity: structured observation 1.0, 5.1, 5.2, 6.3)

Lead students through a cool-down and flexibility exercises appropriate to the physical activity level of the lesson. (Assessment opportunity: structured observation 4.1)

(continued)

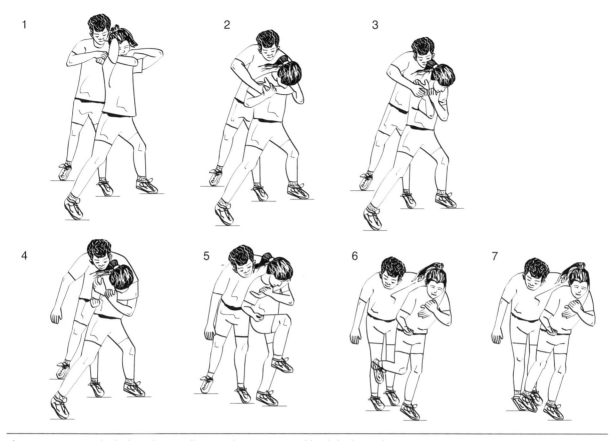

Figure 16.24   Back choke release, elbow strike, stomp, and back kick combination.

Figure 16.25   *(a)* Outside block, *(b)* inside block, and *(c)* side kick.

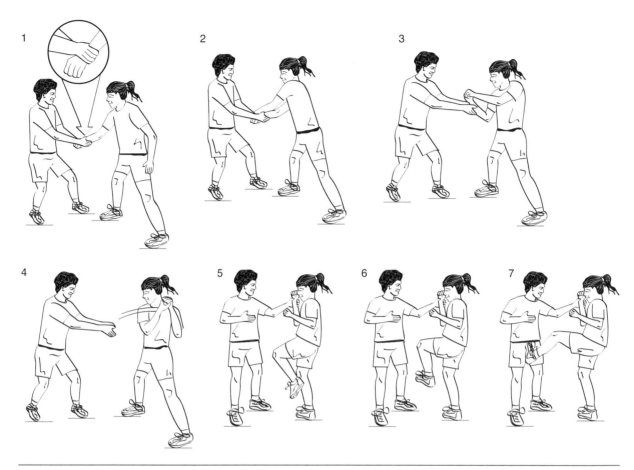

Figure 16.26   Wrist release and front snap kick combination.

Unit 7 Outline *(continued)*

DAY 22

Have students perform a warm-up along with muscular strength and muscular endurance exercises. (Assessment opportunity: structured observation 4.1)

Have students, in groups of four, rotate through striking, kicking, and release stations (elbow strike, stomp, front choke release, rear choke release, knee kick, wrist release, side fall, front snap kick, side kick, rear kick, and palm–heel strike) (see figures 16.23-16.26). (Assessment opportunity: structured observation 1.0, 5.1, 5.2, 6.3)

Lead students through a cool-down and flexibility exercises appropriate to the physical activity level of the lesson. (Assessment opportunity: structured observation 4.1)

DAY 23

Have students perform a warm-up along with a cardiorespiratory workout. (Assessment opportunity: structured observation 4.1)

Have students, in groups of four, rotate through striking, kicking, and release stations (elbow strike, stomp, front choke release, rear choke release, knee kick, wrist release, side fall, front snap kick, side kick, rear kick, and palm–heel strike) (see figures 16.23-16.26). (Assessment opportunity: structured observation 1.0, 5.1, 5.2, 6.3)

Lead students through a cool-down and flexibility exercises appropriate to the physical activity level of the lesson. (Assessment opportunity: structured observation 4.1)

DAY 24

Have students perform a warm-up along with muscular strength and muscular endurance exercises. (Assessment opportunity: structured observation 4.1)

Have students discuss and act out simulation scenarios. Situations could include the following:

- You are walking along a deserted street as an assailant approaches.
- An assailant grabs both of your wrists.
- An assailant grasps one of your wrists and attempts to pull you into his car.
- An assailant grabs you in a rear bear hug.
- An assailant grabs you in a front bear hug.
- An assailant grabs your hair and attempts to pull you into the bushes.
- An assailant pushes you to the ground.
- An assailant grabs your throat in a front choke.
- An assailant grabs your throat in a rear choke.
- An assailant leaps into your car at a stoplight. (Assessment opportunity: structured observation 1.0, 5.1, 5.2, 6.3)

Lead students through a cool-down and flexibility exercises appropriate to the physical activity level of the lesson. (Assessment opportunity: structured observation 4.1)

Review material for tomorrow's quiz (or hand out quiz if you would like for it to be a take home quiz). 2.1, 2.2, 2.3, 2.4, 6.4

DAY 25

Have students take the quiz. (Assessment opportunity: quiz 2.1, 2.2, 2.3, 2.4, 6.4)

Collect student activity logs. (Assessment opportunity: log 3.1)

Collect reports on the description of combative activities during medieval times and the Renaissance. (Assessment opportunity: report 6.1)

Collect essays on the opportunities in the larger community for participation in self-defense activities. (Assessment opportunity: essay 3.2)

Collect reports on critical features of self-defense skills. (Assessment opportunity: report 2.5)

Collect 1-week muscular strength plans. (Assessment opportunity: project 4.2)

Medieval Times Activities — Unit 8

This unit continues our focus on accepting challenges by having students challenge themselves in activities that people participated in during medieval times and the modern-day counterparts of these activities. Like the orienteering unit, this unit dovetails nicely with what my students are studying in history and social science. I conduct this unit at the end of the school year because it lends itself to a culminating interdisciplinary activity in which the school holds a medieval festival, including sporting events.

You can conduct this unit in any open area; however, a grassy area is ideal. Additional medieval times activities can include archery, Rounders (a field game), Jeu de Paume (a form of handball), and Soule (a form of soccer).

Unit 8 Standards

1.0—Demonstrates the mature form for running in armor; juggling; fencing advance, retreat, lunge, ready position, and on-guard; jousting; and use of a lance.

2.1—Explains the process of setting appropriate goals, conducting appropriate practice, and monitoring changes in the development of specialize skills.

2.2—Explains how force can be used to make an object spin.

2.3—Explains offensive and defensive strategies for target sports.

2.4—Explains individual differences that can impact performance in physical activities.

2.5—Explains the critical elements for fencing advance, retreat, lunge, on guard, and ready position.

3.1—Engages in moderate and vigorous physical activity for 60 minutes 6 days each week.

3.2—Describes opportunities in the larger community for participation in individual and dual physical activities.

4.1—Works toward a health-enhancing level of physical fitness.

4.2—Designs a 1-week personal health-related fitness plan.

5.1—Applies problem-solving techniques when working with a person who is differently abled in medieval times activities.

5.2—Accepts responsibility for individual improvement during medieval times activities.

6.1—Describes games, activities, and physical education during medieval times.

6.2—Not applicable.

6.3—Chooses to engage in medieval times activities at the appropriate level of personal challenge.

6.4—Describes the social benefits of regular participation in physical activity.

Unit 8 Assessments

1.0—Structured observation (days 1-19)

2.1—Project (assigned on day 1; collected on day 20)

2.2—Quiz (day 20)

2.3—Quiz (day 20)

2.4—Quiz (day 20)

2.5—Quiz (day 20)

3.1—Log (assigned on day 1; collected on day 20)

3.2—Essay (assigned on day 1; collected on day 20)

4.1—Structured observation (days 1-19)

4.2—Project (assigned on day 6; collected on day 20)

5.1—Structured observation (days 1-19)

5.2—Structure observation (days 1-19)

6.1—Report (assigned on day 1; collected on day 20)

6.2—Not applicable

6.3—Structured observation (days 1-19)

6.4—Quiz (day 20)

Resources

Health-Related Fitness: Tutorial and Portfolio (Bonnie's Fitware, Inc.)

Middle School Physical Education Portfolio (Bonnie's Fitware, Inc.)

Multicultural Games and Activities CD (Bonnie's Fitware, Inc.)

Seventh grade medieval times task cards (Bonnie's Fitware, Inc.)

SimAthlete (Bonnie's Fitware, Inc.)

Seventh grade unit 8 posters (Bonnie's Fitware, Inc.—included in the Middle School Detailed Lesson Plans)

Fitness posters (Bonnie's Fitware, Inc.—included in the Middle School Detailed Lesson Plans)

Equipment

Catcher or football gear for running in armor

Football flags

Flying discs (for shields)

Funnoodles for fencing, lancing, and jousting, stick (loop and stick)

Stilts

Self-defense pads

Deck rings (loop and stick)

Juggling balls

Flag-a-tag rings

Macarena music

Sound system

Mats

Games

Running in armor	Jousting	Tumbling
Melee	Lancing	Self-defense activities
Loop and stick	Juggling	Pad activities
Fencing	Stilts	Flag pull tag
Shields	Hand tap	Knee tag

Unit 8 Outline

DAY 1

Display the posters.

Introduce medieval times unit. 6.1

Assign students to working groups of four.

Discuss problem-solving strategies when working someone who is differently abled. 5.1

Have students record the problem-solving strategies in their notebook. 5.1

Discuss the importance of participating in activities at the appropriate level of personal challenge. 6.3

Discuss the importance of accepting responsibility for one's own improvement. 5.2

Have students perform a warm-up along with a cardiorespiratory workout. (Assessment opportunity: structured observation 4.1)

Review (from sixth grade) juggling and stilt activities. 1.0, 2.5

Have students practice juggling and stilt activities. (Assessment opportunity: structured observation 1.0, 5.1, 5.2, 6.3)

Lead students through a cool-down and flexibility exercises appropriate to the physical activity level of the lesson. (Assessment opportunity: structured observation 4.1)

Assign unit-long homework:

- Have students research and write a description of games, activities, and physical education during medieval times and the Renaissance. (Assessment assignment opportunity: report 6.1)

- Have students keep a log of daily activity. (Assessment assignment opportunity: log 3.1)

- Have students describe the opportunities in the larger community for participation in individual and dual physical activities. (Assessment assignment opportunity: essay 3.2)

- Have students create a practice plan for juggling, stilt walking, tumbling, or self defense using the process for setting goals, appropriate practice, and monitoring changes. (Assessment assignment opportunity: project 2.1)

(continued)

Unit 8 Outline *(continued)*

DAY 2

Review individual differences and their impact on performance in physical activities. 2.4

Review the social benefits of participating in physical activity. 6.4

Explain the role of jesters during medieval times. 6.1

Have students perform a warm-up along with muscular strength and muscular endurance exercises. (Assessment opportunity: structured observation 4.1)

Review juggling and stilt activities. 1.0, 2.5

Demonstrate loop-and-stick activities (see figure 16.27). 1.0, 2.5

Set up three stations (juggling, stilts, loop and stick) and have students participate in activities at each station. (Assessment opportunity: structured observation 1.0, 5.1, 5.2, 6.3)

Lead students through a cool-down and flexibility exercises appropriate to the physical activity level of the lesson. (Assessment opportunity: structured observation 4.1)

Have students brainstorm how their own physical characteristics impacted their learning of the skills taught today. 2.4

Figure 16.27 Loop and stick.

DAY 3

Review the role of jesters during medieval times. 6.1

Have students perform a warm-up. (Assessment opportunity: structured observation 4.1)

Review the Macarena. 1.0

Have students participate in the Macarena. 1.0

Have students, in groups of four, select one multicultural dance to learn and teach the rest of the class. 1.0

Have students rotate through four stations: juggling, stilts, dance, hoop and stick. (Assessment opportunity: structured observation 1.0, 5.1, 5.2, 6.3)

Lead students through a cool-down and flexibility exercises appropriate to the physical activity level of the lesson. (Assessment opportunity: structured observation 4.1)

DAY 4

Explain the role of squires during medieval times. 6.1

Have students discuss how force can be used to make an object spin. 2.2

Review basic tumbling moves from tumbling and gymnastics unit. 1.0, 2.5

Review basic self-defense moves from self-defense unit. 1.0, 2.5

DAY 4 *(continued)*	Demonstrate hand tap (one person pulls hands away as partner tries to make contact). 1.0
	Have students perform a warm-up along with muscular strength and muscular endurance exercises. (Assessment opportunity: structured observation 4.1)
	Set up four stations (tumbling, self-defense, dance, and hand tap) and have students participate in activities at each station. (Assessment opportunity: structured observation 1.0, 5.1, 5.2, 6.3)
	Lead students through a cool-down and flexibility exercises appropriate to the physical activity level of the lesson. (Assessment opportunity: structured observation 4.1)
	Have students brainstorm how their own physical characteristics impacted their learning of the skills taught today. 2.4
DAY 5	Review the roles of squires, jesters, and knights during medieval times. 6.1
	Have students perform a warm-up along with a cardiorespiratory workout. (Assessment opportunity: structured observation 4.1)
	Review tumbling and self-defense moves. 1.0, 2.5
	Review hand tap (one person pulls hands away as partner tries to make contact). 1.0
	Have students rotate through four stations: tumbling, self-defense, dance, and hand tap. (Assessment opportunity: structured observation 1.0, 5.1, 5.2, 6.3)
	Lead students through a cool-down and flexibility exercises appropriate to the physical activity level of the lesson. (Assessment opportunity: structured observation 4.1)
	Have students discuss how force can be used to make an object spin or rotate. 2.2
DAY 6	Review the frequency, intensity, time, and type (FITT) concepts related to each of the five components of health-related fitness using the Health-Related Fitness: Tutorial and Portfolio. 4.2
	Assign the design of a 1-week personal health-related fitness plan. (Assessment assignment opportunity: project 4.2)
	Have students perform a warm-up along with a cardiorespiratory workout. (Assessment opportunity: structured observation 4.1)
	Demonstrate the correct technique for running. 1.0, 2.5
	Demonstrate the correct technique for running in armor. 1.0, 2.5
	Have students practice running in armor. (Assessment opportunity: structured observation 1.0, 5.1, 5.2, 6.3)
	Lead students through a cool-down and flexibility exercises appropriate to the physical activity level of the lesson. (Assessment opportunity: structured observation 4.1)
	Have students brainstorm how their own physical characteristics affected their learning of the skills taught today. 2.4
DAY 7	Review the process of setting appropriate goals, conducting appropriate practice, and monitoring changes in the development of specialized skills. 2.1
	Review appropriate practice using SimAthlete. 2.1
	Have students perform a warm-up along with muscular strength and muscular endurance exercises. (Assessment opportunity: structured observation 4.1)
	Demonstrate knee tag and flag pull tag using Multicultural Games and Activities CD. 1.0
	Have groups rotate through five stations: running in armor, hand tap, knee tag, dance, and flag pull tag. (Assessment opportunity: structured observation 1.0, 5.1, 5.2, 6.3)
	Lead students through a cool-down and flexibility exercises appropriate to the physical activity level of the lesson. (Assessment opportunity: structured observation 4.1)
	Have students brainstorm how their own physical characteristics impacted their learning of the skills taught today. 2.4

(continued)

Unit 8 Outline   *(continued)*

DAY 8

Explain the history of shields. 6.1

Demonstrate shields activities using the Multicultural Games and Activities CD. 1.0, 2.5

Have students create a faceplate for their shield. 6.1

Have students perform a warm-up along with a cardiorespiratory workout. (Assessment opportunity: structured observation 4.1)

Demonstrate shield activities (see figure 16.28). 1.0, 2.5

Discuss the offensive and defensive strategies for shield activities. 2.3

Have students participate in shield activities. (Assessment opportunity: structured observation 1.0, 5.1, 5.2, 6.3) 2.3

Have students work on their dances. 1.0

Lead students through a cool-down and flexibility exercises appropriate to the physical activity level of the lesson. (Assessment opportunity: structured observation 4.1)

Have students brainstorm how their own physical characteristics impacted their learning of the skills taught today. 2.4

Figure 16.28   Shield activities.

DAY 9

Have students perform a warm-up along with muscular strength and muscular endurance exercises. (Assessment opportunity: structured observation 4.1)

Review shield activities. 1.0, 2.5

Have students participate in shield activities. (Assessment opportunity: structured observation 1.0, 5.1, 5.2, 6.3) 2.3

Demonstrate pad activities (see figure 16.29) using the Multicultural Games and Activities CD. 1.0, 2.5

Discuss the offensive and defensive strategies for pad activities. 2.3

Have students participate in pad activities (play shoulder tag using shields for protection). (Assessment opportunity: structured observation 1.0, 5.1, 5.2, 6.3) 2.3

Have students work on their dances. 1.0

Lead students through a cool-down and flexibility exercises appropriate to the physical activity level of the lesson. (Assessment opportunity: structured observation 4.1)

Have students brainstorm how their own physical characteristics impacted their learning of the skills taught today. 2.4

Figure 16.29   Pad activities.

DAY 10

Explain the history of the game of Melee. 6.1

Demonstrate Melee using the Multicultural Games and Activities CD. 2.3

Have students perform a warm-up. (Assessment opportunity: structured observation 4.1)

Have students participate in Melee. (Assessment opportunity: structured observation 1.0, 5.1, 5.2, 6.3)

Have each group teach its dance to the entire class or several other groups. (Assessment opportunity: structured observation 1.0

Lead students through a cool-down and flexibility exercises appropriate to the physical activity level of the lesson. (Assessment opportunity: structured observation 4.1)

Have students brainstorm how their own physical characteristics impacted their learning of the skills taught today. 2.4

DAY 11

Explain the history of fencing. 6.1

Demonstrate fencing. 1.0, 2.5

Have students perform a warm-up along with a cardiorespiratory workout. (Assessment opportunity: structured observation 4.1)

Demonstrate and describe holding the foil. 1.0, 2.5

Have students practice holding the foil. (Assessment opportunity: structured observation 1.0, 5.1, 5.2, 6.3)

Demonstrate and describe the on-guard position (see figure 16.30*a*). 1.0, 2.5

Have students practice the on-guard position. (Assessment opportunity: structured observation 1.0, 5.1, 5.2, 6.3)

Demonstrate and describe advancing. 1.0, 2.5

Have students practice the advance (step-together-step forward). (Assessment opportunity: structured observation 1.0, 5.1, 5.2, 6.3)

Demonstrate and describe the retreat. 1.0, 2.5

Have students practice the retreat (step-together-step backward). (Assessment opportunity: structured observation 1.0, 5.1, 5.2, 6.3)

Demonstrate and describe the lunge (see figure 16.30*b*). 1.0, 2.5

Have students practice the lunge. (Assessment opportunity: structured observation 1.0, 5.1, 5.2, 6.3)

Lead students through a cool-down and flexibility exercises appropriate to the physical activity level of the lesson. (Assessment opportunity: structured observation 4.1)

(continued)

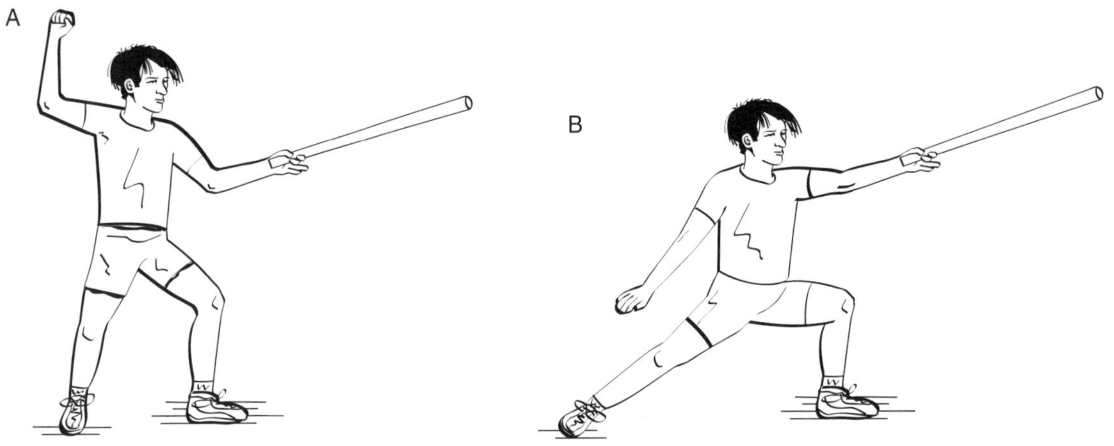

Figure 16.30   Fencing: *(a)* on-guard and *(b)* lunge.

Unit 8 Outline *(continued)*

DAY 12

Have students perform a warm-up along with muscular strength and muscular endurance exercises. (Assessment opportunity: structured observation 4.1)

Review grip. 1.0, 2.5

Review advancing. 1.0, 2.5

Have students practice the advance (step-together-step forward). (Assessment opportunity: structured observation 1.0, 5.1, 5.2, 6.3)

Review the retreat. 1.0, 2.5

Have students practice the retreat (step-together-step backward). (Assessment opportunity: structured observation 1.0, 5.1, 5.2, 6.3)

Review the lunge. 1.0, 2.5

Have students practice the lunge. (Assessment opportunity: structured observation 1.0, 5.1, 5.2, 6.3)

Demonstrate and describe the attack (contacts). 1.0, 2.5

Have students practice attack (contacts). (Assessment opportunity: structured observation 1.0, 5.1, 5.2, 6.3)

Lead students through a cool-down and flexibility exercises appropriate to the physical activity level of the lesson. (Assessment opportunity: structured observation 4.1)

DAY 13

Have students perform a warm-up along with a cardiorespiratory workout. (Assessment opportunity: structured observation 4.1)

Review advancing. 1.0, 2.5

Have students practice the advance (step-together-step forward). (Assessment opportunity: structured observation 1.0, 5.1, 5.2, 6.3)

Review the retreat. 1.0, 2.5

Have students practice the retreat (step-together-step backward). (Assessment opportunity: structured observation 1.0, 5.1, 5.2, 6.3)

Review the lunge. 1.0, 2.5

Have students practice the lunge. (Assessment opportunity: structured observation 1.0, 5.1, 5.2, 6.3)

Review the attack (contacts). 1.0, 2.5

Have students practice attack (contacts). (Assessment opportunity: structured observation 1.0, 5.1, 5.2, 6.3)

DAY 13 *(continued)*

Demonstrate and describe the fencing ready position. 1.0, 2.5

Have students practice the fencing ready position. (Assessment opportunity: structured observation 1.0, 5.1, 5.2, 6.3)

Demonstrate and describe the on-guard position (see figure 16.30a). 1.0, 2.5

Have students practice the on-guard position. (Assessment opportunity: structured observation 1.0, 5.1, 5.2, 6.3)

Explain the sport of fencing. 2.3

Discuss the offensive and defensive strategies for fencing. 2.3

Demonstrate and describe parries. 1.0, 2.5

Have students practice parries. (Assessment opportunity: structured observation 1.0, 5.1, 5.2, 6.3)

Lead students through a cool-down and flexibility exercises appropriate to the physical activity level of the lesson. (Assessment opportunity: structured observation 4.1)

Have students brainstorm how their own physical characteristics impacted their learning of the skills taught today. 2.4

DAY 14

Explain the history of jousting. 6.1

Explain the history of lancing. 6.1

Demonstrate the correct technique for jousting using the Multicultural Games and Activities CD. 1.0, 2.5

Demonstrate the correct technique for lancing (see figure 16.31) using the Multicultural Games and Activities CD. 1.0, 2.5

Discuss the offensive and defensive strategies for lancing and jousting. 2.3

Have students perform a warm-up along with muscular strength and muscular endurance exercises. (Assessment opportunity: structured observation 4.1)

Have students practice jousting. (Assessment opportunity: structured observation 1.0, 5.1, 5.2, 6.3)

Have students practice lancing. (Assessment opportunity: structured observation 1.0, 5.1, 5.2, 6.3)

Lead students through a cool-down and flexibility exercises appropriate to the physical activity level of the lesson. (Assessment opportunity: structured observation 4.1)

Have students brainstorm how their own physical characteristics impacted their learning of the skills taught today. 2.4

(continued)

Figure 16.31   Lancing.

Unit 8 Outline *(continued)*

DAY 15	Have students perform a warm-up along with a cardiorespiratory workout. (Assessment opportunity: structured observation 4.1)
	Review jousting. 1.0, 2.5
	Review lancing. 1.0, 2.5
	Review fencing. 1.0, 2.5
	Have students practice jousting. (Assessment opportunity: structured observation 1.0, 5.1, 5.2, 6.3)
	Have students practice lancing. (Assessment opportunity: structured observation 1.0, 5.1, 5.2, 6.3)
	Have students practice fencing. (Assessment opportunity: structured observation 1.0, 5.1, 5.2, 6.3)
	Lead students through a cool-down and flexibility exercises appropriate to the physical activity level of the lesson. (Assessment opportunity: structured observation 4.1)
	Have students brainstorm how their own physical characteristics impacted their learning of the skills taught today. 2.4
DAY 16	Have students perform a warm-up along with a cardiorespiratory workout. (Assessment opportunity: structured observation 4.1)
	Have groups rotate through stations: stilts, juggling, loop and stick, tumbling skills, shield activities, pad activities, melee, fencing, jousting, and lancing. (Assessment opportunity: structured observation 1.0, 5.1, 5.2, 6.3)
	Lead students through a cool-down and flexibility exercises appropriate to the physical activity level of the lesson. (Assessment opportunity: structured observation 4.1)
DAY 17	Have students perform a warm-up along with muscular strength and muscular endurance exercises. (Assessment opportunity: structured observation 4.1)
	Have groups rotate through stations: stilts, juggling, loop and stick, tumbling skills, shield activities, pad activities, Melee, fencing, jousting, and lancing. (Assessment opportunity: structured observation 1.0, 5.1, 5.2, 6.3)
	Lead students through a cool-down and flexibility exercises appropriate to the physical activity level of the lesson. (Assessment opportunity: structured observation 4.1)
DAY 18	Have students perform a warm-up along with a cardiorespiratory workout. (Assessment opportunity: structured observation 4.1)
	Hold a school-wide medieval festival, in which students have an opportunity to compete in each of the activities taught in the unit or review stations from lessons 16 and 17. (Assessment opportunity: structured observation 1.0, 5.1, 5.2, 6.3)
	Lead students through a cool-down and flexibility exercises appropriate to the physical activity level of the lesson. (Assessment opportunity: structured observation 4.1)
DAY 19	Have students perform a warm-up along with muscular strength and muscular endurance exercises. (Assessment opportunity: structured observation 4.1)
	Hold a school-wide medieval festival, in which students have an opportunity to compete in each of the activities taught in the unit or review stations from lessons 16 and 17. (Assessment opportunity: structured observation 1.0, 5.1, 5.2, 6.3)
	Lead students through a cool-down and flexibility exercises appropriate to the physical activity level of the lesson. (Assessment opportunity: structured observation 4.1)
	Review material for tomorrow's quiz (or hand out quiz if you would like for it to be a take home quiz). 2.1, 2.2, 2.3, 2.4, 2.5, 6.4

DAY 20

Have students take the quiz. (Assessment opportunity: quiz 2.1, 2.2, 2.3, 2.4, 2.5, 6.4)

Collect student activity logs. (Assessment opportunity: log 3.1)

Collect reports on the games, activities, and physical education during medieval times and the Renaissance. (Assessment opportunity: report 6.1)

Collect essays about the opportunities in the larger community for participation in individual and dual physical activities. (Assessment opportunity: essay 3.2)

Collect projects on developing a practice plan. (Assessment opportunity: project 2.1)

Collect fitness plans. (Assessment opportunity: project 4.2)

Closure and Fitness Assessment

This unit, like the fifth and sixth grade closing and fitness postassessment units, provides an opportunity for closure, including the chance to ensure that the students are able to demonstrate the standards. As with the fifth and sixth graders, the seventh graders have worked on projects throughout the year; in this final unit, however, I have them focus on depth over breadth. Direct students to complete their demonstration of learning by collecting and creating work for their portfolios, freeing you to administer the fitness postassessment and to act as a resource for the student projects.

For this unit, I present students with the 16 standards for the seventh grade and ask them to present evidence of their learning related to each standard. For some of the standards, students will be able to demonstrate their learning by looking through their working portfolios and pulling from work that they have already accomplished during the year. For other standards, students will be able to pull from interdisciplinary projects that they have accomplished throughout the year. For still other standards, students will need to create new projects during this closing unit to demonstrate their learning. Once the students have collected their evidence, it goes into their performance portfolios. Then I ask them to write a reflection paper (a one-page essay) on their cumulative learning throughout seventh grade physical education. Ideally, the students then present their portfolios not only to their peers but also to their parents. In this case, during a parent, teacher, and student conference, the student is in charge of the conference as he presents the evidence that he has accumulated during the year and explains how the evidence demonstrates his learning of the various standards. This conference can focus exclusively on physical education or can be a comprehensive conference in which the student explains his learning in all subject areas.

As with the introduction unit, you can conduct this unit in just about any facility. If you are having your students perform exercises on the ground or grass, provide them with carpet squares or some other material so they won't get dirty. An indoor facility is also helpful for the project development phase of this unit. In addition, many teachers reserve the library or arrange for some of their students to do research in the library. Of course, the equipment necessary to implement the unit depends on the type of fitness assessments you plan to administer. I administer the same Fitnessgram tests that I gave at the beginning of the school year. After the postassessments, the students enter their fitness postassessment scores into their own portfolios using the Health-Related Fitness: Tutorial and Portfolio so that you and they can compare these scores to pretests, standards, and goals. Students also need access to reference books, CD-ROMs, DVDs, computers, videotape and DVD players, monitors, camcorders, and other materials to assist in project development.

Sample Assessment for Each Seventh Grade Standard

1.0—Demonstrates the mature form for specialized skills and combinations during individual and dual activities.

Teacher assessment during each instructional unit based on a rubric determines whether a student has reached this standard. The following is a sample rubric for the forehand drive in tennis:

6: Performs a mature forehand drive when striking in a game or activity situation.

5: Performs a mature forehand drive when striking for distance and accuracy.

4: Performs a mature forehand drive:

    _____ Turns trunk to side in anticipation of tossed ball.

    _____ Keeps eyes on ball.

    _____ Keeps dominant hand above nondominant hand.

    _____ Before swing, twists body back.

    _____ Holds elbows up and away from body.

    _____ Shifts weight back and forward during swing.

    _____ Segments body rotation from foot to pelvis to spine to shoulders.

    _____ Swings object level, contacting ball at point of complete extension.

    _____ On contact, ensures forward leg is straight.

    _____ Follows through beyond point of contact.

3: Is moving toward a mature forehand drive.

2: Attempts an immature forehand drive when a ball is tossed to her.

1: Randomly attempts an immature forehand drive.

2.1—Explains the process of setting appropriate goals, conducting appropriate practice, and monitoring changes in the development of specialized skills.

Student writes an explanation of the process for setting appropriate goals, participating in appropriate practice, and monitoring change in the development of a specialized skill.

2.2—Explains how force can be used to make an object spin.

Student writes an explanation of how force can be purposefully used to alter the outcome of specialized skill performance.

2.3—Explains offensive and defensive strategies for net and target sports.

Student writes an explanation of offensive and defensive strategies for net and target sports.

2.4—Explains individual differences and how these differences affect performance in physical activities.

Student writes an essay explaining individual differences and how these differences affect performance in physical activities.

2.5—Explains the critical elements of specialized skills and combinations in individual and dual sports.

Teacher assessment during each instructional unit is based on responses to quiz questions for each motor and movement skill taught.

3.1—Engages in moderate and vigorous physical activity for 60 minutes 6 days each week.

Student maintains a log of participation in physical activity throughout the school year.

3.2—Describes opportunities in the larger community for participation in individual and dual physical activities.

Student writes a description of the opportunities available in the larger community for participation in individual and dual physical activities.

4.1—Works toward a health-enhancing level of physical fitness.

Student submits prefitness assessment data, goals, monitoring logs, and postfitness assessment data.

4.2—Designs a 1-week personal health-related fitness plan.

Student designs a chart, essay, video, or computer program that shows his 1-week personal health-related fitness plan.

5.1—Applies problem-solving techniques when working with another person in physical activity settings.

Teacher assessment during each instructional unit based on a rubric determines whether a student has reached this standard. The following is a rubric for use during this assessment:

6: Demonstrates collaborative problem-solving skills in a real conflict in a physical activity setting.

5: Demonstrates collaborative problem-solving skills in a simulation based on a real conflict.

4: Demonstrates collaborative problem-solving skills in a simulation with friends.

3: Demonstrates some collaborative problem-solving skills in a simulation with friends.

2: Demonstrates a few collaborative problem-solving skills in a simulation with friends.

1: No evidence of collaborative problem solving.

5.2—Accepts responsibility for individual improvement during challenging physical activity.

Teacher assessment throughout the year based on a rubric determines whether a student has reached this standard.

6.1—Describes the development and role of movement-related activities in medieval times and their influences on physical activities today.

Student conducts research and reports on the history of one activity that originated in medieval times and comments on its influence on physical activities today.

6.2—Appreciates one's own stylistic approach to creating a routine.

Student collects journal entries from throughout the year that demonstrate appreciation of his or her own stylistic approach to creating a routine.

6.3—Chooses to engage in activities at the appropriate level of personal challenge.

Teacher assessment throughout the year based on a rubric determines whether a student has reached this standard.

6.4—Describes the social benefits of regular participation in physical activity.

Student writes a description of the social benefits derived from regular participation in physical activity.

Resources

Health-Related Fitness: Tutorial and Portfolio (Bonnie's Fitware, Inc.)

Middle School Physical Education Portfolio (Bonnie's Fitware, Inc.)

Equipment

Fitness assessment equipment

Games

None

Unit 9 Outline

DAY 1	Assign students to working groups of four.
	Remind students why you administer fitness assessments twice a year.
	Remind students how and why you administer the 1-mile run assessment. 4.1
	Have students perform warm-up exercises for the 1-mile run assessment. 4.1
	Administer the 1-mile run assessment. (Assessment opportunity: fitness assessment 4.1)
	Have students input fitness scores in their Health-Related Fitness Portfolios. 4.1
	Lead students through a cool-down and flexibility exercises appropriate to the physical activity level of the lesson. 4.1

(continued)

Unit 9 Outline *(continued)*

DAY 2	Describe the projects and portfolios to be complete in this unit. All
	Describe the project and portfolios design steps. All
	Remind students how and why you administer the curl-up assessment. 4.1
	Have students perform warm-up exercises for the curl-up assessment. 4.1
	Have students begin to work on their projects and Middle School Physical Education Portfolios. (Assessment opportunity: all)
	Administer the curl-up assessment to one group at a time. (Assessment opportunity: fitness assessment 4.1)
	Have students input fitness scores into their Health-Related Fitness Portfolios. 4.1
	Lead students through a cool-down and flexibility exercises appropriate to the physical activity level of the lesson. 4.1
DAY 3	Remind students how and why you administer the skinfold measurement. 4.1
	Have students work on their projects and Middle School Physical Education Portfolios. (Assessment opportunity: all)
	Administer the skinfold measurement privately to one student at a time. (Assessment opportunity: fitness assessment 4.1)
	Have students input fitness scores in their Health-Related Fitness Portfolios. 4.1
DAY 4	Remind students how and why you administer the back-saver sit-and-reach and trunk-lift assessments. 4.1
	Have students perform warm-up exercises for the back-saver sit-and-reach and trunk-lift assessments. 4.1
	Have students work on their projects and Middle School Physical Education Portfolios. (Assessment opportunity: all)
	Administer the back-saver sit-and-reach and trunk-lift assessments to one group at a time. (Assessment opportunity: fitness assessment 4.1)
	Have students input fitness scores in their Health-Related Fitness Portfolios. 4.1
	Lead students through a cool-down and flexibility exercises appropriate to the physical activity level of the lesson. 4.1
DAY 5	Remind students how and why you administer the push-up assessment. 4.1
	Have students perform warm-up exercises for the push-up assessment. 4.1
	Have students work on their projects and Middle School Physical Education Portfolios. (Assessment opportunity: all)
	Administer the push-up assessment to one group at a time. (Assessment opportunity: fitness assessment 4.1)
	Have students input fitness scores in their Health-Related Fitness Portfolios. 4.1
	Lead students through a cool-down and flexibility exercises appropriate to the physical activity level of the lesson. 4.1

DAY 6

Have students perform warm-up exercises for makeup assessments. 4.1

Have students work on their projects and Middle School Physical Education Portfolios. (Assessment opportunity: all)

Administer makeup fitness assessments to one group at a time. (Assessment opportunity: fitness assessment 4.1)

Have students input fitness scores in their Health-Related Fitness Portfolios. 4.1

Lead students through a cool-down and flexibility exercises appropriate to the physical activity level of the lesson. 4.1

DAYS 7-12

Have students work on their projects and Middle School Physical Education Portfolios. (Assessment opportunity: all)

DAY 13

Have each group share their projects and Middle School Physical Education Portfolios. (Assessment opportunity: all)

DAY 14

Have other groups share their projects and Middle School Physical Education Portfolios. (Assessment opportunity: all)

DAY 15

Debrief Middle School Physical Education Portfolios. (Assessment opportunity: all)

17

An Eighth Grade Program: Working as a Team to Develop Strategies for Success

I expect my students to solve various tactical problems within a game. My focus is on using skill to accomplish the tactics. This has resulted in students being highly engaged in skills and tactics that are game-related, rather than working on skills in an isolated situation.

—Rebecca J. Berkowitz, Blendon Middle School, Westerville, Ohio

Eighth Grade Standards

By the end of eighth grade, each student

1.0—Demonstrates the mature form for specialized skills and combinations during modified team and dance activities.

2.1—Analyzes the effect of positive transfer on specialized skill improvement.

2.2—Explains how force can be used to alter the outcome of a skill performance.

2.3—Explains offensive and defensive strategies for invasion, net, and field sports.

2.4—Analyzes the role of physical abilities in the performance of specialized skills.

2. 5—Explains critical elements of specialized skills and combinations in team sports.

3.1—Engages in moderate and vigorous physical activity for 60 minutes 6 days each week.

3.2—Explains ways of increasing physical activity in routine daily activities.

4.1—Works toward a health-enhancing level of physical fitness.

4.2—Designs a 2-week personal health-related fitness plan taking into account the possibility of inclement weather, minor injury, or travel.

5.1—Collaborates with others to solve group problems in physical activity settings.

5.2—Accepts responsibility for one's own actions and decisions during physical activity.

6.1—Explains the development and role of movement-related activities in the United States (19th to 20th centuries) and their influence on physical activities today.

6.2—Appreciates others' stylistic approaches to creating a dance or routine.

6.3—Chooses to engage in physical activities at the appropriate level of social, physical, and emotional challenge.

6.4—Explains the cognitive and psychological benefits of regular participation in physical activity.

In this chapter I describe a sample eighth grade program for the theme Working as a Team to Develop Strategies for Success. As we discussed in chapter 7, students at this grade level are ready for the complex team sports that are played in our society. But you should still set up the practice activities in modified settings. For example, you can teach soccer through practice scrimmages with four players on each team. This gives students a chance to understand the game of soccer while still getting many chances to participate and practice.

I have selected the activity approach for the eighth grade units of instruction. The following are the units for eighth grade:

1. Introduction and Fitness Assessment (3 weeks)

2. Problem-Solving Activities (4 weeks)

3. Team Invasion Sports (11 weeks)

4. Team Net Sports (5 weeks)

5. Team Field Sports (5 weeks)

6. Square Dancing (5 weeks)

7. Closure and Fitness Assessment (3 weeks)

Of course, team invasion sports, team net sports, and team field sports fit in well with the grade-level theme. But so does square dancing, because it's a team activity requiring four couples or eight individuals to work together to achieve the final outcome—successfully dancing to the calls. Problem solving is also a team-building activity, ensuring early in the year that students know how to get along with one another before working together in team sports.

You will notice that throughout each unit, opportunities are noted for assessment and assessment assignments. An assessment assignment refers to the giving of an assignment whereas assignment refers to either the collection of an assessment or the actual lesson in which an assessment occurs. Assessment can be done using paper and pencil or the Middle School Physical Education Portfolio (Bonnie's Fitware, Inc.), which has been listed as a resource for each unit.

Introduction and Fitness Assessment   — Unit 1

This unit is an introductory unit for eighth grade students. It gives students a chance to get reacquainted and to meet new members of the class. I also use this introductory unit to set my expectations, teach the class rules, assess the students' fitness levels, and guide them as they set their yearly goals for fitness development.

You can conduct this unit in just about any facility. If you are performing exercises on the ground or on grass, provide students with carpet squares or some other material so they don't get dirty. The equipment necessary to implement the unit depends on the type of introductory games you choose and the fitness assessments you administer. I administer the Fitnessgram health-related fitness assessment battery, including the back-saver sit-and-reach, curl-ups, skinfold measurements, push-ups, trunk lift, and 1-mile run. You can order the Fitnessgram test administration procedures from Human Kinetics (see appendix C). You will see in the daily agendas that my students prepare for the fitness assessment through various activities. In addition, the students enter their fitness scores into their own electronic portfolios using the Health-Related Fitness: Tutorial and Portfolio (Bonnie's Fitware, Inc.).

Unit 1 Standards

1.0—Demonstrates the mature form for the forearm pass.

2.1—Defines positive and negative transfer.

2.2—Describes the external forces that impact physical performance.

2.3—Explains the elements of a team sport.

2.4—Describes the areas of skill-related fitness.

2.5—Explains the critical elements of the forearm pass.

3.1—Engages in moderate and vigorous physical activity for 60 minutes 6 days each week.

3.2—Explains ways to take physical activity breaks during the day.

4.1—Participates in the fitness assessment.

4.2—Analyzes a 1-week health-related fitness plan.

5.1—Demonstrates working with a partner.

5.2—Accepts responsibility for one's own actions.

6.1—Describes fitness activities in the United States during the 19th and 20th centuries.

6.2—Not applicable.

6.3—Chooses to engage in fitness and cooperative activities.

6.4—Defines physical activity, psychology, and cognition.

Unit 1 Assessments

1.0—Structured observation (days 3-4)

2.1—Quiz (days 14-15)

2.2—Quiz (days 14-15)

2.3—Quiz (days 14-15)

2.4—Quiz (days 14-15)

2.5—Quiz (days 14-15)

3.1—Log (assigned on day 2; collected on day 15)

3.2—Quiz (days 14-15)

4.1—Fitness assessment on days 9-15; food intake and caloric output log collection on days 11-15)

4.2—Essay (assigned on day 3; collected on day 8)

5.1—Structured observation (days 4, 6, 8)

5.2—Essay (assigned on day 3; collected on day 8)

6.1—Report (assigned on day 9; collected on day 15)

6.2—Not applicable

6.3—Structured observation (days 1-15)

6.4—Quiz (days 14-15)

Resources

Health-Related Fitness: Tutorial and Portfolio (Bonnie's Fitware, Inc.)

Fitnessgram testing materials (Human Kinetics)

Middle School Physical Education Portfolio (Bonnie's Fitware, Inc.)

Eighth grade introduction task cards (Bonnie's Fitware, Inc.)

Fitness task cards

Short jump rope task cards

Eighth grade unit 1 posters (Bonnie's Fitware, Inc.—included in the Middle School Detailed Lesson Plans)

Fitness posters (Bonnie's Fitware, Inc.—included in the Middle School Detailed Lesson Plans)

Qualities of Movement chart (Bonnie's Fitware, Inc.—included in the Middle School Detailed Lesson Plans)

Equipment

Fleece balls	Rope	Fitness assessment equipment
Volleyball or balloon	Platform	

Games

Toss-a-Name Game	Moon Ball	Yurt Circle
Toss-and-Catch-a-Name Game	Knots	All Aboard
3-6-9	Rope Pull-Up	

Unit 1 Outline

DAY 1	Display the posters.
	Establish a roll call procedure.
	Introduce the class rules. 5.2
	Have students record the rules in their notebooks.
	Discuss routines and procedures specific for your class.
	Review (from grades 5 to 7) Toss-a-Name Game using a task card. 6.3
	Have students participate in Toss-a-Name Game. Rotate students so they get to know many of the other students. (Assessment opportunity: structured observation 6.3)
DAY 2	Review the class rules. 5.2
	Review (from grades 5 to 7) Toss-and-Catch-a-Name Game using a task card. 6.3
	Have students participate in Toss-and-Catch-a-Name Game. Rotate students so they get to know many of the other students. (Assessment opportunity: structured observation 6.3)
	Review (from grades 5 to 7) how to open lockers.
	Assign lockers to students.
	Instruct students to ensure that their locker combination is working.
	Define physical activity, psychology, and cognition. 6.4
	Have students record in their notebooks the definitions for physical activity, psychology, and cognition in their notebooks. 6.4
	Assign students to keep a log of daily activity. (Assessment assignment opportunity: log 3.1)

DAY 3	Have students dress for physical education. Have students perform a warm-up along with a cardiorespiratory workout. 4.1 Teach students 3-6-9 using the task card. 1.0, 6.3 Have students participate in 3-6-9. (Assessment opportunity: structured observation 1.0, 6.3) Lead students through a cool-down and flexibility exercises appropriate to the physical activity level of the lesson. 4.1 Review the principles of frequency, intensity, time, and type (FITT) for the five components of health-related fitness. 4.2 Discuss what it means to accept responsibility for one's own actions. 5.2 Have students write an essay that reviews their 1-week health-related fitness plan from seventh grade and describes what will help them to make their plans better this year. (Assessment assignment opportunity: essay 4.2, 5.2)
DAY 4	Review the class rules. 5.2 Have students brainstorm what it means to work with a partner. 5.1 Demonstrate, using the ball for Moon Ball, the external forces and rotation principles that impact the ball. 2.2 Review (from grades 5 to 7) the correct technique for the forearm pass. 1.0, 2.5 Have students record in their notebooks the critical elements of the forearm pass. 2.5 Have students perform a warm-up along with muscular strength and muscular endurance exercises. 4.1 Have students practice the forearm pass with a partner. (Assessment opportunity: structured observation 1.0, 5.1, 6.3) Teach students Moon Ball using the task card. 1.0, 6.3 Have students participate in Moon Ball using only the forearm pass. (Assessment opportunity: structured observation 1.0, 6.3) Lead students through a cool-down and flexibility exercises appropriate to the physical activity level of the lesson. 4.1 Have students, in pairs, summarize the external forces and rotation principles that impact the ball. (Assessment opportunity: structured observation 5.1) 2.2 Have students record their summary in their individual notebooks. 2.2
DAY 5	Teach students the rules of Knots using the task card. 6.3 Define positive transfer of learning. 2.1 Have students brainstorm activities they performed in fifth, sixth, and seventh grades that are similar to Knots and may help them to be successful in Knots. 2.1 Define negative transfer of learning. 2.1 Have students brainstorm activities they performed in fifth, sixth, and seventh grades that are different from Knots and that may interfere with their ability to be successful in Knots. 2.1 Have students record in their notebooks the definitions for positive and negative transfer of learning. 2.1 Have students perform a warm-up along with a cardiorespiratory workout. 4.1 Have students participate in Knots (eight people). (Assessment opportunity: structured observation 6.3) Lead students through a cool-down and flexibility exercises appropriate to the physical activity level of the lesson. 4.1

(continued)

Unit 1 Outline *(continued)*

DAY 6

Review the class rules.

Explain the elements of a team sport. 2.3

Have students record in their notebooks the elements of a team sport. 2.3

Have students perform a warm-up along with a cardiorespiratory workout. 4.1

Teach students how to play Rope Pull-Up using the task card. 6.3, 2.3

Have students participate in Rope Pull-Up. (Assessment opportunity: structured observation 6.3)

Lead students through a cool-down and flexibility exercises appropriate to the physical activity level of the lesson. 4.1

Have students discuss whether Rope Pull-Up is a team sport. 2.3

Instruct pairs of students to brainstorm ways to take physical activity breaks during the day. (Assessment opportunity: structured observation 5.1) 3.2

Have students record their ideas in their notebooks. 3.2

DAY 7

Have students perform a warm-up along with muscular strength and muscular endurance exercises. 4.1

Review the elements of a team sport. 2.3

Teach students the rules for Yurt Circle (see figure 17.1) using the task card. 2.3, 6.3

Have students participate in Yurt Circle. (Assessment opportunity: structured observation 6.3) 2.3

Lead students through a cool-down and flexibility exercises appropriate to the physical activity level of the lesson. 4.1

Have students discuss whether Yurt Circle is a team sport. 2.3

Figure 17.1 Yurt Circle.

DAY 8	Have students perform a warm-up. (Assessment opportunity: structured observation 6.3) 4.1
	Teach students the rules for All Aboard using the task card. 2.3, 6.3
	Have students participate in All Aboard. (Assessment opportunity: structured observation 6.3) 2.3
	Have students discuss whether participating in Tarps in earlier grades had a positive or negative effect on their participation in All Aboard. 2.1
	Lead students through a cool-down and flexibility exercises appropriate to the physical activity level of the lesson. 4.1
	Collect students' analyses of their seventh grade 1-week fitness plan. (Assessment opportunity: essay 4.2, 5.2)
DAY 9	Have students perform warm-up exercises for the back-saver sit-and-reach assessment. 4.1
	Assign students randomly to working groups of four for the introduction unit.
	Review the five areas of health-related fitness and the purpose of preassessment. 4.1
	Explain the back-saver sit-and-reach assessment and the purpose of the assessment. 4.1
	Have students participate in an aerobic circuit and, at the computer station (loaded with the Health-Related Fitness Tutorial), go through the information on skill-related fitness. (Assessment opportunity: structured observation 6.3) 4.1, 2.4
	Administer the back-saver sit-and-reach assessment to one group at a time. (Assessment opportunity: fitness assessment 4.1)
	Have students input fitness scores into their Health-Related Fitness Portfolios. 4.1
	Lead students through a cool-down and flexibility exercises appropriate to the physical activity level of the lesson. 4.1
	For homework, instruct students to research the fitness training that occurred in 19th- and 20th-century America. (Assessment assignment opportunity: report 6.1)
DAY 10	Have students perform warm-up exercises for the curl-up assessment. 4.1
	Explain the curl-up assessment and the purpose of the assessment. 4.1
	Have students participate in a flexibility circuit and, at the computer station (loaded with the Health-Related Fitness Tutorial), go through the information on skill-related fitness. (Assessment opportunity: structured observation 6.3) 4.1, 2.4
	Administer the curl-up assessment to two groups at a time. (Assessment opportunity: fitness assessment 4.1)
	Have students input fitness scores into their Health-Related Fitness Portfolios. 4.1
	Lead students through a cool-down and flexibility exercises appropriate to the physical activity level of the lesson. 4.1
	Assign students the task of collecting data on their food intake and caloric output for 3 days. (Assessment assignment opportunity: log 4.1)
DAY 11	Explain the skinfold measurement and the purpose of the assessment. 4.1
	Have students perform warm-up exercises. 4.1
	Have students participate in a jump rope circuit using short jump rope task cards. (Assessment opportunity: structured observation 6.3) 4.1
	Administer the skinfold measurement to students one at a time in private. (Assessment opportunity: fitness assessment 4.1)
	Have students input fitness scores into their Health-Related Fitness Portfolios. 4.1
	Lead students through a cool-down and flexibility exercises appropriate to the physical activity level of the lesson. 4.1

(continued)

Unit 1 Outline *(continued)*

DAY 12

Have students perform warm-up exercises for the push-up assessment. 4.1

Explain the push-up assessment and the purpose of the assessment. 4.1

Have students participate in a flexibility circuit using fitness task cards. (Assessment opportunity: structured observation 6.3) 4.1

Administer the push-up assessment to one group at a time. (Assessment opportunity: fitness assessment 4.1)

Have students input fitness scores into their Health-Related Fitness Portfolios. 4.1

Lead students through a cool-down and flexibility exercises appropriate to the physical activity level of the lesson. 4.1

DAY 13

Have students perform warm-up exercises for the trunk lift. 4.1

Explain the trunk-lift assessment and the purpose of the assessment. 4.1

Have students participate in an aerobics circuit using fitness task cards. (Assessment opportunity: structured observation 6.3) 4.1

Administer the trunk-lift assessment at one station in the circuit. (Assessment opportunity: fitness assessment 4.1)

Have students input fitness scores into their Health-Related Fitness Portfolios. 4.1

Lead students through a cool-down and flexibility exercises appropriate to the physical activity level of the lesson. 4.1

DAY 14

Have students perform warm-up exercises for the 1-mile run. 4.1

Explain the 1-mile run assessment and the purpose of the assessment. 4.1

Administer the 1-mile run assessment to half the class. (Assessment opportunity: fitness assessment 4.1, structured observation 6.3)

Administer the written quiz to the other half of the class. (Assessment opportunity: quiz 2.1, 2.2, 2.3, 2.4, 2.5, 3.2, 6.4)

Administer makeup assessments as needed. (Assessment opportunity: fitness assessment 4.1)

Have students input fitness scores into their Health-Related Fitness Portfolios. 4.1

Lead students through a cool-down and flexibility exercises appropriate to the physical activity level of the lesson. 4.1

DAY 15

Have students perform warm-up exercises for the 1-mile run. 4.1

Explain the 1-mile run assessment and the purpose of the assessment. 4.1

Administer the 1-mile run assessment to half of the class. (Assessment opportunity: fitness assessment 4.1, structured observation 6.3)

Administer the written quiz to the other half of the class. (Assessment opportunity: quiz 6.2, 2.1, 2.2, 2.3, 2.4, 2.5, 3.2, 6.4)

Administer makeup assessments as needed. (Assessment opportunity: fitness assessment 4.1)

Have students input fitness scores into their Health-Related Fitness Portfolios. 4.1

Lead students through a cool-down and flexibility exercises appropriate to the physical activity level of the lesson. 4.1

Collect students' reports on fitness training. (Assessment opportunity: report 6.1)

Collect students' physical activity logs. (Assessment opportunity: log 3.1)

Collect students' food intake and caloric output logs. (Assessment opportunity: log 4.1)

Problem-Solving Activities   — Unit 2

In this unit, I focus on helping students to work in teams to develop strategies for success. You can teach this unit in any open area; however, it is preferable to have access to either a built-in or portable ropes course. This unit works best if you have a ropes course (temporary or permanent); however, you can use low-level cooperative games. You may also want to consider forming a partnership with a local business and sharing the ropes course with that business. The school can use the course during the school day and the business can use and rent out the course during the evenings and on weekends.

This unit links well with the communications unit in health education. To make the connection clear to students, I have them perform the activities in physical education and then debrief their feelings related to the activities during health education. You can also involve the language arts teacher, who can have students write about their feelings after they have discussed them in health education.

Unit 2 Standards

1.0—Not applicable for specific skills; continue to use locomotor and nonlocomotor movement in problem-solving activities.

2.1—Describes the elements of positive transfer.

2.2—Explains the impact of gravity on skill performance.

2.3—Explains the use of strategy in problem-solving situations.

2.4—Describes the variables of physical development and physical abilities that affect motor performance.

2.5—Not applicable.

3.1—Engages in moderate and vigorous physical activity for 60 minutes 6 days each week based on personal goals.

3.2—Explains ways to avoid labor-saving devices in order to increase daily physical activity.

4.1—Works toward a health-enhancing level of physical fitness.

4.2—Creates a 2-week warm-up, cool-down, and flexibility plan.

5.1—Demonstrates the steps for conflict resolution.

5.2—Accepts responsibility for one's own actions and decisions during problem-solving activities.

6.1—Describes modern Olympic movements in the United States during the 19th and 20th centuries.

6.2—Not applicable.

6.3—Chooses to engage in problem-solving activities at the appropriate level of social, physical, and emotional challenge.

6.4—Describes the problem-solving benefits derived from participation in physical activity.

Unit 2 Assessments

1.0—Not applicable

2.1—Quiz (day 20)

2.2—Quiz (day 20)

2.3—Quiz (day 20)

2.4—Quiz (day 20)

2.5—Not applicable

3.1—Log (assigned on day 1; collected on day 20)

3.2—Quiz (day 20)

4.1—Goal setting (day 1); structured observation (days 2-19)

4.2—Project (assigned on day 1; collected on day 20)

5.1—Structured observation (days 1-19)

5.2—Structured observation (days 1-19)

6.1—Report (assigned on day 1; collected on day 20)

6.2—Not applicable

6.3—Structured observation (days 2-19)

6.4—Quiz (day 20)

Resources

Health-Related Fitness: Tutorial and Portfolio (Bonnie's Fitware, Inc.)

Middle School Physical Education Portfolio (Bonnie's Fitware, Inc.)

Eighth grade problem-solving task cards (Bonnie's Fitware, Inc.)

Cooperative and Problem-Solving Activities CD (Bonnie's Fitware, Inc.)

Eighth grade unit 2 posters (Bonnie's Fitware, Inc.—included in the Middle School Detailed Lesson Plans)

Fitness posters (Bonnie's Fitware, Inc.—included in the Middle School Detailed Lesson Plans)

Equipment

Low ropes course (swinging rope, suspended log)	Poles (1.6 inch diameter)
Spiderweb (part of low ropes course or separate item)	Bucket
Web cube	Planks (2 feet by 6 feet)
Trolleys	Broomstick
Rope	Scarves or blindfolds
Foam box or particle board	Hula hoops
Toilet plunger	Poly spots
Foam or PVC cylinders	Short poles
Platform (12 by 12 inches)	

Games

Wordles	Acid Pit	Pharoah's Stone
Trolley	Web Cube	Sherpa Walk
Amazon	Levitation	Quicksand Save
TP Shuffle	Spiderweb	Yeah But
All Aboard	Trust Circle	Two-Person Trust Fall
Human Ladder	Prouty's Landing	

Unit 2 Outline

DAY 1

Display the fitness posters.

Have students discuss ways to avoid labor-saving devices in order to increase daily physical activity. 3.2

Have students record in their notebooks suggestions for increasing daily activity. 3.2

Instruct students to examine the results of their fitness assessment and food and activity logs and to set three long-term goals and three short-term goals for improvement (record goals in the Health-Related Fitness: Tutorial and Portfolio). (Assessment opportunity: goal setting 4.1)

Review concepts related to warm-up, cool-down, and flexibility from the Health-Related Fitness: Tutorial and Portfolio. 4.2

Assign the creation and implementation of a 2-week warm-up, cool-down, and flexibility plan. (Assessment assignment opportunity: project 4.2)

DAY 1 *(continued)*	Introduce problem-solving unit and review safety considerations.
	Assign students to working groups of four for the problem-solving unit.
	Explain the problem-solving benefits derived from participation in physical activity. 6.4
	Have students record the information in their notebooks. 6.4
	Discuss the steps for conflict resolution. 5.1
	Have students summarize the steps for conflict resolution in their notebooks. 5.1
	Discuss taking responsibility for one's own actions and decisions during problem-solving activities. 5.2
	Have student summarize the discussion in their notebooks. 5.2
	Have students work on Wordles in their new groups. 5.1, 5.2
	Debrief activities including effective use of the conflict resolution process; taking responsibility for one's actions; and feelings of challenge, enjoyment, and success. (Assessment opportunity: structured observation 5.1, 5.2)
	Assign unit-long homework:
	• Have students research and write a description of the Olympic movement in the United States during the 19th and 20th centuries. (Assessment assignment opportunity: report 6.1)
	• Have students keep a log of daily activity. (Assessment assignment opportunity: log 3.1)
DAY 2	Discuss with students how participation in problem-solving activities provides personal challenge, enjoyment, and success. 6.3
	Have students record the discussion in their notebooks. 6.3
	Discuss with students the use of strategy in problem-solving situations. 2.3
	Have students take notes during the discussion. 2.3
	Have students work on Wordles in their groups. (Assessment opportunity: structured observation 5.1, 5.2)
	Debrief activities including effective use of the conflict resolution process; taking responsibility for one's actions; and feelings of challenge, enjoyment, and success. (Assessment opportunity: structured observation 5.1, 5.2, 6.3)
	Review ways to avoid labor-saving devices in order to increase daily physical activity. 3.2
DAY 3	Describe the variables of physical development and physical abilities that affect motor performance. 2.4
	Have students record in their notebooks the variables of physical development and physical abilities that affect motor performance. 2.4
	Have students perform a warm-up along with a cardiorespiratory workout. (Assessment opportunity: structured observation 4.1)
	Introduce Trolley, Amazon (see figure 17.2), and TP Shuffle (see figure 17.3) using the Cooperative and Problem-Solving Activities CD. 5.1, 5.2
	Have students rotate through these stations: Trolley, Amazon, and TP Shuffle. (Assessment opportunity: structured observation 1.0, 5.1, 5.2, 6.3)
	Lead students through a cool-down and flexibility exercises appropriate to the physical activity level of the lesson. (Assessment opportunity: structured observation 4.1)
	Debrief the problem-solving strategies used in Trolley, Amazon, and TP Shuffle. 2.3
	Debrief effective use of the conflict resolution process; taking responsibility for one's actions; and feelings of challenge, enjoyment, and success. (Assessment opportunity: structured observation 5.1, 5.2, 6.3).
	Review the problem-solving benefits derived from participation in physical activity. 6.4

(continued)

Figure 17.2   Amazon.

Figure 17.3   TP Shuffle.

Unit 2 Outline   *(continued)*

DAY 4

Describe the impact of gravity on physical performance. 2.2

Have students record in their notebooks the impact of gravity on physical performance. 2.2

Have students perform a warm-up along with muscular strength and muscular endurance exercises. (Assessment opportunity: structured observation 4.1)

Review Trolley, Amazon (see figure 17.2), and TP Shuffle (see figure 17.3). 5.1, 5.2

Have students rotate through these stations: Trolley, Amazon, and TP Shuffle. (Assessment opportunity: structured observation 1.0, 5.1, 5.2, 6.3)

Lead students through a cool-down and flexibility exercises appropriate to the physical activity level of the lesson. (Assessment opportunity: structured observation 4.1)

Review the variables of physical development and physical abilities that affect motor performance. 2.4

Debrief effective use of the conflict resolution process; taking responsibility for one's actions; and feelings of challenge, enjoyment, and success. (Assessment opportunity: structured observation 5.1, 5.2, 6.3)

DAY 5

Have students perform a warm-up along with a cardiorespiratory workout. (Assessment opportunity: structured observation 4.1)

Review Trolley, Amazon (see figure 17.2), and TP Shuffle (see figure 17.3). 5.1, 5.2

Have students rotate through these stations: Trolley, Amazon, and TP Shuffle. (Assessment opportunity: structured observation 1.0, 5.1, 5.2, 6.3)

Lead students through a cool-down and flexibility exercises appropriate to the physical activity level of the lesson. (Assessment opportunity: structured observation 4.1)

Debrief activities including effective use of the conflict resolution process; taking responsibility for one's actions; and feelings of challenge, enjoyment, and success. (Assessment opportunity: structured observation 5.1, 5.2, 6.3)

DAY 6

Have students perform a warm-up along with a cardiorespiratory workout. (Assessment opportunity: structured observation 4.1)

Introduce Human Ladder (see figure 17.4) and Acid Pit using the Cooperative and Problem-Solving Activities CD. 1.0, 5.1, 5.2, 6.3

Review All Aboard (from unit 1). 1.0, 5.1, 5.2, 6.3

Have students rotate through stations: All Aboard, Human Ladder, and Acid Pit. (Assessment opportunity: structured observation 1.0, 5.1, 5.2, 6.3)

Lead students through a cool-down and flexibility exercises appropriate to the physical activity level of the lesson. (Assessment opportunity: structured observation 4.1)

Debrief activities including effective use of the conflict resolution process; taking responsibility for one's actions; and feelings of challenge, enjoyment, and success. (Assessment opportunity: structured observation 5.1, 5.2, 6.3)

(continued)

Figure 17.4 Human Ladder.

Unit 2 Outline (continued)

DAY 7	Have students perform a warm-up along with muscular strength and muscular endurance exercises. (Assessment opportunity: structured observation 4.1)
	Review All Aboard, Human Ladder (see figure 17.4), and Acid Pit. 5.1, 5.2
	Have students rotate through stations: All Aboard, Human Ladder, and Acid Pit. (Assessment opportunity: structured observation 1.0, 5.1, 5.2, 6.3)
	Lead students through a cool-down and flexibility exercises appropriate to the physical activity level of the lesson. (Assessment opportunity: structured observation 4.1)
	Debrief activities including effective use of the conflict resolution process; taking responsibility for one's actions; and feelings of challenge, enjoyment, and success. (Assessment opportunity: structured observation 5.1, 5.2, 6.3)
DAY 8	Have students perform a warm-up along with a cardiorespiratory workout. (Assessment opportunity: structured observation 4.1)
	Review All Aboard, Human Ladder (see figure 17.4), and Acid Pit. 5.1, 5.2
	Have students rotate through stations: All Aboard, Human Ladder, and Acid Pit. (Assessment opportunity: structured observation 1.0, 5.1, 5.2, 6.3)
	Lead students through a cool-down and flexibility exercises appropriate to the physical activity level of the lesson. (Assessment opportunity: structured observation 4.1)
	Debrief activities including effective use of the conflict resolution process; taking responsibility for one's actions; and feelings of challenge, enjoyment, and success. (Assessment opportunity: structured observation 5.1, 5.2, 6.3)
DAY 9	Have students perform a warm-up along with muscular strength and muscular endurance exercises. (Assessment opportunity: structured observation 4.1)
	Explain the elements of positive transfer. 2.1
	Have students record the elements of positive transfer. 2.1
	Introduce Web Cube using the Cooperative and Problem-Solving Activities CD. 5.1, 5.2
	Have students participate in Web Cube. (Assessment opportunity: structured observation 1.0, 5.1, 5.2, 6.3)
	Introduce Levitation (see figure 17.5) using the Cooperative and Problem-Solving Activities CD. 5.1, 5.2
	Have students practice Levitation in their groups. (Assessment opportunity: structured observation 1.0, 5.1, 5.2, 6.3)
	Lead students through a cool-down and flexibility exercises appropriate to the physical activity level of the lesson. (Assessment opportunity: structured observation 4.1)
	Debrief activities including effective use of the conflict resolution process; taking responsibility for one's actions; and feelings of challenge, enjoyment, and success. (Assessment opportunity: structured observation 5.1, 5.2, 6.3)
DAY 10	Have students perform a warm-up along with a cardiorespiratory workout. (Assessment opportunity: structured observation 4.1)
	Review Levitation (see figure 17.5). 5.1, 5.2
	Review Web Cube. 5.1, 5.2
	Describe Spiderweb, Prouty's Landing, and Trust Circle (see figure 17.6) using the Cooperative and Problem-Solving Activities CD. 5.1, 5.2
	Have students rotate through these stations: Spiderweb, Prouty's Landing, Web Cube, and Trust Circle. (Assessment opportunity: structured observation 1.0, 5.1, 5.2, 6.3)

Figure 17.5 Levitation.

DAY 10 *(continued)*	Discuss the elements of positive transfer of learning that exist between Web Cube and Spiderweb. 2.1 Debrief activities including effective use of the conflict resolution process; taking responsibility for one's actions; and feelings of challenge, enjoyment, and success. (Assessment opportunity: structured observation 5.1, 5.2, 6.3) Lead students through a cool-down and flexibility exercises appropriate to the physical activity level of the lesson. (Assessment opportunity: structured observation 4.1)
DAY 11	Have students perform a warm-up along with a cardiorespiratory workout. (Assessment opportunity: structured observation 4.1) Review Spiderweb, Prouty's Landing, Web Cube, and Trust Circle (see figure 17.6). 5.1, 5.2 Have students rotate through these stations: Spiderweb, Prouty's Landing, Web Cube, and Trust Circle. (Assessment opportunity: structured observation 1.0, 5.1, 5.2, 6.3) Debrief activities including effective use of the conflict resolution process; taking responsibility for one's actions; and feelings of challenge, enjoyment, and success. (Assessment opportunity: structured observation 5.1, 5.2, 6.3) Lead students through a cool-down and flexibility exercises appropriate to the physical activity level of the lesson. (Assessment opportunity: structured observation 4.1)
DAY 12	Have students perform a warm-up along with muscular strength and muscular endurance exercises. (Assessment opportunity: structured observation 4.1) Review Spiderweb, Prouty's Landing, Web Cube, and Trust Circle (see figure 17.6). 5.1, 5.2 Have students rotate through these stations: Spiderweb, Prouty's Landing, Web Cube, and Trust Circle. (Assessment opportunity: structured observation 1.0, 5.1, 5.2, 6.3) Debrief activities including effective use of the conflict resolution process; taking responsibility for one's actions; and feelings of challenge, enjoyment, and success. (Assessment opportunity: structured observation 5.1, 5.2, 6.3) Lead students through a cool-down and flexibility exercises appropriate to the physical activity level of the lesson. (Assessment opportunity: structured observation 4.1)

(continued)

Figure 17.6   Trust Circle.

Unit 2 Outline   *(continued)*

DAY 13	Have students perform a warm-up along with a cardiorespiratory workout. (Assessment opportunity: structured observation 4.1)
	Introduce Sherpa Walk (see figure 17.7), Quicksand Save, and Pharaoh's Stone (see figure 17.8) using the Cooperative and Problem-Solving Activities CD. 5.1, 5.2
	Have students rotate through stations: Sherpa Walk, Quicksand Save, and Pharaoh's Stone. (Assessment opportunity: structured observation 1.0, 5.1, 5.2, 6.3)
	Debrief activities including effective use of the conflict resolution process; taking responsibility for one's actions; and feelings of challenge, enjoyment, and success. (Assessment opportunity: structured observation 5.1, 5.2, 6.3)
	Lead students through a cool-down and flexibility exercises appropriate to the physical activity level of the lesson. (Assessment opportunity: structured observation 4.1)
DAY 14	Have students perform a warm-up along with muscular strength and muscular endurance exercises. (Assessment opportunity: structured observation 4.1)
	Review Sherpa Walk (see figure 17.7), Quicksand Save, and Pharaoh's Stone (see figure 17.8). 5.1, 5.2
	Have students rotate through stations: Sherpa Walk, Quicksand Save, and Pharaoh's Stone. (Assessment opportunity: structured observation 1.0, 5.1, 5.2, 6.3)
	Debrief activities including effective use of the conflict resolution process; taking responsibility for one's actions; and feelings of challenge, enjoyment, and success. (Assessment opportunity: structured observation 5.1, 5.2, 6.3)
	Lead students through a cool-down and flexibility exercises appropriate to the physical activity level of the lesson. (Assessment opportunity: structured observation 4.1)

Figure 17.7 Sherpa Walk.

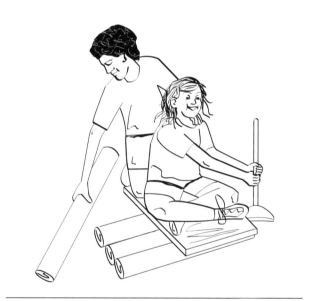

Figure 17.8 Pharaoh's Stone.

DAY 15

Have students perform a warm-up along with a cardiorespiratory workout. (Assessment opportunity: structured observation 4.1)

Review Sherpa Walk (see figure 17.7), Quicksand Save, and Pharaoh's Stone (see figure 17.8). 5.1, 5.2

Have students rotate through stations: Sherpa Walk, Quicksand Save, and Pharaoh's Stone. (Assessment opportunity: structured observation 1.0, 5.1, 5.2, 6.3)

Debrief activities including effective use of the conflict resolution process; taking responsibility for one's actions; and feelings of challenge, enjoyment, and success. (Assessment opportunity: structured observation 5.1, 5.2, 6.3)

Lead students through a cool-down and flexibility exercises appropriate to the physical activity level of the lesson. (Assessment opportunity: structured observation 4.1)

(continued)

Unit 2 Outline *(continued)*

DAY 16

Have students perform a warm-up along with a cardiorespiratory workout. (Assessment opportunity: structured observation 4.1)

Introduce Trust Walk using the Cooperative and Problem-Solving Activities CD. 5.1, 5.2

Have students participate in Trust Walk. (Assessment opportunity: structured observation 1.0, 5.1, 5.2, 6.3)

Introduce Yeah But using the Cooperative and Problem-Solving Activities CD. 5.1, 5.2

Have students participate in Yeah But. (Assessment opportunity: structured observation 1.0, 5.1, 5.2, 6.3)

Introduce the Two-Person Trust Fall from the Cooperative and Problem-Solving Activities CD. 5.1, 5.2

Have students participate in the Two-Person Trust Fall. (Assessment opportunity: structured observation 1.0, 5.1, 5.2, 6.3)

Debrief activities including effective use of the conflict resolution process; taking responsibility for one's actions; and feelings of challenge, enjoyment, and success. (Assessment opportunity: structured observation 5.1, 5.2, 6.3)

Have students discuss the similarities between Trust Walk and Two-Person Trust Fall. 2.1

Lead students through a cool-down and flexibility exercises appropriate to the physical activity level of the lesson. (Assessment opportunity: structured observation 4.1)

DAY 17

Have students perform a warm-up along with muscular strength and muscular endurance exercises. (Assessment opportunity: structured observation 4.1)

Review Trust Walk. 5.1, 5.2

Have students participate in Trust Walk. (Assessment opportunity: structured observation 1.0, 5.1, 5.2, 6.3)

Review Yeah But. 5.1, 5.2

Have students participate in Yeah But. (Assessment opportunity: structured observation 1.0, 5.1, 5.2, 6.3)

Review the Two-Person Trust Fall. 5.1, 5.2

Have students participate in the Two-Person Trust Fall. (Assessment opportunity: structured observation 1.0, 5.1, 5.2, 6.3)

Debrief activities including effective use of the conflict resolution process; taking responsibility for one's actions; and feelings of challenge, enjoyment, and success. (Assessment opportunity: structured observation 5.1, 5.2, 6.3)

Lead students through a cool-down and flexibility exercises appropriate to the physical activity level of the lesson. (Assessment opportunity: structured observation 4.1)

DAY 18

Have students perform a warm-up along with a cardiorespiratory workout. (Assessment opportunity: structured observation 4.1)

Have each group create a problem-solving challenge. (Assessment opportunity: structured observation 1.0, 5.1, 5.2, 6.3)

Lead students through a cool-down and flexibility exercises appropriate to the physical activity level of the lesson. (Assessment opportunity: structured observation 4.1)

DAY 19

Have students perform a warm-up along with muscular strength and muscular endurance exercises. (Assessment opportunity: structured observation 4.1)

Have each group finish their problem-solving challenge. (Assessment opportunity: structured observation 1.0, 5.1, 5.2, 6.3)

Have each group present their problem-solving challenge to another group, asking the other group to solve the challenge. (Assessment opportunity: structured observation 1.0, 5.1, 5.2, 6.3)

DAY 19 *(continued)*	Debrief activities including effective use of the conflict resolution process; taking responsibility for one's actions; and feelings of challenge, enjoyment, and success. (Assessment opportunity: structured observation 5.1, 5.2, 6.3)
	Lead students through a cool-down and flexibility exercises appropriate to the physical activity level of the lesson. (Assessment opportunity: structured observation 4.1)
	Review material for tomorrow's quiz (or hand out quiz if you would like for it to be a take home quiz). 2.1, 2.2, 2.3, 2.4, 3.2, 6.4
DAY 20	Instruct students to take the quiz. (Assessment opportunity: quiz 2.1, 2.2, 2.3, 2.4, 3.2, 6.4)
	Collect descriptions of the modern Olympic movement. (Assessment opportunity: report 6.1)
	Collect students' physical activity logs. (Assessment opportunity: log 3.1)
	Collect 2-week warm-up, cool-down, and flexibility plans. (Assessment opportunity: project 4.2)

Team Invasion Sports

— Unit 3

This unit ties together several invasion games (Ultimate, team handball, soccer, basketball, Speed-a-Way, and football), continuing our focus on working as a team to develop strategies for success. Although this unit takes 11 weeks, by presenting these games collectively we can concentrate on similarities and differences as well as focus on standard 2.1, which stresses the positive transfer of learning to facilitate acquiring new skills. Presenting the games in this manner also allows us to use the tactical approach strategy to teaching games (see Mitchell et al. 2006)

You can teach this unit in any open area, but blacktop is preferable for basketball and team handball skills, and grass is preferable for soccer, Speed-a-Way, and football. Of course, you'll need baskets for basketball and goals for the other sports.

Looking for a way to include math in your interdisciplinary plans? In this unit, students learn about open space and the shortest points between distances on the court and field, which ties in well with their geometry lessons in math class. You can work with the math teacher to help students see the real-life applications of geometry. In addition, you can have students graph their improvements in both distance and accuracy as they continue to refine their motor skills.

Unit 3 Standards

1.0—Demonstrates the mature form for chest pass, one-hand overhead pass, two-hand overhead pass, bounce pass, two-step stop, pivot, catching, jump-stop, hand dribbling, basketball set shot, team handball set shot, team handball jump shot, goal keeping, offensive stance, defensive stance, instep kick, sole-of-foot trap, foot dribbling, layup, rebound, one-foot lift to self, two-foot stationary lift to self, moving ball lift, lift to teammate, centering, forward pass, ball carrying, blocking, lateral, rushing, and handoff.

2.1—Applies transfer of learning principles to the learning of skills used in invasion sports.

2.2—Explains the impact of collision (rebound) on skill performance.

2.3—Explains offensive and defensive strategies for invasion sports.

2.4—Describes how differences in height and weight affect one's performance.

2.5—Explains the critical elements of chest pass, one-hand overhead pass, two-hand overhead pass, bounce pass, two-step stop, pivot, catching, jump-stop, hand dribbling, basketball set shot, team handball set shot, team handball jump shot, goal keeping, offensive stance, defensive stance, instep kick, sole-of-foot trap, foot dribbling, layup, rebound, one-foot lift to self, two-foot stationary lift to self, moving ball lift, lift to teammate, centering, forward pass, ball carrying, blocking, lateral, rushing, and handoff.

3.1—Engages in moderate and vigorous physical activity for 60 minutes 6 days each week based on personal goals.

3.2—Explains ways to get more walking into daily activities.

4.1—Works toward a health-enhancing level of physical fitness.

4.2—Creates a 2-week cardiorespiratory plan.

5.1—Collaborates with team members during invasion sports.

5.2—Accepts responsibility for one's own actions and decisions during invasion sports.

6.1—Describes invasion sports in the United States during the 19th and 20th centuries.

6.2—Not applicable.

6.3—Chooses to engage in invasion sports at the appropriate level of social, physical, and emotional challenge.

6.4—Describes the stress-reduction and relaxation benefits derived from regular participation in physical activity.

Unit 3 Assessments

1.0—Structured observation (days 2-54)

2.1—Quiz (day 55)

2.2—Quiz (day 55)

2.3—Quiz (day 55)

2.4—Quiz (day 55)

2.5—Report (assigned on day 1; collected on day 55)

3.1—Log (assigned on day 1; collected on day 55)

3.2—Essay (assigned on day 1; collected on day 55)

4.1—Structured observation (days 1-54)

4.2—Project (assigned on day 3; collected on 55)

5.1—Structured observation (days 2-54)

5.2—Structured observation (days 2-54)

6.1—Report (assigned on day 1; collected on day 55)

6.2—Not applicable

6.3—Structured observation (days 2-55)

6.4—Quiz (day 55)

Resources

Biomechanics Made Easy (Bonnie's Fitware, Inc.)

Invasion Sports CD (Bonnie's Fitware, Inc.)

Health-Related Fitness: Tutorial and Portfolio (Bonnie's Fitware, Inc.)

Middle School Physical Education Portfolio (Bonnie's Fitware, Inc.)

Eighth grade invasion sports task cards (Bonnie's Fitware, Inc.)

Eighth grade unit 3 posters (Bonnie's Fitware, Inc.—included in the Middle School Detailed Lesson Plans)

Fitness posters (Bonnie's Fitware, Inc.—included in the Middle School Detailed Lesson Plans)

Equipment

Team handballs	Playground balls	Cones
Soccer balls	Kick balls	Targets
Basketballs	Flag belts	Flying discs
Footballs	Pinnies	

Games

Team handball	Dribble tag	Speed-a-Way
Soccer	Keep-Away	Football
Ultimate	Basketball	

Unit 3 Outline

DAY 1

Display the posters.

Introduce team handball, soccer, basketball, Speed-a-Way, and football along with safety rules. 2.3

Assign students to working groups of four for invasion sports unit.

Explain the importance of engaging in invasion sport activities that provide personal challenge, enjoyment, and success. 6.3

Have students record the information in their notebooks. 6.3

Have students perform a warm-up along with a cardiorespiratory workout. (Assessment opportunity: structured observation 4.1)

Have students play Ultimate (which they learned in sixth grade) as an introduction to invasion sports. 2.3

Discuss with students what (e.g., skills, strategies) they found beneficial when playing Ultimate. 2.3

Lead students through a cool-down and flexibility exercises appropriate to the physical activity level of the lesson. (Assessment opportunity: structured observation 4.1)

Assign unit-long homework:

- Have students research and describe invasion sports in the United States during the 19th and 20th centuries. (Assessment assignment opportunity: report 6.1)

- Have students keep a log of daily activity. (Assessment assignment opportunity: log 3.1)

- Have students write an explanation about ways to get more walking into daily activities. (Assessment assignment opportunity: essay 3.2)

- Have students record the critical features for each skill introduced and present their findings to the teacher as a report. (Assessment assignment opportunity: report 2.5)

DAY 2

Explain what it means to accept responsibility for one's own actions. 5.2

Have students record what it means to accept responsibility for one's own actions. 5.2

Explain what it means to abide by the decisions of the officials and to accept the outcome of the game. 5.2

Explain what it means to show appreciation toward participants. 5.2

Have students record what it means to abide by the decisions of the officials, accept the outcome of the game, and show appreciation toward participants. 5.2

Have students perform a warm-up along with muscular strength and muscular endurance exercises. (Assessment opportunity: structured observation 4.1)

Explain how to play team handball and its history. 2.3, 6.1

Have students play modified 4-on-4 team handball to check their current skill level. (Assessment opportunity: structured observation 1.0, 5.2, 6.3)

Lead students through a cool-down and flexibility exercises appropriate to the physical activity level of the lesson. (Assessment opportunity: structured observation 4.1)

Review the importance of engaging in invasion sport activities that provide for personal challenge, enjoyment, and success. 6.3

(continued)

Unit 3 Outline (continued)

DAY 3

Display fitness posters.

Describe stress-reduction and relaxation benefits derived from regular participation in physical activities. 6.4

Have students record in their notebooks stress-reduction and relaxation benefits. 6.4

Explain the frequency, intensity, time, and type (FITT) concepts for cardiorespiratory endurance using the Health-Related Fitness: Tutorial and Portfolio. 4.2

Have students record the FITT concepts for cardiorespiratory endurance in their notebooks. 4.2

Assign a 2-week cardiorespiratory plan that uses a variety of exercises. (Assessment assignment opportunity: project 4.2)

Have students perform a warm-up along with a cardiorespiratory workout. (Assessment opportunity: structured observation 4.1)

Demonstrate and describe the chest pass, one- and two-hand overhead pass, and bounce pass using the Invasion Sports CD. 1.0, 2.5

Provide feedback as pairs practice the chest pass, overhead pass, and bounce pass, using team handballs. (Assessment opportunity: structured observation 1.0, 5.2, 6.3)

Demonstrate passing at stationary and moving targets. 1.0, 2.5

Have students, in pairs, rotate through stations, passing at stationary and moving targets and giving each other feedback. (Assessment opportunity: structured observation 1.0, 5.2, 6.3)

Lead students through a cool-down and flexibility exercises appropriate to the physical activity level of the lesson. (Assessment opportunity: structured observation 4.1)

Review what it means to accept responsibility for one's own actions. 5.2

DAY 4

Describe the elements of positive transfer. 2.1

Emphasize that the more similar two skills are, the easier it is to apply positive transfer of learning. 2.1

Have students summarize the information on positive transfer in their notebooks. 2.1

Have students perform a warm-up along with muscular strength and muscular endurance exercises. (Assessment opportunity: structured observation 4.1)

Demonstrate and describe the two-step stop and the jump-stop using the Invasion Sports CD. 1.0, 2.5

Provide feedback as pairs of students practice the two-step stop and the jump-stop. (Assessment opportunity: structured observation 1.0, 5.2, 6.3)

Demonstrate the pivot using the Invasion Sports CD. 1.0, 2.5

Provide feedback as students practice the pivot. (Assessment opportunity: structured observation 1.0, 5.2, 6.3)

Provide feedback as pairs practice the chest pass, overhead pass, and bounce pass, using team handballs. (Assessment opportunity: structured observation 1.0, 5.2, 6.3)

Review the stress-reduction and relaxation benefits derived from regular participation in physical activities. 6.4

Lead students through a cool-down and flexibility exercises appropriate to the physical activity level of the lesson. (Assessment opportunity: structured observation 4.1)

DAY 5

Have students perform a warm-up along with a cardiorespiratory workout. (Assessment opportunity: structured observation 4.1)

Provide feedback as students participate in passing, catching, stopping, and pivoting drills. (Assessment opportunity: structured observation 1.0, 5.2, 6.3)

Have students play modified 4-on-4 team handball with no dribbling. (Assessment opportunity: structured observation 1.0, 5.2, 6.3)

Lead students through a cool-down and flexibility exercises appropriate to the physical activity level of the lesson. (Assessment opportunity: structured observation 4.1)

Review the elements of positive transfer. 2.1

DAY 6

Explain the impact of collision (rebound) on skill performance using Biomechanics Made Easy. 2.2

Have students summarize the information in their notebooks. 2.2

Have students perform a warm-up along with a cardiorespiratory workout. (Assessment opportunity: structured observation 4.1)

Demonstrate and describe dribbling using the Invasion Sports CD. 1.0, 2.5

Give students feedback as they practice dribbling. (Assessment opportunity: structured observation 1.0, 5.2, 6.3)

Have students, in pairs, rotate through a variety of dribbling stations (stationary, while moving, while defended), giving each other feedback. (Assessment opportunity: structured observation 1.0, 5.2, 6.3)

Have students play dribble tag (see figure 17.9). (Assessment opportunity: structured observation 1.0, 5.1, 5.2, 6.3)

Lead students through a cool-down and flexibility exercises appropriate to the physical activity level of the lesson. (Assessment opportunity: structured observation 4.1)

Have students discuss the application of rebound principles to dribbling. 2.2

(continued)

Figure 17.9 Dribble tag.

Unit 3 Outline *(continued)*

DAY 7	Discuss the elements of collaboration. 5.1
	Have students record in their notebooks the elements of collaboration. 5.1
	Review the impact of collision (rebound) on skill performance using Biomechanics Made Easy. 2.2
	Have students perform a warm-up along with muscular strength and muscular endurance exercises. (Assessment opportunity: structured observation 4.1)
	Review dribbling. 1.0, 2.5
	Give students feedback as they practice dribbling. (Assessment opportunity: structured observation 1.0, 5.1, 5.2, 6.3)
	Have students, in pairs, rotate through a variety of dribbling stations (stationary, while moving, while defended), giving each other feedback. (Assessment opportunity: structured observation 1.0, 5.1, 5.2, 6.3)
	Have students play dribble tag (see figure 17.9). (Assessment opportunity: structured observation 1.0, 5.1, 5.2, 6.3)
	Lead students through a cool-down and flexibility exercises appropriate to the physical activity level of the lesson. (Assessment opportunity: structured observation 4.1)
	Have students discuss the application of rebound principles to dribbling. 2.2
DAY 8	Have students perform a warm-up along with a cardiorespiratory workout. (Assessment opportunity: structured observation 4.1)
	Review passing, catching, stopping, pivoting, and dribbling. 1.0, 2.5
	Have students, in pairs, rotate through stations, practicing pass, catch, stop, pivot; dribbling while stationary; dribbling while moving; playing dribble tag; and dribbling while defended and giving each other feedback. (Assessment opportunity: structured observation 1.0, 5.1, 5.2, 6.3)
	Lead students through a cool-down and flexibility exercises appropriate to the physical activity level of the lesson. (Assessment opportunity: structured observation 4.1)
	Review the elements of collaboration. 5.1
DAY 9	Have students perform a warm-up along with muscular strength and muscular endurance exercises. (Assessment opportunity: structured observation 4.1)
	Review passing, catching, stopping, pivoting, and dribbling. 1.0, 2.5
	Have students rotate through stations, practicing pass, catch, stop, pivot; dribbling while stationary, dribbling while moving; playing dribble tag; and dribbling while defended and giving each other feedback. (Assessment opportunity: structured observation 1.0, 5.1, 5.2, 6.3)
	Lead students through a cool-down and flexibility exercises appropriate to the physical activity level of the lesson. (Assessment opportunity: structured observation 4.1)
DAY 10	Have students discuss how differences in height and weight influence team handball performance. 2.4
	Have students record the information in their notebooks. 2.4
	Have students perform a warm-up along with a cardiorespiratory workout. (Assessment opportunity: structured observation 4.1)
	Demonstrate and describe the set shot (overhand throw) for team handball using the Invasion Sports CD. 1.0, 2.5
	Provide students with feedback as they practice the team handball set shot, aiming at stationary targets. (Assessment opportunity: structured observation 1.0, 5.1, 5.2, 6.3)
	Provide students with feedback as they practice the team handball set shot while moving, aiming at stationary targets. (Assessment opportunity: structured observation 1.0, 5.1, 5.2, 6.3)
	Lead students through a cool-down and flexibility exercises appropriate to the physical activity level of the lesson. (Assessment opportunity: structured observation 4.1)
	Have students discuss the impact of gravity on the set shot. 2.2

DAY 11

Have students perform a warm-up along with a cardiorespiratory workout. (Assessment opportunity: structured observation 4.1)

Review the set shot for team handball. 1.0, 2.5

Demonstrate and describe the set shot block using the Invasion Sports CD. 1.0, 2.5

Have students, in pairs, practice the set shot and set shot block for team handball (see figure 17.10). (Assessment opportunity: structured observation 1.0, 5.1, 5.2, 6.3)

Introduce the jump shot (overhand pass from elevated position) for team handball to students who are ready. 1.0, 2.5

Demonstrate and describe effective goal keeping. 1.0, 2.5

Have students participate in gamelike drills involving the set shot (the jump shot for those who are ready) against a goalie, while giving each other feedback. (Assessment opportunity: structured observation 1.0, 5.1, 5.2, 6.3)

Lead students through a cool-down and flexibility exercises appropriate to the physical activity level of the lesson. (Assessment opportunity: structured observation 4.1)

DAY 12

Have students perform a warm-up along with muscular strength and muscular endurance exercises. (Assessment opportunity: structured observation 4.1)

Demonstrate and describe the basic offensive stance for team handball using the Invasion Sports CD. 1.0, 2.5

Give students feedback as they assume the basic offensive stance. (Assessment opportunity: structured observation 1.0, 5.1, 5.2, 6.3)

(continued)

Figure 17.10 Fake, set shot, and block.

Unit 3 Outline *(continued)*

DAY 12 *(continued)*	Demonstrate and describe the basic defensive stance for team handball using the Invasion Sports CD. 1.0, 2.5
	Give students feedback as they assume the basic defensive stance. (Assessment opportunity: structured observation 1.0, 5.1, 5.2, 6.3)
	Have students play modified 4-on-4 team handball. (Assessment opportunity: structured observation 1.0, 5.1, 5.2, 6.3)
	Lead students through a cool-down and flexibility exercises appropriate to the physical activity level of the lesson. (Assessment opportunity: structured observation 4.1)
DAY 13	Explain the concepts of open and closed space as offensive and defensive strategies. 2.3
	Have students perform a warm-up along with a cardiorespiratory workout. (Assessment opportunity: structured observation 4.1)
	Demonstrate two-player offensive strategies: give-and-go, give-and-screen outside, give-and-screen outside by receiver, give-and-screen inside (see figure 17.11). 2.3
	Have students practice two-player offensive strategies (give-and-go, give-and-screen outside, give-and-screen outside by receiver, give-and-screen inside with their groups. (Assessment opportunity: structured observation 1.0, 2.3, 5.1, 5.2, 6.3)
	Have students practice two-player offensive strategies (give-and-go, give-and-screen outside, give-and-screen outside by receiver, give-and-screen inside) against two-player defense teams. (Assessment opportunity: structured observation 1.0, 2.3, 5.1, 5.2, 6.3)
	Lead students through a cool-down and flexibility exercises appropriate to the physical activity level of the lesson. (Assessment opportunity: structured observation 4.1)
DAY 14	Review the concepts of open and closed space as offensive and defensive strategies. 2.3
	Have students perform a warm-up along with muscular strength and muscular endurance exercises. (Assessment opportunity: structured observation 4.1)
	Review two-player offensive strategies: give-and-go, give-and-screen outside, give-and-screen outside by receiver, give-and-screen inside. 2.3

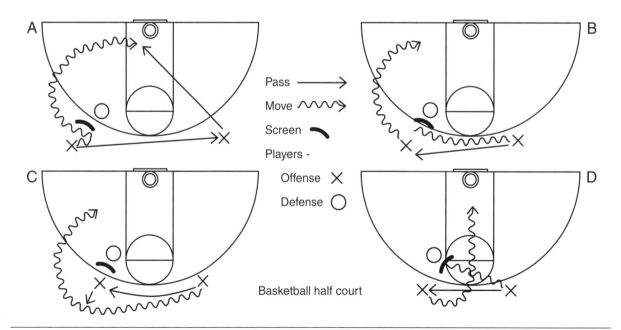

Figure 17.11 Two-on-two basketball plays: *(a)* give-and-go; *(b)* give-and-screen outside; *(c)* give-and-screen outside by receiver; *(d)* give-and-screen inside.

DAY 14 (continued)

Have students practice two-player offensive strategies (give-and-go, give-and-screen outside, give-and-screen outside by receiver, give-and-screen inside) with their groups. (Assessment opportunity: structured observation 1.0, 2.3, 5.1, 5.2, 6.3)

Have students practice two-player offensive strategies (give-and-go, give-and-screen outside, give-and-screen outside by receiver, give-and-screen inside) against two-player defense teams. (Assessment opportunity: structured observation 1.0, 2.3, 5.1, 5.2, 6.3)

Lead students through a cool-down and flexibility exercises appropriate to the physical activity level of the lesson. (Assessment opportunity: structured observation 4.1)

DAY 15

Have students perform a warm-up along with a cardiorespiratory workout. (Assessment opportunity: structured observation 4.1)

Have students play modified 4-on-4 team handball. (Assessment opportunity: structured observation 1.0, 5.1, 5.2, 6.3)

Lead students through a cool-down and flexibility exercises appropriate to the physical activity level of the lesson. (Assessment opportunity: structured observation 4.1)

DAY 16

Have students perform a warm-up along with a cardiorespiratory workout. (Assessment opportunity: structured observation 4.1)

Have students play modified 4-on-4 team handball. (Assessment opportunity: structured observation 1.0, 5.1, 5.2, 6.3)

Lead students through a cool-down and flexibility exercises appropriate to the physical activity level of the lesson. (Assessment opportunity: structured observation 4.1)

DAY 17

Introduce the history and sport of soccer. 2.3, 6.1

Have students perform a warm-up along with muscular strength and muscular endurance exercises. (Assessment opportunity: structured observation 4.1)

Have students play 2-on-2 soccer so that you can see their current skill level. (Assessment opportunity: structured observation 1.0, 5.1, 5.2, 6.3)

Lead students through a cool-down and flexibility exercises appropriate to the physical activity level of the lesson. (Assessment opportunity: structured observation 4.1)

DAY 18

Have students perform a warm-up along with a cardiorespiratory workout. (Assessment opportunity: structured observation 4.1)

Review (from fifth grade) the instep kick and the sole-of-foot trap using the Invasion Sports CD. 1.0, 2.5

Have pairs practice the instep kick and the sole-of-foot trap (see figure 17.12), giving each other feedback. (Assessment opportunity: structured observation 1.0, 5.1, 5.2, 6.3)

Demonstrate and describe the inside-of-foot kick and the leg trap (see figure 17.12) using the Invasion Sports CD. 1.0, 2.5

Have students, in pairs, practice the inside-of-foot kick and the leg trap, giving each other feedback. (Assessment opportunity: structured observation 1.0, 5.1, 5.2, 6.3)

Demonstrate the outside-of-foot pass and inside-of-foot trap (see figure 17.12) using the Invasion Sports CD. 1.0, 2.5

Have students, in pairs, practice the outside-of-foot pass and inside-of-foot trap (see figure 17.12). (Assessment opportunity: structured observation 1.0, 5.1, 5.2, 6.3)

Have students participate in soccer golf (kicking at targets and keeping personal score). (Assessment opportunity: structured observation 1.0, 5.1, 5.2, 6.3)

Lead students through a cool-down and flexibility exercises appropriate to the physical activity level of the lesson. (Assessment opportunity: structured observation 4.1)

(continued)

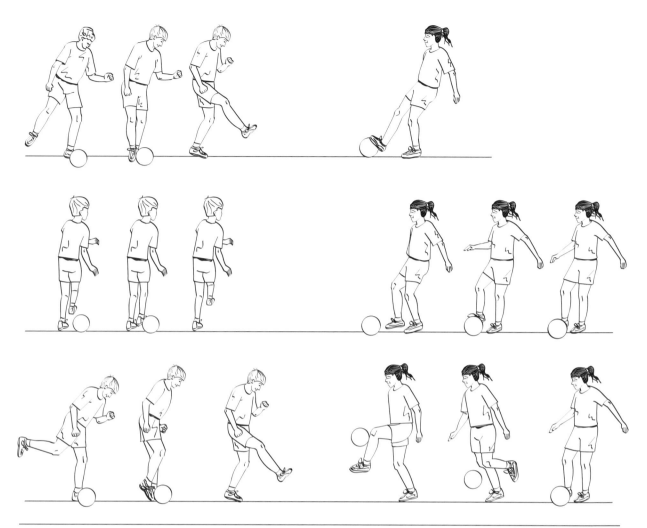

Figure 17.12   Soccer passes and traps.

Unit 3 Outline   *(continued)*

DAY 19

Have students perform a warm-up along with muscular strength and muscular endurance exercises. (Assessment opportunity: structured observation 4.1)

Demonstrate and describe goal keeping and discuss the similarities and differences between goal keeping in team handball and goal keeping in soccer. 1.0, 2.5, 2.1

Demonstrate and describe the instep shot. 1.0, 2.5, 2.1

Have students, in pairs, practice the instep shot. 1.0, 5.1, 5.2, 6.3)

Have students, in groups of four, practice the instep shot against a goalie while partners give feedback. (Assessment opportunity: structured observation 1.0, 5.1, 5.2, 6.3)

Have students, in groups of four, practice the following drill: two students practice the instep kick and shot against a goalie (2-on-1) while the fourth student gives feedback. (Assessment opportunity: structured observation 1.0, 5.1, 5.2, 6.3)

Lead students through a cool-down and flexibility exercises appropriate to the physical activity level of the lesson. (Assessment opportunity: structured observation 4.1)

DAY 20

Have students perform a warm-up along with a cardiorespiratory workout. (Assessment opportunity: structured observation 4.1)

Demonstrate and describe the soccer dribble using the Invasion Sports CD. 1.0, 2.5

Discuss the similarities and differences between dribbling in team handball and dribbling in soccer. 2.1

Provide students with feedback as they practice the soccer dribble. (Assessment opportunity: structured observation 1.0, 5.2, 6.3)

Have students play dribble tag. (Assessment opportunity: structured observation 1.0, 5.1, 5.2, 6.3)

Lead students through a cool-down and flexibility exercises appropriate to the physical activity level of the lesson. (Assessment opportunity: structured observation 4.1)

DAY 21

Have students perform a warm-up along with a cardiorespiratory workout. (Assessment opportunity: structured observation 4.1)

Have students participate in the following gamelike drills:

- dribbling around cones
- dribble tag
- pass and shoot against goalie with feedback
- pass, pass, pass, and shoot against goalie
- dribble, pass, shoot against goalie with feedback
- dribble, pass, dribble, pass, dribble, pass, and shoot against goalie
- outside kick and sole-of-foot trap
- instep kick and instep trap

(Assessment opportunity: structured observation 1.0, 5.1, 5.2, 6.3)

Lead students through a cool-down and flexibility exercises appropriate to the physical activity level of the lesson. (Assessment opportunity: structured observation 4.1)

DAY 22

Have students perform a warm-up along with muscular strength and muscular endurance exercises. (Assessment opportunity: structured observation 4.1)

Demonstrate and describe dodging, feinting, and tackling using the Invasion Sports CD. 1.0, 2.5

Have students practice 1-on-1 feinting and dodging against tackles. (Assessment opportunity: structured observation 1.0, 5.1, 5.2, 6.3)

Have students play Keep-Away (2-on-1 with one student providing feedback) using feet skills. (Assessment opportunity: structured observation 1.0, 5.1, 5.2, 6.3)

Lead students through a cool-down and flexibility exercises appropriate to the physical activity level of the lesson. (Assessment opportunity: structured observation 4.1)

DAY 23

Have students perform a warm-up along with a cardiorespiratory workout. (Assessment opportunity: structured observation 4.1)

Demonstrate and describe punting using the Invasion Sports CD. 1.0, 2.5

Have students, in pairs, practice punting. (Assessment opportunity: structured observation 1.0, 5.1, 5.2, 6.3)

Have students practice 2-on-1 (with one student providing feedback) dribbling, passing, dodging, and feinting against tackles (see figure 17.13). (Assessment opportunity: structured observation 1.0, 5.1, 5.2, 6.3)

Lead students through a cool-down and flexibility exercises appropriate to the physical activity level of the lesson. (Assessment opportunity: structured observation 4.1)

(continued)

Unit 3 Outline *(continued)*

DAY 24

Have students perform a warm-up along with muscular strength and muscular endurance exercises. (Assessment opportunity: structured observation 4.1)

Explain modified 4-on-4 soccer rules. 2.3

Emphasize that students must stay in relative location and not bunch up. 2.3

Have students play modified 4-on-4 soccer. (Assessment opportunity: structured observation 1.0, 5.1, 5.2, 6.3)

Lead students through a cool-down and flexibility exercises appropriate to the physical activity level of the lesson. (Assessment opportunity: structured observation 4.1)

Have students discuss the similarities and differences between team handball and soccer. 2.1

DAY 25

Have students perform a warm-up along with a cardiorespiratory workout. (Assessment opportunity: structured observation 4.1)

Review modified 4-on-4 soccer rules. 2.3

Emphasize that students must stay in relative locations and not bunch up. 2.3

Have students play modified 4-on-4 soccer. (Assessment opportunity: structured observation 1.0, 5.1, 5.2, 6.3)

Lead students through a cool-down and flexibility exercises appropriate to the physical activity level of the lesson. (Assessment opportunity: structured observation 4.1)

(continued)

a

Figure 17.13   Station practice for soccer: *(a)* punting, *(b)* passing , *(c)* 4-on-4 games, *(d)* 2-on-2 games, *(e)* feinting, *(f)* goaltending, and *(g)* 1-on-1 tackles.

Figure 17.13 *(continued)*

Figure 17.13   *(continued)*

Unit 3 Outline   *(continued)*

DAY 26

Have students perform a warm-up along with a cardiorespiratory workout. (Assessment opportunity: structured observation 4.1)

Review basketball. 2.3

Have students play 2-on-2 basketball to review passing, catching, stopping, pivoting, and dribbling. (Assessment opportunity: structured observation 1.0, 5.1, 5.2, 6.3)

Lead students through a cool-down and flexibility exercises appropriate to the physical activity level of the lesson. (Assessment opportunity: structured observation 4.1)

Have students compare basketball to team handball. 1.0, 2.1

DAY 27

Have students perform a warm-up along with muscular strength and muscular endurance exercises. (Assessment opportunity: structured observation 4.1)

Review pass, catch, stop, and pivot. 1.0, 2.5

Have students pass, catch, stop, and pivot. (Assessment opportunity: structured observation 1.0, 5.1, 5.2, 6.3)

Demonstrate the three-person weave. 1.0

Have students perform the three-person weave. (Assessment opportunity: structured observation 1.0, 5.1, 5.2, 6.3)

Review dribbling a basketball. 1.0, 2.5

Have students practice dribbling. (Assessment opportunity: structured observation 1.0, 5.1, 5.2, 6.3)

Demonstrate and describe the one-hand set shot for basketball using the Invasion Sports CD. 1.0, 2.5

Compare the basketball set shot to the team handball set shot. 2.1

Provide students with feedback as they practice the one-hand set shot for basketball. (Assessment opportunity: structured observation 1.0, 5.1, 5.2, 6.3)

Have pairs practice one-hand set shot from various locations, giving each other feedback. (Assessment opportunity: structured observation 1.0, 5.1, 5.2, 6.3)

Lead students through a cool-down and flexibility exercises appropriate to the physical activity level of the lesson. (Assessment opportunity: structured observation 4.1)

DAY 28

Have students perform a warm-up along with a cardiorespiratory workout. (Assessment opportunity: structured observation 4.1)

Review pass, catch, stop, and pivot. 1.0, 2.5

Have students pass, catch, stop, and pivot. (Assessment opportunity: structured observation 1.0, 5.1, 5.2, 6.3)

Review the three-person weave. 1.0

Have students perform the three-person weave. (Assessment opportunity: structured observation 1.0, 5.1, 5.2, 6.3)

Review dribbling a basketball. 1.0, 2.5

Have students practice dribbling. (Assessment opportunity: structured observation 1.0, 5.1, 5.2, 6.3)

Review the one-hand set shot for basketball using the Invasion Sports CD. 1.0, 2.5

Have pairs practice the one-hand set shot from various locations, giving each other feedback. (Assessment opportunity: structured observation 1.0, 5.1, 5.2, 6.3)

Lead students through a cool-down and flexibility exercises appropriate to the physical activity level of the lesson. (Assessment opportunity: structured observation 4.1)

DAY 29

Have students perform a warm-up along with muscular strength and muscular endurance exercises. (Assessment opportunity: structured observation 4.1)

Demonstrate and describe the layup using the Invasion Sports CD. 1.0, 2.5

Provide students with feedback as they practice the layup for basketball. (Assessment opportunity: structured observation 1.0, 5.1, 5.2, 6.3)

Lead students through a cool-down and flexibility exercises appropriate to the physical activity level of the lesson. (Assessment opportunity: structured observation 4.1)

(continued)

Unit 3 Outline *(continued)*

DAY 30

Have students perform a warm-up along with a cardiorespiratory workout. (Assessment opportunity: structured observation 4.1)

Review the layup using the Invasion Sports CD. 1.0, 2.5

Provide students with feedback as they practice the layup for basketball. (Assessment opportunity: structured observation 1.0, 5.1, 5.2, 6.3)

Lead students through a cool-down and flexibility exercises appropriate to the physical activity level of the lesson. (Assessment opportunity: structured observation 4.1)

DAY 31

Have students perform a warm-up along with a cardiorespiratory workout. (Assessment opportunity: structured observation 4.1)

Review the layup. 1.0, 2.5

Demonstrate and describe the rebound using the Invasion Sports CD. 1.0, 2.5

Give students feedback as they practice the layup and rebound for basketball (see figure 17.14). (Assessment opportunity: structured observation 1.0, 5.1, 5.2, 6.3)

Lead students through a cool-down and flexibility exercises appropriate to the physical activity level of the lesson. (Assessment opportunity: structured observation 4.1)

Have students discuss how differences in height and weight influence basketball performance. 2.4

Figure 17.14   Layup and rebound.

DAY 32

Have students perform a warm-up along with muscular strength and muscular endurance exercises. (Assessment opportunity: structured observation 4.1)

Review the offensive and defensive basic stances (see figure 17.15) for basketball and compare with those for soccer and team handball. 1.0, 2.5, 2.1

Provide students with feedback as they practice the defensive basic stance (slide forward, back, right, and left). (Assessment opportunity: structured observation 1.0, 5.2, 6.3)

DAY 32 (continued)

Review the concepts of open and closed spaces. 2.3

Review offensive strategies (give-and-go, give-and-screen outside, give-and-screen outside by receiver, and give-and-screen inside) using a basketball, and compare with team handball. 2.3

Have students practice offensive strategies using a basketball. (Assessment opportunity: structured observation 1.0, 5.1, 5.2, 6.3)

Have students practice offensive strategies against a defense. (Assessment opportunity: structured observation 1.0, 5.1, 5.2, 6.3)

Lead students through a cool-down and flexibility exercises appropriate to the physical activity level of the lesson. (Assessment opportunity: structured observation 4.1)

Figure 17.15 Dribble and defensive stance.

DAY 33

Have students perform a warm-up along with a cardiorespiratory workout. (Assessment opportunity: structured observation 4.1)

Teach basketball the way it was originally played. 2.3

Have students play the original game of basketball. (Assessment opportunity: structured observation 1.0, 5.1, 5.2, 6.3)

Teach basketball the way it was played in the early 1900s. 2.3

Have students play basketball the way it was played in the early 1900s. (Assessment opportunity: structured observation 1.0, 5.1, 5.2, 6.3)

Lead students through a cool-down and flexibility exercises appropriate to the physical activity level of the lesson. (Assessment opportunity: structured observation 4.1)

DAY 34

Have students perform a warm-up along with muscular strength and muscular endurance exercises. (Assessment opportunity: structured observation 4.1)

Teach basketball the way women played it in the 1960s. 2.3

Have students play basketball the way women played it in the 1960s. (Assessment opportunity: structured observation 1.0, 5.1, 5.2, 6.3)

Teach modified 2-on-2 basketball. 2.3

Have students play modified 2-on-2 basketball. (Assessment opportunity: structured observation 1.0, 5.1, 5.2, 6.3)

Lead students through a cool-down and flexibility exercises appropriate to the physical activity level of the lesson. (Assessment opportunity: structured observation 4.1)

(continued)

Unit 3 Outline (continued)

DAY 35	Have students perform a warm-up along with a cardiorespiratory workout. (Assessment opportunity: structured observation 4.1)
	Teach modern basketball. 2.3
	Have students play modern basketball. (Assessment opportunity: structured observation 1.0, 5.1, 5.2, 6.3)
	Lead students through a cool-down and flexibility exercises appropriate to the physical activity level of the lesson. (Assessment opportunity: structured observation 4.1)
	Have students discuss the similarities and differences among soccer, team handball, original basketball, and basketball today. 2.1, 2.3
DAY 36	Have students perform a warm-up along with a cardiorespiratory workout. (Assessment opportunity: structured observation 4.1)
	Introduce Speed-a-Way. 2.3
	Have students play modified 2-on-2 Speed-a-Way, using hand skills only. (Assessment opportunity: structured observation 1.0, 5.1, 5.2, 6.3)
	Lead students through a cool-down and flexibility exercises appropriate to the physical activity level of the lesson. (Assessment opportunity: structured observation 4.1)
DAY 37	Have students perform a warm-up along with muscular strength and muscular endurance exercises. (Assessment opportunity: structured observation 4.1)
	Review passing and trapping using feet. 1.0, 2.5
	Compare passing and trapping with feet for Speed-a-Way to passing and trapping with feet for soccer. 2.1
	Have students practice passing and trapping using feet as teammates give feedback. (Assessment opportunity: structured observation 1.0, 5.1, 5.2, 6.3)
	Review dribbling and compare with the soccer dribble. 1.0, 2.1, 2.5
	Have students practice dribbling. (Assessment opportunity: structured observation 1.0, 5.1, 5.2, 6.3)
	Have students practice dribbling, passing, and trapping. (Assessment opportunity: structured observation 1.0, 5.1, 5.2, 6.3)
	Lead students through a cool-down and flexibility exercises appropriate to the physical activity level of the lesson. (Assessment opportunity: structured observation 4.1)
DAY 38	Have students perform a warm-up along with a cardiorespiratory workout. (Assessment opportunity: structured observation 4.1)
	Demonstrate one-foot lift to self, two-foot stationary lift to self, moving ball lift, and lift to teammate (see figure 17.16) using the Invasion Sports CD. 1.0, 2.5
	Have students, in pairs, rotate through lifting stations, practicing each type of lift and giving each other feedback. (Assessment opportunity: structured observation 1.0, 5.1, 5.2, 6.3)
	Have students play modified 2-on-2 Speed-a-Way. (Assessment opportunity: structured observation 1.0, 5.1, 5.2, 6.3)
	Lead students through a cool-down and flexibility exercises appropriate to the physical activity level of the lesson. (Assessment opportunity: structured observation 4.1)
DAY 39	Have students perform a warm-up along with muscular strength and muscular endurance exercises. (Assessment opportunity: structured observation 4.1)
	Review one-foot lift to self, two-foot stationary lift to self, moving ball lift, and lift to teammate (see figure 17.16). 1.0, 2.5

Figure 17.16 Speed-a-Way lifts: *(a)* lift to teammate, *(b)* moving ball lift, *(c)* two-foot stationary lift to self, and *(d)* one-foot lift to self.

DAY 39 *(continued)*

Have pairs rotate through lifting stations, practicing each type of lift and giving each other feedback. (Assessment opportunity: structured observation 1.0, 5.1, 5.2, 6.3)

Have students play modified 2-on-2 Speed-a-Way. (Assessment opportunity: structured observation 1.0, 5.1, 5.2, 6.3)

Lead students through a cool-down and flexibility exercises appropriate to the physical activity level of the lesson. (Assessment opportunity: structured observation 4.1)

(continued)

Unit 3 Outline   *(continued)*

DAY 40

Have students perform a warm-up along with a cardiorespiratory workout. (Assessment opportunity: structured observation 4.1)

Demonstrate attack options (throwing, juggle, drop dribble, and drop lift to partner—see figure 17.17). 2.3

Have students, in groups of four, practice attack options in 2-on-2 scrimmages. (Assessment opportunity: structured observation 1.0, 5.1, 5.2, 6.3)

Lead students through a cool-down and flexibility exercises appropriate to the physical activity level of the lesson. (Assessment opportunity: structured observation 4.1)

Figure 17.17   Attack options for Speed-a-Way: throwing, juggle, drop dribble, and drop lift to partner.

DAY 41

Have students perform a warm-up along with a cardiorespiratory workout. (Assessment opportunity: structured observation 4.1)

Review dodging, feinting, and tackling; compare these skills for Speed-a-Way with the same skills for soccer. 2.3

Review the concepts of open and closed spaces. 2.3

Demonstrate and describe flag pulling. 1.0, 2.5

Have students work on offense and defense in 1-on-1 scrimmages. (Assessment opportunity: structured observation 1.0, 5.1, 5.2, 6.3)

Have students work on offense and defense in 2-on-2 scrimmages. (Assessment opportunity: structured observation 1.0, 5.1, 5.2, 6.3)

Lead students through a cool-down and flexibility exercises appropriate to the physical activity level of the lesson. (Assessment opportunity: structured observation 4.1)

DAY 42

Teach modified 4-on-4 Speed-a-Way. 2.3

Have students perform a warm-up along with muscular strength and muscular endurance exercises. (Assessment opportunity: structured observation 4.1)

Have students play modified 4-on-4 Speed-a-Way. (Assessment opportunity: structured observation 1.0, 5.1, 5.2, 6.3)

Lead students through a cool-down and flexibility exercises appropriate to the physical activity level of the lesson. (Assessment opportunity: structured observation 4.1)

Have students discuss the similarities and differences among team handball, soccer, basketball, and Speed-a-Way. 2.1, 2.3

DAY 43

Introduce football. 2.3

Have students perform a warm-up along with a cardiorespiratory workout. (Assessment opportunity: structured observation 4.1)

Have students play modified 4-on-4 flag football so that you can assess students' current skill levels. (Assessment opportunity: structured observation 1.0, 5.1, 5.2, 6.3)

Lead students through a cool-down and flexibility exercises appropriate to the physical activity level of the lesson. (Assessment opportunity: structured observation 4.1)

DAY 44

Have students perform a warm-up along with muscular strength and muscular endurance exercises. (Assessment opportunity: structured observation 4.1)

Demonstrate and describe the forward passing and catching of the football using the Invasion Sports CD. 1.0, 2.5

Have students practice the forward pass and catching the football with a partner. (Assessment opportunity: structured observation 1.0, 5.1, 5.2, 6.3)

Demonstrate and describe centering using the Invasion Sports CD. 1.0, 2.5

Have students practice centering with a partner. (Assessment opportunity: structured observation 1.0, 5.1, 5.2, 6.3)

Have students participate in the following stations:

- passing and catching with a partner
- centering with a partner
- passing at a target

(Assessment opportunity: structured observation 1.0, 5.1, 5.2, 6.3)

Lead students through a cool-down and flexibility exercises appropriate to the physical activity level of the lesson. (Assessment opportunity: structured observation 4.1)

DAY 45

Have students perform a warm-up along with a cardiorespiratory workout. (Assessment opportunity: structured observation 4.1)

Demonstrate and describe ball carrying using the Invasion Sports CD. 1.0, 2.5

Demonstrate and describe pass patterns (Z-out, Z-in, and hook out). 1.0, 2.5

Give students feedback as they run through different pass patterns. (Assessment opportunity: structured observation 1.0, 5.1, 5.2, 6.3)

Have students participate in the following stations:

- passing and catching with a partner
- centering with a partner
- passing to a partner who is running pass patterns
- passing at a target (Assessment opportunity: structured observation 1.0, 5.1, 5.2, 6.3)

Lead students through a cool-down and flexibility exercises appropriate to the physical activity level of the lesson. (Assessment opportunity: structured observation 4.1)

DAY 46

Have students perform a warm-up along with a cardiorespiratory workout. (Assessment opportunity: structured observation 4.1)

Demonstrate the basic defensive stance and blocking (see figure 17.18) using the Invasion Sports CD. 1.0, 2.5

Give students feedback as they demonstrate the basic defensive stance and blocking. (Assessment opportunity: structured observation 1.0, 5.2, 6.3)

Demonstrate and describe laterals using the Invasion Sports CD. 1.0, 2.5

(continued)

Unit 3 Outline *(continued)*

Have students participate in centering, lateral, and catching activities (see figure 17.19) while the fourth student provides feedback. (Assessment opportunity: structured observation 1.0, 5.2, 6.3)

Demonstrate and describe rushing using the Invasion Sports CD. 1.0, 2.5

Have students, in groups of four, participate in centering, lateral, and catching activities against a defensive rusher. (Assessment opportunity: structured observation 1.0, 5.1, 5.2, 6.3)

Lead students through a cool-down and flexibility exercises appropriate to the physical activity level of the lesson. (Assessment opportunity: structured observation 4.1)

Figure 17.18   Stances: *(a)* four-point stance, *(b)* three-point stance, and *(c)* blocking.

Figure 17.19   Centering, lateral, and running.

DAY 47

Have students perform a warm-up along with muscular strength and muscular endurance exercises. (Assessment opportunity: structured observation 4.1)

Review laterals. 1.0, 2.5

Have students practice laterals with a partner. 1.0

Demonstrate the two-point stance. 1.0 2.5

Have students demonstrate the two-point stance while you provide feedback. 1.0, 2.5

Demonstrate the three-point stance. 1.0 2.5

Have students demonstrate the three-point stance while you provide feedback. 1.0, 2.5

Demonstrate handoffs (see figure 17.20) using the Invasion Sports CD. 1.0, 2.5

Have students, in groups of four, practice the center, handoff, and run with the ball while the fourth student provides feedback. (Assessment opportunity: structured observation 1.0, 5.1, 5.2, 6.3)

Have students, in groups of four, practice the center, handoff, and run against a defensive rusher. (Assessment opportunity: structured observation 1.0, 5.1, 5.2, 6.3)

Lead students through a cool-down and flexibility exercises appropriate to the physical activity level of the lesson. (Assessment opportunity: structured observation 4.1)

Figure 17.20   Handoff.

DAY 48

Review the concepts of open and closed spaces. 2.3

Demonstrate and describe the basic offensive formation for four players. 2.3

Demonstrate and describe the basic defensive formation for four players. 2.3

Introduce the concept of offensive plays. 2.3

(continued)

Unit 3 Outline *(continued)*

DAY 48 (continued)

Have students perform a warm-up along with a cardiorespiratory workout. (Assessment opportunity: structured observation 4.1)

Demonstrate and describe three additional pass patterns (down and in, down and out, hook in). 1.0, 2.5

Have each group create three offensive plays. (Assessment opportunity: structured observation 1.0, 5.1, 5.2, 6.3)

Lead students through a cool-down and flexibility exercises appropriate to the physical activity level of the lesson. (Assessment opportunity: structured observation 4.1)

DAY 49

Review the concepts of open and closed spaces. 2.3

Review the basic offensive formation for four players. 2.3

Review the basic defensive formation for four players. 2.3

Review the concept of offensive plays. 2.3

Have students perform a warm-up along with muscular strength and muscular endurance exercises. (Assessment opportunity: structured observation 4.1)

Have each group create three additional offensive plays. (Assessment opportunity: structured observation 1.0, 5.1, 5.2, 6.3)

Have each group demonstrate one of its offensive plays for the class. (Assessment opportunity: structured observation 1.0, 5.1, 5.2, 6.3)

Lead students through a cool-down and flexibility exercises appropriate to the physical activity level of the lesson. (Assessment opportunity: structured observation 4.1)

DAY 50

Have students perform a warm-up along with a cardiorespiratory workout. (Assessment opportunity: structured observation 4.1)

Teach modified 4-on-4 flag football. 2.3

Have students play modified 4-on-4 flag football. (Assessment opportunity: structured observation 1.0, 5.1, 5.2, 6.3)

Lead students through a cool-down and flexibility exercises appropriate to the physical activity level of the lesson. (Assessment opportunity: structured observation 4.1)

DAY 51

Have students perform a warm-up along with a cardiorespiratory workout. (Assessment opportunity: structured observation 4.1)

Review modified 4-on-4 flag football. 1.0, 2.3

Have students play modified 4-on-4 flag football. (Assessment opportunity: structured observation 1.0, 5.1, 5.2, 6.3)

Lead students through a cool-down and flexibility exercises appropriate to the physical activity level of the lesson. (Assessment opportunity: structured observation 4.1)

Have students describe similarities and differences among team handball, basketball, soccer, Speed-a-Way, and football. 2.1, 2.3

DAY 52

Have students perform a warm-up along with muscular strength and muscular endurance exercises. (Assessment opportunity: structured observation 4.1)

Have students rotate through stations, playing modified versions of team handball (4-on-4), basketball (3-on-3—two students play 1-on-1 and rotate into the 3-on-3 game), soccer (4-on-4), Speed-a-Way (4-on-4), and football (4-on-4). (Assessment opportunity: structured observation 1.0, 5.1, 5.2, 6.3)

Lead students through a cool-down and flexibility exercises appropriate to the physical activity level of the lesson. (Assessment opportunity: structured observation 4.1)

Have students describe similarities and differences among team handball, basketball, soccer, Speed-a-Way, and football. 2.1, 2.3

DAY 53	Have students perform a warm-up along with a cardiorespiratory workout. (Assessment opportunity: structured observation 4.1)
	Have each group create a new team invasion game. (Assessment opportunity: structured observation 1.0, 5.1, 5.2, 6.3)
	Lead students through a cool-down and flexibility exercises appropriate to the physical activity level of the lesson. (Assessment opportunity: structured observation 4.1)
DAY 54	Have students perform a warm-up along with muscular strength and muscular endurance exercises. (Assessment opportunity: structured observation 4.1)
	Have each group teach another group how to play its game. (Assessment opportunity: structured observation 1.0, 5.1, 5.2, 6.3)
	Lead students through a cool-down and flexibility exercises appropriate to the physical activity level of the lesson. (Assessment opportunity: structured observation 4.1)
	Review material for tomorrow's quiz (or hand out quiz if you would like for it to be a take home quiz). 2.1, 2.2, 2.3, 2.4, 6.4
DAY 55	Have students take the quiz. (Assessment opportunity: quiz 2.1, 2.2, 2.3, 2.4, 6.4)
	Collect student activity logs. (Assessment opportunity: log 3.1)
	Collect reports on the description of invasion sports in the United States during the 19th and 20th centuries. (Assessment opportunity: report 6.1)
	Collect essays about the ways to get more walking into daily activities. (Assessment opportunity: essay 3.2)
	Collect reports on critical features of invasion sport skills. (Assessment opportunity: report 2.5)
	Collect 2-week cardiorespiratory plans. (Assessment opportunity: project 4.2)

Team Net Sports — Unit 4

To continue our focus on working as a team to develop strategies for success, this unit teaches another type of team game: team net sports. We examine volleyball and Takraw, because most of the other net sports fall into the individual and dual sport category (e.g., tennis, badminton, table tennis).

You can teach this unit in any open area; however, blacktop volleyball courts or indoor volleyball courts with nets are preferable. The only pieces of equipment required for this unit are volleyballs and Takraw balls. But which of the many volleyballs available is best? I recommend the Trainer type, because they are lightweight and easy to use. Scientific principles fit in with physical education more often than you might think: Because my students are studying the impact of air resistance in their science classes, I point out how they can apply these science concepts to real-life situations—developing their volleyball skills.

Unit 4 Standards

1.0—Demonstrates the mature form for forearm pass, underhand serve, overhand pass, overhand serve, standing spike, jumping spike, and block.

2.1—Applies transfer of learning to the learning of skills used in net sports.

2.2—Explains the impact of air resistance on physical performance.

2.3—Explains offensive and defensive strategies for net sports.

2.4—Describes how longer limbs provide better leverage if accompanied by increases in strength.

2.5—Explains the critical elements of forearm pass, underhand serve, overhand pass, overhand serve, standing spike, jumping spike, and block.

3.1—Engages in moderate and vigorous physical activity for 60 minutes 6 days each week based on personal goals.

3.2—Explains ways to exercise while playing video games.

4.1—Works toward a health-enhancing level of physical fitness.

4.2—Creates a 2-week muscular endurance and muscular strength plan.

5.1—Collaborates with team members to solve problems during net sports.

5.2—Accepts responsibility for one's own actions and decisions during net sports.

6.1—Describes net sports in the United States during the 19th and 20th centuries.

6.2—Not applicable.

6.3—Chooses to engage in net sports at the appropriate level of social, physical, and emotional challenge.

6.4—Describes the psychological benefits derived from regular participation in physical activity.

Unit 4 Assessments

1.0—Structured observation (days 2-24)

2.1—Essay (assigned on day 16; collected on day 17)

2.2—Quiz (day 25)

2.3—Quiz (day 25)

2.4—Quiz (day 25)

2.5—Quiz (day 25)

3.1—Log (assigned on day 1; collected on day 25)

3.2—Essay (assigned on day 1; collected on day 25)

4.1—Structured observation (days 1-24)

4.2—Project (assigned on day 3; collected on day 25)

5.1—Structured observation (days 18-24)

5.2—Structure observation (days 2-24)

6.1—Report (assigned on day 1; collected on day 25)

6.2—Not applicable

6.3—Structured observation (days 2-24)

6.4—Quiz (day 25)

Resources

Health-Related Fitness: Tutorial and Portfolio (Bonnie's Fitware, Inc.)

Middle School Physical Education Portfolio (Bonnie's Fitware, Inc.)

Team Net Sports CD (Bonnie's Fitware, Inc.)

Eighth grade net sports task cards (Bonnie's Fitware, Inc.)

Eighth grade unit 4 posters (Bonnie's Fitware, Inc.—included in the Middle School Detailed Lesson Plans)

Fitness posters (Bonnie's Fitware, Inc.—included in the Middle School Detailed Lesson Plans)

Equipment

Volleyball trainers

Takraw balls

Volleyballs

Games

Volleyball

Takraw

Unit 4 Outline

DAY 1

Introduce the history and sport of volleyball. 6.1, 2.3

Discuss the importance of engaging in net sports at the appropriate level of social, physical, and emotional challenge. 6.3

Have students perform a warm-up along with a cardiorespiratory workout. (Assessment opportunity: structured observation 4.1)

Review the rules for modified 4-on-4 volleyball. 2.3

Have students play modified 4-on-4 volleyball so that you can evaluate their current skill level. 1.0, 6.3

Assign unit-long homework:

- Have students research and write a description of net sports in the United States during the 19th and 20th centuries. (Assessment assignment opportunity: report 6.1)

- Have students keep a log of daily activity. (Assessment assignment opportunity: log 3.1)

- Have students explain ways to exercise while playing video games. (Assessment assignment opportunity: essay 3.2)

DAY 2

Describe what it means to accept responsibility for one's own actions and decisions during net sports. 5.2

Have students record in their notebooks what it means to accept responsibility for one's own actions and decisions during net sports. 5.2

Have students perform a warm-up along with muscular strength and muscular endurance exercises. (Assessment opportunity: structured observation 4.1)

Demonstrate and describe the ready position using the Team Net Sports CD. 1.0, 2.5

Give students feedback as they assume the ready position. (Assessment opportunity: structured observation 1.0, 5.2, 6.3)

Demonstrate the forearm pass using the Team Net Sports CD. 1.0, 2.5

Give students feedback as they practice the forearm pass (from a toss and from a partner's forearm pass) in pairs. (Assessment opportunity: structured observation 1.0, 5.2, 6.3)

Lead students through a cool-down and flexibility exercises appropriate to the physical activity level of the lesson. (Assessment opportunity: structured observation 4.1)

DAY 3

Display the fitness posters.

Describe the psychological benefits derived from regular participation in physical activity. 6.4

Have students record in their notebooks the psychological benefits derived from regular participation in physical activity. 6.4

Review the muscular endurance and muscular strength frequency, intensity, time, and type (FITT) concepts using the Health-Related Fitness: Tutorial and Portfolio. 4.2

Have students record in their notebooks the concepts of frequency, intensity, time, and type (FITT) as they relate to muscular endurance and muscular strength. 4.2

Have students create a 2-week muscular endurance and muscular strength plan. (Assessment assignment opportunity: project 4.2)

Have students perform a warm-up along with a cardiorespiratory workout. (Assessment opportunity: structured observation 4.1)

Review the forearm pass. 1.0, 2.5

Have students, in groups of four, practice the forearm pass—two practice (from a toss, from a partner's forearm pass, and for accuracy) while the other students give feedback. (Assessment opportunity: structured observation 1.0, 5.2, 6.3)

(continued)

Unit 4 Outline *(continued)*

DAY 3 *(continued)*	Have students participate in a forearm pass game (4-on-4). (Assessment opportunity: structured observation 1.0, 5.2, 6.3)
	Lead students through a cool-down and flexibility exercises appropriate to the physical activity level of the lesson. (Assessment opportunity: structured observation 4.1)
	Review what it means to accept responsibility for one's own actions and decisions during net sports. 5.2
DAY 4	Review the forearm pass. 1.0, 2.5
	Have students perform a warm-up along with muscular strength and muscular endurance exercises. (Assessment opportunity: structured observation 4.1)
	Have students, in groups of four, practice the forearm pass—two practice (from a toss, from a partner's forearm pass, and for accuracy) while the other students give feedback. (Assessment opportunity: structured observation 1.0, 5.2, 6.3)
	Have students participate in a forearm pass game (4-on-4). (Assessment opportunity: structured observation 1.0, 5.2, 6.3)
	Lead students through a cool-down and flexibility exercises appropriate to the physical activity level of the lesson. (Assessment opportunity: structured observation 4.1)
DAY 5	Discuss transfer of learning principle. 2.1
	Have students discuss the application of the transfer of learning principle to the learning of volleyball skills. 2.1
	Have students perform a warm-up along with a cardiorespiratory workout. (Assessment opportunity: structured observation 4.1)
	Demonstrate and describe the underhand serve using the Net Team Sports CD. 1.0, 2.5
	Give students feedback as they practice the underhand serve from as close to the net as they like. (Assessment opportunity: structured observation 1.0, 5.2, 6.3)
	Have students, in pairs, practice the underhand serve from as close to the net as they like, giving each other feedback. (Assessment opportunity: structured observation 1.0, 5.2, 6.3)
	Have students, in pairs, play a serving accuracy game. (Assessment opportunity: structured observation 1.0, 5.2, 6.3)
	Lead students through a cool-down and flexibility exercises appropriate to the physical activity level of the lesson. (Assessment opportunity: structured observation 4.1)
DAY 6	Have students perform a warm-up along with a cardiorespiratory workout. (Assessment opportunity: structured observation 4.1)
	Review the underhand serve. 1.0, 2.5
	Give students feedback as they practice the underhand serve from as close to the net as they like. (Assessment opportunity: structured observation 1.0, 5.2, 6.3)
	Have pairs practice the underhand serve from as close to the net as they like, giving each other feedback. (Assessment opportunity: structured observation 1.0, 5.2, 6.3)
	Have pairs play a serving accuracy game. (Assessment opportunity: structured observation 1.0, 5.2, 6.3)
	Lead students through a cool-down and flexibility exercises appropriate to the physical activity level of the lesson. (Assessment opportunity: structured observation 4.1)
	Review transfer of learning principles. 2.1

DAY 7

Have students perform a warm-up along with muscular strength and muscular endurance exercises. (Assessment opportunity: structured observation 4.1)

Review the forearm pass and underhand serve. 1.0, 2.5

Demonstrate the set (see figure 17.21) using the Net Team Sports CD. 1.0, 2.5

Give students feedback as they practice the set (from a toss and from a partner's forearm pass) in pairs. (Assessment opportunity: structured observation 1.0, 5.2, 6.3)

Lead students through a cool-down and flexibility exercises appropriate to the physical activity level of the lesson. (Assessment opportunity: structured observation 4.1)

Figure 17.21   Set.

DAY 8

Have students perform a warm-up along with a cardiorespiratory workout. (Assessment opportunity: structured observation 4.1)

Review the forearm pass. 1.0, 2.5

Review the set. 1.0, 2.5

Give students feedback as they practice the set (from a toss and from a partner's forearm pass) in pairs. (Assessment opportunity: structured observation 1.0, 5.2, 6.3)

Lead students through a cool-down and flexibility exercises appropriate to the physical activity level of the lesson. (Assessment opportunity: structured observation 4.1)

DAY 9

Have students perform a warm-up along with muscular strength and muscular endurance exercises. (Assessment opportunity: structured observation 4.1)

Review the set and forearm pass. 1.0, 2.5

Have students, in pairs, practice the forearm pass to set. (Assessment opportunity: structured observation 1.0, 5.2, 6.3)

Lead students through a cool-down and flexibility exercises appropriate to the physical activity level of the lesson. (Assessment opportunity: structured observation 4.1)

(continued)

Unit 4 Outline *(continued)*

DAY 10

Demonstrate and describe the overhand serve using the Net Team Sports CD (see figure 17.22). 1.0, 2.5

Discuss the implications of longer limbs on the performance of the overhand serve. 2.4

Have students summarize the information in their notebooks. 2.4

Explain the impact of air resistance on the overhand serve. 2.2

Have students summarize the information in their notebooks. 2.2

Have students perform a warm-up along with a cardiorespiratory workout. (Assessment opportunity: structured observation 4.1)

Give students feedback as they practice the overhand serve from as close to the net as they like. (Assessment opportunity: structured observation 1.0, 5.2, 6.3)

Have students, in pairs, practice the overhand serve from as close to the net as they like, giving each other feedback. (Assessment opportunity: structured observation 1.0, 5.2, 6.3)

Have students, in pairs, play a serving accuracy game. (Assessment opportunity: structured observation 1.0, 5.2, 6.3)

Lead students through a cool-down and flexibility exercises appropriate to the physical activity level of the lesson. (Assessment opportunity: structured observation 4.1)

Figure 17.22   Overhand serve.

DAY 11

Review the implications of longer limbs on the performance of the overhand serve. 2.4

Review the impact of air resistance on the overhand serve. 2.2

Have students perform a warm-up along with a cardiorespiratory workout. (Assessment opportunity: structured observation 4.1)

Review the overhand serve.

Give students feedback as they practice the overhand serve from as close to the net as they like. (Assessment opportunity: structured observation 1.0, 5.2, 6.3)

Have students, in pairs, play a serving accuracy game. (Assessment opportunity: structured observation 1.0, 5.2, 6.3)

Lead students through a cool-down and flexibility exercises appropriate to the physical activity level of the lesson. (Assessment opportunity: structured observation 4.1)

DAY 12

Have students perform a warm-up along with muscular strength and muscular endurance exercises. (Assessment opportunity: structured observation 4.1)

Demonstrate the standing spike using the Net Team Sports CD. 1.0, 2.5

Discuss the implications of longer limbs on the performance of the standing spike. 2.4

Provide students with feedback as they practice the standing spike (from a held ball, from a self-tossed ball, from a partner toss, and from an overhand pass) in groups of four. (Assessment opportunity: structured observation 1.0, 5.2, 6.3)

Lead students through a cool-down and flexibility exercises appropriate to the physical activity level of the lesson. (Assessment opportunity: structured observation 4.1)

DAY 13

Have students perform a warm-up along with a cardiorespiratory workout. (Assessment opportunity: structured observation 4.1)

Demonstrate and describe the jumping spike using the Net Team Sports CD. 1.0, 2.5

Discuss the implications of longer limbs on the performance of the jumping spike. 2.4

Explain the impact of air resistance on the jumping spike. 2.2

Give students feedback as they practice the jumping spike (from a held ball, from a self-tossed ball, from a partner toss, and from an overhand pass) in groups of four. (Assessment opportunity: structured observation 1.0, 5.2, 6.3)

Lead students through a cool-down and flexibility exercises appropriate to the physical activity level of the lesson. (Assessment opportunity: structured observation 4.1)

DAY 14

Have students perform a warm-up along with muscular strength and muscular endurance exercises. (Assessment opportunity: structured observation 4.1)

Review the jumping spike. 1.0, 2.5

Give students feedback as they practice the jumping spike (from a held ball, from a self-tossed ball, from a partner toss, and from an overhand pass) in groups of four. (Assessment opportunity: structured observation 1.0, 5.2, 6.3)

Lead students through a cool-down and flexibility exercises appropriate to the physical activity level of the lesson. (Assessment opportunity: structured observation 4.1)

DAY 15

Have students perform a warm-up along with a cardiorespiratory workout. (Assessment opportunity: structured observation 4.1)

Demonstrate and describe the block using the Net Team Sports CD. 1.0, 2.5

Discuss the implications of longer limbs on the performance of the block. 2.4

Provide students with feedback as they practice the block in pairs. (Assessment opportunity: structured observation 1.0, 5.2, 6.3)

Have students practice spiking and blocking (see figure 17.23) in groups of four. (Assessment opportunity: structured observation 1.0, 5.2, 6.3)

Lead students through a cool-down and flexibility exercises appropriate to the physical activity level of the lesson. (Assessment opportunity: structured observation 4.1)

DAY 16

Review all volleyball skills. 1.0, 2.5

Have students perform a warm-up along with a cardiorespiratory workout. (Assessment opportunity: structured observation 4.1)

Have students rotate through a variety of practice stations: serving, forearm pass, forearm pass to overhand pass, overhand pass, spiking and blocking, and computer (volleyball strategy). (Assessment opportunity: structured observation 1.0, 5.2, 6.3)

Lead students through a cool-down and flexibility exercises appropriate to the physical activity level of the lesson. (Assessment opportunity: structured observation 4.1)

Have students write an essay describing how they applied transfer of learning to the learning of each volleyball skill. (Assessment assignment opportunity: essay 2.1)

(continued)

Figure 17.23 *(a)* Spiking and *(b)* blocking.

Unit 4 Outline *(continued)*

DAY 17

Review open and closed space. 2.3

Discuss the relationship between open space and closed space for invasion team sports and net sports. 2.3

Demonstrate the basic defensive position. 1.0, 2.5

Have students perform a warm-up along with muscular strength and muscular endurance exercises. (Assessment opportunity: structured observation 4.1)

Provide students with feedback as they assume the basic defensive position. (Assessment opportunity: structured observation 1.0, 5.2, 6.3)

Demonstrate the basic rotation. 2.3

Provide students with feedback as they assume positions on the court and walk through the basic rotation. 2.3

Have the center front toss the ball to the back row so that the team can attempt to execute a pass, set, and spike sequence. (Assessment opportunity: structured observation 1.0, 5.2, 6.3)

Lead students through a cool-down and flexibility exercises appropriate to the physical activity level of the lesson. (Assessment opportunity: structured observation 4.1)

Collect essays on transfer of learning. (Assessment opportunity: essay 2.1)

DAY 18

Describe collaboration with team members to solve problems during net sports. 5.1

Have students record the information in their notebooks. 5.1

Demonstrate the 4-2 formation and rotation. 2.3

Have each team determine who will be the setters and who will be the spikers. (Assessment opportunity: structured observation.) 5.1, 2.3

Have students perform a warm-up along with a cardiorespiratory workout. (Assessment opportunity: structured observation 4.1)

Give students feedback as they assume positions on the court and walk through the 4-2 rotation. 2.3

Have the center front toss the ball to the back row so that the group of four can attempt to execute a pass, set, and spike sequence. (Assessment opportunity: structured observation 1.0, 5.2, 6.3)

Lead students through a cool-down and flexibility exercises appropriate to the physical activity level of the lesson. (Assessment opportunity: structured observation 4.1)

DAY 19

Teach the game and rules of volleyball. 2.3

Have students perform a warm-up along with muscular strength and muscular endurance exercises. (Assessment opportunity: structured observation 4.1)

Have students play volleyball. (Assessment opportunity: structured observation 1.0, 5.1, 5.2, 6.3)

Lead students through a cool-down and flexibility exercises appropriate to the physical activity level of the lesson. (Assessment opportunity: structured observation 4.1)

DAY 20

Review the game and rules of volleyball. 2.3

Have students perform a warm-up along with a cardiorespiratory workout. (Assessment opportunity: structured observation 4.1)

Have students play volleyball. (Assessment opportunity: structured observation 1.0, 5.1, 5.2, 6.3)

Lead students through a cool-down and flexibility exercises appropriate to the physical activity level of the lesson. (Assessment opportunity: structured observation 4.1)

(continued)

Unit 4 Outline *(continued)*

DAY 21

Have students perform a warm-up along with a cardiorespiratory workout. (Assessment opportunity: structured observation 4.1)

Review (from sixth grade circus unit) the instep kick pass. 1.0, 2.5

Practice the instep kick. (Assessment opportunity: structured observation 1.0, 5.1, 5.2, 6.3)

Lead students through a cool-down and flexibility exercises appropriate to the physical activity level of the lesson. (Assessment opportunity: structured observation 4.1)

DAY 22

Have students perform a warm-up along with muscular strength and muscular endurance exercises. (Assessment opportunity: structured observation 4.1)

Review the instep kick pass. 1.0

Practice the instep kick. (Assessment opportunity: structured observation 1.0, 5.1, 5.2, 6.3)

Describe the game of Takraw to the students. 2.3

Have students play 3-on-3 Takraw. (Assessment opportunity: structured observation 1.0, 5.1, 5.2, 6.3)

Lead students through a cool-down and flexibility exercises appropriate to the physical activity level of the lesson. (Assessment opportunity: structured observation 4.1)

Discuss the similarities and differences between Takraw and volleyball. 2.3

Discuss the offensive and defensive strategies common to Takraw and volleyball. 2.3

DAY 23

Have students perform a warm-up along with a cardiorespiratory workout. (Assessment opportunity: structured observation 4.1)

Have students rotate from playing volleyball to playing Takraw. (Assessment opportunity: structured observation 1.0, 5.1, 5.2, 6.3)

Lead students through a cool-down and flexibility exercises appropriate to the physical activity level of the lesson. (Assessment opportunity: structured observation 4.1)

DAY 24

Have students perform a warm-up along with muscular strength and muscular endurance exercises. (Assessment opportunity: structured observation 4.1)

Have students rotate from playing volleyball to playing Takraw. (Assessment opportunity: structured observation 1.0, 5.1, 5.2, 6.3)

Lead students through a cool-down and flexibility exercises appropriate to the physical activity level of the lesson. (Assessment opportunity: structured observation 4.1)

Review material for tomorrow's quiz (or hand out quiz if you would like for it to be a take home quiz). 2.2, 2.3, 2.4, 2.5, 6.4

DAY 25

Have students take the quiz. (Assessment opportunity: quiz 2.2, 2.3, 2.4, 2.5, 6.4)

Collect student activity logs. (Assessment opportunity: log 3.1)

Collect reports on net sports played in the United States during the 19th and 20th centuries. (Assessment opportunity: report 6.1)

Collect essays about ways to exercise while playing video games. (Assessment opportunity: essay 3.2)

Collect 2-week muscular endurance and muscular strength plans. (Assessment opportunity: project 4.2)

Team Field Sports  — Unit 5

In this unit, as we continue to work as a team to develop strategies for success, we focus on another type of team game: team field sports. We examine softball only, because the other field sports are more elementary-level recess games (e.g., kickball and sockball). You can teach this unit in any open area; however, grass is preferable. Softball diamonds and backstops help, too.

Because my students are studying the 1800s in their history class, I have them study the history of softball and other team sports that developed during the 1800s to create an especially interesting interdisciplinary link. Have you heard about the controversies about who created baseball? I like to cooperate with my students' history teachers and create an interdisciplinary project by asking students to research the history of baseball, having them determine who, in fact, invented it and the reasons for the controversy.

Unit 5 Standards

1.0—Demonstrates the mature form for pitch, bat, bunt, sidearm whip throw, fielding ground balls and flies, and baserunning.

2.1—Applies transfer of learning to the learning of skills used in field sports.

2.2—Explains the impact of friction on physical performance.

2.3—Explains offensive and defensive strategies for field sports.

2.4—Explains why different positions require different physical abilities.

2.5—Explains the critical elements of pitch, bat, bunt, sidearm whip throw, fielding ground balls and flies, and baserunning.

3.1—Engages in moderate and vigorous physical activity for 60 minutes 6 days each week based on personal goals.

3.2—Explains ways to exercise while watching television.

4.1—Works toward a health-enhancing level of physical fitness.

4.2—Creates a 2-week body composition plan.

5.1—Collaborates with team members to solve problems during field sports.

5.2—Accepts responsibility for one's own actions and decisions during field sports.

6.1—Describes field sports in the United States during the 19th and 20th centuries.

6.2—Not applicable.

6.3—Chooses to engage in field sports at the appropriate level of social, physical, and emotional challenge.

6.4—Describes the cognitive benefits derived from regular participation in physical activity.

Unit 5 Assessments

1.0—Structured observation (days 1-24)

2.1—Essay (assigned on day 4; collected on day 5)

2.2—Quiz (day 25)

2.3—Quiz (day 25)

2.4—Quiz (day 25)

2.5—Quiz (day 25)

3.1—Log (assigned on day 1; collected on day 25)

3.2—Essay (assigned on day 1; collected on day 25)

4.1—Structured observation (days 1-24)

4.2—Project (assigned on day 3; collected on day 25)

5.1—Structured observation (days 19-24)

5.2—Structure observation (days 1-24)

6.1—Report (assigned on day 1; collected on day 24)

6.2—Not applicable

6.3—Structured observation (days 1-24)

6.4—Quiz (day 25)

Resources

SimAthlete (Bonnie's Fitware, Inc.)

Health-Related Fitness: Tutorial and Portfolio (Bonnie's Fitware, Inc.)

Middle School Physical Education Portfolio (Bonnie's Fitware, Inc.)

Field Sports CD (Bonnie's Fitware, Inc.)

Eighth grade softball task cards (Bonnie's Fitware, Inc.)

Eighth grade unit 5 posters (Bonnie's Fitware, Inc.—included in the Middle School Detailed Lesson Plans)

Fitness posters (Bonnie's Fitware, Inc.—included in the Middle School Detailed Lesson Plans)

Equipment

Softballs	Catcher's protective equipment (chest protector, mask, leg protectors)
Softball bats	Batting tees
Softball gloves	Batting helmets
Bases	Targets

Games

Softball

Three-team softball

Pickleball

Unit 5 Outline

DAY 1

Display the posters.

Introduce softball, discussing equipment and safety.

Discuss the importance of engaging in field sport activities at the appropriate level of social, physical, and emotional challenge. 6.3

Have students record the information in their notebooks. 6.3

Discuss the importance of accepting responsibility for your own actions and decisions during field sports. 5.2

Have students record the information in their notebooks. 5.2

Have students perform a warm-up along with a cardiorespiratory workout. (Assessment opportunity: structured observation 4.1)

Demonstrate and describe the overhand throw and catch using the Field Sports CD. 1.0, 2.5

Have students practice the overhand throw and catch with a partner. (Assessment opportunity: structured observation 1.0, 5.2, 6.3)

Lead students through a cool-down and flexibility exercises appropriate to the physical activity level of the lesson. (Assessment opportunity: structured observation 4.1)

Assign unit-long homework:

- Have students research and write a description about field sports in the United States during the 19th and 20th centuries. (Assessment assignment opportunity: report 6.1)

- Have students keep a log of daily activity. (Assessment assignment opportunity: log 3.1)

- Have students explain the ways to exercise while watching television. (Assessment assignment opportunity: essay 3.2)

DAY 2

Assign students to work in groups of four.

Have students perform a warm-up along with muscular strength and muscular endurance exercises. (Assessment opportunity: structured observation 4.1)

Review the overhand throw and catch. 1.0, 2.5

Have students, in pairs, practice the overhand throw and catch (throwing at stationary object, throwing at moving object, throwing for distance, throwing for accuracy, throwing while moving, and throwing while moving at a moving target). (Assessment opportunity: structured observation 1.0, 5.2, 6.3)

Lead students through a cool-down and flexibility exercises appropriate to the physical activity level of the lesson. (Assessment opportunity: structured observation 4.1)

Review transfer of learning and its application to learning softball skills. 2.1

Have students record in their notebooks the transfer of learning information. 2.1

DAY 3

Display fitness posters.

Explain the cognitive benefits derived from regular participation in physical activity. 6.4

Have students view the body composition section on the Health-Related Fitness software. 4.2

Review the concepts of frequency, intensity, time, and type (FITT) as they relate to body composition. 4.2

Have students record in their notebooks the FITT concepts as they relate to body composition. 4.2

Assign students the creation of a 2-week body composition plan. (Assessment assignment opportunity: project 4.2)

Have students perform a warm-up along with a cardiorespiratory workout. (Assessment opportunity: structured observation 4.1)

Review the overhand throw and catch. 1.0, 2.5

Have students, in pairs, practice the overhand throw and catch (throwing at stationary object, throwing at moving object, throwing for distance, throwing for accuracy, throwing while moving, and throwing while moving at a moving target). (Assessment opportunity: structured observation 1.0, 5.2, 6.3)

Lead students through a cool-down and flexibility exercises appropriate to the physical activity level of the lesson. (Assessment opportunity: structured observation 4.1)

Review transfer of learning and its application to learning softball skills. 2.1

DAY 4

Have students perform a warm-up along with muscular strength and muscular endurance exercises. (Assessment opportunity: structured observation 4.1)

Demonstrate the sidearm whip throw and catch using the Field Sports CD. 1.0, 2.5

Have students brainstorm how transfer of learning applies to learning the sidearm whip throw. 2.1

Have students, in pairs, practice the sidearm whip throw and catch (throwing at stationary object, throwing at moving object, throwing for distance, throwing for accuracy, throwing while moving, and throwing while moving at a moving target). (Assessment opportunity: structured observation 1.0, 5.2, 6.3)

Lead students through a cool-down and flexibility exercises appropriate to the physical activity level of the lesson. (Assessment opportunity: structured observation 4.1)

Have students write essays on how they used transfer of learning to learn the sidearm whip throw. (Assessment assignment opportunity: essay 2.1)

(continued)

Unit 5 Outline *(continued)*

DAY 5	Have students perform a warm-up along with a cardiorespiratory workout. (Assessment opportunity: structured observation 4.1)

Review overhand throw and sidearm whip throw and catch. 1.0, 2.5

Demonstrate and describe the underhand toss and catch using the Field Sports CD. 1.0, 2.5

Have students, in pairs, practice throwing and catching (underhand throwing at stationary object, underhand throwing at moving object, underhand throwing for accuracy, underhand throwing while moving, underhand throwing while moving at a moving target, overhand throwing and catching, and sidearm throwing and catching). (Assessment opportunity: structured observation 1.0, 5.2, 6.3)

Lead students through a cool-down and flexibility exercises appropriate to the physical activity level of the lesson. (Assessment opportunity: structured observation 4.1)

Collect essays on how transfer of learning helped with improving softball throws. (Assessment opportunity: essay 2.1) |
| **DAY 6** | Have students perform a warm-up along with a cardiorespiratory workout. (Assessment opportunity: structured observation 4.1)

Review the overhand throw, sidearm whip throw, and underhand toss. 1.0, 2.5

Have students play Pickleball. (Assessment opportunity: structured observation 1.0, 5.2, 6.3)

Demonstrate and describe fielding ground balls using the Field Sports CD. 1.0, 2.5

Explain the impact of friction on physical performance. 2.2

Have students record in their notebooks the explanation of the impact of friction on physical performance. 2.2

Have students, in pairs, practice fielding ground balls (from a toss and from a toss to the side). (Assessment opportunity: structured observation 1.0, 5.2, 6.3)

Lead students through a cool-down and flexibility exercises appropriate to the physical activity level of the lesson. (Assessment opportunity: structured observation 4.1)

Have students discuss the impact of friction on fielding ground balls. 2.2 |
| **DAY 7** | Explain why different positions require different physical abilities. 2.4

Have students record in their notebooks why different positions require different physical abilities. 2.4

Have students perform a warm-up along with muscular strength and muscular endurance exercises. (Assessment opportunity: structured observation 4.1)

Demonstrate and describe fielding fly balls using the Field Sports CD. 1.0, 2.5

Have students, in pairs, practice fielding fly balls (from a toss and from a toss to the side), giving each other feedback. (Assessment opportunity: structured observation 1.0, 5.2, 6.3)

Review fielding ground balls. 1.0, 2.5

Have students, in pairs, practice fielding ground balls (from a toss and from a toss to the side). (Assessment opportunity: structured observation 1.0, 5.2, 6.3)

Lead students through a cool-down and flexibility exercises appropriate to the physical activity level of the lesson. (Assessment opportunity: structured observation 4.1)

Review the impact of friction on physical performance. 2.2 |

DAY 8	Have students perform a warm-up along with a cardiorespiratory workout. (Assessment opportunity: structured observation 4.1) Review fielding ground balls and fly balls and throwing. 1.0, 2.5 Have students practice throwing the ball from the shortstop position to the catcher, to first, to second, to third, and back to the catcher (also other sequences). (Assessment opportunity: structured observation 1.0, 5.2, 6.3) Lead students through a cool-down and flexibility exercises appropriate to the physical activity level of the lesson. (Assessment opportunity: structured observation 4.1) Have students brainstorm the physical abilities used in throwing, fielding, and catching. 2.4
DAY 9	Have students perform a warm-up along with muscular strength and muscular endurance exercises. (Assessment opportunity: structured observation 4.1) Review fielding ground balls and fly balls and throwing. 1.0, 2.5 Have students practice throwing the ball from the shortstop position to the catcher, to first, to second, to third, and back to the catcher (also other sequences). (Assessment opportunity: structured observation 1.0, 5.2, 6.3) Lead students through a cool-down and flexibility exercises appropriate to the physical activity level of the lesson. (Assessment opportunity: structured observation 4.1)
DAY 10	Have students perform a warm-up along with a cardiorespiratory workout. (Assessment opportunity: structured observation 4.1) Demonstrate and describe pitching using the Field Sports CD. 1.0, 2.5 Have students, in pairs, practice pitching (first technique, then accuracy). (Assessment opportunity: structured observation 1.0, 5.2, 6.3) Lead students through a cool-down and flexibility exercises appropriate to the physical activity level of the lesson. (Assessment opportunity: structured observation 4.1) Have students brainstorm the physical abilities used in pitching. 2.4
DAY 11	Have students perform a warm-up along with a cardiorespiratory workout. (Assessment opportunity: structured observation 4.1) Review pitching. 1.0, 2.5 Have students, in pairs, practice pitching (first technique, then accuracy). (Assessment opportunity: structured observation 1.0, 5.2, 6.3) Lead students through a cool-down and flexibility exercises appropriate to the physical activity level of the lesson. (Assessment opportunity: structured observation 4.1) Have students brainstorm the physical abilities used in pitching. 2.4
DAY 12	Have students perform a warm-up along with muscular strength and muscular endurance exercises. (Assessment opportunity: structured observation 4.1) Demonstrate and describe batting using the Field Sports CD. 1.0, 2.5 Have students practice batting (off tee, from a toss, from a pitch, for distance, and for accuracy) in groups of four, rotating from retriever to pitcher to batter to catcher. (Assessment opportunity: structured observation 1.0, 5.2, 6.3) Lead students through a cool-down and flexibility exercises appropriate to the physical activity level of the lesson. (Assessment opportunity: structured observation 4.1) Have students brainstorm the physical abilities used in batting off a tee. 2.4

(continued)

Unit 5 Outline *(continued)*

DAY 13

Have students perform a warm-up along with a cardiorespiratory workout. (Assessment opportunity: structured observation 4.1)

Review batting. 1.0, 2.5

Have students practice batting (off tee, from a toss, from a pitch, for distance, and for accuracy) in groups of four, rotating from retriever to pitcher to batter to catcher. (Assessment opportunity: structured observation 1.0, 5.2, 6.3)

Lead students through a cool-down and flexibility exercises appropriate to the physical activity level of the lesson. (Assessment opportunity: structured observation 4.1)

Have students brainstorm the physical abilities used in batting. 2.4

DAY 14

Have students perform a warm-up along with muscular strength and muscular endurance exercises. (Assessment opportunity: structured observation 4.1)

Demonstrate and describe bunting (see figure 17.24) using the Field Sports CD. 1.0, 2.5

Have students practice bunting (off tee, from a toss, from a pitch, for distance, and for accuracy) in groups of four, rotating from retriever to pitcher to batter to catcher. (Assessment opportunity: structured observation 1.0, 5.2, 6.3)

Review batting. 1.0, 2.5

Have students practice batting (off tee, from a toss, from a pitch, for distance, and for accuracy) in groups of four, rotating from retriever to pitcher to batter to catcher. (Assessment opportunity: structured observation 1.0, 5.2, 6.3)

Lead students through a cool-down and flexibility exercises appropriate to the physical activity level of the lesson. (Assessment opportunity: structured observation 4.1)

Have students brainstorm the physical abilities used in bunting. 2.4

Figure 17.24   Bunting.

DAY 15

Have students perform a warm-up along with a cardiorespiratory workout. (Assessment opportunity: structured observation 4.1)

Review bunting (see figure 17.24). 1.0, 2.5

Have students practice bunting (off tee, from a toss, from a pitch, for distance, and for accuracy) in groups of four, rotating from retriever to pitcher to batter to catcher. (Assessment opportunity: structured observation 1.0, 5.2, 6.3)

DAY 15 (continued)	Review batting. 1.0, 2.5 Have students practice batting (off tee, from a toss, from a pitch, for distance, and for accuracy) in groups of four, rotating from retriever to pitcher to batter to catcher. (Assessment opportunity: structured observation 1.0, 5.2, 6.3) Lead students through a cool-down and flexibility exercises appropriate to the physical activity level of the lesson. (Assessment opportunity: structured observation 4.1)
DAY 16	Have students perform a warm-up along with a cardiorespiratory workout. (Assessment opportunity: structured observation 4.1) Review bunting. 1.0, 2.5 Have students practice bunting (off tee, from a toss, from a pitch, for distance, and for accuracy) in groups of four, rotating from retriever to pitcher to batter to catcher. (Assessment opportunity: structured observation 1.0, 5.2, 6.3) Review baserunning. 1.0, 2.5 Have students practice bunting and baserunning. (Assessment opportunity: structured observation 1.0, 5.2, 6.3) Lead students through a cool-down and flexibility exercises appropriate to the physical activity level of the lesson. (Assessment opportunity: structured observation 4.1) Have students brainstorm the physical abilities used in baserunning. 2.4
DAY 17	Have students perform a warm-up along with muscular strength and muscular endurance exercises. (Assessment opportunity: structured observation 4.1) Review how to practice in stations. Have students review skills by practicing in a variety of softball stations (throwing and catching, fielding fly balls, fielding grounders, pitching, batting, bunting, and baserunning). Also set up the computer as one station with SimAthlete loaded so students can reinforce their understanding of transfer of learning. (Assessment opportunity: structured observation) 1.0, 2.1, 6.3, 5.2 Lead students through a cool-down and flexibility exercises appropriate to the physical activity level of the lesson. (Assessment opportunity: structured observation 4.1)
DAY 18	Have students perform a warm-up along with a cardiorespiratory workout. (Assessment opportunity: structured observation 4.1) Review how to practice in stations. Have students review skills by practicing in a variety of softball stations (throwing and catching, fielding fly balls, fielding grounders, pitching, batting, bunting, and baserunning). Also set up the computer as one station with SimAthlete loaded so students can reinforce their understanding of transfer of learning. (Assessment opportunity: structured observation 1.0, 2.1, 6.3, 5.2) Lead students through a cool-down and flexibility exercises appropriate to the physical activity level of the lesson. (Assessment opportunity: structured observation 4.1)
DAY 19	Discuss what it means to collaborate with team members when solving problems during field sports. 5.1 Have students record the information in their notebooks. 5.1 Explain the development of offensive and defensive strategies in softball and other field sports. 2.3 Have students summarize in their notebooks the description of offensive and defensive strategies. 2.3 Give students, in groups of four, a variety of scenarios for which they must collectively determine the best offensive or defensive strategy. (Assessment opportunity: structured observation 5.1, 2.3) Have students discuss the role each group member played in the resolution of strategic scenarios. 5.1

(continued)

Unit 5 Outline *(continued)*

DAY 20

Assign students to groups of nine.

Have students perform a warm-up along with a cardiorespiratory workout. (Assessment opportunity: structured observation 4.1)

Teach three-team softball and regulation softball. 1.0

Have students try one inning of each game. 2.3, 1.0, 5.2, 6.3

Lead students through a cool-down and flexibility exercises appropriate to the physical activity level of the lesson. (Assessment opportunity: structured observation 4.1)

Review the role of group members in the resolution of group problems. 5.1

Have students meet with their softball teams to determine who will play which position. 5.1, 2.3

Have students discuss the role each group member played in the position selection process. 5.1

DAY 21

Have students perform a warm-up along with a cardiorespiratory workout. (Assessment opportunity: structured observation 4.1)

Have students play three-team softball. (Assessment opportunity: structured observation 1.0, 5.2, 6.3, 2.3, 5.1)

Lead students through a cool-down and flexibility exercises appropriate to the physical activity level of the lesson. (Assessment opportunity: structured observation 4.1)

DAY 22

Have students perform a warm-up along with muscular strength and muscular endurance exercises. (Assessment opportunity: structured observation 4.1)

Have students play three-team softball. (Assessment opportunity: structured observation 1.0, 5.2, 6.3, 2.3, 5.1)

Lead students through a cool-down and flexibility exercises appropriate to the physical activity level of the lesson. (Assessment opportunity: structured observation 4.1)

DAY 23

Have students perform a warm-up along with a cardiorespiratory workout. (Assessment opportunity: structured observation 4.1)

Have students play regulation softball. (Assessment opportunity: structured observation 1.0, 5.2, 6.3, 2.3, 5.1)

Lead students through a cool-down and flexibility exercises appropriate to the physical activity level of the lesson. (Assessment opportunity: structured observation 4.1)

Have students discuss which softball game they like the best and why. 2.3

DAY 24

Have students perform a warm-up along with muscular strength and muscular endurance exercises. (Assessment opportunity: structured observation 4.1)

Have students play regulation softball. (Assessment opportunity: structured observation 1.0, 5.2, 6.3, 2.3, 5.1)

Lead students through a cool-down and flexibility exercises appropriate to the physical activity level of the lesson. (Assessment opportunity: structured observation 4.1)

Have students discuss transfer of learning and how it can be used to learn regulation softball after learning three-team softball. 2.1

Review material for tomorrow's quiz (or hand out quiz if you would like for it to be a take home quiz). 2.2, 2.3, 2.4, 2.5, 6.4

DAY 25

Have students take the quiz. (Assessment opportunity: quiz 2.2, 2.3, 2.4, 2.5, 6.4)

Collect student activity logs. (Assessment opportunity: log 3.1)

Collect reports on the description of field sports in the United States during the 19th and 20th centuries. (Assessment opportunity: report 6.1)

Collect essays explaining the ways to exercise while watching television. (Assessment opportunity: essay 3.2)

Collect body composition plans. (Assessment opportunity: project 4.2)

Square Dancing

— Unit 6

By looking at how individuals need to work together to square dance successfully, this unit continues our focus on working as a team to develop strategies for success. And because square dance developed in America during the 1800s, this unit dovetails nicely with what my students are studying in history. This unit also reinforces the concept of the transfer of learning because dance skills used in one dance positively transfer to other dances.

You can teach this unit in any open area; however, an indoor facility is preferable. Of course, you'll need compact discs, audiotapes, or MP3 sound files for each dance you teach, as well as the appropriate player. A microphone will ensure that students can hear your voice over the music. A heart rate monitor interface to a computer will help you teach about cardiorespiratory endurance.

Naturally, this unit ties in well with music education. My students learn more about the history of American square dance and the type and development of music that goes with the dancing in their music classes. Then in physical education, the students actually participate in the dances and learn the history from a physical education perspective.

Unit 6 Standards

1.0—Demonstrates the mature form for circle left, right, shuffle step, do-si-do, swing, promenade, right-hand star, allemande left, single-file promenade, split ring, grand right and left, courtesy turn, forearm turn, right and left through, pass partner, circle to line, allemande left from a line of four, two ladies chain, four ladies chain, chain straight across, seesaw, grand square, half sashay, and shoot the star.

2.1—Applies transfer of learning to the learning of steps in new dances.

2.2—Explains how force can be used to alter the outcome of a dance performance.

2.3—Not applicable.

2.4—Analyzes the role of physical abilities in the performance of specialized skills.

2.5—Explains critical elements of specialized skills and combinations for circle left and right, shuffle step, do-si-do, swing, promenade, right-hand star, allemande left, single-file promenade, split ring, grand right and left, courtesy turn, forearm turn, right and left through, pass partner, circle to line, allemande left from a line of four, two ladies chain, four ladies chain, chain straight across, seesaw, grand square, half sashay, and shoot the star.

3.1—Engages in moderate and vigorous physical activity for 60 minutes 6 days each week based on personal goals.

3.2—Explains ways of increasing physical activity in routine daily activities.

4.1—Works toward a health-enhancing level of physical fitness.

4.2—Designs a 2-week personal health-related fitness plan.

5.1—Collaborates with others to solve group problems in physical activity settings.

5.2—Accepts responsibility for one's own actions and decisions during square dancing.

6.1—Describes dancing in the United States during the 19th and 20th centuries.

6.2—Appreciates other's stylistic approach to creating a dance.

6.3—Chooses to engage in square dance activities at the appropriate level of social, physical, and emotional challenge.

6.4—Explains the cognitive and psychological benefits of regular participation in physical activity.

Unit 6 Assessments

1.0—Structured observation (days 3-25)

2.1—Essay (assigned on day 24; collected on day 25)

2.2—Quiz (day 23)

2.3—Not applicable

2.4—Quiz (day 23)

2.5—Quiz (day 23)

3.1—Log (assigned on day 1; collected on day 25)

3.2—Essay (assigned on day 2; collected on day 5)

4.1—Structured observation (days 1-22, 24-25)

4.2—Project (assigned on day 4; collected on day 25)

5.1—Structured observation (days 19, 24)

5.2—Structured observation (days 2-25)

6.1—Report (assigned day 1; collected on day 25)

6.2—Essay (assigned on day 25; collected the first day of the new unit)

6.3—Structured observation (days 2-25)

6.4—Quiz (day 23)

Resources

Heart rate monitors

Health-Related Fitness: Tutorial and Portfolio (Bonnie's Fitware, Inc.)

Middle School Physical Education Portfolio (Bonnie's Fitware, Inc.)

Dance Instruction CD (Bonnie's Fitware, Inc.)

Eighth grade square dance task cards (Bonnie's Fitware, Inc.)

Eighth grade unit 6 posters (Bonnie's Fitware, Inc.—included in the Middle School Detailed Lesson Plans)

Fitness posters (Bonnie's Fitware, Inc.—included in the Middle School Detailed Lesson Plans)

Qualities of Movement chart (Bonnie's Fitware, Inc.—included in the Middle School Detailed Lesson Plans)

Music

Fundamental Square Dancing—Volumes 1 and 2 (Bonnie's Fitware, Inc.)

Square Dance Now—Volume 1 (Bonnie's Fitware, Inc.)

Square Dance Now—Volume 2 (Bonnie's Fitware, Inc.)

Equipment

Sound system

Dances

Gentle on My Mind—set; couples; circle left, right; shuffle step; do-si-do; swing; promenade; right hand star

Bad Bad Leroy Brown—single file promenade; allemande left

Engine 9—single-file promenade; split ring; grand right and left;

Hey Li Lee Li Lee—same as Engine 9

If They Could See Me Now—back to back; courtesy turn; forearm turn; pass partner

Long Lonesome Highway—circle to line; do-si-do opposite; allemande left from a line of four

Robinson Crusoe—two ladies chain; couples face right; four ladies chain

Glendale Train—chain straight across

Shindig in the Barn—review

King of the Road—weave the ring

Mississippi—seesaw

Houston—review

Sweet Personality—grand square; half sashay; shoot the star

Unit 6 Outline

DAY 1

Introduce square dancing. 1.0

Discuss participating in square dance activities at the appropriate level of social, physical, and emotional challenge. 6.3

Have students record the information in their notebooks. 6.3

Assign students to work in groups of eight.

Review with students how to wear a heart monitor and transfer data to the computer. 4.2

Review locomotor skills. 1.0

Have students perform a warm-up. (Assessment opportunity: structured observation 4.1)

Have students perform locomotor skills to music while wearing heart monitors. 1.0, 6.3

Review the qualities of movement (force, space, relationships). 6.2

Have students perform locomotor skills to music using a variety of qualities. 1.0, 6.2, 6.3

Lead students through a cool-down and flexibility exercises appropriate to the physical activity level of the lesson. (Assessment opportunity: structured observation 4.1)

Assign unit-long homework:

- Have students research and write a description of dancing in the United States during the 19th and 20th centuries. (Assessment assignment opportunity: report 6.1)

- Have students keep a log of daily activity. (Assessment assignment opportunity: log 3.1)

DAY 2

Display the posters.

Review transfer of learning concept (concept covered in previous units). 2.1

Have students brainstorm the role of transfer of learning in the learning of new dance steps. 2.1

Have students record their brainstorming in their notebooks. 2.1

Discuss taking responsibility for one's own actions. 5.2

Have students take notes on accepting responsibility. 5.2

Have students perform a warm-up along with muscular strength and muscular endurance exercises. (Assessment opportunity: structured observation 4.1)

Set up a square set and describe the different positions using the Dance Instruction CD. 1.0

Have students set up in a square and identify the different positions. (Assessment opportunity: structured observation 1.0, 5.2, 6.3)

Have students teach one another the following moves: shuffle step, circle left and right, do-si-do, swing, promenade, and right-hand star using a jigsaw strategy. (Assessment opportunity: structured observation 1.0, 5.2, 6.3) 2.5

Lead students through a cool-down and flexibility exercises appropriate to the physical activity level of the lesson. (Assessment opportunity: structured observation 4.1)

For homework, have students write an essay explaining ways to increase physical activity in daily routines. (Assessment assignment opportunity: essay 3.2)

DAY 3

Have students perform a warm-up. (Assessment opportunity: structured observation 4.1)

Explain how force can be used to alter the outcome of a dance performance. 2.2

Have students record the information in their notebooks. 2.2

Have students perform a warm-up. (Assessment opportunity: structured observation 4.1)

Demonstrate and describe swing, promenade, and right-hand star.

(continued)

Unit 6 Outline *(continued)*

DAY 3 *(continued)*

Review the shuffle step, circle left and right, do-si-do, swing, promenade, and right-hand star using the Dance Instruction CD. 1.0, 2.5

Walk students through Gentle on My Mind. (Assessment opportunity: structured observation 1.0, 5.2, 6.3)

Lead students through a cool-down and flexibility exercises appropriate to the physical activity level of the lesson. (Assessment opportunity: structured observation 4.1)

Review transfer of learning related to dance. 2.1

DAY 4

Display the fitness posters.

Explain the cognitive and psychological benefits of regular participation in physical activity. 6.4

Have students record in their notebooks the cognitive and psychological benefits. 6.4

Review the concepts of frequency, intensity, time, and type (FITT) as they relate to all five health-related fitness components using the Health-Related Fitness: Tutorial and Portfolio. 4.2

Assign students a 2-week fitness plan. (Assessment assignment opportunity: project 4.2)

Have students perform a warm-up along with muscular strength and muscular endurance exercises. (Assessment opportunity: structured observation 4.1)

Walk students through Gentle on My Mind (see figure 17.25). 1.0

Have students dance to Gentle on My Mind. (Assessment opportunity: structured observation 1.0, 5.2, 6.3)

Lead students through a cool-down and flexibility exercises appropriate to the physical activity level of the lesson. (Assessment opportunity: structured observation 4.1)

Review how force can be used to alter the outcome of a skill performance. 2.2

(continued)

Figure 17.25   Gentle on My Mind: *(a)* starting set, *(b)* circle left, *(c)* circle right, *(d)* allemande left corner, *(e)* allemande right partner, *(f)* do-si-do corner, and *(g)* right elbow swing partner.

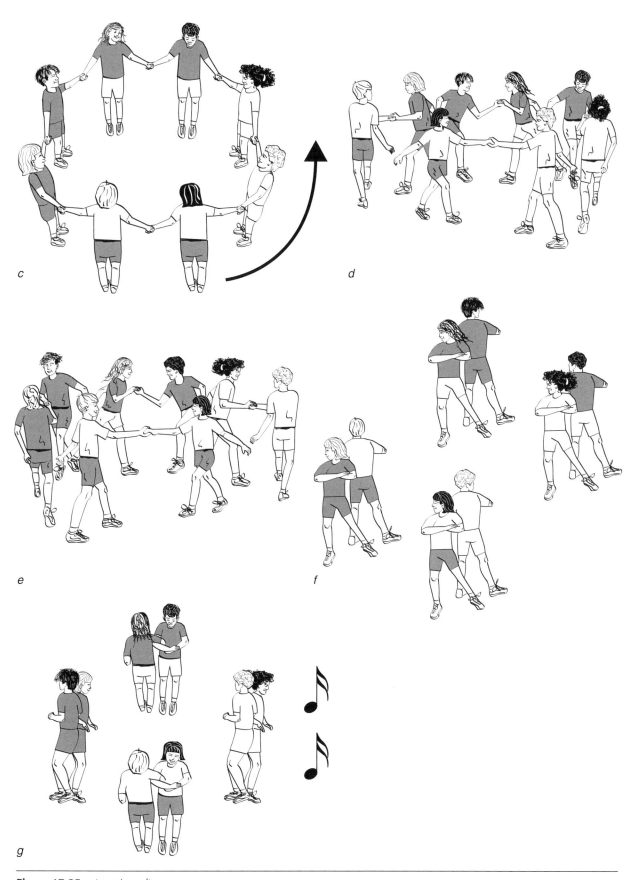

Figure 17.25   *(continued)*

Unit 6 Outline *(continued)*

DAY 5	Discuss the role of physical abilities in the performance of dance skills. 2.4
	Have student take notes on the role of physical abilities. 2.4
	Have students perform a warm-up. (Assessment opportunity: structured observation 4.1)
	Have students review Gentle on My Mind (see figure 17.25). (Assessment opportunity: structured observation 1.0, 5.2, 6.3)
	Demonstrate and describe the allemande left using the Dance Instruction CD. 1.0, 2.5
	Have students practice the allemande left. (Assessment opportunity: structured observation 1.0, 5.2, 6.3)
	Demonstrate and describe single-file promenade using the Dance Instruction CD. 1.0, 2.5
	Have students practice single-file promenade. (Assessment opportunity: structured observation 1.0, 5.2, 6.3)
	Walk students through Bad Bad Leroy Brown. 1.0
	Have students dance to Bad Bad Leroy Brown. (Assessment opportunity: structured observation 1.0, 5.2, 6.3)
	Lead students through a cool-down and flexibility exercises appropriate to the physical activity level of the lesson. (Assessment opportunity: structured observation 4.1)
	Collect essays on increasing physical activity. (Assessment opportunity: essay 3.2)
DAY 6	Have students perform a warm-up. (Assessment opportunity: structured observation 4.1)
	Have students review Bad Bad Leroy Brown. (Assessment opportunity: structured observation 1.0, 5.2, 6.3)
	Demonstrate and describe split the ring using the Dance Instruction CD. 1.0, 2.5
	Have students practice split the ring. (Assessment opportunity: structured observation 1.0, 5.2, 6.3)
	Demonstrate and describe the grand right and left using the Dance Instruction CD. 1.0, 2.5
	Have students practice the grand right and left. (Assessment opportunity: structured observation 1.0, 5.2, 6.3)
	Walk students through Engine 9 (see figure 17.26). 1.0
	Have students dance to Engine 9. (Assessment opportunity: structured observation 1.0, 5.2, 6.3)
	Lead students through a cool-down and flexibility exercises appropriate to the physical activity level of the lesson. (Assessment opportunity: structured observation 4.1)
	Review the role of physical abilities in the performance of dance skills. 2.4
DAY 7	Have students perform a warm-up along with muscular strength and muscular endurance exercises. (Assessment opportunity: structured observation 4.1)
	Have students review Engine 9. (Assessment opportunity: structured observation 1.0, 5.2, 6.3)
	Walk students through Hey Li Lee Li Lee. 1.0
	Have students dance to Hey Li Lee Li Lee. (Assessment opportunity: structured observation 1.0, 5.2, 6.3)
	Lead students through a cool-down and flexibility exercises appropriate to the physical activity level of the lesson. (Assessment opportunity: structured observation 4.1)
DAY 8	Have students perform a warm-up. (Assessment opportunity: structured observation 4.1)
	Have students review Gentle on My Mind, Bad Bad Leroy Brown, Engine 9, and Hey Lei Lee Lei Lee. (Assessment opportunity: structured observation 1.0, 5.2, 6.3)
	Lead students through a cool-down and flexibility exercises appropriate to the physical activity level of the lesson. (Assessment opportunity: structured observation 4.1)

(continued)

(continued)

Figure 17.26 Engine 9: *(a)* starting set; *(b)* grand right and left, phase 1; *(c)* grand right and left, phase 2; *(d)* grand right and left, phase 3; *(e)* grand right and left, phase 4; *(f)* twirl; and *(g)* promenade.

g

Figure 17.26 *(continued)*

Unit 6 Outline *(continued)*

DAY 9	Have students perform a warm-up along with muscular strength and muscular endurance exercises. (Assessment opportunity: structured observation 4.1)
	Demonstrate and describe courtesy turn using the Dance Instruction CD. 1.0, 2.5
	Have students practice courtesy turn. (Assessment opportunity: structured observation 1.0, 5.2, 6.3)
	Demonstrate and describe forearm turn using the Dance Instruction CD. 1.0, 2.5
	Have students practice forearm turn. (Assessment opportunity: structured observation 1.0, 5.2, 6.3)
	Walk students through If They Could See Me Now. 1.0
	Have students dance to If They Could See Me Now. (Assessment opportunity: structured observation 1.0, 5.2, 6.3)
	Lead students through a cool-down and flexibility exercises appropriate to the physical activity level of the lesson. (Assessment opportunity: structured observation 4.1)
DAY 10	Have students perform a warm-up. (Assessment opportunity: structured observation 4.1)
	Have students review If They Could See Me Now. (Assessment opportunity: structured observation 1.0, 5.2, 6.3)
	Demonstrate and describe moving from a circle to line using the Dance Instruction CD. 1.0, 2.5
	Have students practice circle to line. (Assessment opportunity: structured observation 1.0, 5.2, 6.3)
	Demonstrate and describe allemande left from a line of four using the Dance Instruction CD. 1.0, 2.5
	Have students practice allemande left from a line of four. (Assessment opportunity: structured observation 1.0, 5.2, 6.3)
	Walk students through Long Lonesome Highway. 1.0
	Have students dance to Long Lonesome Highway. (Assessment opportunity: structured observation 1.0, 5.2, 6.3)
	Lead students through a cool-down and flexibility exercises appropriate to the physical activity level of the lesson. (Assessment opportunity: structured observation 4.1)

DAY 11

Have students perform a warm-up. (Assessment opportunity: structured observation 4.1)

Have students review Long Lonesome Highway. (Assessment opportunity: structured observation 1.0, 5.2, 6.3)

Demonstrate the ladies chain using the Dance Instruction CD. 1.0, 2.5

Have students practice the ladies chain. (Assessment opportunity: structured observation 1.0, 5.2, 6.3)

Demonstrate the four ladies chain using the Dance Instruction CD. 1.0, 2.5

Have students practice the four ladies chain. (Assessment opportunity: structured observation 1.0, 5.2, 6.3)

Walk students through Robinson Crusoe (see figure 17.27). 1.0

Have students dance to Robinson Crusoe. (Assessment opportunity: structured observation 1.0, 5.2, 6.3)

Lead students through a cool-down and flexibility exercises appropriate to the physical activity level of the lesson. (Assessment opportunity: structured observation 4.1)

(continued)

(continued)

Figure 17.27 Robinson Crusoe: *(a)* starting set; *(b)* side couples front and back; *(c)* head couples right and left through, phase 1; *(d)* head couples right and left through, phase 2.

Figure 17.27 Robinson Crusoe *(continued)*: *(e)* side ladies chain, phase 1; *(f)* side ladies chain, phase 2; *(g)* head ladies chain, phase 1; *(h)* head ladies chain, phase 2; *(i)* all four ladies chain, phase 1; *(j)* all four ladies chain, phase 2; and *(k)* all four ladies chain, phase 3.

Unit 6 Outline *(continued)*

DAY 12

Have students perform a warm-up along with muscular strength and muscular endurance exercises. (Assessment opportunity: structured observation 4.1)

Have students review Robinson Crusoe. (Assessment opportunity: structured observation 1.0, 5.2, 6.3)

Demonstrate right and left through using the Dance Instruction CD. 1.0, 2.5

Have students practice right and left through. (Assessment opportunity: structured observation 1.0, 5.2, 6.3)

Walk students through Glendale Train. 1.0

Have students dance to Glendale Train. (Assessment opportunity: structured observation 1.0, 5.2, 6.3)

Lead students through a cool-down and flexibility exercises appropriate to the physical activity level of the lesson. (Assessment opportunity: structured observation 4.1)

DAY 13

Have students perform a warm-up. (Assessment opportunity: structured observation 4.1)

Have students review If They Could See Me Now, Long Lonesome Highway, Robinson Crusoe, and Glendale Train. (Assessment opportunity: structured observation 1.0, 5.2, 6.3)

Lead students through a cool-down and flexibility exercises appropriate to the physical activity level of the lesson. (Assessment opportunity: structured observation 4.1)

DAY 14

Have students perform a warm-up along with muscular strength and muscular endurance exercises. (Assessment opportunity: structured observation 4.1)

Walk students through Shindig in the Barn. 1.0

Have students dance to Shindig in the Barn. (Assessment opportunity: structured observation 1.0, 5.2, 6.3)

Lead students through a cool-down and flexibility exercises appropriate to the physical activity level of the lesson. (Assessment opportunity: structured observation 4.1)

DAY 15

Have students perform a warm-up. (Assessment opportunity: structured observation 4.1)

Have students review Shindig in the Barn. (Assessment opportunity: structured observation 1.0, 5.2, 6.3)

Demonstrate weave the ring using the Dance Instruction CD. 1.0, 2.5

Have students practice weave the ring. (Assessment opportunity: structured observation 1.0, 5.2, 6.3)

Walk students through King of the Road. 1.0

Have students dance to King of the Road. (Assessment opportunity: structured observation 1.0, 5.2, 6.3)

Lead students through a cool-down and flexibility exercises appropriate to the physical activity level of the lesson. (Assessment opportunity: structured observation 4.1)

DAY 16

Have students perform a warm-up. (Assessment opportunity: structured observation 4.1)

Have students review King of the Road. (Assessment opportunity: structured observation 1.0, 5.2, 6.3)

Demonstrate the seesaw using the Dance Instruction CD. 1.0, 2.5

Have students practice the seesaw. (Assessment opportunity: structured observation 1.0, 5.2, 6.3)

Walk students through Mississippi. 1.0

Have students dance to Mississippi. (Assessment opportunity: structured observation 1.0, 5.2, 6.3)

Lead students through a cool-down and flexibility exercises appropriate to the physical activity level of the lesson. (Assessment opportunity: structured observation 4.1)

(continued)

Unit 6 Outline *(continued)*

DAY 17	Have students perform a warm-up along with muscular strength and muscular endurance exercises. (Assessment opportunity: structured observation 4.1) Have students review Shindig in the Barn, King of the Road, and Mississippi. (Assessment opportunity: structured observation 1.0, 5.2, 6.3) Lead students through a cool-down and flexibility exercises appropriate to the physical activity level of the lesson. (Assessment opportunity: structured observation 4.1)
DAY 18	Have students perform a warm-up. (Assessment opportunity: structured observation 4.1) Walk students through Houston. 1.0 Have students dance to Houston. (Assessment opportunity: structured observation 1.0, 5.2, 6.3) Lead students through a cool-down and flexibility exercises appropriate to the physical activity level of the lesson. (Assessment opportunity: structured observation 4.1)
DAY 19	Describe collaborative group problem-solving. 5.1 Have students take notes on collaborative group problem solving. 5.1 Have students perform a warm-up along with muscular strength and muscular endurance exercises. (Assessment opportunity: structured observation 4.1) Demonstrate the grand square (see figure 17.28) using the Dance Instruction CD. 1.0, 2.5

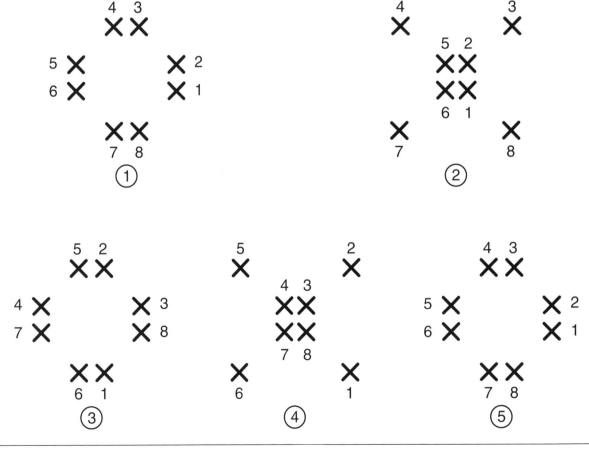

Figure 17.28   Grand square call in square dancing.

DAY 19 *(continued)*	Have students practice the grand square. (Assessment opportunity: structured observation 1.0, 5.2, 6.3) Have students learn how to dance to Sweet Personality by reading and following written directions for the dance. (Assessment opportunity: structured observation 1.0, 5.1, 5.2, 6.3) Have students dance to Sweet Personality. (Assessment opportunity: structured observation 1.0, 5.1, 5.2, 6.3) Lead students through a cool-down and flexibility exercises appropriate to the physical activity level of the lesson. (Assessment opportunity: structured observation 4.1)
DAY 20	Have students perform a warm-up. (Assessment opportunity: structured observation 4.1) Review the grand square (see figure 17.28). 1.0, 2.5 Have students practice the grand square. (Assessment opportunity: structured observation 1.0, 5.2, 6.3) Have students dance to Sweet Personality. (Assessment opportunity: structured observation 1.0, 5.2, 6.3) Lead students through a cool-down and flexibility exercises appropriate to the physical activity level of the lesson. (Assessment opportunity: structured observation 4.1) Review collaborative group problem solving. 5.1
DAY 21	Have students perform a warm-up. (Assessment opportunity: structured observation 4.1) Have students review Mississippi, Houston, and Sweet Personality. (Assessment opportunity: structured observation 1.0, 5.2, 6.3) Lead students through a cool-down and flexibility exercises appropriate to the physical activity level of the lesson. (Assessment opportunity: structured observation 4.1)
DAY 22	Have students perform a warm-up along with muscular strength and muscular endurance exercises. (Assessment opportunity: structured observation 4.1) Review all dances learned in this unit. (Assessment opportunity: structured observation 1.0, 5.2, 6.3) Lead students through a cool-down and flexibility exercises appropriate to the physical activity level of the lesson. (Assessment opportunity: structured observation 4.1) Review material for tomorrow's quiz (or hand out quiz if you would like for it to be a take home quiz). 2.2, 2.4, 2.5, 6.4
DAY 23	Have students take a quiz. (Assessment opportunity: quiz 2.2, 2.4, 2.5, 6.4) Review collaborative group problem-solving process. 5.1 Review stylistic differences. 6.2 Explain square dance creation project to students. (Assessment opportunity: structured observation 1.0, 5.1, 5.2, 6.3)
DAY 24	Have students perform a warm-up along with muscular strength and muscular endurance exercises. (Assessment opportunity: structured observation 4.1) Review stylistic differences and what account for them. 6.2 Have each group work on their square dance creation. (Assessment opportunity: structured observation 1.0, 5.1, 5.2, 6.3) 6.2 Lead students through a cool-down and flexibility exercises appropriate to the physical activity level of the lesson. (Assessment opportunity: structured observation 4.1) For homework, have students write an essay, explaining how they used transfer of learning to learn steps in new dances. (Assessment assignment opportunity: essay 2.1)

(continued)

Unit 6 Outline *(continued)*

DAY 25

Have students perform a warm-up. (Assessment opportunity: structured observation 4.1)

Have each group teach their dance to another group. (Assessment opportunity: structured observation 1.0, 5.1, 5.2, 6.3) 6.2

Lead students through a cool-down and flexibility exercises appropriate to the physical activity level of the lesson. (Assessment opportunity: structured observation 4.1)

Collect student logs of participation in physical activity outside of physical education. (Assessment opportunity: log 3.1)

Collect the 2-week fitness plans. (Assessment opportunity: project 4.2)

Collect essays on the history of square dance. (Assessment opportunity: report 6.1)

Collect essays on transfer of learning. (Assessment opportunity: essay 2.1)

Have students write essays describing what they appreciated about other's stylistic approach to creating a dance. (Assessment assignment opportunity: essay 6.2)

Closure and Fitness Assessment — Unit 7

This unit, similar to the fifth, sixth, and seventh grade closing and fitness assessment units, gives students the opportunity to demonstrate whether they have reached the eighth grade standards. Although students have been working on projects throughout the year, I give them the chance to focus on depth over breadth in this unit. Have students focus on completing their demonstrations of learning by collecting and creating work for their portfolios, freeing you to administer the fitness assessment and to act as a resource for the student projects.

For this unit, I present students with the 16 standards for the eighth grade and ask them to present evidence of their learning related to each standard. For some of the standards, students will be able to demonstrate their learning by looking through their working portfolios and pulling from work that they have already accomplished during the year. For other standards, students will be able to pull from interdisciplinary projects that they have accomplished throughout the year. For still other standards, students will need to create new projects during this closure unit to demonstrate their learning. Once the students have collected their evidence, it goes into their performance portfolios. Then I ask students to write a reflection paper (a one-page essay) on their cumulative learning throughout eighth grade physical education.

Ideally, you and your students' other teachers should assign a final eighth grade project that incorporates all subject areas, affording students the opportunity to demonstrate their learning in all subject areas. Teachers in all subject areas should give students time to work on the eighth grade project as well as offer appropriate guidance. Thus, this closure unit is not only an opportunity for students to complete their physical education or comprehensive portfolios but also an opportunity to complete their eighth grade projects. To link the eighth grade project to real life, you and your colleagues should allow students to select the content they wish to investigate and create an opportunity to exhibit the projects. Often, schools invite community members to attend the presentations of the eighth graders' final projects. These presentations can take the form of speeches, multimedia presentations, video reports, and demonstrations.

As with the introductory unit, you can conduct this unit in just about any facility. But if you have students perform exercises on the ground or grass, provide them with carpet squares or some other material so they don't get dirty. An indoor facility is also helpful for the project development phase of this unit. Many times, teachers also reserve the library or arrange for some of their students to do research in the library. Of course, the equipment necessary to implement the unit depends on the fitness assessments you plan to administer. I administer the same Fitnessgram tests that I gave at the beginning of the school year and during fifth, sixth, and seventh grades. Once again, I have the students enter their fitness assessment scores into their own electronic portfolios so that they and I can compare the latest scores with preassessment, standards, and goals and calculate their progress over the last 4 years. You'll also need to make sure students have access to reference books, CD-ROMs, DVDs, computers, videotape or DVD players, monitors, camcorders, and other materials to assist with project development.

Sample Assessment for Each Eighth Grade Standard

1.0—Demonstrates the mature form for specialized skills and combinations during modified team and dance activities.

Teacher assessment during each instructional unit based on a rubric determines whether a student has reached this standard. The following is a sample rubric for the soccer kick:

6: Performs a mature soccer kick when kicking in a game or activity situation.

5: Performs a mature soccer kick when kicking for distance and accuracy.

4: Performs a mature soccer kick.

_____ Stands behind ball slightly to nonkicking side of the ball.

_____ Runs to ball and takes a small leap to get kicking foot in position.

_____ Keeps eyes on ball.

_____ Swings kicking leg back and then forcefully forward from hip.

_____ Leans trunk backward.

_____ Extends knee.

_____ Contacts center of ball with instep.

_____ Swings arm opposite kicking leg forward.

_____ Follows through in an upward motion.

_____ Takes small step forward on support foot after contact.

3: Is moving toward mature soccer kick.

2: Attempts an immature soccer kick when a ball is rolled to her.

1: Randomly attempts an immature soccer kick.

2.1—Analyzes the effect of positive transfer on specialized skill improvement.

Student writes an essay analyzing the effect of positive transfer for identified specialized skills.

2.2—Explains how force can be used to alter the outcome of a skill performance.

Student writes an explanation of how external forces affect the outcome of identified specialized skills.

2.3—Explains offensive and defensive strategies for invasion and field sports.

Student writes an explanation of offensive and defensive strategies for invasion and field sports.

2.4—Analyzes the role of physical abilities in the performance of specialized skills.

Student writes an analysis of the role of physical abilities in the performance of identified specialized skills.

2.5—Explains critical elements of specialized skills and combinations in team sports.

Teacher assessment during each instructional unit is based on responses to quiz questions for each motor and movement skill taught.

3.1—Engages in moderate and vigorous physical activity for 60 minutes 6 days each week.

Student maintains a log of participation in physical activity throughout the school year.

3.2—Explains ways of increasing physical activity in routine daily activities.

Student writes an explanation of ways to increase physical activity in routine daily activities.

4.1—Works toward a health-enhancing level of physical fitness.

Student submits fitness preassessment data, goals, monitoring logs, and fitness postassessment data.

4.2—Designs a 2-week personal health-related fitness plan taking into account the possibility of inclement weather, minor injury, or travel.

Student designs a chart, essay, video, or computer program that shows her 2-week personal health-related fitness plan.

5.1—Collaborates with others to solve group problems in physical activity settings.

Teacher assessment throughout the year based on a rubric determines whether a student has reached this standard.

5.2—Accepts responsibility for one's own actions and decisions during physical activity.

Teacher assessment throughout the year based on a rubric determines whether a student has reached this standard.

6.1—Explains the development and role of movement-related activities in the United States (19th to 20th centuries) and their influence on physical activities today.

Student conducts research and reports on the history of one activity that originated in the United States during the 19th and 20th centuries and comments on its influence on physical activities today.

6.2—Appreciates others' stylistic approaches to creating a dance or routine.

Student writes an essay comparing the stylistic approaches to movement routines and dances created by peers.

6.3—Chooses to engage in physical activities at the appropriate level of social, physical, and emotional challenge.

Teacher assessment through the year based on a rubric determines whether or not a student has reached this standard.

6.4—Explains the cognitive and psychological benefits of regular participation in physical activity.

Student writes an explanation of the cognitive and psychological benefits of regular participation in physical activity.

Resources

Health-Related Fitness: Tutorial and Portfolio (Bonnie's Fitware, Inc.)

Middle School Physical Education Portfolio (Bonnie's Fitware, Inc.)

Equipment

Fitness assessment equipment

Games

None

Unit 7 Outline

DAY 1	Assign students to working groups of four.
	Remind students why you administer fitness assessments twice a year.
	Remind students how and why you administer the 1-mile run assessment. 4.1
	Have students perform warm-up exercises for the 1-mile run assessment. 4.1
	Administer the 1-mile run assessment. (Assessment opportunity: fitness assessment 4.1)
	Have students input fitness scores into their Health-Related Fitness Portfolios. 4.1
	Lead students through a cool-down and flexibility exercises appropriate to the physical activity level of the lesson. 4.1

DAY 2	Describe the projects and portfolios you expect students to complete in this unit. All
	Describe the project and portfolios design steps. All
	Remind students how and why you administer the curl-up assessment. 4.1
	Have students perform warm-up exercises for the curl-up assessment. 4.1
	Have students begin to work on their projects and Middle School Physical Education Portfolios. (Assessment opportunity: all)
	Administer the curl-up assessment to one group at a time. (Assessment opportunity: fitness assessment 4.1)
	Have students input fitness scores into their Health-Related Fitness Portfolios. 4.1
	Lead students through a cool-down and flexibility exercises appropriate to the physical activity level of the lesson. 4.1
DAY 3	Remind students how and why you administer the skinfold measurement. 4.1
	Have students work on their projects and Middle School Physical Education Portfolios. (Assessment opportunity: all)
	Administer the skinfold measurement privately to one student at a time. (Assessment opportunity: fitness assessment 4.1)
	Have students input fitness scores into their Health-Related Fitness Portfolios. 4.1
DAY 4	Remind students how and why you administer the back-saver sit-and-reach and trunk-lift assessments. 4.1
	Have students work on their projects and Middle School Physical Education Portfolios. (Assessment opportunity: all)
	Have students perform warm-up exercises for the back-saver sit-and-reach and trunk-lift assessments. 4.1
	Administer the back-saver sit-and-reach and trunk-lift assessments to one group at a time. (Assessment opportunity: fitness assessment 4.1)
	Have students input fitness scores into their Health-Related Fitness Portfolios. 4.1
	Lead students through a cool-down and flexibility exercises appropriate to the physical activity level of the lesson. 4.1
DAY 5	Remind students how and why you administer the push-up assessment. 4.1
	Have students perform warm-up exercises for the push-up assessment. 4.1
	Have students work on their projects and Middle School Physical Education Portfolios. (Assessment opportunity: all)
	Administer the push-up assessment to one group at a time. (Assessment opportunity: fitness assessment 4.1)
	Have students input fitness scores into their Health-Related Fitness Portfolios. 4.1
	Lead students through a cool-down and flexibility exercises appropriate to the physical activity level of the lesson. 4.1
DAY 6	Have students perform warm-up exercises for the makeup assessments. 4.1
	Have students work on their projects and Middle School Physical Education Portfolios. (Assessment opportunity: all)
	Administer makeup fitness assessments to one group at a time. (Assessment opportunity: fitness assessment 4.1)
	Have students input fitness scores into their Health-Related Fitness Portfolios. 4.1
	Lead students through a cool-down and flexibility exercises appropriate to the physical activity level of the lesson. 4.1

(continued)

Unit 7 Outline *(continued)*

DAYS 7-12	Have students work on their projects and Middle School Physical Education Portfolios. (Assessment opportunity: all)
DAY 13	Have some groups share their projects and Middle School Physical Education Portfolios. (Assessment opportunity: all)
DAY 14	Have remaining groups share their projects and Middle School Physical Education Portfolios. (Assessment opportunity: all)
DAY 15	Debrief Middle School Physical Education Portfolios. (Assessment opportunity: all)

Appendix A

Characteristics of Middle School Students

Intellectual Development

1. Display a wide range of individual intellectual development as their minds experience transition from the concrete–manipulatory stage to the capacity for abstract thought. This transition ultimately makes the following possible:
   - Propositional thought
   - Consideration of ideas contrary to fact
   - Reasoning with hypotheses involving two or more variables
   - Appreciation for the elegance of mathematical logic expressed in symbols
   - Insight into the nuances of poetic metaphor and musical notation
   - Analysis of the power of a political ideology
   - Ability to project thought into the future, to anticipate, and to formulate goals
   - Insight into the sources of previously unquestioned attitudes, behaviors, and values
   - Interpretation of larger concepts and generalizations of traditional wisdom expressed through sayings, axioms, and aphorisms

2. Are intensely curious.

3. Prefer active over passive learning experiences; favor interaction with peers during learning activities.

4. Exhibit a strong willingness to learn things they consider to be useful; enjoy using skills to solve real-life problems.

5. Are egocentric; argue to convince others; exhibit independent, critical thought.

6. Consider academic goals as a secondary level of priority; personal–social concerns dominate thoughts and activities.

7. Experience the phenomenon of metacognition—the ability to know what one knows and does not know.

8. Are intellectually at risk; face decisions that have the potential to affect major academic values with lifelong consequences.

Physical Development

1. Experience accelerated physical development marked by increases in weight, height, heart size, lung capacity, and muscular strength.

2. Mature at varying rates of speed. Girls tend to be taller than boys for the first 2 years of early adolescence and are ordinarily more physically developed than boys.

3. Experience bone growth faster than muscle development; uneven muscle and bone development results in lack of coordination and awkwardness; bones may lack protection of covering muscles and supporting tendons.

4. Reflect a wide range of individual differences that begin to appear in prepubertal and pubertal stages of development. Boys tend to lag behind girls. There are marked individual differences in physical development for boys and girls. The greatest

variability in physiological development and size occurs at about age 13.

5. Experience biological development 5 years sooner than adolescents of the last century; the average age of menarche has dropped from 17 to 12 years of age.

6. Face responsibility for sexual behavior before full emotional and social maturity has occurred.

7. Show changes in body contour including temporarily large noses, protruding ears, and long arms; have posture problems.

8. Are often disturbed by body changes.

   • Girls are anxious about physical changes that accompany sexual maturation.

   • Boys are anxious about receding chins, cowlicks, dimples, and changes in their voices.

9. Experience fluctuations in basal metabolism that can cause extreme restlessness at times and equally extreme listlessness at other moments.

10. Have ravenous appetites and peculiar tastes; may overtax digestive system with large quantities of improper foods.

11. Lack physical health; have poor levels of endurance, strength, and flexibility; as a group are fatter and unhealthier.

12. Are physically at risk; major causes of death are homicide, suicide, accident, and leukemia.

Psychological Development

1. Are often erratic and inconsistent in their behavior; anxiety and fear are contrasted with periods of bravado; feelings shift between superiority and inferiority.

2. Have chemical and hormonal imbalances that often trigger emotions that are frightening and poorly understood; may regress to more childish behavior patterns at this point.

3. Are easily offended and are sensitive to criticism of personal shortcomings.

4. Tend to exaggerate simple occurrences and believe that personal problems, experiences, and feelings are unique to themselves.

5. Are moody and restless; often are self-conscious and alienated; lack self-esteem; are introspective.

6. Are searching for adult identity and acceptance even in the midst of intense peer group relationships.

7. Are vulnerable to naive opinions and one-sided arguments.

8. Are searching to form a conscious sense of individual uniqueness—"Who am I?"

9. Have emerging sense of humor based on increased intellectual ability to see abstract relationships; appreciate the "double entendre."

10. Are basically optimistic and hopeful.

11. Are psychologically at risk; at no other point in human development is an individual likely to encounter so much diversity in relation to oneself and others.

Social Development

1. Experience often traumatic conflicts attributable to conflicting loyalties to peer groups and family.

2. Refer to peers as sources for standards and models of behavior; media heroes and heroines are also singularly important in shaping both behavior and fashion.

3. May be rebellious toward parents but still strongly dependent on parental values; want to make own choices, but the authority of the family is a critical factor in ultimate decisions.

4. Are affected by high level of mobility in society; may become anxious and disoriented when peer group ties are broken because of family relocation to other communities.

5. Are often confused and frightened by new school settings that are large and impersonal.

6. Act out unusual or drastic behavior at times; may be aggressive, daring, boisterous, or argumentative.

7. Are fiercely loyal to peer group values; sometimes are cruel or insensitive to those outside the peer group.

8. Want to know and believe that significant adults, including parents and teachers, love and accept them; need frequent affirmation.

9. Sense negative impact of adolescent behaviors on parents and teachers; realize thin edge between tolerance and rejection; feelings of adult rejection drive the adolescent into the relatively secure social environment of the peer group.

10. Strive to define sex role characteristics; search to establish positive social relationships with members of the same and opposite sex.

11. Experience low risk–trust relationships with adults who show lack of sensitivity to adolescent characteristics and needs.

12. Challenge authority figures; test limits of acceptable behavior.

13. Are socially at risk; adult values are largely shaped conceptually during adolescence; negative interactions with peers, parents, and teachers may compromise ideals and commitments.

Moral and Ethical Development

1. Are essentially idealistic; have a strong sense of fairness in human relationships.

2. Experience thoughts and feelings of awe and wonder related to their expanding intellectual and emotional awareness.

3. Ask large, unanswerable questions about the meaning of life; do not expect absolute answers but are turned off by trivial adult responses.

4. Are reflective, analytical, and introspective about their thoughts and feelings.

5. Confront hard moral and ethical questions for which they are unprepared to cope.

6. Are at risk in the development of moral and ethical choices and behaviors; primary dependency on the influences of home and church for moral and ethical development seriously compromises adolescents for whom these resources are absent; adolescents want to explore the moral and ethical issues that are confronted in the curriculum, in the media, and in the daily interactions they experience in their families and peer groups.

Appendix B
Content Related to Grade-Level Standards

This appendix contains the competencies related to the grade-level standards at fifth, sixth, seventh, and eighth grade.

Fifth Grade

1.0 Demonstrates speed, accuracy, and control using the mature form for fundamental movement and manipulative skills.

- Overhand pattern—overhand throw, throw using an implement, strike with an implement
- Sidearm pattern—forehand strike with implement, sidearm throw, batting
- Backhand pattern—backhand strike with implement
- Underhand pattern—toss, underhand strike with one hand, underhand strike with two hands, hockey strike
- Overhand pattern—overhand strike with one hand, overhand strike with two hands, throw with implement
- Catch pattern—catch, catch using an implement
- Kick pattern—outside of foot kick, punt, instep kick
- Hand dribble pattern—dribble
- Foot dribble pattern—dribble
- Static balance pattern—front scale, knee scale, tripod, tip-up
- Dynamic balance pattern—squat forward roll, squat backward roll

- Locomotor patterns—jump, run, walk, leap, hop, skip, gallop, slide, dance steps, pivot
- Trapping—instep trap, sole-of-foot trap
- Passing—chest pass
- Stopping—jump stop, two-step stop

2.1 Explains the types of practice that improve motor skill performance for speed and accuracy.

Mental and Physical Practice
- Mental rehearsal can increase skill performance.
- Physical practice must come before mental practice.
- Physical practice is better than mental practice.

Speed–Accuracy Trade-Off
- If a skill requires speed in a game situation, then practice for speed.
- If a skill requires accuracy in a game situation, then practice for accuracy.
- If a skill requires both speed and accuracy, then place equal emphasis on practicing for both speed and accuracy.
- There is a speed–accuracy trade-off in many striking and throwing skills.

Whole and Part Practice
- Most skills should be practiced as a whole in order to maintain the rhythm of the skill.
- If a skill is practiced in parts, it should be practiced as a whole as quickly as possible.

- Whole practice is used when the skill has highly dependent (integrated) parts, is simple, is not meaningful in parts, or is made up of simultaneously performed parts.

- Whole practice is used when the learner is highly skilled, is able to remember long sequences, and has a long attention span.

- Part practice is used when the skill has highly independent parts, is made up of individual skills, is very complex, or if the limited work on certain parts is necessary.

- Part practice is used when the learner has a limited memory span, is unable to concentrate for a long period of time, is having difficulty with a particular part, or cannot succeed with the whole method.

Mass and Distributed Practice

- Mass practice is used when the skill is complex, has many elements, requires warm-up, or is a new skill for the performer.

- Distributed practice is used when the skill is simple, is repetitive, is boring, demands intense concentration, is fatiguing, or demands close attention to detail.

- Mass practice is used when the learner is older or more mature, is able to concentrate for long periods of time, or has good ability to focus attention.

- Distributed practice is used when the learner is young or immature, has a short attention span, has poor concentration skills, or tires quickly.

2.2 Describes how to generate and absorb force when performing movement and motor skills.

- Force is a push or pull exerted on a body or an object.

Type of Force

- An internal force is the contraction of a muscle.

- An external force is a push or pull that originates outside the body (another performer, gravity, friction, air resistance, wind, water).

Generate Force

- Enough force must be applied to change the object's state of motion (Newton's first law).

- More force is required to move a stationary object.

Absorbing Force

- Force can be absorbed by increasing the surface area or the distance or time over which it is absorbed.

2.3 Describes how the qualities of movement (e.g., space, time, force) are used in basic game tactics.

- A game has purpose, equipment, organization pattern, movement, limitations, and means of scoring.

- Game tactics or strategies refer to decisions about what to do in a competitive situation (against an opponent or against a standard).

- Game tactics in a cooperative game involve working together as a group, brainstorming possible solutions, trying the solutions that seem to have the best possibility of solving the problem, and arriving at the best possible solution.

Change Speed

- Chasing (to overtake a person) involves speeding up to catch an opponent.

- Fleeing (trying to avoid a person) involves speeding up to elude an opponent.

Change Force

- Dodging (changing direction) involves movement in atypical patterns to elude an opponent.

- Feinting (pretending movement in one direction followed by a quick maneuver in a different direction) is used to elude an opponent.

Use Space

- Create space (open) when on offense (send ball to open space on opponent's space).

- Close space when on defense.

- Pass effectively using spatial patterns based on the positioning of teammates and opponents.

2.4 Describes changes from birth through puberty along with their impact on physical performance.

Changes

- After birth, bone growth in length occurs at each end of the bone shaft called the growth plate.

- Arms and legs grow faster than the rest of the body between age 1 and puberty.

- There are virtually no differences between boys and girls in body proportions throughout childhood.

- Girls are typically taller than boys from 10 to 13 and boys are typically taller after 13 years of age.

- Adolescent boys have wider shoulders and adolescent girls have wider hips.

Impact

- Preadolescents may need concrete instruction regarding how to perform specific skills or playing strategies.

- The potential exists for severe injury to the epiphyseal plate because an accident can cut off the blood supply, resulting in early cessation of growth at the site.

- During the adolescent growth spurt, more time may be necessary to adjust motor patterns to rapidly changing body dimensions and physical attributes.

- Increases in height create the potential for greater leverage if accompanied by an increase in strength.

- Improved cognitive abilities help with complex skill performance.

2.5 Describes critical elements of fundamental movement and manipulative skills.

The critical elements for each skill taught in grade 5 are available on the task cards from Bonnie's Fitware, Inc. Samples are included on the CD.

3.1 Engages in moderate physical activity for 60 minutes 5 days each week.

- The student chooses the activities in which to engage.

- The student monitors participation.

- Moderate physical activity generally requires sustained rhythmic movements and refers to a level of effort a healthy individual might expend while, for example, walking briskly, dancing, swimming, or bicycling on level terrain. A person should feel some exertion but should be able to carry on a conversation comfortably during the activity.

3.2 Describes opportunities in the school setting for regular participation in physical activity.

- The student identifies physical activities that are available in and out of school.

- Knowing the available activities helps to determine the activities of interest.

4.1 Works toward a health-enhancing level of physical fitness.

- The assessment and analysis of health-related fitness provide information on the student's current status.

- Setting goals leads to greater improvement.

- Monitoring progress leads to greater improvement.

- Performing warm-up activities, such as flexibility, muscular endurance and strength, and cardiorespiratory endurance exercises according to frequency, intensity, time, and type (FITT) guidelines, and cooling down after exercising lead to greater improvement.

4.2 Designs a cardiorespiratory and body composition fitness plan including a warm-up and cool-down for 1 day.

Principles

- Principles of training include overload, specificity, regularity, progression, and individual differences.

- Following the principles of training leads to improvement of the five health-related fitness areas.

- Principles of specificity: There are specific exercises for each area of health-related fitness.

- Principle of regularity: Each exercise must be performed on a regular basis.

- Principle of individuality: Each person's exercise program is different.

- Principle of progression: The performer should start off slow and increase gradually.

- Principle of overload: The performer should increase intensity gradually over time.

Cardiorespiratory Endurance

- Cardiorespiratory endurance refers to the ability of the heart and lungs to function for a long period of time.

- Aerobic activities (exercise with oxygen) increase cardiorespiratory endurance; these include jogging, cycling, and swimming.

- Cardiorespiratory endurance is increased by performing aerobic exercises three to five times per week for a minimum of 15 to 20 minutes while in the target heart rate zone.

- A simple equation for calculating target heart rate zone is maximum heart rate [208 – (0.7 × age)] multiplied by the workout zone range (e.g., 70% to 80%).

- The heart rate is calculated by counting heartbeats with the index and middle fingers placed on the radial artery (wrist) for 15 seconds and then multiplying that number by four to determine heart rate for 1 minute.

- A health-related fitness assessment for cardiorespiratory endurance is the 1-mile run.

Body Composition

- Body composition refers to lean and fat components of the human body.

- One pound of fat is measured by 3,500 calories.

- To increase body fat, more calories (food) need to be consumed compared with the number of calories burned through daily activities (exercise, sleeping, sitting, playing).

- To reduce body fat, fewer calories need to be consumed compared with the number of calories burned through daily activities.

- A health-related fitness assessment for body composition is the skinfold measurement.

- The food pyramid should be used when planning meals.

Warm-Up

- Warm-up exercises occur at the beginning of the exercise period and consist of slowly increasing body temperature.

Cool-Down

- Cool-down occurs at the end of the exercise period and consists of slowly decreasing body temperature and performing static stretching.

5.1 Works with an individual who is differently abled in physical activity settings.

- *Differently abled* refers to individuals who are physically challenged (e.g., visually impaired, hearing impaired, mobility impaired). Sometimes the term *person with disabilities* is used.

- Inclusion refers to modifying an activity or situation so that everyone can be included.

- Contributing ideas for modifying activities for others helps the contributor build self-esteem.

- Displaying empathy helps develop effective communication skills.

- Modifying tasks to fit needs of differently abled students helps those students to feel included.

- Listening to the ideas of others and acknowledging their contributions and strengths help those students feel included.

5.2 Accepts responsibility for personal safety during physical activity.

- Responsibility refers to an individual's being answerable for the situation.

- Rules provide for fairness of play and safety. Procedures help to ensure safe and effective use of instructional time.

- Knowing the correct response helps when the student is confronted with negative peer pressure.

6.1 Describes the development and role of movement-related activities in the United States during the 17th and 18th centuries.

- Education in early colonial America was left to parents.

- Health and physical education were not included in the curriculum because the frontier society did not appreciate their value.

- The idea of physical education as an essential part of American education was not considered until Noah Webster presented his views on the positive effects of physical education in 1790.

- Acceptable physical activities during this period were fishing, hunting, and walking because it was through these activities that an individual's health was improved and his or her spirit renewed.

- The Quakers enjoyed bowling and golf along with early versions of croquet, tennis, and cricket.

- Immigrants had an impact on the sports and leisure-time recreational activities played in their communities.

6.2 Expresses personal feelings through a movement-based routine.

- Movement-based routines refer to a combination of dance steps, gymnastics and tumbling moves, locomotor skills, or manipulative skills. Movement qualities include relationships, space, and effort.

- Movement qualities are used to express feelings.

- Personal feelings are what an individual knows (understand), likes (taste or preference), and can do (experience).

- To express personal feelings is to show one's understanding, taste, and experience.

6.3 Chooses to engage in skill competencies at a level that leads to personal satisfaction, success, and enjoyment.

- Feelings of competence lead to a willingness to try new activities.

- *Success* refers to an event that accomplishes its intended purpose.

- *Personal satisfaction* means that the result of the experience meets certain criteria.

- *Enjoyment* is the pleasure one feels when having a good time.

6.4 Describes the physical benefits of regular participation in physical activity.

Physical Benefits

- Helps control weight by lowering the risk of becoming obese by 50%.

- Helps build and maintain healthy bones, muscles, and joints.

- Improves stamina.

- Improves muscular strength and endurance so that the individual can accomplish more.

- Increases flexibility.

- Improves cardiorespiratory endurance.

Sixth Grade

1.0 Demonstrates the mature form for specialized skills and combinations during cooperative activities; lead-up or simple target, invasion, field, and net activities; stunts and tumbling; and dance activities.

- Overhand pattern—javelin throw, shot put, basketball shooting (set shot), softball overhand throw

- Sidearm pattern—Pickleball continuous forearm strike, discus, batting, Pickleball serve

- Underhand pattern—bowling, forearm pass, juggling (one-hand juggle, basic cascade juggle), softball pitching

- Backhand pattern—flying disc backhand, Pickleball continuous backhand strike

- Catch pattern—flying disc pancake catch, flying disc thumb-up catch, flying disc thumb-down catch, softball catch, field fliers, field grounders

- Kick pattern—footbag instep kick, footbag knee kick, footbag outside kick, footbag heel kick

- Hand dribble pattern—basketball dribble and pass

- Static balance pattern—headstand, handstand

- Dynamic balance pattern—handstand roll out, cartwheel, squat turn on beam, walk on beam with dip, pike forward roll, straddle roll, stilt walking

- Locomotor patterns—run; jump; long jump; sprint; step hop; elbow swing; toes out, heels out, heels in, toes in; 1/4 pivot; turn under; step swing; schottische; bleking.

- Unicycle—mounting and riding

- Coordination—ball spinning

2.1 Explains how to provide appropriate feedback to a partner who is developing or improving specialized skills.

- Feedback improves the learning of motor skills by providing error detection and motivation for the learner.

- Feedback is based on the critical elements for each skill.

- Only one or two corrections should be identified for feedback after each performance.

- Feedback is delayed for a few seconds after the performance to give the performer an opportunity to reflect on his or her own performance.

- Feedback is given when the performer cannot see the result of the performance (e.g., technique).

- Feedback is not given when the performer can see the result of the performance (e.g., accuracy, speed, or distance).

- Feedback is most helpful when it is specific and meaningful.

- Feedback should be given frequently in the early stages of learning and then tapered off.

2.2 Explains ways to use force to increase speed or distance of a body or propelled object.

Increasing Force

- The stronger the action, the greater is the reaction (Newton's Third Law).

- The speed of an object affects the amount of force developed (increases in the speed of muscle contraction result in greater force).

Increasing Distance

- The angle of release affects the distance an object or body travels (45° when the release is at ground level and 30° when the release level is higher result in greater distances).

- The higher the release, the greater the distance an object travels.

- Stabilizing the body segments involved in the motion increases the distance an object travels.

- Increasing the range of movement of the body segments imparting force increases the distance an object travels.

- Using sequential muscle movement increases the distance an object travels.

- Increasing the distance through which force is applied (putting the muscle on stretch, extension of joints, longer lever) increases the distance an object travels.

- Using more muscles increases the distance an object travels.

- Using stronger muscles increases the distance an object travels.

- Using heavier implements increases the distance an object travels.

Review Reducing Force

- Force is reduced by increasing the surface area or the distance or time over which it is reduced.

2.3 Describes offensive strategies for cooperative and bowling activities and offensive and defensive strategies for simple invasion, field, and net activities.

Offensive Strategies for Cooperative Games

- A cooperative game requires players to work together for a common goal.

- There is at least one way of scoring or completing the task.

Offensive Strategies for Bowling Activities

- The primary strategy in bowling is to always bowl a strike and, if that cannot occur, then to bowl a spare or at least down the greatest number of pins.

Offensive Strategies for Simple Invasion, Field, and Net Activities

- Creating space is basic to any offensive strategy.

- The selection of an offensive game tactic depends on what your teammates and opponents do in a game.

- The primary purposes of an offensive system are to build on the strengths of the players, shift the balance of power away from the defense, and capitalize on defensive weaknesses.

- Individual players assume offensive positions based on their strengths and limitations.

Defensive Strategies for Simple Invasion, Field, and Net Activities

- Closing space is basic to any defensive strategy.

- The selection of a defensive game tactic depends on what your teammates and opponents do in a game.

- The primary purposes of a defensive system are to increase the odds of intercepting an object or blocking an offensive player.

- Individual players assume defensive positions based on their strengths and limitations.

2.4 Describes the characteristics of physical activities appropriate for early adolescents.

- The selection of games and activities for early adolescents should be based on their mental, physical, social, and cognitive development.

- Physical activities with concrete rules and directions are best for early adolescents.

- Physical activities that avoid repetitive motions are best for early adolescents.

- Physical activities that include the lifting of overly heavy objects should be avoided by early adolescents.

• Noncompetitive activities should be selected more frequently than competitive activities for early adolescents.

• Games played with fewer players are best for early adolescents.

• Games played on small fields are best for early adolescents.

• Games played with equipment appropriate for early adolescents are best.

• Enjoyable games are best for early adolescents.

• Attempting to teach physical skills to early adolescents before they are physically ready is often frustrating and can sometimes be harmful if the students have not yet developed the skeletal and muscular strength necessary for the skills.

2.5 Describes the critical elements of specialized skills and combinations in cooperative activities; lead-up or simple target, invasion, field, and net activities; stunts and tumbling; and dance activities.

The critical elements for each skill taught in grade 6 are available on the task cards from Bonnie's Fitware, Inc. Samples are included on the CD.

3.1 Engages in moderate and vigorous physical activity for 60 minutes 5 days each week.

• The student chooses the activities in which to engage.

• The student monitors participation.

• Moderate physical activity generally requires sustained rhythmic movements and refers to a level of effort a healthy individual might expend while, for example, walking briskly, dancing, swimming, or bicycling on level terrain. A person should feel some exertion but should be able to carry on a conversation comfortably during the activity.

• Vigorous-intensity physical activity generally requires sustained, rhythmic movements and refers to a level of effort a healthy individual might expend while, for example, jogging, participating in high-impact aerobic dancing, swimming continuous laps, or bicycling uphill. Vigorous-intensity physical activity may be intense enough to result in a significant increase in heart and respiration rate.

3.2 Describes opportunities in the local community for regular participation in physical activity.

• The student identifies physical activities that are available in the local community (within a distance that can be traveled independently).

• Knowing the available activities helps to determine the activities of interest.

4.1 Works toward a health-enhancing level of physical fitness.

• The assessment and analysis of health-related fitness provide information on the student's current status.

• Setting goals leads to greater improvement.

• Monitoring progress leads to greater improvement.

• Warming up; performing flexibility, muscular endurance and strength, and cardiorespiratory endurance exercises according to frequency, intensity, time, and type (FITT) guidelines; and cooling down after exercising lead to greater improvement.

4.2 Designs a 1-day personal health-related fitness plan.

Principles

• Principles of training include overload, specificity, regularity, progression, and individual differences.

• Following the principles of training leads to improvement of the five health-related fitness areas.

• Principles of specificity: There are specific exercises for each area of health-related fitness.

• Principle of regularity: Each exercise must be performed on a regular basis.

• Principle of individuality: Each person's exercise program is different.

• Principle of progression: The performer should start off slow and increase gradually.

• Principle of overload: The performer should increase intensity gradually over time.

Cardiorespiratory Endurance

• Cardiorespiratory endurance refers to the ability of the heart and lungs to function for a long period of time.

- Aerobic activities (exercise with oxygen) increase cardiorespiratory endurance; these include jogging, cycling, and swimming.

- Cardiorespiratory endurance is increased by performing aerobic exercises three to five times per week for a minimum of 15 to 20 minutes while in the target heart rate zone.

- A simple equation for calculating target heart rate zone is maximum heart rate [208 − (0.7 × (age)] multiplied by the workout zone range (e.g., 70% to 80%).

- The heart rate is calculated by counting heartbeats with the index and middle fingers placed on the radial artery (wrist) for 15 seconds and then multiplying that number by four to determine heart rate for 1 minute.

- A health-related fitness assessment for cardiorespiratory endurance is the 1-mile run.

Body Composition

- Body composition refers to lean and fat components of the human body.

- Body composition is a result of food intake and exercising.

- To lose 1 pound of fat, you must decrease your caloric intake by 3,500 calories or increase your calorie expenditure by 3,500 calories, or undergo a combination of decreasing caloric intake and increasing caloric expenditure that equals 3,500 calories (e.g., decrease your caloric intake by 1,500 and increase your caloric expenditure by 2,000).

- A health-related fitness assessment for body composition is the skinfold measurement.

- The food pyramid should be used when planning meals.

Flexibility

- Flexibility exercises are held to the point of strain, but not pain, for 30 to 60 seconds.

Muscular Fitness

- Muscular strength is the ability to lift something very heavy one time.

- Muscular strength exercises involve lifting a heavy object between five and eight times for three sets.

- Muscular endurance is the ability to lift something light many times.

- Muscular endurance exercises involve lifting a light object between 8 and 20 times for three sets.

Warm-Up

- Warm-up exercises occur at the beginning of the exercise period and consist of slowly increasing body temperature.

Cool-Down

- Cool-down occurs at the end of the exercise period and consists of slowly decreasing body temperature and performing static stretching.

5.1 Works cooperatively with a small group in physical activity settings.

- Each individual in a group has a role to play, as does the leader in a group. The group must first identify the goal before it can be achieved.

- Setting goals is based on the group's level of ability.

- Groups often progress through four stages of development: forming, norming, storming, and conforming.

- Cooperative skills are social skills that help a group achieve its goal and build positive feelings among group members.

- Examples of cooperative skills include active listening, encouragement, courtesy, positive disagreement, and acceptance of personal differences.

5.2 Accepts responsibility for safely completing assigned role when working with a small group during physical activity.

- Responsibility refers to an individual being answerable for the situation.

- Small group refers to three or four individuals.

- Each individual has a role in a group.

- There are safe procedures for each activity.

- Each individual must hold himself accountable to predetermined standards of behavior that affect the safety of other group members and himself.

6.1 Describes the development and role of movement-related activities in the ancient world and their influences on physical activities today.

Ancient World Activities and Fitness

- The purpose of games, dance, and sport in the ancient world was to maintain the culture, train for combat, perform religious ceremonies, and respond to a need for physical activity.

Ancient World Physical Education

• In Rome, the training or physical education of youth had one purpose: to make them obedient, disciplined, and ready to be a warrior.

• In ancient Athens, gymnastics and music (academics) were the two components of the curriculum.

• Physical education activities in Athens commenced at about age 7 and began with general physical conditioning.

• Physical education in Athens included boxing, wrestling, jumping, ball games, games with hoops, military skills, running, dancing, javelin and discus throwing, and the pancratium (a combination of boxing and wrestling).

• Wealthy Athenian families hired a paidotribe (physical education teacher) who owned his own palaestra (wrestling center) and charged a fee similar to today's private health clubs.

• Athenian women did not receive instruction in physical education.

Ancient World Dance

• The role of games, sports, and dance helps us know and understand people of diverse cultures.

Ancient Babylon

• In Babylon about 5,000 years ago, boys and girls played with spinning tops.

• A game very much like field hockey was played thousands of years ago in ancient Egypt and Persia according to paintings in tombs in the Nile River Valley.

Ancient China

• The teachings of Confucius encouraged participation in physical activity.

• Kung Fu, gymnastics, archery, badminton, dancing, fencing, and wrestling were popular activities in ancient China.

Ancient Egypt

• Archaeologists have found a set of nine stone pins (bowling) in a child's tomb in Egypt dated 5200 BC.

• A game very much like field hockey was played thousands of years ago in ancient Egypt and Persia according to paintings in tombs in the Nile River Valley.

Ancient Olympics

• Early Olympic Games had only one event, the stade, a footrace of about 200 meters; additional events were added each year (wrestling, pentathlon, chariot races, boxing, race in armor).

• The ancient Olympics were considered both a sport and a religious festival.

Ancient Athens

• Athenian men spent much of their day at the gymnasium, where they took part in sports such as boxing, discus and javelin throwing, and wrestling.

• Children in ancient Greece swung in swings.

• It is believed that the ancient Greeks began the sport of gymnastics.

Ancient Rome

• Romans enjoyed ball games based on throwing and catching and a form of handball.

• The skill of kicking was introduced by the Romans.

• Roman bath houses, where men participated in strenuous types of exercises like swinging lead weights, were popular between 4 BC and 65 AD.

• In Rome, the training of youth had one purpose: to make them obedient, disciplined, and ready to be a warrior.

• In Rome, children were taught running, jumping, swimming, wrestling, horsemanship, boxing, fencing, and archery.

Sparta

• Physical training was strictly for military purposes.

• Spartan youth were instructed in swimming, running, fighting, wrestling, boxing, ball games, horsemanship, archery, discus and javelin throwing, field marches, and pancratium.

• Spartan women participated in gymnastic exercises (military and physical training).

6.2 Expresses personal feelings through a manipulative or movement-based routine.

• Movement-based routines refer to a combination of dance steps, gymnastics and tumbling moves, locomotor skills, or manipulative skills.

- Movement qualities include time, space, effort, and flow.
- Manipulative based routines refer to the combination of ball-handling skills.
- Movement qualities are used to express feelings.
- Personal feelings are what an individual knows (understand), likes (taste or preference), and can do (experience).
- To express personal feelings is to show one's understanding, taste, and experience.

6.3 Chooses to engage in new activities.

- New activities are those which the performer has not yet attempted.

6.4 Describes the health benefits of regular participation in physical activity.

Health Benefits of Physical Activity

- Reduces the risk of dying prematurely from heart disease or stroke.
- Reduces the risk of developing heart disease or colon cancer by up to 50%.
- Reduces the risk of developing type II diabetes by 50%.
- Helps to prevent or reduce hypertension.
- Helps to prevent or reduce osteoporosis.
- Reduces the risk of developing low back pain.
- Reduces the risk of developing high cholesterol levels.
- Improves mood.
- Lowers stress.
- Improves sleep.

Seventh Grade

1.0 Demonstrates the mature form for specialized skills and combinations during individual and dual activities.

- Overhand pattern—tennis volley
- Sidearm pattern—tennis forehand strike, tennis drop serve
- Backhand pattern—tennis backhand strike
- Underhand pattern—underhand toss, putt, iron stroke, juggling

- Catch pattern—catching, juggling catch
- Kick pattern—foot pass
- Dynamic balance and coordination patterns—long horse vaulting (straddle dismount from croup, straddle vault); vaulting (squat vault); pommels (jump front support, hand walk, leg cut); floor exercises (front walkover, back extension); balance beam (straddle support mount, walk with dip, squat turn, jump dismount); horizontal bar (knee hang, front pullover, penny drop, forward hip circle); parallel bars (forward hand walk, half-turn, back hand walk, forward hand jump, swing a straight-arm support, series of straddle seats, front dismount from straight-arm support)
- Trap pattern—foot trap
- Swimming activities—survival float, prone glide with flutter kick, beginning crawl with breathing, back glide with sculling, back glide with kick, reverse directions, jump into deep water, tread water with scissor kick, feet-first surface dive
- Outdoor education activities—hold compass, read compass, take bearing, follow bearing, read topographic maps
- Combative activities—stance, stomp, knee kick, front snap kick, side kick, rear kick, elbow strike, palm–heel strike, side fall, wrist release, front choke release, rear choke release, hair release, fencing advance, fencing retreat, fencing lunge, fencing ready position, fencing on-guard, jousting, lance activities, running in armor

2.1 Explains the process of setting appropriate goals, conducting appropriate practice, and monitoring changes in the development of specialized skills.

Goals

- Setting goals, based on current ability, improves the learning of motor skills.
- Monitoring change in motor skill development based on the type of improvement desired (e.g., accuracy, distance, technique) improves the learning of motor skills.
- Goals should be clear, measurable, and achievable.

Whole or Part Practice

- Most skills should be practiced as a whole to maintain the rhythm of the skill.
- If a skill is practiced in parts, it should be practiced as a whole as quickly as possible.

- Whole practice is used when the skill has highly dependent (integrated) parts, is simple, is not meaningful in parts, or is made up of simultaneously performed parts.

- Whole practice is used when the learner is highly skilled, is able to remember long sequences, and has a long attention span.

- Part practice is used when the skill has highly independent parts, is made up of individual skills, or is very complex or if the limited work on certain parts is necessary.

- Part practice is used when the learner has a limited memory span, is unable to concentrate for a long period of time, is having difficulty with a particular part, or cannot succeed with the whole method.

Mass or Distributed Practice

- Mass practice is used when the skill is complex, has many elements, requires warm-up, or is a new skill for the performer.

- Distributed practice is used when the skill is simple, is repetitive, is boring, demands intense concentration, is fatiguing, or demands close attention to detail.

- Mass practice is used when the learner is older or more mature, is able to concentrate for long periods of time, or has good ability to focus attention.

- Distributed practice is used when the learner is young or immature, has a short attention span, has poor concentration skills, or tires quickly.

Constant or Variable Practice

- Variable practice involves practicing one skill in a variety of settings or conditions.

- Constant practice involves practicing one skill in same way for the entire practice session.

- Constant practice enhances the learning of open skills for beginners and closed skills.

- Variable practice enhances learning of open skills for intermediate and advanced learners.

Blocked or Random Practice

- Blocked practice refers to practicing one skill for a certain amount of time, then a second skill for the same amount of time, and then the third skill for the same amount of time.

- Random practice refers to practicing one skill for a few minutes, then a second skill for a few minutes, then the first skill again, and then the third skill (or some other random order).

- Blocked practiced leads to short-term success.

- Random practice leads to long-term success.

2.2 Explains how force can be used to make an object spin.

- Spin results when force is applied away from an object's center of gravity.

- Force applied below the center of gravity causes backward rotation (back spin), which results in the ball staying in the air longer, bouncing higher, and rolling a shorter distance along with a decrease in velocity after impact.

- Force applied above the center of gravity causes forward rotating (top spin), which results in a quick drop with a longer but lower bounce and lengthened roll along with an increase in velocity after impact.

- Force to the left of the center of gravity results in counterclockwise spin, and force to the right of the center of gravity results in clockwise spin.

- The shorter the radius of rotation, the greater is the angular velocity or speed of rotation.

- The longer the radius of rotation, the greater the force.

- When two forces are applied, the result is a combination of the two forces in proportion to the strength of each force.

2.3 Explains offensive and defensive strategies for net and target sports.

Offensive Strategies for Net Sports

- Players should be aware of their positions within the playing area.

- Offensive strategies are based on a particular plan of spatial arrangement.

- Creating spaces and sending the ball to the open spaces on the court are keys to a strong offense.

- Sending the ball to weaknesses in the opponent's defense is also a key to a strong offense.

- Interchanging of positions is often necessary to take advantage of players' strengths.

Defensive Strategies for Net Sports

- Players should be aware of their positions within the playing area.

- Defensive strategies are based on a particular plan of spatial arrangement.

- Closing space is key to a strong defense.

- Interchanging of positions is often necessary to take advantage of players' strengths.

Offensive Strategies for Target Sports

- Aim to get the object to the target as quickly as possible (e.g., golf).

- Aim to get the object to the center of the target (e.g., archery).

- Plan the most effective path to the target ahead of time (e.g., golf).

Defensive Strategies for Target Sports

- Block the path to the target for an opponent (e.g., shuffle board).

2.4 Explains individual differences and how these differences affect performance in physical activities.

- Individuals proceed through similar stages on their way to learning skills, but each progresses at a different rate.

- Some children begin puberty earlier than others, resulting in dramatic physical differences between same-aged individuals.

- Longer limbs provide better leverage if accompanied by an increase in strength (e.g., run faster, throw farther).

- There are three body type variations: endomorph (spherical), mesomorph (muscular), and ectomorph (linear).

- A person's body type helps to determine capabilities and limitations.

- People of different body types tend to be more effective at different skills and activities (i.e., basketball players tend to be tall and lean, gymnasts tend to be short, and wrestlers tend to be stout).

2.5 Explains the critical elements of specialized skills and combinations in individual and dual sports.

The critical elements for each skill taught in grade 7 are available on the task cards from Bonnie's Fitware, Inc. Samples are included on the CD.

3.1 Engages in moderate and vigorous physical activity for 60 minutes 6 days each week.

- The student chooses the activities in which to engage.

- The student monitors participation.

- Moderate physical activity generally requires sustained rhythmic movements and refers to a level of effort a healthy individual might expend while, for example, walking briskly, dancing, swimming, or bicycling on level terrain. A person should feel some exertion but should be able to carry on a conversation comfortably during the activity.

- Vigorous-intensity physical activity generally requires sustained, rhythmic movements and refers to a level of effort a healthy individual might expend while, for example, jogging, participating in high-impact aerobic dancing, swimming continuous laps, or bicycling uphill. Vigorous-intensity physical activity may be intense enough to result in a significant increase in heart and respiration rate.

3.2 Describes opportunities in the larger community for participation in individual and dual physical activities.

- Identifies physical activities that are available in the larger community (students would need assistance from an adult to travel out into the larger community).

- Knowing the available activities helps to determine the activities of interest.

4.1 Works toward a health-enhancing level of physical fitness.

- The assessment and analysis of health-related fitness provide information on the student's current status.

- Setting goals leads to greater improvement.

- Monitoring progress leads to greater improvement.

- Warming up; performing flexibility, muscular endurance and strength, and cardiorespiratory endurance exercises according to FITT guidelines; and cooling down lead to greater improvement.

4.2 Designs a 1-week personal health-related fitness plan.

Principles

- Principles of training include overload, specificity, regularity, progression, and individual differences.

- Following the principles of training leads to improvement of the five health-related fitness areas.

- Principles of specificity: There are specific exercises for each area of health-related fitness.

- Principle of regularity: Each exercise must be performed on a regular basis.

- Principle of individuality: Each person's exercise program is different.

- Principle of progression: The performer should start off slow and increase gradually.

- Principle of overload: The performer should increase intensity gradually over time.

Cardiorespiratory Endurance

- Cardiorespiratory endurance refers to the ability of the heart and lungs to function for a long period of time.

- Aerobic activities (exercise with oxygen) increase cardiorespiratory endurance; these include jogging, cycling, and swimming.

- Cardiorespiratory endurance is increased by performing aerobic exercises three to five times per week for a minimum of 15 to 20 minutes while in the target heart rate zone.

- A simple equation for calculating target heart rate zone is maximum heart rate [208 − (0.7 × age)] multiplied by the workout zone range (e.g., 70% to 80%).

- The heart rate is calculated by counting heartbeats with the index and middle fingers placed on the radial artery (wrist) for 15 seconds and then multiplying that number by four to determine heart rate for 1 minute.

- A health-related fitness assessment for cardiorespiratory endurance is the 1-mile run.

Body Composition

- Body composition refers to lean and fat components of the human body

- Body composition is a result of food intake and exercising.

- To lose 1 pound of fat, you must decrease your caloric intake by 3,500 calories or increase your calorie expenditure by 3,500 calories, or undergo a combination of decreasing caloric intake and increasing caloric expenditure that equals 3,500 calories (e.g., decrease your caloric intake by 1,500 and increase your caloric expenditure by 2,000).

- A health-related fitness assessment for body composition is the skinfold measurement.

- The food pyramid should be used when planning meals.

Flexibility

- Flexibility exercises are held to the point of strain, but not pain, for 30 to 60 seconds.

Muscular Fitness

- Muscular strength is the ability to lift something very heavy one time.

- Muscular strength exercises involve lifting a heavy object between five and eight times for three sets.

- Muscular endurance is the ability to lift something light many times.

- Muscular endurance exercises involve lifting a light object between 8 and 20 times for three sets.

Warm-Up

- Warm-up exercises occur at the beginning of the exercise period and consist of slowly increasing body temperature.

Cool-Down

- Cool-down occurs at the end of the exercise period and consists of slowly decreasing body temperature and performing static stretching.

5.1 Applies problem-solving techniques when working with another person in physical activity settings.

- The problem-solving process includes the following steps:
  - Define the problem.
  - Generate a possible list of solutions.
  - Select and implement one solution at a time.
  - Compare the results from testing several solutions.
  - Select the best solution.

5.2 Accepts responsibility for individual improvement during challenging physical activity.

- Responsibility refers to an individual's being answerable for the situation.

- Challenging activities require physical courage but don't offer an undue risk.

- Achievement is directly related to the effort and motivation put forth.

• Setting and achieving goals based on personal strengths and weaknesses creates a sense of personal responsibility for one's own learning.

• Consistent use of short-term goals and self-evaluation when learning a new skill or activity makes it easier for people to recognize and appreciate the things they are doing well.

6.1 Describes the development and role of movement-related activities in medieval times and their influences on physical activities today.

Medieval Times

• Physical education was virtually nonexistent during medieval times.

• Fitness was a requirement for survival during medieval times.

• Orienteering began as a Swedish military exercise.

• Ball games, such as mob football (unlimited number of players on opposing teams competing to drag an inflated pig's bladder by any possible means to the markers at each end of a town), Soule (a game similar to soccer played by an unlimited number of players), Jeu de Paume (a form of handball), and a game similar to tennis (played with an open hand) continued to be popular.

• The Romans, during the reign of Caesar, played a game resembling golf by striking a feather-stuffed ball with club-shaped branches. In 1457, golf was banned in Scotland because it interfered with archery practice, which was more important for national defense.

• During medieval times, jesters, squires, and knights participated in different activities; the knights and squires were preparing for combat whereas the jesters were entertainers.

• Popular tournaments during medieval times included jousting (two mounted horsemen charging one another with long, wooden lances with the object to knock each other off the horse) and Melee (groups of opposing knights engaging in hand-to-hand combat with dull swords).

Renaissance

• Leading educators of the Renaissance incorporated physical education into their educational curricula.

• During the Renaissance, physical education began to be considered for both military and health benefits.

• In physical education, students participated in games, riding, running, leaping, fencing, playing ball, hiking, and camping.

• During the Renaissance, new concern for hygiene brought an emphasis on swimming and water safety.

6.2 Appreciates one's own stylistic approach to creating a routine.

• Stylistic differences are reflected by altering the qualities of movement (space, effort, relationships).

• Stylistic approaches to creating movement reflect individual differences.

• Past experiences influence one's stylistic approach.

6.3 Chooses to engage in activities at the appropriate level of physical challenge.

• Challenging activities require physical courage but don't offer an undue risk.

• The student chooses to engage in activities.

6.4 Describes the social benefits of regular participation in physical activity.

• Regularly active individuals are less likely to withdraw from society and more likely to actively contribute to the social milieu.

• Participation in physical activity, particularly in small groups and other social environments, stimulates new friendships and acquaintances.

• Physical activity frequently provides individuals with an opportunity to widen social networks.

• A physically active lifestyle helps foster the stimulating environment necessary for maintaining an active role in society as well as for acquiring positive new roles.

• In many societies, physical activity is a shared activity that provides opportunities for intergenerational contact, thereby diminishing stereotypic perceptions about aging and the elderly.

Eighth Grade

1.0 Demonstrates the mature form for specialized skills and combinations

during modified team and dance activities.

- Overhand pattern—overhand pass, overhand serve, standing spike, jumping bike, one-hand overhead pass, two-hand overhead pass, set shot, layup, team handball set shot, team handball jump shot, forward pass, rebound

- Sidearm pattern—bat, bunt, sidearm whip throw, handoff

- Underhand pattern—forearm pass, pitch, lateral, centering, underhand serve

- Catch pattern—catching, fielding ground ball, fielding flies, blocking, football catch, goalkeeping

- Kick pattern—instep kick, one-foot lift to self, lift to teammate, two-foot stationary lift to self, moving ball lift

- Hand dribble pattern—hand dribble

- Foot dribble pattern—foot dribble

- Trapping patterns—sole-of-foot trap, instep trap

- Static balance pattern—defensive stance, offensive stance

- Dynamic balance pattern—defensive stance, offensive stance, pivot

- Passing pattern—chest pass, bounce pass

- Stopping pattern—two-step stop, jump stop

- Locomotor patterns—circle left and right, shuffle step, do-si-do, swing, promenade, right-hand star, allemande left, single-file promenade, split ring, grand right and left, courtesy turn, forearm turn, right and left through, pass partner, circle to line, allemande left from a line of four, two ladies chain, four ladies chain, chain straight across, seesaw, grand square, half sashay, shoot the star, baserunning, ball carrying, rushing

- Nonlocomotor patterns—lifting, swinging

- Trap—instep trap, sole of foot trap

2.1 Analyzes the effect of positive transfer on specialized skill improvement.

- Positive transfer occurs when previous learning has a favorable effect on new learning.

- Negative transfer occurs when prior learning interferes with learning new information or skills or new skills interfere with previously learned tasks.

- The more closely related one skill is to another, the more likely is the transfer of learning (e.g., throwing a variety of objects).

- Greater positive transfer occurs when the first task is well learned.

- Greater positive transfer occurs when similarities are pointed out to the learner.

- Transfer from practice to the game is subject to the same element issues as transfer from skill to skill.

2.2 Explains how force can be used to alter the outcome of a skill performance.

- External forces that can alter the outcome of a skill performance include gravity, collision (e.g., rebound), friction, and air resistance.

- Bouncing an object with no spin causes it to rebound at an opposite angle equal to that at which it strikes the surface.

- Gravity decelerates an object or the body on its upward flight.

- Gravity causes objects dropped from the same height to fall at the same speed (discounting air resistance).

- Increases in contact force or surfaces' roughness produce more friction between two objects.

- Streamlined shapes and smooth surfaces reduce air and water resistance on a moving body.

- The larger the object, the greater is the resistance.

- As velocity increases, resistance is increased (squared).

- When two forces are applied, the result is a combination of the two forces in proportion to the strength of each force.

2.3 Explains offensive and defensive strategies for invasion and field sports.

Offensive Invasion Strategies

- Players can create space by moving into open space. Players can create time by moving away from the defense.

- Players choose to pass, shoot, dribble, or run based on defensive positioning.

- Players should follow up on all shots at the goal.

Offensive Strategies for Net Sports

- Players should be aware of their positions within the playing area.
- Strategies are based on a particular plan of spatial arrangement.
- Creating spaces and sending the ball to the open spaces on the court are keys to a strong offense.
- Sending the ball to weaknesses in the opponent's defense is also a key to a strong offense.
- Interchanging of positions is often necessary to take advantage of players' strengths.

Defensive Strategies for Net Sports

- Players should be aware of their positions within the playing area.
- Strategies are based on a particular plan of spatial arrangement.
- Closing space is key to a strong a defense.
- Interchanging of positions is often necessary to take advantage of players' strengths.

Defensive Invasion Strategies

- Respond instantly to a change of possession.
- Ensure there is always pressure on the ball.
- Cover the defender who is putting pressure on the ball.
- Closely mark opponents who move into dangerous position.
- Close space to the offense.
- Clear the ball away from the goal area quickly.
- Use player to player defense or spatial pattern (zone) defense.

Offensive Field Strategies

- The selection of an offensive game tactic depends on what your teammates and opponents do in a game.
- The prime purposes of an offensive system are to build on the strengths of the players, shift the balance of power away from the defense, and capitalize on defensive weaknesses.
- Individual players assume offensive positions (batting order) based on their strengths and limitations.
- The ball should be directed toward open space or weak defensive players.

Defensive Field Strategies

- Individual players assume defensive positions based on their strengths and limitations.
- Backing up affords a second line of attack.
- The selection of a defensive game tactic depends on what your teammates and opponents do in a game.
- The defensive team should close up as much space as possible.

2.4 Analyzes the role of physical abilities in the performance of specialized skills.

- The variables of physical abilities that affect motor performance include skill-related fitness (coordination, balance, agility, reaction time, power, and speed) and physical characteristics (body build, height, weight, vision, hearing, and touch).
- Different skills require different physical abilities that can be developed through training programs.
- Tall people tend to perform better in skills like the high jump.
- Shorter people tend to perform better at skills like gymnastics.
- Differences in weight distribution cause a higher or lower center of gravity (an individual with a lower center of gravity is more stable than an individual with a higher center of gravity).
- Longer limbs provide better leverage if accompanied by an increase in strength.

2.5 Explains critical elements of specialized skills and combinations in team sports.

The critical elements for each skill taught in grade 8 are available on the task cards from Bonnie's Fitware, Inc. Samples are included on the CD.

3.1 Engages in moderate and vigorous physical activity for 60 minutes 6 days each week.

- The student chooses the activities in which to engage.
- The student monitors participation.
- Moderate physical activity generally requires sustained rhythmic movements and refers

to a level of effort a healthy individual might expend while, for example, walking briskly, dancing, swimming, or bicycling on level terrain. A person should feel some exertion but should be able to carry on a conversation comfortably during the activity.

- Vigorous-intensity physical activity generally requires sustained, rhythmic movements and refers to a level of effort a healthy individual might expend while, for example, jogging, participating in high-impact aerobic dancing, swimming continuous laps, or bicycling uphill. Vigorous-intensity physical activity may be intense enough to result in a significant increase in heart and respiration rate.

3.2 Explains ways of increasing physical activity in routine daily activities.

- Take the stairs.

- Walk or ride bike to school.

- Park away from final destination to encourage more activity.

- Play video games that require physical activity.

- Take fitness breaks—walk or do desk exercises.

- Perform gardening or home repair activities.

- Avoid labor-saving devices—turn off the self-propel option on your lawn mower or vacuum cleaner.

- Use leg power—take small trips on foot to get your body moving.

- Exercise while watching TV (e.g., use hand weights, stationary bicycle, treadmill, or stair climber, or stretch).

- Walk while doing errands.

4.1 Works toward a health-enhancing level of physical fitness.

- The assessment and analysis of health-related fitness provide information on the student's current status.

- Setting goals leads to greater improvement.

- Monitoring progress leads to greater improvement.

- Warming up; performing flexibility, muscular endurance and strength, and cardiorespiratory endurance exercises according to frequency, intensity, time, and type (FITT) guidelines; and cooling down after exercising lead to greater improvement.

4.2 Designs a 2-week personal health-related fitness plan taking into account the possibility of inclement weather, minor injury, or travel.

Principles

- Principles of training include overload, specificity, regularity, progression, and individual differences.

- Following the principles of training leads to improvement of the five health-related fitness areas.

- Principles of specificity: There are specific exercises for each area of health-related fitness.

- Principle of regularity: Each exercise must be performed on a regular basis.

- Principle of individuality: Each person's exercise program is different.

- Principle of progression: The performer should start off slow and increase gradually.

- Principle of overload: The performer should increase intensity gradually over time.

Cardiorespiratory Endurance

- Cardiorespiratory endurance refers to the ability of the heart and lungs to function for a long period of time.

- Aerobic activities (exercise with oxygen) increase cardiorespiratory endurance; these include jogging, cycling, and swimming.

- Cardiorespiratory endurance is increased by performing aerobic exercises three to five times per week for a minimum of 15 to 20 minutes while in the target heart rate zone.

- A simple equation for calculating target heart rate zone is maximum heart rate [208 − (0.7 × age)] multiplied by the workout zone range (e.g., 70% to 80%).

- The heart rate is calculated by counting heartbeats with the index and middle fingers placed on the radial artery (wrist) for 15 seconds and then multiplying that number by four to determine heart rate for 1 minute.

- A health-related fitness assessment for cardiorespiratory endurance is the 1-mile run.

Body Composition

- Body composition refers to lean and fat components of the human body

- Body composition is a result of food intake and exercising.

- To lose 1 pound of fat, you must decrease your caloric intake by 3,500 calories or increase your calorie expenditure by 3,500 calories, or undergo a combination of decreasing caloric intake and increasing caloric expenditure that equals 3,500 calories (e.g., decrease your caloric intake by 1,500 and increase your caloric expenditure by 2,000).

- A health-related fitness assessment for body composition is the skinfold measurement.

- The food pyramid should be used when planning meals.

Flexibility

- Flexibility exercises are held to the point of strain, but not pain, for 30 to 60 seconds.

Muscular Fitness

- Muscular strength is the ability to lift something very heavy one time.

- Muscular strength exercises involve lifting a heavy object between five and eight times for three sets.

- Muscular endurance is the ability to lift something light many times.

- Muscular endurance exercises involve lifting a light object between 8 and 20 times for three sets.

Warm-Up

- Warm-up exercises occur at the beginning of the exercise period and consist of slowly increasing body temperature.

Cool-Down

- Cool-down occurs at the end of the exercise period and consists of slowly decreasing body temperature and performing slow static stretching.

Personal Situation

- Activities for each area of health-related fitness should be selected based on personal preferences.

- Alternative activities should be included in case of inclement weather, travel, or a minor injury.

- Alternatives for conditioning should be included for different physical activities.

5.1 Collaborates with others to solve group problems in physical activity settings.

- Collaboration means working together.

- There are five basic steps in negotiating a resolution for a conflict of interests or problem:

  - Jointly define the conflict or problem.
  - Exchange reasons and rationale for opinions or ideas.
  - Revise perspectives.
  - Invent options for mutual benefit.
  - Reach a wise agreement.

- Each member of a group has a role, including the leader.

5.2 Accepts responsibility for one's own actions and decisions during physical activity.

- Responsibility refers to an individual's being answerable for the situation.

- The student accepts responsibility for developing skills, acquiring knowledge, and achieving fitness.

6.1 Explains the development and role of movement-related activities in the United States (19th to 20th centuries) and their influence on physical activities today.

Physical Education

- Between the War of 1812 and the Civil War, a variety of physical education programs were instituted in U.S. schools.

- Public schools showed little interest in physical education until the 1850s, when some cities allowed a few minutes of calisthenics in the daily curriculum.

- In 1853, Boston became the first city to require daily exercise for school children.

- The Morrill Act of 1862 required military instruction in all state colleges and affected physical education in the schools and colleges because of the inclusion of military drill as a form of physical activity.

- After the Civil War, attention shifted to a strong emphasis toward physical exercise for the purpose of improving and maintaining a healthy body.

- Physical education programs in the United States during the 19th century reflected the various cultures in which immigrants originated, especially Germany and Sweden.

- During the 19th century, three major programs influenced American physical education: English sports and games, German gymnastics, and Swedish calisthenics.

- During the late 1800s, training institutions specifically trained individuals for roles in physical education.

- During the late 1800s, medicine began to specialize into subdisciplinary groups including physical education.

- By 1921, there was compulsory public school physical education in 28 states.

Recreational Activities

- The playground and recreation movements developed as an outgrowth of the Industrial Revolution with a concern about the poor health of children and the lack of space in which they could play.

- Sports and games became more popular as leisure time increased for the general population.

- In the 19th century, American culture became increasingly urban and technical, providing both the necessary numbers of people to be athletes and spectators and the technology necessary for sports as we know them today.

- Many American sports and games have their roots in other countries; this accounts for many of the similarities between sports in different cultures.

Modern Olympics

- The year 1896 marked the revival of the Olympic Games in Athens, Greece.

- The modern Olympics has its roots in furthering the cause of world peace, highlighting athletes from different parts of the world, and preparing individuals to become highly trained athletes.

Invasion Sports

- In 1863, soccer became an official school game, complete with rules and regulations.

- The modern game of football began at Harvard University in the spring of 1871, using a soccer ball and many of the soccer rules except that football players could pick up the ball and run with it.

- Dr. James A. Naismith introduced basketball to a class at the YMCA in Springfield, Massachusetts, in 1891 as an indoor activity during bad weather and used peach baskets on a gym rail as the first baskets.

- Team handball originated in Europe in late 1920s.

- Speed-a-Way was created in the 1940s at Edison High School in Stockton, California, as a game that would serve as a lead-up game for field hockey.

Net Sports

- Volleyball originated in the United States in 1895 by William C. Morgan of Springfield College. It served as a less strenuous alternative to basketball for businessmen at the YMCA.

- Volleyball was first played with the bladder of a basketball over a tennis net. Early versions of the game allowed for any number of players on the court; each server had three outs, and the game was played for nine innings.

Field Sports

- Rounders, an older form of baseball, was around in the 1500s. Indoor baseball with larger balls, smaller bats, and modified rules originated in 1887 because baseball players wanted some sort of winter activity. When indoor baseball moved outdoors, it was first named playground ball and later softball.

Dancing

- John Playford's epochal book *English Dancing Master,* published March 19, 1651, is credited with producing the movement from which American square dancing emerged.

- In the early 1800s, dancing masters worked out sequences of moves that were memorized by the dancers.

- During the War of 1812, an American invented "calling" by a fiddler in the orchestra, which made it unnecessary to memorize the dance steps.

- By 1890, a decline in square dancing began as conservative masters of dance attacked swinging and dancers had to listen for the next step.

- In 1925, Henry Ford started a movement to bring back square dancing to counteract what he considered the evils of jazz.

6.2 Appreciates others' stylistic approaches to creating a dance or routine.

- Stylistic differences are reflected by altering the qualities of movement (time, space, effort, relationships).
- Assessment of another's performance is influenced by personal preference.
- Assessment of another's performance is influenced by one's educational experience.
- Assessment of another's performance is based on one's cultural background.

6.3 Chooses to engage in physical activities at the appropriate level of social, physical, and emotional challenge.

- The student chooses to engage in activities.
- Challenging activities require courage.

- The activities should stretch the individual socially, physically, and emotionally.

6.4 Explains the cognitive and psychological benefits of regular participation in physical activity.

Psychological Benefits

- Reduces anxiety and stress.
- Increases self-esteem.
- Enhances relaxation.
- Elevates mood.
- Improves psychological functioning.
- Contributes to the treatment of several mental illnesses, including depression and anxiety neuroses.
- May help postpone age-related declines in central nervous system processing speed and improve reaction time.

Cognitive Benefits

- May improve cognitive functioning.

Appendix C
Recommended Resources

Amazon.com
Variety of books, videos, and software programs. www. amazon.com

American Alliance for Health, Physical Education, Recreation and Dance, 1900 Association Dr., Reston, VA 20191-1598; 800-213-7193
Professional organization and publications. www. aahperd.org

American Heart Association, 7272 Greenville Ave., Dallas, TX 75231; 800-242-8721
Instructional materials on health and fitness. www. americanheart.org

American Red Cross; contact local chapter
Instructional materials and videos on first aid and water safety. www.redcross.org

Apple Computer, Inc., 20525 Mariani Ave., Cupertino, CA 95014-6299; 408-996-1010
Macintosh hardware and software. www.apple.com

Association for American Health Education, 1900 Association Dr., Reston, VA 20191; 800-213-7193
Professional organization and publications. www. aahperd.org

Association for Supervision and Curriculum Development, 1703 N. Beauregard St., Alexandria, VA 22311-1714; 800-933-2723
Professional organization and publications. www. ascd.org

Bonnie's Fitware, Inc., 18832 Stefani Ave., Cerritos, CA 90703; 419-828-2144
Macintosh and Windows software, books, instructional materials, and sporting goods for physical education and health education. shop.pesoftware.com

The Brain Store, Corwin Press, 2455 Teller Rd., Thousand Oaks, CA 91320; 800-233-9936
Instructional CDs. www.corwinpress.com/brainstore. htm

Bureau of Education & Research, P.O. Box 96068, Bellevue, WA 98009-9668; 800-735-3503
Building a Quality Physical Education Program audiotape. www.ber.org

Christy Lane Enterprises, P.O. Box 4040, Palm Springs, CA 92263-4040; 800-555-0205
Music videos, books, and CDs. www.christylane. com

DINE Systems, Inc., 163 Brunswick Electric Rd., Whiteville, NC 28472; 800-688-1848
Nutrition software. www.dinesystems.com

Discovering The World Inc., 6455 Roland St., Buena Park, CA 90621; 714-522-2202
New games materials. www.dtworld.com

Human Kinetics, P.O. Box 5076, Champaign, IL 61825-5076; 800-747-4457
Books, journals, videos, and Fitnessgram materials. www.HumanKinetics.com

Hunter Textbooks Inc., 701 Shallowford St., Winston-Salem, NC 27101; 336-725-0608
Student textbooks. www.huntertextbooks.com

Kendall/Hunt Publishing Company, 4050 Westmark Dr., P.O. Box 1840, Dubuque, IA 52004; 800-228-0810
Student textbooks. kendallhunt.com

Macmillan Education Australia, 627 Chapel St., South Yarra, VIC 3141, Australia; +61 3 9825 1000
Student textbooks. www.macmillan.com.au

Microsoft, One Microsoft Way, Redmond, WA 98052-6399; 800-642-7676
Software and hardware. www.microsoft.com

National Association for Sport & Physical Education (NASPE), 1900 Association Dr., Reston, VA 20191-1598; 800-213-7193
Professional organization and publications. www. aahperd.org

National Cartography & Geospatial Center, Fort Worth Federal Center, 501 W. Felix St., Bldg. 23, P.O. Box 6567, Fort Worth, TX 76115; 817-509-3200
Maps. www.ncgc.nrcs.usda.gov

Orange County Department of Education, 200 Kalmus Dr., Costa Mesa, CA 92626; 714-966-4000.
Video on sheltered instruction in physical education. www.ocde.k12.ca.us

PGA Foundation, 100 Avenue of the Champions, Palm Beach Gardens, FL 33418; 888-532-6661
Instructional materials for golf. www.pgafoundation. com

Project Adventure, 701 Cabot St., Beverly, MA 01915; (978) 524-4500
Books and materials for new games and ropes courses. www.pa.org

Rollerblade USA, 3705 Quakerbridge Rd., Hamilton, NJ 08619; 800-232-7655
Rollerblading equipment. www.rollerblade.com

Silva Orienteering Services, 625 Conklin Rd., Binghamton, NY 13903; 607-779-2264
Instructional materials for orienteering

Spilsbury, P.O. Box 1408, Ottawa, IL 61350-6408; 800-772-1760
Virtual reality games. www.spilsbury.com

SyberVision, One Sansome St., Suite 1610, San Francisco, CA 94104; 800-648-5095
Audio cassettes and videos. www.sybervision2000. com

Unicycling Society of America, P.O. Box 49534, Redford, MI 48240; 800-783-2425
Instructional materials for unicycling. www.unicycling. org/usa

United States Bowling Congress, 5301 S. 76th St., Greendale, WI 53129; 800-943-2399
Instructional videos and materials. www.bowl.com

United States Orienteering Federation, P.O. Box 1444, Forest Park, GA 30298; phone number unavailable
Videos and books on orienteering. www.us.orienteering. org

United States Team Handball Association, 1 Olympic Plaza, Colorado Springs, CO 80909; 719-632-5551
Instructional materials for team handball. www. usateamhandball.org

United States Tennis Association, 70 W. Red Oak Lane, White Plains, NY 10604; 914-696-7000
Instructional materials for tennis. www.usta.com

United States Volleyball Association, 715 S. Circle Dr., Colorado Springs, CO 80910; 719-228-6800
Instructional materials for volleyball. www.usavolleyball.org

U.S. Games, P.O. Box 7726, Dallas, TX 75209; 1-800-327-0484
Heart challenge course simulation. www.usgames. com

USA Pickleball Association, P.O. Box 7354, Surprise, AZ 85374; phone number unavailable
Instructional materials for Pickleball. www.usapa. org

Wagon Wheel Records, 1612 Pembroke Lane, Huntington Beach, CA 92649; 714-846-8169
Music. www.wagonwheelrecords.net

Wittek Golf Supply Company, 3865 Commercial Ave., Northbrook, IL 60062; 847-943-2399
Cayman golf balls. www.wittekgolf.com

Bibliography

Adams, S.H. 1993. Duty to properly instruct. *JOPERD* 64(2):22-23.

Allen, J., E. McNeill, and V. Schmidt. 1992. *Cultural awareness for children*. Menlo Park, CA: Addison-Wesley.

Amabile, T. 1989. *Growing up creative*. New York: Crown.

American Alliance for Health, Physical Education, Recreation and Dance (AAHPERD). 1994. *New physical best educational kit*. Reston, VA: Author.

———. 1995. *Including students with disabilities in physical education*. Reston, VA: Author.

———. 1998. *Physical activity for children: A statement of guidelines*. Council for Physical Education for Children (COPEC) of the NASPE, an Association of the AAHPERD. Reston, VA: Author.

———. 1999a. *Physical best activity guide/elementary level*. Champaign, IL: Human Kinetics.

———. 1999b. *Physical best activity guide/secondary level*. Champaign, IL: Human Kinetics.

American College of Sports Medicine. 1988. Physical fitness and youth. *Medicine and Science in Sports and Exercise* 20(4):422-423.

———. 1990. The recommended quantity and quality of exercise for developing and maintaining cardiorespiratory and muscular fitness in healthy adults. *Medicine and Science in Sports and Exercise* 22(2):265-274.

———. 1993. Summary statement: Workshop on physical activity and public health. *Sports Medicine Bulletin* 28(4):7.

American Heart Association. 1986. *The corporate heart*. Needham, MA: Author.

———. 1988. *Heart facts*. Dallas: Author.

———. 1991. *Heart and stroke facts*. Dallas: Author.

———. 2001. *Heart and stroke facts: 2001 Statistical supplement*. Dallas: Author.

———. 2006. Cardiovascular disease statistics.www.americanheart.org/presenter.jhtml?identifier=4478

American Psychological Association. 2006. Adolescent mental disorder rate.www.apa.org/ppo/issues/echccra.html

Anglin, G.J., ed. 1991. *Instructional technology: Past, present, and future*. Englewood, CO: Libraries Unlimited.

Apple, M.W., and J.A. Beane, eds. 1995. *Democratic schools*. Alexandria, VA: Association for Supervision and Curriculum Development (ASCD).

Ardovino, J., J. Hollingsworth, and S. Ybarra. 2000. *Multiple measures: Accurate ways to assess student achievement*. Thousand Oaks, CA: Corwin Press.

Armstrong, T. 1994. *Multiple intelligences in the classroom*. Alexandria, VA: ASCD.

Asher, J.J. 1977. *Learning another language through actions: The complete teacher's guidebook*. Los Gatos, CA: Sky Oak Productions.

Association for Supervision and Curriculum Development. 1975. *The middle school we need*. Washington, DC: ASCD.

Asthana, A. 2006. Single-sex schools no benefit for girls.http://education.guardian.co.uk/schools/story/0,,1805641,00.html

Aukstakalnis, S., and D. Blatner. 1992. *Silicon mirage: The art and science of virtual reality*. Berkeley, CA: Peachpit Press.

Baker, E.T., M.C. Wang, and H.J. Walberg. 1994. The effects of inclusion on learning. *Educational Leadership* 52(4):33-35.

Balan, C.M., and W.E. Davis. 1993. Ecological task analysis—an approach to teaching physical education. *JOPERD* 64(9):54-61.

Bassett, D. 2000. Validity and reliability issues in objective monitoring of physical activity. *Research Quarterly for Exercise and Sport* 71(2): 30-36.

Bassett, D.R., B.E. Ainsworth, S.R. Leggett, C.A. Mathien, J.A. Main, D.C. Hunter, and G.E. Duncan. 1996. Accuracy of five electronic pedometers for measuring distance walked. *Medicine and Science in Sports and Exercise* 28: 1071-1077.

Bassett, D.R., B.E. Ainsworth, A.M. Swartz, S.J. Strath, W.L. O'Brien, and G.A. King. 2000. Validity of four motion sensors in measuring moderate intensity physical activity. *Medicine and Science in Sports and Exercise* 32: S471-S480.

Bassin, S., D. Davidson, R. Deitrick, G.S. Morris, N. Wong, and A. Crecelius. 1989. Montebello health and fitness research project: A three-year school-based assessment and intervention. Paper presented at the AAHPERD National Convention, April 19-23, 1989, Boston.

Batesky, J. 1988. Teacher performance self appraisal for physical educators. *Strategies* 1(4):19-22.

BBC News. 2006. Children need more exercise.http://news.bbc.co.uk/1/hi/health/5198154.stm

Benjamin, R. 1981. *Making schools work: A reporter's journey through some of America's most remarkable classrooms.* New York: Continuum.

Benjamin, S. 1989. An ideascape for education: What futurists recommend. *Educational Leadership* 47(1):8-12.

Bensen, J. 1982. An alternative direction for middle school physical education. *Physical Educator* 39(2):75-77.

Berkowitz, R.J. 1996. A practitioner's journey: From skill to tactics. *JOPERD* 67(4):44-45.

Berliner, D.C., and U. Casanova. 1993. *Putting research to work in your school.* New York: Scholastic.

Berman, P. 1994. *Mobilizing for competitiveness: Linking education and training to jobs.* San Francisco: California Business Roundtable.

Birdwell, D. 1980. The effects of modification of teacher behavior on the academic learning time of selected students in physical education. PhD dissertation, Ohio State University, Columbus.

Blackall, B. 1987. *Australian physical education: Book 1.* South Melbourne: Macmillan Company of Australia.

Blackall, B., and D. Davis. 1987. *Australian physical education: Book 2.* South Melbourne: Macmillan Company of Australia.

Blake, A. 2006. *Why PE is the secret to your child's success at school work.* Cardiff, Wales: Western Mail.

Blakemore, C.L., and J.K. Rogers. 1995. Learn how middle school students think. *Strategies* (February):11-14.

Block, M.E. 1994. *A teacher's guide to including students with disabilities in regular physical education.* Baltimore: Brookes.

———. 2000. *A teacher's guide to including students with disabilities in general physical education* (2nd ed.). Baltimore: Brookes.

Bloom, B.S., ed. 1956. *Taxonomy of educational objectives, handbook I: Cognitive domain.* New York: McKay.

Boyce, B.A. 1990. Grading practices—How do they influence students' skill performance? *JOPERD* 61(6):46-48.

Brandt, R. 1993. On restructuring roles and relationships: A conversation with Phil Schlechty. *Educational Leadership* 51(2):9-11.

———. 1998. *Assessing student learning: New rules, new realities.* Alexandria, VA: ASCD.

Brewer, C., and D. Campbell. 1991. *Rhythms of learning.* Tucson, AZ: Zephyr Press.

Briggs, J.C. 2002. Virtual reality is getting real: Prepare to meet your clone. *The Futurist* (May/June):34-41.

Brooks, J.G., and M.G. Brooks. 1993. *In search of understanding: The case for constructivist classrooms.* Alexandria, VA: ASCD.

Brown, J. 1995. *Tennis: Steps to success* (2nd ed.). Champaign, IL: Human Kinetics.

———. 1996. *Tennis instructor guide: Steps to success.* Champaign, IL: Human Kinetics.

Brown, L., and S. Grineski. 1992. Competition in physical education: An educational contradiction. *JOPERD* 63(1):17-19, 77.

Brown, S.C. 1993. Selecting safe equipment—What do we really know? *JOPERD* 64(2):33-35.

Bruder, I. 1993. Alternative assessment: Putting technology to the test. *Electronic Learning* (January):22-23, 26-28.

Bruer, J.T. 1998. Brain science, brain fiction. *Educational Leadership* 56(3):8-13.

Buchanan, D. 1992. Outward Bound goes to the inner city. *Educational Leadership* 50(4):38-41.

Buck, M.M. 2002. *Assessing heart rate in physical education.* Reston, VA: National Association for Sport and Physical Education (NASPE).

Burgeson, C.R., H. Wechsler, N.D. Brener, J.C. Young, and C.G. Spain. 2001. Physical education and activity: Results from the School Health Policies and programs Study, 2000. *Journal of School Health* 71(7), 279-293.

Burrus, D. 1993. *Techno trends.* New York: HarperBusiness.

Bushweller, K. 1995. The resilient child. *American School Board Journal* (May):18-24.

Butler, L.F., and G.C. Mergardt. 1994. The many forms of administrative support. *JOPERD* 65(7):43-47.

Bycura, D., and P. Darst. 1991. Motivating middle school students: A health-club approach. *JOPERD* 72(7):24-29.

Caine, R.N., and G. Caine. 1990. Understanding a brain-based approach to learning and teaching. *Educational Leadership* 48(2):66-70.

———. 1991. *Making connections: Teaching and the human brain.* Alexandria, VA: ASCD.

———. 1997a. *Education on the edge of possibilities.* Alexandria, VA: ASCD.

———. 1997b. *Unleashing the power of perceptual change: The potential of brain-based teaching.* Alexandria, VA: ASCD.

California Department of Education. 1986. *Handbook for physical education: Framework for developing a curriculum for California public schools.* Sacramento, CA: Author.

———. 1987. *Caught in the middle: Educational reform for young adolescents in California public schools.* Sacramento, CA: Author.

———. 1991. *Not schools alone: Guidelines for schools and communities.* Sacramento, CA: Author.

———. 1994a. *Health framework for California public schools: Kindergarten through grade twelve.* Sacramento, CA: Author.

———. 1994b. *Physical education framework for California public schools: Kindergarten through grade twelve.* Sacramento, CA: Author.

———. 2008. *Taking center stage.* Sacramento: Author.

California Department of Health Services. 1994. *Vital statistics of California 1992 (preliminary data).* Sacramento, CA: Author.

California Department of Health Services and UCSF Institute for Health and Aging. 1994. *Cardiovascular disease awareness survey of California adults.* Sacramento, CA: Authors.

California—Region 9. 1994. *Physical education curriculum.* San Diego: San Diego County Office of Education.

California School Leadership Academy (CSLA). 1991a. *Structuring the school for student success.* Sacramento, CA: Author.

———. 1991b. *Thinking/meaning-centered curriculum module.* Sacramento, CA: Author.

———. 1994a. *Accountability and assessment program for improving student performance.* Sacramento, CA: Author.

———. 1994b. *Physical education for lifelong well being.* Sacramento, CA: Author.

Campbell, D. 1992. *100 ways to improve your teaching using your voice and music.* Tucson, AZ: Zephyr Press.

Cannings, T., and L. Finkel, eds. 1993. *The technology age classroom.* Wilsonville, OR: Franklin, Beedle and Associates.

Carlson, R.P. 1984. *Ideas II for secondary school physical education.* Reston, VA: NASPE.

Carnegie Council on Adolescent Development. 1989. *Turning points: Preparing American youth for the 21st century.* Washington, DC: Author.

———. 1992. *A matter of time: Risk and opportunity in the nonschool hours.* Report of the Task Force on Youth Development and Community Programs. New York: Carnegie Corporation of New York.

———. 1994a. *Consultation on afterschool programs.* New York: Carnegie Corporation of New York.

———. 1994b. *A matter of time: Risk and opportunity in the out-of-school hours. Recommendations for strengthening community programs for youth.* New York: Carnegie Corporation of New York.

———. 1995. *Great transitions: Preparing adolescents for a new century. Concluding report of the Council.* New York: Carnegie Corporation of New York.

Carnegie Forum on Education and the Economy. 1986. *A nation prepared: Teachers for the 21st century. The report of the Task Force on Teaching as a Profession.* Washington, DC: The Forum.

Carpenter, L.J. 2000. *Legal concepts in sport: A primer.* Champaign, IL: Sagamore.

Carr, G. 1997. *Mechanics of sport.* Champaign, IL: Human Kinetics.

Carr, J.F., and D.E. Harris. 2001. *Succeeding with standards: Linking curriculum, assessment, and action planning.* Alexandria, VA: ASCD.

Cassidy, J. 1982. *The hacky sack book.* Stanford, CA: Klutz Press.

Cawelti, G., ed. 1993. *Challenges and achievements of American education.* Alexandria, VA: ASCD.

Centers for Disease Control and Prevention. 1996. Guidelines for school health programs to promote lifelong healthy eating. *Morbidity and Mortality Weekly Report* 45(RR-9):1-41.

———. 1997a. Guidelines for school and community programs to promote lifelong physical activity among young people. *Morbidity and Mortality Weekly Report* 46(RR-6):1-36.

———. 1997b. *Nutrition and the health of young people: Fact sheet.* Washington, DC: U.S. Department of Health and Human Services, National Center for Chronic Disease Prevention and Health Promotion.

———. 1997c. *Physical activity and the health of young people: Fact sheet.* Washington, DC: U.S. Department of Health and Human Services, National Center for Chronic Disease Prevention and Health Promotion.

———. 1999. Neighborhood safety and the prevalence of physical inactivity—selected states, 1996. *Morbidity and Mortality Weekly Report* 48(7):143-146.

———. 2000a. *Promoting better health for young people through physical activity and sports: A report to the President from the Secretary of Health and Human Services and the Secretary of Education.* Atlanta: Author.

———. 2000b. *School health policies and programs study 2000.* Atlanta: Author.

———. 2005. *School health index: A self-assessment and planning guide. Middle school/high school version.* Atlanta: Author.

———. 2006. *Physical education curriculum analysis tool.* Atlanta: Author.

———. n.d. Fact sheet: Youth risk behavior trend—from CDC's 1991, 1993, 1995, and 1997 Youth Risk Behavior Surveys.www.cdc.gov/nccdphp/dash/yrbs/trend.htm

———. n.d. Unpublished mortality data from the National Center for Health Statistics (NCHS) mortality data tapes.

Centers for Disease Control and Prevention and the American College of Sports Medicine. 1995. *Physical activity and public health—a recommendation.* Atlanta: Authors.

Chadwick, I., and A. Gathright. 1990. Middle school frameworks: The implications for elementary schools. *Florida Journal of Health, Physical Education, Recreation, Dance, and Driver Education* 28(1):37-38.

Chandler, G.L., and W.W. Purkey. 1986. Invitational physical education. *Physical Educator* 43(3):123-128.

Chandler, T. 1996. Teaching games for understanding: Reflections and further questions. *JOPERD* 67(4):49-51.

Chepko, S., and R.K. Arnold. 2000. *Guidelines for physical education programs: Grades K-12 standards, objectives, and assessments.* Boston: Allyn & Bacon.

Clancy, M.E. 2006. *Active bodies, active brains.* Champaign, IL: Human Kinetics.

Clarke, J.H., S.D. Sanborn, J.A. Aiken, N.A. Cornell, J.B. Goodman, and K.K. Hess. 1998. *Real questions, real answers.* Alexandria, VA: ASCD.

Cohen, P. 1995. Schooling away from school: Some districts work with home educators. *Education Update* 37(6):1, 6, 8.

Collins, L.M. 1988. Youth problems are frightening. *Desert News*, September 13.

Cooper Institute for Aerobics Research. 1999. *Fitnessgram: Test administration manual* (2nd ed.). Champaign, IL: Human Kinetics.

Corbin, C.B. 1993a. Clues from dinosaurs, mules, and the bull snake: Our field in the 21st century. *Quest* 45(4):546-556.

———. 1993b. The field of physical education—common goals, not common roles. *JOPERD* 64(1):79, 84-87.

Corbin, C.B., G. Le Masurier, and D.D.. Lambdin. 2007. *Fitness for life—middle school.* Champaign, IL: Human Kinetics.

———. 2005. *Fitness for life: Teacher's resource book* (5th ed.). Champaign, IL: Human Kinetics.

Cornish, E., ed. 1994. *Outlook '95.* Bethesda, MD: World Future Society.

Costa, A.L. 1991. *Teaching for intelligent behavior: Outstanding strategies for strengthening your students' thinking skills.* Bellevue, WA: Bureau of Education and Research.

Cradler, J. 1991. Authentic assessment: Finding the right tools. *Thrust for Educational Leadership* 49(2):20-25.

Cradler, J., and M. Melendez. 1991. In with the new. *Thrust for Educational Leadership* 49(2):8-11.

Crouter, S.E., P.L. Schneider, M. Karabulut, and D.R. Bassett, 2003. Validity of 10 electronic pedometers for measuring steps, distance, and energy cost. *Medicine and Science in Sports and Exercise* 35(8):1455-1460.

Cuesta, J.G. 1981. *Team handball techniques.* Colorado Springs, CO: United States Team Handball Federation.

Curtner-Smith, M.D. 1996. Teaching for understanding: Using games invention with elementary children. *JOPERD* 67(3):33-37.

Curwin, R.L., and A.N. Mendler. 1988. *Discipline with dignity.* Alexandria, VA: ASCD.

Dale, D., C.B. Corbin, and T.F. Cuddihy. 1998. Can conceptual physical education promote physically active lifestyles? *Pediatric Exercise Science* 10:97-109.

Davies, J., R. Davies, and S. Heacock, 2003. A wellness program for faculty. *Educational Leadership* (May): 68-70.

Davis, G.A., and A.W. Jackson. 2000. Turning points: A decade later. *Middle Ground* (October):10-16.

Davis, S. 1987. *Future perfect.* New York: Addison-Wesley.

Davis, S., and J. Botkin. 1994. *The monster under the bed.* New York: Simon & Schuster.

Davison, B. 1998. *Creative physical activities and equipment.* Champaign, IL: Human Kinetics.

Day, J.C., A. Janus, and J. Davis, 2005. *Computer and Internet use in the United States.* Washington DC: US Department of Commerce.

Deal, T.B., and L.O. Deal. 1995. Heart to heart: Using heart rate telemetry to meet physical education outcomes. *JOPERD* 66(3):30-35.

Dede, C. 1998. *Learning with technology.* Alexandria, VA: ASCD.

Delisle, R. 1997. *How to use problem-based learning in the classroom.* Alexandria, VA: ASCD.

Dennison, P.E. 1981. *Switching on: A guide to edu-kinesthetics.* Ventura, CA: Edu-Kinesthetics.

Dennison, P.E., and G. Dennison. 1988. *Brain gym.* Ventura, CA: Edu-Kinesthetics.

Dewey, J. [1915] 1990. *The school and society.* Chicago: University of Chicago Press.

Dienstbier, R. 1989. Periodic adrenaline arousal boosts health, coping. *Brain-Mind Bulletin* 14:9A.

Diez, M.E., and C.J. Moon. 1992. What do we want students to know? . . . and other important questions. *Educational Leadership* 49(8):38-41.

Dodds, P., ed. 1987. *Basic stuff series I.* Reston, VA: AAHPERD.

Doolittle, S., and T. Fay. 2002. *Authentic assessment of physical activity for high school students.* Reston, VA: NASPE.

Dougherty, N.J., ed. 1993. *Principles of safety in physical education and sport.* Reston, VA: NASPE.

———. 2002. *Principles of safety in physical education and sport* (2nd ed.). Reston, VA: NASPE.

Dougherty, N.J., A.S. Goldberger, and L.J. Carpenter. 2002. *Sport, physical activity, and the law* (2nd ed.). Champaign, IL: Sagamore.

Duffy, T.M., and D.H. Jonassen. 1992. *Constructivism and the technology of instruction: A conversation.* Hillsdale, NJ: Erlbaum.

Dusenbury, L., and M. Falco. 1995. Eleven components of effective drug abuse prevention curricula. *Journal of School Health* 65:420-425.

Dwyer, T., J.F. Sallis, L. Blizzard, R. Lazarus, and K. Dean. 2001. Relation of academic performance to physical acativity and fitness in children. *Pediatric Exercise Science* 13(3):225-237.

Echevarria, J., and A. Graves. 1997. *Sheltered content instruction: Teaching English-language learners with diverse abilities.* Needham Heights, MA: Allyn and Bacon.

Echevarria, J., M. Vogt, D. Short, and M. Vogt. 1999. *Making content comprehensible for English language learners.* Needham Heights, MA: Allyn and Bacon.

Educational Amendment Act of 1972. United States.

Elmore, R.F., and S.H. Fuhrman, eds. 1994. *The governance of curriculum.* Alexandria, VA: ASCD.

Ethnier, J.L., W. Salazar, D.M. Landers, S.J. Petruzzello, M. Han, and P. Nowell. 1997. The influence of physical fitness and exercise upon cognitive functioning: A meta-analysis. *Journal of Sport and Exercise Psychology* 19(3):249-277.

Evertson, C.M., E.T. Emmer, J.P. Sanford, and B.S. Clements. 1983. Improving classroom management: An experiment in elementary classrooms. *Elementary School Journal* 84(2):173-188.

Fenwick, J.J. 1993. *The middle school years.* San Diego: Fenwick Associates.

———. 1992. *Managing middle grade reform: An America 2000 agenda.* Sacramento: California Department of Education.

Finnigan, D. 1987. *Scarf juggling.* n.p.: The Complete Juggler.

Fitts, P.M., and M.I. Posner. 1967. *Human performance.* Belmont, CA: Brooks/Cole.

Fleming, M., and W.H. Levie, eds. 1993. *Instructional message design: Principles from the behavioral and cognitive sciences.* Englewood Cliffs, NJ: Educational Technology.

Fluegelman, A. 1976. *The new games book.* New York: Doubleday.

———. 1981. *More new games.* New York: Doubleday.

Fogarty, R. 1991a. Ten ways to integrate curriculum. *Educational Leadership* 49(2):61-65.

———. 1991b. *The mindful school: How to integrate the curricula.* Palatine, IL: IRI/Skylight.

Fothergill, K. 1998. *Update 1997: School-based health centers.* Washington, DC: Advocates for Youth, Support Center for School-Based and School-Linked Health Care.

Fredericksen, E., A. Pickett, P. Shea, W. Pelz, and K. Swan. 2000. Student satisfaction and perceived learning with online courses: Principles and examples from the SUNY learning network. *Journal of Asynchronous Learning Networks* 4(2).www.aln.org/publications/jaln/index.asp

Freedman, D.S., L.K. Khan, W.H. Dietz, S.R. Srinivason, and G.S. Berenson. 2001. Relationship of childhood obesity to coronary heart disease risk factors in adulthood. The Bogalusa heart study. *Pediatrics* 108(3):712-718.

Fronske, H. 1997. *Teaching cues for sport skills.* Needham Heights, MA: Allyn and Bacon.

Fronske, H., and R. Wilson. 2002. *Teaching cues for basic sport skills for elementary and middle school students.* Boston: Cummings.

Fullan, M. 1993. *Change forces: Probing the depths of educational reform.* Bristol, PA: Falmer Press.

———1996. *10 assumptions about change.* Toronto: OISE/UT Press.

Gabbard, C. 2000. Physical education: Should it be in the core curriculum. *Principal* (January):29-31.

Gagne, R.M., L.J. Briggs, and W.W. Wager. 1992. *Principles of instructional design.* Fort Worth, TX: Harcourt Brace Jovanovich College.

Gall, S.L. 1991. The fit miss less work. *Physician and Sports Medicine* 19(4):28.

Galyean, B.C. 1984. *Mindsight: Learning through imaging.* Berkeley, CA: Center for Integrative Learning.

Gamoran, A. 1992. Is ability grouping equitable? *Educational Leadership* 50(2):11-17.

Gardner, H. 1983. *Frames of mind: The theory of multiple intelligences.* New York: Basic Books.

———. 1993a. *Frames of mind: The theory of multiple intelligences* (2nd ed.). New York: Basic Books.

———. 1993b. *Multiple intelligences: The theory in practice.* New York: Basic Books.

———. 2000. *Intelligence reframed: Multiple intelligences for the 21st century.* New York: Basic Books.

Gaskin, L.P. 1993. Establishing, communicating, and enforcing rules and regulations. *JOPERD* 64(2):26-27, 63-64.

Gates, B. 1995. *The road ahead.* New York: Viking.

Gaugler, W.M., A.F. Nadi, and L.C. Lobo. 1997. *The science of fencing.* New York: Laureate Press.

Gawronski, J.D. 1991. Ready or not, assessment, here it comes. *Thrust for Educational Leadership* 49(2):12-15.

Gentile, L. 1983. *Using sports for reading and writing activities: Middle and high school years.* Phoenix: Onyx Press.

George, P.S. 2001. The evolution of middle schools. *Educational Leadership* (December/January):40-44.

George, P.S., C. Stevenson, J. Thomason, and J. Beane. 1992. *The middle school—and beyond.* Alexandria, VA: ASCD.

Gibbons, S.L., B. Robinson, P. Bruce, K. Bremen, L. Lundeen, J. Mouritzen, J. Perkins, T. Stogre, and C.

Wejr. 2002. Using rubrics to support assessment and evaluation of personal and social outcomes in physical education. *Strategies* 15(4):28-33.

Gibbs, J. 1987. *Tribes: A process for social development and cooperative learning.* Santa Rosa, CA: Center Source.

Glover, D.R., and D.W. Midura. 1992. *Team building through physical challenges.* Champaign, IL: Human Kinetics.

Gold, R.S. 1991. *Microcomputer applications in health education.* Dubuque, IA: Brown.

Goldberger, M. 1992. The spectrum of teaching styles: A perspective for research on teaching physical education. *JOPERD* 63(1):42-46.

Goodlad, J. 1984. *A place called school.* New York: McGraw-Hill.

Graham, G., S. Holt-Hale, and M. Parker. 1993. *Children moving: A reflective approach to teaching physical education.* Mountain View, CA: Mayfield.

Gray, G.R. 1995. Safety tips from the expert witness. *JOPERD* 66(1):18-21.

Grehaigne, J., D. Bouthier, and P. Godbout. 1997. Performance assessment in team sports. *Journal of Teaching in Physical Education* 16:500-516.

Griss, S. 1994. Creative movement: A language for learning. *Educational Leadership* 51(5):78-80.

Gros, V. 1979. *Inside field hockey.* Chicago: Contemporary Books.

Grunbaum, J.A., L. Kann, S. Kinchen, J. Ross, J.Hawkins, R. Lowry, W.A. Harris, T. McManus, D. Chyen, and J. CollinsJ. 2004. Youth risk behavior surveillance—US, 2004. *Morbidity and Mortality Weekly Report* 53(SS-2):1-95.

Guglielmo, C. 1994. Forecast '95. *New Media* 4(16):41-45.

Guiton, G., J. Oakes, J. Gong, K.H. Quartz, M. Lipton, and J. Balisok. 1995. Teaming: Creating small communities of learners in the middle grades. In J. Oakes and K.H. Quartz (eds.), *Creating new educational communities: 94th yearbook of the National Society for the Study of Education* (pp. 87-107). Chicago: University of Chicago Press.

Hackmann, D.G. 1996. Student-led conferences at the middle level: Promoting student responsibility. *NASSP Bulletin* 80(578):31-36.

Hafner, K. 1995. Wiring the ivory tower. *Newsweek* (January 30):62-63, 66.

Hall, G.E., R.C. Wallace, and W.A. Dossett. 1973. *A developmental conceptualization of the adoption process within educational institutions.* Austin, TX: Research and Development Center for Teacher Education.

Hall, S. 2007. *Basic biomechanics* (5th ed.). Boston: WCB/McGraw-Hill.

Halpern, S. 1985. *Sound health.* New York: Harper & Row.

Hannaford, C. 1995. *Smart moves: Why learning is not all in your head.* Arlington, VA: Great Ocean.

Hanvey, R.G. 1976. *An attainable global perspective.* Denver: Center for Teaching International Relations.

Harris, D., and J.F. Carr. 1996. *How to use standards in the classroom.* Alexandria, VA: ASCD.

Harris, J.A., A.M. Pittmann, and M.S. Waller. 1999. *Dance a while* (8th ed.). Boston: Benjamin/Cummings.

Harrison, J.M., and C.L. Blakemore. 1992. *Instructional strategies for secondary school physical education.* Dubuque, IA: Brown.

Harrison, J.M., C.L. Blakemore, and M.M. Buck. 2001. *Instructional strategies for secondary school physical education* (5th ed.). Boston: McGraw-Hill.

Hart, J.E., and R.J. Ritson. 2002. *Liability and safety in physical education and sport.* Reston, VA: NASPE.

Hay, J.G. 1993. *The biomechanics of sports techniques.* Englewood Cliffs, NJ: Prentice Hall.

Haywood, K.M., and N. Getchell. 2001. *Learning activities for life span motor development.* Champaign, IL: Human Kinetics.

Healthy Kids Healthy California Committee. 1989. *A comprehensive approach to improving the health and well-being of California's students.* Sacramento, CA: California Department of Education.

Hedley, A.A., C.L. Ogden, C.L. Johnson, M.D. Carroll, L.R. Curtin, and K.M. Flegal. 2004. Overweight and obesity among U.S. children, adolescents, and adults, 1999-2002. *Journal of the American Medical Association* 291(23):2847-2850.

Hellison, D.R. 1985. *Goals and strategies for teaching physical education.* Champaign, IL: Human Kinetics.

Henderson, A. 1987. *The evidence continues to grow: Parent involvement improves student achievement.* Columbia, MD: NCCE.

Henderson, A.T., and N. Berla. 1994. *A new generation of evidence: The family is critical to student achievement.* Washington, DC: Center for Law and Education.

Herdman, P. 1994. When the wilderness becomes a classroom. *Educational Leadership* 52(3):15-19.

Hermann, D.J., and J.R. Hanwood. 1980. More evidence for the existence of the separate semantic and episodic stores in long-term memory. *Journal of Experimental Psychology: Human Learning and Memory* 6(5):467-478.

Heterick, R.C., and J. Gehl. 1995. Information technology and the year 2000. *Educom Review* (January/February):23-25.

Hichwa, J. 1998. *Right fielders are people too.* Champaign, IL: Human Kinetics.

Himberg, C., G.E. Hutchinson, J.M. Roussell. 2003. *Teaching secondary physical education: Preparing adolescents to be active for life.* Champaign, IL: Human Kinetics.

Holt/Hale, S.A. 1999. *Assessing and improving fitness in elementary physical education.* Reston, VA: NASPE.

———. 1999. *Assessing motor skills in elementary physical education.* Reston, VA: NASPE.

Holyoak, C., and H. Weinberg. 1986. *Meeting needs and pleasing kids: A middle school physical education curriculum.* Dubuque, IA: Kendall/Hunt.

Horowitz, J., and B. Bloom. 1987. *Frisbee: More than a game of catch.* La Mirada, CA: Discovering the World.

Hough, D. 1997. A bona fide middle school: Programs, policy, practice, and grade span configurations. In J.L. Irvin (ed.), *What current research says to the middle level practitioner* (pp. 285-294). Columbus, OH: National Middle School Association.

Hough, D., and J.L. Irvin. 1997. Setting a research agenda. In J.L. Irvin (ed.), *What current research says to the middle level practitioner* (pp. 351-356). Columbus, OH: National Middle School Association.

Housner, L.D. 1995. Physical education: Visions for the future. In *Proceedings of the AAHPERD Southwest District/Hawaii Convention* (pp. 93-94). Turtle Bay, Oahu: Southwest AAHPERD.

———. 2001. Teaching physical education with the brain in mind. *Teaching Elementary Physical Education* (September):38-40.

Housner, L.D., and D.C. Griffey. 1994. Wax on, wax off. *JOPERD* 65(2):63-68.

Houston, J. 1982. *The possible human: A course in enhancing your physical, mental and creative abilities.* Los Angeles: Jeremy Tarcher.

Hovell, M.F., J.F Sallis, B. Kolody, and T.L. McKenzie. 1999. Children's physical activity choices: A developmental analysis of gender, intensity levels, and time. *Pediatric Exercise Science* 11:158-168.

Humberstone, B. 1990. Warriors or wimps? Creating alternative forms of physical education. In M.A. Messner and D.F. Sabo (eds.), *Sport, men, and the gender order: Critical feminist perspectives* (pp. 201-210). Champaign, IL: Human Kinetics.

Hunter, M. 1982. *Mastery teaching.* El Segundo, CA: TIP.

Hurrelmann, K., and A. Klocke. 1997. The role of the school in comprehensive health promotion. In R. Takanishi and D.A. Hamburg (eds.), *Preparing adolescents for the twenty-first century: Challenges facing Europe and the United States* (pp. 82-107). Cambridge: Cambridge University Press.

Hutchinson, G.E. 1995. Gender-fair teaching in physical education. *JOPERD* 66(1):42-47.

Inlay, L. 2005. Safe schools for the roller coaster years. *ASCD* (April):41-43.

International Society of Sport Psychology. 1992. Physical activity and psychological benefits. *Physician and Sports Medicine* 20:179-180.

Issacs, K.R. 1992. Exercise and the brain: Angiogenesis in the adult rate cerebellum after vigorous physical activity and motor skill learning. *Journal of Cerebral Blood Flow and Metabolism* 12(1):110-119.

Jackson, A.W. 1997. Adapting educational systems to young adolescents and new conditions. In R. Takanishi and D.A. Hamburg (eds.), *Preparing adolescents for the twenty-first century: Challenges facing Europe and the United States* (pp. 13-37). Cambridge: Cambridge University Press.

Jackson, A.W., and G.A. Davis. 2000. *Turning points 2000: Educating adolescents in the 21st century.* New York: Teachers College Press.

Jacobs, H.H., ed. 1989. *Interdisciplinary curriculum: Design and implementation.* Alexandria, VA: ASCD.

———. 1991. Planning for curriculum integration. *Educational Leadership* 49(2):27-28.

———. 1997. *Mapping the big picture.* Alexandria, VA: ASCD.

Jambor, E.A., and E.M. Weekes. 1995. Videotape feedback: Make it more effective. *JOPERD* 66(2):48-50.

Jensen, E. 1994. *The learning brain.* Del Mar, CA: Turning Point.

———. 1995. *Brain-based learning and teaching.* Del Mar, CA: Turning Point.

———. 1998. *Teaching with the brain in mind.* Alexandria, VA: ASCD.

Jewett, A.E., L.L. Bain, and C.D. Ennis. 1995. *The curriculum process in physical education.* Dubuque, IA: Brown.

Johnson, C. 1991. *Teaching orienteering.* Binghamton, NY: Johnson Camping.

Johnson, D.W., and R.T. Johnson. 1991. *Teach students to be peacemakers.* Edina, MN: Interaction Book.

———. 1998. *Learning together and alone: Cooperative, competitive, and individualistic learning* (5th ed.). Needham Heights, MA: Allyn & Bacon.

Johnson, D.W., R.T. Johnson, and E.J. Holubec. 1994. *Cooperative learning in the classroom.* Alexandria, VA: ASCD.

Johnson, J., and C. Deshpande. 2000. Health education and physical education: Disciplines preparing students as productive, healthy citizens for the challenges of the 21st century. *Journal of School Health* 70(2):66-68.

Johnston, L.D., P.M O'Malley, and J.G. Bachman. 1999. Drug use by American young people begins to turn downward. In L.D. Johnston, P.M. O'Malley, and J.G. Bachman (eds.), *National survey results on drug use from the Monitoring the Future study, 1975-1998. Volume 1: Secondary school students.* NIH Publication No. 99-4660. Rockville, MD: National Institute on Drug Abuse.

Joint Committee on National Health Education Standards. 1995. *National health education standards.* Reston, VA: Association for the Advancement of Health Education.

Joyce, B., ed. 1990. *Changing school culture through staff development.* Alexandria, VA: ASCD.

Joyce, B., and B. Showers. 1995. *Student achievement through staff development.* New York: Addison-Wesley.

Joyce, B., and M. Weil. 1999. *Models of teaching* (6th ed.). Needham Heights, MA: Allyn & Bacon.

The Juggle Bug. 1979. *The joy of juggling.* Champaign, IL: Human Kinetics.

Kagan, S. 1991. *Cooperative learning: Resources for teachers.* Laguna Niguel, CA: Kagan Cooperative.

———. 1997. *Cooperative learning.* Laguna Niguel, CA: Kagan Cooperative.

Kagan, S., and L. Kagan. 1992. *Cooperative learning workshops for teachers.* Laguna Niguel, CA: Kagan Cooperative.

Kaku, M. 1997. *Visions: How science will revolutionize the 21st century.* New York: Anchor Books.

Kalakanis, L.E., G.S. Goldfield, R.A. Paluch, and L.H. Epstein. 2001. Parental activity as a determinant of activity level and patterns of activity in obese children. *Research Quarterly for Exercise and Sport* 72(3):202-209.

Kane, W.M. 1993. *Step by step to comprehensive school health: The program planning guide.* Santa Cruz, CA: ETR Associates.

Kentucky Department of Education. 1990. *Transformations: Kentucky's curriculum framework.* Frankfort, KY: Author.

Kentucky Education Reform Act of 1990, House Bill 940.

Kerman, S. 1979. Teacher expectations and student achievement. *Phi Delta Kappa* 36(2):14-15.

Kimiecik, S.J., K.R. Demas, and C.B. Demas. 1994. Establishing credibility: Proactive approaches. *JOPERD* 65(7):38-42.

King, D. 2000. Exercise seen boosting children's brain function. PELINKS4U (May).www.pelinks4u.org/news/bgbrain.htm

Kirchner, G. 1991. *Children's games from around the world.* Dubuque, IA: Brown.

Kirchner, G., and G.J. Fishburne. 1995. *Physical education for elementary school children.* Dubuque, IA: Brown and Benchmark.

Kirkpatrick, B. 1987. Ultra physical education in middle schools. *JOPERD* 58(6):46-49.

Kirkpatrick, B., and M.M. Buck. 1995. Heart adventures challenge course: A lifestyle education activity. *JOPERD* 66(2):17-24.

Kittleson, S. 1992. *Racquetball: Steps to success.* Champaign, IL: Human Kinetics.

———. 1993. *Teaching racquetball: Steps to success.* Champaign, IL: Human Kinetics.

Knop, N., D. Tananehill, and M. O'Sullivan. 2001. Making a difference for urban youths. *JOPERD* 72(7):38-44.

Knudson, D. 1993. Biomechanics of the basketball jump shot—six key teaching points. *JOPERD* 64(2):67-73.

Kohn, A. 1987. *No contest: The case against competition.* New York: Houghton Mifflin.

———. 1991a. Caring kids: The role of the schools. *Phi Delta Kappa* 48(1):498-506.

———. 1991b. Don't spoil the promise of cooperative learning. *Educational Leadership* 48(5):93-94.

———. 1991c. Group grade grubbing versus cooperative learning. *Educational Leadership* 48(5):83-87.

———. 1994. Grading: The issue is not how but why. *Educational Leadership* 52(2):38-41.

———. 1999. *Punished by rewards: The trouble with gold stars, incentive plans, A's, praise, and other bribes.* New York: Houghton Mifflin.

Kounin, J. 1977. *Discipline and group management in classrooms.* Melbourne, FL: Krieger.

Kuykendall, C. 1992. *From rage to hope: Strategies for reclaiming black and Hispanic students.* Bloomington, IN: National Educational Service.

Lambert, L.T. 1999. *Standards-based assessment of student learning: A comprehensive approach.* Reston, VA: NASPE.

Lane, C. 2000. *Complete book of line dancing* (2nd ed.). Champaign, IL: Human Kinetics.

Lauffenburger, S.K. 1992. Efficient warm-ups: Creating a warm-up that works. *JOPERD* 63(4):21-25.

Laughlin, N., and S. Laughlin. 1992. The myth of measurement in physical education. *JOPERD* 63(4):83-85.

Lavroff, N. 1992. *Virtual reality playhouse.* Corte Madera, CA: Waite Group.

Lebow, D., and D. Johnson. 1993. Integrating emerging technologies into fitness education. *Florida Journal of Health, Physical Education, Recreation, Dance, and Driver Education* 31(3):38-45.

Lemaster, K.J., and A.C. Lacy. 1993. Relationship of teacher behaviors to ALT-PE in junior high school physical education. *Journal of Classroom Interaction* 28(1):21-25.

Lepper, M., and D. Green, eds. 1978. *The hidden cost of rewards: New perspectives on the psychology of human motivation.* New York: Erlbaum.

Levy, J.R., and H. Bjellan. 1995. *Create your own virtual reality system.* New York: Windcrest/McGraw-Hill.

Lewin, L. 2001. *Using the Internet to strengthen curriculum.* Alexandria, VA: ASCD.

Lieberman, L.J., and C. Houston-Wilson. 2002. *Strategies for inclusion: A handbook for physical educators.* Champaign, IL: Human Kinetics.

Lohrmann, D.K., and S.F. Wooley. 1998. Comprehensive school health education. In E. Marx and S.F. Wooley with D. Northrop (eds.), *Health is academic: A guide to coordinated school health programs* (pp. 43-66). New York: Teachers College Press.

Los Angeles Unified School District and Office of the Los Angeles County Superintendent of Schools. 1983. *Multicultural games for elementary school children.* Los Angeles: Authors.

Lund, J.L. 2000. *Creating rubrics for physical education.* Reston, VA: NASPE.

Luxbacher, J. 1996. *Soccer instructor guide: Steps to success.* Champaign, IL: Human Kinetics.

———. 1996. *Soccer: Steps to success* (2nd ed.). Champaign, IL: Human Kinetics.

Magill, R.A. 2007. *Motor learning and control: Concepts and applications* (8th ed.). New York: McGraw-Hill.

Maina, M. 2003. Attitudes of middle school students toward their physical education teachers. *The Physical Educator* March 2003.

Maloy, B.P. 1993. Legal obligations related to facilities. *JOPERD* 64(2):28-30, 64.

Martin, R.M. 1975. *Gravity guiding system.* San Marino, CA: Essential.

Martinek, T.J., and J.B. Griffith. 1993. Working with the learned helpless child. *JOPERD* 64(6):17-20.

Martinek, T.J., P.B. Crowe, and W.J. Rejeski. 1982. *Pygmalion in the gym: Causes and effects of expectations in teaching and coaching.* West Point, NY: Leisure Press.

Maryland State Department of Education. 1989. *Better physical education.* Baltimore: Author.

Marzano, R.J. 1992. *A different kind of classroom: Teaching with dimensions of learning.* Alexandria, VA: ASCD.

———. 2000. *Transforming classroom grading.* Alexandria, VA: ASCD.

———. 2003. *Classroom management that works: Research based strategies for every teacher.* Alexandria, CA: ASCD.

Marzano, R.J., and J.S. Kendall. 1996. *A comprehensive guide to designing standards-based districts, schools, and classrooms.* Alexandria, VA: ASCD and Aurora, CO: Mid-Continent Regional Educational Laboratory.

Marzano, R.J., and D.J. Pickering. 1997. *Dimensions of learning: Teacher's manual* (2nd ed.). Alexandria, VA: ASCD and Aurora, CO: Mid-Continent Regional Education Laboratory.

Marzano, R.J., D. Pickering, and J. McTighe. 1993. *Assessing student outcomes: Performance assessment using the dimensions of learning model.* Alexandria, VA: ASCD.

Marzano, R.J., D.J. Pickering, and J.E. Pollock. 2001. *Classroom instruction that works.* Alexandria, VA: ASCD.

McCracken, B. 2001. *It's not just gym anymore: Teaching secondary school students how to be active for life.* Champaign, IL: Human Kinetics.

McDonald, J.P., S. Smith, D. Turner, M. Finney, and E. Barton. 1993. *Graduation by exhibition: Assessing genuine achievement.* Alexandria, VA: ASCD.

McEwin, C.K., T.S. Dickinson, and D.M. Jenkins. 1996. *America's middle schools: Practices and progress—a 25 year perspective.* Columbus, OH: National Middle School Association.

McNeill, C., J. Cory-Wright, and T. Renfrew. 1998. *Teaching orienteering* (2nd ed.). Champaign, IL: Human Kinetics.

Mechikoff, R., and S. Estes. 2006. *A history and philosophy of sport and physical education: From ancient civilizations to the modern world* (4th ed). Madison, WI: Brown and Benchmark.

Mechikoff, R.A., and S.G. Estes. 2002. *A history and philosophy of sport and physical education.* New York: McGraw-Hill.

Melograno, V.J. 1994. Portfolio assessment: Documenting authentic student learning. *JOPERD* 65(8):50-55, 58-61.

———. 1996. *Designing the physical education curriculum* (3rd ed.). Champaign, IL: Human Kinetics.

———. 1999. *Preservice professional portfolio system.* Reston, VA: NASPE.

———. 2000. *Portfolio assessment for K-12 physical education.* Reston, VA: NASPE.

Mendon, K. 1994. Outstanding middle school physical education program. *CAHPERD Journal/Times* 56(8):10, 34.

Mercier, R. 1992. Beyond class management—teaching social skills through physical education. *JOPERD* 63(6):83-87.

———. 1993. Student-centered physical education—Strategies for teaching social skills. *JOPERD* 64(5):60-65.

Merriman, J. 1993. Supervision in sport and physical activity. *JOPERD* 64(2):20-21, 23.

Midura, D.W., and D.R. Glover. 1995. *More team building challenges.* Champaign, IL: Human Kinetics.

Miller, B., B. Lord, and J. Dorney. 1994. *Summary report. Staff development for teachers. A study of configurations and costs in four districts.* Newton, MA: Education Development Center.

Milliken, L. 1995. *Medieval times activity book.* New York: Edupress.

Mitchell, D. and Hutchinson, C.J. 2003. Using graphic organizers to develop the cognitive domain in physical education. *JOPERD* 47(9): 42-47.

Mitchell, S., and J. Oslin. 1999. *Assessment in games teaching.* Reston, VA: NASPE.

Mitchell, S.A., J.L. Oslin, and L.L. Griffin. 2003. *Sport foundations for elementary physical education: A tactical games approach.* Champaign, IL: Human Kinetics.

Mitchell, S.A., J.L. Oslin, and L.L. Griffin. 2006. *Teaching sport concepts and skills: A tactical games approach* (2nd ed.). Champaign, IL: Human Kinetics.

Mohnsen, B.S. 1987. *Physical education playground and field safety for grades K-12.* Downey, CA: Los Angeles County Office of Education.

———. 1990a. Physical education: Caught in the middle and forgotten. *Journal of Supervision and Curriculum Improvement* 3(3):10-16.

———. 1990b. Quality physical education: A three-part series. *CAHPERD Journal* 53(2):7-8.

———. 1991. Quality physical education: Part 2. *CAHPERD Journal* 53(4):3-4.

———, ed. 1998. *Concepts of physical education: What every student needs to know.* Reston, VA: NASPE.

———, ed. 1999. *The new leadership paradigm for physical education: What we need to lead.* Reston, VA: NASPE.

———. 2001. *Building a quality physical education program (grades 6-12).* Medina, WA: Institute for Educational Development.

———, ed. 2003a. *Concepts and principles of physical education: What every student needs to know.* Reston, VA: NASPE.

———. 2003b. *Teaching middle school physical education: A standards-based approach for grades 5–8* (2nd ed.). Champaign, IL: Human Kinetics.

———. 2003c. *Using technology in physical education* (4th ed.). Cerritos, CA: Bonnie's Fitware.

Mohnsen, B.S., and B. Hennessy. 1991. Quality physical education: Part 3. *CAHPERD Journal* 53(6):3-4, 6.

Mohnsen, B.S., and C. Thompson. 1995. Authentic assessment in physical education. *Teaching High School Physical Education* 1(1):6-8.

Moore, M.G., and M.M. Thompson with A.B. Quigley, G.C. Clark, and G.G. Goff. 1990. *The effects of distance learning: A summary of the literature. Research Monograph No. 2* (ED 330 321). University Park, PA: The Pennsylvania State University, American Center for the Study of Distance Education.

Morford, L. 1996. Can you believe this? *Teaching Secondary Physical Education* 2(2):2.

Morris, G., and J. Stiehl. 1998. *Changing kids' games* (2nd ed.). Champaign, IL: Human Kinetics.

Morrow, J.R., H.B. Falls, and H.W. Kohl. 1994. *The Prudential Fitnessgram: Technical reference manual.* Dallas: Cooper Institute for Aerobics Research.

Mosston, M., and S. Ashworth. 1994. *Teaching physical education.* New York: Macmillan College.

Mustain, W.C. 1996. Navigating with assessment. *Teaching Secondary Physical Education* 2(2):4-6.

Naisbitt, J. 1984. *Megatrends: Ten new directions transforming our lives.* New York: Warner Books.

Naisbitt, J., and P. Aburdene. 1985. *Re-inventing the corporation.* New York: Warner Books.

National Association for Sport and Physical Education. 1990. *Definition of the physically educated person: Outcomes of quality physical education programs.* Reston, VA: Author.

———. 1994. *NASPE sport and physical education advocacy kit.* Reston, VA: Author.

———. 1995a. *Moving into the future: National physical education standards, a guide to content and assessment.* Reston, VA: Author.

———. 1995b. *National standards for beginning physical education teachers.* Reston, VA: Author.

———. 1998. *Physical education program improvement and self study guide: Middle school.* Reston, VA: Author.

———. 1999. *NASPE sport and physical education advocacy kit II.* Reston, VA: Author.

———. 2000. *Teaching physical education in a block schedule.* Reston, VA; author.

———. 2001a. *Appropriate practices for middle school physical education.* Reston, VA: Author.

———. 2001b. *Physical education is critical to a complete education. A position paper from the Council of Physical Education for Children and the National Association for Sport and Physical Education.* Reston, VA: author.

———. 2002. *Co-curricular physical activity and sport programs for middle school students: A position paper of the Middle and Secondary School Physical Education Council and the National Association for Sport and Physical Education.* Reston, VA: Author.

———. 2003. *Parents' views of children's health and fitness: A summary of results* [executive summary]. Reston, VA: Author.

———. 2004a. *Opportunity to learn standards for middle school physical education.* Reston, VA: Author.

———. 2004b. *Physical activity for children: A statement of guidelines for children ages 5-12* (2nd ed.). Reston, VA: Author.

———. 2004c. *Moving into the future: National standards for physical education* (2nd ed.). Reston, VA: NASPE.

———. 2006a. *Shape of the nation report.* Reston, VA: Author.

———. 2006b. *Opposing substitution and waiver/exemptions for required physical education.* Reston, VA: Author.

———. n.d. *Position on dodgeball in physical education.* Reston, VA: author.

National Association of School Nurses. 1990. *Resolutions and policy statements.* Scarborough, ME: Author.

National Association of State Boards of Education. 2000. *Fit, healthy and ready to learn.* Alexandria, VA: Author.

National Board for Professional Teaching Standards. 1999. *Physical education standards.* Arlington, VA: Author.

———. 2002. National Board for Professional Teaching Standards history.www.nbpts.org/about/history.html

National Center for Education Statistics. 2005. Digest of education statistics.http://nces.ed.gov/programs/digest/d05/tables/dt05_416.asp

National Coalition on Health Care. 2006. Health care costs.www.nchc.org/facts/cost.shtml

National Consortium for Physical Education and Recreation for Individual with Disabilities. 1995. *Adapted physical education national standards.* Champaign, IL: Human Kinetics.

National Staff Development Council. 1994. *Standards for staff development.* Oxford, OH: Author.

Negroponte, N. 1995. *Being digital.* New York: Knopf.

Neil, G. 1976. *Modern team handball: Beginner to expert.* Montreal: McGill University.

Nelson, J.M. 1991. *Self-defense: Steps to success.* Champaign, IL: Human Kinetics.

———. 1994. *Teaching self-defense: Steps to success.* Champaign, IL: Human Kinetics.

Nelson, J., J. Moore, and J. Dorociak. 1983. A survey of grading practices in physical education in Louisiana. *Louisiana Journal for Health, Physical Education, Recreation and Dance* 28:18-21.

Nelson, W.E., and H. Glass. 1992. *International playtime: Classroom games and dances from around the world.* Carthage, IL: Fearon Teacher Aids.

Newmann, F.M. 1991. Linking restructuring to authentic student achievement. *Phi Delta Kappa* 48(1):35-40.

Nichols, B. 1994. *Moving and learning: The elementary school physical education experience.* St. Louis, MO: Mosby.

Nieto, S. 1992. *Affirming diversity: The sociopolitical context of multicultural education.* White Plains, NY: Longman.

Noland, R. 2003. The effectiveness of the ropes challenge course on the enhancement of critical thinking skills. *Research Quarterly for Exercise and Sport* 74.

Office of Applied Studies. 2006. Highlights of recent reports on substance abuse and mental health.www.oas.samhsa.gov/highlights.htm#2k6Pubs

Ogden, C.L., K.M. Flegal, M.D. Carroll, and C.L. Johnson. 2002. Prevalence and trends in overweight among U.S. children and adolescents, 1999-2000. *Journal of the American Medical Association* 288(14):1728-1732.

Orlick, T. 1978. *The cooperative sports and games book.* New York: Pantheon Books.

———. 1982. *The second cooperative sports and games book.* New York: Pantheon Books.

Ostrow, A.C. 1990. *Directory of psychological tests in the sport and exercise sciences.* Morgantown, WV: Fitness Information Technology.

O'Sullivan, M., and M. Henninger. 2000. *Assessing student responsibility and teamwork.* Reston, VA: NASPE.

Owens, D., and L.K. Bunker. 1995. *Golf: Steps to success* (2nd ed.). Champaign, IL: Human Kinetics.

———. 1996. *Golf instructor guide: Steps to success.* Champaign, IL: Human Kinetics.

Palmer, J.M. 1991. Planning wheels turn curriculum around. *Educational Leadership* 49(2):57-60.

Pangrazi, R. 2001. *Dynamic physical education for elementary school children.* Boston: Allyn and Bacon.

Pangrazi, R., and C. Corbin. 1994. *Teaching strategies for improving youth fitness.* Reston, VA: AAHPERD.

Parker, M., and D. Hellison. 2001. Teaching responsibility in physical education: Standards, outcomes, and beyond. *JOPERD* 72(9):25-28.

Pastore, M. 2001a. Net users worldwide taking commerce online.cyberatlas.internet.com/big_picture/geographics/article/0,,5911_783851,00.html

Pastore, M. 2001b. Number of U.S. households online grows in second quarter. http://cyberatlas.internet.com/big_picture/geographics/article/0,,5911_783851,00.html

Patterson, J.L. 1993. *Leadership for tomorrow's schools.* Alexandria, VA: ASCD.

Paulson, F.L., P.R. Paulson, and C.A. Meyer. 1991. What makes a portfolio a portfolio? *Educational Leadership* 48(5):60-63.

Peddiwell, J.A. 1939. *The saber-tooth curriculum.* New York: McGraw-Hill.

Pellett, T.L., H.A. Henschel-Pellet, and J.M. Harrison. 1994. Feedback effects: Field-based findings. *JOPERD* 65(9):75-78.

Perelman, L.J. 1992. *School's out: Hyperlearning, the new technology, and the end of education.* New York: Morrow.

Petersen, S.C., V.L. Allen, and V.L. Minotti. 1994. Teacher knowledge and reflection. *JOPERD* 65(7):31-37.

Petray, C.K., and S.L. Blazer. 1986. *Health-related physical fitness: Concepts and activities for elementary school children.* Edina, MN: Bellwether Press.

Philipp, J.A., and J.D. Wilkerson. 1990. *Teaching team sports: A coeducational approach.* Champaign, IL: Human Kinetics.

Pickle-Ball, Inc. 1972. *Pickle-Ball.* Seattle: Pickle-Ball.

Pimentel, K., and K. Teixeira. 1993. *Virtual reality: Through the new looking glass.* Carlsbad, CA: Windcrest Books.

Placek, J. 1983. Conceptions of success in teaching: Busy, happy, and good? In *Research on teaching in physical education* (pp. 46-56). Champaign, IL: Human Kinetics.

———. 1992. Rethinking middle school physical education curriculum: An integrated thematic approach. *Quest* 44(3):330-341.

Polin, L. 1991. Portfolio assessment. *The Writing Notebook* (January/February):25-27, 42.

Popcorn, F., and L. Marigold. 1996. *Clicking: 16 trends to future fit your life, your work, and your business.* New York: HarperCollins.

Poplin, M.S. 1988. Holistic/constructivist principles of the teaching/learning process: Implications for the field of learning disabilities. *Journal of Learning Disabilities* 21(7):402-416.

Potter, D.L., and G. Brockmeyer. 1999. *Softball: Steps to success* (2nd ed.). Champaign, IL: Human Kinetics.

Professional Golfers' Association of America Junior Golf Foundation. 1987. *First swing manual.* Palm Beach Gardens, FL: National Golf Foundation.

Prusak, K.A., S.D. Vincent, and R.P. Pangrazi. 2005. Teacher talk. *JOPERD* 76(5):21-25.

Randall, L.E. 1992a. *The student teacher's handbook for physical education.* Champaign, IL: Human Kinetics.

———. 1992b. *Systematic supervision for physical education.* Champaign, IL: Human Kinetics.

Ratey, J.J. 2001. *A user's guide to the brain.* New York: Pantheon Books.

Ratliffe, T., L. Ratliffe, and B. Bie. 1991. Creating a learning environment: Class management strategies for elementary PE teachers. *JOPERD* (November/December):24-27.

Ray, O.M. 1992. *Encyclopedia of line dances: The steps that came and stayed.* Reston, VA: AAHPERD.

Reauthorized U.S. Public Law 99-057, 1986. Section 504 of the Rehabilitation Act of 1973.

Redican, K.J., L.K. Olsen, and C.R. Baffi. 1986. *Organization of school health programs.* New York: Macmillan.

Reeves, D. 2000. Standards are not enough: Essential transformations for successful middle schools. Workshop given for the California Department of Education, October 16-17, 2000, Sacramento, CA.

Renfrew, T. 1997. *Orienteering.* Champaign, IL: Human Kinetics.

Rhodes, R.E. and Courneya, K.S. 2003. Investigating multiple components of attitude, subjective norm, and perceived control: An examination of the theory of planned behavior in the exercise domain. *British Journal of Social Psychology* 42:129-146.

Richard-Amato, P.A., and M.A. Snow. 1992. *The multicultural classroom: Reading for content-area teachers.* White Plains, NY: Longman.

Rink, J.E. 1993a. *Teaching physical education for learning.* St. Louis: Mosby.

———, ed. 1993b. *Critical crossroads: Middle and secondary school physical education.* Reston, VA: NASPE.

———. 1998a. Motor learning. In B. Mohnsen (ed.), *Concepts of physical education: What every student needs to know* (pp. 15-37). Reston, VA: NASPE.

———. 1998b. *Teaching physical education for learning* (3rd ed.). Boston: McGraw-Hill.

Robert Wood Johnson Foundation. 2003. National poll shows parents and teachers agree on solutions to childhood obesity [News release]. Princeton, NJ: Author.

Roblyer, M.D., and J. Edwards. 2000. *Integrating educational technology into teaching.* Upper Saddle River: Merrill.

Rohnke, K. 1989a. *Cowtails and cobras II.* Hamilton, MA: Project Adventure.

———. 1989b. *Silver bullets.* Hamilton, MA: Project Adventure.

———. 1989c. *The bottomless bag: This one.* Dubuque, IA: Kendall/Hunt.

———. 1994. *The bottomless bag: Again.* Dubuque, IA: Kendall/Hunt.

Romijn, T. 1995. *TPR is more than commands.* New York: Command Performance.

Rosenshine, B. 1983. Teaching functions in instructional programs. *Elementary School Journal* 83:335-351.

Ross, J.G., and R.P. Pate. 1987. The national children and youth fitness study: A summary of findings. *JOPERD* 58(9):51-56.

Rowland, T.W. 1992. *Pediatric laboratory exercise testing: Clinical guidelines.* Champaign, IL: Human Kinetics.

Ryan, S., R. Voss, and M. Maina. 2001. The first step towards a climbing wall: Writing a proposal. *JOPERD* 72(7):45-48.

Ryser, O.E., and J.R. Brown. 1989. *A manual for tumbling and apparatus stunts* (8th ed.). Dubuque, IA: Brown.

Sallis, J.F., and K. Patrick. 1994. Physical activity guidelines for adolescents: Consensus statement. *Pediatric Exercise Science* 6:302-314.

Sallis, J.F., T.L. McKenzie, B. Kolody, M. Lewis, S. Marshall, and P. Rosengard. 1999. Effects of health-related physical education on academic achievement: Project SPARK. *Research Quarterly for Exercise and Sport* 70(2):127-134.

Sander, A.N., M. Harageones, T. Ratliffe, and D. Pizzaro. 1993. Florida's fit to achieve program. *JOPERD* 64(7):26-28.

Scherer, M. 2001. How and why standards can improve student achievement. *Educational Leadership* (September):14-18.

Schmidt, R.A., and C.A. Wrisberg. 2000. *Motor learning and performance* (2nd ed.). Champaign, IL: Human Kinetics.

Schmoker, M. 1996. *Results: The key to continuous school improvement.* Alexandria, VA: ASCD.

Schneider, P.L., Crouter, S.E., and Bassett, D.R. 2004. Pedometer measures of free-living physical activity: Comparison of 13 models. *Medicine and Science in Sports and Exercise* 36(2):331-335.

Schneider, P.L., S.E. Crouter, O. Lukajic, and D.R. Bassett. 2003. Accuracy and reliability of 10 pedometers for measuring steps over a 400-m walk. *Medicine and Science in Sports and Exercise* 35(10):1779-1784.

Schneider, R.E. 1992. Don't just promote your profession—market it! *JOPERD* 63(5):70-73.

Schnitzer, S. 1993. Designing an authentic assessment. *Educational Leadership* 50(7):32-35.

School Improvement Office, California Department of Education. 1994. *Guide and criteria for program quality review middle level.* Sacramento, CA: Author.

Schurr, S. 1999. *Authentic assessment: Using product, performance, and portfolio, measures from A to Z.* Westerville, OH: National Middle School Association.

Seaman, J.A. 1995. *Physical best and individuals with disabilities: A handbook for inclusion in fitness programs.* Reston, VA: AAHPERD.

Sebren, A. 1994. Reflective thinking—integrating theory and practice in teacher preparation. *JOPERD* 65(6):23-24, 57-59.

Secretary's Commission on Achieving Necessary Skills (SCANS). 1991. *What work requires of schools: A SCANS report for America 2000.* Washington, DC: U.S. Department of Labor.

———. 2000. What work requires of schools. Washington, DC: U.S. Department of Labor.

Seefeldt, V., and P. Vogel. 1986. *The value of physical activity.* Reston, VA: AAHPERD.

Seidler, T.L. 2006. Planning and designing safe facilities. *JOPERD* 77(5):32-37, 44.

Shakarian, D.C. 1995. Beyond lecture: Active learning strategies that work. *JOPERD* 66(5):21-24.

Shulman, L.S. 1987. Knowledge and teaching: Foundations of the new reform. *Harvard Educational Review* 57(1):1-22.

Sibley, B.A. and Ethnier, J.L. 2003. The relationship between physical activity and cognition in children: A meta-analysis. *Pediatric Exercise Science* 15(30):243-256.

Siedentop, D. 1983. *Developing teaching skills in physical education.* Mountain View, CA: Mayfield.

———. 1991. *Developing teaching skills in physical education* (2nd ed.). Mountain View, CA: Mayfield.

Siedentop, D., J. Herkowitz, and J. Rink. 1984. *Elementary physical education methods.* Englewood Cliffs, NJ: Prentice Hall.

Siedentop, D., C. Mand, and A. Taggart. 1986. *Physical education: Teaching and curriculum strategies for grades 5-12.* Mountain View, CA: Mayfield.

Silverman, S. 1991. Research on teaching in physical education: Review and commentary. *Research Quarterly for Exercise and Sport* 62(4):352-364.

Sizer, T.R., and B. Rogers. 1993. Designing standards: Achieving the delicate balance. *Educational Leadership* 50(5):24-26.

Slavin, R.E. 1990. Achievement effects of ability grouping in secondary schools: A best-evidence synthesis. *Review of Educational Research* 60:471-499.

———. 1991. Synthesis of research on cooperative learning. *Educational Leadership* 48(5):71-82.

Smith, M.D. 1993. Physical education in the British national curriculum. *JOPERD* 64(9):21-32.

Solipaz. n.d. *Basic circus skills.* Lodi, CA: Author.

———. n.d. *How to ride a unicycle.* Lodi, CA: Author.

Solmon, M.A. 2005. Pedagogy research through the years in RQES. *Research Quarterly for Exercise and Sport* 76(2 Suppl): S108-S121.

Sondag, K.A., L.A. Curry, and M. Thomas. 1997. Integrating physical and health education into one course: Is it working in Montana? *Physical Educator* 54:105-112.

Sosa, D. 1995. *How the brain learns.* Reston, VA: National Association of Secondary School Principals.

Spady, W.G. 1994. Choosing outcomes of significance. *Educational Leadership* 51(6):19-22.

Spalding, A., L. Kelly, J. Posner-Mayer, and J. Santopietro. 1999. *Kids on the ball: Using Swiss balls in a complete fitness program.* Champaign, IL: Human Kinetics.

Spickelmier, D., T. Sharpe, C. Deibler, C. Golden, and B. Krueger. 1995. Use positive discipline for middle school students. *Strategies* 8(8):5-8.

Spindt, G.B., W.H. Monti, and B. Hennessy. 2002a. *Moving as a team.* Dubuque, IA: Kendall/Hunt.

———. 2002b. *Moving as a team physical education portfolio.* Dubuque, IA: Kendall/Hunt.

———. 2002c. *Moving with confidence.* Dubuque, IA: Kendall/Hunt.

———. 2002d. *Moving with confidence physical education portfolio.* Dubuque, IA: Kendall/Hunt.

———. 2002e. *Moving with skill.* Dubuque, IA: Kendall/Hunt.

———. 2002f. *Moving with skill physical education portfolio.* Dubuque, IA: Kendall/Hunt.

Sprenger, M. 1999. *Learning and memory: The brain in action.* Alexandria, VA: ASCD.

Staff writer. 2002. The incredible shrinking technology. www.jamesline.com/news/publications/frontiers/archives/?ID=716andCID=0

Stevens-Smith, D.A. 2002. Why your school needs a quality physical education program. *Principal* (May):30-31.

———. 2006. Brain games. *Strategies* (July/August):19-23.

Stevenson, H.W., and J.W. Stigler. 1992. *The learning gap: Why our schools are failing and what we can learn from Japanese and Chinese education.* New York: Touchstone.

Stiehl, J. 1993. Becoming responsible—theoretical and practical considerations. *JOPERD* 64(5):38-40, 57-59, 70-71.

Stiggins, R.J. 1998. *Classroom assessment for student success.* Washington, DC: National Education Association.

Stokes, R., C. Moore, and S.L. Schultz. 2002. *Personal fitness and you.* Winston-Salem, NC: Hunter Textbooks.

Strand, B., and S. Reeder. 1993. P.E. with a heartbeat—Hi-tech physical education. *JOPERD* 64(3):81-84.

Strand, B.N., and R. Wilson. 1993. *Assessing sport skills.* Champaign, IL: Human Kinetics.

Strickland, R.H. 1996. *Bowling instructor guide: Steps to success.* Champaign, IL: Human Kinetics.

———. 1996. *Bowling: Steps to success* (2nd ed.). Champaign, IL: Human Kinetics.

Superintendent Bill Honig's Middle Grade Task Force. 1987. *Caught in the middle: Educational reform for young adolescents in California public schools.* Sacramento, CA: California State Department of Education.

Sutliff, M. 1996. The duty to warn of inherent dangers. *Teaching Secondary Physical Education* 2(2):18-19.

Swaim, D., and S. Edwards. 2002. *Middle school healthy hearts in the zone.* Champaign, IL: Human Kinetics.

Sylvester, R. 1993. What the biology of the brain tells us about learning. *Educational Leadership* 51(4):46-51.

Tannehill, D., and D. Zakrajsek. 1993. Student attitudes towards physical education: A multicultural study. *Journal of Teaching in Physical Education* 13(1):78-84.

Tapscott, D. 1998. *Growing up digital: The rise of the net generation.* New York: McGraw-Hill.

The Educational Kinesiology Foundation. 2003. *A chronology of annotated research study summaries in the field of educational kinesiology.* Ventura, CA: Author.

The state of innovation. 2002. *Technology Review* (June):55-63.

Thomas, D.G. 1996. *Swimming instructor guide: Steps to success.* Champaign, IL: Human Kinetics.

———. 1996. *Swimming: Steps to success* (2nd ed.). Champaign, IL: Human Kinetics.

Thornburg, D.D. 1992. *Edutrends 2010: Restructuring, technology, and the future of education.* San Francisco: Starson.

———. 2002. *The new basics: Education and the future of work in the telematic age.* Alexandria, VA: ASCD.

Tip, C., and D. Roddick. 1985. *Frisbee games.* La Mirada, CA: Discovering the World.

Toch, T. 1991. *In the name of excellence: The struggle to reform the nation's schools, why it's failing, and what should be done.* Philadelphia, PA: American Philological Association.

Toffler, A. 1968. *The schoolhouse in the city.* New York: Praeger.

Tripp, A. and W. Zhu. 2005. Assessment of students with disabilities in physical education: Legal perspectives and practices. *JOPERD* 76(20):41-47.

Tucker, P.D. and J.H. Stronge. 2005. *Linking teacher evaluation and student learning.* Alexandria, VA: ASCD.

Tuckman, B.W. 1965. Developmental sequence in small groups. *Psychological Bulletin* 63:384-389.

Turner, A. 1996. Teaching for understanding: Myth or reality? *JOPERD* 67(4):46-47, 55.

Tye, K.A., ed. 1990. *Global education: From thought to action.* Alexandria, VA: ASCD.

United States Census Bureau. 2000a. *World population.* Washington, DC: Author.

———. 2000b. *Home computers and internet use in the US.* Washington, DC: Author.

———. 2001. *Health.* Washington, DC: Author.

United States Consumer Product Safety Commission. 2005. *Public playground handbook for safety.* Washington, DC: Author.

United States Department of Education. 2002. *No child left behind: A desktop reference.* Washington, DC: author.

United States Department of Health and Human Services. 1985. National children and youth fitness study. *JOPERD* 56:44-90.

———. 1987. National children and youth fitness study II. *JOPERD* 58:49-96.

———. 1990. *Healthy people 2000: National health promotion and disease prevention objectives.* Washington, DC: Author.

———. 1996. *Physical activity and health: A report of the Surgeon General.* Atlanta: Author.

———. 1998. *National vital statistics reports* (Vol. 48, No. 11). Hyattsville, MD: Author.

———. 2000. *Healthy people 2010: Understanding and improving health.* Washington, DC: Author.

———. 2001. *The Surgeon General's call to action to prevent and decrease overweight and obesity 2001.* Rockville, MD: Office of the Surgeon General.

United States National Commission on Excellence in Education. 1983. *A nation at risk: The imperative for education reform. A report to the Nation and the Secretary of Education, United States Department of Education.* Washington, DC: Author.

United States Team Handball Federation. 1981. *Team handball—official rules of the game.* Colorado Springs, CO: Author.

United States Tennis Association Schools Program. 1993. *United States Tennis Association schools program curriculum.* White Plains, NY: Author.

U.S. Public Law 94-142. Education for All Handicapped Children Act of 1975.

Valentine, B., and B. Valentine. 1991. *Self-defense for life.* Glendale, CA: Self-Defense.

van der Smissen, B. 1990. *Legal liability and risk management for public and private entities.* Cincinnati, OH: Anderson.

Van Nagel, C., R. Siudzinski, and R. Bandler. 1993. *Mega-teaching and learning: Neurolinguistic programming applied to education.* Portland, OR: Metamorphous Press.

Verduin, J.R., and T.A. Clark. 1991. *Distance education: The foundations of effective practice.* San Francisco: Jossey-Bass.

Viera, B.J., and B.J. Ferguson. 1996. *Volleyball instructor guide: Steps to success.* Champaign, IL: Human Kinetics.

————. 1996. *Volleyball: Steps to success* (2nd ed.). Champaign, IL: Human Kinetics.

Vincent, S.D., and R.P. Pangrazi. 2002. An examination of the activity patterns of elementary school children. *Pediatric Exercise Science* 14: 432-452.

Vogel, P., and V. Seefeldt. 1988. *Program design in physical education.* Indianapolis: Benchmark Press.

Wang, M.C., G.D. Haertel, and H.J. Walberg. 1993. What helps students learn? *Educational Leadership* 51(4):46-51.

Wechsler, H., R. Devereaux, M. Davis, and J. Collins. 2000. Using the school environment to promote physical activity and healthy eating. *Preventive Medicine* 31:S121-S137.

Weidel, B.L., F.R. Biles, G.E. Figley, and B.J. Neuman. 1980. *Sports skills: A conceptual approach to meaningful movement.* Dubuque, IA: Brown.

Welk, G.J. (Ed.). 2002. *Physical activity assessments for health-related research.* Champaign, IL: Human Kinetics.

Welk, G.J., S.N. Blair, K. Wood, S. Jones, and R. Thompson. 2000. A comparative evaluation of three accelerometry-based physical activity monitors. *Medicine and Science in Sports and Exercise* 32:S489-S497.

Welk, G.J. and C.B. Corbin. 1995. The validity of the Tritrac-R3D activity monitor for the assessment of physical activity in children. *Research Quarterly for Exercise and Sport* 66:202-209.

Welk, G., C. Corbin, and D. Dale. 2000. Measurement issues in the assessment of physical activity in children. *Research Quarterly for Exercise and Sport* 71(2):59-73.

Welk, G., J. Differding, R. Thompson, S. Blair, J. Dziura, and P. Hart. 2000. The utility of the digi-walker step counter to assess daily physical activity patterns. *Medicine and Science in Sports and Exercise* 32(9 Suppl):S481-S488.

Welk, G.J. and Wood, K. 2000 Physical activity assessment in physical education. *Journal of Physical Education, Recreation, and Dance* 71(1):30-40.

Werner, P., R. Thorpe, and D. Bunker. 1996. Teaching games for understanding: Evolution of a model. *JOPERD* 67(1):28-33.

Wheatley, M.J. 1994. *Leadership and new science: Learning about organization from an orderly universe.* San Francisco: Berrett-Koehler.

White House document outlines President's education goals. 1990. *Education Daily Bulletin* 23(14).

Wiburg, K. 1995. Becoming critical users of multimedia. *Computing Teacher* 22(7):59-61.

Wiggins, G. 1994. Toward better report cards. *Educational Leadership* 52(2):28-37.

Wiggins, G., and J. McTighe. 1998. *Understanding by design.* Alexandria, VA: ASCD.

Wikgren, S. 1995. Coeducational physical education: Seeking quality and equity for all students. *Teaching Middle School Physical Education* 1(4):1, 4-5.

————. 1996. Are you a "C"? *Teaching Secondary Physical Education* 2(2):7.

Wiley, J. n.d. *Complete book of unicycling.* Lodi, CA: Solipaz.

————. n.d. *Unicycling society of America.* Lodi, CA: Solipaz.

Williamson, K.M. 1993. Is your inequity showing? Ideas and strategies for creating a more equitable learning environment. *JOPERD* 64(8):15-23.

Wilmore, J.H., and D.L. Costill. 2004. *Physiology of sport and exercise* (3rd ed.). Champaign, IL: Human Kinetics.

Winnick, J.P., and F.X. Short. 1999. *The Brockport physical fitness test manual.* Champaign, IL: Human Kinetics.

————. 1999. *The Brockport physical fitness training guide.* Champaign, IL: Human Kinetics.

————. 1996. *Basketball instructor guide: Steps to success.* Champaign, IL: Human Kinetics.

Wissel, H. 1994. *Basketball: Steps to success.* Champaign, IL: Human Kinetics.

Wlodkowski, R. 1985. *Enhancing adult motivation to learn.* San Francisco: Jossey-Bass.

Wolfe, P. 2001. *Brain matters: Translating research into classroom practice.* Alexandria, VA: ASCD.

Wolfe, P., and R. Brandt. 1998. What do we know from brain research? *Education Leadership* 56(3):8-13.

Wolk, S. 1994. Project-based learning: Pursuits with a purpose. *Educational Leadership* 52(3):42-45.

Wong, F., M. Huhman, C. Heitzler, L. Asbury, R. Bretthauer-Mueller, S. Mccarthy, and P Londe. 2004. VERB™—A social marketing campaign to increase physical activity among youth. Preventing Chronic Disease [serial online] 2004 July. www.cdc.gov/pcd/issues/2004/jul/04_0043.htm

Wong-Fillmore, L. 1980. *Language learning through bilingual instruction.* Berkeley, CA: University of California, Berkeley.

Wood, K., C. Fisher, T. Huth, and P. Graham. 1995. Opening the door to tomorrow's classroom. *Teaching Middle School Physical Education* 1(1):1, 4-5, 8.

Woodard, R., V. Wayda, M. Buck, J. Lund, and J Pauline. 2004. Daily physical education, physical fitness, and middle school students. *Journal of ICHPER-SD* XL(4):20-24.

World Health Organization. 2006. Adolescent suicide rate.www.medscape.com/viewarticle/540353

Wuest, D.A., and B.J. Lombardo. 1994. *Curriculum and instruction: The secondary school physical education experience.* St. Louis: Mosby.

Yessis, M. 1992. *Kinesiology of exercise.* Indianapolis, IN: Masters Press.

Zakrajsek, D., and L.A. Carnes. 1986. *Individualizing physical education: Criterion materials.* Champaign, IL: Human Kinetics.

Zhu, W., A.Cohen, and M. Safrit. 1999. *FitSmart.* Champaign, IL: Human Kinetics.

Zorfass, J.M., and H. Copel. 1998. *Teaching middle school students to be active researchers.* Alexandria, VA: ASCD.

Index

Note: The italicized *f* following page numbers refers to figures.

About the Author

Bonnie Mohnsen, PhD, CEO and president of Bonnie's Fitware, Inc., taught middle school physical education for 13 years and has served as a middle school department chair and mentor–teacher in the Los Angeles Unified School District. She also has worked as a physical education consultant for the Los Angeles County Office of Education, Orange County Department of Education, and Montebello Unified School District. She has consulted with numerous state departments of education on curriculum, including those in California and Maine, and served as the primary consultant for the *Physical Education Curriculum Analysis Tool* from the Centers for Disease Control and Prevention.

Dr. Mohnsen has presented in Japan, Germany, Canada, and the United Arab Emirates. In the United States, she has presented at more than 300 workshops and in-services, speaking on a variety of topics, including teaching middle school physical education, curriculum development, assessment, and using technology in physical education. Dr. Mohnsen is the author of *Using Technology in Physical Education, Fifth Edition; Building a Quality Physical Education Program (Grades 6-12); Integrating Technology and Physical Education; Assessing Student Understanding of Motor Learning Concepts; Strengthening Your Physical Education Program Through Grading and Assessment;* and *Assessing Concepts: Secondary Biomechanics.* She has also authored numerous articles. Dr. Mohnsen is the editor of NASPE's *Concepts of Physical Education: What Every Student Needs to Know,* a follow-up to the National Standards for Physical Education and the *New Leadership Paradigm for Physical Education.*

Dr. Mohnsen was Southern California Middle School Physical Educator of the Year in 1989. She was also named the 1997 Physical Education Administrator of the Year for the Council of School Leadership for Physical Education. In her spare time, she enjoys swimming, reading, and digital electronics.

User Instructions for CD-ROM

System Requirements

You can use this CD-ROM on either a Windows®-based PC or a Macintosh computer.

Windows

- IBM PC compatible with Pentium® processor
- Windows® 98/2000/XP
- Adobe Reader® 8.0
- 4x CD-ROM drive

Macintosh

- Power Mac® recommended
- System 10.4 or higher
- Adobe Reader®
- 4x CD-ROM drive

User Instructions

Windows

1. Insert the *Teaching Middle School Physical Education CD-ROM, Third Edition.* (Note: The CD-ROM must be present in the drive at all times.)

2. Select the "My Computer" icon from the desktop.
3. Select the CD-ROM drive.
4. Open the "Start.pdf" file.

Macintosh

1. Insert the *Teaching Middle School Physical Education CD-ROM, Third Edition.* (Note: The CD-ROM must be present in the drive at all times.)
2. Double-click the CD icon located on the desktop.
3. Open the "Start.pdf" file.

For customer support, contact Technical Support:

Phone: 217-351-5076 Monday through Friday (excluding holidays) between 7:00 a.m. and 7:00 p.m. (CST).

Fax: 217-351-2674

E-mail: support@hkusa.com

For customer support regarding software trial downloads that are listed in the Software Demonstrations file, contact Bonnie's Fitware, Inc. E-mail: bmohnsen@pesoftware.com